Corporations

BLACK LETTER OUTLINES

Corporations

by Robert W. Hamilton

Minerva House Drysdale Regents Chair in Law
University of Texas School of Law

Richard A. Booth

Marbury Research Professor of Law
University of Maryland School of Law

FIFTH EDITION

THOMSON

WEST

Mat #18229951

Thomson/West have created this publication to provide you with accurate and authoritative information concerning the subject matter covered. However, this publication was not necessarily prepared by persons licensed to practice law in a particular jurisdiction. Thomson/West are not engaged in rendering legal or other professional advice, and this publication is not a substitute for the advice of an attorney. If you require legal or other expert advice, you should seek the services of a competent attorney or other professional.

Black Letter Series and Black Letter Series design appearing on the front cover are trademarks registered in the U.S. Patent and Trademark Office.

 PRINTED ON 10% POST CONSUMER RECYCLED PAPER

Preface

This "Black Letter" is designed to help law students recognize and understand the basic principles and issues of law covered in a law school course. It can be used both as a study aid when preparing for classes and as a review of the subject matter when studying for an examination.

Each "Black Letter" is written by experienced law school teachers who are recognized national authorities on the subject covered.

The law is succinctly stated by the authors of this "Black Letter." In addition, the exceptions to the rules are stated in the text. The rules and exceptions have purposely been condensed to facilitate quick and easy recollection. For an in-depth study of a point of law, citations to major student texts are given.

FORMAT

The format of this "Black Letter" is specially designed for review. (1) **Text.** First, it is recommended that the entire text be studied and, if deemed necessary, supplemented by the student texts cited. (2) **Capsule Summary.** The Capsule Summary is an abbreviated review of the subject matter which can be used both before and after studying the main body of the text. The headings in the Capsule Summary follow the main text of the "Black Letter." (3) **Table of Contents.** The Table of Contents is in outline form to help you organize the details of the subject and the Summary of Contents gives you a final overview of the materials.

In addition, a number of other features are included to help you understand the subject matter and prepare for examinations:

Perspective: In this feature, the authors discuss their approach to the topic, the approach used in preparing the materials, and any tips on studying for and writing examinations.

Analysis: This feature, at the beginning of each section, is designed to give a quick summary of a particular section to help you recall the subject matter and to help you determine which areas need the most extensive review.

Examples: This feature is designed to illustrate, through fact situations, the law just stated. This, we believe, should help you analytically approach a question on the examination.

We believe that the materials in this "Black Letter" will facilitate your study of a law school course and assure success in writing examinations not only for the course but for the bar examination. We wish you success.

THE PUBLISHER

Introduction

A major statute, the Sarbanes–Oxley Act of 2002, imposed sweeping changes in corporate governance and required the SEC to adopt implementing rules and procedures to make effective these changes. These changes, summarized below, impose federal standards on many issues that were formerly the sole responsibility of state law.

Historically, state law controlled corporations were formed only under the statutes of each state. The enactment of the Securities Act of 1933 and the Securities Exchange Act of 1934 in the depth of the great depression imposed nation-wide federal registration of publicly held corporations for the first time, but the detailed rules governing the activities of public corporations, to the extent they existed at all, continued to be supplied by the laws of the state of incorporation of the specific corporation.

This reliance on state law proved inadequate in the period from the late 1990s through 2002, a tumultuous period that involved disclosure of significant misconduct and fraud on the part of many publicly held corporations: Enron, Adelphia, Berlin Metals, Cendant, Computer Associates, Dynegy, Global Crossing, Homestore.com, Reliant Resources, Inc., Rite Aid, Sunbeam, Waste Management, WorldCom, Xerox and others. In January, 2003, the SEC published a report documenting that over 100 blue chip companies had "cooked their books" during this period.[1]

The result of these disclosures was the enactment of the Sarbanes–Oxley Act in 2003. This statute imposes sweeping changes in corporate governance at the

---

1. Securities and Exchange Commission, Report Pursuant to Section 704 of the Sarbanes–Oxley Act of 2002, at 38. (January 24, 2003).

national level for the first time and requires the SEC to adopt implementing rules and procedures to make these changes effective. At the same time, new listing and rating requirements have been created by several state agencies, including:

1) New listing requirements for publicly traded corporations governed by the New York Stock Exchange which are described as "Corporate Governance Rules" and often abbreviated as the "NYSE CG Rules;"

2) Detailed and stringent corporate governance rating systems that have been devised by private governance rating agencies and proxy advisors, including International Shareholder Services ("ISS"), Government Metrics, International ("GMI"), the Corporate Library, Moody's, and Standard & Poor's. In addition, agencies such as Glass, Lewis, & Company now provide significant targeted advice when voting issues are to be considered by individual corporations.

3) Changes in the tone and emphasis of judicial opinions, particularly in the Delaware Courts (where more than half of all American publicly held corporations are incorporated).

In addition to these permanent changes, a number of smaller corporations have restated downward their announced earnings during this period: Berlin Metals, Computer Associates, Dynegy, HomeStore, Livent, PNC Financial, Reliant Resources, Sunbeam, Waste Management, and others.

In addition, section 201 of Sarbanes–Oxley (which adds section 10A(g) to the 1934 Act), prohibits external auditors from providing a number of traditional business-related services to the companies they are auditing: corporate auditors may not create financial information systems, design, and implementation; and they may not help clients in choosing, installing, and operating accounting-related computer and software systems. Furthermore, they are prohibited from providing a number of other services, including provision of book-keeping services, appraisal and evaluation services, actuarial services, internal audit outsourcing services, management functions, human resource sources, investment banking services, and legal and related services. In addition, they must separately hire companies and rating agencies to test their balance-sheet goodwill amounts, pension payment estimates; they must also review the assumptions used to compute the company's determinations of pension plan assets and liabilities. In connection with these services, public companies must also disclose the dollar amount of audit and audit-related services separately from permitted non-audit services. These determinations may be evaluated by governance rating agencies, and investors are advised to take this data into account when making investments or casting votes. In the current environment, some shareholder activists have also sponsored resolutions asking companies to discontinue providing non-audit services.

Section 301 of Sarbanes–Oxley provides that the power to hire, fire, and compensate internal auditors must reside in the corporation's audit committee rather than in the board of directors or corporate management. Members of this committee must be "independent" under standards set forth by the audit committee. Prior to Sarbanes–Oxley, the usual practice was to have the board of directors select corporate auditors; under Sarbanes–Oxley, individual auditors who deal with the company's executives must be independent, and furthermore, must be rotated off the engagement after five years. Section 206 further requires the SEC to adopt rules requiring the principal executive and financial officers to certify quarterly and annual reports with respect to the following:

- That they have actually reviewed the report in question;

- That to their knowledge the report does not contain material falsehoods or omissions;

- That the financial statements present the company's condition and operating results in a way that is "fair and complete" in all material respects;

- That they are responsible for, and have evaluated, the adequacy of internal controls;

- That they have disclosed any significant control deficiencies to the external auditors and to the audit committee; and

- That they have disclosed significant changes in controls and corrective actions that have been taken.

Presumably, the intended effect of these statutory certifications is that they will make officers and directors more focused on reports and more diligent and assiduous in their dealings with subordinates. Whether or not this will have the intended effect is probably questionable.

Sarbanes–Oxley sections 301 and 407 also require that at least one member of the audit committee have financial expertise and financial literacy.

Sarbanes–Oxley also requires the creation of a new independent regulatory body, the "Public Company Accounting Oversight Board ("PCAOB"), the function of which is to oversee and regulate external auditing firms and their auditing processes. Sections 101–109. Section 404 sets forth the standards for such oversight and regulation. The PCAOB began the process of overseeing and regulating external auditing firms and their auditing processes and experienced decidedly mixed results: On the positive side, and number of CEOs have expressed the view that the process of meeting the requirements of section 404 attestation has improved their management information systems, and have led to better internal controls. On the other hand, there is a real risk that mandatory attestation requirement will become so routine as to be ineffective.

The risks of potential criminal liability imposed by sections 404 and 906 have led to the development of intensive and expensive evaluations of internal review processes and procedures. The cost of these procedures has been one of the major criticisms of Sarbanes–Oxley. These procedures involve the following steps:

1) Review, and if necessary, adopt new liability assessment and reporting practices;

2) Obtain and evaluate all insurance company risk assessments for company properties;

3) Discuss with appropriate corporate officials pending and threatened litigation and regulatory enforcement issues referred to in periodic reports;

4) Include a discussion of environmental matters;

5) Discuss and evaluate potential contingent liability issues in financial statements, including operational, warranty and environmental issues;

6) Implement and periodically evaluate all section 404 controls;

7) Perform periodic actions required by internal controls and procedures, including the evaluation of known problem areas, the search for new problem areas, and a report of the results to participants in the management chain;

8) Have all of the preceding steps reviewed, evaluated, and certified by appropriate senior managers; and

9) Require a review of the foregoing and its audit by company accountants.

If these steps are consistently followed, they should generate information that is much greater in both quality and reliability than that generally available previously. This information should also be valuable in connection with internal review and the assessment of public information. However, the cost of such an evaluation will be substantial.

The Sarbanes–Oxley Act also contains a number of sections of minor importance: Sections 406–498 requires a code of ethics for senior financial officers, the determination of a financial expert, enhanced review criteria, and a requirement of "real time" disclosures under sections 13(a) and 15(d).

A minor section, section 806 of Title VIII, makes employees, employers, and other specified persons civilly and criminally liable if they retaliate against whistle blowers.

Finally, despite all of these mandated controls, there is always a slight risk that cannot be avoided that trusted corporate officers may have engaged in misconduct ranging from embezzlement of funds from the company, to receipt of improper payments from vendors, or the disclosure of sensitive information to competitors in exchange for cash payments.

*

Summary of Contents

■ III. PREINCORPORATION TRANSACTIONS

■ IV. PIERCING THE CORPORATE VEIL

■ V. CORPORATION FINANCE

■ VI. CORPORATE GOVERNANCE

■ IX. STOCKHOLDER DERIVATIVE LITIGATION

■ X. DISCLOSURE & CORPORATE RECORDS

■ XI. CLOSELY HELD CORPORATIONS

■ XII. PUBLICLY HELD CORPORATIONS

■ XIII. SECURITIES FRAUD & INSIDER TRADING

*

Table of Contents

III. PREINCORPORATION TRANSACTIONS

IV. PIERCING THE CORPORATE VEIL

■ VI. CORPORATE GOVERNANCE

VII. DIRECTORS & OFFICERS

■ VIII. FIDUCIARY DUTIES OF DIRECTORS, OFFICERS & STOCKHOLDERS

■ IX.   STOCKHOLDER DERIVATIVE LITIGATION

■ X. DISCLOSURE & CORPORATE RECORDS

■ XI. CLOSELY HELD CORPORATIONS

APPENDICES

Capsule Summary

■ I. CORPORATION LAW IN GENERAL

A corporation is form of organization that provides (1) limited liability for its owners, (2) perpetual existence independent of its owners, (3) centralization of management in persons who need not be owners (directors and officers), and (4) free transferability of ownership interests (shares). The owners of a corporation are the *shareholders* or *stockholders*. The stockholders elect the board of directors, which in turn sets general policies for the corporation and elects the officers who carry out those policies day to day and generally manage the corporation.

A. THEORETICAL FOUNDATION

Several different theories have been proposed to describe the corporation. Each is to some degree a useful picture of what a corporation is.

1. Entity Theory

A corporation may be most readily envisioned as an entity created for the purpose of conducting a business. The basic elements are:

a. The entity has the power to conduct its business in its own name, including entering into contracts, buying or selling land, bringing suits or being sued, filing tax returns, paying taxes, and the like.

b.   The entity is formed by a grant of authority by a government agency, in most states, the secretary of state. A basic governing document usually called the *articles of incorporation* must be filed with the state and a filing fee paid. The grant of authority may be evidenced by a *certificate of incorporation* or other document issued by the government agency. Subsequent formal steps may also be required to complete formation.

c.   The entity is generally recognized as an entity separate from its owners by the states, the federal government, and those who deal with the corporation.

d.   In some limited situations courts may refuse to follow the artificial entity analysis to its logical conclusions, if it leads to fraudulent or significantly unfair consequences, frustration of clearly defined statutory policies, or other undesirable results. These situations are discussed in somewhat greater detail below under the doctrine of *piercing the corporate veil*.

2.   Concession Theory

A second theory is that a corporation is a grant or concession from the state. Cf. *Association for the Preservation of Freedom of Choice, Inc. v. Shapiro,* 214 N.Y.S.2d 388, 174 N.E.2d 487 (N.Y. 1961). This theory is based on the role of the state in the formation of a corporation.

This theory was more accurate earlier when corporate charters were granted one at a time by act of the state legislature for a specified purpose and were subject to significant restrictions or limitations.

3.   Contract Theory

A third theory of corporateness is that the charter of a corporation represents a contract (a) between the state and the corporation, or (b) between the corporation and its stockholders, or (c) among the stockholders.

The argument that a corporate charter represents a contract between the state and the corporation was relied upon by the United States Supreme Court in *Trustees of Dartmouth College v. Woodward,* 17 U.S. (4 Wheat) 518 (1819) to prevent the state of New Hampshire from enacting a statute amending the charter of the College. The case is primarily of historical interest today, because following a suggestion in an opinion in that case, all modern state statutes specifically reserve the power to subject outstanding charters to subsequent statutory amendments.

4. Nexus of Contracts

Economists have developed a theory of corporateness that permits analysis of the corporation as an economic phenomenon. This theory rejects the notion that the stockholders are the ultimate owners of the enterprise but treats them, along with bondholders and other creditors, as providers of capital in anticipation of receiving a desired return. The *nexus of contracts* arises because the corporate managers obtain all the requirements of the corporation for capital, labor, materials, and services through a series of contracts.

5. Process Theories

Scholars have also suggested that a corporation may be viewed as a process by which various inputs of capital, services, and raw materials are combined to produce desirable products. It may also be viewed as a form of private governance for persons involved in a business.

B. CONSTITUTIONAL INCIDENTS OF THE CORPORATE PERSONALITY

A corporation is viewed as a person entitled to some but not all of the constitutional protections available to individuals. The process of deciding which constitutional protections are available to corporations and which are not is a matter of constitutional construction. The test is whether the protection is a 'purely personal [guarantee]' . . . whose 'historic function' has been limited to the protection of individuals. *First National Bank of Boston v. Bellotti*, 435 U.S. 765, 779, 98 S.Ct. 1407, 1417 (1978).

C. SOURCES OF LAW

The law of corporations is derived from several sources.

1. State Corporation Statutes

Every state has a general corporation statute that describes the incorporation process, defines generally the rights and duties of stockholders, directors, and officers and provides rules about fundamental corporate changes. While these statutes vary from state to state, there is a substantial trend toward liberalization with the result that variations from state to state are declining in importance. Three sources of statutes have been particularly influential:

   a. The Model Business Corporation Act (MBCA) is published by the Committee on Corporate Laws of the ABA Section of Business Law. The original version of this statute was published in 1950 and was substantially revised in 1969. The MBCA has been quite influential and has been followed substantially by many states (sometimes called *model act states*). A major revision was completed in 1984 and was for a time called the Revised Model Business Corporation Act (RMBCA). It is now again called simply the Model Business Corporation Act and it is more or less continually under revision. Most references here are to the MBCA as revised through 2002. References to earlier versions of the MBCA are identified as MBCA (1969) or MBCA (1984).

b. The Delaware General Corporation Law (DGCL). Most large publicly traded corporations are incorporated in Delaware and are therefore subject to Delaware law with regard to their internal affairs such as governance and finance. The reasons for the peculiar concentration of the largest corporations in one small state can be traced to an accident of history. But for a variety of reasons, Delaware is and is likely to remain the most influential jurisdiction in the area of corporation law. And because of its stature in corporation law, Delaware law is also widely followed for some other forms of organization such as limited liability companies (LLCs).

c. The New York Business Corporation Law (NYBCL), California Corporation Code (CCC), and the laws of other important commercial states. Because of the commercial importance of these states, their statutes have been influential in the enactment or amendment of statutes in a limited number of smaller states.

d. Because of the importance of statutory provisions in the law of corporations, the common law is now less important than in some other subjects. Many judicial decisions are interstitial in nature, either supplying supplementary principles when the statutes are silent or construing statutory provisions. Nevertheless, in some areas broad common law principles are still generally applied on the theory that they define basic rights and duties within a corporation and were not affected by statutory enactments. One important area that common law principles continue to have relevance is the articulation of duties of directors and officers. One of the most important such principles is the business judgment rule, which in essence provides a presumption of propriety for decisions of the board of directors in the absence of a conflict of interest.

2. Federal Statutes

The Securities Act of 1933 and the Securities Exchange Act of 1934 are the major federal statutes applicable to broad categories of corporations. The 1933 Act regulates the public offer and sale of securities, while the 1934 Act generally regulates securities markets, securities trading, and the public dissemination of information by publicly held corporations. Under these statutes, the Securities and Exchange Commission (SEC) has broad rule making power. A significant portion of the law applicable to publicly held corporations is based on these statutes, and rules promulgated thereunder. Other federal statutes relating to securities law include the Investment Advisers Act of 1940, Investment Company Act of 1940, and the Trust Indenture Act of 1939.

a. There is no general federal common law of corporations. See Kamen v. Kemper Financial Services, Inc., 500 U.S. 90, 111 S.Ct. 1711 (1991). Prior to 1970 several federal cases and law review commentaries suggested that a federal law of corporations was developing under the federal securities acts. In particular, Rule 10b–5, the catch-all antifraud rule adopted in 1943 by the SEC under the Exchange Act has been applied in a wide variety of circumstances ranging from insider trading to corporate level mismanagement. But as a result of a series of restrictive decisions by the United States Supreme Court beginning in about 1975, the trend has reversed. The principal cases involved in the growth and decline of federal corporation law during this period are set forth in Part XV. In the 1980s, many commentators argued that a market for corporate control existed that was interstate in character and beyond the power of states to limit or control. The decision in *CTS Corporation v. Dynamics Corp. of America,* 481 U.S. 69, 107 S.Ct. 1637 (1987), rejected this argument and held that state law controlled corporations formed under the laws of that state. As the CTS case makes clear, federal securities law is focused primarily on disclosure of material information to the market and investors, whereas state corporation law provides the substantive rights and duties of stockholders, directors, and officers.

b. There have been several important amendments to federal securities law over the years.

- The Williams Act (1968) (relating to tender offers) is a part of the Securities Exchange Act.

- The Insider Trading Sanctions Act (ITSA)(1984) and the Insider

Trading and Securities Fraud Enforcement Act (ITSFEA)(1988), both relating to penalties for insider trading, are also part of the Securities Exchange Act.

- The Private Securities Litigation Reform Act (PSLRA) regulates class actions under federal securities law. PSLRA amended both the 1933 Act and the 1934 Act to make it more difficult for private plaintiffs to file a class action based on federal securities law. It was adopted in response to the perception that numerous frivolous actions had been filed primarily to generate legal fees for plaintiff attorneys.

- The Securities Litigation Uniform Standards Act (SLUSA) was adopted in 1998 to plug a loophole in PSLRA and to require that all class actions based on theories of misrepresentation or nondisclosure be brought in federal court.

- The Sarbanes Oxley Act is the most substantive general regulatory statute adopted since the 1933 Act and the 1934 Act. Formally titled the Public Company Accounting Reform and Investor Protection Act of 2002, the Sarbanes Oxley Act was adopted in response to the collapse of Enron, WorldCom, and several other major corporations. It focuses primarily on the accounting profession which sets the rules by which financial reports are prepared and which is responsible for auditing the reports of publicly traded companies to assure their accuracy. But the Sarbanes Oxley Act also includes many provisions that directly govern public companies and the stock exchanges.

3. Stock Exchange Listing Standards

In addition to state and federal law, a publicly traded company must comply with elaborate rules adopted by stock exchanges as a condition of being listed for trading. Stock exchange listing standards often impose requirements beyond those of state and federal law. For example, they typically require a stockholder vote in connection with the issuance of a significant number of new shares even though such a vote is not required by state law. Moreover, stock exchange rules require that the board of directors of all listed companies have an audit committee composed of independent (non officer) directors. The SEC has general regulatory authority over the stock exchanges and must approve any rule changes. Many of the reforms imposed by the Sarbanes Oxley Act take the form of instructions to the SEC to require the stock exchanges to adopt new rules in areas related to corporate governance, for example, the composition of the audit committee of the board of directors. Thus, although state law is the primary source of substantive corporation law, federal law has become increasingly significant in connection with the regulation of publicly traded companies.

4. State Securities Laws (Blue Sky Laws)

Every state has enacted statutes that regulate the public distribution of securities within that state. Many of these statutes are similar to, and overlap, the federal Securities Act of 1933. In 1996, Congress significantly reduced the overlap that traditionally existed between the federal securities acts and the state blue sky laws with passage of the National Securities Markets Improvement Act (NSMIA), which in essence preempts state securities laws to the extent that they impose duplicative regulation of securities offerings. State law continues to apply, however, in wholly intrastate offerings.

D. FUNCTIONAL CLASSIFICATION OF CORPORATIONS

The basic distinction underlying much of the law of corporations is between the *closely held corporation* and the *publicly held corporation*. While the same general corporation statutes are applicable to both classes of corporations, the problems and concerns are usually quite different and in most courses are discussed separately.

1. Closely Held Corporations

A closely held corporation is a corporation with most of the following attributes: It has a few stockholders, all or most of whom are usually active in the management of the business; there is no public market for its shares; its shares are subject to one or more contractual restrictions on transfer.

2. Publicly Held Corporations

A publicly held corporation is a corporation with most of the following attributes: Its shares are widely held by members of the general public and the overall number of stockholders is large; there is a public market for its shares; the corporation is subject to reporting and disclosure requirements under federal law.

3. Significance of the Distinction

While many publicly held corporations are relatively large in terms of assets and many closely held corporations are relatively small in terms of assets, the importance of the distinction is not size as much as the number of stockholders and the marketability of shares.

a. The presence or absence of a public market for the corporation's shares is the most important difference between the two types of corporations.

b. A second major difference is that in a closely held corporation, most of the stockholders are likely to be employed by the corporation while in a publicly held corporation, most of the stockholders are not connected with management and have only a limited say in the policies adopted by the corporation. As a result, ownership and control are likely to be separated in a publicly held corporation but closely interconnected in a closely held corporation.

c. A third difference is that the presence of public stockholders unconnected with the business of a publicly held corporation is thought to present a strong case for governmental regulation of internal affairs, while in a closely held corporation, there is usually thought to be only a relatively weak (or nonexistent) case for governmental regulation of the internal affairs of the corporation.

E. EFFICIENT MARKET THEORY

The *efficient capital market hypothesis* (ECMH) posits that prices move rapidly—indeed almost instantaneously—to reflect information about publicly traded securities. In an efficient market, there are many purchasers and sellers all seeking to make a profit. Traders seek to take advantage of information, using increasingly sophisticated analysis. The most commonly cited version of the ECMH is the semi-strong form, which posits that all public information is incorporated into security prices. The strong form of the ECMH posits that even nonpublic (inside) information is reflected quickly in security prices. The weak form of the ECMH posits only that it is impossible to predict the next change in price for a security on the basis of past changes.

1. Implications of the ECMH

A number of inferences, some of which are counter-intuitive, may be drawn from the ECMH:

a. Price movements are random in the absence of new market information. It is not possible to predict from a previous transaction whether the next transaction will be higher or lower.

b. Those who analyze historical changes in prices, often called technical analysts or chartists, are engaged in a futile and irrelevant exercise, because market price already incorporates that information. Moreover, because all public information is incorporated in the current price of the shares, one cannot systematically improve one's investment success by studying publicly available information about investment alternatives.

c. It is not possible to develop and apply a trading strategy that consistently outperforms the market. Large institutional investors cannot hope in the long run to perform better than the broad-based market indexes.

2. Judicial Recognition of the ECMH

The ECMH was accepted by the United States Supreme Court as creating a rebuttable presumption that investors relied on a false press release in *Basic Inc. v. Levinson*, 485 U.S. 224, 108 S.Ct. 978 (1988) by virtue of the fact that the false press release affected the market price and the investors in turn relied on the fairness of the market price. This doctrine is usually referred to as the fraud on the market theory. The ECMH has also been cited and relied upon by the Securities & Exchange Commission and lower federal courts.

F. STATE COMPETITION FOR CORPORATIONS

Since the late 1800s the states have competed to attract businesses to incorporate under their statutes. The undisputed winner of this competition is the state of Delaware. The incorporation business provides filing fees and tax revenues for the state, fees for members of the local bar, and other economic benefits. More than half of the fortune 500 corporations are incorporated in Delaware. Over one-third of all the corporations listed on the New York Stock Exchange are incorporated in Delaware. Every year several publicly held corporations incorporated in other states reincorporate in Delaware. There are few (if any) examples of movement in the opposite direction. The Delaware Legislature and the Delaware Supreme Court are therefore important sources of corporation law.

1. Race to the Bottom

The earliest explanation of Delaware's success was that the DGCL was permissive and permitted management the maximum freedom to operate without constraint. It was also argued that the Delaware judiciary made decisions favorable to management in order to preserve the economic benefits of the incorporation business. In this view, put forth by Professor Cary in 1974, Delaware was leading a race for the bottom.

2. Race to the Top

The reason for the popularity and primacy of the state of Delaware may be explained partially by history, partially by the continued efforts by the bar of that state to provide an effective body of corporate law, and partially by the familiarity of corporate lawyers around the country with the DGCL. Also contributing to Delaware's primacy is the existence of a sophisticated judiciary and a sophisticated filing office that assures reasonable and knowledgeable decision making.

G. ALTERNATIVES TO THE CORPORATION

Publicly held businesses are almost always corporations. Traditional alternative business forms for closely held businesses are the partnership and limited partnership. A major disadvantage of these forms was that they did not provide limited liability for all participants. Since the 1980s a new business form, the limited liability company, has achieved wide acceptance. The LLC provides limited liability for all members, flexibility in internal operation similar to that provided by partnerships, and, of paramount importance, partnership tax treatment. It is possible that the LLC will become the predominant business form for newly created closely held businesses. But because there is usually a tax cost for converting from corporations to LLCs, it is likely that many closely held corporations will continue in existence indefinitely. Because the LLC provides limited liability for all members, it is probable that many corporate principles, such as piercing the corporate veil, will be applicable to LLCs. Similarly, in a manager managed LLC, principles applicable to directors of corporations may be applied by analogy. The extent to which principles of closely held corporations will be applied to this new business form is uncertain.

■ II. FORMING A CORPORATION

A. STATE OF INCORPORATION

The first question that must be resolved in forming a new corporation is what state should be the state of incorporation. For small enterprises planning to transact business primarily in one state, the corporation should usually be incorporated in that state. For larger enterprises transacting business in many states, incorporation in any one of several states is usually feasible; incorporation in Delaware is attractive for these businesses, though many remain incorporated in the state in which originated.

B. VARIATIONS IN STATUTORY REQUIREMENTS AND NOMENCLATURE

1. Statutory Requirements

It is essential to comply with the specific statutory requirements of the state chosen for the state of incorporation.

2. Nomenclature

The MBCA (1984) nomenclature is followed in most states. The document filed with the secretary of state is called articles of incorporation. Under earlier versions of the Model Act (and the statutes of many states), the secretary of state thereafter issues a document called a certificate of incorporation when he accepts the articles of incorporation for filing. In the MBCA (1984) (and the statutes of an increasing number of states), the paperwork is simplified by requiring the Secretary of State simply to issue a fee receipt as indicating acceptance of the filing.

a. In Delaware and several other states the document filed with the secretary of state is called a *certificate of incorporation*.

b. In some states, the document issued by the secretary of state is called a *charter*.

C. DOCUMENTS FILED IN THE OFFICE OF THE SECRETARY OF STATE

The basic requirement is that articles of incorporation conforming to the statutory requirements of the specific state be filed in a specified government office and be accompanied by the appropriate filing fee. The state official charged with accepting corporate filings is usually the Secretary of State, but some states use a different designation for the filing officer.

D. INCORPORATORS

Articles of incorporation are executed by one or more persons called *incorporators*. Historically, three incorporators who were natural persons were required and many states imposed special residency or other requirements for incorporators. The signatures of incorporators usually were required to be verified or acknowledged under oath before a notary public.

The principal function of incorporators is to execute the articles of incorporation and receive back the certificate of incorporation or receipt for the filing fee. They generally serve no other function, although in some states, the incorporators may also meet to complete the formation of the corporation.

a. In most states, only a single incorporator is required, who may be a corporation, trust, estate or partnership. There are usually no residency requirements for incorporators who are individuals. A secretary or employee of the law firm creating the corporation, a low level employee of a corporation service company, or any other person unconnected with the future business may serve as an incorporator.

b. Requirements of oaths, verifications, and seals have been eliminated in most states by statute or judicial decision.

c. In some states the incorporators meet to complete the formation of the corporation. In other states, initial directors named in the articles of incorporation complete the formation of the corporation. MBCA 2.02(b)(1) and 2.05(a) give each corporation the option of having the formation completed by the incorporators or by initial directors named in the articles of incorporation. Initial directors may be used if they will be the permanent board of directors and there is no objection to the public disclosure of their identity.

E. ARTICLES OF INCORPORATION

1. Mandatory Requirements

There is a trend toward simplifying the mandatory disclosure requirements for articles of incorporation. In many states the required information comfortably fits on a post card.

a. Older state statutes generally require the following minimum information to appear in the articles of incorporation:

- The name of the corporation.

- Its duration, which may be perpetual.

- Its purpose or purposes which may be, or include, the conduct of any lawful business.

- The stock it is authorized to issue.

- The name of its registered agent and the street address of its registered office.

- The names and addresses of its initial board of directors.

- The name and address of the incorporator or incorporators.

b. Virtually all corporations elect the duration to be perpetual and their purposes to be the conduct of any lawful business. As a result, many states provide that every corporation has perpetual duration unless a shorter period is chosen and a purpose of engaging in any lawful business unless a more limited purpose is set forth in the articles of incorporation.

2. Discretionary Provisions

In addition to the required minimum provisions, state statutes permit additional provisions to be included in the articles of incorporation at the election of the corporation.

a. State statutes typically provide that specified rules of corporate governance are automatically applicable unless the corporation elects to eliminate or modify them by specific provision in the articles of incorporation. These are called *opt out* provisions.

b. State statutes also may provide that a corporation may elect to make specific rules of corporate governance applicable by making specific provision in the articles of incorporation for the application of those rules. These are called *opt in* provisions.

c. State statutes authorize additional discretionary provisions to be placed either in the articles of incorporation or the bylaws. Typically bylaws may be amended either by the board of directors or by the stockholders. Many jurisdictions, however, limit the power of the board of directors to amend bylaws adopted by the stockholders. The decision to place a given provision in articles of incorporation or in bylaws thus affects the ease with which amendments may be made. Because of these technical differences, it is important to keep track of the way in which bylaws or articles of incorporation may be amended.

d. State statutes generally authorize corporations to include in the articles of incorporation provisions relating to corporate powers. Though it is unnecessary (and, indeed, undesirable) to refer to powers specifically and unambiguously granted to corporations by statute, references to specific powers may be helpful where the state statute is silent or unclear on whether corporations generally possess the specific power.

e. Special clauses relating to the purposes of a corporation are sometimes included in articles of incorporation even in states where the statute, like MBCA 3.01, automatically grants every corporation the power to engage in any lawful business.

3. Name

Under most state statutes, a corporate name (i) must contain a reference to the corporate nature of the entity (using the words Corporation, Incorporated, Inc. or a similar word or abbreviation), (ii) must not be the same as or deceptively similar to a name already in use or reserved for use, and (iii) must not imply that a corporation is engaged in a business in which corporations may not lawfully engage. The MBCA substitutes the test of distinguishable upon the records of the Secretary of State for the same or deceptively similar test. Filing authorities maintain lists of names that are reserved or currently in use (and hence unavailable) and also may have internal rules about name availability. As a result, it is desirable to check whether a specific name is available with the filing authority before it is used.

4. Duration

Most statutes authorize a corporation to have perpetual existence. Although it is possible to specify a shorter period of existence, it is almost never desirable to do so. A shorter period of existence creates the risk that the corporate existence may expire without renewal with uncertain rights and liabilities of participants thereafter.

5. Purpose

Most statutes authorize very general purposes clauses, e. g., the purpose of the corporation is to engage in any lawful business or businesses. The use of such clauses is a recent phenomenon. The MBCA and the statutes of several states go even further and provide that every corporation automatically has a broad purpose to engage in any lawful business unless a narrower purpose is specified in the articles of incorporation.

a. The nature of purposes clauses has evolved over a long period of time, reflecting varying attitudes of mistrust toward the corporation. They were formerly of much greater importance than they are today. Before 1875, most corporations were formed by special legislative enactment. Each purposes clause was separately developed in the legislative process.

b. Under early general incorporation statutes corporation could be formed only for a limited and specific purpose, for example, to operate a mill for the grinding of wheat, corn, and other grain. Corporations were usually limited to a single specific purpose, though ancillary powers might be implied from such a purposes clause.

c. Many early statutes restricted the power of corporations to amend articles of incorporation to broaden purposes clauses. Over time, state statutes were amended to permit corporations to include an unlimited number of specific purposes clauses. This quickly eliminated any significance that purpose clauses might have, and restrictions on amendments were gradually eliminated as the practice of using multiple purposes clauses grew. Now corporations with limited purposes clauses may freely amend them to include whatever purposes are permitted under the applicable state statute.

d. Today, there is usually no reason to have a purposes clause at all, and doctrines based on the premise that a corporation is formed for a specific purpose, such as *ultra vires* or implied powers, have little modern relevance. Nevertheless, purposes clauses may be necessary or desirable in some situations. A recitation of the purpose of a corporation may be required by a regulatory statute or agency if the corporation is to engage in a specific business. Some business people and investors may prefer that articles of incorporation provide information about the purpose of the corporation. A purposes clause that describes in general terms the business in which the corporation plans to engage may be coupled with a clause such as and any other lawful business in order to assure that the corporation may enter into new lines of business without going to the expense of amending its purposes clause.

e.   A limited purposes clause may be used today (despite broader statutory authorization) as a planning device or to limit corporate activities as a protection for investors. A corporation that pursues a business that exceeds such a limited purposes clause is acting *ultra vires.*

6.   Authorized Shares

The articles of incorporation must state the number of shares that the corporation is authorized to issue. If shares with special rights are to be issued (such as shares that carry a fixed dividend), those special rights must be described in detail. If no special rights are specified, each share is entitled to one vote per share on each matter put up to a stockholder vote and to a pro rata share of each distribution made to the stockholders generally. Such shares are called *common shares* or *common stock.*

a.   MBCA 2.02(a)(2) requires only that the corporation set forth the number of shares the corporation is authorized to issue. But MBCA 6.01(a) provides that if a corporation is to issue more than one class of shares, the articles of incorporation must prescribe the classes of shares and the number of shares of each class that the corporation is authorized to issue.

b.   The number of authorized shares is a ceiling not a floor. The corporation is under no obligation to issue the entire number of authorized shares, but it may not exceed that number unless it first amends the articles of incorporation to increase the number of authorized shares. Thus, it is standard practice to authorize significantly more shares than it is planned to issue immediately in order to assure the corporation flexibility in future financing. In many states, however, the annual fee paid to maintain a corporation (sometimes called a *franchise tax*) increases as the number of authorized shares increases.

c.   The statutes of about half of the states also require that the articles of incorporation set forth the par value of the authorized shares or a statement that the shares are issued without par value. Par value refers to the minimum price for which shares may be sold and is typically set very low: one cent per share is common but even lower amounts are often used. No par shares may usually be sold for any amount. Par value is a floor not a ceiling. A corporation may sell its shares for the highest price it can get, and indeed the board of directors may be held liable for issuing shares for inadequate consideration. Par value has other implications in connection with dividends and distributions. Some states that continue to require that par value be specified in the articles of incorporation have eliminated most of the restrictions that flow from it. For example, in some jurisdictions shares may be sold for any amount even if the amount is less than par value.

d. Most states do not require any provision in the articles of incorporation authorizing the corporation to issue debt securities except to the extent that such securities may be convertible into shares.

7. Registered Office and Agent

The registered office and registered agent must be specified in the articles of incorporation. They serve the purposes of providing a location where the corporation may be found for service of process, tax notices, and the like and a person on whom process may be served. State statutes require filings to reflect changes in the registered office or registered agent. Corporation service companies serve as registered agents for many corporations. MBCA 5.03 addresses how a registered agent may resign. MBCA 5.02(b) also sets forth a simplified procedure in the event that case the corporation service company moves its office to another location. This procedure avoids the need for each of the company's clients to file a change of registered address.

F. COMPLETING FORMATION

The filing of articles of incorporation is only the first step in forming a corporation. In most jurisdictions the existence of the corporation begins at the moment of the filing of the articles of incorporation. A filed copy of the articles of incorporation is deemed to be conclusive proof of corporate existence against any challenge to corporate existence (other than by the attorney general of the state of incorporation). Nevertheless, the law of most states provides that an organizational meeting *shall* be held following the filing of the articles of incorporation. For example, the MBCA 2.05 provides that after incorporation: (1) if initial directors are named in the articles of incorporation, the initial directors shall hold an organizational meeting, at the call of a majority of the directors, to complete the organization of the corporation by appointing officers, adopting bylaws, and carrying on any other business brought before the meeting; (2) if initial directors are not named in the articles, the incorporator or incorporators shall hold an organizational meeting at the call of a majority of the incorporators: (i) to elect directors and complete the organization of the corporation; or (ii) to elect a board of directors who shall complete the organization of the corporation. These actions may be taken without a meeting in most states if all of the directors or incorporators sign written consents describing the actions taken. If a meeting is held, it is common for the lawyer handling the formation of the corporation to prepare minutes of the meeting in advance and to use them as a script for the actual meeting.

1. Additional Steps

Lawyers generally are expected to complete the formation of a corporation on behalf of a client. The following additional steps may be necessary to complete the formation of a corporation:

- Prepare bylaws.

- Prepare minutes of the various organizational meetings, including waivers of notice or consents to action without formal meetings.

- Obtain a minute book and seal.

- Obtain blank share certificates and make sure they are properly prepared and issued for the consideration specified for those shares.

- Prepare stockholders' agreement, if any.

- Obtain necessary tax identification numbers and comply with other state and federal legal requirements.

- Determine whether the S Corporation tax election should be made, and, if so, make that election.

- Make sure the directors and officers understand the nature of their duties and responsibilities.

These steps may require additional meetings or signatures of the incorporators, the board of directors or the stockholders. It is customary to act by written consent rather than actually conducting meetings.

2. Consequences of Failure to Complete Formation

The consequences of a partial formation of a corporation usually arise in the context of a suit against officers, directors, or stockholders seeking to hold them personally liable for an obligation incurred in the name of the corporation. Although the organizational meeting is mandatory under a literal reading of the statutes of many states, failure to hold the meeting does not affect the existence of the corporation which begins with the filing of the articles of incorporation. Thus, it is unlikely that failure to hold an organizational meeting carries any negative consequences. *See In re Whatley*, 874 F.2d 997 (5th Cir. 1989) A number of cases hold that no personal liability is created so long as articles of incorporation were properly filed. *See Moe v. Harris*, 172 N.W. 494 (Minn.1919). If personal liability is imposed after the filing of articles of incorporation, it is likely to be based either on a contract or other action for the benefit of the corporation that occurred before the filing of the articles of incorporation (promoter liability) or as a result of piercing the corporate veil. Both are discussed in detail in subsequent chapters. On the other hand, failure to hold the organization meeting may be viewed as a breach of duty on the part of the directors or cited for the proposition that an officer or other agent of the corporation was not authorized to act on behalf of the corporation.

G. INITIAL CAPITALIZATION

Prior to 1970, many states required that a corporation have a minimum amount of capital (often $1,000 in cash or property) before it could commence doing business.

1. Current Trend

The modern trend is clearly in the direction of eliminating such requirements. Most states today have eliminated all minimum capitalization requirements. The theory is that minimum capitalization requirements are arbitrary and unrelated to the true capital needs of the corporation, and therefore do not provide meaningful protection to creditors.

2. Failure to Meet Minimum Initial Capital Requirements

In states that retain minimum capitalization requirements, directors are usually personally liable if business is commenced without the required minimum capital. This liability is limited to the difference between the minimum required capitalization and the amount of capital actually contributed.

a. A few early state statutes were construed to impose unlimited liability on directors for all debts incurred before the minimum capitalization is paid in.

b. There is no requirement that a corporation *maintain* any specified minimum capital after incorporation.

H. BYLAWS

The bylaws of a corporation are a set of rules for governing the internal affairs of the corporation. They are typically adopted as part of the formation of a new corporation, and generally may be modified thereafter either by the board of directors or by the stockholders subject to (1) limitations on the ability of the directors to change bylaws adopted by the stockholders and (2) supermajority requirements that may be imposed in the case of bylaws that themselves require a supermajority for certain actions. MBCA 10.20 – 10.22.

1. Legal Effect of Bylaws

Bylaws are binding on intra-corporate matters. They may be viewed as a contract between the corporation and its members, or as a set of binding internal rules of governance. Amendments to the bylaws that have the effect of changing the rules in the middle of a controversy may be found to be invalid even if appropriate procedures have been followed. For example, if the board of directors attempts to change a bylaw that permits 10% of the stockholders to call a special meeting to increase the requirement to 20% (having already received a proper demand signed by 10% of the stockholders), the amendment is probably ineffective even if duly adopted. *See Schnell v. Chris–Craft Industries, Inc.,* 285 A.2d 437 (Del., 1971); *Blasius Industries, Inc. v. Atlas Corporation,* 564 A.2d 651 (Del. Ch. 1988). In addition, bylaws that restrict the discretion of the board of directors to manage the corporation may be held to be invalid. *See Quickturn Design Systems, Inc. v. Shapiro,* 721 A.2d 1281 (Del. 1998).

2. Practical Effect of Bylaws

Bylaws essentially are an operating manual of basic rules for the conduct of the ordinary business of the corporation. They may be relied upon by the corporate officers as a checklist in administering the affairs of the corporation.

a. Corporate officers and directors are likely to be more conversant with the bylaws than the articles of incorporation.

b. Procedural matters and mandatory provisions that appear in the articles of incorporation relating to corporate governance should normally also appear in the bylaws.

I. CORPORATE POWERS

MBCA 3.02 provides that every corporation has the same powers as an individual to do all things necessary or convenient to carry out its business and affairs, including without limitation a list of specific powers. Most states have an enumeration of specific powers but without the quoted, broadening language, which was drawn from the California statute.

1. Enumerated Powers

Every state statute enumerates general powers that every corporation possesses. Generally, it is unnecessary and undesirable to list these powers in the articles of incorporation. The traditional enumerated powers possessed by corporations under modern statutes include the power:

- To sue and be sued.

- To have a corporate seal.

- To purchase, receive, lend, sell, invest, convey and mortgage personal and real property.

- To make contracts, borrow and lend money, and guarantee the indebtedness of third persons.

- To conduct its business within or without the state.

- To elect or appoint officers or agents, define their duties, and fix their compensation.

- To purchase shares or interests in, or obligations of, any other entity.

- To make charitable, scientific or education contributions or donations for the public welfare.

- To be a partner or manager of a partnership or other venture.

- To make and alter bylaws for the administration and regulation of its internal affairs.

- To indemnify directors and officers against liabilities imposed on them while acting on behalf of the corporation, and to provide liability insurance for them.

MBCA 3.02(15) also permits a corporation to make payments or donations, or do any other act, not inconsistent with law, that furthers the business and affairs of the corporation. This power permits corporations to make political donations or contributions to influence elections to the extent permitted by state law.

2. Acts in Excess of Powers

If a corporation does an act which it does not have power to do, it is acting *ultra vires*.

J. ULTRA VIRES

The phrase *ultra vires* means beyond the power. It is used to describe acts that exceed the stated purposes of the corporation or restrictions on the power of the board of directors. See California Public Employees' Retirement System v. Coulter, 2002 WL 31888343 (Del.Ch.2002).

1. Common Law

The early common law view was that an *ultra vires* transaction was void because the corporation lacked the power to enter into the transaction. Such a doctrine, however, led to potentially undesirable results and was gradually modified:

a. A transaction that was purely executory might be enjoined if it was *ultra vires* with respect to either party.

b. If the transaction was wholly executed by both parties, the transaction could not be attacked on the ground of *ultra vires*. *Herbert v. Sullivan*, 123 F.2d 477 (1st Cir.1941).

c. If the transaction was partially executed, *ultra vires* might be raised, but doctrines of estoppel, unjust enrichment, or fairness might mitigate the strict common law view. *Goodman v. Ladd Estate Co.*, 427 P.2d 102 (Ore.1967).

d. An *ultra vires* transaction might be ratified by all the stockholders. See *Lurie v. Arizona Fertilizer & Chemical Co.*, 421 P.2d 330 (Ariz.1966) (corporation entering partnership.)

e. Generally, the defense of *ultra vires* is not available to a corporation in a suit based on tort or in a prosecution for criminal conduct.

f. Directors and officers causing the corporation to enter into *ultra vires* transactions were not automatically liable for losses suffered thereby, although the fact that the conduct was *ultra vires* might cause courts to be more willing to pierce the corporate veil or otherwise impose personal liability on the stockholders. *See Lurie v. Arizona Fertilizer & Chemical Co.*, 421 P.2d 330 (Ariz.1966).

g. The attorney general of the state may enjoin corporations engaging in *ultra vires* transactions, seek a writ of *quo warranto*, or bring a suit to dissolve the corporation. As a practical matter, such actions are extremely rare.

2. Statutory Law

The *ultra vires* doctrine has been narrowly confined by statute. For example, MBCA 3.04 provides that the validity of a corporate action may not be challenged on the ground that the corporation lacks to act, except (1) in a proceeding by a stockholder against the corporation to enjoin the act, (2) in a proceeding by the corporation, directly, derivatively, or through a receiver, trustee, or other legal representative, against an incumbent or former director, officer, employee, or agent of the corporation, or (3) in a proceeding by the attorney general.

K. FOREIGN CORPORATIONS

Corporations that do business in one state but that are formed under the laws of another state are called as *foreign corporations*. Corporations formed under the law of foreign countries are also called foreign corporations, but the discussion here focuses primarily on issues of interstate commerce. The various states are required to recognize each other's corporations under the full faith and credit clause of the Constitution. But a state also has the constitutional right to regulate foreign corporations doing business within its borders. Thus, every state has a procedure by which a foreign corporation may qualify to do business in that state. But a state may not exclude foreign corporations from entering into transactions with its citizens in interstate commerce. Thus, the question of what constitutes doing business is an important one.

1. Qualification to Transact Business

A foreign corporation qualifies to transact business by obtaining a certificate of authority to transact business in the state.

2. Qualification Requirement

Qualification is required when the foreign corporation's local business activities are such that it is deemed to be transacting business in the foreign state. Transactions involving interstate commerce are not considered in this determination.

3. Effect of Qualification

A foreign corporation that qualifies to transact business in a state generally obtains the rights and privileges of domestic corporations formed within that state. MBCA 15.05(b).

4. Failure to Qualify

State statutes provide a variety of sanctions applicable to corporations that are required to qualify to transact business but fail to do so.

a. The corporation may be disqualified from suing in the courts of that state or from interposing the statute of limitations in litigation brought against it within the state. MBCA 15.02(a) (courts of state closed to proceedings brought by unqualified foreign corporations). State statutes usually prohibit a successor to an unqualified foreign corporation, or an assignee, to maintain a suit that would be barred if brought directly by the predecessor or assignor. MBCA 15.02(b). The MBCA and the statutes of many states provide that qualification after suit is filed permits the suit to be maintained. In other words, the closure of the courts is designed to assure qualification rather than being a sanction for failing to qualify.

b. The statutes of some states make unenforceable contracts entered into by a nonqualified corporation that should have qualified to transact business. This is a true sanction for failing to qualify. The MBCA does not contain such a sanction.

c. Most states impose a monetary penalty on the corporation for each year that it should have qualified to transact business but did not. MBCA 15.02(d). Some states also impose penalties on officers or directors who are within the state.

5. Amenability of Nonqualified Corporation to Suit

A corporation that is not required to qualify to transact business in the state may nevertheless have sufficient contacts with that state to be subject to service of process within that state on suits arising out of those contacts. *International Shoe Co. v. Washington,* 326 U.S. 310 (1945); *Helicopteros Nacionales de Colombia, S.A. v. Hall,* 466 U.S. 408 (1984).

6. Liability of Nonqualified Corporation to State Taxation

A corporation that is not required to qualify to transact business in the state may also be subject to taxation in that state but the tax must be commensurate with the corporation's activities in that state. Requirements include a sufficient nexus with the taxing state, fair relationship of tax to benefits received, nondiscrimination against interstate commerce and fair apportionment. *Mobil Oil Corp. v. Commissioner* 445 U.S. 425, 100 S.Ct. 1223 (1980). The Federal Interstate Income Act of 1959 limits the application of state income tax laws to foreign corporations where the only contact with the state is solicitation of orders in interstate commerce.

7. Internal Affairs Rule

Litigation involving corporate issues may be filed in states other than the state of incorporation. The general rule is that the internal affairs of a corporation are governed by the laws of the state of incorporation. This rule is statutory in many states. MBCA 15.05(c).

a. The internal affairs rule means that many issues of Delaware law are resolved in federal or state courts other than in Delaware.

b. New York and California have adopted statutes that require courts to apply domestic principles to a limited number of issues to corporations that are incorporated in other states but have dominant economic contacts with New York of California.

c. New York requires corporations doing business in New York to be subject to New York statutory provisions imposing liability on directors for cash or property distributions to stockholders that is unlawful under New York law. NYBCL 1315 – 1319.

d. California requires corporations incorporated in other states that have their predominant business activities in California and more than half of their outstanding shares held by persons resident in California to provide procedural protections to stockholders, including cumulative voting, permitting removal of directors without cause, defining the directors' duty of care, and providing for dissenters' rights in specified situations. Corporations subject to these provisions are sometimes called pseudo-foreign corporations. CCC 2115.

e. The constitutionality of these statutes has never been definitively resolved. In recent decisions by the Supreme Court, the power of the state of incorporation to regulate the affairs of domestic corporations has been cast in near constitutional terms.

8. **Domestication and Conversion**

The MBCA was amended in 2002 to add provisions permitting domestication and conversion into other entities without merger. Domestication refers to a change in the state of incorporation and is so-called because from the point of view of the new state of incorporation the corporation is converted from a foreign corporation to a domestic corporation. In the absence of a statute providing for this process, the usual practice is for the foreign corporation to merge with a newly formed domestic corporation which survives the merger. The new provisions eliminate the need for a merger and accomplish domestication by means of a simple filing, thus avoiding the dangers that may be associated with using the merger statute (such as triggering appraisal rights). Similarly, the provisions relating to conversion permit a corporation to convert into a partnership or LLC (or other non corporation) or into a non profit corporation, again without the need for a merger. Such transactions may also be accomplished by merger, although the possibility of a merger between different forms of organization is a relatively recent development. As with domestication, the provisions relating to conversion provide a simpler alternative for internal changes in corporate governance as to which the use of the merger statute is somewhat strained.

■ III. PREINCORPORATION TRANSACTIONS

A. PROMOTERS

A *promoter* is someone who undertakes to form a new business. Although the term *promoter* sometimes has a pejorative connotation, promoters are often shrewd, visionary individuals who serve important social and economic functions. In promoting a new venture, a promoter may arrange for the necessary business assets and personnel so that the new business may function effectively. This may include obtaining or renting a plant, assembling work and sales forces, finding sources of raw materials and supplies, finding retail outlets, making long term commitments of various types, and so forth. A promoter may also obtain the necessary capital to finance the venture. The sources of initial capital include (i) equity capital contributed by investors, (ii) loans from third parties, either secured or unsecured, and (iii) loans from the investors supplying the equity capital.

B. PROMOTER CONTRACTS

Promoters may enter into contracts on behalf of the venture being promoted either before or after articles of incorporation have been filed. Most problems are created by preincorporation contracts because under modern statutes the corporate existence begins when articles of incorporation are accepted for filing, and contracts entered into by the promoter in the corporate name after that date will normally bind only the corporation. The legal consequences of preincorporation contracts entered into by promoters vary, depending in part on the form of the contract itself.

1. Contracts in the Name of a Corporation to Be Formed

In contracts of this type, the promoter enters into a preincorporation contract which on its face shows that the corporation has not yet been formed. Such a contract may be analyzed in several different ways, depending on the facts and the context, which have widely different legal consequences.

a. The most traditional analysis is that the promoter is personally liable on the contract and is not relieved of liability if the corporation is later formed and adopts the contract. Assuming that the corporation is formed and adopts the contract, both the promoter and the corporation are thereafter liable on the contract. Presumably the promoter may look to the newly formed corporation for indemnification if the contract benefits the corporation but the promoter remains personally liable.

b. A related analysis is that the promoter is personally liable on the contract, but is thereafter relieved of liability if the corporation is later formed and adopts the contract. This is an example of a novation.

c. Another possible analysis that leads to a diametrically different result is that the promoter is not personally liable on the contract because the third party intended to deal only with the corporation. While the corporation may become liable if it is later formed and enters into the contract, no one is liable under this analysis until that event occurs.

d. Another possible analysis is that the promoter is not personally liable on the contract but has agreed to use best efforts to cause the corporation to be formed and to adopt the contract. The promoter's best efforts promise may be consideration for the third party's promise under the contract. This differs from (c) in that both parties have incurred liability: the promoter may be liable on the promise if no steps are taken to form the corporation though not liable on the contract itself.

e. The question of which of these four alternatives is the appropriate one to apply in a specific case depends on the intention of the parties. Where the intention is not clearly expressed uncertainty may exist as to the appropriate legal analysis. Most cases find the promoter personally liable on one theory or another. A lawyer should normally recommend that the contract specify who is liable and under what circumstances.

2. Contracts in the Corporate Name

In these cases, a contract is entered into in the name of a corporation even though it has not been formed. One or both of the parties to the corporation erroneously believe the corporation has been formed. The factual patterns under this heading may vary because the contract may be entered into at various times during the incorporation process. For example, the contract may be entered into when no steps at all toward incorporation have been taken, or it may be entered into after articles of incorporation have been prepared but not filed, or after the articles of incorporation have been mailed to the secretary of state but before the certificate of incorporation is issued.

a. If a promoter represents that she is acting on behalf of a corporation when she knows no steps have been taken to form a corporation, she is usually personally liable on the contract. This result may be justified on various grounds. A person who purports to act as an agent for a nonexistent principal is personally liable on the contract. Or a person who purports to act as an agent for a principal warrants his authority.

b. The common law developed concepts of *de facto* corporations and *de jure* corporation to deal with preincorporation problems. In a suit brought by a private plaintiff against a promoter, the conclusion that either a *de facto* or a *de jure* corporation existed effectively absolved the promoter of liability.

c. A *de jure* corporation has sufficiently complied with the incorporation requirements so that a corporation is legally in existence for all purposes. A *de jure* corporation exists if there is compliance with all mandatory statutory requirements; failure to comply with less important require-ments (called directory requirements) do not affect the *de jure* status of a corporation. The distinction between mandatory and directory require-ments is a matter of degree. *People v. Ford,* 128 N.E. 479 (Ill.1920) holds (over one dissent) that the statutory requirement of a seal is a directory requirement. In evaluating this case it should be noted that the contrary conclusion would have called into question the validity of over 4,300 corporations.

d. A *de facto* corporation is a corporation that is partially but defectively or incompletely formed. It is sufficiently formed, however, to be immune from attack by everyone but the state. Because virtually all litigation in this area involves private plaintiffs rather than the state, a holding that a corporation is *de facto* is virtually as good as a holding that it is *de jure.* The traditional test of *de facto* existence is threefold: (1) there is a valid statute under which the corporation might incorporate; (2) there has been a good faith or colorable attempt to comply with the statute; and (3) There has been actual use of the corporate privilege.

e. Most states now have statutes that substitute a more objective test that upon the issuance of the certificate of incorporation the corporate existence shall begin. MBCA (1969) § 50. MBCA 2.03(a) is similar. It provides that unless a delayed effective date is specified, the corporate existence begins when the articles of incorporation are filed. Under these provisions it would appear that all transactions entered into in the corporate name after the certificate of incorporation has been issued or the articles of incorporation filed would be corporate obligations.

f. Several state statutes contain a provision based on MBCA (1969) § 139 that addresses the status of preincorporation obligations: All persons who assume to act as a corporation without authority so to do shall be jointly and severally liable for all debts and liabilities incurred or arising as a result thereof. Some courts have read § 139 literally to provide that the issuance of the certificate of incorporation is the bright line that distinguishes the corporation from the noncorporation. Under this reasoning, personal liability automatically exists on all obligations that antedate the time the secretary of state issues the certificate of incorporation.

g. Under MBCA (1969) § 139, some courts have distinguished between active participants and passive investors with the usual result that; the latter are not personally liable on transactions entered into before the certificate of incorporation is issued. This view is based on the statutory language referring only to persons who assume to act on behalf of the corporation as being liable under § 139. *Timberline Equipment Co., Inc. v. Davenport*, 514 P.2d 1109 (Ore. 1973).

h. Some statutes contain provisions making the issuance of the certificate of incorporation conclusive of the existence of the corporation but do not contain language similar to that appearing in MBCA (1969) § 139, referring to persons who assume to act on behalf of the corporation. In these states, an argument may be made that the traditional common law concept of the *de facto* corporation continues to exist because the statute does not purport to deal explicitly with precorporation transactions.

i. MBCA 2.04 provides that all persons purporting to act as or on behalf of a corporation, knowing there was no incorporation under this Act, are jointly and severally liable for all liabilities created while so acting. This provision is consistent with the results reached in most of the above cases.

j. Some cases have applied a concept of *corporation by estoppel* that appears to be independent of both statutes and the common law *de facto* corporation concept.

k. If carried to its logical conclusion, the concept of corporation by estoppel would permit stockholders to obtain the benefits of limited liability simply by consistently representing the corporation's existence. Notions of public policy and the need to preserve the incorporation process therefore dictate that only persons who honestly but erroneously believe that articles have been filed should be able to take advantage of the corporation by estoppel concept. MBCA 2.04 accepts this view.

l. The failure to complete the formation of the corporation usually is discovered long after the transaction in question. Discovery following the commencement of litigation usually leads to information that reveals that the corporation was not fully formed when the transaction was entered into. Some courts have accepted the windfall argument and refuse to impose personal liability even in circumstances where no steps toward incorporation have been taken. *Frontier Refining* Co. *v. Kunkel's Inc.*, 407 P.2d 880 (Wyo.1965).

m. This area of the law of corporations reflects the interplay of conflicting general principles. In such situations, unpredictability of result and irreconcilable precedents often result. The statutes and common sense say no certificate of incorporation, no corporation. Under this approach there should be unlimited personal liability for all obligations entered into in the corporate name before the corporation is formed. But where third persons deal with an apparent corporation, they receive a windfall if they may subsequently hold promoters or investors liable.

3. Liability of Corporation on Promoter's Contracts

The corporation is not automatically liable on contracts made for its benefit before it came into existence. Rather, a newly formed corporation may accept or reject preincorporation contracts.

a. Technically, an acceptance of a preincorporation contract by a corporation is an adoption not a ratification. Ratification assumes that the principal was in existence when the agent entered into the unauthorized contract. When a principal ratifies a contract, the principal is deemed bound on the contract from the time the contract formed. Because a corporation is not in existence when a preincorporation contract formed, ratification is not the proper concept. Some courts, however, loosely use the word ratification to describe the corporate adoption of a preincorporation contract.

b. This rule allows subsequent investors in some cases to review promoters' contracts and reject those that seem improvident. The rule works unevenly however, because the time for adoption may occur before the outside investors appear or while the promoter is the dominant force in the newly formed corporation.

c. Adoption may be express or implied and presupposes knowledge of the terms of the contract. A recovery in quasi contract is normally available where benefits are accepted even if the contract has not been adopted.

d. Where the contract relates to services leading to the formation of the corporation (, the lawyer's fee for forming the corporation), mere existence of the corporation does not constitute adoption of the contract. The lawyer may recover in quasi contract for the reasonable value of his services.

4. Relationship Between Promoter's Liability and Corporate Adoption

Generally, corporate adoption of a contract releases the promoter from further liability if the parties expressly agree that a novation will occur.

a. Williston argued that a novation is almost always contemplated on the theory that the third person usually intends to look solely to the corporation after it is formed.

b. This complete novation theory may lead to promoters deciding to form shell corporations solely to escape personal liability even after it is clear that the promotion will fail. In other words, the complete novation theory permits a promoter to obtain an option at no cost, a deal to which the contracting party would not likely agree.

C. FIDUCIARY DUTIES

Promoters of a venture owe fiduciary duties to each other and to the corporation. The duty is essentially the same as the duties owed by a partner to a partnership or partners. A duty of full disclosure is owed to subsequent investors.

1. **To Corporation**

    After the corporation is formed it may obtain from the promoter any benefits or rights the promoter obtained on its behalf.

2. **To Fellow Promoters**

    Promoters are essentially partners in the promotion of the venture, and any benefits or rights one promoter obtains must be shared with co-promoters.

3. **To Subsequent Investors**

    A major issue relating to promoters' fiduciary duties is the extent to which *subsequent* stockholders or investors are protected by fiduciary duties.

    a. According to the Massachusetts rule the corporation may attack the earlier transaction if the subsequent sale to public investors was contemplated at the time of the earlier transaction. *Old Dominion Copper Mining & Smelting* Co. *v. Bigelow,* 89 N.E. 193 (Mass.1909).

    b. According to the federal rule the corporation may not attack the earlier transaction because all the stockholders at the time consented to the transaction. *Old Dominion Copper Mining & Smelting* Co. *v. Lewisohn,* 210 U.S. 206, 28 S.Ct. 634 (1908).

    c. These rules were both established in the early 1900s. The Massachusetts rule has been followed more widely than the Federal rule.

    d. Arguably, the real issue in these cases is whether there was full disclosure of the transaction at the time the public investors decided to make their investments. If there was full disclosure, the public investors should have reduced the price they agreed to pay for the shares to reflect the transactions in question.

    e. Cases of this nature usually are litigated today as disclosure or securities fraud cases rather than as promoters fraud cases. Cases such as these, together with the market crash of 1929 and the Great Depression, provided much of the original impetus for the passage of federal Securities Act of 1933.

4. To Creditors

Fiduciary concepts may also protect creditors against unfair or fraudulent transactions by promoters. *Frick v. Howard*, 126 N.W.2d 619 (Wis.1964). Most of these transactions also may be attacked on the ground they constitute fraud on creditors.

D. AGREEMENT TO FORM CORPORATION

A preincorporation agreement to create a corporation is enforceable to the same extent as any other contract. Today promotions are usually cast in the form of such a contract.

E. PREINCORPORATION SUBSCRIPTIONS

A preincorporation subscription is a written promise by a person prior to the formation of a corporation to purchase a specific number of shares of the corporation at a specific price after the corporation is formed. Such promises may be obtained by promoters as part of their capital-raising efforts.

1. Use of Preincorporation Subscriptions

Historically most capital for new ventures was raised through preincorporation subscriptions. Their public use was made impractical by the enactment of the securities acts which impose registration requirements on both the subscription itself and on the subsequent sale of shares. Subscription agreement may still be used in connection with the formation of a closely held corporation, though simple contractual agreements are now more common.

2. Enforceability in Absence of Statute

Preincorporation subscriptions may be obtained independently from each other. If so, promises of individual subscribers are not likely to be viewed as made in consideration of the promises of other subscribers and, because the corporation has not yet been formed, such subscriptions may not be enforceable as contracts. As a result, in the absence of statute, a subscriber may withdraw a subscription at any time before it is accepted by the corporation.

3. Statutory Treatment of Preincorporation Subscriptions

The statutes of most states provide that preincorporation subscriptions are irrevocable for a stated period, often six months, without regard to whether they are supported by consideration. *See* MBCA 6.20(a). The six month period may be extended or shortened by specific provision in the subscription itself.

■ IV. PIERCING THE CORPORATE VEIL

When a court refuses to recognize the separate existence of a valid corporation and holds the stockholders personally liable for the obligations of the corporation, it is said to *pierce the corporate veil*. The phrase is often abbreviated to PCV. Piercing is a remedy that is asserted by *creditors* of the corporation—usually against stockholders—when the corporation is unable or unwilling to make good on its obligations whether arising in contract or tort. An aggrieved stockholder has other remedies available against fellow stockholders who may have extracted excessive benefits from the corporation. A stockholder may sue derivatively for the benefit of the corporation for the return of an improper distribution or may sue directly on the theory that the distribution should have been *pro rata* to all stockholders. On the other hand, a stockholder may also be a creditor of the corporation.

A. GENERAL CONSIDERATIONS

Many courts state that the general rule is that the corporation is separate and independent from its stockholders and that its separate existence should be recognized. *Billy v. Consolidated Machine Tool Corp.,* 412 N.E.2d 934 (N.Y. 1980); *Port Chester Elec. Corp. v. Atlas,* 357 N.E.2d 983 (N.Y. 1976). Courts also state that one should be reluctant to pierce, *Eagle v. Benefield–Chappell, Inc.,* 476 So.2d 716 (Fla.App.1985), or that piercing should be applied only with great caution and in extreme circumstances. *Amason v. Whitehead,* 367 S.E.2d 107 (Ga.App.1988); *Farmers Warehouse v. Collins,* 137 S.E.2d 619 (Ga.1964).

1. Nature of Liability

Although it is often assumed that piercing is more common in nonconsensual tort cases in which the plaintiff has had little or no practical ability to conduct a credit check of the defendant in advance, empirical studies of judicial opinions have found that it is in fact somewhat more common for piercing to be ordered in cases based on contractual relationships. On the other hand, most litigated cases involve only the sufficiency of a complaint to withstand a motion to dismiss rather than review of a judgment on the merits. Settlement statistics may reflect that tort cases are settled more often than contract cases.

2. Publicly Held and Closely Held Corporations

Piercing is exclusively a doctrine applicable to closely held corporations. But piercing may be applied to subsidiary corporations owned by a publicly held parent corporation. However, in these cases the separate existence of the subsidiary and not the parent is being ignored. A one person corporation is treated no differently than other corporations in piercing cases. While piercing is probably more likely to occur in small corporations with one or two stockholders than in corporations with more stockholders, essentially the same tests are applied, and in appropriate cases the separate existence of one person corporations will be recognized.

3. Sibling Corporations

Piercing cases are not limited to the liability of individual or corporate stockholders for corporate obligations. In appropriate cases, the separate existence of related corporations—corporations with common stockholders— may be ignored so that the two corporations are treated as a single entity. This may occur even though the common stockholders are not found to be personally liable for corporate obligations under a piercing theory. These cases are discussed in more detail below.

4. Motive for Incorporation

Motive is unimportant in the sense that the separate corporate existence may be recognized even though the corporation was formed solely for the purpose of avoiding unlimited liability.

5. Inactive Stockholders

Piercing is not an all-or-nothing principle. In appropriate cases, active stockholders may be held liable for corporate debts on a piercing theory but inactive stockholders may be found not to be personally liable on such obligations.

6. **Estoppel**

Piercing is basically an equitable doctrine available to creditors of the corporation. It generally is not available to the corporation itself or its stockholders. Similarly, piercing may not be available to a bankruptcy trustee who stands in the shoes of the corporation and may assert claims on the name of the corporation. Individual creditors may, however, be able to assert a claim under the piercing doctrine even through a bankruptcy trustee cannot do so. *Stodd v. Goldberger*, 141 Cal.Rptr. 67 (Cal.App.1977).

B. LEGAL TESTS

The law relating to piercing is quite confused. There is no widely agreed test. Rather the courts tend to refer to the goals such as to prevent fraud or oppression, to avoid illegality, or to achieve equity. These tests are result-oriented and give little indication of the circumstances in which a court will refuse to recognize the separate existence of a corporation. There are several factors that tend to be cited in piercing cases.

1. **Alter Ego and Instrumentality**

The phrase *alter ego* literally means *other self.* Courts hold that piercing is proper under the alter ego doctrine where (a) such unity of ownership and interest exists between corporation and stockholder that the corporation has ceased to have separate existence, and (b) recognition of the separate existence of the corporation sanctions fraud or leads to an inequitable result. A corporation becomes the *instrumentality* of a stockholder where there has been an excessive exercise of control by the stockholder that leads to wrongful or inequitable conduct that in turn causes the plaintiff a loss.

2. **Misrepresentation and Fraud**

Piercing may be ordered if information about the corporation is misrepresented or if a third party is in some way misled or tricked into dealing with the corporation. An affirmative misrepresentation by a stockholder might also constitute actionable fraud independent of the piercing doctrine.

3. **Personal Guaranty**

Piercing may also be ordered if the stockholder orally promises to be personally responsible for corporate obligations under circumstances where it is inequitable to permit the stockholder to rely on the statute of frauds. Except for the possible applicability of the statute of frauds, enforcement of a personal guaranty is not really an example of piercing. Indeed, it is quite common for creditors such as banks to require a personal guaranty when dealing with a small corporation.

4. Undercapitalization

Lack of adequate capitalization is a major factor in tort cases, but in most cases there is also some additional justification for piercing. If capital was originally adequate but has been reduced by business reverses, a piercing argument is likely to be rejected. A piercing argument is more likely to be accepted where the original capital is nominal or clearly inadequate in light of contemplated business risks.

a. Piercing is more likely to be ordered where the corporation is formed with minimal capital specifically to engage in hazardous activities that cause the injury. To recognize the separate corporate existence of a nominally capitalized (judgment proof) corporation engaged in a hazardous activity in effect shifts the risk of loss or injury to random members of the general public who happen to be injured by the activity.

b. Liability insurance should be viewed as the equivalent of capital for purposes of piercing in torts cases because such insurance provides readily available funds to tort victims. *Radaszewski v. Telecom Corp.*, 981 F.2d 305 (8th Cir.1992).

c. Inadequate or nominal capitalization should not usually be a factor in contract cases. Absent unusual circumstances, a contract creditor assumes the risk that the corporation will be unable to meet its obligations when dealing voluntarily with the corporation and in the absence of a personal guarantee from the stockholder. Indeed, the formation of a nominally capitalized corporation may be an integral part of a carefully devised plan by the parties to allocate the risk of loss. The courts should not change allocations of risks that are worked out by the parties in the absence of fraud or other abuse. In cases involving nonconsensual transactions (torts) there is usually no element of voluntary dealing. As a result, one cannot usually argue that the third person assumed the risk by dealing with a nominally capitalized corporation. *See Consumer's Co-op. of Walworth Co. v. Olsen*, 419 N.W.2d 211 (Wis.1988).

5. **Operation on the Edge of Insolvency**

   Piercing may be ordered if the corporation is operated so that it can never make a profit, or available funds are siphoned off to the stockholder without regard to the needs of the corporation, or it is operated so that it is always insolvent. *Iron City Sand & Gravel Div. v. West Fork Towing Corp.*, 298 F.Supp. 1091 (N.D.W.Va.1969); *DeWitt Truck Brokers, Inc. v. W Ray Flemming Fruit Co.*, 540 F.2d 681 (4th Cir.1976).

6. **Commingling and Confusion**

   Piercing may be ordered if the stockholder conducts business in such a way as to cause confusion between individual and corporate finances. *See Zaist v. Olson*, 227 A.2d 552 (Conn.1967).

7. **Artificial Division of Business Entity**

   In many PCV cases, an important factor is whether a single business is artificially divided into several different corporations to reduce exposure of assets to liabilities. The normal response to an artificial division of a single business entity should be to hold the entire entity responsible for the debts of the business rather than to hold the stockholders personally liable for such debts. One might also argue in such cases that the various related corporations are in partnership with each other and thus liable for the business debts of each other. Two or more corporations owned by a single stockholder or owned more or less proportionally by several stockholders are often referred to as *sibling corporations*. Such a relationship may be analyzed in a similar fashion as *parent and subsidiary* corporations discussed below.

8. **Mere Continuation**

   A situation that is closely related to artificial division may arise if a stockholder conducts a single business under a succession of corporations, abandoning one and forming the next whenever he needs a fresh start. Again, the logical result should be to hold the successor corporation liable for the debts of the predecessor corporation(s). But in some cases, the courts hold the stockholder personally liable, possibly on a theory of abuse or misuse of the corporate form. *See K.C. Roofing Center v. On Top Roofing, Inc.*, 807 S.W.2d 545 (Mo.App.1991).

9. **Failure to Follow Corporate Formalities**

   A piercing argument is somewhat more likely to be accepted if the plaintiff can show (in addition to other factors) failure to follow corporate formalities.

Many cases rely to some extent on the failure of the corporation and the stockholder to follow corporate formalities (such as holding an annual meeting or keeping proper minutes) as a basis for piercing. But it is unlikely that failure to follow corporate formalities alone will suffice as grounds for piercing unless failure to follow formalities (such as statutory restrictions on distributions) caused the loss. *See Zaist v. Olson,* 227 A.2d 552 (Conn.1967).

C. LIABILITY OF PARENT FOR OBLIGATIONS OF SUBSIDIARY

Many piercing cases involve corporations as stockholders. In other words, the issue involves the responsibility of a parent corporation for the actions of a subsidiary (or vice versa). Most publicly held corporations have numerous subsidiaries engaged in a variety of businesses. Subsidiaries are usually wholly owned by the parent corporation but they may also be partially owned. It is often stated that courts are more likely to pierce when the stockholder is itself a corporation than when the stockholder is an individual, but there is little empirical evidence supporting this assertion. Most courts appear to apply the same piercing principles to parent-subsidiary relationships as are applied to stockholders who are individuals. Still, with the continued growth of corporate groups in the future and the increased number of regulatory and environmental laws, it is possible that a unique set of principles for piercing in corporate groups will evolve.

1. Issues That May Arise

Piercing in the parent-subsidiary context may arise in several ways. The issue may be whether transactions between parent and subsidiary or between two subsidiaries must be recognized by third persons who are affected by the transaction.

a. The issue may involve a question of statutory or contract construction. For example, does the relevant statute or contract refer to the corporation or to the owner or operator of the business? Depending on the precise language of the statute or contract it may apply only narrowly to a single corporation or it may apply broadly to affiliated corporations.

b. It is common for a single corporation with several lines of business to separate the businesses by *dropping* the assets and liabilities of a particular business into a newly formed subsidiary. In some cases, shares in the newly formed corporation are then distributed (*spun off*) to the stockholders of the parent corporation with the result that there are now two separate corporations that over time may become wholly unrelated as a result of decisions by various stockholders to hold or sell parent or subsidiary stock. Often such *spin-offs* result in an increase in total stockholder wealth because the two corporations may have more focused competitive businesses. But such transactions may raise questions if one of the corporations is left with a greater share of the liabilities. *See HB Korenvaes Inv., L.P. v. Marriott Corp.*, 1993 WL 205040; 1993 WL 257422 (Del.Ch.). And if one of the corporations fails after the spin-off, the creditors may argue that the other corporation remains responsible for the excess liabilities of the failed corporation.

2. Confusion of Affairs

A parent corporation may be held liable for its subsidiary's obligations if it fails to maintain a clear separation between parent and subsidiary affairs. A failure to maintain a clear separation between affairs of different subsidiary corporations may result in the separate existence of those corporations being ignored as well. Conduct that may lead to parental liability includes: referring to the subsidiary as a department or division of the parent; mixing business affairs, such as using parental stationery to respond to inquiries addressed to the subsidiary; having common officers who do not clearly delineate the capacity in which they are acting; mixing assets, such as having the subsidiary sign a pledge of assets to secure parental indebtedness, transferring funds informally from one entity to the other without the formalities normally involved in a loan, or having a common bank account. *See Bernardin, Inc. v. Midland Oil Corp.*, 520 F.2d 771 (7th Cir.1975).

3. Permissible Activities

As long as affiliated corporations avoid commingling of affairs, a piercing argument should be rejected even though: one corporation owns all the shares of the corporation; the corporations have common officers or directors; the corporations file a consolidated tax return or report their earnings to their stockholders on a consolidated basis; the parent corporation maintains a cash management function by which all cash accounts are centralized to obtain the most favorable interest rates and minimize borrowing costs, so long as records are carefully kept and each subsidiary has immediate access to its funds as needed for its operations; the parent corporation provides centralized accounting and legal services for all subsidiaries, charging for such services on an even-handed and reasonable basis; the parent and subsidiary have a common office or share common office space so long as the terms of the arrangement are reasonable and the separate identities are maintained by appropriate signs, telephone listings, and the like; the board of directors of the subsidiary consists of employees of the parent, actions by employees of the subsidiary are reviewed by employees of the parent, and the organizational chart of the parent includes the subsidiary. *See Berger v. Columbia Broadcasting System, Inc.*, 453 F.2d 991 (5th Cir.1972).

4. Fraud or Injustice

Some cases have concluded that in a contract case a parent is liable for its subsidiary's liabilities only upon a showing of fraud or injustice. *Edwards Co., Inc. v. Monogram Industries, Inc.*, 730 F.2d 977 (5th Cir.1984).

D. ALTERNATIVES TO PIERCING

There are many ways other than piercing doctrine to hold individual stockholders liable for unsatisfied claims against a corporation.

1. As a matter of corporation law, a stockholder may be held liable to the corporation by statute for failure to contribute capital as agreed or for knowing receipt of an illegal dividend (including an illegal liquidating dividend following dissolution). A stockholder may also be held liable for mismanagement or misappropriation as a matter of fiduciary duty. Although these claims may ordinarily be asserted only by the corporation itself or a stockholder suing derivatively, a corporation that has failed to pay a valid obligation to a creditor is presumably bankrupt, and these claims of the corporation may be asserted by a bankruptcy trustee for the ultimate benefit of creditors.

2. In addition, recent case law suggests that the benefits of fiduciary duty extend to creditors in a corporation on the edge of insolvency. It may also be possible to argue in many cases that a stockholder exerted such control over a corporation as to make the corporation an agent under principles of agency law. Or it may be possible to argue that benefits extracted by a stockholder from a corporation constituted a fraudulent conveyance or transfer or a voidable preference under bankruptcy law.

3. There is also a growing body of case law in which buyers of assets and even lenders have been held liable for the unsatisfied obligations of the seller or borrower corporation.

4. The individual tortfeasor who actually caused the injury is personally liable whether or not he was acting as an agent of the corporation. If he was acting as a corporate agent, the corporation is also liable for the tort under the theory of *respondeat superior*. If the tortfeasor is also a corporate stockholder, officer or agent, he is liable because he is a tortfeasor and it is unnecessary to argue for piercing.

5. If the corporation may be viewed as the agent of a stockholder, the stockholder may be liable for corporate torts on a *respondent superior* theory. In a typical case, however, the tortfeasor is a judgment proof employee, the corporation is also unable to satisfy the claim, and attempts are made to hold stockholders personally liable on a piercing theory.

6. In some cases, actual domination and control of a subsidiary's affairs may be sufficient to justify piercing and hold the parent liable. *See Craig v. Lake Asbestos of Quebec, Ltd.*, 843 F.2d 145 (3d Cir.1988) (control found insufficient to hold parent liable for asbestos injury to employee of subsidiary.)

E. SUCCESSOR LIABILITY

Piercing of a sort may arise if a business is transferred from one corporation to another particularly by means of a sale of assets in which the seller corporation retains the long term liabilities of the business and where the seller stockholder then distributes the proceeds to himself.

1. Tests for Successor Liability

The courts generally recognize four situations in which a successor business may be held liable for the obligations of the transferor business:

a. Contract: The successor corporation agrees to assume the liabilities of the transferor.

b. Merger: The successor corporation assumes the liabilities of the transferor by operation of law.

c. Mere Continuation: The successor corporation is so similar to the old business (in terms of stock ownership, control, employees, etc.) that it is deemed to be the same business and is therefore liable for the obligations of the old business. (In such cases, there will not likely have been a formal transfer and the original business may remain in existence as a formal matter in order to bolster the argument that the two businesses are separate.)

d. Fraud: Fraud comes in many forms, but one example is the scenario above where the parties agree to transfer the business for what appears to be a bargain price. In effect, the parties conspire with each other to the detriment of future creditors. In a good faith transaction, the buyer will presumably seek some form of assurance from the seller that the proceeds will be held in escrow or insurance obtained so as to guard against subsequent allegations of fraud. Thus, the absence of any such assurance or efforts to enforce such provisions may be evidence of a conspiracy.

2. De Facto Merger

In some cases, the courts will resort to a theory known as the *de facto merger doctrine* and hold that the two companies in fact engaged in a merger even though the transaction was structured as a sale of assets. If the transaction is ruled to be a merger *de facto* the successor corporation is liable for the debts of the transferor. These issues have arisen with some frequency in recent years in products liability cases and in cases involving environmental harms. *See Patin v. Thoroughbred Power Boats, Inc.*, 294 F.3d 640 (5th Cir. 2002) (products liability); *Nettis v. Levitt*, 241 F.3d 186 (2d Cir. 2001) (wrongful discharge of employee); *Knapp v. North American Rockwell Corporation*, 506 F.2d 361 (3d Cir. 1974) (products liability). In cases involving environmental harms, a common pattern is for a company engaged in several lines of business to sell off a clean business leaving the dirty business behind. *See North Shore Gas Company v. Salomon, Inc.*, 152 F.3d 642 (7th Cir. 1998) (CERCLA).

F. USE OF CORPORATION TO DEFEAT PUBLIC POLICY

The flexibility of the corporate fiction often permits it to be used in a way that arguably tends to defeat or undercut statutory policies. The issue generally revolves more around the strength and purpose of the statutory policy than any abuse of the corporate form. Piercing analysis may also be used to determine whether a parent corporation is bound by a subsidiary's union contract. *United Paperworkers Intl. Union v. Penntech Papers, Inc.*, 439 F.Supp. 610 (D.Me.1977), *aff'd*, 583 F.2d 33 (1st Cir.1978).

G. CHOICE OF LAW IN PIERCING THE CORPORATE VEIL

Some states are more liberal than others in permitting piercing. A question may arise in the case of a foreign corporation whether the law of the state of incorporation or the law of the state in which the transaction occurred should apply in determining whether the court should pierce.

H. THE FEDERAL LAW OF PIERCING THE CORPORATE VEIL

Federal courts often hold that where the enforcement of a federal statute is involved, and a uniform federal policy of piercing will further the federal policies, the federal courts should establish a federal law of piercing.

1. CERCLA

The Comprehensive Environmental Response Compensation and Liability Act (CERCLA) imposes responsibility for clean-up and response costs on all owners and operators of hazardous waste disposal sites. Much of the current litigation involving the federal law of piercing arises under this statute. In *United States v. Bestfoods,* 524 U.S. 51, 118 S.Ct. 1876 (1998), the Supreme Court held that CERCLA did not change the settled law of piercing the corporate veil. A parent-subsidiary relationship standing alone is not enough to hold the parent liable for the acts of the subsidiary even though (1) the parent controls the subsidiary through stock ownership, (2) places its representatives on the board of directors of the subsidiary, and (3) some individuals are actively involved in the management of both corporations. In other words, the parent is liable under a piercing theory only if there is some *misuse* of the corporate form to accomplish a wrongful purpose. A parent corporation may be held liable, however, for its own actions as an owner-operator if its agents participate directly in the operation of the subsidiary's facility. In such a case, the parent corporation may be seen as a joint venturer with the subsidiary. In addition, a court may pierce if agents of the parent corporation become directly involved in the operation and management of the subsidiary without regard to the customary norms of corporate behavior applicable to parent and subsidiary as separate corporations. *See also North Shore Gas Company v. Salomon, Inc.,* 152 F.3d 642 (7th Cir. 1998).

2. Fair Housing Act

In *Meyer v. Holley,* 537 U.S. 280, 123 S.Ct. 824 (2003), the Supreme Court addressed another important issue arising under the Fair Housing Act which forbids racial discrimination with respect to the sale or rental of a dwelling. In that case, a salesperson for the defendant real estate brokerage company was alleged to have prevented the plaintiffs from buying a house for racially discriminatory reasons. The plaintiffs sued the president, sole stockholder, and licensed officer/broker of the brokerage company claiming that he was vicariously liable individually in one or more of these capacities for the salesman's unlawful actions. The Ninth Circuit held that the strong public policy behind the Fair Housing Act requires the imposition of strict liability principles beyond those traditionally associated with principal-agent or employer-employee relationships.

The Supreme Court held that the Fair Housing Act imposes liability without fault upon the employer corporation in accord with traditional agency principles but not on its individual officers or owners. Consistent with its holding in *Bestfoods*, the Court expressly rejected the idea that corporate owners and officers may be held liable for an employee's unlawful act simply because they control or have the power to control the employee's actions. In addition, the Court rejected the argument that the act creates a nondelegable duty not to discriminate that is so strong that an officer may be held liable even if he acts reasonably and within his actual authority. The court did not, however, reject the idea that a corporate officer may be held liable for failure to supervise or negligent hiring, although it is unclear whether a third party would alone have standing to assert such a claim.

I. PIERCING IN TAX CASES

Under the Internal Revenue Code the government has broad power to ignore or restructure transactions that have as their sole or principal purpose the avoidance or minimization of taxes.

1. Recognition of Corporation in General

Generally, the separate existence of a corporation is recognized for tax purposes if it is carrying on a bona fide business and is not merely a device to avoid taxes.

    a.   In some cases, high tax bracket individuals may seek to use a corporation as a repository for income primarily to avoid paying tax at the individual level. Several sections of the IRC address such practices. See IRC §§ 531–537 (accumulated earnings tax on corporations); IRC §§ 541–547 (personal holding companies).

b.   Similarly, if a single business is conducted by a series of sibling corporations as a way of splitting income in order to keep each corporation in a low tax bracket, the IRS may treat the business as a single corporation for tax purposes. *See United States v. Vogel Fertilizer Co.,* 455 U.S. 16, 102 S.Ct. 821 (1982).

c.   In addition, stockholders will sometimes seek to avoid tax at the corporate level by attempting to zero out corporate income by paying themselves large salaries and bonuses. In such cases, the IRS may recharacterize corporate expenses as distributions from corporate income that should have been taxed at the corporate level. *See Hatt v. CIR,* 457 F.2d 499 (7th Cir. 1972). In effect this amounts to a reverse piercing.

2.   Estoppel Against Taxpayer

If a taxpayer selects the corporate form of business, the taxpayer is generally bound by that selection and cannot argue that the separate existence of the corporation should be ignored. Prior to 1995, the IRS often scrutinized unincorporated businesses to determine if they had the characteristics of corporations and should be taxed as such. (Under tax law the word *association* is used to denote such a business). In 1995, the IRS adopted the *check the box* rules that allow unincorporated business to choose whether to be taxed as a corporation (association) or as a partnership. (An unincorporated business with a single owner is ignored for tax purposes, and its income is treated as income of the owner.) The check the box rules apply only to unincorporated businesses. A corporation may not elect to be taxed other than as a corporation. Moreover, under IRC 7704 a business whose ownership interests are publicly traded must be taxed as a corporation no matter what formal structure it has adopted.

J.   PIERCING IN BANKRUPTCY

Under the Federal Bankruptcy Code, courts have considerable flexibility in dealing with corporations and stockholders for the purpose of protecting and preserving the rights of creditors.

1.   Complete Piercing

The court may ignore the separate corporate existence and hold the stockholders liable for all corporate obligations.

2. Reclassification of Transaction

The court may refuse to recognize, may reclassify, or change the form of a transaction between stockholder and corporation where it is equitable or reasonable to do so.

3. Subordination

The court may subordinate claims of stockholders to claims of other creditors where the claim of the stockholder is inequitable. This power was viewed by the Supreme Court as inherent in the bankruptcy jurisdiction of federal courts. *Pepper v. Litton*, 308 U.S. 295, 60 S.Ct. 238 (1939). It is now codified in § 510(c)(1) of the Bankruptcy Reform Act of 1978.

a.   The power to subordinate inequitable claims is known as the Deep Rock doctrine from the name of the subsidiary in the leading case applying the doctrine. *Taylor v. Standard Gas & Electric Co.*, 306 U.S. 307, 59 S.Ct. 543 (1939).

b.   Subordination theoretically simply changes the order of payment so that the stockholder's claim may be paid after other creditors are satisfied in full. As a practical matter, however, the claims of other creditors usually exhaust the estate so that if a claim is subordinated under the Deep Rock doctrine, it is seldom paid evening part.

c.   Where both the parent and subsidiary are bankrupt, proceedings may be consolidated and priorities between the parent's and subsidiary's creditors determined on an equitable basis. *Stone v. Eacho*, 127 F.2d 284 (4th Cir.1942).

d.   It may be important whether a claim is merely subordinated or the supposed debt obligation is deemed to be equity. In the latter case, an otherwise valid security interest in connection with the obligation will presumably be cancelled. It is also possible for a court to invalidate a security interest without expressly subordinating the underlying obligation.

e.   In many cases, a bona fide creditor may assume a large degree of control over a debtor in an effort to rehabilitate the debtor pursuant to a workout plan. If the creditor assumes too much control, however, there is a risk that the creditor's claim will be subordinated to the claims of other creditors or in extreme cases that the creditor will be held liable for the claims of other creditors on the theory that the controlling creditor assumed the status of principal and the debtor corporation the status of agent. *See A. Gay Jenson Farms Co. v. Cargill, Inc.,* 309 N.W.2d 285 (Minn. 1981). *Cf. Martin v. Peyton,* 246 N.Y. 213 (1927) (question whether lender became partner).

K. OTHER USES OF PIERCING DOCTRINE

While piercing is usually limited to the liability of a stockholder for corporate obligations, the same issue arises in other contexts. The principles applied in these other contexts appear to be the same as those applied in traditional piercing cases, but the nature of the issue involved dictates whether the doctrine should be narrowly or broadly applied.

■ V. CORPORATION FINANCE

Capital is the money or property that must be invested more or less permanently in a business in order for the business to start up and continue to operate. Capital may take the form of either equity or debt. Capital that is contributed by stockholders in exchange for shares of stock is equity capital. Capital that is borrowed is debt capital. Equity holders are generally thought of as the owners of the business, whereas debtholders have no ownership interest in the business but rather are viewed as third party creditors. Roughly speaking, the difference between equity and debt is that there is generally no maturity date for equity and return is dependent on the profitability of the business. Moreover, the board of directors retains the discretion to make distributions subject to statutory limitations. In contrast, debt must be repaid at some point and the periodic return is fixed. Payment of interest is mandatory and not subject to limitations under corporation law. Default may trigger bankruptcy. Because the return on equity fluctuates with the fortunes of the business, equity may enjoy increasing returns (growth) if the business does well. Thus, stockholders (equity holders) are sometimes said to have a residual claim. But because equity is paid a return only if debt is paid first, equity is naturally riskier than debt. Thus, equity holders generally require a higher rate of return. In addition to borrowed funds and funds contributed by stockholders, a corporation may use internally generated funds (retained earnings) as a third source of capital. But these funds also constitute stockholder equity and may therefore be seen as contributed by the stockholders in the form of forgone dividends. The mix of debt and equity (including both common stock and preferred stock) is sometimes called the *capital structure* of the business.

A. SHARES AND STOCK

Shares and stock are synonyms for the basic units of ownership of a corporation. If the corporation is authorized to issue more than one class of shares, the number of shares of each class and a detailed description of each class, (other than common shares) must be set forth in the articles of incorporation (or equivalent governing document).

1. Common Shares or Common Stock

When shares are authorized in the articles of incorporation without any specified rights, such shares are common shares. Such shares are entitled to (1) one vote per share on any matter submitted to a vote of the stockholders and (2) a pro rata share of any distribution of cash or property to the stockholders generally. These rights are automatic and need not be described in the articles of incorporation.

2. Preferred Shares or Preferred Stock

Preferred means that shares have preference over common shares either as to dividends or on liquidation or both. A *preference* simply means that the preferred shares are entitled to a payment of a specified amount before the common shares are entitled to anything. Most preferred shares have both dividend and liquidation preferences. The MBCA (1984) does not use the terms common shares and preferred shares but these terms are widely used in practice and in many state statutes.

3. Authorized Shares

The articles of incorporation define the *authorized shares* the corporation may issue. MBCA 2.02(a)(2) provides that the articles of incorporation must set forth the number of shares the corporation is authorized to issue. MBCA 6.01(a) provides that the articles of incorporation must prescribe the classes of shares and the number of shares of each class that the corporation is authorized to issue. In addition, if more than one class of shares is authorized, the articles of incorporation must prescribe a distinguishing designation for each class, and, prior to the issuance of shares of a class, the preferences, limitations, and relative rights of that class must be described in the articles of incorporation.

4. Issued Shares

Issued shares are the shares of one or more classes actually held by stockholders as distinct from merely being authorized but unissued. Under the MBCA the terms *issued* and *outstanding* are synonymous. It is customary in modern corporate practice to authorize more shares than the number planned to be issued initially. Additional capital may be needed at a later date, and authorized shares may be issued to raise that capital without amending the articles of incorporation. Shares authorized but not issued may be issued at a later date by the board of directors acting alone without approval of the stockholders.

5. Treasury Shares

Treasury shares are shares of the corporation that have been issued and reacquired by the corporation. Under traditional statutes, treasury shares have an intermediate status. They are not *outstanding* for purposes of voting or dividend payments but are viewed as *issued* for some purposes as discussed further below. MBCA 6.31(a) provides that when a corporation acquires its own shares, they automatically become authorized but unissued shares. This change was made in recognition of the fact that with the elimination of restrictions on the issuance of shares, there is no reason to retain the concept of treasury shares.

6. Par Value and Stated Capital

In some jurisdictions, a corporation must specify a *par value* for its shares in the articles of incorporation. Par value is the minimum price for which shares may be issued by the corporation. It is an arbitrary number. Shares may always be sold for more than par value. Par value rules apply only to the original issue of shares by the corporation. A stockholder may resell for any amount, whether more or less than par value. After shares are issued, the aggregate par value of the outstanding shares constitutes the *stated capital* or *legal capital* of the corporation. As a general rule, the corporation may not invade stated capital to make a distribution to stockholders. In other words, assets must be at least equal to liabilities plus stated capital after giving effect to the dividend. In effect, the capital accounts created from the par value concept control the extent to which distributions of capital may be made in these states. Most of these rules have been abolished under the MBCA.

B. COMMON STOCK

Common shares reflect the ownership of the residual interest in the corporation. The two basic rights of common shares are: (1) entitlement to vote for directors and on basic corporate matters, and (2) entitlement to the net assets of the corporation when distributions are made or upon dissolution. Common shares reflect the residual ownership of the corporation. All corporations must have at least one share outstanding with such rights. MBCA 6.03(b) also requires that at least one share with each of these basic attributes must always be outstanding. Common stock may be issued in different classes. There are virtually no restrictions or limitations on the rights that may be varied from class to class. Because of this flexibility, classes of common shares are widely used as planning devices in closely held corporations.

a. A class of nonvoting common shares may be created under the statutes of most states. Historically, some states have prohibited non voting shares (in some cases in the state constitution).

b. In many states, classes may be created with identical financial rights but with multiple or fractional votes per share. Traditionally, the NYSE refused to list the shares of any such company, but those rules were relaxed in the 1990s, and variable voting shares have become common even among publicly traded companies.

c. It is also possible to create a class of shares with full voting power but with little or no financial interest in the corporation. *Stroh v. Blackhawk Holding Corp.*, 272 N.E.2d 1 (Ill. 1971); *Lehrman v. Cohen*, 222 A.2d 800 (Del.1966). *But see Telvest, Inc. v. Olson*, 1979 WL 1759 (enjoining issue of piggyback preferred stock solely with supermajority voting right in connection with mergers). *See also Moran v. Household International, Inc.*, 500 A.2d 1346 (Del. 1985) (suggesting that poison pill rights must have economic substance).

d. Different classes of common shares are often designated by alphabetical notation: Class A, Class B, Class C, etc. When used as a planning device, all Class A shares might be issued to one stockholder, all Class B shares to another stockholder, and so forth. Class A shares may have the right to elect two directors, whereas Class B and Class C shares may have the right to elect one director each. This arrangement would permit Class A to elect half of a four person board even though Class A shares might represent only one-third of the financial interest in the company. Or Class A may have twice the dividend right per share of Class B. This arrangement permits two stockholders to share equal voting control but unequal dividend rights by issuing the same number of class A and class B shares.

e. In most jurisdictions, all shares of a class or series must have identical rights with those of other shares of the same class or series. *See Asarco Incorporated v. M.R.H. Holmes a Court*, 611 F. Supp. 468 (D.N.J. 1985).

C. PREFERRED STOCK

Common shares are the residual ownership interests in the corporation. Corporations may also issue classes of shares that have rights that must be satisfied before the common shares are entitled to distributions. These shares are called *preferred* (or *preference*) shares or *preferred* stock. Preferred stock and debt securities have many similar characteristics and may be used to achieve similar results. Thus, the term *senior securities* is sometimes used to refer to preferred stock and debt securities collectively. With minor exceptions the MBCA does not use these terms because it is possible to create classes of shares that have some characteristics of both types of shares and there is no precise dividing line. These terms, however, are widely used in corporate practice and have well understood meanings.

1. Distributions

Preferred shares typically have a preference over common shares either as to dividends or on liquidation or both. That is, preferred shares are entitled to a payment of a specified amount before the common shares. Most preferred shares have both dividend and liquidation preferences. Most traditional preferred shares are nonvoting shares that are limited to a right to receive a specified amount and no more, no matter how profitable the corporation may be.

a. Preferential rights must be defined in the articles of incorporation, and the attributes of preferred shares may include some rights normally associated with common shares.

b. A dividend preference may be *cumulative* or *non-cumulative*, or *cumulative-to-the-extent-earned*. Generally, cumulative rights must be described with particularity in the articles of incorporation. If no such rights are set forth in the articles of incorporation, then the shares are presumed to be non-cumulative except in jurisdictions that follow the New Jersey dividend credit rule described below. A cumulative dividend that is not paid in one year carries over to the next year and following years and must be satisfied in addition to the next year's preferred dividend before any dividend can be paid on the common stock. A non-cumulative dividend not declared for a given period is gone. A cumulative-to-the-extent-earned dividend is cumulative only to the extent of earnings in a specified period. If earnings fail to cover the preferred dividend, the portion of the dividend that is not covered does not cumulate and is gone.

2. Redemption and Conversion

Preferred shares may be made *redeemable* at a price set forth in the articles of incorporation. Upon redemption, the holder of redeemable shares is entitled only to the redemption price set forth in the articles of incorporation. Preferred shares also may be made *convertible* at the option of the holder into common shares and sometimes other classes of securities (*conversion securities*) at a ratio set forth in the articles of incorporation.

a. The conversion ratio is usually subject to adjustment for dilution that may occur if the number of outstanding conversion securities is increased through a share split, share dividends, or recapitalizations prior to conversion.

b. In some cases, conversion rights only arise upon a call for redemption. If so, the conversion right typically continues to exist for a limited period after the call for redemption is announced. In such cases, the corporation may induce conversion by calling the preferred for redemption at a time when the market value of the conversion security is greater than the redemption value of the convertible security.

3. Other Features

a. In states with par value statutes, preferred shares are assigned a par value (or are issued without par value) in the same way as common shares and are subject to the same rules as common shares.

b. A corporation may issue several classes of preferred shares, each having varying dividend and other rights specified in the articles of incorporation. While a class of preferred shares may be junior to other classes of preferred, it is nevertheless a preferred stock it is preferred in comparison to common stock.

c. The 1980s saw the development of novel classes of preferred shares. Most of these novel preferreds were designed to give corporate holders the benefit of the tax credit for intercorporate dividends while providing economic terms similar to debt instruments.

4. Preferred Issued in Series

Most state statutes authorize the creation of preferred shares *in series*, with terms that may vary from series to series. Specific authorization to create one or more series of preferred shares out of a larger class of preferred shares must appear in the articles of incorporation. (The term *series* refers in effect to a subset of the class of stock specifically authorized in the articles of incorporation.) If series issue is authorized, the board of directors has the authority to set the terms of each series from time to time by resolution. Some statutes limit the discretion of the board in certain respects. Preferred shares that may be issued in series are often called *blank check stock* because the board may fill in the terms.

a. The rationale for series issue is that the board of directors may set the financial terms of the series just before the shares are marketed in order to obtain the best price for the shares. In a publicly held corporation, it is not practical to create a new class of preferred shares by amendment to the articles of incorporation because of the need for a stockholders' meeting to approve the amendment. Typically, a meeting of the stockholders requires several days notice and, in the case of a publicly traded corporation, the filing of proxy materials with the SEC. During this period market conditions may change, requiring a change in the terms of the preferred stock to be issued. For example, interest rates may rise or fall, and because preferred stock is usually a fixed income security, the dividend rate must usually be adjusted accordingly. Although the corporation could in theory sell the stock at a different price—for example, at a lower price if interest rates have risen—preferred stock also typically carries a liquidation preference so that investors who paid the lower price would become entitled to a liquidation preference in excess of the price paid. In other words, the various terms of preferred stock are quite precisely coordinated with each other. These problems do not arise with respect to common stock because common stock generally has no terms that are specified in the articles of incorporation.

b. A formal certificate describing the terms of the series must be filed with the secretary of state after the series has been established. This certificate becomes a formal amendment of the articles of incorporation even though it does not require action by the stockholders. This amendment is often called the *certificate of designation.*

c. There is no difference between *classes* and *series* of shares except in method of creation. MBCA 6.02 permits the board of directors to fix the terms of classes as well as series of shares if that power is granted to the board of directors by the articles of incorporation.

5. Alteration of Rights

At one time, the rights attaching to shares were viewed as vested and unchangeable except possibly by unanimous consent of the affected stockholders. Today, it is clear in most jurisdictions that the rights attaching to preferred shares (or any class or series of shares) may be changed by amendment to the articles of incorporation. Such an alteration of rights is sometimes called a *recapitalization* because in effect it constitutes a change in the capital structure of the business.

a. A recapitalization usually take one of two forms: either an amendment to the articles of incorporation or a merger into a wholly owned subsidiary or that has the same economic effect. There may be different procedural rules applicable to these transactions depending on how they are structured and the precise language of the applicable state statute. *Bove v. Community Hotel Corp. of* Newport, R.I., 249 A.2d 89 (R.I. 1969).

b. These transactions are not subject to a frontal attack on the ground they impair vested rights. *McNulty v. W. & J. Sloane,* 54 N.Y.S.2d 253 (1945). Some courts have construed narrowly the amendment and reservation of power sections of the business corporation act to invalidate transactions deemed by the court to be of questionable fairness. *Bowman v. Armour & Co.,* 160 N.E.2d 753 (Ill.1959). Most courts, however, have rejected arguments that in effect would restore the vested rights theory. *Langfelder v. Universal Laboratories, Inc.,* 163 F.2d 804 (3d Cir.1947).

c. One protection to stockholders often applicable in such transactions is the right to vote by separate voting groups. A stockholder objecting to the recapitalization also may have the statutory right of dissent and appraisal. Some courts have reviewed such transactions for fraud or unfairness so great as to constitute fraud, *Porges v. Vadsco Sales Corp.*, 32 A.2d 148 (Del.Ch.1943); *Barrett v. Denver Tramway Corp.*, 53 F.Supp. 198 (D.Del.1943).

D. ISSUING SHARES UNDER THE MBCA

MBCA 6.21(b) authorizes shares to be issued for consideration consisting of any tangible or intangible property or benefit to the corporation, including cash, promissory notes, services performed, contracts for services to be performed, or other securities of the corporation. MBCA 6.21(c) provides that before the corporation issues shares, the board of directors must determine that the consideration received or to be received for shares to be issued is adequate. That determination by the board of directors is conclusive insofar as the adequacy of consideration for the issuance of shares relates to whether the shares are validly issued, fully paid, and non-assessable. MBCA 6.21(d) provides that when the corporation receives the consideration for which the board of directors authorized the issuance of shares, the shares issued therefor are fully paid and non-assessable.

1. Amount of Consideration

The traditional par value requirement has been eliminated in the MBCA. There is no minimum issue price for shares. The price at which shares are issued is set by the board of directors and any price may be set by the board. Shares may be issued for any tangible or intangible property or benefit to the corporation. MBCA § 6.21(b).

2. Optional Par Value

Par value may be used on an optional basis at the election of the corporation. MBCA 2.02(b). The Official Comment to the MBCA explains that such provisions may be of use to corporations which are to be qualified in foreign jurisdictions if franchise or other taxes are computed upon the basis of par value. Optional par value may also be given effect or meaning essentially as a matter of contract between the parties. In other words, the par value rules described below may be elected by a corporation.

3. Conclusive Valuation

The MBCA and most state statutes provide that in the absence of fraud, the judgment of the board of directors as to the value of the consideration received for shares shall be conclusive and that when that value is received by the corporation in exchange for shares the shares are validly issued. This rule is designed to protect the stockholder any from challenge that the price paid is inadequate and that the shares have not been validly issued. It does not protect the board of directors from a challenge (for example) that it failed to exercise its business judgment in connection with setting the price.

4. Permissible Consideration

Traditional rules in most par value jurisdictions prohibited payment for shares by a promise to pay in the future or to render future services or a future benefit. These rules create anomalous results and have been eliminated in the MBCA. On the other hand, a corporation may escrow shares issued for such consideration until the consideration is received. MBCA 6.21(e).

5. Tax Implications

a. The contribution of property to a corporation in exchange for its shares is not a taxable disposition of the property contributed, if immediately after the exchange the persons contributing the property own at least 80 per cent of the voting and nonvoting shares of the corporation. This nonrecognition of gain is limited to shares received by the contributor and only to the extent that the liabilities assumed by the corporation do not exceed the basis of the property in the hands of the contributor. IRC 351, 357. No gain or loss is recognized by the corporation by the issuance of shares. IRC 1032.

b. If shares are issued for services already performed or to be performed, the fair value of the shares so received is subject to federal income tax at ordinary income tax rates. This tax liability may create problems for the stockholder who must find the cash to pay the tax if shares cannot be sold. IRC 83.

E. ISSUING SHARES IN PAR VALUE STATES

Several states retain the concept of par value to some extent. In these states, the articles of incorporation must state the par value of the shares of each class (or state that the shares are issued "with no par value" or "without par value"). The current trend is toward the elimination of the concept of par value as an historical anomaly.

1. **Par Value**

    Par value is an arbitrary value associated with shares. The par value of shares is set forth in the articles of incorporation and appears on the face of certificates for shares. In states with par value statutes, the board of directors may set the price at which shares are issued, but shares may not be issued for less than par value. Shares may always be issued for more than par value.

    a. If par value shares are issued for consideration worth less than par, the recipient remains obligated to pay to the corporation the difference between par value and the amount actually paid. Shares so issued are usually called *watered shares* or *watered stock* as discussed further below.

    b. It is customary to use *low par* shares rather than *high par* shares. High par value leads to undesirable consequences: (i) no shares of the corporation can be issued by the corporation at less than par even if the fair market value is less than par, (ii) some state taxes are computed on the basis of par value so that a high par value simply increases tax liabilities with no offsetting benefits; and (iii) the transaction is reflected in the capital accounts of the corporation in a way that is less advantageous to the corporation than if nominal par shares are used. as discussed further below.

    c. Par value, once set in the articles of incorporation, cannot be changed except by formal amendment to the articles of incorporation.

    d. There is no benefit to the corporation from using high par shares in dealing with creditors because creditors do not rely on par value in deciding whether or not to extend credit.

    e. The requirement to pay at least par value for shares generally applies only to the purchase of newly issued shares directly from the corporation. It does not apply to a purchase of shares from an existing stockholder, unless the purchaser knows that the shares are not fully paid. When the full agreed consideration equal to or greater than par value is paid to the corporation, the shares are said to be *fully paid and non assessable.*

    f. In most jurisdictions the requirement that shares be sold for at least par value does not apply to the resale of treasury shares by the corporation. It is not clear that this latter exception has been accepted in Delaware. *See Byrne v. Lord*, 1996 WL 361503 (Del.Ch.). A stockholder who purchases shares for less than par value remains liable for the difference between the price paid and the par value even if the stockholder sells the shares.

2. Par Value and Capital Accounts

Corporation statutes that retain the concept of par value provide that the aggregate par value of issued shares constitutes the *stated capital* of the corporation and that any excess received for the issuance of shares over par value is *capital surplus*.

a. Capital accounts are based on *issued* shares, not *authorized* shares.

b. A major advantage of reflecting the bulk of the capital contributions as capital surplus is that under most state statutes stated capital is locked in while capital surplus may be distributed to the stockholders or used to reacquire outstanding shares.

3. No Par Shares

Most states that have par value statutes authorize *no par* shares. Although no par shares may be issued at any price that the board of directors may set in the exercise of its business judgment, they are otherwise subject to par value rules relating to stated capital, the payment of dividends, etc. In other words, no par shares are a variation of nominal par value shares. They are very different from common shares issued under statutes such as the MBCA (1984) which have eliminated mandatory par value.

a. No par shares may be issued for any amount of consideration specified by the directors. There is no minimum price. Watered stock liability may arise if shares are issued for cash or property worth less then the price set by the board of directors.

b. The entire consideration is initially allocated to stated capital but in most states the directors may allocate a specified amount to capital surplus. If no part of the consideration is allocated to capital surplus, the no par alternative is equivalent to the high par alternative. If all or nearly all of the consideration is allocated to capital surplus, the no par alternative is equivalent to the low par alternative. No par shares have no significant advantage over low par shares in most states.

c. Where property (other than cash) is received for no par shares, the directors must usually specify in dollars the consideration received. In some states, the directors may simply specify the property to be received without a dollar value. Thus, no par shares may have an advantage where property of highly uncertain value is contributed because the directors may be able to specify the property that is to be received now without setting a dollar value on it.

d.   Under the now-repealed federal documentary stamp tax, no par shares were valued at the price at which the shares were actually issued while par value shares were valued at par value. Some state continue to use this model in connection with franchise taxes. In these states there is a strong tax incentive to issue low par rather than no par shares.

F. PERMISSIBLE CONSIDERATION

Under many state statutes, only certain types of property qualify as valid consideration for shares. A typical statute provides that consideration may be paid, in whole or in part, in cash, in other property, tangible or intangible, or in labor or services actually performed for the corporation. MBCA (1969) § 19. Many statutes add that neither promissory notes nor future services shall constitute payment or part payment for the issuance of shares of a corporation. MBCA (1969) § 19.

G. WATERED STOCK

Watered stock is a generic term generally used to describe the issuance of shares at a price below par value. The phrase *watered stock* originated from the practice of getting cattle to drink large amounts of water immediately before being weighed for sale. If stock is issued for no consideration at all, it is sometimes called *bonus stock*. If stock is issued for some consideration but less than par value, such shares are often called *discount shares*. In either case, under common law and the statutes of states that still follow the par value system, one who purchases stock directly from an issuing corporation and pays less than par value is liable to the corporation (or in some cases creditors) for the difference between the price paid and the par value.

1. Theories of Watered Stock Liability

Several different theories have been advanced to explain stockholder liability for watered stock.

a.   The par value of issued shares was early viewed as a public representation that at least that amount of equity capital has been received by the corporation. From this it may be argued that stockholders who know-ingly receive watered shares are involved in a potential misrepresenta-tion to creditors and should be liable to them for any short-fall between the par value and the amount actually paid for shares. This is the historical explanation for watered stock liability.

b.   Watered stock liability has also been rationalized on the theory that the capital of a corporation is a trust fund for creditors who rely on the capital of the corporation when extending credit to it. Under this theory any creditor might bring suit against the recipient of watered shares for failing to make the required payment to this trust fund. This theory is largely a fiction. The capital of a corporation is not a trust fund in any meaningful sense. The capital of a corporation may be invested in the business and may be lost if the business does not succeed. No one is liable if the capital is lost. The creditors simply go unpaid.

c.   In an early case, watered stock liability was based on a *holding out* theory. *Hospes v. Northwestern Mfg. & Car Co.*, 50 N.W. 1117 (Minn.1892). The practical differences between the holding out and the trust fund or classic theories are that under a holding out theory are: (i) only creditors who extend credit subsequent to the issuance of the watered shares may enforce the liability, (ii) creditors who know that the shares were watered when they extended credit may not recover at all., and (iii) the burden is on the plaintiffs to establish that they qualify under (i) and (ii), but they do not have the burden of establishing that they in fact relied on the capital of the corporation in extending credit.

d.   Another rationale for enforcing minimum pay-in requirements is that it affords some guaranty to the stockholders that other stockholders have contributed a similar amount for their shares. In other words, watered stock liability may protect stockholders from dilution to some extent. Par value works well in this way, however, only when par is set at or near selling price, which may create other problems over time. Nevertheless, watered stock liability probably made some sense to promoters and investors at a time when the use of pre-incorporation subscriptions was common and par value was thought of as a target price.

e.   Some par value statutes substitute a statutory liability for the common law theories. These statutes obligate every stockholder to pay at least par value for shares, and if a stockholder fails to do so, the corporation or any creditor may enforce this statutory liability.

f.   The issuance of watered stock leads to the creation of fictitious assets, or the inflation of asset values, on the balance sheet.

2.   Other Situations Giving Rise to Watered Stock

a.   Depending on the language of the statute, watered stock liability may also arise if shares are issued for any price below the price set by the directors for the issuance of such shares. In other words, under some statutes, shares may be viewed as watered whenever the consideration for which the shares are actually issued is less than the price set by the board of directors. *Milberg v. Baum*, 25 N.Y.S.2d 451 (1941) (low par shares); *G. Loewus & Co. v. Highland Queen Packing Co.*, 6 A.2d 545 (N.J.Ch.1939) (no par shares).

b.   Shares issued in exchange for ineligible property or services may also be said to be watered.

H.   USES OF TREASURY STOCK

Corporations often use treasury stock to circumvent the par value rules.

a.   Treasury shares, having once been issued for at least par value and still outstanding for legal capital purposes, may be resold by the corporation without regard to par value.

b.   Treasury shares, having once been issued for eligible consideration, may be resold by the corporation in exchange for future services, promissory notes, or other consideration that is not eligible consideration for new shares.

c.   Stated capital is not reduced by the par value of treasury shares. Rather, such shares are reflected on the balance sheet by a special (negative) entry showing that they are held as treasury shares and restrictions are placed on a surplus account (such as earned surplus) to reflect the purchase price of the treasury shares. Accounting for treasury shares is based on the assumption that the shares are not permanently retired but will be reissued at a later date.

I.   ISSUANCE OF SHARES BY A GOING CONCERN

A corporation may issue shares at any time during its life—not simply at the time of organization. Shares issued by a going concern affect outstanding stockholders. Shares issued at bargain prices may *dilute* the financial interests of existing stockholders. When shares are issued at fair market value, the voting rights of existing stockholders are diluted if the shares issued are voting shares.

1. Preemptive Rights

A *preemptive right* gives holders of outstanding shares the right to buy a proportionate part of any new issue of securities by the corporation. *Stokes v. Continental Trust Co.,* 78 N.E. 1090 (N.Y.1906). Preemptive rights may protect existing stockholders against dilution of their control interest or financial interest in the issuing corporation. If all stockholders exercise their preemptive rights, no dilution occurs and the additional capital needed by the corporation is entirely raised from its present stockholders.

a. In about half of the states, a stockholder has a preemptive right unless a specific opt out provision appears in the articles of incorporation. MBCA 6.30 and the statutes of states make preemptive rights an opt in provision. Corporations in these states have preemptive rights only if the articles of incorporation or the bylaws so provide.

b. MBCA 6.30 contains a model provision relating to preemptive rights that may be elected by a simple clause in the articles of incorporation, for example: "This corporation elects to have preemptive rights."

c. In some states preemptive rights do not apply to treasury shares on the theory that the dilution has already occurred. Some statutes extend preemptive rights to treasury shares. And some cases reject the exception for treasury shares in the absence of express statutory language. *Fuller v. Krogh,* 113 N.W.2d 25 (Wis.1962).

d. Preemptive rights generally do not extend to shares issued for consideration other than money. Some courts have construed this exemption narrowly if the corporation can sell shares for cash and use the cash to acquire the property. *Dunlay v. Avenue M Garage & Repair Co.,* 170 N.E. 917 (N.Y.1930).

e. Preemptive rights do not extend to authorized but unissued shares to the extent they represent part of the contemplated initial capitalization of the corporation. For example, MBCA 6.30 exempts of sales during the first six months after incorporation.

f. Preemptive rights generally do not extend to shares of different classes unless the other class is convertible into the class held by the stockholder.

g. Preemptive rights serve little purpose in publicly held corporations because they complicate the raising of capital. Also, the availability of a public market for shares renders the preemptive right less important because any stockholder may add to shareholdings simply by purchasing shares in the open market.

2. Fiduciary Restrictions on the Oppressive Issuance of Shares

Where preemptive rights are unavailable (either because the transaction falls within an exception to the preemptive right or because the right itself has been eliminated by the corporation), the power of the board of directors of a closely held corporation to issue new shares on terms that are unfair to minority stockholders may be limited by a general fiduciary duty. *Schwartz v. Marien*, 373 N.Y.S.2d 122, 335 N.E.2d 334 (N.Y. 1975); *Ross Transport, Inc. v. Crothers*, 45 A.2d 267 (Md.1946).

a. Fiduciary duty may preclude issuance of shares in the absence of a compelling business purpose even where preemptive rights exist but circumstances are such that it is unreasonable to expect some stockholders to exercise their preemptive rights.

b. Issuance of shares to controlling stockholders at unfair prices may be set aside even though the transaction has a valid business purpose. *Adelman v. Conotti Corp.*, 213 S.E.2d 774 (Va.1975); *Bennett v. Breuil Petroleum Corp.*, 99 A.2d 236 (Del.Ch.1953).

c. Transactions that affect the balance of power within a corporation may also be set aside if they have no apparent business purpose. *Schwartz v. Marien*, 335 N.E.2d 334 (N.Y. 1975).

d. If there is a good faith business purpose and no personal benefit to controlling stockholders, shares may be issued on terms that benefit one class at the expense of another. *Bodell v. General Gas & Electric Corp.*, 140 A. 264 (Del. 1927).

3. Stockholder Approval Requirements

In 1999, the MBCA was amended to require that any new issue of shares that increases aggregate voting power of stockholders by 20 percent or more (including increases that may result from conversion) must be approved by the existing stockholders.

a. This provision closely tracks the rules of the stock exchanges that require a stockholder vote in similar situations. It is arguable, however, that stock exchange rules are designed primarily to give the markets a chance to absorb information about the new issue of shares in order to allow prices to adjust in an orderly fashion. In contrast, the MBCA rule is intended to apply to all corporations whether or not they are publicly traded.

b. The amendment to MBCA 6.21 was adopted in conjunction with a change in the rules regarding stockholder voting in connection with mergers. Formerly, the MBCA required a vote of the stockholders of the surviving corporation only if the surviving corporation proposed to issue new shares in connection with the merger equal to 20 percent or more of those outstanding before the merger. The MBCA no longer requires a vote by the stockholders of the surviving corporation in connection with the merger, but it does require a vote whenever additional shares are issued that increase voting power by 20 percent or more regardless of the reason for the new issue.

J. DEBT SECURITIES

Corporations and other businesses usually raise a significant portion of their capital by borrowing rather than by selling stock. Generally, such capital is called *debt capital*. A corporation may borrow debt capital from individuals (including stockholders), a bank, other companies, or any other source. A corporation may also borrow debt capital by issuing *debt securities*. Debt securities may be sold in a public offering (in which case a registration statement must be filed with the SEC) or they may be privately placed with a limited number of large investors (often institutional investors such as insurance companies, pension plans, and mutual funds). With debt securities, the corporation in effect borrows from a group of lenders, although in some cases a single investor may buy an entire issue of debt securities. Debt securities may be of any duration. Debt financing may be short term (for example, bank loans or lines of credit) or long term (for example, bonds that may have maturity dates 20 to 50 years or more in the future). A short term debt security with a maturity of nine months or less from the date of issue is called *commercial paper* and is generally exempt from SEC registration. Corporations also issue a variety of medium term notes that may be publicly traded. Longer term debt securities are called *bonds* or *debentures* and often have maturities of ten years or more. A stockholder may also be a creditor, particularly in a small closely held corporation. That is, a stockholder may choose to lend some portion of his or her investment (capital contribution) to the corporation rather than invest it in the form of equity. Stockholder loans may have many of the characteristics of equity capital and may be treated as equity capital for some purposes. There is little chance that a bona fide loan from a third party creditor will be treated as equity capital, even though some bonds (such as *junk bonds*) have economic characteristics that make them similar to equity capital.

1. Bonds and Debentures

Technically a *bond* is secured whereas a *debenture* is unsecured. But in practice the word *bond* is used to refer generically to all long term debt securities issued by a corporation whether secured or not. Bonds are typically secured by a lien on specific property of the issuer (land, buildings, equipment, inventory, receivables, *etc.*).

a. Bonds and debentures are written obligations to pay a specific amount at a future date usually with periodic interest payments due in the interim.

b. Bonds and debentures are usually negotiable instruments. Historically, debt securities were payable to the *bearer* (that is, the person in possession of the certificate) and the obligation to pay periodic interest was represented by *coupons* that could be clipped from the bond certificate and cashed much as an ordinary check and which were themselves negotiable instruments payable to bearer. Such debt securities are typically called *bearer bonds*. Because of changes in tax law, bonds and debentures today are issued in registered form in the name of a specific holder. Interest payments are not represented by coupons but rather are paid by check directly to the registered holder. Registered debt instruments are transferable only by endorsement rather than by mere delivery.

c. The rights of holders of debt securities are set forth in an *indenture* which typically vests in a *trustee* the rights to enforce the terms of the indenture, including the right to foreclose on security. *United States Trust Co. v. First Nat. City Bank*, 394 N.Y.S.2d 653 (App.Div.1977). An indenture (sometimes called a *trust indenture*) is essentially a contract between the issuer and investors. Because bondholders are not viewed as owners of the corporation, they do not have the right to vote on matters of corporate governance as stockholders do. Bondholders may sometimes have the right to vote on matters relating solely to the bonds, such as whether to permit the issuer to delay an interest payment. It is fairly clear as a matter of case law that the board of directors owes no fiduciary duty to bondholders (although there are a few cases in which courts have held that a limited fiduciary duty is owed to the holders of bonds that may be converted into stock). Bondholders are not entitled to information about the issuer and its business except to the extent specified in the indenture or as may be required by the registration statement (if any) filed with the SEC. In other words, the rights of bondholders are purely contractual. But these contractual rights include an obligation of *good faith* (as under any contract) on the part of the issuer, which means that the issuer agrees implicitly not to subvert the terms of the contract. As a result of these limited rights, bondholders must depend on a trustee to monitor the finances of the issuer. The federal Trust Indenture Act of 1939 (administered by the SEC) sets minimum standards for indentures under which $10 million or more in bonds may be issued.

d. Debt securities are usually issued in units of $1,000 or larger round numbers. If they are publicly traded, their market price is a function of prevailing interest rates and the risk of default by the issuer. Bonds are generally traded by and among dealers for their own account rather than on a formal centralized exchange such as the New York Stock Exchange. Thus, an investor who wants to buy or sell a bond, typically buys from or sells to a dealer rather than having the transaction handled by a broker who finds an investor to take the other side of the trade. Such market is called a *dealer market* or an *over the counter* (OTC) market. Because of this market structure, there is less reliable information about bond prices than about stock prices (although technically NASDAQ is an OTC market).

e. Bonds are usually rated by a rating agency such as Moody's or Standard & Poors. The highest ratings (A through AAA) are *investment grade* and institutional investors are sometimes prohibited by law or contract from investing in any lower grade instruments. Preferred stock may also be rated.

f. Debt securities are usually issued at or close to the face amount $1,000 per unit, also called par value. Market prices of debt instruments fluctuate with market conditions. When interest rates rise, bond prices fall because (other things being equal) the fixed interest payment on a bond becomes less attractive compared to other investments when those other investments offer a higher rate of return. As the price of a bond falls, however, the fixed interest rate relative to par become a higher interest rate relative to market price. Similarly, when interest rates fall, bond prices generally rise. But regardless of movements in market price during the life of a bond, when the bond matures the issuer must repay the face amount.

g. The fixed relationship between the face amount of a debt security and the amount the issuer must pay each year in interest is called the *coupon rate*. When market prices fluctuate an investment in a debt security will yield an effective return of return that may be greater or less than the coupon rate.

h. Debt securities are usually redeemable by the corporation at a premium over the face amount of the instrument. They may also be made convertible into common stock at the election of the holder. The price of a convertible bond will depend on value of the bond as a debt instrument and the value of the securities into which it can be converted. Generally speaking, the bond will trade at the greater of the two and possibly slightly more if it cannot be redeemed immediately.

i. In the 1980s, numerous types of novel debt instruments were developed.

- *zero coupon bonds* or *zeroes* are debentures that do not carry interest payments. They are issued at deep discounts from par and interest is reflected in the discount.

- *income bonds* are debt instruments, but the obligation to pay interest is conditioned on the existence of earnings to cover the interest.

- *participating bonds* are debt instruments, but the obligation to pay interest fluctuates with the earnings of the corporation.

- *PIK (payment in kind)* bonds pay interest in the form of promissory notes or additional bonds for a stated period of time.

- *reset bonds* are bonds that require the issuer to adjust (reset) the interest rate on a specific date in the future if the bonds are selling below par so as to return the bonds' market value to par value.

- *junk bonds* (or high yield bonds) are bonds that are below investment grade when issued.

2. Debt Instruments Compared with Preferred Shares

Bonds (and debentures) are debt securities. They differ from preferred shares, which are equity securities, in several basic respects:

a. Interest on bonds (sometimes called *debt service*) is an unconditional obligation of the corporation while dividends on preferred shares are discretionary with the board of directors. But dividend payments may be made mandatory under circumstances specified in the articles of incorporation subject to statutory limitations on distributions to stockholders.

b. A bond usually has a maturity date at which time the principal becomes due while preferred shares never becomes due. But preferred shares may be made subject to mandatory redemption at a specified time or at the option of the holder (in effect on demand) subject again to statutory limitations on distributions to stockholders.

c. A bond may have legal rights of foreclosure in the event of default while preferred stock does not.

d. Bonds are created pursuant to indentures that usually appoint a trustee to handle the rights of security holders whereas classes of preferred stock are created by provision in the articles of incorporation of the corporation. Debt securities need not be authorized in the articles of incorporation. A corporation has the inherent power to borrow money. But if debt is to be convertible into stock, there must be explicit authorization in the articles of incorporation to issue the conversion securities.

e. Despite these legal differences the economic differences between these two types of securities may be slight.

K. ADVANTAGES OF DEBT CAPITAL

There are both tax and non-tax advantages in using a judicious amount of debt to capitalize a corporation. The ratio between a corporation's equity capital and its long term debt is called the *debt/equity ratio*. A corporation with a high debt/equity ratio is said to be *thinly capitalized or highly leveraged.*

1. Tax Advantages of Debt

a. Interest on debt is deductible by the corporation whereas dividends on stock are not. Thus, the use of debt permits the corporation to pay out more of its available cash to investors, because interest payments are a deductible business expense and are therefore paid in pretax dollars. In a closely held corporation, stockholder debt is an important way to zero out corporate income, minimize income tax, and increase ultimate return for owners.

b. A repayment of debt may be a tax-free return of capital rather than a taxable dividend. The use of debt may therefore permit the tax-free return of a portion of a stockholder's investment, whereas a partial redemption of a taxpayer's common or preferred shares gives rise to ordinary income or capital gain.

c. Because the existence of stockholder debt in the capital structure reduces taxes, the stockholder usually desires the greatest amount of debt possible in the structure.

2. Non Tax Advantages of Debt

a. An important advantage of debt financing is that it simplifies planning where some investors contribute more capital than others.

b. Debt financing may permit the stockholders to obtain parity with general trade creditors if the business fails. But, as in the tax context, if too much of the stockholders' investment is in the form of debt, a court may recharacterize the debt as equity, that is, *subordinate* it to obligations owed to third-party creditors. *See Costello v. Fazio,* 256 F.2d 903 (9th Cir.1958).

c. Corporations (and other businesses) often borrow some portion of their capital to create *leverage* and increase return on common stock. For example, if a company can generate a 10 percent return on its total capital, and it can borrow half of its capital at 8 percent, then the excess 2 percent generated on the debt goes to the common stock increasing its return to 12 percent. (The same end can be accomplished by issuing preferred stock at 8 percent.) But because debt and interest thereon must generally be paid no matter how the business fares, debt also increases the risk in the common stock. For example, if the business above were to generate a total return of 6 percent, the debt would still need to be paid at 8 percent, and the return on the common stock would be reduced to 4 percent.

L. FEDERAL AND STATE SECURITIES LAWS

The federal Securities Act of 1933 is designed to protect the public investors from fraud and misrepresentation in connection with the offer and sale of securities in interstate commerce by requiring the registration of public offerings. State securities laws (blue sky laws) serve a similar purpose for small issues of securities within each state. The goal of federal securities law is full disclosure of all <u>material</u> facts about the securities being sold. The federal Securities Act is a disclosure statute. No evaluation of the investment quality of securities is involved. The federal Securities Exchange Act of 1934 focuses on trading and publicly traded companies (as opposed to the offering of securities). It mandates periodic reporting by publicly held companies, establishes various rules relating to trading and stockholder voting, and provides for regulation of the securities business.

1. Registration of Securities Offerings

The 1933 Act generally requires registration of securities before they may be publicly offered. Registration involves the filing of detailed information about the offering, its review by the SEC, and public dissemination of that information to potential investors in the form of a prospectus. The federal registration process is expensive and thus impractical for most offerings of less than $20 million. As a result, for small offerings it is essential to find an applicable exemption from registration. Most *initial public offerings* (IPOs) of stocks to be listed on an exchange must be registered on the SEC's long form registration statement called an S–1. Forms S–2 and S–3 are shorter and simpler than Form S–1 and are available to issuers who are already publicly held. Such issuers must register for purposes of continuous reporting under the Securities Exchange Act of 1934 and reports filed under that act may be incorporated by reference in the short form registration statements under the *integrated disclosure system*.

    a.   The sale of unregistered securities when registration is required gives rise to substantial civil liabilities to purchasers of the securities and may give rise to criminal prosecution as well. Under § 11 of the 1933 Act, if the registration statement contains a material misrepresentation of fact or fails to disclose a material fact, the company is absolutely liable in damages and all signers of the registration statement, together with all directors of the issuer, the CEO, the CFO, the underwriters, and the various experts (including accountants and attorneys) whose opinions are incorporated into the registration statement are liable in damages unless they demonstrate that they exercised due diligence or reasonably relied on another to do so depending on the circumstances. Under § 12, one who sells securities by means of a false prospectus is liable for rescission or damages.

b. Under federal law those who prepare and sign a registration statement represent not only that they believe the registration statement to be correct but also that they have conducted an investigation into the facts (that is, they have exercised *due diligence*) and that the registration statement contains all *material information* (that is, information that would be important to a reasonably investor in deciding whether to invest).

2. Exemptions from Registration Requirement

There are several exemptions from the registration requirement. The two primary exemptions are known as Regulation A and Regulation D. Roughly speaking, Regulation A focuses on small offerings, whereas Regulation D focuses on private offerings. There are several other more specialized exemptions, as well as several open-ended statutory exemptions.

a. Regulation A, adopted by the SEC under section 3(b) of the Securities Act, exempts offerings of up to $5,000,000 following a simplified registration scheme. Under Regulation A an issuer may *test the waters* by distributing a written document to prospective issuers to determine whether there is investor interest in the contemplated offering without fear that the document will itself be deemed to constitute an offer.

b. SEC Regulation D set forth the primary exemptions from registration. It contains three discrete parts, together with accompanying definitions, terms, and conditions. Regulation D and particularly Rule 406 is often used in connection with the *private placement* of securities with large institutional investors. Regulation D applies only to sale by issuers. It is not available to investors for purposes of resale. Securities sold under Rule 505 and 506 are *restricted*. They may not be resold by the purchaser except pursuant to an exemption permitting their sale. Regulation D is a *safe harbor* rule. It sets forth the conditions that the SEC views as sufficient to qualify for various statutory exemptions (as well as establishing other exemptions). The statutory exemptions remain available, but it is relatively uncommon for issuers to rely on them when a safe harbor rule is available.

- Rule 504 exempts sales of up to $1,000,000 in any one year. If the offer is registered under state law and that law requires delivery of a disclosure document.

- Rule 505 exempts sales of up to $5,000,000 in any one year to a maximum 35 accredited investors. No general solicitation or advertising is used. Under Rule 505, there is no limit on the number of accredited investors. Specified information about the issue must be given to all unaccredited investors.

- Rule 506 permits sales in unlimited amounts to accredited investors and to not more than 35 unaccredited investors. Each purchaser who is not an accredited investor must have such knowledge and experience in financial and business matters that the purchaser is capable of evaluating the merits and risks of the prospective investment. No general solicitation or general advertising may be used, and specified information must be delivered to each purchaser who is not an accredited investor. Rule 501(a) lists eight categories of accredited investors, including institutional investors, private business development companies, tax exempt organizations, directors, executive officers or general partners of the issuer, large purchasers high net worth individuals and trusts, and entities owned by accredited investors.

c. Section 4(2) of the Securities Act of 1933, exempts transactions by an issuer not involving any public offering. Offerings not complying with Regulation D may nevertheless be exempt under section 4(2) if they meet the tests established by case law for the availability of the exemption. The test is not dependent on the mathematical number of offerees. The basic requirement is that all offerees must have sufficient access and sophistication so that they do not need the protection of the act. *SEC v. Ralston Purina Co.*, 346 U.S. 119, 73 S.Ct. 981 (1953).

d. Section 4(6) of the Securities Act, added in 1980, exempts offerings or sales solely to one or more accredited investors if the aggregate amount does not exceed $5 million and there is no advertising or public solicitation. Most offerings exempt under this section are also exempt under Regulation D, but there are a number of technical differences.

e. Section 3(a)(11) of the Securities Act exempts securities which are part of an issue offered and sold only to persons resident within a single state where the issuer is incorporated and doing business in that state.

f.   Rule 701 provides an exemption for specified offers of securities by an employer to employees as compensation or pursuant to employment contracts. Such issues may not exceed the lesser of 15 percent of the employer's assets or $5,000,000 and must be made subject to limitations on resale.

3.   **Restrictions on Transfer of Unregistered Securities**

In order to ensure that buyers of exempt securities are the ultimate investors and do not buy with a view toward further distribution, SEC regulations require restrictions to be imposed on resale of securities sold pursuant to many exemptions. Securities that must be made subject to such restrictions are called *restricted securities*. The restrictions are noted by a *legend* on certificates issued pursuant to the exemption, and *stop transfer* orders are issued to the issuer's transfer agent to prevent unauthorized transfers.

a.   Rule 144 permits limited resales of restricted securities after one year and unlimited sales by unaffiliated investors after two years if the company is registered under the 1934 Act for purposes of continuous reporting. The term *affiliate* includes directors, officers, controlling stockholders, employees, and agents of the issuer or of a controlling or related entity and family members of those persons.

b.   Rule 144A permits unlimited resales of restricted securities to *qualified institutional buyers,* often referred to as *QIBs*.

4.   **What Constitutes a Security**

Innumerable investment schemes may be imagined. As a result, the question whether a specific scheme or economic arrangement constitutes a security under federal or state law is an issue that is often litigated.

a.   The term *security* includes investment contracts and other instruments that evidence a financial investment. The term *investment contract* has been construed to include any contract, transaction, or scheme by which a person invests money in a common enterprise with the expectation that profits will be derived primarily from the efforts of others. A scheme may involve a security even if the investor is required to exert some individual effort.

b.   In *Landreth Timber Co. v. Landreth,* 471 U.S. 681, 105 S.Ct. 2297 (1985), the Supreme Court rejected the *sale of a business doctrine* and held that the sale of all or a majority of the shares of a closely held corporation constituted the sale of a security subject to the federal securities acts. Even though a controlling interest in a business arguably does not meet the *Howey* test, the Court held that common stock was plainly within the class of instruments Congress intended to include within the category of securities. The holding in cases such as *Landreth* is of importance primarily because it makes available the protections of federal antifraud provisions to all sales of closely held shares (assuming that the facilities of interstate commerce are used) even where the purchaser is intent on acquiring control of the business rather than making a passive investment.

c.   In *Reves v. Ernst & Young,* 494 U.S. 56, 110 S.Ct. 945 (1990), the Court held that a promissory note is presumptively a security, but that the presumption may be rebutted by a showing that the transaction in which the note was issued was not of a type normally used for raising capital, and that the note was not an instrument likely to give rise to trading for speculation or investment by the general public. The court also considered the expectation of the trading public as to whether the note in question was within the coverage of the securities acts, and whether other regulatory schemes provide protection to the investing public similar to that provided by the securities acts.

5.   State Blue Sky Laws

Most state blue sky statutes roughly parallel the federal securities acts. Many states have adopted the Uniform Securities Act in whole or part.

a.   Some state statutes do not require registration of issues sold within the state but only contain antifraud provisions. or provisions requiring the registration of securities professionals. But many state securities statutes apply to the provision of financial services beyond those involving securities.

b.   The definition of security under many state statutes is broader than that under federal law.

c.   Some states impose substantive standards over and above the full disclosure philosophy of the federal law. These *merit review* states permit distributions to be registered and sold in the state only if the terms are *fair, just, and equitable.*

d. The National Securities Markets Improvements Act of 1996 preempts many aspects of blue sky statutes.

M. DIVIDENDS AND DISTRIBUTIONS

Traditionally, the word *dividend* refers to a payment to stockholders out of current or past undistributed earnings that is distributed in proportion to the number of shares owned. In other words, traditionally a dividend is a periodic or special payment out of earnings made by a corporation in some specified amount per share—a *pro rata* payment to stockholders. In some cases, a dividend may also be paid out of capital. In other words, a corporation may make a distribution to stockholders even though the corporation has no earnings. Such a distribution amounts in effect to a return of capital to the stockholders. Typically, dividends and distributions are discretionary with the board of directors. A dividend may be paid in the form of cash or property or even a promise to pay cash or property in the future—a distribution of indebtedness. In other words, a dividend may take the form of a distribution of just about anything of value. In addition, a stockholder may receive cash or property from a corporation in connection with the repurchase or redemption of shares. Such payments are not usually pro rata. But a pro rata repurchase of shares is economically equivalent to a dividend. Thus, the MBCA uses the word *distribution* to refer to both dividends and repurchases. And the rules relating to distributions are more or less unified in MBCA 6.40. In contrast, many state statutes, particularly those in par value jurisdictions, contain two separate provisions that deal with dividends and repurchases respectively. In the MBCA, the word *dividend* is used primarily in connection with *stock dividends*, that is, distributions of additional stock to existing stockholders. Although stock dividends are similar in form to cash and property dividends, stock dividends do not involve the distribution of property by the corporation. In other words, a stock dividend is usually a *paper transaction* in which the primary effect is simply to increase the number of shares outstanding. Thus, stock dividends are typically regulated by a separate provision. *See* MBCA 6.23.

1. Dividend Policies in Publicly Held Corporations

Publicly held corporations generally adopt stable dividend policies that permit regular periodic distributions even though corporate income fluctuates. Changes in dividend payment rates by publicly held corporations are, not made lightly. They tend to reflect only important and usually permanent changes in the profitability of the business. An action to compel the payment of a dividend is rarely successful in a publicly held corporation because the payment of dividends is a matter of business judgment and thus within the discretion of the board of directors. *Sinclair Oil Corp. v. Levien*, 280 A.2d 717 (Del.1971). But it is clear that a court has authority to order that a dividend be paid in an appropriate case.

2. Dividend Policies in Closely Held Corporations

In a closely held corporation dividend policies are heavily influenced by the tax status of the corporation. The disadvantage of dividends in C corporations is that they lead to double taxation: the corporate income is subject to the corporate income tax and amounts paid in dividends to stockholders are subject to a second tax when the dividends are included in individual stockholder tax returns.

a. In a C Corporation, the payment of dividends carries a higher tax cost than the payment of the same amount in the form of salaries, rents, interest, or other payments that are deductible by the corporation. If the entire potential income of the corporation can be distributed to stockholders in the form of payments that are deductible by the corporation, the taxable income of the corporation can be *zeroed out* and the corporation will pay no income tax.

b. In a corporation that has elected S Corporation treatment, all corporate income is directly taxed to the stockholders, whether or not distributed, so that payment of dividends has no effect on the aggregate tax bill.

c. The distribution of corporate income in the form of salaries, rent, etc. in order to zero out corporate income may give rise to internal dispute because some stockholders may receive larger payments than others and the payments may bear no relationship to relative shareholdings. Excluded stockholders may prefer distributions in the form of dividends despite the additional tax cost.

d. In the context of a closely held corporation, the courts have ordered dividends to be paid in many cases if the plaintiff has been able to show (i) the availability of surplus cash not needed in the corporate business and (ii) affirmative indications of bad faith on the part of management. *Keough v. St. Paul Milk Co.*, 285 N.W. 809 (Minn.1939); *Dodge v. Ford Motor Co.*, 170 N.W. 668 (Mich.1919); *Miller v. Magline, Inc.*, 256 N.W.2d 761 (Mich.App.1977).

e. Language in articles of incorporation may be construed as requiring the mandatory payment of dividends, particularly on preferred stock. *Crocker v. Waltham Watch Co.,* 53 N.E.2d 230 (Mass.1944); *New England Trust Co. v. Penobscot Chemical Fibre Co.,* 50 A.2d 188 (Me.1946); *Arizona Western Insurance Co. v. L.L. Constantin & Co.,* 247 F.2d 388 (3d Cir.1957). *But see L.L. Constantin & Co. v. R.P. Holding Corp.,* 153 A.2d 378 (N.J.Super.Ch.Div. 1959).

3. **Legal Restrictions on Dividends and Distributions**

    State statutes impose widely varying tests for the legality of dividends and distributions. The tests differ depending on whether the state retains the par value system and the related concepts of *stated capital* and *capital surplus* or rather has eliminated the par value system as under the MBCA. Even among states that retain the par value system in whole or part, the tests may differ significantly in detail.

    a. MBCA 6.40 imposes two tests to determine whether a distribution may be lawfully made: (1) an *equity insolvency test* that requires the corporation to be able to pay its debts as they become due in the ordinary course of business after giving effect to the distribution, and (2) a *balance sheet test* that prohibits a distribution if, after giving it effect, the corporation's total assets would be less than the sum of its total liabilities plus (unless the articles of incorporation provide otherwise) the amount that would be needed to satisfy preferential liquidation rights of senior classes of shares.

    b. All states apply some form of equity insolvency test for distributions. The equity insolvency test is the only test under Massachusetts law. Other states combine the insolvency test with some form of balance sheet test. In states that continue to follow the par value system, the balance sheet test requires reference to the various capital accounts that make up stockholder equity. In effect, the capital accounts created under the par value system control the extent to which distributions of capital may be made in these states.

    c. A few states continue to follow the MBCA (1969) and permit dividends to be paid only out of *earned surplus,* a term that is defined as the sum of net accumulations of income from all earlier periods reduced by dividends paid in earlier years and similar items. The theory of the earned surplus test is to permit dividends to be paid from earnings but not from contributed capital. These states usually also permit distributions out of *capital surplus* or other surplus accounts (subject to certain limitations) but not from *stated capital*. For example, the corporation may be required to identify distributions other than those from earned surplus so that the stockholders will know that the distribution does not necessarily indicate that the corporation has been profitable. Some statutes refer to such a dividend as a *partial liquidation*.

d. Some state statutes permit dividends or distributions that do not *impair capital*. Generally these statutes permit dividends to be paid as long as assets exceed liabilities plus stated capital. These states may be called *simple surplus jurisdictions* in that a dividend may be paid out of any form of surplus. Delaware and New York are such jurisdictions.

e. Some state statutes may not fit neatly into the above classification. For example, California requires assets to be equal to 125 percent or more of liabilities after giving effect to a dividend.

f. Under the par value system, there are several well recognized wrinkles in the general rules that may affect the dividend-paying capacity of a corporation depending on the language of the specific statute.

• Many statutes permit a so-called *nimble dividend* to be paid out of current earnings (or earnings from the immediately preceding year) even though a deficit exists from prior years. *United States v. Riely*, 169 F.2d 542 (4th Cir.1948); *Goodnow v. American Writing Paper Co.*, 69 A. 1014 (N.J.Err. & App.1908); *Morris v. Standard Gas & Electric Co.*, 63 A.2d 577 (Del.Ch.1949).

• In most jurisdictions, a company that is engaged in exploiting natural resources (*wasting assets*) may pay dividends to the extent of accumulated depletion.

• In most jurisdictions, dividends may be paid out of *reduction surplus* created by the reduction of stated capital by amendment to the articles of incorporation or by the retirement and cancellation of shares.

• A *quasi reorganization* is essentially a bookkeeping entry by which a deficit of earned surplus is eliminated by the transfer of capital surplus to earned surplus. Future earnings are thereafter available for the payment of dividends without requiring that they be first applied against any deficit in earned surplus.

- In some jurisdictions, a dividend may be paid out of *revaluation surplus* created by a *write up* in the value of appreciated assets. *Randall v. Bailey,* 23 N.Y.S.2d 173 (1940); *Dominguez Land Corp. v. Daugherty,* 238 P. 697 (Cal.1925).

- Surplus may also be created by recognizing and placing a value on goodwill or other intangible assets not previously shown in the corporation's books. The use of such surplus for distributions has been permitted in some cases. *See Klang v. Smith's Food & Drug Centers, Inc.,* 702 A.2d 150 (Del. 1997).

4. Contractual Restrictions on Dividends and Distributions

Because state statutes provide few practical restrictions on distributions and therefore little or no protection for creditors, creditors often impose contractual restrictions on dividends and distributions in loan agreements.

N. REDEMPTIONS AND REPURCHASES OF OUTSTANDING SHARES

A corporation may repurchase its own shares by negotiating with a stockholder. A redemption of shares by a corporation is a reacquisition that occurs pursuant to the terms of the shares themselves, with the redemption price established by, or in the manner specified by, the articles of incorporation. Redemptions are usually at the option of the issuer but may also be at the option of the holder. A redemption or repurchase by a corporation has the same economic effect as a dividend or distribution in that it constitutes a transfer of property to stockholders. Repurchases and redemptions usually are not pro rata.

1. Relationship Between Repurchases and Distributions

When a corporation repurchases or redeems some of its own shares, the assets of the corporation are reduced by the purchase price of the shares. But such shares do not constitute an asset in the hands of the corporation. Such shares are akin to authorized but unissued shares (and are so treated under the MBCA). A redemption or repurchase of its own shares by a corporation is thus similar to a dividend in that it constitutes a gratuitous transfer of cash to one or more stockholders in exchange for their shares. Indeed, a pro rata redemption or repurchase has the same economic effect as a dividend.

    a. The MBCA uses the term *distribution* to refer to all transfers of cash or property in respect of shares. MBCA § 1.40(6). The legal restrictions applicable to dividends are also generally applicable to share repurchases or redemptions. MBCA § 6.40. Thus, as with dividends, redemptions and repurchases are subject to a balance sheet test and a solvency test.

b. Under the MBCA (1969), dividends were treated under a separate section (§ 45) from repurchases (§ 6) and redemptions (§ 66). Each section included a balance sheet test and a solvency test albeit with slight variations. Many states continue to follow this pattern.

c. Unlike a distribution, a redemption or repurchase may affect the voting power of the remaining shares.

2. Repurchases of Shares by Publicly Held Corporations

Share repurchases may occur in publicly held corporations for several reasons and by several methods.

a. A corporation may redeem redeemable shares if the terms of redemption are attractive. Or the corporation may repurchase the shares of a particular stockholder by agreement.

b. A corporation may engage in open market repurchases as an alternative to paying dividends if the corporation has no better internal use for the funds or if the board of directors believes that the prevailing market price is attractive. Both of these justifications are usually problematic.

c. A corporation may repurchase shares in order to limit dilution created by the issuance of shares pursuant to stock options or conversion rights.

d. A corporation may announce a public offer to repurchase its own shares. Such an offer is called a *self tender offer.* A self tender offer is often made at a range of prices slightly above the prevailing market price, with the ultimate price to dependent on how many shares are offered to the corporation at various prices. Such an offer is called a *Dutch Auction.*

e. A self tender offer may also be undertaken as a defense to a hostile takeover bid. *See Unocal Corporation v. Mesa Petroleum Co.,* 493 A.2d 946 (Del.1985). By purchasing shares from its own stockholders, a target corporation may be able to reduce the number of shares available for a hostile bidder to purchase (sometimes called the *public float)* and at the same time increase the relative voting power of controlling stockholders or those who may have agreed to support management. On the other hand, by purchasing its own shares, the target corporation also increases the relative voting power of a hostile bidder.

f.   A self tender offer may be used when a corporation seeks to buy back enough shares to reduce the number of stockholders below some specified number.

g.   There are a few situations in which a corporation is permitted (or even required) to reacquire its own shares even though the corporation does not meet the statutory tests for making a distribution. In many states a corporation may repurchase fractional shares for cash. Fractional shares may be created by a *reverse stock split*. For example, one new share may be issued for every 10,000 shares outstanding. All holders of less than 10,000 shares end up owning a fractional share of the corporation, and in most states those fractional shares may be bought back by the corporation. *See* MBCA § 6.04. A reverse stock split may be undertaken as a way of going private by creating fractional shares that the corporation must purchase at a specified fair price.

h.   Every state provides a right of dissent and appraisal for stockholders who object to the terms of a merger (and other transactions in some cases). *See* MBCA 13.02. Under these statutes, a stockholder may be entitled to have his or her shares be purchased at fair value by the corporation. Generally, the requirement that the corporation repurchase a dissenting stockholder's shares is not subject to statutory limitations on distributions.

3.   Repurchases of Shares by Closely Held Corporations

Because there is no public market for shares in a closely held corporation, a stockholder who wishes to sell shares has only limited options. Usually the only potential buyers are other stockholders or the corporation itself. In a closely held corporation, repurchase of shares by the corporation may serve several purposes, including retirement of a stockholder from active employment, the cash out of a stockholder who has agreed to a limited term investment, or the resolution of disagreements about business policy between stockholders. One of the most common disagreements relates to whether the corporation will pay dividends or reinvest available cash to grow the business. If the corporation has elected S Corporation status, the failure to pay dividends may create a financial hardship for stockholders who must nonetheless pay tax on their share of corporate income. In some cases, controlling stockholders may cause the corporation to withhold dividends in order to force minority stockholders to sell their shares to the corporation at a bargain price.

a. It is important in most settings for stockholders in a closely held corporation to enter into an agreement governing the purchase and sale of shares. Such an agreement is usually called a *buy-sell agreement*. A buy-sell agreement may be incorporated in the articles of incorporation, the bylaws, or a separate contract between the stockholders. A stockholder agreement may also cover many other matters including election of directors and officers, dividend policy, etc. Most buy-sell agreements address restrictions on transfer by stockholders, circumstances under which the corporation or the stockholder may compel repurchase of shares by the corporation, and valuation.

b. Many states have statutes that permit stockholders in closely held corporations to seek judicial dissolution on the grounds that fellow stockholders have engaged in oppressive conduct. *See* MBCA 14.34. In a case in which dissolution is sought, the corporation or the non petitioning stockholders may have the right to redeem the shares of the petitioning stockholder. The right of redemption is not subject to statutory restrictions on distributions.

c. By definition, there is no public market price by which the fairness or reasonableness of repurchase prices for minority shares in a closely held corporation can be judged. Thus, both buy/sell agreements and judicial dissolution may require valuation of the company or its shares—which can be expensive, time-consuming, and subject to widely varying opinions—unless the parties have agreed in advance on a valuation formula or method.

d. If several stockholders plan to remain involved with the corporation and one stockholder desires to sell his shares, the purchase of those shares by any other single stockholder will affect the relative voting power of all the remaining stockholders. Thus, repurchase by the corporation is usually preferable to purchase by a remaining stockholder, because it preserves the balance of power among the remaining stockholders. Repurchase by the corporation also solves the problems that may arise if some stockholders find it difficult or impossible to raise the funds to purchase their pro rata part of the shares.

e.	The corporation may acquire life insurance policies on the lives of its stockholders to have funds available to acquire their shares on their death. The premiums may be deductible by the corporation.

f.	Repurchases by the corporation may be made on an installment basis over a period of years with the stockholder accepting a promissory note of the corporation for part of the purchase price. The payment of the purchase price by the corporation over time may allow the corporation to pay for the shares out of future cash flow.

## 4.	Statutory Restrictions on Repurchases

In order for a corporation to repurchase its own shares, the corporation must meet essentially the same tests that would be applicable to a dividend or distribution of the amount of the purchase price. In par value states the corporation must have available earned surplus or capital surplus to back up the repurchase, and the corporation must not be rendered insolvent by the transaction. In some states, repurchases may be made on the basis of available capital surplus, whereas ordinary dividends may be paid without stockholder approval only on the basis of earned surplus. MBCA 6.40 applies the same balance sheet and solvency test to all distributions, including both dividends and repurchases.

## 5.	Repurchase by Promissory Note

If the corporation repurchases shares in part by issuing a promissory note to the selling stockholder, the statutory tests may be applied in either of two ways: (i) once, at the time of the note is issued, or (ii) repeatedly, at the time of each payment on the note. It is common in connection with such a repurchase over time for the selling stockholder to negotiate for some sort of security interest in connection with the note because

a.	Early case law generally tested the validity of each payment separately. *In re Trimble Co.*, 339 F.2d 838 (3d Cir.1964); *Robinson v. Wangemann*, 75 F.2d 756 (5th Cir.1935).

b.	MBCA 6.40(e) and some cases take the position that the tests should be applied only once, at the time of the original purchase. *Mountain State Steel Foundries, Inc. v. C.I.R.*, 284 F.2d 737 (4th Cir.1960) (holding that a promissory note covered by earned surplus when it came due was enforceable even if not covered by earned surplus at the time it was issued); *Williams v. Nevelow*, 513 S.W.2d 535 (Tex.1974); *Neimark v. Mel Kramer Sales, Inc.*, 306 N.W.2d 278 (Wis.App.1981). Under the MBCA a promissory note representing the purchase price of shares has the same status as any other ordinary corporate obligation if there is sufficient surplus to cover the note at the time it is issued.

c. The rationale for the rule adopted by the MBCA is that the corporation might obtain a loan from a third party and use the proceeds to repurchase the shares. Such a loan would typically be on parity with other creditors. The same should arguably be true of a loan made by the selling stockholder. The opposing theory is that the selling stockholder knows that each payment on the notes is essentially a distribution by the corporation and should be evaluated as though it were a distribution.

d. California apparently takes an intermediate position and invalidates the note if there is not available earned surplus at the time of payment but allows a lien securing the note to be enforced. *Matter of National Tile & Terrazzo Co., Inc.*, 537 F.2d 329 (9th Cir.1976).

e. Arguably, these same issues arise with regard to any distribution of indebtedness by a corporation to its stockholders, but no statutes expressly address the issue outside the context of repurchase debt.

f. Contractual obligations by the corporation to repurchase shares at fixed prices are enforceable despite the potential unfairness to the selling stockholder or to other stockholders.

g. If remaining stockholders have agreed to contribute additional funds to the corporation to enable it to purchase shares consistent with legal capital requirements, the courts have ordered specific performance if the remaining stockholders are able to make the necessary contributions. *Neimark v. Mel Kramer Sales, Inc.*, 306 N.W.2d 278 (Wis.App.1981).

6. Status of Reacquired Shares

Under the MBCA reacquired shares become authorized but unissued shares. If the articles of incorporation prohibit the reissue of reacquired shares, reacquired shares are cancelled, and the number of authorized shares is reduced. In par value states, reacquired shares become treasury shares and remain on the balance sheet as issued but not outstanding shares. Surplus in an amount equal to the repurchase amount is restricted from use to back up other distributions. When treasury shares are cancelled, the stated capital attributable to those shares is also cancelled together with enough surplus to equal the amount for which the shares were reacquired. Any further restriction on the use of surplus with respect to the cancelled shares is removed.

7. Redeemable Shares in General

State statutes expressly permit corporations to issue preferred shares that are redeemable by the corporation upon terms set forth in the articles of incorporation.

a. In many states common shares may not be made redeemable at all or may be made redeemable only if there exists another class of common shares that is not redeemable. *See Lewis v. H.P. Hood & Sons, Inc.,* 121 N.E.2d 850 (Mass.1954).

b. MBCA 6.01 permits redeemable common shares without limitation or restriction.

c. If redeemable shares have voting power, the redemption may affect control of the corporation. Such redemptions, however, have been permitted if made in good faith. *Hendricks v. Mill Engineering & Supply Co.,* 413 P.2d 811 (Wash.1966).

d. Some commentators have argued that redeemable voting shares should be prohibited as a matter of public policy because of their potential to be used coercively.

e. Many states prohibit the repurchase of redeemable shares at a price higher than the redemption price.

f. The corporation may purchase redeemable shares from individual stockholders at a negotiated price below the redemption price without necessarily triggering the redemption obligation. *Snyder v. Memco Engineering & Mfg. Co.,* 257 N.Y.S.2d 213 (App.Div. 1965).

8. Redemptions at Option of Stockholder

The MBCA and the statutes of many states permit shares to be made redeemable at the option of the stockholder. In some states the statutes are silent on this question. Presumably, such rights are permitted if not specifically prohibited. Such shares are sometimes called *putable* shares because they give the holder the power to compel the issuer to repurchase the shares at a designated price. Shares that are redeemable by the corporation are *callable* in the sense that the corporation has a call option that permits it to require the holder of the shares to sell them to the corporation at a designated price. These features may also be incorporated into debt securities.

a.   Such shares have many of the characteristics of debt. Nevertheless, distributions in respect of such shares must be consistent with the applicable balance sheet and solvency tests. Payments in respect of debt are mandatory in the sense that they must be made as agreed irrespective of operating results with two possible exceptions: (i) agreement by the debtholder to defer payment or (ii) a declaration of bankruptcy by the corporation. Accounting rules require that putable shares be listed on the balance sheet in a special category of quasi-liabilities falling between true liabilities and equity.

b.   Putable shares may be more attractive than debt if the investor is a corporation entitled to the dividend received deduction under federal tax law.

9.   Fiduciary Duties in Connection with Repurchases of Shares

Caselaw in most jurisdictions holds that controlling stockholders in a closely held corporation a subject to a strong fiduciary duty to minority stockholders when redeeming shares. The leading case is *Donahue v. Rodd Electrotype Co.,* 328 N.E.2d 505 (Mass.1975), in which shares owned by the retiring CEO (and father) of the controlling stockholder were redeemed by the corporation. No similar offer was made to the minority stockholders, although the corporation had offered on earlier occasions to buy back shares owned by the minority at significantly lower prices. The court held this conduct violated the fiduciary duty that majority stockholders owe to the minority. Many subsequent cases have followed this holding. *See Estate of Meller v. Adolf Meller Co.,* 554 A.2d 648 (R.I.1989); *Sundberg v. Abbott,* 423 N.W.2d 686 (Minn.App.1988); *Balvik v. Sylvester,* 411 N.W.2d 383 (N.D.1987). *But see Toner v. Baltimore Envelope Co.,* 498 A.2d 642 (Md.1985), where the court rejected a *per se* rule that selective repurchase was improper and held that an examination of all relevant facts was necessary. *See also Nixon v. Blackwell,* 626 A.2d 1366, 1376 (Del. 1993).

a. The holding in *Donahue* is premised on the fact that the corporation is closely held. The primary feature of a closely held corporation is the lack of a public market for shares, a feature that requires stockholders to rely on the good faith of controlling stockholders for access to the financial return of the business. Some commentators have likened the *Donahue* rule to a *reverse preemptive right*.

b. *Donahue* holds that the controlling stockholder owes a duty of good faith and loyalty directly to other stockholders. This duty permits an aggrieved stockholder to maintain a direct action against a fellow stockholder and does not limit his remedies to a derivative action on behalf of the corporation seeking to compel the return of the distribution to the corporation.

c. The *Donahue* rule has been modified by subsequent case law in Massachusetts. *See Wilkes v. Springside Nursing Home, Inc.* 353 N.E. 2d 657 (Mass. 1976) (founding stockholder is not necessarily entitled to continuing employment where the majority shows a business purpose for dismissal but aggrieved stockholder may show that tactics of majority exceeded business need); *Merola v. Exergen Corp.*, 648 N.E.2d 1301, 1305 (Mass.App. 1995) (an arrangement under which an employee is permitted to purchase shares subject to the condition that the shares may be sold back to the corporation upon termination of employment does not entitle the stockholder to continuing employment).

O. ILLEGAL DIVIDENDS OR DISTRIBUTIONS

Generally, a director is jointly and severally liable to the corporation for any amount distributed in excess of the amount that could legally be distributed unless the director formally objects to the distribution if it is established that the director did not comply with the required standard of conduct. MBCA 8.33. Some caselaw holds stockholders who receive an illegal dividend or distribution must return it to the corporation if they know the distribution was unlawful when they received it. *Reilly v. Segert*, 201 N.E.2d 444 (Ill.1964). In contrast, MBCA 8.33 provides that a director is entitled to contribution from a stockholder who knowingly receives an illegal dividend.

1. Reliance by Directors

Directors who rely in good faith on officers, employees, board committees, or outside experts retained by the corporation (such as lawyers or accountants) in determining whether a distribution may be made, usually do not incur liability for an illegal dividend. MBCA 8.30, 8.33.

2. Recovery by Creditors

Liability for illegal dividends or distributions generally run to the corporation rather than to individual creditors. *Schaefer v. DeChant,* 464 N.E.2d 583 (Ohio App.1983). Creditors may be able to force a defaulting corporation into bankruptcy or receivership in order to compel the corporation to recover illegal dividends or distributions for the benefit of creditors.

3. Settlement Payments

Courts have held that amounts distributed to stockholders in a self-tender offer or in a going private merger cannot be recovered from the recipients because such distributions are protected under § 546 of the Bankruptcy Code as settlement payments made through the securities clearing system. *See Kaiser Steel Corp. v. Charles Schwab & Co., Inc.,* 913 F.2d 850 (10th Cir., 1990) (paying agents not personally liable); *Kaiser Steel Corporation v. Pearl Brewing Co.,* 952 F.2d 1230 (10th Cir. 1991) (recipients not liable). *But see Munford, Inc. v. Valuation Research Corp.,* 97 F.3d 456 (11th Cir. 1996) (directors liable). *Cf. C–T of Virginia, Inc. v. Barrett,* 958 F.2d 606 (4th Cir. 1992) (payment in connection with merger is not a distribution).

P. SHARE DIVIDENDS AND SHARE SPLITS

Unlike dividends or distributions that are payable in cash or property, a *share dividend* or *share split* does not dissipate corporate assets. Rather, the total number of shares is increased but corporate assets are neither increased nor decreased.

1. Definitions

The terms *share dividend* and *share split* (or *stock dividend* and *stock split*) connote subtly different transactions, but it is quite common even for sophisticated corporate lawyers to use the terms somewhat interchangeably.

a. In par value states, a share split differs from a share dividend. In a share split, the par value of each old share is divided among the new shares whereas in a share dividend the par value of each share is unchanged and the stated capital of the corporation is increased by the number of shares issued. MBCA 6.23 refers only to *share dividends* and does not address *share splits*.

b. The New York Stock Exchange defines a *stock dividend* as a distribution of less than 25 per cent of the outstanding shares (as calculated prior to the distribution). A *partial stock split* is defined as a distribution of 25 per cent or more but less than 100 per cent of the outstanding shares (as calculated prior to the distribution). And a *stock split* is defined as a distribution of 100 per cent or more of the outstanding shares (as calculated prior to the distribution).

c. A share dividend is usually described as a percentage increase in the number of shares while a share split is usually described in the form of a new-for-old ratio.

2. Effect of Share Splits or Share Dividends on Market Prices

Market price after a share dividend or share split may be somewhat greater than one might expect simply from the mechanical adjustment for dilution. For example, following a two-for-one split shares often trade at more than half of the price of the old shares. Similarly, following a five percent share dividend shares may continue to trade at the pre-dividend price even though one would expect the price to fall to about 95 percent of the pre-dividend price. Several explanations have been offered for these anomalies. Share dividends and share splits may be viewed as signals to the market that the corporation is doing better than anticipated. Also, corporations often maintain a constant per share dividend even though the number of outstanding shares has been increased. Another plausible explanation is that investors prefer shares that trade in the $20 to $30 range because that range permits the purchase of round lots of 100 shares for a reasonable total investment. Shares that trade at lower prices may be viewed as risky because a relatively small decline in the price represents a larger loss on one's investment. Also, shares that trade for less than $5 per share usually may not be used as collateral for a loan. Thus, share dividends and share splits may be used by management as a signal that they believe that the share price is more likely to rise than to fall. Finally, some stockholders may choose to sell dividend shares as a way of rolling their own dividend and nonetheless maintaining an investment in a round lot of shares. This strategy was especially attractive when capital gains rates were lower than dividend rates, but it may still make sense in that it permits stockholders to choose whether to withdraw some cash and pay tax or let it ride, whereas a cash dividend visits a tax on all including those who would prefer to reinvest returns.

3. Treatment of Share Dividends and Splits as Principal or Income

Share dividends or splits have some characteristics of income and some of principal. Litigation has arisen over the proper classification of such distributions in various contexts. The intention of the creator of the interest, if clearly expressed, controls; litigation arises because no intention is expressed or the expression is ambiguous.

a. A recurring question that arises in trusts or testamentary bequests is whether a share dividend should be awarded to the life tenant or to the remainderperson when the instrument is silent on the subject. One view is that share dividends should be classified as income and not principal if earnings are capitalized (on the corporation's books) to reflect the dividend. In *re Fosdick's Trust*, 176 N.Y.S.2d 966, 152 N.E.2d 228 (N.Y. 1958). A second view is that share dividends should be classified as income to the extent they are paid out of income that accrued subsequent to the creation of the life interest. This is referred to as the Pennsylvania rule. A third view is that share dividends should be treated as income up to an amount equal to six per cent of the principal each year. A fourth view is simply that share dividends should be treated as principal. This is referred to as the Massachusetts rule.

b. A similar issue is whether a testamentary gift of a specified number of shares should be deemed to carry with it shares later received in a share split. Again, the intent of the testator ultimately controls. Was it intended to give a specified number of shares or a specified interest in the corporation? *Compare In re Marks' Estate*, 255 A.2d 512 (Pa.1969) *with In re Howe's Will*, 224 N.Y.S.2d 992 (App.Div.1962).

c. Under federal tax law, share dividends are generally not regarded as income, but there are important exceptions to this rule. For example, a dividend of common stock paid on preferred stock constitutes taxable income to the extent of the value of the common shares. Moreover, where a stockholder has the option to receive either a cash dividend or a stock dividend, the stock dividend is taxable on the theory that the stockholder could have opted for the cash dividend and used the cash to buy the stock. See generally IRC 305. A dividend of preferred stock on common is not taxable at the time of receipt but is taxed as if the entire value of the stock is a dividend at the time of sale. IRC 306.

d. The issue may also arise in community property states where dividends are typically viewed as community income irrespective of who brought the stock to the marital estate, but capital gains typically remain the property of the spouse who originally owned the shares.

e. Under GAAP, a stock dividend of 20 percent or less must be treated as an expense for income statement purposes, whereas a stock dividend of 25 percent or more is treated as a capital transaction. The amount in the middle is a matter of discretion for the accountant.

■ VI. CORPORATE GOVERNANCE

A. THE STATUTORY SCHEME IN GENERAL

State corporation statutes provide for a standard distribution of the powers of management and control among the three tiers of a corporation: stockholders, directors and officers. But this scheme can be varied considerably in the articles of incorporation, the bylaws, and by stockholder agreement. The statutory scheme described here is an idealized model of corporate governance that does not accurately reflect the exercise of power in either large publicly held corporations (where shares may be owned by thousands of stockholders) or in a closely held corporation (with few stockholders). Moreover, there are many corporations that have some characteristics of both.

1. Stockholders

The stockholders are generally regarded as the owners of a corporation. Nevertheless, the stockholders have only limited powers of management and control in the corporation, including:

a. The power to elect directors.

b. The power to remove (and replace) directors.

c. The power to make recommendations to the board of directors about business and personnel matters. *Auer v. Dressel,* 118 N.E.2d 590 (N.Y.1954).

d. The power to amend or repeal bylaws. MBCA 10.20.

e. The power to approve fundamental corporate changes as proposed by the board of directors, including amendments to articles of incorporation (MBCA 10.03), mergers, consolidations or share exchanges with other corporations (MBCA 11.03), sales of substantially all the assets of the corporation (MBCA 12.02), and dissolution (MBCA 14.02).

f. The power to inspect corporate books and records for proper purposes. MBCA 16.02.

g. The power to elect (or ratify the appointment of) the corporate auditor (in corporations subject to SEC regulation).

h. The power maintain a derivative action on behalf of the corporation subject to numerous substantive and procedural restrictions.

i. Standing to attend and participate in a meeting of the stockholders (either in person or by proxy).

2. Directors

The role of directors is specified statute. The board of directors is entrusted with the power of management of the business and affairs of the corporation. *Continental Securities Co. v. Belmont,* 99 N.E. 138 (N.Y.1912). The board may delegate authority to make many decisions to officers or agents. Individual directors are not agents or representatives of stockholders. Rather, they are *members* of the board of directors. They may act only as a board or as a committee of the board appointed by the board. The corporation acts by action of the board of directors. The role of directors is discussed in more detail in a separate chapter.

a. More traditional statutes provide that powers of the corporation *shall be exercised by* and the business and affairs of a corporation *shall be managed by* the board of directors. This description may reflect the role of the board of directors in some small closely held corporations in which day to day management by the board of directors is feasible. In a closely held corporation, directors are usually substantial stockholders and principal officers. But typically they act informally without clearly designating in which capacity they act.

b. In many states, statutory language has been modified to state that the powers of the corporation may be *exercised by or under authority of* and its business and affairs may be *managed by or under the direction of* the board of directors. *See* MBCA 8.01; DGCL 141(a). This broader language reflects the role of the board of directors in a publicly held corporation where control and management is largely entrusted to professional managers. In a publicly held corporation most directors are not officers of the corporation and neither the officers nor the directors typically owns a controlling interest in the stock of the corporation.

c. The board of directors selects the corporate officers and has the power to remove them. The board also may employ employees or agents, or create new officers and employ persons to fill them. It is customary for boards of directors to delegate the power of employing lower level employees and agents to the corporate officers.

d. Certain corporate decisions, such as determining the amount that should be distributed as dividends to stockholders, must be made by the board directors and may not be delegated to officers or a committee of the board.

e. The directors are not agents of the stockholders and may not be compelled to approve transactions merely because a majority or even all the stockholders approve them. *Continental Securities Co. v. Belmont,* 99 N.E. 138 (N.Y.1912). The sole remedy of the majority stockholders in this situation is to elect different directors.

3. Officers

Officers of the corporation have a limited statutory role. They carry out the policies and decisions of the board of directors. They are not themselves formulators of policy. The role of officers is discussed in more detail in a separate chapter.

a. Officers have limited ministerial authority to bind the corporation. For example, the secretary of the corporation typically has the power to certify that the board has adopted a resolution. This power is not broadly construed.

b. In most corporations, the actual role and discretion of officers is greater than contemplated by the statutory scheme. Modern statutes relating to the roles of directors indirectly support this greater role and discretion.

B. STOCKHOLDER MEETINGS & VOTING

The rules with respect to stockholder meetings are rather straight-forward. There is a considerable degree of uniformity from state to state in these statutory requirements.

1. Annual Meetings

Annual meetings are required to be held for the purpose of electing directors and conducting other business. The time and place of the annual meeting may be specified in or fixed in accordance with the bylaws. The failure to hold an annual meeting does not affect the validity or continued existence of the corporation. The failure to hold an annual meeting does not affect the incumbency of sitting directors. MBCA 7.01.

2. Special Meetings

All meetings other than the annual meeting are special meetings. Special meetings may be called by the board of directors, and under many state statutes by the President, the holders of a specified number of shares (often 10 percent), and other persons named in the bylaws. MBCA 7.02.

3. Notice

Stockholders who are entitled to vote must be given written notice of annual or special meetings as provided in the statute or in the bylaws. Many statutes require 10 to 50 days notice. MBCA 7.05 requires 10 to 60 days notice.

a. The purposes of a special meeting must be stated in the notice and the business to be conducted at the meeting is limited to what is specified in the notice. MBCA 7.02(d). No purpose needs to be specified for an annual meeting, and any business may be conducted at such a meeting.

b. Notice may be waived by a written document executed before, at, or after the meeting in question. MBCA 7.06.

c. In the absence of statute or SEC regulation, there is no common law requirement that matters not required to be considered by stockholders be noticed or submitted to a vote of stockholders. *Carter v. Portland General Electric Co.*, 362 P.2d 766 (Ore.1961).

C. QUORUM AND VOTING REQUIREMENTS

In order for action to be taken at a stockholders' meeting, there must be a quorum at the meeting and the action must be approved by the required percentage of the votes of stockholders.

1. Quorum Requirements

A quorum is typically a majority of the voting shares although some statutes allow the quorum to be reduced either without limitation or to a specified fraction (e.g. one third) by provision in the articles of incorporation. MBCA 7.25(a) permits the quorum requirement to be reduced without limitation.

  a. Statutes permit the quorum requirement to be increased up to and including unanimity. Unanimity is a popular control device in closely held corporations because it assures minority participation. A unanimity requirement for a quorum enables any stockholder to prevent undesired action simply by refusing to attend the meeting. It thereby increases the likelihood of deadlock.

  b. Shares represented by proxy are deemed present for purposes of a quorum. *Duffy v. Loft, Inc.*, 151 A. 223 (Del.Ch.1930).

  c. The majority view is that if a quorum is once present, the meeting may continue even though a faction leaves the meeting in an effort to break the quorum. MBCA 7.25(b) codifies the majority view. *See Levisa Oil Corp. v. Quigley*, 234 S.E.2d 257 (Va.1977) (minority view).

2. Shares Entitled to Vote and Class Voting

All shares are entitled to vote one vote per share on any matter to be voted on by the stockholders unless the articles of incorporation specify that a class of shares shall have no voting rights. Generally, shares other than common shares are non-voting. A corporation may also issue non-voting common shares. But if the corporation has issued any shares, there must be outstanding at all times at least one common share with plenary voting rights. MBCA 6.03. (Similarly, there must be outstanding at least one common share with residual financial rights.) Preferred shares are typically non-voting.

  a. Treasury shares and shares owned by a majority-owned subsidiary of the corporation are not eligible to vote under most state statutes. But if a corporation holds shares of its own stock in a fiduciary capacity (for example, in a pension plan), those shares may be voted. (Voting of shares in a pension plan may be subject to regulation under laws governing such plans, primarily ERISA). Shares called for redemption generally cannot vote. MBCA 7.21.

b.   A class or series of nonvoting shares may be entitled to vote on specific matters that affect the rights of the class or series in ways specified by statute. Most state statutes refer to such voting as *class voting*. The MBCA uses the phrase *voting by voting groups* to describe the same concept. *See* MBCA 1.40(26). Where class voting on a specific matter is required, that matter is approved only if it receives the necessary affirmative votes from stockholders of that class as well as the necessary affirmative votes of all shares entitled to vote generally on matters coming before the meeting.

c.   Under the MBCA only shares may vote. The statutes of some states permit corporations to grant voting power to bond or debenture holders. *See* DGCL 221. Authorization for non stockholders to vote under these statutes must appear in the articles of incorporation.

3. Vote Required

The traditional rule is that the affirmative vote of a majority of the votes present at a meeting at which a quorum is present is necessary to adopt a measure.

a.   MBCA 7.25(c) changes the approval requirement from a simple majority to the votes cast favoring the action exceed the votes cast opposing the action. This change was designed to eliminate the treatment of abstentions as votes against the question.

b.   Many states and MBCA 7.28 establish a plurality vote requirement for the election of directors in order to take into account the possibility of three or more factions competing for directorships. Many states do not have a special rule for elections of directors.

4. Supermajority Requirements

Statutes generally permit the quorum and voting requirements to be increased up to and including unanimity. *See* MBCA 7.27.

a. One case finding such an increase in voting or quorum requirements to be against public policy, *Benintendi v. Kenton Hotel*, 60 N.E.2d 829 (N.Y.1945), was promptly over-ruled by legislative enactment.

b. Supermajority requirements may be imposed in closely held corporations to ensure that a minority stockholder has a veto power over matters coming before the stockholders.

c. Supermajority requirements are also used as defensive weapons to protect publicly held corporations against unwanted takeover attempts. *See Centaur Partners IV v. National Intergroup, Inc.*, 582 A.2d 923 (Del.1990).

d. Statutes often require a greater majority for fundamental corporate actions, including amendments to articles of incorporation, mergers, dissolution, and similar transactions. Until 1999, the MBCA required a majority of all outstanding shares. Some states require a higher percentage of votes (typically 2/3) and may permit nonvoting as well as voting shares to vote on such matters. The MBCA was amended in 1999 to permit mergers and other fundamental changes to be approved by the affirmative vote of a majority of the shares voted.

5. Action without a Meeting

In lieu of a meeting, the stockholders may act by written consent signed by all the stockholders. MBCA 7.04. The requirement of unanimity ensures that this procedure is used only by corporations with relatively few stockholders.

6. Action by Majority Consent

Delaware and a few other states provide that a consent signed by the percentage of shares needed to approve a transaction is effective. DGCL 228. This majority consent procedure may be used in publicly held as well as closely held corporations and permits a purchaser of a majority of the shares of a publicly held corporation immediately to replace the board of directors and take control of the corporation.

7. Multiple or Fractional Votes per Share

The traditional rule is one vote per share. A number of state statutes now permit multiple or fractional votes per share. In these states all computations including quorum counts must be based on aggregate votes rather than aggregate shares. MBCA 6.01, 7.21.

Publicly held corporations with strong minority interests held by a single family often create classes of shares with multiple votes per share. Shares with multiple votes are then assigned to family members. Generally, these shares may be sold to third persons only after conversion to shares with a single vote per share.

8. Manipulation of Meeting Dates

Cases are divided on whether a court should intervene if those in control of a corporation manipulate the meeting date in order to make a proxy fight more difficult.

a. *Schnell v. Chris–Craft Industries, Inc.*, 285 A.2d 437 (Del.1971) holds that such manipulation may constitute a breach of fiduciary duty by those in control of the corporation. *See Stahl v. Apple Bancorp., Inc.*, 579 A.2d 1115 (Del.Ch.1990) (decision to defer meeting date and rescind record date when faced with threatened proxy fight and tender offer not a breach of duty when no proxies had been solicited and the place of meeting not yet established); see also *Alabama By–Products Corp. v. Neal*, 588 A.2d 255, 258 (Del.1991) (*Schnell* "should be reserved for those instances that threaten the fabric of the law or which by an improper manipulation of the law would deprive a person of a clear right.")

b. *In re Unexcelled, Inc.*, 281 N.Y.S.2d 173 (App.Div. 1967) permits such manipulation based on a literal reading of the applicable business corporation act.

D. AMENDMENTS TO THE ARTICLES OF INCORPORATION

Under the law of most states, the articles of incorporation may be freely amended by board resolution followed by stockholders ratification. In a few situations, the board of directors may amend the articles of incorporation without stockholder action. In most states, an amendment to the articles of incorporation must be approved by a majority of the stockholders eligible to vote. But under the MBCA as amended in 1999, a simple majority suffices. MBCA 10.03(d). A few states continue to follow the traditional rule which requires a two-thirds majority. In most states, the articles of incorporation may be amended so as to include any provision that may be included in the articles of incorporation or to eliminate any provision that may be omitted. MBCA 10.01. That is, the articles of incorporation may be amended to read in any way that would be legal if the corporation were being formed at the time of the amendment. In other words, the articles of incorporation does not create any *vested rights* that cannot be changed by subsequent amendment. As a general rule, only shares with voting rights may vote on an amendment to the articles of incorporation. But if the amendment would change the rights of a particular class of shares, that class may vote as a class on the amendment. In some states, an amendment of the articles of incorporation that changes certain fundamental stockholder rights, triggers appraisal rights for shares eligible to vote on the amendment. In 1999, the MBCA eliminated appraisal rights in most such situations.

1. **Constitutional and Substantive Limitations**

   MBCA 10.01 states that a shareholder of the corporation does not have a vested property right resulting from any provision in the articles of incorporation, including provisions relating to management, control, capital structure, dividend entitlement, or purpose or duration of the corporation. Many state statutes contain similar provisions.

   a. The argument that rights in the articles of incorporation are *vested rights* or *property rights* is basically a constitutional argument. In *Trustees of Dartmouth College v. Woodward*, 17 U.S. (4 Wheat.) 518 (1819), the Supreme Court held that a state to could not adopt a statute that had the effect of amending previously issued articles of incorporation. But the Court also recognized that states might avoid this problem by a reservation of power to amend statutes applicable to all corporations created thereafter. Today, all states reserve the power of to amend state law even if the amendment has the effect of changing fundamental stockholder rights. *Dentel v. Fidelity Sav. & Loan Ass'n*, 539 P.2d 649 (Or.1975).

   b. Nevertheless, some cases have adopted the view (on non constitutional grounds) that certain provisions of articles of incorporation may not be altered by stockholder vote. In effect, these cases require unanimous agreement by the stockholders to amend the articles of incorporation in certain ways. *See Cowan v. Salt Lake Hardware Co.*, 221 P.2d 625 (Utah 1950). It is probable that most of these cases have been overruled by statutes similar to MBCA 10.01(b), but the doctrine may continue to have limited vitality in a few states.

   c. One issue on which this theory was applied as late as the 1930s is whether arrearages of cumulative dividends on preferred stock may be eliminated by amendment to the articles of incorporation. *Keller v. Wilson & Co.*, 190 A. 115 (Del.1936). An amendment that runs afoul of the vested rights theory may nonetheless be valid if it is accomplished by merger of a corporation into a newly created and wholly owned subsidiary. See *Federal United Corporation v. Havender*, 11 A.2d 331 (Del. 1940); *Hottenstein v. York Ice Machinery Corp.*, 136 F.2d 944 (3d Cir. 1943); *Bove v. Community Hotel Corp. of* Newport, R. I., 249 A.2d 89 (R.I.1969).

 d. The requirement of unanimous consent for amendments to the articles of incorporation permits individual stockholders to block amendments unless they receive special consideration or payment. *See, e.g., Matteson v. Ziebarth*, 242 P.2d 1025 (Wash. 1952). Thus, in lieu of the vested rights theory, some courts have developed a broad equitable principle that an amendment may be challenged if it is not reasonable or in good faith or if it does not serve a valid business purpose. *Dentel v. Fidelity Sav. & Loan Ass'n*, 539 P.2d 649 (Or.1975). *See also Singer v. Magnavox Co.*, 380 A.2d 969 (Del. 1977) (freezeout merger on grounds that stockholders were entitled to maintain investment in shares in the absence of business purpose for merger). *But see Weinberger v. UOP, Inc.*, 457 A.2d 701 (Del. 1983) (overruling Singer on this point).

2. Procedural Requirements

State statutes relating to the amendment process vary widely. And most states permit amendments to be made in different ways.

 a. In most states, the board of directors must initiate a proposal to amend the articles of incorporation. (In Delaware and a few other states, shareholders may act by majority written consent without preliminary action by the board of directors.) After proposal by the board of directors, the proposed amendments must be submitted to the shareholders for approval. Notice of the proposed amendment and a copy or summary thereof must be given to all shareholders (voting and nonvoting). MBCA 10.03(d).

 b. MBCA requires approval by a simple majority of shares present and voting at a meeting of the stockholders. MBCA 10.03 Some states require a two-thirds vote of *outstanding* shares to approve an amendment. Other states require a majority of *outstanding* shares.

 c. The board of directors, when it approves amendments to be presented to shareholders, may condition the submission on such terms as it desires, e.g., that the amendment be approved by each class of shares, voting as separate voting groups, even though not specifically required by statute.

d. Most states permit minor amendments to be made by the incorporators or initial directors before shares have been issued. MBCA 10.05. Many states also authorize the board of directors, acting alone, to adopt certain minor amendments. *See* MBCA 10.02 (authorizing amendment by the board of directors acting alone to extend the duration of the corporation if incorporated at a time when limited duration was required by law, to delete the names and addresses of the initial directors and the initial registered agent, to change each issued share of the only outstanding class of shares into a greater number of whole shares of the same class, to reduce the number of authorized shares to reflect the reacquisition of shares that may not be reissued, to eliminate classes of shares of which none are outstanding, and to make minor changes to the corporation's name). In addition, when the corporation issues shares with rights specified by the board of directors pursuant to blank check authority under MBCA 6.02, the articles of incorporation must be amended by the board of directors in effect to record the rights of the shares issued. Such an amendment is sometimes called a certificate of designation, but it nonetheless becomes part of the articles of incorporation.

e. The statutes of many states authorize amendments to articles of incorporation of corporations in bankruptcy or reorganization to be made by order of court without requiring approval of either shareholders or directors. MBCA 10.08.

f. After an amendment is approved, articles of amendment must be filed with the secretary of state. If an amendment makes a change in outstanding shares or rights of shareholders, or an exchange, reclassification or cancellation of shares or rights is to be made pursuant to the amendment, the articles of amendment must set forth the provisions necessary to effect the transaction. For example, it may be required that holders of reclassified shares surrender old shares before new shares may be issued. Such implementing provisions may appear in the articles of amendment rather than in the amendments themselves. MBCA 10.06.

g. A corporation that has filed several articles of amendments at various times may restate the articles of incorporation so as to create a unified document and eliminate superseded provisions. MBCA 10.07. Restated articles of incorporation that do not make any substantive change may be approved by the board of directors acting alone.

3. Procedural Protections Against Abusive Amendments

An amendment to the articles of incorporation may adversely affect the holders of one class of shares to the advantage of holders of another class. For example, an amendment to the articles of incorporation may eliminate the right of a class of preferred stock to cumulative dividends and may even do so retroactively.

a.   The primary protection against abuse is the requirement that such an amendment be approved by the separate vote of any class of shares that would be adversely affected by the amendment or that would be affected in a specified way. The MBCA refers to this procedure as *voting by voting group.*

b.   Under Delaware law, a class is entitled to vote as a class only if it would be adversely affected by the amendment. This can give rise to nice questions of whether a change constitutes an adverse change. *See Dalton v. American Investment Co.,* 490 A2d 574 (Del.Ch. 1985).

c.   Under MBCA 10.04, a class is entitled to vote as a separate group only if the amendment would: (1) effect an exchange or reclassification of all or part of the shares of the class into shares of another class; (2) effect an exchange or reclassification, or create the right of exchange, of all or part of the shares of another class into shares of the class; (3) change the rights, preferences, or limitations of all or part of the shares of the class; (4) change the shares of all or part of the class into a different number of shares of the same class; (5) create a new class of shares having rights or preferences with respect to distributions or to dissolution that are prior or superior to the shares of the class; (6) increase the rights, preferences, or number of authorized shares of any class that, after giving effect to the amendment, have rights or preferences with respect to distributions or to dissolution that are prior or superior to the shares of the class; (7) limit or deny an existing preemptive right of all or part of the shares of the class; or (8) cancel or otherwise affect rights to distributions that have accumulated but not yet been authorized on all or part of the shares of the class.

d.   The underlying objective of class voting is to require voting by voting groups on all amendments that are uniquely burdensome to the voting group. *Levin v. Mississippi River Fuel Corp.*, 386 U.S. 162 (1967). The basic idea of voting by voting groups is that if a majority of a class of shares adversely affected by an amendment is willing to accept that amendment, it should be approved. For example, where an amendment is proposed that would eliminate dividend arrearages on a class of cumulative preferred stock by converting that stock into common stock constituting a majority of the common stock that would be outstanding if the merger is approved, the transaction may be seen as akin to a sale of control to the preferred as a class in exchange for giving the prospect of payment sometime in the future. *See Bove v. Community Hotel Corp. of Newport, R. I.*, 249 A.2d 89 (R.I.1969). Whether the transaction is fair or desirable may be a matter of differing opinion among the affected preferred stockholders. A majority vote in favor would seem to indicate that the tradeoff represents a gain for the affected class and should go forward. In other words, the requirement of a class vote may be a good substitute for a market based resolution.

e. Where a class of shares is specially affected by an amendment, a vote of that class is required even if shares are otherwise nonvoting shares. MBCA 10.04. Similarly, when two corporations merge and the non surviving corporation has a class of nonvoting preferred stock outstanding, the preferred stock may usually vote as a class on the merger if its rights under the articles of incorporation of the surviving corporation would differ from its existing rights.

f. Many statutes extend the right to vote by class only to classes of shares and not to series within a class. The theory is that the class of blank shares (out of which series are created) is itself a single class of shares. This theory is unrealistic as a practical matter since differences between series may be as great as or greater than differences between classes. MBCA 10.04 extends the right to vote by voting groups to classes or series that are affected in different ways but states that if an amendment affects two or more classes or series in essentially the same way, the classes or series vote as a single voting group on the amendment.

4. Appraisal Rights

Many states provide for appraisal rights instead of the right to vote as a voting group on an amendment to the articles of incorporation. This right permits certain dissenting shareholders to have the value of their shares ascertained by judicial proceeding and paid to them in cash by the corporation. Prior to 1999, the MBCA provided for the right of dissent and appraisal with respect to an amendment of the articles of incorporation that materially and adversely affects rights in respect of a dissenter's shares because it: (1) alters or abolishes a preferential right of the shares; (2) creates, alters, or abolishes a right in respect of redemption, including a provision respecting a sinking fund for the redemption or repurchase, of the shares; (3) alters or abolishes a preemptive right of the holder of the shares to acquire shares or other securities; (4) excludes or limits the right of the shares to vote on any matter, or to cumulate votes, other than a limitation by dilution through issuance of shares or other securities with similar voting rights; or (5) reduces the number of shares owned by the shareholder to a fraction of a share if the fractional share so created is to be acquired for cash (effects a freezeout by reverse stock split).

E. AMENDMENTS TO THE BYLAWS

In most jurisdictions, the bylaws of a corporation may be amended either by the board of directors or by the stockholders. In some jurisdictions, power to amend the bylaws may reside exclusively in the stockholders or the board of directors unless the articles of incorporation provide otherwise. Under the MBCA, the articles of incorporation may reserve the power to amend the bylaws, exclusively to the stockholders but not to the board of directors. MBCA 10.20. Moreover, the stockholders in adopting a bylaw may provide that it may not be amended by the board of directors.

a. Where the stockholders have the power to amend the bylaws, there is no need for an amendment to be proposed by the board of directors as there is with an amendment to the articles of incorporation. Thus, the stockholders may amend the bylaws by the solicitation of consents. Under the MBCA, however, the stockholders may not act outside a meeting except unanimously. Thus, the power to amend by consent is limited. There is no such limitation under Delaware law.

b. Under the MBCA, a stockholder-adopted bylaw that increases a quorum or voting requirement for the board of directors may be amended only by the stockholders unless the bylaw provides otherwise. (The bylaw may provide that it may be amended only by a specified vote of the stockholders or the board of directors.) A director-adopted bylaw that increases a quorum or voting requirement for the board of directors may be amended by the directors but only if the board of directors meets the same quorum and voting requirements specified in the bylaw. MBCA 10.21.

c. Although statutory law appears to permit amendments to the bylaws for virtually any purpose, the courts have limited the power of the board of directors and even the stockholders where they seek to exercise this power for purposes of entrenchment or unduly limiting the power of the board of directors to manage the corporation. *See Black v. Hollinger International, Inc.*, 872 A.2d 559 (Del. 2005); *Blasius v. Atlas Corp.*, 564 A.2d 651 (Del. Ch. 1988); *Schnell v. Chris-Craft Industries, Inc.*, 285 A.2d 437 (Del. 1971). *See also Carmody v. Toll Bros., Inc.*, 723 A.2d 1180 (Del. Ch. 1998); *Quickturn Design Systems, Inc. v. Mentor Graphics Corp.*, 721 A.2d 1281 (Del. 1998).

F. VOTING FOR DIRECTORS

Elections of directors may be by *straight voting* or *cumulative voting*. In a few states constitutional or statutory provisions mandate cumulative voting in all elections of directors. In most states a corporation may elect by appropriate provisions in its articles of incorporation whether or not to have cumulative voting. MBCA 7.28. Default rules vary by state. The default rule in most commercially important states is straight voting. In some states, cumulative voting is permitted (even if apparently mandated by the articles of incorporation) only if proxy materials state that the election will be so conducted or a stockholder notifies the corporation of intent to vote cumulatively at least 48 hours before the meeting. In elections for directors, all directors run at large and not for a particular seal. Thus, stockholders may not vote against a candidate except by voting in favor of other candidates.

1. **Straight Voting**

In straight voting, a stockholder may cast the number of votes equal to the number of shares held for candidates for each position to be filled on the board of directors.

a. Under straight voting, stockholders holding a majority of the voting shares can always elect the entire board of directors.

b. Straight voting is simple and easy to understand. As a result, it is widely used in publicly held corporations.

2. **Cumulative Voting**

In cumulative voting, each stockholder determines the aggregate number of votes by multiplying the number of shares held by the number of positions to be filled. Each stockholder may cast that number of votes for one or more candidates. MBCA 7.28(a).

a. Cumulative voting permits minority stockholders to elect one or more directors in certain circumstances.

b. The formula for determining the number of shares required to elect one director under cumulative voting is:

$$N=S/(D+1)+1$$

where N equals the required number of shares, S equals the total number of shares outstanding, and D equals the total number of directors standing for election. For example, if there are 1000 shares outstanding and four directors to be elected, the formula shows that the number of shares required to elect one director is (1000/5) + 1 or 201. The formula may be modified to determine the number of votes to be cast to assure the election of one director:

$$N=V/(D+1)+1$$

where V equals the total number of votes to be cast at the meeting: For example, if there are 1000 shares outstanding, there are 4000 total votes that may be cast in an election for four directors, and the formula shows that the number of votes required to elect a single director is (4000/5) + 1 or 801. Whether solving for shares or votes, the required number for the election of one director is a fraction of the total votes to be cast equal to $1/(D+1)$ plus one vote. Thus, if twelve directors are to be elected, the number of shares or votes required to assure the election of one particular person to the board of directors is 1/13 plus one vote.

3. Advantages and Disadvantages of Cumulative Voting

The primary advantage of cumulative voting is that it is more democratic in that it permits minority representation on the board. It also may permit the election of a watchdog director to oversee the majority's management of the corporation. The primary disadvantage is that it may increase partisanship on the board. Moreover, cumulative voting is complex and may be confusing to stockholders.

a. Although the general rule is that a director may be removed without cause by a majority vote of the stockholders, most states limit the power to remove a director elected by cumulative voting to situations in which the vote to retain the director is insufficient to have elected him if the vote were cast in an election for directors in which cumulative voting was permitted. MBCA 8.08(c).

b. The effects of cumulative voting can be minimized in several ways.

- In states where it is not mandatory, the stockholders may amend the articles of incorporation to eliminate cumulative voting. *Maddock v. Vorclone Corp.*, 147 A. 255 (Del.Ch.1929).

- The board of directors may be reduced in size to reduce the impact of cumulative voting.

- The work of the board may be delegated to a committee that does not have a minority-elected member.

- The board may be stage managed so that all important decisions are made through informal discussions that do not include the minority directors. The formal meeting thereafter may be entirely *pro forma* without discussion and conducted with a quick gavel.

4. Staggered Terms for Directors

Under many state statutes, if the board of directors consists of nine or more members, the board may be or *staggered* or *classified* so that members are elected for two or three year terms with one half or one third being elected each year. Under MBCA 8.06 there is no minimum size board required. Even a board of three may be staggered so that each director serves a three year term. Some state statutes provide that a board of directors consisting of three or more members may be classified if cumulative voting is not permitted.

a. Usually the formal justification for classification is to ensure continuity of service on the board of directors. *Bohannan v. Corporation Com'n*, 313 P.2d 379 (Ariz.1957). The practical justification may be to minimize the effect of cumulative voting. *Stockholders Committee v. Erie Technological Products, Inc.*, 248 F.Supp. 380 (W.D.Pa.1965).

b. In the 1980s, staggered boards of directors removable only for cause became a popular defense against unwanted takeover attempts in publicly held corporations. These provisions prevent the purchasers of a majority of the shares through a cash tender offer from immediately replacing a majority of the board of directors.

G. RECORD OWNERSHIP AND RECORD DATES

Eligibility to vote shares at a stockholders' meeting is determined by *record ownership* on a specified date called the *record date*.

1. Record Ownership

Corporations traditionally issue share certificates in the name of each stockholder and the names and addresses of stockholders are recorded in the share register of the corporation. That person is called the record owner.

a. A person who buys shares becomes a record owner by obtaining possession of the certificate (endorsed by the selling stockholder) and presenting the certificate to the corporation, which cancels the old certificate and issues a new certificate in the name of the purchaser. The purchaser thereby becomes the new record owner. The mechanics of share transfer are generally governed by UCC Article 8. Publicly held corporations usually retain a share transfer agent (often a commercial bank) to process transactions and maintain the share register. Most corporations do not issue a formal certificate for shares unless specifically requested. The common practice is to issue to the stockholder a written statement of the information required to be contained in the certificate. *See* MBCA 6.26.

b. Most stockholders in publicly held corporations leave their shares on deposit with a broker-dealer. And most broker-dealers leave their shares on deposit with a clearing house or share depository (usually the Depository Trust Corporation (DTC)) which officially registers the shares in the name of a nominee corporation (Cede & Company in the case of DTC). In most cases the clearing house or depository is the *record owner* of the shares and the individual stockholder is the *beneficial owner* or *equitable owner* of the shares. Such shares are usually described as being held in *street name*. Ownership of the shares can be transferred simply by a *book entry* in the records of the broker, the clearing house, or the depository. No delivery of certificates is required.

c. Under current practice, securities transactions settle on the third day after execution, a practice known as T + 3 (*trade plus three*). If a customer places an order to buy or sell, payment or delivery of the certificate or documentation must occur no later than the third day after the trade. And the trade is posted in the customer account on that date. The book entry system permits much more efficient trading and transfer of shares. If an individual owner of shares keeps shares registered in his own name, the sale of the shares requires additional paper-work. The stockholder must endorse the certificates and deliver them to the broker-dealer (within three days). Shares held in book entry form may be bought and sold by a phone call. No physical signature and delivery of certificates is necessary. Moreover, the broker-dealer may lend shares left on deposit to traders who want to effect a short sale. Thus, broker-dealers strongly encourage their customers to keep shares on deposit in book entry form, and may even impose a fee for obtaining a share certificate on behalf of a customer.

2. Record Date for Voting

The identity of stockholders entitled to vote at a meeting is determined by the ownership of shares of the corporation on a specific date called the *record date*. The record date may be established by a provision in the bylaws or by designation by the board of directors (which may not set it more than 70 days before the meeting). If no record date is set, the record date is the day before the notice of meeting is delivered to stockholders of record. MBCA 7.05. A similar record date system governs the payment of dividends.

a. Holders of shares transferred on the books of the corporation after the record date do not receive notice of the meeting and are not entitled to vote shares in their own name. The vote of the record owner is viewed by the corporation as the vote of those shares. *See Salgo v. Matthews*, 497 S.W.2d 620 (Tex.Civ.App.1973) (rules relating to record ownership are designed to simplify stockholder voting process and to minimize disputes).

b. In a few states, the corporation may also establish entitlement to vote by closing the transfer books on a specific date and refusing to recognize all subsequent transfers of shares until after the meeting. This procedure is seldom used today and has been eliminated as an option in the MBCA.

c. The beneficial owner of shares on the meeting date may compel the record owner to vote shares as the beneficial owner directs. This is usually done by the record owner granting a proxy to the beneficial owner to permit the beneficial owner to vote the shares. In addition, a court may compel the record owner to execute a proxy appointment in favor of the beneficial owner.

d. The book entry system complicates communication between corporations and their stockholders because corporations do not know the true identity of most stockholders. Thus, in order to hold a stockholder vote, the corporation ordinarily must send proxy materials in bulk to the various brokerage firms that maintain the records of beneficial owners.

The brokerage firms then forward the materials to the beneficial stock-holders (as required by SEC rule) who then mail in the proxy forms. Obviously, this procedure takes time, and in the case of a meeting to be held after minimal notice, there may not be time to complete the process. Thus, SEC rules allow for the record owner to vote the shares in circumstances in which it is unlikely that the beneficial owners will be able to return proxy forms in time to be counted. There are several proxy solicitation firms that are in the business of assisting corporations in connection with finding and communicating with stockholders particularly in the context of a proxy fight or tender offer.

e. The SEC has adopted regulations that permit issuers of publicly held shares to communicate directly with assenting beneficial owners of shares held in book entry form by brokerage firms on behalf of their customers. The brokerage firms must poll their customers stating that their identities and addresses will be provided to the issuer unless the beneficial owner objects to that disclosure. Beneficial owners who do not object are known as NOBOs (non objecting beneficial owners). An issuer may be compelled to create a list of NOBOs at the request of a person also seeking the stockholder list as a prelude to mounting a takeover attempt. *Sadler v. NCR Corporation*, 928 F.2d 48 (2d Cir.1991). SEC also amended its rules in 2000 to permit delivery of one set of proxy materials to any given household.

f. Given that most shares are held in street name, each record owner usually represents many beneficial owners. As a result, a company may have relatively few record owners. Under SEC rules, a company with fewer than 300 stockholders which is not listed for trading on a stock exchange may deregister as a public company and cease filing public reports as well as complying with numerous SEC rules that are triggered by the requirement to report. Given that reporting is expensive and creates a variety of opportunities for stockholder litigation, several companies have chosen to deregister under these circumstances.

g. The MBCA also has addressed the problems of book ownership to some extent by permitting corporations to adopt rules by which beneficial stockholders may register with the corporation and exercise the rights of record owners. MBCA 7.23. The laws of many states, however, confer rights only on record owners. Thus, only a record owner may bring a derivative action or exercise the right of dissent and appraisal. Under Delaware law, for example, an appraisal proceeding must be commenced in the name of the record owner. On the other hand, not all beneficial owners may want to exercise their appraisal rights. Thus, Delaware law allows the record owner to seek appraisal on behalf of some stockholders but not others, but only for all of the shares held by an individual beneficial stockholder.

h. Prior to 1986, practically all corporate bonds were issued in bearer form and could be sold or negotiated only by physical delivery of the certificate itself. Typically, neither the issuer nor the bond trustee had any record of who actually owned specific bonds. This system created serious problems in communicating with bondholders other than by newspaper notice. But because bondholders cannot vote on matters of corporate governance, this seldom mattered to the issuing corporation except in limited circumstances relating to the modification of bond terms or if the bonds were called for redemption. The 1986 Tax Act prohibited deduction of interest payments on bearer bonds issued thereafter because it was difficult to determine who received the interest and was subject to tax thereon. As a result, virtually all corporate bonds are now issued in registered form, which has also greatly simplified the notice and communication process for bondholders.

3. Voting Lists

Corporations must prepare an accurate voting list of the record owners entitled to vote at a meeting. This list must be available for inspection at the meeting, and under most statutes must also be available for inspection for a period of time before the meeting. MBCA 7.20. The failure to prepare this list does not affect the validity of any action taken at a meeting. Some state statutes impose a penalty on the corporate officer who is obligated to prepare a voting list but fails to do so.

4. Miscellaneous Voting Rules

Statutes of many states set forth rules as to who may vote shares in certain circumstances. MBCA 7.24 contains more elaborate rules than most statutes addressing acceptance of votes of shares owned by other entities, fiduciaries, pledges, beneficial owners, and co-owners.

5. Inspectors of Election

In a publicly traded corporation, it is standard practice to appoint inspectors of election to determine the number of shares outstanding and the voting power of each, the number of shares represented at the meeting, and the validity of ballots and proxies. Inspectors of election also count the votes and determine the result. Under the MBCA it is required for a public corporation to appoint inspectors of election. MBCA 7.29. A non public corporation may also appoint inspectors of election, but it is not required. Inspectors of election may be officers or employees of the corporation. Disputes as to entitlement to vote are usually resolved by inspectors of election on the basis of statutory voting rules and records of the corporation. *Salgo v. Matthews*, 497 S.W.2d 620 (Tex.Civ.App. 1973).

H. PROXY VOTING

A *proxy* is the grant of authority by a stockholder to someone else to vote the shares. The relationship is one of principal and agent.

1. Terminology

Depending on the context, the term *proxy* may refer to the piece of paper granting the authority, to the grant of authority itself, or to the person holding the authority. The MBCA uses the term in the last sense. The MBCA uses the term *proxy appointment* and *proxy appointment form*, respectively, to refer the other senses. *See* MBCA 7.22. Voting by proxy is the norm in publicly held corporations where the large number of stockholders makes personal voting impractical. Voting by proxy may also be used in closely held corporations if a stockholder will not attend a meeting.

2. Formal Requirements

A proxy appointment must be in writing. Under many statutes a proxy appointment is valid for eleven months only, thus necessitating a new appointment for each annual meeting. Under MBCA 7.22(c) a proxy appointment is valid for a longer period if specified in the appointment form.

3. Revocability

The general rule is that a proxy appointment is revocable.

a. The act of revocation may consist of any action inconsistent with the continued existence of the grant of authority.

b. To be irrevocable a proxy appointment must (i) state that it is irrevocable; and (ii) be *coupled with an interest*. Examples of appointments that are coupled with an interest include:

- A proxy who is a pledgee under a valid pledge of the shares.

- A proxy who is a person who has agreed to purchase the shares under an executory contract of sale.

- A proxy who is a person who has lent money or contributed valuable property to the corporation.

- A proxy who is a person who has contracted to perform services for the corporation as an officer.

- A proxy appointment given in order to effectuate the provisions of a valid pooling agreement (described below).

c. Some courts have upheld irrevocable proxy appointments that do not squarely fall within any of the above categories or meet the above requirements, but some statutes provide that the five situations described above are the only ones in which an irrevocable proxy appointment may be recognized.

d. A proxy appointment is revocable even if it is stated to be irrevocable and even if consideration for the appointment is paid. *Stein v. Capital Outdoor Advertising, Inc.,* 159 S.E.2d 351 (N.C.1968).

e. Vote selling is generally thought to be against public policy and unenforceable. There are relatively few cases addressing naked vote selling, but most hold that purchased votes are void. NYBCL § 609(e) expressly prohibits a stockholder from selling his vote. But in *Schreiber v. Carney,* 447 A.2d 17 (Del.Ch.1982), the court refused to invalidate an arrangement in which a major stockholder contracted, for consideration, to vote in the same manner as a majority of the independent stockholders. There was full disclosure of the arrangement to the independent stockholders.

I. STOCKHOLDER VOTING AGREEMENTS

Agreements among stockholders that they will vote their shares cooperatively or as a unit generally enforceable. MBCA 7.31. These are often called *pooling agreements* or *pooling arrangements* in older cases.

1. Scope of Valid Stockholders Agreements

Stockholder voting agreements are valid so long as they relate to issues, such as the election of directors, on which stockholders may vote. *E. K. Buck Retail*

Stores v. Harkert, 62 N.W.2d 288 (Neb.1954); *Weil v. Beresth*, 220 A.2d 456 (Conn.1966); *Ringling Brothers-Barnum & Bailey Combined Shows v. Ringling*, 53 A.2d 441 (Del.1947). If the agreement deals with issues that are within the discretion of directors, the agreement may be invalid.

2. Formal Requirements

A few states have adopted statutes regulating voting agreements, limiting the period during which a voting agreement may continue (*e.g.*, to ten years), requiring that copies of the voting agreement be deposited at the principal office of the corporation, and so forth. In most states, a voting agreement is seen as a simple private contract subject to few limitations.

3. Determination of How Shares Should be Voted

Voting agreements may provide that the shares be voted on a specified proposal or motion. Or such matters may be the subject of subsequent negotiation and decision by the stockholders with some method of determining how the shares are to be voted in the event of a failure to agree. Resolution of disagreements is often by arbitration.

4. Enforcement of Voting Agreements

Enforcement of a voting agreement creates special problems because the shares are registered in the names of the individual stockholders on the books of the corporation.

a. In one leading case the Delaware Supreme Court enforced a voting agreement by disqualifying the shares sought to be voted in violation of the agreement. *Ringling Brothers-Barnum & Bailey Combined Shows v. Ringling*, 53 A.2d 441 (Del.1947). The effect was to permit a minority stockholder to elect half of the board under cumulative voting even though the minority stockholder would ordinarily have been able only to elect two of seven directors.

b. Some state statutes specifically address the enforcement issue by authorizing specific performance of pooling agreements. *See* MBCA 7.31(b).

c. New York makes a proxy granted in connection with a pooling agreement irrevocable. To take advantage of this enforcement device, the agreement should contain specific reference to the irrevocable nature of the proxy appointment, and should designate who may exercise the irrevocable proxy and under what circumstances.

J. VOTING TRUSTS

A voting trust is a device by which the power to vote may be temporarily but irrevocably severed from title to shares. A voting trust is a formal arrangement by which shares are registered in the name of one or more voting trustees on the books of the corporation. In most jurisdictions, a voting trust is the only way one may effectively create an irrevocable proxy without coupling it with an economic interest. A voting trust is a control mechanism that may be abusive but generally no more so than other control devices. *Oceanic Exploration Co. v. Grynberg*, 428 A.2d 1 (Del.1981).

1. Common Law

At common law there was suspicion of voting trusts. While this attitude has been partially reversed by state statutes recognizing and validating voting trusts, some of the rules discussed below can be traced to early judicial hostility to this device. *See Tankersley v. Albright*, 514 F.2d 956 (7th Cir.1975) (refusing to grant summary judgment on the validity of a common law voting trust.)

2. Statutory Requirements

State statutes uniformly recognize the validity of voting trusts that meet statutory requirements. *See* MBCA 7.30. The most common such requirements are:

a. The agreement may not extend beyond ten years.

b. The agreement must be in writing.

c. A copy of the agreement must be deposited with the corporation at its registered office and be available for inspection by stockholders and holders of beneficial interests in the trust.

d. Some states have imposed the further requirement that the essential purpose of the trust must be a proper one.

e. Because of the common law attitude toward voting trusts, discussed above, a voting trust agreement that fails to comply with all statutory requirements is considered invalid in its entirety in most states. Even though these requirements are simple ones that may be easily satisfied, there are numerous cases in which the requirements have been ignored with the result that the voting trust has been struck down.

f. An arrangement that has most of the characteristics of a voting trust must fully meet the applicable statutory requirements if it is to be upheld even though it is formally a voting agreement or proxy appointment rather than a voting trust. *Abercrombie v. Davies*, 130 A.2d 338 (Del.1957). A limited partnership formed in order to obtain voting control of a corporation may be a voting trust and is valid only if statutory requirements are complied with. *Hall v. Staha*, 800 S.W.2d 396 (Ark.1990).

g. A voting trust may be set aside if later events frustrate its essential purpose. *Selig v. Wexler*, 247 N.E.2d 567 (Mass.1969).

3. Financial Rights

Voting trust agreements usually provide that all dividends or other corporate distributions pass through to the beneficial owners of the shares so that all attributes of ownership other than the power to vote remain in the beneficial owners. Trustees may issue voting trust certificates to represent the beneficial interests; these certificates may be traded much as shares of stock are traded.

4. Uses of Voting Trusts

Voting trusts may be used for a wide variety of purposes:

a. The preservation, retention or securing of control.

b. Assurance of temporary stability in control of a corporation coming out of bankruptcy or receivership or being created as the result of divestment from another corporation pursuant to the anti-trust laws. *Brown v. McLanahan*, 148 F.2d 703 (4th Cir.1945).

c. Elimination of a troublesome stockholder from participation in control of a corporation.

d. Obtaining credit, when required by creditors as a condition of providing needed financing to the corporation.

5. Voting Trusts in Publicly Held Corporations

Voting trusts are generally considered to be inconsistent with corporate democracy in corporations with publicly traded securities. The New York Stock Exchange usually refuses to list for trading a security that is partially held in a voting trust.

6. Powers of Trustees

The power of trustees to vote on fundamental corporate matters depends on the specific language of the voting trust, *Clarke Memorial College v. Monaghan Land Co.*, 257 A.2d 234 (Del.Ch.1969). Some decisions have imposed equitable limitations on the power of trustees to approve fundamental changes despite clear and broad language in the governing document. *Brown v. McLanahan*, 148 F.2d 703 (4th Cir.1945).

K. CLASSES OF SHARES

The simplest and most effective device by which the control rights of particular shares may be assured is to create multiple classes of shares. This is a particularly useful device in cases in which it is necessary to allocate voting power in different proportions from financial interests, as when one stockholder contributes cash and one contributes services but both desire equal control rights. Classes of shares may be created without voting rights, with fractional or multiple votes per share, with power to select one or more directors, or with limited financial interests in the corporation. MBCA § 6.01 provides that the articles of incorporation may authorize shares with special voting rights, and MBCA 8.04 provides that if the articles authorize dividing shares into classes, the articles may also authorize the election of all or a specified number of directors by the holders of one or more classes.

■ VII. DIRECTORS & OFFICERS

A. NUMBER AND QUALIFICATIONS OF DIRECTORS

In most states today the board of directors may consist of one or more members. MBCA 8.03(a). Residence and shareholding requirements for directors, while once common, have been largely eliminated. MBCA 8.02. MBCA 8.03 states expressly that only individuals may serve as directors. Delaware law was amended in 2002 to make it clear that only natural persons may be directors. DGCL 141(b). In some European legal systems an entity may serve as a director. Although it is common practice in the United States for a corporation to serve as a general partner in a limited partnership, it does not appear that any states permit non natural persons to serve as directors. Directors need not be full-time employees of the corporation and are not required to devote their efforts exclusively to the corporation. (Of course, a full-time employee may also be a director, but the role of director as such is not a full-time responsibility.)

1. Board Size

Historically, three directors were required and a few states retain this requirement.

a. NYBCL 702, and the statutes of a few other states allow boards of one or two directors only where there are one or two stockholders.

b. Most states simply state that the board may consist of one or more members without qualification.

c. The number of directors is usually established in the bylaws; if the bylaws are silent the number may be set by the statute as either the minimum permitted in the state or the number of initial directors set forth in the articles of incorporation.

2. Increase or Decrease

The number of directors may be increased or decreased by amendments to the bylaws, but a decrease does not have the effect of eliminating or shortening the term of any sitting director.

a. Because the board of directors generally has power to amend bylaws, the board of directors in effect has power to determine its own size under most state statutes.

b. The statutes of some states impose limits on the extent to which a board of directors may exercise its power to amend bylaws to increase or decrease its own size without stockholder approval.

B. MEETINGS OF DIRECTORS

Regular meetings of the board occur at the times specified in the bylaws. Special meetings may be called as specified in the bylaws.

1. Notice

No notice of regular meetings is required. MBCA 8.22(a). Special meetings may be called upon two days notice unless a longer or shorter notice is required or permitted by the bylaws. MBCA 8.22(b).

2. Quorum

A quorum of directors consists of a majority of the directors except that a greater or lesser number (but no less than one-third) may be specified by the bylaws. MBCA 8.24(b).

a. Generally, only lawfully elected directors may be counted toward quorum or voting requirements. *Dillon v. Scotten, Dillon Co.*, 335 F.Supp. 566 (D.Del.1971).

b. A board of directors may act on a specific matter only if a quorum is present when the action is taken. MBCA 8.24(c). Many state statutes are silent on this question.

c. The board of directors may sometimes be able to act even though a quorum is not present where vacancies exist and the action to be taken is the filling of those vacancies. Depending on the language of the specific statute, this power may exist only when the number of directors *in office* is less than a quorum; or when the number of directors *acting* is less than a quorum even though the number *in office* is greater than a quorum. *Jacobson v. Moskowitz*, 313 N.Y.S.2d 684, 261 N.E.2d 613 (N.Y. 1970). MBCA 8.10(a)(3) adopts the former position.

d. Some courts have treated a willful refusal to attend a meeting as a breach of fiduciary duty. *Gearing v. Kelly*, 227 N.Y.S.2d 897, 182 N.E.2d 391 (N.Y. 1962). Other courts have recognized that this tactic may be part of a struggle for control and have held that it should not be treated as improper.

e. In a closely held corporation, an important planning device that creates a veto power on the part of minority stockholders is to increase the quorum requirement for the board of directors to all of the directors, and to require a unanimous vote to approve specific actions. If a minority stockholder has power to elect at least one director, these provisions assure minority participation on all matters, but they also increase the likelihood of deadlock.

3. Voting

Directors traditionally vote on a per capita basis. A majority vote of those present at a meeting where a quorum is present is necessary for the board to act. MBCA 8.24(c). The bylaws may increase the vote necessary for approval of an action up to and including unanimity. DGCL 141(d) permits certificates of incorporation to provide that some directors may have a fractional vote or multiple votes based on shareholdings rather than a per capita one. These voting arrangements may mirror the relative shareholdings of individual stockholders.

4. Objection

A director waives objection to the adequacy of notice of a meeting by attending the meeting, unless he or she attends for the sole purpose of objecting to the transaction of any business and does not participate in the business undertaken at the meeting. Even minimal participation is likely to be construed as a waiver. MBCA 8.23(b).

5. Delegation of Duties

The directors may not delegate their duties to third persons and agreements entered into by the corporation which purport to do so may be unenforceable.

6. Voting Agreements and Directions

a. The directors may not enter into agreements among themselves relating to how they will vote and generally may not vote by proxy.

b. A majority stockholder may seek to guide the fortunes of a corporation after death by testamentary directions to their trustees. Such directions are generally unenforceable on the ground they restrict the discretion of directors.

C. COMPENSATION

Traditionally, directors served without compensation on the assumption that their financial interest in the corporation was sufficient inducement. In publicly held corporations today, outside directors receive significant compensation as an inducement to devote substantial attention to corporate affairs and in recognition of the danger of liability. *See* MBCA 8.11. Typically, director compensation consists of an annual payment and a per meeting fee (plus expenses). It may also include grants of stock or the right to participate in a retirement plan. In the 1990s, there was a trend toward compensating outside directors with options. That trend appears to have abated as a result of criticism that it tended to induce directors to approve business strategies that were too risky.

D. REMOVAL AND RESIGNATION

1. Removal

Directors may be removed by stockholders, with or without cause, under the statutes of most states. MBCA 8.08. The articles of incorporation, however, may limit the power of removal to removal for cause. Removal by judicial action is also authorized under the statutes of some states.

a. The power to remove directors without cause tends to assure fealty by the board to the majority stockholder.

b. Many publicly held corporations have eliminated the power of stockholders to remove directors without cause as a defensive measure against hostile takeovers. This provision is usually coupled with the staggering of the term of directors.

c. Under the statutes of some states, a court may also remove a director for cause specified in the statute. MBCA 8.09, for example, permits court removal for fraudulent or dishonest conduct, or gross abuse of authority or discretion. Removal for cause by judicial action is appropriate in at least two types of situations. In a publicly held corporation, a judicial proceeding to remove a director for cause, when the director refuses to resign, may be simpler and less expensive than holding a stockholders' meeting to remove the director, an action that must be preceded by a proxy solicitation. In a closely held corporation, judicial removal may be used where the director charged with misconduct declines to resign and possesses the voting power as a stockholder to prevent his own removal.

2. Resignation

The resignation of directors in most states is not expressly covered by statute. MBCA 8.07 permits resignation either immediately or at a future date. A resignation at a future date permits the departing director to participate in the selection of a successor.

E. FILLING VACANCIES

Vacancies created by resignation, death or removal of a director, may be filled either by the board of directors or the stockholders. MBCA 8.10(a). Under older statutes, vacancies created by increasing the size of the board could only be filled by the stockholders, but most modern state statutes permit all vacancies to be filled by the board of directors without regard to the way the vacancies is created.

F. TERM OF OFFICE

Directors serve for the term for which they are elected and a director continues to serve, despite the expiration of the term, until a successor is elected and qualifies or until there is a decrease in the number of directors. MBCA 8.05(e).

G. HOLDOVER DIRECTORS

If directors are not elected at an annual meeting for any reason, or the required annual meeting is never held, the directors then in office hold over until their successors are selected. This principle applies (1) where meetings are held erratically, if at all, and (2) in deadlock situations where the stockholders are evenly divided and unable to elect successors. *Gearing v. Kelly*, 227 N.Y.S.2d 897, 182 N.E.2d 391 (N.Y. 1962).

H. MEETING REQUIREMENT

The common law rule is that the power invested in directors to control and manage the affairs of a corporation is not joint and several, but joint only, and that directors may take action only as a body at a properly constituted meeting. The theory is that stockholders are entitled to a decision reached only after group discussion and deliberation. Views may be changed as a result of discussion, and the sharpening of minds as a result of joint deliberation improves the decisional process. Moreover, unlike stockholders who may vote based on self-interest, a director is required to exercise business judgment on behalf of the corporation. As a result, the board of directors is effectively required to reach a decision, whereas a stockholder may simply decline to vote.

1. Implications

This rule has several important implications. Perhaps most important is that directors may not vote by proxy. Moreover, formalities as to notice, quorum, and similar matters must be fully observed.

a. The rule has the undesirable consequence of permitting a corporation to use its own internal procedural defects as a sword to undo undesired transactions even though a person dealing with a corporation usually has no way of verifying that formalities were in fact completely and fully followed. *Mosell Realty Corp. v. Schofield*, 33 S.E.2d 774 (Va.1945).

b. Several exceptions have been created, including estoppel, ratification, and acquiescence. *See Meyers v. El Tejon Oil & Refining* Co., 174 P.2d 1 (Cal.1946).

c. The common law rule will likely be applied today in situations where it appears that no benefit was received from the transaction by the corporation. *Hurley v. Ornsteen*, 42 N.E.2d 273 (Mass.1942); *Mosell Realty Corp. v. Schofield*, 33 S.E.2d 774 (Va.1945).

2. Variations

a. Most state statutes permit the board of directors or a committee of the board to participate in a meeting by conference call or similar means enabling all persons participating in the meeting to hear each other at the same time. MBCA 8.20(b). Such participation constitutes presence in person at a meeting so as to satisfy the quorum requirement.

b. Most state statutes now permit directors to act by unanimous written consent without a formal meeting. MBCA 8.21. A written consent has the same effect as a unanimous vote.

I. DIRECTOR LIABILITY

Under some circumstances a director can be held personally liable for decisions that cause a loss to the corporation or that are otherwise illegal. In general, all members of the board are presumed to have assented to the action of the board (even if voting against the resolution in question) and are jointly and severally liable in such cases.

1. Written Dissent

Statutes provide that a director is presumed to have assented to an action unless he or she votes against the action or abstains and his or her dissent appears in the written minutes or a written dissent is thereafter timely filed. MBCA 8.24(d).

    a.   Abstention or silence without registering a formal dissent is taken is the equivalent of voting in favor of the action.

    b.   A written dissent must be filed with the presiding officer of the meeting or with the corporation immediately after the meeting.

2. Resignation

The director fearing liability may resign as director, though if the resignation occurs after the objectionable transaction is approved, liability may be avoided only if the director files the appropriate dissent.

3. Limitation of Liability

The statutes of many states permit corporations to limit the liability of directors by specific provision in articles of incorporation. MBCA 2.02(b)(4); DGCL 102(b)(7).

J. RELIANCE ON ADVICE OF OTHERS

Depending on the language of the specific statute, a director may be able to avoid liability in some situations by showing good faith reliance on the advice of others. MBCA 8.30(c).

Generally, reliance defense is not available to a director who has actual knowledge about, or expertise with respect to, the issue in question. MBCA 8.30(c). Statutes permit reliance on one or more of the following:

- The written opinion of legal counsel for the corporation.

- Financial reports prepared by the corporation or by its auditors or accountants.

- Statements by officers or employees of the corporation with respect to matters within their authority.

- Reports by committees of the board other than committees on which the director serves.

K. COMMITTEES

It may be convenient to appoint one or more committees to perform certain of the functions of the board of directors. MBCA 8.25. The committee may specialize on one area of concern to the board (for example, a compensation committee or an audit committee) or may function as a substitute for the full board between meetings (an executive committee).

1. Committee Authority

MBCA 8.25 authorizes only committees composed exclusively of members of the board of directors which are authorized to exercise functions of the board of directors.

a. The board of directors may create advisory committees that may consist of directors and possibly others. These committees may render advice or make recommendations to the board of directors but do not have power to exercise directorial function.

b. A committee formed under MBCA 8.25 may be created only by board action.

c. A committee formed under MBCA 8.25 may have a single member. Some statutes require that a committee have at least two members.

d. The creation of a committee and the delegation to it of authority does not of itself constitute compliance with the directors' statutory duty of care.

e. MBCA 8.25(e) lists four functions that must be exercised by the full board of directors and may not be delegated to a committee:

- declaration of distributions except pursuant to a formula

- proposal of matters requiring a stockholder ratification vote

- filling vacancies on the board or committees

- adoption, amendment, or repeal of bylaws

All other matters may be decided by committees acting on behalf of the board of directors.

2. Executive Committee

An executive committee generally provides oversight over general corporate matters during periods when the board of directors is not sitting.

a. An executive committees usually consists only of directors who are executive officers of the corporation.

b. Under older statutes, an executive committee may be created only if specific provision therefor appears in the articles of incorporation or bylaws. Under MBCA 8.25, any committee, including an executive committee, may be created by a corporation unless the articles of incorporation or bylaws specifically provide otherwise.

c. Some statutes that specifically refer to executive committees impose limitations on the powers of such committees.

d. Delegation of authority to an executive committee generally does not relieve the board of directors, or any member, of any responsibility imposed upon it or them.

3. Audit Committee

An audit committee is now required by SEC rules for publicly held companies. The audit committee perform functions such as the following:

a. Recommends the accounting firm to be employed by the corporation as its independent auditor.

b. Consults with the accounting firm so chosen to be the independent auditors with regard to the plan of audit.

c.   Reviews, in consultation with the independent auditors, the report of audit and the accompanying management letter of response, if any.

d.   Consults with the independent auditors (out of the presence of management) with regard to the adequacy of the internal accounting controls and similar matters.

e.   Reports to the full board of directors the results of the audit and make recommendations for changes to improve the adequacy of the control processes.

4.   Nominating Committee

Most publicly held corporations have a nominating committee that performs some or all of the following functions:

a.   Establish qualifications for directors.

b.   Establish procedures for identifying possible nominees who meet these criteria.

c.   Review the performance of current directors and recommend, where appropriate, that sitting directors be removed or not reappointed.

d.   Recommend the appropriate size and composition of the board of directors.

5.   Compensation Committee

Most publicly held corporations have a compensation committee whose role is to set compensation and retirement benefits for high level executive officers. Most compensation committees consist entirely of non-management directors. The compensation committee may perform some or all of the following functions:

a.   Review and approve (or recommend to the full board) the annual salary, bonus and other benefits, direct and indirect, of the CEO and other designated members of senior management.

b.   Review and submit to the full board of directors recommendations concerning new executive compensation plans.

c. Establish and periodically review the corporation's policies with regard to management perquisites.

d. Review compensation policies relating to members of the board of directors.

e. Review the operation of retirement plans for employees.

f. Review conflict of interest transactions between the corporation and a director.

6. Special Litigation Committee

When derivative litigation is filed by a stockholder on behalf of the corporation, a special litigation committee composed of disinterested directors may be created to review the litigation and determine whether its pursuit is in the best interest of the corporation. The courts generally respect the decision of an independent special litigation committee and may dismiss derivative litigation based on the decision of such a committee. As discussed further below, if the derivative action is based on a claim of negligence, the courts will usually apply the business judgment rule to the decision of the special litigation committee. If the derivative action is based on a duty of loyalty claim, however, the court may review the substance of the committee decision to seek dismissal. In both cases, the court will review whether the committee has conducted an adequate investigation into the matter. *Aronson v. Lewis*, 473 A.2d 805 (Del. 1984).

L. STATUTORY DESIGNATIONS OF CORPORATE OFFICERS

State corporation statutes contain only skeletal provisions dealing with corporate officers. The officers of a corporation, and the functions they are to perform, are usually defined in the bylaws or in resolutions adopted by the board of directors rather than by statute.

1. Traditional Statutes

Traditional statutes such as the MBCA (1969) provide that each corporation shall have a president, a treasurer, a secretary, and (usually) one or more vice-presidents.

a. Under these statutes a person may fill two or more offices simultaneously except the offices of president and secretary. This exception was based on the belief that execution of documents required signatures of two officers, one executing the document and the other attesting to the execution.

b. These statutes also grant unlimited authority to the board of directors to create such additional offices as the board deems appropriate.

2. Flexible Statutes

Neither the MBCA nor the DGCL specifies officer titles. Both grant the corporation freedom to determine which officers it chooses to have. MBCA 8.40(a); DGCL 142. Problems of implied or apparent authority based on titles are avoided under these statutes.

a. Both statutes recognize that there must be an officer performing the functions usually associated with the office of the corporate secretary. MBCA 1.40(20), 8.40(c); DGCL 142(a).

b. Both statutes permit any individual to hold two or more offices at the same time without limitation or restriction. MBCA 8.40(d); DGCL 142(a).

M. NON–STATUTORY OFFICERS

Boards of directors or bylaw provisions may create new or different offices under both types of statutes. These various offices are sometimes created by specific provisions in the bylaws. But more typically these titles are created by a simple resolution of the board of directors.

1. Publicly Held Corporations

Publicly held corporations typically use functional designations such as: Chairman of the Board of Directors, Chief Executive Officer (CEO), Chief Financial Officer (CFO), Chief Legal Officer (CLO), and Chief Operations Officer (COO). If the corporation is formed in a state that requires that every corporation have a "president," the person holding that office may be a senior officer subordinate to other officers such as the CEO.

2. Assistant Officers

Most corporations find it convenient to designate numerous assistant officers, particularly assistant secretaries or treasurers. In a corporation with several officers in different locations a vice president and assistant officers may be named for each office to permit decision-making and the execution of documents at the local level.

N. AUTHORITY OF OFFICERS IN GENERAL

Corporate officers, including the president, have relatively little inherent power by virtue of their offices. The principal repository of power to conduct the business and affairs of the corporation is in the board of directors not the officers.

1. Sources of Authority

Corporate officers may draw authority from the following sources:

a. Statutes (to a limited extent).

b. Articles of incorporation (though provisions dealing with officers in this document are uncommon).

c. Bylaws (which usually outline the functions of officers in some detail).

d. Resolutions of the board granting authority to officers.

e. Specific resolutions of the board authorizing corporate officers to enter into specific transactions reviewed and approved by the board.

f. Course of conduct.

g. Many cases recognize that some authority may be implied from the office held by the person acting. This is referred to as inherent authority.

h. Many cases find that authority exists in specific circumstances by the application of amorphous doctrines such as ratification, estoppel, or implied consent inferred from inaction by the board of directors. MBCA 8.41 provides that an officer has such authority as is set forth in the bylaws or, to the extent consistent with the bylaws, the duties prescribed by the board of directors or by direction of an officer authorized by the board of directors to prescribe the duties of other officers.

2. Inherent Authority from Description of Office

The bylaws of the corporation usually describe in general terms the roles of traditional corporate officers. The brief descriptions that follow, taken from typical bylaw provisions, define the authority of corporate officers.

a. The president is the principal executive officer of the corporation, and, subject to the control of the board, in general supervises and controls the business and affairs of the corporation.

b. The vice president performs the duties of the president in his absence or in the event of his death, inability or refusal to act. Vice presidents act in the order designated at the time of their election, or in the absence of designation, in the order of their election.

c. The secretary keeps the minutes of meetings of the stockholders and the board of directors, sees that all notices are duly given as required by the bylaws, is custodian of the corporate records and of the corporate seal, sees that the seal of the corporation is properly affixed on authorized documents, attests to the execution by the president or vice president of certificates for shares of the corporation, important contracts, and other documents, and has charge of the stock register and transfer books of the corporation if there is no transfer agent.

d. The treasurer has charge and custody of and is responsible for all funds and securities of the corporation, and receives, gives receipts for, and deposits, all moneys due and payable to the corporation. The treasurer may be required to give a bond to ensure the faithful performance of his duties. The treasurer, however, does not have inherent or apparent authority to execute a loan guarantee. *General Overseas Films, Ltd. v. Robin Intern., Inc.*, 542 F.Supp. 684 (S.D.N.Y.1982).

3. Inherent Authority of the President

It is a popular belief that the president of a corporation has wide discretion to enter into not only ordinary business transactions, but extraordinary transactions as well.

a. Most courts have held that this view is erroneous. The traditional position is that the president has only limited authority. *Black v. Harrison Home Co.*, 99 P. 494 (Cal.1909); *In re Westec Corp.*, 434 F.2d 195 (5th Cir.1970). The power to approve significant transactions is in the board of directors, not the president. *Schwartz v. United Merchants & Manufacturers*, 72 F.2d 256 (2d Cir.1934).

b. This construction of the president's authority may lead to injustice because persons relying on appearances may discover that their reliance was ill-advised. Persons aware of the limited authority of a president are forced to demand an exhibit of the president's authority before dealing with him.

c. There is a trend to broaden the implied authority of the president. Some courts have concluded that a president presumptively has any powers which the board of directors could give him. Others have held that the president has authority to enter into transactions "arising in the usual and regular course of business," and have construed that phrase broadly.

4. DETERMINATION OF AN OFFICER'S AUTHORITY

A person dealing with a corporate officer who purports to represent the corporation should verify the officer's authority.

a. Reliance on oral representations is hazardous because an agent's representation about his or her authority without more is not binding on the principal.

b. Reliance on the office held by an individual is also hazardous because of the common law view described above that such offices carry with them only very limited authority to bind the corporation.

c. The formal way to ensure that the corporation is bound is to require the person purporting to act for the corporation to deliver, prior to the closing of the transaction, a certified copy of a resolution of the board of directors authorizing the transaction (although such formalities may be uneconomic in a small transaction). The certificate should be executed by the secretary of the corporation. There is no reason to go behind the certificate. The corporation is estopped to deny the secretary's certificate, because keeping and certifying corporate records is within the actual authority of the secretary. *In re Drive–In Development Corp.,* 371 F.2d 215 (7th Cir.1966). Nevertheless, lawyers often conduct *due diligence* reviews of contemplated transactions which may include verification of the authority of the officer entering into the transaction. This review may include examination of the corporation's minute book to ensure that an appropriate resolution has been entered in the official corporate records.

O. APPARENT AND IMPLIED AUTHORITY OF OFFICERS

Where the authority of a person purporting to act for a corporation has not been specifically granted by action of the board of directors, the following doctrines may be available to a third person seeking to bind the corporation.

1. Ratification

The board of directors of a corporation may learn that an officer has entered into a transaction without being specifically authorized to do so. If the board of directors does not promptly repudiate the transaction, the corporation may be bound on a theory of *ratification*. Or the knowledge of the officer-agent may be imputed to the corporation. *See generally Scientific Holding Co., Ltd. v. Plessey Incorporated*, 520 F.2d 15 (2d Cir. 1974). Acquiescence by the board of directors may also indicate that an an actual grant of authority was informally made. *Hessler, Inc. v. Farrell*, 226 A.2d 708 (Del.1967). It is sometimes said that ratification is merely an after-the-fact grant of authority. An officer may also be deemed to have implied authority to take action necessary to complete actions that are in fact authorized by the board. Such authority is actual authority and sometimes described as *implied actual authority* (or *lesser included authority*).

2. Estoppel or Unjust Enrichment

When the corporation retains the benefit of a transaction or a third party relies to its detriment, concepts of *unjust enrichment* or *estoppel* may be applied. Estoppel differs from ratification primarily because of reliance by third persons.

3. Implied Authority

An officer may be deemed to have implied authority to take action necessary to complete actions that are in fact authorized by the board. Such authority is *actual* authority and thus is sometimes called *implied actual authority.*

4. Apparent Authority

Apparent authority exists where there is conduct on the part of the principal that leads a reasonable person to suppose that the agent has the authority he purports to exercise.

a. A classic example of apparent authority involves a third person who knows that an officer has exercised authority in the past with the consent of the board of directors.

b. Apparent authority involves conduct on the part of the *principal* (the corporation) which creates the appearance of authority. A mere representation by a corporate officer that he possesses the requisite authority is not sufficient.

c.   Apparent authority differs from implied actual authority. For apparent authority, the third person must show that she was aware of the prior acts or holding out and that she relied on appearances, while implied actual authority may be found even in the absence of knowledge on the part of the third person.

P. DUTIES OF OFFICERS

Corporate officers and agents owe a fiduciary duty to the corporation of honesty, good faith, and diligence. The scope of an officer's or agent's obligation to the corporation is determined in part by the nature of his employment with the corporation. MBCA 8.42 imposes a duty of care on officers analogous to the duty of care imposed on directors. Other duties of officers are not codified. State statutes permitting corporations to limit monetary liability for due care violations may cover officers as well as directors.

Q. OFFICERS' LIABILITY ON CORPORATE OBLIGATIONS

An officer or agent who acts within the scope of authority in a consensual transaction is not personally liable on the transaction solely by virtue of so acting. MBCA 8.42. The common law of agency is the same.

1. Express Guarantee

The officer or agent may expressly guarantee the performance by the corporation, intending to be personally bound on the obligation.

a.   To be enforceable, a guarantee must be supported by consideration.

b.   Whether or not a guarantee must also be in writing may depend on the statute of frauds as applied to promises to answer for the indebtedness of another.

2. Confusion of Roles

An officer or employee may not intend to be personally bound, but may become bound by creating the impression that she is negotiating as an individual rather for the corporation or if the agreement is executed in such a way as to indicate personal liability.

   a.   If a person negotiates a transaction without disclosing that she is acting on behalf of a corporation, she is liable to the third person on general agency principles relating to undisclosed principals.

   b.   If the existence of the corporation is disclosed, the corporation and the officer may both be bound because of carelessness in the manner of execution. *Harris v. Milam*, 389 P.2d 638 (Okl.1964). *Benjamin Plumbing, Inc. v. Barnes*, 470 N.W.2d 888 (Wis.1991).

3.   Statutory Liability

Liability may be imposed by statute. For example, some state statutes impose personal liability for corporate obligations if officers fail to pay franchise taxes or to publish a notice upon incorporation.

4.   Personal Participation in Tortious Conduct

An officer or agent is personally liable if he or she personally participates in tortious conduct.

5.   Authority

An officer or agent may be personally liable on contracts or other obligations entered into in the name of the corporation if the officer or agent exceeds his actual authority to bind the corporation. The corporation is bound if the action is within apparent authority, but the corporation may have an action over against the officer or agent for exceeding his actual authority.

R.   CORPORATE NOTICE OR KNOWLEDGE

A corporation can *know* or *have notice of* something only if one or more persons who represent the corporation know or have notice. The issue is whether knowledge or notice should be imputed to the corporate entity.

1.   General Rule

Knowledge acquired by a corporate officer or employee while acting in furtherance of the corporate business or in the course of employment is imputed to the corporation.

2. Agent Acting Adversely to Principal

Difficult problems arise when it is sought to impute knowledge of an agent to the corporation if the agent is acting adversely to the corporation. Generally, information or knowledge may be imputed from an agent who has ultimate responsibility for the transaction to his corporation even if the agent is acting adversely to the corporation.

3. Corporate Criminal Responsibility

An agent's wrongful intent may be imputed to a corporation so that a corporation may be subject to criminal prosecution, including prosecution for traditional crimes such as murder or rape. For the corporation to be prosecuted, such acts must be connected with or in furtherance of the corporation's business.

S. TENURE OF OFFICERS AND AGENTS

Corporate officers and agents serve at the will of the board of directors. Corporate officers are elected by the board of directors and may be removed by the board of directors with or without cause. MBCA 8.43(b). Agents appointed by officers or other agents may be discharged by the persons with authority to employ them.

1. Employment Contracts in General

An officer or agent may be given an employment contract, and removal of that officer or agent may give rise to a cause of action for breach of contract.

a. The mere election or appointment of an officer or agent, even for a definite term, does not of itself give rise to a contract of employment. MBCA 8.44(a).

b. Bylaws sometimes provide that specified officers shall be elected by the board of directors for a term of one year. A provision of this nature does not prevent a corporation from granting an officer an employment contract extending beyond the term of office.

c. Despite a contract, the officer may be relieved at any time (as is the general rule for agents). *But see Staklinski v. Pyramid Elec. Co.,* 188

N.Y.S.2d 541, 160 N.E.2d 78 (N.Y. 1959). The corporation may be liable for breach of contract for the premature termination of the employment period if the officer is discharged without cause. MBCA 8.44(b).

d. Long-term employment contracts for officers may be upheld on the same theory applied to other long-term contracts, such as long term leases that bind subsequent boards of directors. *Staklinski v. Pyramid Elec. Co.,* 188 N.Y.S.2d 541, 160 N.E.2d 78 (N.Y. 1959); *In re Paramount Publix Corp.,* 90 F.2d 441 (2d Cir.1937).

e. Even if a bylaw provision is deemed to be a restraint on the power of the board of directors to grant an officer a long term employment contract, a long term employment contract may be deemed to be an implied amendment of the bylaws. *Realty Acceptance Corp. v. Montgomery,* 51 F.2d 636 (3d Cir.1930). This assumes that the board of directors has power to amend the bylaws.

2. Lifetime Employment Contracts

The claim that an officer or agent has been given a lifetime employment contract by a corporation has been treated with hostility by courts. Such contracts are usually oral and arise within the context of a family-run business.

a. Although such a contract is not invalidated by the statute of frauds, courts have found such open-ended commitment to be inherently implausible.

b. Many cases that have refused to enforce lifetime arrangements have done so on the ground that the officer making the arrangement had no actual or apparent authority to enter into the arrangement. *See Lee v. Jenkins Bros.,* 268 F.2d 357 (2d Cir.1959).

3. Discharge for Cause

An officer or employee with an employment contract may always be discharged for cause.

a. Cause may consist of dishonesty, negligence, refusal to obey orders, refusal to follow rules, or a variety of other acts such as engaging in an unprovoked fight.

b.   In effect, such conduct constitutes a breach of an implied (or express) covenant in the employment contract.

c.   If an officer does not have an employment contract, it is irrelevant whether or not cause for discharge exists.

4.   Executive Compensation

High level officers are often compensated based on earnings or sales or on an increase in the market price of the corporation's shares rather than at a flat salary. No legal problem is raised by such contracts so long as the total amount of compensation is not so excessive as to constitute waste.

a.   A common question arising with respect to bonus arrangements based on earnings or profits is one of computation. Profits may be computed in various ways and may lead to different results.

b.   Corporate officers and employees may also be paid with stock or options to purchase stock. Some executive compensation plans measure compensation on the basis of stock price but do not involve the actual purchase of shares. These devices are often called *phantom stock options* or *stock appreciation rights* (SARs).

c.   Such equity compensation arrangements are designed to give officers employees a long term investment interest in the corporation that is similar to the interest of stockholders and that will thus induce the officers to maximize stockholder value. They are more common in publicly held corporations (where a market for shares exists) than in closely held corporations.

d.   Long term employees of closely held corporations may be granted or permitted to buy a small number of shares of the corporation as an incentive. Typically, these shares are subject to an agreement between the corporation and the officers by which the officer agrees to sell them back to the corporation and the corporation agrees to repurchase them when the employment arrangement ends often at a preset price or a price determined by a formula.

e.   Employment contracts for highly paid officers usually provide for deferred compensation, fringe benefits, reimbursement of business expenses, and other benefits. Such benefits may also be provided to lower paid employees on a more limited basis.

f. In a closely held corporation, an employment agreement may be an integral part of the basic understanding between stockholders. Terms relating to employment are often included in stockholder agreements so that they will be binding on all other stockholders as well as on the corporation. In the absence of such an agreement or an employment agreement, the majority may be able to exclude the minority from financial and managerial participation in the business, although such tactics may constitute a breach of fiduciary duty or grounds for dissolution in many states.

■ VIII. FIDUCIARY DUTIES OF DIRECTORS, OFFICERS & STOCKHOLDERS

A. DUTIES IN GENERAL

Directors and officers owe fiduciary duties to the corporation and to the stockholders and in some cases to other constituencies such as creditors. Controlling stockholders may also owe a fiduciary duty to the corporation and other stockholders not to use their power inappropriately. These duties are generally a matter of state law, but federal securities law may also impose duties that are similar to state law duties.

1. Directors

Directors have the broad responsibility of overseeing the management of the corporation. They occupy a unique position within the corporate structure, and owe both a duty of care and a duty of loyalty to the corporation.

a. The duties of directors are sometimes analogized to those of a trustee of a trust. *Guth v. Loft, Inc.*, 5 A.2d 503 (Del.1939); *Litwin v. Allen*, 25 N.Y.S.2d 667 (1940). Directors of corporations are not strictly trustees, because they are not automatically liable for consequences of actions which exceed their powers. Further, the area of their discretion and judgment is considerably greater than that possessed by traditional trustees. Directors may enter into transactions with the corporation under some circumstances.

b. In most instances, directors owe duties to the corporation as a whole rather than to individual stockholders or to individual classes of stockholders. Moreover, directors act as a group, although in some cases a court may conclude that one or more individual directors have breached a duty to the corporation.

2. Officers and Agents

The duties owed by corporate officers and agents to the corporation depend to some extent on the position occupied by the officer or agent and the type of liabilities that are being imposed. A full-time, high-level managing officer may owe substantially the same duties to the corporation as a director. Agents or employees in subordinate or limited positions owe a correspondingly lesser degree of duty, though even the lowest agent owes the principal certain minimum duties of care, skill, propriety in conduct, and loyalty in matters connected with his agency.

3. Stockholders

Stockholders as such have no power to manage the business and affairs of the corporation and do not perform services for the corporation in that capacity. But they do select the directors and have power to approve or ratify certain transactions. Their fiduciary relationship to the corporation therefore differs from the relationship of a director or officer.

a. Many cases state that a stockholder owes no fiduciary duty to the corporation. Such statements are too broad, because stockholders, particularly controlling stockholders, clearly owe a duty to the corporation or fellow stockholders in some circumstances.

b. A number of states hold that controlling stockholders in a closely held corporation owe a duty to other stockholders that is akin to that owed by partners to each other. *See Matter of TJ Ronan Paint Corp.*, 469 N.Y.S.2d 931, 936 (App.Div. 1984); *Fender v. Prescott*, 476 N.Y.S.2d 128 (App.Div. 1984).

c. Controlling stockholders may also owe duties to minority stockholders when they transfer control of the corporation to a third party. *See Perlman v. Feldmann*, 219 F.2d 173 (2d Cir.1955); *Jones v. H. F. Ahmanson & Co.*, 1 Cal.3d 93 (1969).

d. Transactions between a controlling stockholder and the corporation must be fair to the corporation and the controlling stockholder has the burden of proving entire fairness unless the transaction has been ratified by the stockholders after full disclosure of all material facts. *Kahn v. Lynch Communication Systems*, 638 A.2d 1110 (Del.1994); *Lewis v. S.L. & E., Inc.*, 629 F.2d 764 (2d Cir.1980); *Sinclair Oil Corp. v. Levien*, 280 A.2d 717 (Del.1971); *Weinberger v. UOP, Inc.*, 457 A2d 701 (Del. 1983).

e. Even though a stockholder is under no general obligation to vote in the best interest of the corporation and may vote with a view to personal interests or indeed on the basis of whim or caprice, a stockholder may not sell his or her vote. *Ringling v. Ringling Brothers–Barnum & Bailey Combined Shows*, 53 A.2d 441 (Del. 1947); *Schreiber v. Carney*, 447 A.2d 17, 22 (Del. 1982).

f. Stockholders are not subject to the same conflict-of-interest rules as directors, but the courts have generally declined to count the votes of stockholders who vote their shares in favor of ratification of their own self-dealing transactions. *Fliegler v. Lawrence*, 361 A.2d 218, 222 (Del.1976). *See also Weinberger v. UOP, Inc.*, 457 A2d 701 (Del. 1983) (endorsing majority of minority vote). This rule has been codified in MBCA 8.63.

B. DUTY OF CARE

Directors and officers owe a duty to the corporation to exercise reasonable care in performing their duties with respect to the corporation's affairs.

1. General Tests

MBCA 8.30 states that the standard test for directors' duty of care is that the duties must be discharged (1) in good faith (2) with the care an ordinarily prudent person in a like position would exercise under similar circumstances, and (3) in a manner he reasonably believes to be in the best interests of the corporation.

a. This standard of care is justified on various grounds. A stricter test might unduly discourage individuals from serving as directors. And the courts are reluctant to second-guess corporate managers with the benefit of hindsight.

b. A number of older cases state that bank directors owe a higher degree of care than directors of ordinary business corporations. *See Bates v. Dresser*, 251 U.S. 524, 251 U.S. 524 (1920). On the other hand, this rule may simply be a reflection of the nature of the banking business, that is, that the business of a bank is among other things to provide a safe depository.

   c.   The test of skill and prudence is based on an average person of reasonable intelligence and competence. *See Selheimer v. Manganese Corp. of America,* 224 A.2d 634 (Pa.1966).

2. Business Judgment Rule

The business judgment rule is a common law principles that provides that honest business decisions made in good faith and on the basis of reasonable investigation are not actionable, even though the decision is mistaken, unfortunate, or even disastrous. *Shlensky v. Wrigley,* 237 N.E.2d 776 (Ill.App.1968) (decision not to play night games at Wrigley Field); *Kamin v. American Express Co.,* 383 N.Y.S.2d 807 (1976), *aff'd,* 387 N.Y.S.2d 993 (decision to pay dividend in property on which tax loss was available).

   a.   Section 4.01(c) of the ALI Principles of Corporate Governance (PCG) codifies the business judgment rule: A director or officer who makes a business judgment in good faith fulfills [the duty of care] if (1) He is not interested in the subject of his business judgment; (2) He is informed with respect to the subject of his business judgment to the extent he reasonably believes to be appropriate under the circumstances; and (3) He rationally believes that his business judgment is in the best interests of the corporation.

   b.   The relationship between the duty of care and the business judgment rule is unclear. The business judgment rule may be seen as a presumption or burden shifting device. That is, in the absence of the business judgment rule it is not clear that the plaintiff would bear the burden of proof given that the defendant director controls the evidence. Under the business judgment rule, the burden of pleading specific facts thus falls to the plaintiff. Otherwise, the court will dismiss the case without discovery.

   c.   As a practical matter, the most common way to overcome the business judgment rule has been to show that the decision in question was tainted by a conflict of interest and thus may not have been made in good faith.

   d.   There are a few cases in which plaintiffs have prevailed by showing that the decision in question was a no win proposition or could only lead to a financial loss.

e. An *ultra vires* act is probably not protected by the business judgment rule.

f. The business judgment rule is not applicable unless a decision has been made. A failure to manage is not protected by the business judgment rule.

g. Issues relating to dividend policies and distributions are often said to be especially appropriate for the application of the business judgment rule. *Kamin v. American Express Co.*, 383 N.Y.S.2d 807 (1976).

3. Failure to Manage

A director may be liable for failure to manage. Liability is not precluded by the business judgment rule because no judgment or decision is involved.

4. Knowing Authorization of Wrongful Act

Liability has sometimes been imposed where a director knowingly authorizes or participates in a wrongful act, for example, where a director authorizes the improper use of corporate funds, knowing that the use is not in furtherance of corporate affairs.

a. Attempts to hold non-participating directors or officers personally liable for antitrust fines imposed on the corporation, or for bribes, improper payments or illegal campaign contributions made by the corporation, have generally been unsuccessful. *Graham v. Allis–Chalmers Mfg. Co.*, 188 A.2d 125 (Del.1963).

b. In *Miller v. American Telephone & Telegraph Co.*, 507 F.2d 759 (3d Cir.1974), the court upheld a stockholder's complaint against AT & T that that corporation had failed to try to collect a debt of $1,500,000 owed to the company by the Democratic National Committee for communications service provided during the 1968 Democratic Convention. The decision was based in part on a statute prohibiting campaign contributions by corporations to political parties.

c. In some cases, the courts appear to be reluctant to hold a director liable for a wrongful or illegal action on the part of the corporation, because the action may nonetheless have generated a benefit for the corporation. This does not mean, however, that the corporation itself cannot be held liable for the wrongful or illegal act. In this situation, the status of the director is similar to that of an agent who negotiates a contract on behalf of a principal who later breaches the contract. In such a case, the agent cannot be held liable as long as the principal was disclosed and the contract was made in good faith.

5. Reliance on Experts and Committees

MBCA 8.30(b) permits directors to rely on information, opinions, reports, or statements, including financial statements and other financial data prepared or presented by responsible corporate officers, employees, legal counsel, public accountants, or committees of the board of directors. Liability cannot be imposed on directors if the conditions of MBCA 8.30 are met.

a. Reliance is justified only if the director reasonably believes that the officers or directors are reliable and competent on the matters presented, and in the case of legal counsel, public accountants, and other professionals, the director reasonably believes that the matters are within the person's professional or expert competence.

b. A director may also rely on the reports of committees of the board of directors (of which the director is not a member) if the director reasonably believes the committee merits competence.

c. If the director makes a judgment that the source of information on which she proposes to rely is reliable and competent, then the decision to rely is itself protected by the business judgment rule.

6. *Smith v. Van Gorkom* and its Consequences

Prior to 1985, relatively few cases imposed liability upon directors for failure to comply with their duty of care. But in *Smith v. Van Gorkom*, 488 A.2d 858 (Del.1985), the Delaware Supreme Court imposed liability upon the directors of TransUnion Corporation for accepting an outside offer to purchase the corporation without investigating whether a higher price might be obtained and without making an investigation into the value of the company. The directors relied on the opinion of Van Gorkom, the CEO, that the price being offered was a reasonable one and approved a sale of the corporation within a three day period with virtually no discussion of possible alternatives and no assistance from outside experts. The corporation was sold at $55 per share.

While the sale was pending it received an inquiry that indicated that a sale at $60 per share might be possible. Since there were more than 12,000,000 shares outstanding, the potential liability of the directors arising from this $5 differential was more than $60,000,000.

a. The Delaware Supreme Court held that the test for applying the business judgment rule was gross negligence. Further, the business judgment rule did not protect the directors of TransUnion because they had been grossly negligent in not adequately informing themselves of the transaction they approved.

b. The court decided that all directors, outside as well as inside directors, were responsible for the potential loss to stockholders but did not consider the measure of damages.

c. The decision in *Smith v. Van Gorkom* came at the height of a takeover boom involving immense transactions and was widely criticized by practicing lawyers on several grounds.

- The possibility of director liability with respect to such transactions was a deterrent to any outside person agreeing to serve as a director.

- Directors' and officers' liability insurance premiums soared, though whether caused by the decision or independent factors was disputed.

- Many feared that the decision would lead to overly cautious decision-making by directors, to emphasis on creating a paper trail that would appear to demonstrate informed decision-making, and to increased reliance on experts, including legal counsel.

- Many commentators were appalled that liability could be imposed on directors for simply following the recommendation of the CEO for whom they had great respect with respect to a transaction that did not involve self dealing by directors.

7. Director Liability Statutes

In 1986, in direct response to *Smith v. Van Gorkom*, the Delaware General Assembly enacted DGCL 102(b)(7), which authorizes in a certificate of incorporation:

> A provision eliminating or limiting the personal liability of a director to the corporation or its stockholders for monetary damages

for breach of fiduciary duty as a director, provided that such provision shall not eliminate or limit the liability of a director (i) for any breach of the director's duty of loyalty to the corporation or its stockholders, (ii) for acts or omissions not in good faith or which involve intentional misconduct or a knowing violation of law, (iii) under [the section of the Delaware GCL making directors liable for unlawful distributions] or (iv) for any transaction from which the director derived an improper personal benefit. No such provision shall eliminate or limit the liability of a director for any act or omission occurring prior to the date when such provision becomes effective.

The requirement that such a provision appear in a certificate of incorporation means a stockholders' vote is necessary in connection with existing corporations if the liability of directors is to be eliminated or limited.

a. Virtually all states have enacted similar statutes since 1986. A few states, including Indiana, have adopted self executing statutes that automatically limit the liability of directors without requiring an amendment to the articles of incorporation.

b. Thousands of corporations incorporated in Delaware, including most publicly held corporations, have taken advantage of DGCL 102(b)(7) and eliminated directorial liability to the maximum extent permitted by that section.

c. This section makes it clear that the directors of a corporation adopting an appropriate provision are not personally liable for damages even in the case of gross negligence. *Boeing Co. v. Shrontz*, 1992 WL 81228 (Del.Ch.1992).

d. DGCL 102(b)(7) applies only to actions for monetary damages. An action for equitable relief to enjoin a transaction is not precluded. As a result litigation in due care cases continue to arise despite the enactment of DGCL 102(b)(7). Similar statutes in a few other states apply to actions for equitable relief as well as to actions for monetary damages.

e. MBCA 2.02(b)(4) permits a provision in the articles of incorporation providing for the limitation or elimination of liability of directors for gross negligence. The exceptions are narrower than DGCL 102(b)(7): liability may not be eliminated or limited for (A) the amount of a financial benefit received by a director to which he is not entitled; (B) an intentional infliction of harm on the corporation or the stockholders; (C) a violation of section 8.33 (relating to illegal distributions); or (D) an intentional violation of criminal law.

f. MBCA 8.31(a) provides in essence that a director may not be held liable to the corporation unless it is established that the director's conduct (1) is not immune and has not been ratified, and (2) is either a violation of the duty of care, or a violation of the duty of loyalty, or the result sustained inattention, or involves the receipt of a financial benefit to which the director was not entitled or which resulted from unfair dealing with the corporation. MBCA 8.31(b) provides that it must also be established that the corporation suffered harm (presumably financial harm) and that the harm was proximately caused by the conduct challenged.

C. DUTY OF LOYALTY

Whereas the duty of care focuses on the responsibility of directors and officers to manage a corporation competently, the duty of loyalty (sometimes called the duty of fairness) focuses on the responsibility of directors and officers to avoid or at least scrutinize conflicts of interest. Conflicts of interest may take many forms.

- In a self-dealing case, a director or officer enters into a transaction with the corporation. For example, a director may sell a piece of property to the corporation. The obvious danger is that the director may use his position to cause the corporation to overpay.

- In a corporate opportunity case, a director or officer may come across a valuable business opportunity in his capacity as a director or officer and may seek to exploit the opportunity for his own benefit rather than offering it to the corporation. The harm to the corporation is lost profits.

- In a competition case, a director or officer engages in a new business venture that seeks to exploit the same market as the old corporation. The harm to the corporation comes in the form of reduced profits.

1. In General

If a transaction is tainted by a conflict of interest that triggers duty of loyalty analysis, the burden shifts to the defendant to prove that the transaction is fair to the corporation. Some courts use the phrase *entire fairness* or *inherent fairness* or *intrinsic fairness*.

a. The key question in many cases is whether or not the transaction in question should be analyzed as a duty of care case or a duty of loyalty case. Often the answer to this question is outcome determinative, because the business judgment rule does not apply if a director or officer has a personal financial interest in the transaction. PCG 4.01(c).

b. The burden of proof may be shifted back to the plaintiff if the decision is ratified by unconflicted directors (or a committee thereof) or by the stockholders in a fully informed vote (without counting the votes that may be cast by a conflicted stockholder).

c. Generally speaking, the remedy in a duty of care case is damages, whereas the remedy in a duty of loyalty case is rescission or the equivalent. The pattern is the same as under the common law of agency. An agent must account to the principal. In cases in which it is impossible to rescind the transaction, the courts may apply a constructive trust on the proceeds from the offending transaction or award the monetary equivalent of rescission–sometimes called *rescissory damages*. In some cases, a transaction may give rise to both types of liability. If rescission is ordered, the corporation will ordinarily also be required to surrender whatever it received in connection with the transaction.

d. Proof of fairness of a complex transaction may be difficult and expensive, involving a protracted trial. Moreover, the potential liability may be significant in that a fiduciary may be required to disgorge all profits from a transaction occurring years before judgment is finally rendered. Hence, there is a strong incentive to obtain review and approval of the transaction by directors or stockholders rather than requiring the interested director to establish the fairness of the transaction.

2. Self–Dealing

A self-dealing transaction is one between a director and corporation. The test for self-dealing transactions developed by the courts in absence of statute combines procedural and substantive requirements. Some courts describe the test as requiring both fair dealing and fair price.

a. The early common law took the position that because of the risk inherent in self-dealing transactions, all such transactions were void or voidable at the election of the corporation. *Stewart v. Lehigh Valley R. Co.*, 38 N.J.L.

505 (1875). This approach has been abandoned as overbroad, because many self-dealing transactions are entirely fair and reasonable. Indeed, directors may give their corporations terms that are more favorable than the corporation might obtain elsewhere. *Robotham v. Prudential Ins. Co. of America*, 53 A. 842 (N.J.Ch.Div.1903). Moreover, the strict approach has the effect of precluding a director or officer from a mutually beneficial deal simply because of status and effectively creating a presumption in favor of outsiders who presumably are less well informed.

b. Generally speaking, there are three ways that a tainted transaction may be upheld or ratified. First, if the transaction is approved by the board of directors after full disclosure of material terms and without the partici-pation of the interested director (except possibly for purposes of establishing a quorum), the transaction is deemed to be ratified. Second, if the transaction is approved by the stockholders after full disclosure of material terms, the transaction is deemed to be ratified and enforceable. Third, in the absence of ratification, the transaction may be upheld if a court determines that the terms of the transaction are fair. Some authorities would require ratification or approval even for fair transac-tions.

3. Ratification by Stockholders

Ratification by stockholders of a transaction between a director and the corporation may validate a self-dealing transaction. At common law, inter-ested directors may vote their shares as stockholders in favor of the transaction. *North-West Trans. Co. v. Beatty*, 12 App.Cas. 589 (Eng. 1887); *Gamble v. Queens County Water Co.*, 25 N.E. 201 (N.Y.1890); *Allaun v. Consolidated Oil Co.*, 147 A. 257 (Del.Ch.1929). The modern view is to disqualify the vote of the interested stockholder and permit ratification by a majority of the remaining stockholders. This may lead to ratification by a *majority of the minority*.

4. Statutory Treatment of Self–Dealing Transactions

Statutes in many states address the issue of self-dealing transactions. Most such statutes are similar to MBCA (1984) 8.31 though individual state statutes vary widely in details MBCA (1984) 8.31 provided:

Director Conflict of Interest

(a) A conflict of interest transaction is a transaction with the corporation in which a director of the corporation has a direct or indirect interest. A conflict of interest transaction is not voidable by the corporations solely because of the director's interest in the transaction if any one of the following is true: (1) the material facts of the transaction and the director's interest were disclosed or known to the board of directors or a committee of the board of directors and the board of directors or committee authorized, approved, or ratified the transaction; (2) the material facts of the transaction and the director's interest were disclosed or known to the stockholders entitled to vote and they authorized, approved, or ratified the transaction; or (3) the transaction was fair to the corporation.

(b) For purposes of this section, a director of the corporation has an indirect interest in a transaction if (1) another entity in which he has a material financial interest or in which he is a general partner is a party to the transaction, or (2) another entity of which he is a director, officer, or trustee is a party to the transaction and the transaction is or should be considered by the board of directors of the corporation.

(c) For purposes of subsection (a)(1), a conflict of interest transaction is authorized, approved, or ratified if it receives the affirmative vote of a majority of the directors on the board of directors (or on the committee) who have no direct or indirect interest in the transaction, but a transaction may not be authorized, approved, or ratified under this section by a single director. If a majority of the directors who have no direct or indirect interest in the transaction vote to authorize, approve, or ratify the transaction, a quorum is present for the purpose of taking action under this section. The presence of, or a vote cast by, a director with a direct or indirect interest in the transaction does not affect the validity of any action taken under subsection (01) if the transaction is otherwise authorized, approved, or ratified as provided in that subsection.

(d) For purposes of subsection (a)(2), a conflict of interest transaction is authorized, approved, or ratified if it receives the vote of a majority of the shares entitled to be counted under this subsection. Shares owned by or voted under the control of a director who has a direct or indirect interest in the transaction, and shares owned by or voted under the control of an entity described in subsection (b)(1), may not be counted in a vote of stockholders to determine whether to authorize, approve, or ratify a conflict of interest transaction under subsection (a)(2). The vote of those shares, however, shall be counted in determining whether the transaction is approved under other sections of this Act. A majority of the shares, whether or not present, that are entitled to be counted in a vote on the transaction under this subsection constitutes a quorum for the purpose of taking action under this section.

a. MBCA (1984) 8.31 was withdrawn in 1988 and replaced by MBCA 8.60 – 8.63, discussed below.

b. These statutes simply exonerate or remove a cloud from self-dealing transactions based on the early common law rule of automatic void-ability. It merely removes an interested director cloud when its terms are met and provides against invalidation of an agreement solely because such a director or officer is involved. *Fliegler v.* Lawrence, 361 A.2d 218, 222 (Del.1976); *Cookies Food Products, Inc. v. Lakes Warehouse Distributing, Inc.,* 430 N.W.2d 447 (Iowa, 1988).

c. These statutes involve the business judgment rule. The conditions for approval set forth in MBCA 8.31(a)(1) and 8.31(c) are similar to the requirements of the business judgment rule. In *Marciano v. Nakash,* 535 A.2d 400 (Del.1987), the Delaware Supreme Court stated that under DGCL 144 approval by fully-informed disinterested directors or disinterested stockholders permits invocation of the business judgment rule and limits judicial review to issues of gift or waste with the burden of proof upon the party attacking the transaction.

d. Compliance with these statutes generally requires full disclosure of both the existence of conflicting interests and the details of the transaction.

e. MBCA (1984) 8.31 excluded interested stockholders from voting to approve conflict-of-interest transactions but many state statutes do not expressly do so. In *Fliegler v.* Lawrence, 361 A.2d 218 (Del.1976), interested stockholders voted to ratify a transaction as literally permitted by DGCL 144. The court applied an intrinsic fairness test and set aside the transaction, stating that nothing in the statute sanctions unfairness * * * or removes the transaction from judicial scrutiny.

f. Under the California statute (which differs significantly from MBCA (1984) 8.31 in that fairness is the sole test for invalidity), unfair or unreasonable transactions may not be validated. *Remillard Brick Co. v. Remillard–Dandini Co.*, 241 P.2d 66 (Cal.App.1952); *Kennerson v. Burbank Amusement Co.*, 260 P.2d 823 (Cal.App.1953).

5. MBCA Subchapter F

In 1988, the Committee on Corporate Laws withdrew MBCA (1984) 8.31, discussed above, and substituted a new and more comprehensive statute dealing with conflict of interest transactions. This new treatment appears in MBCA 8.61-8.63, and is usually referred to as Subchapter F.

a. Subchapter F is structured similarly to MBCA (1984) 8.31: a conflict of interest transaction is not voidable by the corporation if (a) it has been approved by disinterested directors or stockholders, or (b) the interested director establishes the fairness of the transaction. Unlike MBCA (1984) 8.31, however, Subchapter F is designed to create a series of bright line principles that increase predictability and enhance practical administration.

b. Subchapter F deals only with transactions between a director and the corporation.

c. MBCA 8.60(1) defines a conflicting interest in terms that are exclusive. MBCA 8.60(1)(i) defines a direct conflicting interest to be when the director knows at the time of commitment that he or a related person is a party to the transaction or has a beneficial interest in or so closely linked to the transaction and of such financial significance to the director or a related person that the interest would reasonably be expected to exert an influence on the director's judgment if he were called upon to vote on the transaction. MBCA 8.60(1)(ii) adds limited classes of indirect interests to the definition of conflicting interest: transactions that would in the normal course of events be brought to the board of directors for decision and involve (i) an entity of which the director is a director, general partner, agent, or employee or (ii) an entity that controls, is controlled by, or is under common control with one of those entities or (iii) a person who is a general partner, principal, or employer of the director. MBCA 8.60(2) defines a related person to include spouses, children, grandchildren, siblings, parents, and any trust of which the director is a trustee.

d. A director's conflicting interest transaction is a transaction effected or proposed to be effected by the corporation in which a director of the corporation has a conflicting interest, MBCA 8.60(2). This definition is also exclusive, MBCA 8.61(a) provides that a court may not enjoin, set aside or award damages or impose another sanction with respect to a transaction that is not a director's conflicting interest transaction on the ground that the director has a personal interest in the transaction.

e. MBCA 8.61(b)(1) provides that approval of a transaction by disinterested directors, following full disclosure by the interested director, is protected by the business judgment rule and MBCA 8.30.

6. Loans to Directors or Officers

Most state statutes contain a provision restricting or prohibiting loans to directors or officers. MBCA 8.32 contained a liberalized prohibition similar to these state statutes, but that section was withdrawn in 1988 when subchapter F was approved. That subchapter now governs loans to directors or officers.

7. Waiver by Provision in the Articles of Incorporation

Provisions may be placed in the articles of incorporation of a corporation to validate transactions between directors and the corporation that otherwise might be voidable under the above principles. These clauses are not construed literally, and do not validate fraudulent or manifestly unfair acts. *Spiegel v. Beacon Participations*, 8 N.E.2d 895 (Mass.1937). Such clauses may be effective to permit an interested director to be counted in determining whether a quorum is present and exonerate transactions between corporation and director from adverse inferences which might be drawn against them. *Everett v. Phillips*, 43 N.E.2d 18 (N.Y.1942).

D. CORPORATE OPPORTUNITIES

As a fiduciary, a director owes a duty to further the interest of the corporation and to give it the benefit of her uncorrupted business judgment. She may not take a secret profit in connection with corporate transactions, compete unfairly with the corporation, or take personally profitable business opportunities which belong to the corporation. If the opportunity is not a corporate opportunity the director may take advantage of it personally for his or her own private gain and need not share it with the corporation or with other participants in the corporation.

1. What is a Corporate Opportunity?

Several competing tests exist as to when an opportunity should be considered a corporate opportunity.

a.   An early test was that the opportunity must involve property wherein the corporation has interest already existing or in which it has an expectancy growing out of an existing right. *See Burg v. Horn*, 380 F.2d 897 (2d Cir.1967); *Litwin v. Allen*, 25 N.Y.S.2d 667 (N.Y. 1940). This narrow test of corporate opportunity and has been rejected by most courts. *See Kerrigan v. Unity Sav. Ass'n*, 317 N.E.2d 39 (Ill. 1974).

b.   Some courts have adopted a test that the opportunity must arise out of the corporation's business as it is then conducted. The *line of business* test compares the opportunity to the businesses in which the corporation is engaged. The more similar the opportunity, the more likely it is to be seen as a corporate opportunity. This test tends to be expansive and has been categorized as too broad. *Burg v. Horn*, 380 F.2d 897 (2d Cir.1967).

c.   Some courts simply apply a test of fairness. *Durfee v. Durfee & Canning, Inc.*, 80 N.E.2d 522 (Mass.1948). This test has been rejected by most courts as providing little or no practical guidance. *Northeast Harbor Golf Club, Inc. v. Harris*, 661 A.2d 1146 (Me.1995)

d.   A leading Minnesota case combines a line of business test with consideration of whether it is fair for the director under the circumstances to appropriate the opportunity. *Miller v. Miller*, 222 N.W.2d 71 (Minn.1974).

e.   Delaware law holds that an opportunity is a corporate opportunity if (1) the corporation is financially able to exploit the opportunity, (2) the opportunity is within the corporation's line of business, (3) the corporation has an interest or expectancy in the opportunity and (4) by taking the opportunity for his own, the corporate fiduciary will thereby be placed in a position inconsistent with his duties to the corporation. *Broz v. Cellular Information Systems, Inc.*, 673 A.2d 148 (Del.1996), *citing Guth v. Loft, Inc.*, 5 A.2d 503 (Del.1939).

f.   PCG 5.05 defines a corporate opportunity *for director or officer* as an opportunity offered with the expectation that it would be offered to the corporation or discovered with the use of corporate information or property, and for an officer as an opportunity that is reasonably closely related to the business in which the corporation is engaged or expects to engage. *See Northeast Harbor Golf Club v. Harris*, 661 A.2d 1146 (Me.1995) (reviewing competing tests and adopting PCG test). *See also Klinicki v. Lundgren*, 695 P.2d 906 (Ore.1985) (adopting earlier and stricter version of test).

g.   Several factors are considered in evaluating the status of an opportunity.

- Whether there were prior negotiations with the corporation about the opportunity.

- Whether the opportunity was offered to the corporation or to the director as an agent of the corporation. *See Rapistan Corp. v. Michaels*, 511 N.W.2d 918 (Mich.App.1994) (Delaware law).

- Whether the director disclosed the opportunity to the corporation or took advantage of it secretly.

- Whether the director learned of the opportunity by reason of his or her position with the corporation.

- Whether the director used corporate facilities or property in taking advantage of the opportunity.

- Whether as a result of taking advantage of the opportunity the director is competing with the corporation, thwarting corporate policy, or acting unfairly with respect to the corporation (*Zidell v. Zidell, Inc.*, 560 P.2d 1091 (Or.1977));

- Whether the director acquired at a discount claims against the corporation when the corporation could have done so. *See Weissman v. A. Weissman, Inc.*, 97 A.2d 870 (Pa.1953); *Manufacturers Trust Co. v. Becker*, 338 U.S. 304, 70 S.Ct. 127 (1949).

- Whether the need of the corporation for the opportunity was substantial; and

- Whether the director was involved in several ventures and the opportunity in question was not uniquely attributable to one such venture. *See Johnston v. Greene*, 121 A.2d 919 (Del.1956).

2. Rejection of Corporate Opportunity

Even if an opportunity is a corporate opportunity, directors may take advantage of it if the corporation elects not to do so. *Zidell v. Zidell, Inc.*, 560 P.2d 1091 (Ore.1977).

    a.   The corporation may voluntarily relinquish a corporate opportunity, though such a relinquishment is a self-dealing transaction and is scrutinized by the courts on the basis of principles described earlier. *Johnston v. Greene*, 121 A.2d 919 (Del.1956).

    b.   A persuasive reason for the relinquishment helps to make it clear that the corporation voluntarily decided not to pursue the opportunity.

    c.   As is the case with self-dealing transactions generally, effective approval by the board of directors requires compliance with the standards of the business judgment rule as applied to self dealing transactions. Requirements include full disclosure of all the surrounding facts by the interested directors and their non-participation in the decision-making process.

3. Inability or Incapacity of Corporation

Directors may take advantage of a corporate opportunity if the corporation is unable or incapable of taking advantage of the opportunity.

    a.   Most courts permit directors to take advantage of a corporate opportunity if the corporation is financially unable to capitalize on the opportunity. *A. C. Petters Co. v. St. Cloud Enterprises, Inc.*, 222 N.W.2d 83 (Minn.1974). The financial inability defense is troublesome because it may tempt directors to refrain from exercising best efforts on behalf of the corporation if they thereafter may take advantage personally of a profitable opportunity. *Irving Trust Co. v. Deutsch*, 73 F.2d 121 (2d Cir.1934). Thus, when courts permit a director to utilize a corporate opportunity on this basis, they require a convincing showing that the corporation indeed lacks the independent assets to take advantage of its opportunity.

    b.   The PCG does not recognize a defense of financial inability. *See Klinicki v. Lundgren*, 695 P.2d 906 (Ore.1985). Under the PCG, before a director or officer may take advantage of an opportunity, the corporation must voluntarily renounce its interest in the opportunity or unreasonably fail to act on the proposal.

c.   An absolute prohibition on directors taking advantage of a corporate opportunity may be directors would have to forgo an opportunity entirely if they are unable to persuade the corporation to forgo the transaction and are unwilling to lend the necessary funds to the corporation.

E.   COMPETITION WITH THE CORPORATION

Directors may engage in a similar line of business in competition with the corporation's business where it is done in good faith and without injury to the corporation. A director is not a full-time employee and may utilize his or her time as the director sees fit.

a.   Cases have found a competing director or officer guilty of a breach of fiduciary duty on several possible theories: conflict of interest, corporate opportunity, misappropriation of trade secrets or customer lists, or wrongful interference with contractual relationships. *Duane Jones Co. v. Burke*, 117 N.E.2d 237 (N.Y.1954).

b.   Tort concepts **of** unfair competition in this area are close to fiduciary duties.

c.   Judicial notions of fairness or fair play seem dominant, and cases require a close appraisal of the fiduciary's conduct in light of ethical business practice. *Aero Drapery of Kentucky, Inc. v. Engdahl*, 507 S.W.2d 166 (Ky.1974).

F.   EXECUTIVE COMPENSATION

Decisions regarding executive compensation by their very nature raise duty of loyalty issues. The board of directors must approve the compensation paid to the CEO, who is invariably a director and usually is also chairman of the board of directors. Most publicly held corporations have created compensation committees composed of independent directors to review all compensation issues for highly compensated executives. Because the conflicts of interest involved are structural and cannot be avoided, and because most publicly traded corporations have established standing compensation committees composed solely of outside directors, decisions regarding executive compensation are not usually treated as duty of loyalty problems.

1.   Test for Excessive Compensation

Courts are reluctant to inquire into issues of executive compensation in publicly held corporations. In such corporations, the test for excessive compensation is whether the payments are so large as to constitute spoliation or waste. *Rogers v. Hill,* 289 U.S. 582, 53 S.Ct. 731 (1933).

2. Compensation Issues in Publicly Held Corporations

A controversial aspect of modern corporation law is the level of the compensation paid to senior executives of publicly held corporations. In the 1990s average salaries of senior executives were in the high six or low seven figures usually supplemented by stock options and incentive compensation arrangements. Incomes of senior executives were increasing more rapidly than average income levels throughout society and the spread between average wage levels and the salaries of senior executives was increasing.

a. In 1992, the SEC mandated more elaborate and complete descriptions of executive compensation in disclosure documents, including a specific discussion of compensation levels.

b. The SEC required corporations to place stockholder proposals with respect to compensation levels in proxy statements under Rule 14a–8.

c. The SEC required footnote disclosure of the value of stock options granted to senior executives.

d. In 1993, Congress enacted IRC 162(m) capping the deductibility of executive compensation at $1,000,000 million per year. Performance based compensation such as bonuses and stock options is excluded from the cap. This provision has not reduced the level of executive compensation and may actually have encouraged increases in compensation levels from the high six figures to the limit.

3. Compensation Based on Stock Performance

Courts have upheld compensation arrangements based on the price or value of shares. Economists generally favor these arrangements because they tend to align management interests with the maximization of stockholder wealth.

a. Stock option plans, stock purchase plans, and stock bonus plans may have special tax benefits. Such plans are upheld if approved by disinterested directors or by stockholders, and the benefits being conferred bear a reasonable relationship to the services being performed. *Beard v. Elster,* 160 A.2d 731 (Del. 1960); *Eliasberg v. Standard Oil Co.,* 92 A.2d 862

(N.J.Super.Ch.Div. 1952). *See also Cohen v. Ayers*, 596 F.2d 733 (7th Cir.1979) (cancellation of out-of-money options and substitution of valuable options valid if effectively ratified by disinterested directors or stockholders).

b. A *phantom stock plan* provides compensation that is computed over a period of time as though the officer had owned a specified number of shares. Such an arrangement is a legitimate form of compensation. *Lieberman v. Koppers Co., Inc.*, 149 A.2d 756 (Del.Ch.1959); *Berkwitz v. Humphrey*, 163 F.Supp. 78 (N.D.Ohio 1958).

c. *Stock appreciation rights* (SARs) are bonus payments computed on the basis of growth of value of the corporation's shares. In recent years bonus payments based on the attainment of a predetermined goal (e.g. a ten per cent increase in gross sales of the division) have become popular. These are sometimes called *performance unit payments* (PUPs).

4. Benefit to Corporation

Services must be given or promised in exchange for compensation. A post-death payment to the estate of a deceased employee or surviving spouse not made pursuant to a preexisting plan has been invalidated on this ground. *Adams v. Smith*, 153 So.2d 221 (Ala.1963); *Alexander v. Lindsay*, 152 So.2d 261 (La.App.1963).

G. CONTROLLING STOCKHOLDERS

Minority stockholders in a corporation may be injured by a variety of transactions authorized by the controlling stockholder or by the board of directors elected by such stockholders. The test usually applied to such transactions is fairness or intrinsic fairness. However, to an increasing extent, courts are willing to accept the decision of disinterested directors as to the reasonableness of such transactions under the business judgment rule.

1. Transactions with a Partially Owned Subsidiary

A clear example of a potentially injurious transaction is a transaction between a corporation and its partially owned subsidiary. The minority stockholders of the subsidiary are injured by any transaction that in effect transfers assets from the subsidiary to the parent on less than a fair and equivalent exchange.

a. The parent corporation usually has the power to nominate and elect all the directors of the subsidiary and thereby to name all members of the subsidiary's management.

b. If the transaction involves a proportionate distribution of assets by the subsidiary to all of its stockholders, the minority has no basis for complaint on the ground of domination of the management by the parent corporation.

c. The proper standard for evaluating transactions between parent and subsidiary is that it must be entirely fair or intrinsically fair to the subsidiary.

d. A common problem is the allocation of tax benefits resulting from the filing of a consolidated, return. As a result of the consolidation of the financial operations of the subsidiary with the parent, it is possible that valuable tax benefits owned by the partially owned subsidiary will be realized by the parent corporation. *Case v. New York Central R. Co.,* 256 N.Y.S.2d 607, 204 N.E.2d 643 (N.Y. 1965). In order to avoid conflicts of interest in this situation, parent corporations usually enter into tax sharing agreements with their partially owned subsidiaries, requiring each subsidiary to pay the portion of the total tax shown on the consolidated return resulting from the subsidiary's operations and requiring the parent corporation to compensate the subsidiary for any tax benefits utilized by the parent to reduce or eliminate its tax obligation as reflected in the consolidated return.

e. Similar allocation problems may arise whenever parent and partially owned subsidiary share office space or utilize common services. They also arise whenever the parent corporation provide services to subsidiaries. To avoid claims of conflict of interest, parent and subsidiary usually enter into formal agreements providing how these costs should be shared and reimbursements made.

f. Because of conflict of interest problems, a parent corporation with a partially owned subsidiary may place outside unaffiliated directors on the board of directors of the subsidiary. When a transaction between subsidiary and parent is proposed, the subsidiary may be represented solely by the outside directors. In this way, the transaction may be subject to the business judgment rule rather than the rule of intrinsic or entire fairness.

g. A parent corporation with a partially owned subsidiary may lawfully eliminate the minority stockholders in the subsidiary through a cash-out merger, thereby making the subsidiary wholly owned rather than partially owned.

2. Miscellaneous Transactions

The fairness test is applicable to a variety of transactions which defy precise categorization and are best illustrated by example. These situations also generally involve duties of controlling stockholders or of directors named by controlling stockholders.

H. STATE STATUTORY LIABILITIES

State business corporation acts may impose personal liability on directors for transactions that violate specific statutory provisions. This liability is usually in addition to other liabilities and not dependent on bad faith.

1. Acts for Which Liability Is Imposed

While provisions vary from state to state, liability for the following actions are typical:

a. Paying dividends or making distributions in violation of the act or in violation of restrictions in the articles of incorporation. MBCA 8.33. Liability is usually limited to the excess of the amount actually distributed over the amount which could have been distributed without violating the act or restriction.

b. Authorizing the purchase of its own shares by a corporation in violation of statute. The liability is usually limited to the consideration paid for the shares which is in excess of the maximum amount that could have been paid without violating the statute.

c. Distributing assets to stockholders during the dissolution and winding up of the corporation without paying and discharging, or making adequate provision for the payment and discharge of, all known debts, obligations, and liabilities of the corporation.

d. Permitting the corporation to commence business before it has received the minimum required consideration for its shares.

e.   Permitting the corporation to make a loan to an officer or director, or to make a loan secured by shares of the corporation when such transactions are prohibited. The liability is limited to the amount of the loan until it is repaid.

2. Directors Who Are Liable

Business corporation acts usually provide that joint and several liability is imposed on all directors present at the meeting at which the action in violation of the statute is taken, unless a director's negative vote is duly entered in writing in the corporate records or the secretary is notified in writing by registered mail of the negative vote.

■ IX.   STOCKHOLDER DERIVATIVE LITIGATION

A.   DERIVATIVE ACTIONS GENERALLY

A *derivative action* is a lawsuit brought by one or more stockholders to remedy or prevent a wrong *to the corporation*, rather than a wrong to the stockholders individually. In contrast, a *direct* action involves the enforcement by a stockholder of a claim based on injury to the stockholder as an individual as an owner of shares. This is a fundamental distinction, but it is fuzzy at the edges because some types of claims may be characterized either as direct actions or as derivative actions depending on the way the claim is described.

1.   The ultimate rationale for the derivative action as a procedural device is that in a case in which the corporation has a claim against a director, officer, or controlling stockholder, the claim may not be pursued directly because it would in effect require these parties to sue themselves. In other words, there is an inherent conflict of interest in such situations. The plaintiff stockholder thus serves as an outside agent (similar to an independent prosecutor) to protect the rights of the corporation. In addition, a derivative action brought in the corporation's name avoids a multiplicity of actions by stockholders. Thus, some courts have questioned whether the derivative action makes much sense in the context of a closely held corporation.

2.   In a derivative action, a stockholder sues in a representative capacity on a cause of action that belongs to the corporation. Accordingly, the

stockholder must be an adequate representative of all the stockholders. The real party in interest is the corporation. But for most procedural purposes the corporation is treated as a defendant in derivative litigation. *Koster v. Lumbermens Mut. Cas. Co.*, 330 U.S. 518, 67 S.Ct. 828 (1947). The rules relating to derivative actions are sometimes found in corporation law and sometimes included in procedural rules of court. MBCA 7.40-7.47; FRCP 23.1. (Many states have adopted the FRCP and retain its numbering.) In some cases these two authorities may conflict. The rules relating to class actions are found primarily in procedural rules, but many rules relating specifically to federal securities fraud actions are incorporated into federal securities law by PSLRA and SLUSA.

3. In a derivative action, the claim belongs to the corporation and recovery if any should usually go to the corporation rather than to the stockholders individually, although in extraordinary cases individual recovery may be ordered. The rationale for the general rule is that where an injury is done to the corporation each stockholder is made whole if the corporation recovers damages from the wrongdoer. If the stockholder suffered damage in the form of a decrease in share price, share price should increase when the corporation recovers. In addition, damages recovered by the corporation derivatively are available for the payment of claims by the corporation's creditors while a direct recovery by stockholders may adversely affect creditors.

4. A derivative action may be settled or dismissed only with the approval of the court because of the danger that in a privately negotiated settlement, the corporation may in effect bribe the plaintiff, or the plaintiff's attorney, to drop the action. MBCA 7.45; FRCP 23.1.

5. Commentators disagree about the ultimate value of the derivative action as a device for protecting stockholder interests. Some observers see the derivative action as an important check on management discretion. Others argue that most derivative litigation is without substantive merit and is instituted primarily for the settlement value and for the benefit of the plaintiff attorneys whose fee must be paid by the corporation if the action is successful. Critics often refer to derivative actions as *strike actions.*

a. Plaintiff attorneys may look for and find possible litigation situations and then seek to find a plaintiff in whose name action may be brought. Plaintiff attorneys usually advance the expenses of litigation costs and accordingly have a substantial financial interest in the litigation that usually exceeds that of any single stockholder. The litigation is directed and controlled by the plaintiffs' attorneys who are motivated at least in part by their financial interest in the litigation.

b. Most derivative actions are dismissed or settled. Few cases are litigated to final judgment. The corporation usually receives some benefit, either in the form of monetary recovery or changes in management practices. Nevertheless, most studies have found little or no financial benefit from successful derivative litigation in terms of share price movement.

c. Where the action is settled without payment but rather in the form of agreed changes in management practices, the plaintiff attorney is nevertheless entitled to recover a fee from the corporation for the benefit conferred on the corporation. This is an exception to the usual American rule regarding attorney fees. The rationale is that because all of the stockholders benefit from the recovery by the corporation, all should pay proportionally, which they do in effect by charging attorney fees against corporate assets which in theory results in a pro rata charge against the value of each stockholder's shares. The same rationale applies in connection with a (direct) class action where attorney fees are paid out of the class recovery.

B. DISTINGUISHING DERIVATIVE ACTIONS AND DIRECT ACTIONS

One of the key questions in many cases is whether the action is derivative or direct, because if the action is derivative, the corporation is the real party in interest and the board of directors may be able to assume control of the action. In *Tooley v. Donaldson, Lufkin, & Jenrette, Inc.*, 845 A.2d 1031 (Del.2004), the Delaware Supreme Court held that the issue of whether an action is direct or derivative must turn *solely* on (1) who suffered the alleged harm (the corporation or the suing stockholders, individually), and (2) who would receive the benefit of any recovery or other remedy (the corporation or the stockholders, individually). Tooley involved a claim by a stockholder that a delay in completing a merger deprived the stockholders of the interest on the consideration paid during the delay. The court held that because the stockholders had no right to receive the consideration until the merger was accomplished, they had no right to interest thereon. The claim, if any belonged to the corporation and the stockholders lost the right to pursue it by virtue of having been cashed out in the merger.

1. Anything that harms the corporation also harms its stockholders by reducing the value of their shares. But a stockholder cannot transmute a derivative claim into a direct one merely by alleging that he suffered a reduction in value of his shares as a result of injury to the corporation. *Armstrong v. Frostie Co.*, 453 F.2d 914 (4th Cir.1971).

2. Usually a direct action is pursued as a class action on behalf of all stockholders. Stockholders who are members of the class in those cases may claim they were injured by an act which did not itself injure the corporation. *Green v. Wolf Corporation,* 406 F.2d 291 (2d Cir. 1968). Nevertheless, a derivative action usually has some aspects of a class action because a stockholder, when suing to right a wrong done to the corporation, is also usually suing to protect the interest of all stockholders who are not plaintiffs. In other words, in both types of actions, the plaintiff is acting as a representative, and therefore must qualify as an adequate representative of the stockholders.

3. In actions under the proxy rules, Federal courts have tended to ignore the distinction between direct and derivative actions. *See J.I. Case Co. v. Borak,* 337 U.S. 426, 69 S.Ct. 1410 (1964). On the other hand, it is clear that the courts treat securities fraud class actions under Rule 10b–5 as direct rather than derivative actions.

C. PREREQUISITES FOR MAINTAINING DERIVATIVE ACTION

The procedural rules governing derivative actions are extensive and complicated. The purpose of these rules is to assure that the plaintiff is a faithful representative of the stockholders and to prevent the purchase of claims or claims brought solely for their settlement value.

1. Demand on the Corporation or Board of Directors

Generally in a derivative action, the plaintiff must allege and prove a good faith effort to obtain redress from the corporation. A demand on the board of directors is the traditional device that satisfies this requirement.

a. The traditional rule still followed in many states and in federal courts is that a demand must be made unless it would be futile because members of the board of directors are interested in the transaction in question and a demand would in effect require the directors to sue themselves. MBCA 7.42 and the statutes of several states require that demand be made in every case.

b.   Statutes generally require that the plaintiff allege in his complaint either that a demand has been made on the board of directors or that such a demand would be futile. Historically, this was only a pleading requirement: The worst that could happen is that the court might conclude that a demand should have been made and that the proceeding should be suspended until a demand was actually made. As a result, the demand requirement usually did not significantly affect the progress of the litigation. More recent cases require more than *pro forma* allegations. An action that recites only conclusory reasons for not making a demand will likely be dismissed. *Grossman v. Johnson*, 674 F.2d 115 (1st Cir. 1982); *Gonzalez Turul v. Rogatol Distributors, Inc.*, 951 F.2d 1 (1st Cir. 1991).

c.   Delaware is the most important single state with respect to derivative litigation because of the number of corporations organized there. In Delaware, the distinction between cases in which demand is required and cases in which demand is excused often determines the outcome of the case. If demand is required, the board of directors or a committee thereof (usually called a *special litigation committee*) may decide whether to pursue the action and its decision will usually be protected by the business judgment rule. Many Delaware cases consider the circumstances when demand is required and when it is excused. *Aronson v. Lewis*, 473 A.2d 805 (Del.1984); *Rales v. Blasband*, 634 A.2d 927 (Del.1993). Litigation over the demand issue in Delaware is time-consuming. It requires a virtual trial on the merits before discovery is undertaken. *Starrels v. First Nat. Bank of* Chicago, 870 F.2d 1168 (7th Cir.1989) (concurrence by Easterbrook stating that the Delaware demand rule creates more litigation than it avoids.) *See also Kaplan v. Wyatt*, 484 A.2d 501 (Del.Ch.1984), *aff'd*, 499 A.2d 1184 (Del.1985).

d.   MBCA 7.42 and the statutes of several states require that demand be made in all cases.

e.   FRCP 23.1 requires that a plaintiff must allege with particularity the efforts, if any, made by the plaintiff to obtain the action he or she desires from the directors or comparable authority and the reasons for his or her failure to obtain the action or for not making the effort. In *Kamen v. Kemper Financial Services, Inc.*, 500 U.S. 90, 111 S.Ct. 1711 (1991), the Court held that the demand futility exception, as defined in the law of the state of incorporation, applies to derivative actions brought under federal statutes. State law also controls in actions brought on the basis of diversity of citizenship. *RCM Securities Fund Inc. v. Stanton*, 928 F.2d 1318 (2d Cir.1991); *Hausman v. Buckley*, 299 F.2d 696 (2d Cir.1962).

f.   Although some older statutes require demand upon stockholders, the MBCA and most states have dropped this requirement. The FRCP and the statutes of several states provide that if a demand on stockholders is not made, the plaintiff must show some adequate reason for not making the effort. Expense or difficulty may be justifiable reasons. In most states with stockholder-demand requirements, cases have held that demand may be omitted in appropriate circumstances. *Levitt v. Johnson*, 334 F.2d 815 (1st Cir. 1964). Courts generally have proceeded on a case-by-case basis, not requiring a demand when there are thousands of stockholders, and considering other factors such as the motives of the plaintiff, the number of stockholders joining in the action, and the proximity to the next stockholders' meeting.

g.   Massachusetts appears to have adopted the most stringent rule, requiring a demand in every case where a majority of stockholders are not wrongdoers. *S. Solomont & Sons Trust v. New England Theatres Operating Corp.*, 93 N.E.2d 241 (Mass.1950); *Pomerantz v. Clark*, 101 F.Supp. 341 (D.Mass. 1951).

h.   If a demand is made on stockholders, and the stockholders reject the demand, the action may nevertheless be brought by the minority stockholders in many cases. *Rogers v. American Can Co.*, 305 F.2d 297 (3d Cir.1962). For example, demand may be excused if the wrongdoers own a majority of the shares and hence favorable stockholder action is unlikely. In addition, if the challenged transaction cannot be ratified by the stockholders, demand on the stockholders is useless. *Mayer v. Adams*, 141 A.2d 458 (Del.1958). *But see Claman v. Robertson*, 128 N.E.2d 429 (Ohio 1955).

2.   Contemporaneous Ownership

MBCA 7.41 provides that one may not commence a derivative action unless one was a stockholder of the corporation at the time the cause of action arose or one became a stockholder through transfer by operation of law from a person who was a stockholder at that time. This statute is typical of requirements in many states. This is usually referred to as the contemporaneous ownership rule.

a.   The contemporaneous ownership rule is often justified as necessary to prevent buying into a lawsuit. If buying into a lawsuit is the concern, the contemporaneous ownership requirement might be safely liberalized to allow action by plaintiffs who discover the facts giving rise to the lawsuit only after becoming a stockholder. *Pollitz v. Gould*, 94 N.E. 1088 (N.Y. 1911). California has adopted this approach. CCC 800(b)(1). Most state statutes, however, have not accepted this liberalizing principle. *Goldie v. Yaker*, 432 P.2d 841 (N.M. 1967); *Jepsen v. Peterson*, 10 N.W.2d 749 (S.D.1943). On the other hand, where an action seems reasonable, the time of the transaction has been construed flexibly to permit the action to be maintained. *Maclary v. Pleaant Hills, Inc.*, 109 A.2d 830 (Del.Ch. 1954).

b. Another rationale for the contemporaneous ownership rule is that a stockholder is presumed to have bought shares at a fair price. Thus, in cases in which the cause of action is known to the market at the time of purchase, the market price should already reflect the harm and the stockholder pays a fair discounted price. This rationale, however, assumes that the market is efficient.

c. A principle related to the contemporaneous ownership rule prohibits a stockholder (who purchases all or substantially all the shares of a corporation at a fair price) from causing the corporation to bring action against the selling stockholders on grounds of prior corporate misman-agement. *Bangor Punta Operations, Inc. v. Bangor & Aroostook R. Co.*, 417 U.S. 703, 94 S.Ct. 2578 (1974); *In re REA Express, Inc.*, 412 F.Supp. 1239 (E.D.Pa. 1976); *Courtland Manor, Inc. v. Leeds*, 347 A.2d 144 (Del.Ch.1975); *Capitol Wine & Spirit Corp. v. Pokrass*, 98 N.Y.S.2d 291(App.Div.1950). This is an equitable principle that bars action *by the corporation* after the sale rather than simply barring a stockholder from serving as a plaintiff. In *Rifkin v. Steele Platt*, 824 P.2d 32 (Colo.App.1991) the court held that subsequent stockholders could sue on a pre-existing claim only if the purchase price did not reflect the prior wrongdoings.

d. A stockholder plaintiff who sells or disposes of his shares during the pendency of derivative litigation thereafter loses the right to maintain or continue the action. *Tenney v. Rosenthal*, 189 N.Y.S.2d 158, 160 N.E.2d 463 (N.Y.1959).

e. A stockholder plaintiff who is cashed out by merger may not thereafter continue a derivative action. *Lewis v. Anderson*, 477 A.2d 1040 (Del.1984); *Kramer v. Western Pacific Industries, Inc.*, 546 A.2d 348 (Del.1988). On the other hand, a stockholder plaintiff who receives stock in the surviving corporation following the merger may be able to continue the action on the theory that the action belongs to the surviving corporation by virtue of the merger. *See Schreiber v. Carney.* If the original corporation survives as a subsidiary, the stockholder may be able to maintain the action as a *double derivative* action.

3. Security for Expenses

Many state statutes require that the plaintiff stockholder post security for expenses as a condition of maintaining a derivative action. These statutes authorize the corporation and individual defendants to recover their expenses (including attorney fees) from such security in some circumstances. These statutes were designed to deter derivative actions in that plaintiffs may be unable or unwilling to post security. The constitutionality of security-for-expenses statutes was upheld in *Cohen v. Beneficial Indus. Loan Corp.*, 337 U.S. 541, 69 S.Ct. 1221 (1949). These statutes have not been particularly effective, and some states have repealed them.

a. Under statutes requiring security for expenses, the amount of the security is fixed by the court in light of reasonable expenses that the corporation may incur, including the expenses of other defendants for which the corporation may become liable by indemnification or otherwise. The security is usually in the form of a bond, but it may also be in the form of cash or securities.

b. Stockholder plaintiffs who are required to post security-for-expenses are defined in different ways in state statutes. In the older statutes (where the purpose to discourage derivative litigation is most manifest), the size of the plaintiff's holding is determinative. A typical provision is that plaintiffs must post security-for-expenses unless their holdings are more than five percent of the outstanding shares or exceed a specified market value, $25,000. MBCA (1969) § 49. This provision was eliminated in MBCA (1984) in part on the ground that basing the requirement on the size or value of the plaintiff's holdings rather than on the apparent good faith of the claim unreasonably discriminates against small stockholders. Some state statutes require security for expenses only upon a finding that the action appears to lack merit.

c. Security-for-expenses statutes usually provide that the corporation may have recourse to such security in such amount as the court thereafter determines. Under such statutes, courts usually allow reimbursement only if the plaintiff is unsuccessful and the action was brought without reasonable cause. Where reimbursement is allowed, an unsuccessful stockholder plaintiff posting security-for-expenses ends up paying the expenses of both sides of the litigation. If no security is posted and the case is dismissed, the plaintiff is not liable for the defendant's expenses in securing the dismissal. *Tyler v. Gas Consumers Assn.*, 231 N.Y.S.2d 15 (N.Y. 1962).

d. MBCA 7.46(2) provides that the court, upon termination of a derivative action, may require the plaintiff to pay any defendants reasonable expenses (including counsel fees) incurred in defending the proceeding if it finds that the proceeding was commenced or maintained without reasonable cause or for an improper purpose.

e. Security-for-expenses statutes are not applicable to actions in federal court based on violations of the federal securities acts, though a state claim made in connection with a federal claim under the doctrine of pendent jurisdiction may be subject to the security-for-expenses requirement.

f. Security-for-expenses statutes are not applicable to class actions. *Eisenberg v. Flying Tiger Line, Inc.*, 451 F.2d 267 (2d Cir. 1971); *Knapp v. Bankers Securities Corp.*, 230 F.2d 717 (3d Cir.1956).

D. DEFENDING A DERIVATIVE ACTION

The defendant in a derivative action has all of the defenses that would be available in a direct action based on the same claim. For example, the corporation may establish that the claim is barred by the statute of limitations. Because the corporation is the nominal plaintiff in a derivative action, these defenses may need to be asserted by the defendant. But the corporation may also argue that the individual plaintiff is an inadequate representative of the stockholders based on laches, participation in the fraud, or conflicts of interest. The most common and effective defensive tactic is for the board of directors to seek dismissal of the lawsuit on the grounds that the action ultimately belongs to the corporation and thus may be *voluntarily* dismissed by the corporation because it is contrary to the best interests of the corporation to pursue it. This is a relatively recent development, and although it remains controversial, it now appears to be well established.

1. Dismissal by the Corporation

A derivative action is a lawsuit for the benefit of the corporation. The right to pursue the action is an asset like any other under the authority of the board of directors. As a general rule the corporation acting through the board of directors may choose whether or not to pursue the action on behalf of the corporation.

a. Where a derivative action seeks recovery by the corporation from third persons unrelated to the corporation, it is clear that a decision by the directors not to pursue such litigation is protected by the business judgment rule.

b. If the cause of action is one that is based on a decision by the board of directors itself or on the actions of one more individual directors, an adverse decision by the board may be seen as conflicted and therefore subject to scrutiny under the duty of loyalty. Under well-established rules, however, the board of directors may nonetheless act even when conflicted. Conflicted directors may be required to recuse themselves, or the matter may be referred to a committee of directors who are free of conflict, or the stockholders may ratify the matter, or a court may determine that the action of the board was fair. The most common practice is for the board of directors to appoint a special litigation committee (SLC).

c. Early decisions on the dismissal issue involved actions in which stockholders sought to recover improper foreign payments or domestic political contributions from the directors or officers who authorized them (or who failed to prevent them). The courts initially ruled with little reservation that the decision to seek dismissal of derivative litigation was no different than other questions to be resolved by disinterested directors as a matter of business judgment. *Gall v. Exxon Corp.*, 418 F.Supp. 508 (S.D.N.Y. 1976); *Auerbach v. Bennett*, 419 N.Y.S.2d 920 (N.Y. 1979); *Burks v. Lasker*, 441 U.S. 471, 99 S.Ct. 1831 (1979). It is doubtful that the plaintiffs in some of these cases would have prevailed if a trial on the merits had been held.

d. The primary argument against the uncritical application of the business judgment rule is based on *structural bias*—that directors may be reluctant to sue each other. This argument has been consistently rejected by the courts. See *Auerbach v. Bennett*, 47 N.Y. 2d 619, 631–633, 393 N.E. 994, 1001–1002, 419 N.Y.S.2d 920 (1979); *Beam ex rel. Martha Stewart Living*

Omnimedia, Inc. v. Stewart, 833 A.2d 961 (Del.Ch. 2003); *Beam v. Stewart*, 845 A.2d 1040 (personal friendship or family relationship alone is insufficient to show interestedness). *Cf. United States v. Chestman*, 947 F.2d 551, 566 (2d Cir. 1991) (en banc) (family relationship insufficient to establish a fiduciary duty not to use inside information). Rather, one must show a financial interest. MBCA 7.44(c) specifically rejects structural bias as grounds for interestedness.

f.   Either the board of directors itself (excluding directors who are defendants in the proceedings) or a special litigation committee composed of independent directors who are not involved in the matters complained of should investigate the matters complained of in the stockholders complaint.

- Where a special litigation committee is formed, the full powers of the board of directors are delegated to the SLC without any express reservation by the board to review the recommendation of the committee. In other words, the SLC is authorized to act on its own recommendations.

- The board of directors or the committee may hire independent counsel to investigate the complaint and make a recommendation as to the position the board of directors or the litigation committee should take.

- If the board of directors or litigation committee concludes that it is not in the best interests of the corporation to pursue the derivative action, the corporation may file a motion to dismiss the stockholders' action on the ground that the decision whether or not to pursue litigation is itself an important business decision that is subject to the business judgment rule.

g.   Delaware courts have developed a complex set of rules with respect to the dismissal of derivative litigation. The test for the application of the business judgment rule in Delaware depends on whether the case is a *demand excused* or a *demand required* case.

- *Zapata Corp. v. Maldonado*, 430 A.2d 779 (Del.1981), holds that where a demand on directors is excused, the action is properly filed without a demand, but the corporation may thereafter appoint a committee to consider the merits of the plaintiff's claim. If the committee recommends that the litigation be dismissed (as litigation committees almost invariably do) the court should review the independence of the committee and may thereafter exercise its own independent business judgment to determine whether litigation should be dismissed over the objection of the plaintiff on the basis of the recommendation of the litigation committee.

- *Aronson v. Lewis*, 475 A.2d 805 (Del.1984), holds that the *Zapata* rule is applicable only where demand is excused. Where demand is required, the decision whether or not to pursue the litigation is vested in the board of directors, and the business judgment rule applies. If action was filed without making a demand, it should be dismissed for failing to make a demand. If a demand was made, the decision by the litigation committee should be evaluated under the business judgment rule.

- Under *Aronson,* demand is excused only if (1) there is a reasonable doubt that the board of directors has the independence and disinterestedness necessary for application of the business judgment rule, or (2) if the facts (alleged with particularity) when taken as true, support a reasonable doubt that the challenged transaction was the product of a valid exercise of business judgment. To avoid the business judgment rule the plaintiff must overcome one of the two requirements set forth in *Aronson.* If both requirements have been met, a demand is required and the decision of the board or committee is thereafter entitled to the protections of the business judgment rule. *See also Levine v. Smith,* 591 A.2d 194, 205–208 (Del.1991): The premise of a stockholder claim of futility of demand is that a majority of the board of directors either has a financial interest in the challenged transaction or lacks independence or otherwise failed to exercise due care. . . . When lack of independence is charged, a plaintiff must show that the Board is either dominated by an officer or director who is the proponent of the challenged transaction or that the board is so under his influence that its discretion is sterilize[d]. Assuming a plaintiff cannot prove that directors are interested or otherwise incapable of exercising independent business judgment, a plaintiff in a demand futility case must plead particularized facts creating a reasonable doubt as to the soundness of the challenged transaction sufficient to rebut the presumption that the business judgment rule attaches to the transaction.

h. Most Delaware cases since *Aronson* have concluded that demand is required and therefore that the business judgment rule is applicable to the decision of the independent litigation committee or the board of directors to discontinue the litigation even though the cause of action is based on a business decision that appears to be questionable. In *Aronson,* demand was required even though the challenged decision by the board was to grant to the controlling stockholder a lucrative employment and consulting contract that did not require the performance of any specific services. The controlling stockholder did not himself sit on the board, but had hand-picked each of the directors. *See also Grobow v. Perot,* 539 A.2d 180 (Del.1988)(decision to repurchase shares of dissenting stockholder and director Ross Perot at a premium was described by Perot as obscene.) *But see RCM Securities Fund, Inc. v. Stanton,* 928 F.2d 1318 (2d Cir. 1991)(decision to borrow heavily against corporate assets in order to buy back shares of stock to be contributed to employee share ownership plan (ESOP) that would then control corporation and insulate it from a threatened takeover).

i. The Delaware approach has led to extensive pretrial skirmishing because the decision as to whether demand is excused is likely to be outcome-determinative. Some judges have questioned the desirability of the Delaware approach. *See Starrels v. First Nat. Bank of Chicago,* 870 F.2d 1168 (7th Cir. 1989) (concurrence by Easterbrook); *Kaplan v. Wyatt,* 484 A.2d 501 (Del.Ch. 1984), aff'd, 499 A.2d 1184 (Del.1985).

j. Delaware law applies in federal cases that involve Delaware corporations. *Kamen v. Kemper Financial Services, Inc.,* 500 U.S. 90, 111 S.Ct. 1711 (1991); *RCM Securities Fund, Inc. v. Stanton,* 928 F.2d 1318 (2d Cir. 1991). *See also Joy v. North,* 692 F.2d 880 (2d Cir. 1982) (construing Connecticut law and applying the *Zapata* test rather than the *Auerbach* test; the court also rejected the decision to seek dismissal as unlikely to be a valid exercise of business judgment).

k. MBCA 7.42 requires a written demand on the corporation in all cases. A derivative action may nonetheless be commenced despite a refused demand. Also the board of directors or a committee of two or more independent directors thereof may seek to have the action dismissed if after a reasonable investigation they conclude in good faith that the action is not in the best interests of the corporation. If a majority of the board is independent at the time the determination to seek dismissal is made, the plaintiff bears the burden of proof with regard to the determination to seek dismissal. If a majority of the board is not disinterested at the time the determination is made, the committee bears the burden of proof as to the determination to seek dismissal. The business judgment rule does not appear to apply even when the board is majority independent. Thus, the MBCA appears to favor derivative actions more than Delaware law. *See also Beneville v. York,* 769 A.2d 80,

85–86 (Del.Ch. 2000), holding that demand may be excused where a board is evenly divided between interested and disinterested directors.

l. The PCG also requires demand be made in virtually all cases unless irreparable injury to the corporation would result from delay. Under PCG § 7.04, if the board rejects a demand, it must deliver a written reply to the plaintiff stating the reasons for the rejection and identifying the directors who reviewed the demand. PCG 7.09 provides that the board may appoint a committee of two or more disinterested directors to review the action. Although the comments suggest that disinterested directors should appoint the committee, the Principles do not specifically so require. PCG 7.10 provides that the standard of review upon a motion to dismiss generally should be the same as that which applies to the challenged transaction.

m. Note that the business judgment rule does not appear to apply even when the board is majority independent. Thus, the MBCA appears to favor derivative actions slightly more than Delaware law. *See also Beneville v. York,* 769 A.2d 89, 85–86 (Del.Ch. 2000)(holding that demand is excused where a board is evenly divided between interested and disinterested directors).

n. The PCG also requires demand in virtually all cases unless irreparable injury to the corporation would result from delay. Under PCG 7.04, if the board rejects a demand, it must deliver a written reply to the plaintiff stating the reasons for the rejection and identifying the directors who reviewed the demand. PCG 7.09 provides that the board may appoint a committee of two or more disinterested directors to review the action. Although the comments suggest that the committee should be appointed by disinterested directors, the Principles do not specifically so require. PCG 7.10 provides that the standard of review upon motion to dismiss should generally be the same as that which applies to the transaction challenged.

o. Both the MBCA and the Principles of Corporate Governance contain provisions permitting the Court to stay discovery proceedings on motion by the corporation if the corporation undertakes to review the merits of the action with a view toward seeking dismissal. As a practical matter, the stay of discovery often precludes the representative plaintiff from obtaining information that would permit pleading with particularity. Similar provisions apply in connection with securities fraud class actions.

p. *Miller v. Register & Tribune Syndicate, Inc.*, 336 N.W.2d 709 (Iowa 1983) holds that if a majority of directors are named as defendants, the board of directors may not establish a litigation committee with the power of the board to terminate derivative litigation. Rather, the board must apply to a court for the appointment of a trustee or receiver if it wishes to discontinue the litigation. *See also* MBCA 7.44(f) (authorizing the court to appoint an independent panel to determine whether to seek dismissal); PCG 7.12 (same).

FRCP 23.1 requires that a plaintiff must allege with particularity the efforts, if any, made by the plaintiff to obtain the action he or she desires from the directors or comparable authority and the reasons for his or her failure to obtain the action, or for not making the effort. In *Kamen v. Kemper Financial Services, Inc.*, 500 U.S. 90, 111 S.Ct. 1711 (1991), the Court held that the demand futility exception, as defined in the law of the state of incorporation, applies to derivative actions brought under federal statutes. State law also controls actions brought on the basis of diversity of citizenship. *RCM Securities Fund Inc. v. Stanton*, 928 F.2d 1318 (2d Cir. 1991); *Hausman v. Buckley*, 299 F.2d 696 (2d Cir. 1962).

E. SETTLEMENT

A derivative action may be settled only with judicial approval. In the absence of such a requirement, the corporation might attempt to settle with a representative plaintiff alone, in effect paying a bribe to the plaintiff to drop his action.

a. Notice of the proposed dismissal or compromise must be given to stockholders or members in such manner as the court directs. *Saylor v. Bastedo*, 594 F.Supp. 371 (S.D.N.Y.1984); *Lewis v. Newman*, 59 F.R.D. 525 (S.D.N.Y.1973); *Perrine v. Pennroad Corp.*, 47 A.2d 479 (Del.1946); *Shlensky v. Dorsey*, 574 F.2d 131 (3d Cir.1978).

b. Where a secret settlement has led to a payment to a derivative plaintiff, other stockholders may bring derivative actions in the name of the corporation against the settling stockholder to recover the payment. *Clarke v. Greenberg*, 71 N.E.2d 443 (N.Y. 1947).

c. The corporation itself may settle a claim without court approval and
    without the consent of the plaintiffs' attorneys, but a sweetheart settle-
    ment may become the basis of a later derivative action. *Wolf v. Barkes,* 348
    F.2d 994 (2d Cir.1965).

F. RECOVERY

Recovery in a derivative action is usually payable to the corporation rather
than to individual stockholders. The theory is that payment to the corporation increases the value of the corporation and its shares for the benefit of all
stockholders. In some cases, courts have ordered a pro rata recovery to be
paid to the stockholders if payment to the corporation would effectively
result in payment to the wrongdoers. See PCG 7.18.

a. Most courts are reluctant to order stockholder recovery. Indeed, some
    have suggested that pro rata recovery is inconsistent with the idea of a
    derivative action and can never be awarded.

b. A pro rata recovery often gives rise to practical and conceptual problems.
    Keenan v. Eshleman, 2 A.2d 904 (Del.1938); *Norte & Co. v. Huffines,* 4126
    F.2d 1189 (2d Cir. 1969); *Schachter v. Kulik,* 547 N.Y.S.2d 816, 547 N.E.2d
    71 (N.Y. 1989)[recovery should go to the corporation even where there
    were only two stockholders]. *See also Tooley v. Donaldson, Lufkin, &
    Jenrette,* 845 A.2d 1031 (Del.2004) (determination of whether claims are
    direct or derivative depends on who suffered harm and who will
    recover). *Cf. Bangor Punta Operations, Inc. v. Bangor & Aroostook R. Co.,* 417
    U.S. 703 (174) (rejecting pro rata recovery on behalf of holdover minority
    stockholders and dismissing action brought by injured corporation on
    theory that control had changed hands at a fair price following misman-
    agement by former controlling stockholder and that new stockholders
    could not therefore have maintained derivative action because of the
    contemporaneous ownership rule).

c. A direct recovery for a derivative injury has a mandatory dividend
    feature. Arguably, the courts should thus determine that a distribution
    would be permissible under the circumstances.

d. In appropriate cases plaintiffs may obtain non-monetary relief. *White v.
    Perkins,* 189 S.E.2d 315 (Va. 1972) (dissolution); *Robinson v. Thompson,* 466
    S.W.2d 626 (Tex.Civ.App.1971) (receiver).

G. RES JUDICATA

The *res judicata* effect of the termination of a derivative action depends on the manner or basis for the termination. A final judgment on the merits is *res judicata* and binding on all other stockholders.

1. Settlement

A court-approved settlement ordinarily has the same effect as a final judgment on the merits. *Berger v. Dyson*, 111 F.Supp. 533 (D.R.I.1953). But stockholders may not be bound if they were not notified of the proposed settlement or if the settlement was based on nondisclosure of relevant evidence or collusion between plaintiff and defendant. *Manufacturers Mut. Fire Ins. Co. of Rhode Island v. Hopson*, 25 N.Y.S.2d 502 (N.Y. 1940); *Shlensky v. Dorsey*, 574 F2d 131 (3d Cir. 1978); *Alleghany Corp. v. Kirby*, 333 F.2d 327 (2d Cir.1964).

2. Dismissal

The *res judicata* effect of a dismissal of a derivative action depends on the reason for the dismissal. A voluntary dismissal, or a dismissal because the plaintiff stockholder does not qualify as a proper plaintiff is usually without prejudice and does not bind the class. For example, dismissal for failure to post security for expenses or to answer interrogatories does not bind the class. *Papilsky v. Berndt*, 466 F.2d 251 (2d Cir. 1972).

a. In some situations, the court may order that notice be given to all other stockholders before a derivative action is dismissed voluntarily. Such action may then be continued by intervening stockholders. If none appear, the action may be dismissed with prejudice.

b. A dismissal on the merits, as where the complaint does not state a claim on which relief can be granted or where the decision of a litigation committee not to pursue the litigation is protected by the business judgment rule, binds all members of the class.

H. LITIGATION EXPENSES

If the plaintiff is successful, the court usually awards expenses, including attorney fees, to be paid by the corporation. Expenses are typically paid out of the award or settlement obtained by the corporation as a result of the action. Expenses may also be paid by the corporation where the corporation receives no money as a result of the litigation if the action was of some benefit to the corporation. *Bosch v. Meeker Co–Op Light & Power Assn.*, 101 N.W.2d 423 (Minn.1960); *Fletcher v. A.J. Industries, Inc.*, 72 Cal.Rptr. 146 (1968). MBCA 7.46(1) adopts a substantial benefit standard.

1. Amount

The amount of the attorney fees to be awarded to a successful plaintiff counsel depends on a variety of factors: the nature and character of the litigation, the skill required, the amount of work actually performed, the size of the recovery, the nature of the harm prevented, and other factors.

a. The fee must be reasonable. Its size is determined or approved by the court and is a question of fact on which evidence may be taken.

b. Where derivative litigation is settled, attorney fees may be negotiated as part of the settlement. Such fees are subject to judicial review and approval. As a practical matter, it may be difficult for a judge to review the reasonableness of an agreed fee if all settling parties support the negotiated fee.

2. Defendant Expenses

In limited circumstances defendants may be entitled to have their fees and expenses paid by the plaintiffs or by the corporation.

a. If the plaintiff has posted security for expenses, the defendants may have recourse to that security if authorized by the court. Or if a court determines that the plaintiff has filed action or pleadings not in good faith, expenses may be recoverable from the plaintiff or plaintiff's attorney if authorized by the court.

b. Individual defendants may be entitled to be indemnified *by the corporation* for their expenses. Defendants may also be protected by a directors and officers (D&O) insurance policy obtained by the corporation. Such policies usually cover litigation expenses.

3. Miscellaneous Procedural Issues

The corporation is the nominal plaintiff in a derivative action. And often the board of directors is the defendant. In such a case, the corporation and the board of directors are technically adverse parties. But the reality is that the corporation and the board are usually allied at least in the early stages of litigation. This gives rise to several peculiar problems.

a. The corporation is technically the plaintiff in a derivative action and its interest is therefore technically adverse to the interest of the other defendants. *Cannon v. U.S. Acoustics Corp.*, 398 F.Supp. 209 (N.D.Ill.1975); *Marco v. Dulles*, 169 F.Supp. 622 (S.D.N.Y. 1959). Nevertheless, a single attorney may represent both the corporation and the directors or officers who are defendants in the early stages of a derivative action until it becomes clear that the interests of the two are in fact adverse. Multiple representation may be permitted only if it is clear that there are no possible conflicts. *Seifert v. Dumatic Industries, Inc.*, 197 A.2d 454 (Pa.1964).

b. The attorney-client privilege between corporation and counsel usually may not be invoked by management defendants. *Garner v. Wolfinbarger*, 430 F.2d 1093 (5th Cir. 1970).

c. An attorney involved in an investigation of wrongdoing for a client corporation may be disqualified to serve later as a derivative plaintiff based on that wrongdoing. *Richardson v. Hamilton Intern. Corp.*, 469 F.2d 1382 (3d Cir.1972); *Cannon v. U.S. Acoustics Corp.*, 398 F.Supp. 209 (N.D.Ill. 1975).

d. Although a derivative action is technically an action at equity, in *Ross v. Bernhard*, 396 U.S. 531, 90 S.Ct. 733 (1970), the Supreme Court held that a right to jury trial may exist in a derivative action in federal court where the ultimate issue is one at law rather than at equity.

e. If the independent existence of the corporate plaintiff disappears by merger or similar transaction during the pendency of the action, the action must be dismissed unless the surviving entity is added as a party defendant. *Niesz v. Gorsuch*, 295 F.2d 909 (9th Cir. 1961). A representative plaintiff who has been cashed-out ceases to be a stockholder and may no longer maintain a derivative action.

f. A stockholder in a parent corporation may maintain a derivative action on behalf of a wholly-owned subsidiary corporation. Such an action is often called a *double derivative action.*

g. The corporation is a necessary party; without it the action cannot proceed. *Dean v. Kellogg*, 292 N.W. 704 (Mich. 1940).

h. A derivative action has class as well as derivative aspects; multiple derivative actions may be filed by several different stockholders. Courts may consolidate proceedings, or permit one proceeding to continue and stay the others. *Res judicata* applies to preclude retrial of issues previous decided.

i. The representative plaintiff in a derivative action may be seen as a fiduciary which may give rise to a duty not to enter into other transactions with the corporation that entail special benefits not enjoyed by all stockholders.

I. INDEMNIFICATION GENERALLY

In the context of corporation law, indemnification refers to payment or reimbursement by the corporation of a director, officer, or agent for expenses incurred in defending against a civil claim or criminal prosecution that arises in connection with service to the corporation, including claims by the corporation itself in the context of a derivative action. If indemnification is permitted or required, it normally covers legal fees and other expenses. It may also cover a monetary award or settlement, amounts needed to satisfy a judgment entered against defendant officers or directors, or even a criminal fine. A corporation may also advance expenses to a defendant prior to a determination of liability. Liability insurance for directors and officers (D&O insurance) is also available. There are fundamental policy questions posed by indemnification. On he one hand, the practice encourages responsible persons to accept a position as a director. Given litigation costs today, few responsible persons would be willing to serve as directors in the absence of indemnification. Moreover, it encourages innocent directors to resist unjust charges, and it discourages groundless stockholder litigation. There can be little objection to indemnification of expenses if a director is absolved of liability or misconduct. *In re E. C. Warner Co.*, 45 N.W.2d 388 (Minn.1950). On the other hand, indemnification in connection with some wrongful acts such as self-dealing would effectively nullify fiduciary duty and would presumably therefore violate public policy. The trick is to sort out the situations where indemnification is proper and should be encouraged and situations where it is against public policy and should be prohibited.

J. SCOPE OF INDEMNIFICATION UNDER STATE STATUTES

State statutes attempt to work out a compromise of these various competing considerations. Statutes on indemnification vary from skeletal authorization to elaborate procedural and substantive requirements.

1. Mandatory Indemnification

A defendant is entitled to indemnification as a matter of statutory right if he is wholly successful, on the merits or otherwise. MBCA 8.52.

2. Permissive Indemnification

Indemnification is permitted as a matter of discretion but not as a matter of right in a variety of situations. Directors cannot compel corporations to grant indemnification for conduct falling within the category of permissive indemnification. *Tomash v. Midwest Technical Development Corp.*, 160 N.W.2d 273 (Minn.1968). Permissive indemnification is authorized in the following situations:

a. Liabilities that may be indemnified against include the obligation to pay a judgment, settlement, penalty, fine, tax, or reasonable expenses. For actions in the official capacity of a person, indemnification is permitted only if the person acted in good faith and can establish that she reasonably believed that her conduct was in the corporation's best interest. MBCA 8.51(a)(2)(i). For all other actions, indemnification is permitted only if the person acted in good faith and can establish that she reasonably believed that her conduct was *at least not opposed to* the corporation's best interest. MBCA 8.51(a)(2)(ii).

b. In the case of a director, official capacity means only the office of director in a corporation. In other cases, official capacity means the office in the corporation or the employment or agency relationship undertaken by that individual for or on behalf of the corporation. All relationships other than the foregoing do not involve actions in official capacity.

c. In the case of a criminal proceeding, the person must also have had no reasonable cause to believe her conduct was unlawful. MBCA 8.51(a)(3).

d. Even though an individual meets these standards, indemnification is not permitted in two situations: (1) in a action or proceeding by or in the name of the corporation in which the person is adjudged liable to the corporation; and (2) in a proceeding charging the receipt of an improper personal benefit in which the person is adjudged liable for receiving that personal benefit.

e. Many corporations, by bylaw provision, grant a contractual right of indemnification in all cases in which indemnification is permissive. Some state statutes make this the default rule unless the articles of incorporation provide the contrary.

3. Court–Approved Indemnification

MBCA 8.54(2) recognizes that a person ineligible for indemnification under the technical requirements of the statute may in some circumstances be fairly entitled to indemnification and provides that a person otherwise not eligible for indemnification may petition a court (which may be either the court in which the proceeding occurred or another court) for a determination that the person is fairly and reasonably entitled to indemnification. Court-approved indemnification is limited to the indemnification of reasonable expenses.

4. Advance for Expenses

MBCA 8.53 authorizes a corporation to pay or reimburse the expenses of a proceeding *as* they are incurred without waiting for a final determination that the person is eligible for indemnification. This provision recognizes that as a practical matter, adequate legal representation and adequate preparation of a defense often requires substantial payments of expenses before a final determination. If advances are not permitted less affluent officers and directors might be unable to finance their own defense. On the other hand, advances for expenses may lead to payments to defendants who are ultimately determined to be ineligible for indemnification.

5. Officers, Employees & Agents

Officers, employees, and agents of a corporation may have rights of indemnification based on contract, corporation policy, or general principles of agency that are broader than the right of directors. MBCA 8.56.

6. Modification of Statutory Indemnification Policies

Delaware and several other states provide that the indemnification statute is not exclusive. That means that a corporation may include broader indemnification provisions in its articles of incorporation or bylaws.

a.   In states with non-exclusive statutes, the only limitation on indemnification rights granted by contract or bylaw provision is public policy.

b.   MBCA 8.58(a) makes the statute exclusive, but provides that a contractual or voluntary provision relating to indemnification that goes beyond the statute is valid only to the extent the provision is consistent with the statute. The Official Comment states that this position is believed to be a more accurate description of the limited validity of nonstatutory indemnification provisions. As a practical matter there may be little difference between the Model Act and non-exclusive statutes, because public policy probably does not permit indemnification significantly broader than that permitted by the Model Act.

7. Indemnification of Witnesses

MBCA 8.50-8.58 applies only when a director is named or threatened to be named as a defendant in a proceeding. MBCA 8.50(6).

8. Notification of Indemnification

MBCA 16.21(a) requires the corporation to notify stockholders of all indemnifications or advances of expenses to defendants in connection with actions brought by or in the name of the corporation.

9. Indemnification in Federal Proceedings

Indemnification of liabilities incurred under federal statutes may raise additional questions of public policy.

a.   The SEC has long taken the position that it is against public policy for a corporation to indemnify officers or directors against liabilities imposed by the Securities Act of 1933. Rule 460 provides that acceleration of the effective date of a registration statement may be denied unless a waiver of right to indemnification is filed.

b.   Some cases indicate that indemnification is also less broadly available for liabilities imposed by federal securities law than under common law or state statutory provisions. *See Globus v. Law Research Serv. Inc.*, 418 F.2d 1276 (2d Cir.1969). *S.E.C. v. Continental Growth Fund, Inc.*, 1964 Fed.Sec.L.Rep. ¶ 91,437 (S.D.N.Y.Oct. 7, 1964). *See also Gould v. American–Hawaiian Steamship Co.*, 387 F.Supp. 163 (D.Del.1974), *vacated on other grounds*, 535 F.2d 761 (3d Cir.1976).

K.   D & O LIABILITY INSURANCE

Directors and officers (D&O) liability insurance provides useful but limited protection against costs and liabilities for negligence or misconduct not involving dishonesty or knowing bad faith, and for false or misleading statements in disclosure documents. Most candidates would decline to serve as a director of a publicly held corporation unless protected by a D&O policy.

1. **Structure of D&O Policies**

   D&O policies are complementary to indemnification. Most publicly held corporations provide both indemnification and insurance for its directors.

   a. D&O insurance is *claims made* insurance. It insures only for claims that are presented to the insurer during the period of insurance (and a short period thereafter if the insurance is not renewed) even though the actions giving rise to the claim may have occurred months or years earlier. When the period of insurance ends, if no claim has been made the insurer has no responsibility for events occurring during the period. *McCullough v. Fidelity & Deposit Co.*, 2 F.3d 110 (5th Cir.1993).

   b. D&O insurance consists of two different parts. (1) The Corporate Reimbursement portion of the policy insures the corporation against payments it is obligated or permitted to make to officers or directors under its indemnification obligations. This portion of the policy does not insure the corporation against direct claims made by stockholders or others. (2) The Directors and Officers portion of the policy insures directors and officers against obligations that are not indemnifiable by the corporation as long as they are not excluded by the policy.

2. **Policy Exclusions**

   Policy exclusions in D&O policies fall into three broad categories.

   a. Conduct exclusions deal with conduct that is sufficiently self-serving or egregious that it is not insurable.

   b. Other insurance exclusions cover conduct for which insurance is available under other policies.

   c. Laser exclusions are exclusions unique to the specific firm or industry.

   d. Reckless, willful, or criminal conduct may not be insurable as a matter of law. *Raychem Corp. v. Federal Ins. Co.*, 853 F.Supp. 1170 (N.D.Cal.1994).

3. **State Statutes**

   Many state statutes specifically authorize corporations to purchase D&O insurance. *See* MBCA 8.57. Where no statutory authorization exists, the power to purchase such insurance is usually thought to be implicit in the general corporate power to provide executive compensation. Corporate bylaws often specifically authorize the purchase of such insurance.

■ X. DISCLOSURE & CORPORATE RECORDS

Under federal securities law, a publicly held company is required to file periodic reports with the Securities & Exchange Commission (SEC or Commission). Most of the information contained in these reports is also required to be distributed to stockholders. A corporation subject to these rules is often called a *reporting company*. State law also requires corporations to maintain certain books and records and to make them available to stockholders under specified conditions. State law relating to books and records applies to all corporations, whether or not publicly traded. But state law also imposes disclosure obligations in connection with particular transactions.

A. CORPORATIONS SUBJECT TO FEDERAL PERIODIC REPORTING REQUIREMENTS

Periodic reporting requirements under federal securities law are applicable to corporations (1) that must register under Section 12 of the Securities Exchange Act of 1934, or (2) that have made a public offering of securities registered under the Securities Act of 1933. The latter requirement is found in § 15(d) of the 1934 Act. The distinction between the two reporting requirements is important. A company that is registered under § 12 is also subject to a variety of other SEC rules including the rules governing proxy solicitations. Section 15(d) does not trigger these requirements. Thus, for example, a company that has registered only an offering of debt securities is not required to comply with the proxy rules.

1. Section 12 Registration

Section 12 of the 1934 Act requires registration by corporations (1) that have securities that are registered on a national securities exchange, or (2) that have a class of equity securities held of record by 500 or more persons and assets of $10 million or more. In order to register under § 12 a company must file SEC Form 10.

2. Section 15(d) Reporting

If a company issues securities pursuant to a registration statement filed under the 1933 Act, it must file and distribute periodic reports under § 15(d) of the 1934 Act. Whereas § 12(g) is triggered by the equity securities only, the reporting requirement under § 15(d) is triggered by any offering of securities, including debt securities.

3. Implications of § 12 Registration

Registration under § 12 of the 1934 Act triggers the applicability of several other requirements under the 1934 Act, including:

- the proxy solicitation rules under § 14.

- the tender offer rules under §§ 13 and 14.

- reporting and trading rules under § 16.

- beneficial ownership rules under § 13.

In other words, these rules apply only to companies that are registered under § 12 of the 1934 Act. They do not apply to companies that are required to file reports under § 15(d).

4. Termination of Section 12 Registration

Once a corporation is required to register under § 12, it remains subject to that section even though the number of stockholders drops below 500. Registration under § 12 may be terminated if the corporation has no class of shares held of record by more than 300 persons. A corporation may also terminate registration if it has fewer than 500 stockholders and if its assets are valued at less than $10,000,000 on the last day of its fiscal year for the last three years. SEC Rule 12g–4. In order to terminate registration, a company must file SEC Form 15. Reporting requirements are immediately suspended, but the termination becomes effective 90 days later after SEC review.

5. Termination of Section 15 (d) Reporting

The reporting requirement under § 15(d) is automatically suspended if a company has fewer than 300 stockholders of any class as of the beginning of any fiscal year after the year of an offering. There is no asset standard. A company must file SEC Form 15 within 30 days in order to notify the SEC of the suspension.

B. PERIODIC REPORTING REQUIREMENTS

Companies subject to § 12 or § 15 (d) are required to file periodic reports with the SEC. These reports, are designed to update continually the information that is publicly available about the company. These reports are publicly available. They are on file in SEC reading rooms and are available electronically under the SEC's Electronic Data Gathering and Retrieval (EDGAR) system. These reports are subject to detailed formal requirements set forth in § 13 of the 1934 Act and rules thereunder. The SEC does not routinely review 1934 Act reports, but may do so if the report is incorporated by reference in a 1933 Act registration statement or in connection with selective enforcement program.

1. Form 10–K

Form 10–K is annual report provide the same information about the issuer that appears in a 1933 Act registration statement except for information that would relate to an offering of securities (such as stockholder rights, use of proceeds, underwriting arrangements, method of offering, pricing, and so forth). It must include full audited financial statements. Information required in Form 10–K includes:

- description of business and properties.

- management's discussion and analysis of financial condition and results of operations.

- full audited financial information together with independent auditor opinion

- description of material legal proceedings.

- quantitative and qualitative disclosures about market risk.

- information regarding directors and officers and their compensation.

In addition, the Sarbanes Oxley Act requires that Form 10–K include:

- information relating to the company's code of ethics (if any).

- information relating to financial experts on the company's audit committee and whether they are independent.

- a table of contractual obligations.

- information relating to internal controls over financial reporting.

Many companies also include a discussion of risk factors in the 10–K (and 10–Q). By doing so, the company can take advantage of statutory defenses for forward looking statements (whether in the filed form or elsewhere) that turn out to be incorrect. Form 10–K must be signed by the CEO, CFO, principal accounting officer, and a majority of the members of the board of directors. Moreover, under the Sarbanes Oxley Act, the CEO and CFO both must certify (1) that they have reviewed the report and that the report is fair and accurate to their knowledge, and (2) that the company has designed and implemented internal controls over financial reporting and disclosure. In addition the CEO and CFO must certify that the report complies with the requirements of the 1934 Act.

2. Form 10–Q

Form 10–Q is a quarterly report containing unaudited interim financial data. It must also disclose material nonrecurring events that occurred during the quarter, such as commencement of significant litigation. Under the Sarbanes Oxley Act, Form 10–Q reports must be certified by the CEO and CFO in the same fashion as Form 10–K reports.

3. Form 8–K

Form 8–K is a report that must be filed only when event occurs. A reportable event generally involves matters of major significance such as significant financial developments, changes in control, material acquisitions or dispositions of assets, changes in and resignations of directors. Generally, a Form 8–K must be filed within two days of a reportable event. Specifically, a company must file a Form 8–K if any of the following events occur:

- change in control.

- acquisition or disposition of significant assets other than in the normal course of business.

- bankruptcy or receivership.

- resignation or dismissal of auditor or engagement of new auditor.

- resignation of director or principal officer and reasons therefore

- election of new director or appointment of principal officer

- change in fiscal year.

- material events regarding employee benefit plans including temporary suspension of trading under employee stock ownership plan.

- earnings release under Regulation G.

- amendment to or waiver under code of ethics.

- establishment or termination of material agreement or business relationship.

- change in securities rating.

- amendments to articles of incorporation or bylaws.

A company may voluntarily file a Form 8–K relating to any other material event.

4. Management's Discussion and Analysis (MD&A)

One of the most important items of information provided in periodic reports and proxy statements is the Management Discussion and Analysis of Financial Condition and Results of Operations (MD&A). SEC rules require that the MD&A focus specifically on material events and uncertainties known to management that would cause reported information not to be necessarily indicative of future results or conditions.

a.   The MD&A must include a discussion of liquidity, capital resources and results of operations, including any unusual or infrequent events or transactions, as well as any other information necessary to understanding a company's financial condition and changes therein. SEC Regulation S–K, Item 303.

b.   The SEC tends to focus on the MD&A in reviewing periodic reports and has identified several common deficiencies including:

- failure to discuss revenue recognition policies, one-time charges, and assumptions used.

- failure to discuss or quantify reasons for material changes year to year in financial report line items.

- failure to discuss known material trends and uncertainties that diverge from historical patterns.

- failure to discuss business segment information.

Matter of Caterpillar, Inc., 50 S.E.C. 903 (1992) (SEC enforcement proceeding resulting from failure to disclose and discuss significance of profits from Brazilian subsidiary on overall financial results).

c. As a result of the Sarbanes Oxley Act, the MD&A must now include a discussion of material off balance sheet financings, critical accounting estimates, and adoption of new accounting policies.

C. OTHER DISCLOSURE RULES

The reporting requirements discussed above are mandatory for companies subject to § 12 or § 15(d). There are, however, other disclosure requirements that may be triggered in situations in which the company chooses to speak.

1. Regulation FD

Regulation FD, adopted in 1999, requires that when a company discloses material nonpublic information to certain stockholders or investment professionals—whether intentionally or inadvertently—it must also disclose the information to all stockholders unless the original disclosure is subject to a confidentiality agreement. The rule is designed to prevent selective disclosure. (FD stands for *fair disclosure*.) The disclosure may be made by via Form 8–K.

2. Regulation G

Regulation G requires that a company that issues an earnings report using non GAAP methods furnish the information to the SEC on Form 8–K. It is common for companies to issue so-called *pro forma* earnings reports that show what earnings from ordinary operations would have been but for the inclusion of extraordinary items.

3. Press Releases

Public companies often issue press releases to the public in addition to filing required reports. Although such press releases may not be required as a technical matter, they may be required, practically speaking, if the company or its directors, officers, agents, or controlling stockholders engage in trading company shares. In the absence of disclosure, a transaction in shares may give rise to liability for insider trading. A company may also be required to issue a press release to correct an earlier statement that has become incorrect or to deal with rumors that may have originated from a source within the company. In addition, the company may be required by exchange or NASDAQ rules to make disclosures to stockholders or the public beyond those required by SEC rules. When a company to communicates with its stockholders or the public via press release or otherwise, it may be liable under SEC Rule 10b–5 for any misstatement or omission of a material fact in the press release or communication.

D. BOOKS & RECORDS UNDER STATE LAW

State law requires corporations to maintain a record of stockholders' (insert A) In addition many states require corporations to keep certain minimum records, such as minutes of meetings, and books and records of account. Unlike most state statutes the MBCA (1984) contains detailed rules with respect to the maintenance of minimum records.

1. Mandatory and Discretionary Records

    a.   MBCA 16.01(a) requires every corporation to *keep* certain basic records, such as minutes of meetings and records of actions taken by directors and stockholders. MBCA 16.01(b) and (c) require every corporation to *maintain* appropriate accounting records and a record of stockholders. MBCA 16.01(e) also requires that specified records be kept at its principal office where they may be inspected by stockholders. MBCA 16.02(a).

    b.   Most records maintained by corporations, financial records, tax returns, samples of advertising, are not covered by corporation statutes, but their retention may be required by other statutes. Depending on their character and the purpose of the stockholder, discretionary records may be subject to inspection by a stockholder.

2. **Record of Stockholders**

    MBCA 16.01(c) requires that a corporation maintain a record of its stockholders, in a form that permits preparation of a list of the names and addresses of all stockholders, in alphabetical order by class of shares showing the number and class of shares held by each.

    a. Many states require a voting list to be compiled immediately before the meeting. The voting list must be available to stockholders for inspection for a limited period of time during or immediately before a meeting.

    b. The record of stockholders consists of the names of record owners only. It does not attempt to list beneficial owners. Where shares are held in the names of nominees, only the name of the nominee appears.

3. **Disclosure to Stockholders**

    a. MBCA 16.20 requires every corporation to furnish stockholders with annual financial statements, containing at a minimum an income statement, a balance sheet, and a statement of changes in stockholders' equity.

    b. MBCA 16.21 requires disclosure to stockholders of (1) transactions involving issuance of shares for promissory notes or promises of future services and (2) indemnification transactions in proceedings in which the corporation is a party.

    c. MBCA 16.22 requires every corporation to file an annual report with the Secretary of State. The annual report must disclose the nature of the corporation's business, the identity of its directors and officers, and the number and classes of outstanding shares. MBCA 16.01(e)(7) also requires corporations to maintain a copy of its most recent annual report at its principal office where it must be made available for inspection by stockholders.

    d. Most states do not contain these disclosure requirements, though many states require disclosure of various types of information, usually by way of a required annual report of the corporation. There is great diversity of requirements in this regard. Some states require disclosure of franchise tax reports or other documents that provide basic financial information.

E. INSPECTION OF BOOKS & RECORDS

1. Inspection by the Public

Corporations that are not registered under the federal securities acts generally need not make public disclosures except to the extent required by corporation and state tax statutes.

a. Documents typically available at the Secretary of State's office include articles of incorporation, designation of registered office and agent, articles of amendment, and articles of merger. The MBCA also requires every corporation to file an annual report with the Secretary of State containing current information about the corporation's business, directors, and capitalization.

b. Information may also be publicly available from franchise tax returns and other filings, but in most states relatively little information is available. Information may also be obtained from state securities commissions.

2. Inspection by the Government

The government of the state of incorporation has broad visitorial powers under many state incorporation statutes, but as a practical matter, those powers are seldom exercised. Specific state or federal offices may also have visitorial powers under substantive statutes.

3. Inspection by Directors

A director has a broad right of inspection of books and records. A director is a manager of the corporation and owes certain duties to it and to all the stockholders. A director has a duty to be acquainted with the business and affairs of the corporation. Some decisions state that the directors' right of inspection is absolute and unqualified. *See Pilat v. Broach Systems, Inc.*, 260 A.2d 13 (N.J.Super.Law Div. 1969); *Brenner v. Hart System, Inc.*, 493 N.Y.S.2d 881 (App.Div. 1985); *Davis v. Keilsohn Offset Co.*, 79 N.Y.S.2d 540 (App.Div.1948). Other courts have sometimes denied inspection rights to directors where it was clear that the director was acting with improper motives.

4. Inspection by Stockholders

The right of a stockholder to inspect corporate books and records is narrower than the right of a director. A stockholder has a financial interest in the corporation and the law recognizes a right to inspect books and records to protect this interest. But a stockholder is not charged with management responsibility, is not subject to a broad fiduciary duty, and may have conflicting or inconsistent financial interests. As a result, a stockholder's right to inspect is limited to inspection for a *proper purpose*.

a.   A stockholder may have either a common law or a statutory right of inspection, or both. A stockholder may also have rights of discovery if in litigation with the corporation. In many states, stockholders also have a special statutory right to inspect a list of stockholders before or during a stockholder meeting. MBCA 7.20. The right of stockholders to inspect books and records may not be eliminated in the articles of incorporation. *Cochran v. Penn–Beaver Oil Co.*, 143 A. 257 (Del.1926).

b.   A common law inspection right is available to any stockholder of record who establishes a proper purpose for examining the books and records of the corporation. The burden of proof of a proper purpose is on the stockholder. *Fleisher Dev. Corp. v. Home Owners Warranty Corp.*, 856 F.2d 1529 (D.C.Cir.1988).

c.   In an effort to make the right of inspection available without litigation, the statutes of many states supplement the common law right of inspection with a statutory right of inspection.

- The statutory right of inspection is typically available to persons (a) who have been stockholders of record for at least six months prior to the demand or (b) who own a specified number of shares.

- The statutory right of inspection often also requires a proper purpose for the inspection which must be stated in a written demand. But the corporation has the burden of showing the plaintiff does not have a proper purpose.

- Some statutes specifically provide that a record of stockholders need not be produced if the applicant has sold or offered for sale a stockholders list within the preceding five years.

- Under many statutes a corporate officer or agent who refuses to grant a statutory right of inspection maybe liable for a penalty equal to a specified per cent of the value of the shares owned by the stockholder or some other fixed amount.

d.   MBCA 16.01–16.04 adopts a somewhat different approach toward inspection rights than traditional statutes. Stockholders have an unrestricted and unqualified right to inspect documents that the corporation must preserve at its principal office. MBCA 16.02(a). This right of inspection is absolute and not subject to a proper purpose limitation. The documents are listed in MBCA 16.01(e) and include:

- Articles or restated articles of incorporation.

- Bylaws.

- Resolutions creating classes or series of shares.

- Minutes of stockholders' meetings and records of action taken by consent of the stockholders for the past three years.

- Written communications to stockholders within the past three years, including financial statements required to be provided to stockholders.

- A list of the names and business addresses of directors and officers.

- The corporation's most recent annual report.

MBCA 16.02(b) authorizes a stockholder to inspect and copy additional records only upon a showing of proper purpose and good faith, and upon providing a statement setting forth with reasonable particularity his purpose and the records he desires to inspect. The records must be directly connected with that purpose. The records subject to this additional inspection right include:

- Excerpts from minutes of the board of directors, records of actions of committees of the board of directors, and minutes of stockholders meetings more than three years old.

- Accounting records of the corporation.

- The record of stockholders.

e. The rights of inspection set forth in MBCA 16.02 are other inspection rights. They may not be restricted or eliminated by provisions in the articles of incorporation or bylaws.

f. The inspection right includes the right to make copies. MBCA 16.03. The corporation may impose a reasonable charge for making copies but may not limit the inspection right to taking notes or making longhand copies. The stockholder is entitled to be accompanied by an attorney or accountant.

g. A stockholder who is denied the right of inspection may seek a summary judicial order compelling inspection. MBCA 16.04. Further, the court must order the corporation to pay the stockholder's costs in compelling inspection unless the corporation proves that it refused inspection in good faith because it had a reasonable basis for doubt about the right of the stockholder to inspect the records demanded.

h. A court may impose restrictions on the use of information by a stockholder. It may, for example, prohibit the stockholder from disclosing it to a competitor. Courts have inherent power to restrict the use of information obtained by stockholders independent of specific statutory authority to do so. *See CM & M Group, Inc. v. Carroll*, 453 A.2d 788 (Del.1982); *Helmsman Management Services, Inc. v. A & S Consultants, Inc.*, 525 A.2d 160 (Del.Ch.1987).

i. A purpose is proper if it is directed toward obtaining information bearing upon or seeking to protect the stockholder's interest and that of other stockholders of the corporation. A stockholder may have a proper purpose even though this could be unfriendly to management.

j. A person who is a beneficial owner of shares but not the record owner has a common law right of inspection. Whether or not a beneficial owner has a statutory right depends on the precise wording of the statute. Under some state statutes, pledgees or judgment creditors have a statutory right to inspect. Under the MBCA 16.02(f), a beneficial owner of shares has a statutory right of inspection. Holders of voting trust certificates also have a statutory right to inspect under the MBCA and many state statutes.

F. FEDERAL REGULATION OF PROXY SOLICITATIONS

Under § 14(a) of the 1934 Act, it is unlawful to solicit proxies with respect to corporations registered under § 12 in contravention of SEC rules and regulations as the Commission may prescribe as necessary or appropriate in the public interest or for the protection of investors. Pursuant to this broad grant of authority to regulate proxies, the SEC has issued comprehensive and detailed regulations. Historically, the proxy solicitation rules were particularly important because they forced public companies to communicate directly with stockholders. Although federal securities law focuses on disclosure and not substantive rights of stockholders, the proxy solicitation rules work because state law requires an annual meeting of stockholders to elect directors. Thus, the theory behind federal regulation of proxy solicitations is that stockholders should be informed as to the matters on which they may vote. Moreover, and perhaps more important today, the proxy rules tend to focus on the financial interests of the soliciting group. They require detailed disclosures on such matters as conflicting interest transactions and executive compensation. Thus, the proxy statement is a major source of stockholder information about corporate affairs. Federal law also requires that if a solicitation is made on behalf of management, the company must also distribute an annual report to stockholders (ARS). In contrast to Form 10–K which is filed with the SEC and available for review, the proxy statement and annual report are sent directly to stockholders (although for the majority of stockholders who hold their shares in street name they are sent through a broker-dealer). The proxy solicitation rules are collected in Regulation 14A which comprises Rules 14a–1 through 14b–2.

1. PROXY STATEMENTS

a. SEC rules provide that with certain exceptions solicitation of a proxy must be accompanied or preceded by the delivery of a proxy statement setting forth detailed information about the solicitation and the group soliciting proxies. Schedule 14A of the SEC rules sets forth the matters that must be addressed in the proxy statement:

- date, time, and place of meeting, and deadline for submitting stockholder proposals.

- identity and detailed background information relating to nominee and incumbent directors.

- voting information including matters subject to a vote (if any), the manner of voting, the required vote for each matter, shares entitled to vote, method for counting votes, and the record date.

- the identity of the party for whom proxies are being solicited (for example, incumbent management), revocability of proxies, and the cost of the solicitation

- detailed information about compensation of the CEO and the four next most highly compensated officers, about stock performance compared to the market and peer companies, about equity compensation plans generally and whether such plans have been approved by a stockholder vote.

- related party transactions (a related party is defined as a director, officer, five-percent stockholder, or family member)

As a result of the Sarbanes Oxley Act and beginning in 2004, NYSE and NASDAQ companies must have boards comprising a majority of independent (non-management) directors and must disclose in their proxy statements the basis on which that determination is made. Moreover, independent directors must meet in regular executive sessions, and the proxy statement must disclose who presides at those sessions. Proxy statements must also include a description of and report by the company's audit committee and compensation committee.

b. The proxy statement usually also incorporates the state-law-required notice of the meeting to stockholders. Most states require notice at least 10 days (but no more than 60 days) in advance of the meeting. Thus, state law effectively dictates when the proxy statement will be distributed.

c. The proxy rules apply to all solicitations seeking stockholder approval. Thus, they apply to the solicitation of stockholder consents as permitted under Delaware law even though such consents are not proxies.

d. The rules apply in connection with all solicitations not just those in connection with a regular annual meeting. Thus, the rules apply whenever a vote of the stockholders is to be taken, including in connection with mergers and other fundamental changes, amendments to the articles of incorporation or bylaws, ratification of board actions, and removal of directors. The proxy rules are thus particularly important in connection with mergers and acquisitions in that they provide stockholders with material information about the merits of the deal. (In a merger in which the stockholders of both corporations must vote, it is common for the two corporations to issue a joint proxy statement in order to avoid inconsistencies.) Proxy materials may thus also be important as a matter of state law in connection with an appraisal proceeding or an action challenging the validity of a corporate level transaction. Moreover, as discussed further below, there is a private cause of action under federal law for violations of the proxy rules, which may also give rise to parallel federal litigation.

2. **Annual Report to Stockholders**

The proxy regulations require the distribution of an annual report to stockholders (ARS).

a. Rule 14a–3 provides that if a solicitation is made on behalf of management relating to an annual meeting of stockholders at which directors are to be elected, the proxy statement must be accompanied or preceded by an annual report of the corporation.

b. Rule 14c–3 extends this requirement to registered companies that do not solicit proxies.

c. SEC rules specify the minimum content of the ARS:

    *   financial statements for the two most recent years

    *   stock and dividend information

    *   operation and industry segment information

    *   director and officer information

d. NYSE rules require that annual reports also include information relating to corporate governance, the charters of important committees of the board of directors, a certification by the CEO that the company meets NYSE listing standards. NYSE rules require that the annual report be distributed no later than 120 days after the close of the fiscal year or 15 in advance of the annual meeting. Thus, the annual report may be distributed separately from the proxy statement.

e. Because the ARS serves a public and stockholder relations function in addition to a disclosure function (as distinct from the Form 10–K), companies may and usually do include additional information in the annual report.

f. The annual report must be furnished to the SEC but is not technically a filed document unless it is incorporated by reference in Form 10–K. If the company is listed for trading, the annual report must also be filed with the NYSE or NASDAQ.

g. Most state statutes do not require the distribution of annual information to stockholders.

3. Form of Proxy

SEC regulations prescribe the form of proxy appointments by specifying the information that must appear on the proxy card to be returned by the stockholder (as well as details about the form of its presentation) and prohibit certain tactics such as undated or post-dated appointments or broad grants of discretionary power to proxy holders. Stockholders must be given the option to vote for candidates for directors (or to withhold a vote for some or all of the candidates). The persons appointed as proxy (the proxy holder) must vote as directed by the appointing stockholders for the election of directors and on other issues presented for decision to the stockholders. In short, the proxy holder is simply an agent for the appointing stockholder. Thus, the proxy holder is typically required to vote some shares FOR and some shares AGAINST any given proposition. (The individual who is to serve as proxy holder is typically designated by the soliciting group. The proxy holder may be a lower level officer of the company or an attorney or accountant retained by the company or group.)

4. Presolicitation Review

Prior to 1992, the SEC required a presolicitation review of all for proxy documents. Drafts of proxy statements and other soliciting materials (such as letters, press releases, and the like), were required to be filed with the SEC at least ten days prior to the date it is proposed to mail definitive copies to securities holders. In 1992, the SEC sharply reduced the scope of presolicitation review to out-of-the-ordinary matters. While the SEC does not pass upon the accuracy or adequacy of the disclosures, it does indicate that revisions should be made if it concludes that some materials are incomplete or inaccurate.

5. What is a Solicitation?

The SEC has consistently argued, and most courts have agreed, that the definitions of *solicitation* and *proxy* should be broadly construed to ensure the widest protection provided by the proxy regulations. Thus, any communication that is reasonably calculated to result in the granting, withholding, or revocation of a proxy, consent, authorization, or other action by a stockholder is covered by Regulation 14A.

6. Exempt Proxy Solicitations

a. SEC proxy rues exempt certain narrow classes of solicitations. The principal exceptions are:

- Solicitations other than or behalf of registrant to fewer than 10 persons.

- Solicitations by a record owner to beneficial owner to obtain instructions on how to vote.

- Solicitation by a beneficial owner to obtain proxy materials from the record owner.

- Newspaper advertisements that merely describe how holders may obtain copies of the proxy documents.

- Proxy advice furnished by a person who renders financial advice in the ordinary course of business and receives no special remuneration for the proxy advice.

b. In 1992 the SEC amended rules 14a–1 and 14a–2 to exempt most communications by persons do not seek the power to act as proxy. The amendments permit communications that state how a stockholder intends to vote and communicates directed to persons to whom the stockholder owes a fiduciary duty or is in response to an inquiry from another stockholder. These amendments are designed to permit discussion of corporate governance issues among institutional investors such as mutual funds and pension plans. Prior to these amendments institutional investors—who own more than 60 percent of all shares—were effectively precluded from communicating with each other about how to vote, because such communications would have been deemed to be proxy solicitations subject to all of the formalities of Regulation 14A. (Failure to comply with the proxy rules may result in votes being voided.) Thus, SEC rules originally designed to promote stockholder democracy arguably impeded the process and conferred an additional advantage on management beyond the considerable edge afforded by incumbency and the ability to use corporate funds to solicit proxies.

7. Corporations That Need Not Solicit Proxies

Most publicly held corporations need to solicit proxies if there is to be a quorum at a stockholders' meeting. In some corporations, one or a few stockholders may own or control an outright majority of shares and accordingly may not need to solicit proxies from other stockholders. Section 14(c) of the 1934 Act requires corporations that do not solicit proxy appointments to supply stockholders with information substantially equivalent to the information that would have been required if a proxy solicitation to its stockholders had been made.

8. Problems Created by Book Entry and Nominee Holdings

The widespread practice of holding shares in street names creates problems for the proxy solicitation process because beneficial owners of shares are not the record owners.

a. Under § 14(b) of the 1934 Act and SEC rules, a broker-dealer, bank, or other entity that exercises fiduciary powers (street name holder) must forward proxy materials to beneficial owners and afford them a reasonable opportunity to vote either by executing proxy forms in blank (and delivering them to the beneficial owners so that the shares may be voted) or by soliciting directions as to how to vote the shares and voting them as the beneficial owners direct.

b. A street name holder transmits proxy information to beneficial owners if the solicitor reimburses forwarding expenses. The solicitor must provide sufficient copies of the proxy materials so that a copy can be transmitted to each beneficial owner.

c. SEC regulations require street name holders to determine whether a beneficial owner objects to disclosure of their names to the issuer in order to permit direct communication.

- Beneficial owners who do not object are known as non-objecting beneficial owner (NOBOs.)

- Many brokerage firms recommend that customers do not elect to become NOBOs in part because of concern that the customers may be solicited by other brokerage firms if their names appear on a NOBO list.

- Some investors prefer to maintain their anonymity in order to avoid unwanted communications or pressure or recrimination in connection with voting decisions.

- A corporation may be required to prepare a NOBO list and make it available to a stockholder for inspection. *Sadler v. NCR Corp.*, 928 F.2d 48 (2d Cir.1991).

d.   Studies by the SEC reveal that beneficial owners generally receive proxy solicitation material on a timely basis and that there are not widespread abuses of the proxy solicitation process as a result of street name ownership. Thus, although there have been various proposals to create a direct registration system for beneficial owners, none have progressed far.

e.   Because of the difficulties created by holdings in street name as well as the complexity of the SEC proxy rules, many companies find it useful to retain one of the several proxy solicitation firms to help organize and conduct the process, particularly if a proxy fight is likely.

9.   Stockholder Proposals

Rule 14a–8 establishes procedure by which a stockholder may submit one proposal each year for inclusion in a company's proxy statement.

a.   If the proposal is an appropriate one for stockholder action, the company is required to include the proposal even if opposed to it.

b.   The stockholder submitting the proposal must have owned for a period of at least one year either (i) one per cent of the outstanding shares or (ii) shares with a market value of at least $2,000. The shares may be owned beneficially or of record.

c.   A stockholder submitting a proposal may also submit a supporting statement which the company is required to publish if the proposal and the supporting statement do not exceed 500 words in the aggregate. Management may explain the basis of its opposition to a proposal without limitation on the number of words.

d.   Proposals that fail in one year may be resubmitted within the following five years only if they meet specific standards based on votes received in the past.

e.   Because stockholders may seek action on proposals of dubious relevance or propriety, or simply for personal publicity, the SEC has imposed specific requirements and limitations on stockholders' proposals. A proposal may be omitted if.

• It is not a proper subject for action by stockholders.

• It would require the company to violate any law, if implemented.

- It is contrary to proxy regulations.

- It relates to the redress of a personal claim or grievance or is designed to result in a benefit to the proponent not shared with other security holders.

- It deals with operations which account for less than 5 per cent of the company's total assets net earnings, and gross sales and is not otherwise significantly related to the registrant's business.

- It deals with a matter that is beyond the company's power to effectuate.

- It deals with a matter relating to the conduct of ordinary business operations.

- It relates to election of a director or officer.

- It is moot the company has substantially implemented the proposal.

- It is either counter to a proposal by management or substantially the same as a proposal by another stockholder which will be included in the proxy materials.

- It relates to specific amounts of cash or stock dividends.

f.   The SEC has issued numerous rulings applying these exclusions. As a result, phrases such as *proper subject* or *ordinary business operations* have been given considerable practical content, and the tests are not as vague and open-ended as the language might indicate. In *SEC v. Transamerica Corp.*, 163 F.2d 511 (3d Cir.1947) the court rejected the argument that these terms should be construed restrictively or legalistically.

g.   In 1989, the SEC ruled that a proposal recommending that a company dismantle its affirmative action program must be included in the company's proxy statement. In 1991, the SEC held that a company could omit a proposal that required the registrant to report on its equal employment opportunity programs, including data on work force composition and affirmative action timetables and programs. On the ground it dealt with the ordinary business operations of the registrant. The SEC staff subsequently agreed that employment matters concerning the work force could be omitted even though they involved social as well as economic issues. *In re Cracker Barrel Old Country Store, Inc.*, 1992 WL 289095 (1992). A court subsequently refused to accept this conclusion on the ground that *Cracker Barrel* was inconsistent with a published policy statement of the SEC. *Amalgamated Clothing & Textile Workers v. Wal–Mart Stores, Inc.*, 821 F.Supp. 877 (S.D.N.Y.1993). In a subsequent case involving the same corporation, an injunction requiring the inclusion of a proposal that Cracker Barrel not discriminate on the basis of sexual orientation was overturned on the ground that this interpretation by the staff was a legislative rule that could not be implemented without notice and comment. *New York City Employees' Retirement System v. SEC*, 45 F.3d 7 (2d Cir.1995).

h. *Roosevelt v. E.I. Du Pont de Nemours & Co.*, 958 F.2d 416 (D.C.Cir.1992) holds that stockholders have a private cause of action to enforce Rule 14a-8. But *Roosevelt* also held that a proposal relating to the defendant's plan to phase out chlorofluorocarbons was excludable as involving ordinary business operations.

i. Institutional investors have submitted numerous proposals. In many instances, these proposals have been voluntarily implemented by without a vote by stockholders. In other instances these proposals have been adopted outright or have received significant stockholder support. Proposals made by institutional investors include:

- confidential voting.

- independent tabulation of votes.

- requiring stockholder approval for poison pills and other defensive tactics relating to takeovers.

- requiring stockholder approval of management compensation arrangements following a takeover (so-called golden parachutes).

- requiring issuers to opt out of undesirable provisions of state law.

- requiring the redemption of poison pills when faced with a desirable tender offer.

j. Proposals by institutional investors under rule 14a–8 have declined since 1992 in favor of direct contact with directors.

k. Some academic commentary during the 1980s and early 1990s has been critical of the stockholder proposal rule. Here too SEC rules extend somewhat beyond the narrow principle of mandating disclosure where stockholder action is sought. Some SEC Commissioners have expressed concern that the numerous social policy proposals being included in proxy statements provide little or no benefit to stockholders generally.

10. Extension of SEC Authority over Stockholder Voting

The SEC has attempted to use its power to regulate proxy solicitation as a foundation for protecting stockholder democracy generally.

a. In 1990, an SEC rule purporting to require the stock exchanges to adopt listing standards prohibiting alterations in stockholder voting rights was struck down as an unwarranted intrusion on state corporation law and beyond the Commission's authority to foster disclosure.

b. In 2003, the SEC proposed new rules that would require disclosures about the process of nominating candidates for election as director and about stockholder communications with the board of directors. In addition the SEC staff recommended that stockholders be permitted access to the company's proxy machinery to nominate candidates for director after certain triggering events, including failure of the company to act on stockholder proposals that receive a majority of votes or the election of an unopposed director by fewer than 65 percent of votes cast. These proposals have been quite controversial, and have prompted counter proposals that state law be amended instead to require election of directors by majority vote. The proposals may have contributed to several campaigns by institutional investors to withhold votes from specific directors, including Michael Eisner of Disney and Warren Buffett of Coca Cola.

G. FALSE AND MISLEADING STATEMENTS IN PROXY COMMUNICATIONS

Rule 14a-9 makes it unlawful to solicit proxies by means of communication that contains any statement that is false or misleading with respect to any material fact, or which omits to state any material fact.

1. Private Cause of Action

This broad prohibition creates an implied private cause of action by stockholders. *J. I. Case Co. v. Borak*, 377 U.S. 426, 84 S.Ct. 1555 (1964). *Borak* held that

Rule 14a-9 created a private cause of action because, private enforcement of the proxy rules provides a necessary supplement to Commission action. This is sometimes called the *private attorney general* doctrine.

a. Since the mid 1970s the courts have been reluctant imply further private causes of action (particularly for damages) under the federal securities laws. It is, however, clear that there is also a private cause of action under Rule 10b-5 relating to misstatements and omissions of material facts in connection with the purchase or sale of securities (such as insider trading and the like) as discussed further in the chapter on transactions in shares. Generally speaking, the law relating to what constitutes a material fact under Rule 14a-9 also applies to actions under Rule 10b-5 (and vice versa). State courts also rely heavily on federal case law relating to materiality in opinions dealing with the validity of stockholder ratification votes and the like. On the other hand, although it is clear that some level of *scienter* (knowingness) is required to state a cause of action under Rule 10b-5, it appears that negligence will suffice under Rule 14a-9. *Wilson v. Great Am. Indus.,* 855 F.2d 987 (2d Cir. 1988); *Herskowitz v. Nutri/System,* 857 F.2d 179 (3d Cir. 1988).

b. Actions arising under the 1934 Act are subject to exclusive federal jurisdiction. See § 27. But the settlement of state class actions dealing with related claims may include within the settlement claims based on federal law such as Rule 14a-9. *Matsushita Electric Industrial Co. v. Epstein* 516 U.S. 367, 116 S.Ct. 873 (1996).

c. A private action under Rule 14a-9 may take the form of either a derivative action or a direct action (usually a class action), depending on the precise nature of the claim. In either case, federal law also applies to the procedural aspects of the case. Thus, a state law requirement that a bond be posted in connection with a derivative action does not apply.

d. The SEC may maintain a civil enforcement action under any of the proxy rules. Willful violations may be prosecuted criminally by a United States Attorney.

2. Materiality

Most of the leading cases regarding private actions under Rule 14a-9 have dealt with stockholder votes in connection with mergers and have focused on whether an alleged failure of disclosure involved a material fact.

a. In *Mills v. Electric Auto–Lite Co.*, 396 U.S. 375, 90 S.Ct. 616 (1970), the Court held that it is not necessary to show that the omission of a material fact actually influenced votes. Rather, it is enough to establish that the vote itself was an *essential link* in the transaction being questioned. This is sometimes called *transaction causation* and is distinct from *loss causation*. *Mills* also suggested that a fact is material if it might be of interest to a stockholder.

b. In *TSC Industries, Inc. v. Northway, Inc.*, 426 U.S. 438, 96 S.Ct. 2126 (1976), the Court held that a fact is material if there is a substantial likelihood that a reasonable stockholder *would* consider it important in deciding how to vote and rejected the *might* test. TSC also held that in order to be material a fact must change the *total mix* of information available to stockholders. Thus, proxy materials need not provide characterizations and interpretations but rather should set forth just the facts. The Court also held that it was error to grant summary judgment on the issue is favor of the plaintiff, although a warning to lower courts to limit Rule 14a-9 to substantial misstatements. Prior to this decision some courts had tended to find relatively minor misstatements or omissions to be material and therefore violations of Rule 14a-9. The test adopted in *TSC* is generally accepted as the definition of materiality in securities litigation as well as under state law cases relating to stockholder voting.

c. In *Virginia Bankshares, Inc. v. Sandberg*, 501 U.S. 1083, 111 S.Ct. 2749 (1991), the Court held (1) that a statement couched in terms of opinion or belief may be materially misleading in violation of Rule 14a-9, but (2) that a false statement in a proxy solicitation may not meet the essential link (transaction causation) test if it is addressed solely to stockholders whose combined votes are not sufficient to prevent the action being taken.

3. Remedies in Rule 14a–9 Cases

As a practical matter the test in *TSC* seems to turn on whether the fact in question would have affected the price of the transaction, even though in *Mills* the Court reversed a decision that no cause of action had been stated because the price was fair. Ironically, after remand, the court in *Mills* found that even though a cause of action had been stated and the plaintiff established liability, the stockholders had not suffered financial harm and no damages were awarded because § 28 of the 1934 Act limits awards to actual damages (which has generally been interpreted as requiring an out-of-pocket measure (OOPs)). Some federal courts have suggested that injunctive relief should be the norm in order to avoid this result.

a. A court may grant injunctive relief in a Rule 14a-9 case, but it rarely happens, because the plaintiff must show irreparable harm, and because the plaintiff may be required to post a large bond in order to obtain a TRO or temporary injunction. Moreover, most Rule 14a-9 cases involve stockholder votes in connection with mergers and similar transactions in which the ultimate issue is the price paid for the acquired company. The usual remedy in such cases is money damages.

b. Many state courts (in particular the Delaware courts) award *rescissory damages* (benefit of the bargain (BOBs)) in such cases, making state law more attractive than federal law even though it may be more difficult to establish liability in a state law action than in a federal action under the proxy rules in which mere negligence will suffice. (If a cause of action based on Rule 10b–5 is also asserted, that claim must allege that the defendant acted with *scienter,* that it, at least recklessly.) In addition, a state court in an appraisal action may sometimes include a premium for control. Moreover, some state courts (including those of Delaware and California) have held that failure to disclose a material fact may be actionable even in the absence of any action in reliance thereon by a stockholder. On the other hand, the federal courts have awarded BOBs in a few cases in which the deal promised a specific amount higher than the consideration actually paid.

c. In some cases, the courts may order that improperly obtained votes be sterilized and not counted. This remedy may be favored where it is workable because of judicial reluctance to mandate that a stockholder vote in a particular way (possibly because of concern that such an order would run afoul of the general rule that proxies are revocable). Sterilization may also be favored because of reluctance to attach a dollar value to stockholder votes (which might be likened to illegal vote selling).

d. In theory, a court may order that a merger be reversed (or *unwound*), but this remedy is seldom if ever used, because once a merger is effected, it quickly becomes impossible to determine which assets and liabilities would go with which predecessor business. In other words, it is extremely difficult to unscramble eggs.

e. If a derivative action or class action is successful (or partially successful), attorney fees may be awarded to the plaintiff attorneys against the defendant even though the action does not result in the award of damages. Although *Mills* suggested that attorney fees might be awarded based on the private attorney general theory, that rationale has since been rejected by the Supreme Court. In an action in which damages are awarded or a monetary settlement results, attorney fees are typically paid out of the damages or settlement.

H. PROXY CONTESTS

In a proxy context, an insurgent group competes with management in an effort to obtain proxy appointments. In the classic proxy fight the goal of insurgents is to elect a majority of the board of directors and thereby obtain control, but in some cases contests are waged solely to obtain representations on the board.

1. Strategy and Tactics

a. It is important for an insurgent group to obtain a stockholder's and NOBO list so that substantial stockholders may be identified and contacted personally. A court proceeding under state law may be necessary to obtain these lists. An insurgent group also has limited rights under SEC Rule 14a-7, which requires management to provide minimal assistance either by providing a list of stockholder names and addresses or by mailing a communication directly to stockholders at the expense of the insurgent group. Large stockholders may be courted individually. In addition mutual funds and many other institutional investors are required regularly to disclose their portfolio holdings showing their beneficial ownership in all corporations.

b. An insurgent group usually purchases a substantial block of shares in the open market before announcing its intentions. Under the 1934 Act an insurgent group must file schedule 13D with the SEC within ten days if it acquires over five percent of any class of the target corporation's equity securities. The Schedule 13D must also be furnished to the target company and to the relevant stock exchange and must be amended within ten days of any purchase of additional shares (or sale of shares).

c. Within a broad range, management may finance its solicitation from the assets of the corporation, because management controls the proxy machinery and is free to use it to seek reelection, while the insurgent group must finance its campaign from outside sources. In addition, many stockholders routinely vote as recommended by management (or not at all). Although, SEC rules are often said to be intended to protect stockholder democracy, stockholder apathy is arguably rational on the part of a well diversified investor.

d.   Although incumbent management may use its control over the proxy machinery with relative freedom in an attempt to defeat a challenger, such tactics are permissible only if supported by a reasonable business purpose.

e.   There are several firms that specialize in proxy solicitations, which are available to assist both management and insurgents in connection with a proxy contest.

2.   Regulation of Proxy Contests

Proxy contests in corporations registered under § 12 of the Securities Exchange Act of 1934 are subject to regulation by the SEC under its proxy regulations.

a.   SEC regulations require all participants in a proxy contest (including non-management groups) to file a proxy statement with the SEC and the relevant exchange at least ten days before it is disseminated.

b.   A proxy statement in connection with a proxy fight must contain all of the information required in an ordinary proxy statement (as specified in SEC Schedule 14A) although an insurgent group need not include information about incumbent management that would appear in an ordinary proxy statement. In addition, a proxy statement in connection with a proxy contest must include disclosures relating to the identity and background of the participants, their interests in securities of the corporation and when they were acquired, financing arrangements, participation in other proxy contests, and understandings with respect to future employment with the corporation. Other materials such as advertisements, press releases, and direct mailings must be filed with the SEC as they are disseminated.

c.   SEC regulations reject the view that proxy contests should be viewed as political contests with each side free to hurl charges with comparative unrestraint on the assumption that the opposing side may refute misleading charges. Rather, each participant's statements are subject to objective standards of accuracy and truthfulness. *SEC v. May*, 229 F.2d 123 (2d Cir.1956).

    d.   State law is applicable to proxy contests in unregistered corporations but there are few reported state cases dealing with proxy fights. *Salgo v. Matthews*, 497 S.W.2d 620 (Tex.Civ.App.1973).

3. Who Pays the Cost of a Proxy Contest?

The corporation usually pays the costs of the defense of a proxy contest. Where a change in control occurs, the corporation may also pay the costs of the successful campaign to oust incumbent management.

    a.   It is clear that the corporation should pay for the cost of printing and mailing the notice of meeting, the proxy statement required by federal law, and the proxy appointment forms themselves. These are legitimate corporate expenses necessary to ensure the existence of a quorum of stockholders.

    b.   Most courts have allowed management also to charge to the corporation the reasonable expenses of educating stockholders if the controversy involves a *policy* question rather than a mere *personal* struggle for control. *Rosenfeld v. Fairchild Engine and Airplane Corp.*, 128 N.E.2d 291 (N.Y.1955); *Levin v. Metro–Goldwyn–Mayer, Inc.*, 264 F.Supp. 797 (S.D.N.Y.1967). Virtually every issue may be dressed up as a policy rather than personal issue. The effect of a. and b. is probably to permit the deduction of all reasonable management expenses.

    c.   A successful challenger may seek to have the corporation reimburse expenses. As with management expenses, the reimbursement of successful insurgents are permitted if the dispute can be characterized as one over business policy. involved policy rather than personalities. *Rosenfeld v. Fairchild Engine and Airplane Corp.*, 128 N.E.2d 291 (N.Y.1955). As a result the corporation may end up paying for the expenses of both sides if the challenger is successful.

    d.   Although one might argue that the system is biased against insurgents, it would be difficult to structure an unbiased system. Although proxy fights arguably constitute an important check on managerial behavior, a system that required insurgents to be reimbursed would arguably encourage too many proxy fights, while a system that prohibited management from using corporate resources to defend itself might discourage competent managers from agreeing to serve and would operate as an effective presumption that an insurgents is as worthy as incumbent management.

■ XI. CLOSELY HELD CORPORATIONS

A. CHARACTERISTICS OF CLOSELY HELD CORPORATIONS

The statutory scheme does not accurately reflect the manner of operation of closely held corporations owned by a very small number of stockholders. The stockholders in closely held corporations are usually simultaneously officers and directors. Business decisions may be made by consensus and without regard to whether the person is acting as officer, director, or stockholder. Requirements of meetings, appointments, elections, and so forth are all likely to be considered meaningless formalities. Indeed, many such corporations go for years without ever having a formal stockholders' or directors' meeting. Accordingly, a number of states have adopted statutes relaxing the statutory requirements applicable to closely held corporations.

1. Stockholder Domination of Management

In a closely held corporation, the controlling stockholders usually operate the business in an informal manner, more as though it were a partnership rather than a corporation. Indeed, closely held corporations are sometimes called *incorporated partnerships* to reflect the close similarity in management that exists between partnerships and closely held corporations. The majority stockholders name the board of directors, and through them, the officers and employees. Usually they name themselves as directors and officers, including to the most important and highest paying positions. A major aspect of planning is to develop devices that assure minority stockholders of meaningful participation in management despite the power of majority stockholders to name a majority or all of the directors, officers and employees.

    a.   Stockholders' meetings may be held infrequently if at all. Unanimous consents may be prepared to record who is serving on the board of directors from time to time.

b. Formal directors meetings may also be held infrequently. Meetings may consist of informal discussions or simple decision making by the majority stockholder (who may also be the sole director of the corporation) or by the controlling stockholders. The controlling stockholders may or may not consult with other officers, directors, or stockholders.

c. The attorney for a closely held corporation should assure that minimal records are kept as to the identity of stockholders, directors, and officers, the manner of their election or appointment, and the periods they serve. The attorney should also assure that documents executed on behalf of the corporation clearly reflect corporate execution by the persons who hold the positions described in the form of execution.

2. No Market for Shares

Because a closely held corporation has only a relatively small number of stockholders, there is no public trading in, or public market for, its shares. Majority or controlling shares are salable to the same extent the underlying business is salable, because they represent control of that business. Minority or non-controlling shares, however, have only very limited marketability even if the business is highly profitable. The power of minority stockholders to participate in the business and its profits may be at the sufferance of the majority or controlling stockholder.

a. Potential purchasers of minority blocks of shares usually must be found among the corporation, present stockholders, or rarely, among outsiders willing to take a gamble.

b. The market for minority blocks of shares is at worst non-existent and at best a buyer's market. Because there are few alternative purchasers there is little or no incentive for buyers to offer reasonable prices for shares. Minority shares have some value because they constitute a nuisance, may serve as the basis for litigation, and have residual rights in the event the corporation is dissolved or sold.

c. If the minority shares offered for sale represent the balance of control between factions, they are readily salable to one faction or another.

d. Transferability of shares is usually restricted by contractual restrictions limiting free transferability. A stockholder desiring to sell his shares may have to comply with the restrictions before offering shares to outsiders.

3. Dividend Policy

In a closely held corporation, dividend policy is heavily influenced by the tax status of the corporation and is often manipulated to favor controlling stockholders.

a. Large salary payments may be designed to limit the double tax problem of doing business as a C corporation. But the IRS may disallow excessive payments of salaries, bonuses, or fringe benefits as business expenses (deductions) of the corporation treating the excess as income to the corporation and as a dividend to the recipient stockholder. The test is whether the compensation is for services and is reasonable. *Charles McCandless Tile Service v. United States*, 422 F.2d 1336 (Ct.Cl.1970), *Herbert G. Hatt*, 28 T.C.M. 1194 (1969). Minority stockholders may use such a tax determination in an effort to obtain a court order requiring the payment of a dividend or the return of the excess funds to the corporation. *See, Wilderman v. Wilderman*, 315 A.2d 610 (Del.Ch.1974); *Fendelman v. Fenco Handbag Mfg. Co.*, 482 S.W.2d 461 (Mo.1972).

b. Controlling stockholders may divert the bulk of corporate income to themselves by adopting a no dividend policy, refusing to employ the minority stockholders in the business, and paying the bulk of the earnings to themselves in the form of salaries, bonuses, benefit plan contributions, and fringe benefits (free use of automobiles, country club memberships and the like). These policies may be adopted in an effort to soften up minority stockholders and persuade them to sell their shares at a low price either to the corporation or to other stockholders. Such a strategy—often called a freeze out or squeeze out—may lead to litigation seeking the payment of a dividend or other relief against the controlling stockholders on grounds of oppressive conduct.

4. Stockholder Oppression

In the absence of a binding stockholder agreement, the foregoing factors may result in oppression of minority stockholders who are locked into the corporation but excluded from management and deprived of investment return. Minority stockholders in a closely held corporation ordinarily have no power to force dissolution of the corporation because corporation statutes typically require the consent of at least a majority of the outstanding shares. In this respect a closely held corporation differs significantly from a partnership, in which each partner possesses inherent power to dissolve the partnership.

a. Advance planning—usually in the form of a buy/sell agreement—may avoid many of these problems. Important functions of stockholder agreements are they assure minority stockholders that (i) they will be able to dispose of their shares when they die, retire, or wish to leave the corporation, (ii) they will have a voice in management, (iii) they will be entitled to a financial return from their investment, and (iv) they will have the benefits of estate planning.

b. Nonetheless, there are many cases in which advance planning may not occur. Over the long haul, the possibility that hostility will develop within a closely held corporation as a result of falling out, withdrawal, or death among the stockholders is fairly high. These situations include family businesses which have devolved down through one or two generations, particularly when deaths of controlling stockholders occur unexpectedly and without adequate planning, and situations where the participants enter the venture fully trusting each other and believe it is unnecessary to provide legal protection.

B. ALLOCATION OF CONTROL IN A CLOSELY HELD CORPORATION

In the absence of special statutory treatment of closely held corporations, such corporations must establish control devices through the use of traditional and accepted stockholder control techniques.

1. Traditional Control Techniques

There are many planning devices that may be used to allocate control in a closely held corporation, including multiple classes of shares, supermajority quorum and voting requirements (at both the stockholder level and the board level), stockholder voting agreements, voting trusts, proxy appointments, employment agreements between stockholders and the corporation, and share transfer restrictions. These devices are discussed in more detail in subsequent chapters.

2. Supermajority Quorum & Voting Requirements

Minority participation may be assured by increased voting and quorum requirements in order to give minority interests effectively a veto power. This veto power may be applicable at the stockholder level, at the board level, or at both levels.

a. It is usually important to increase both the quorum requirement and the minimum vote requirement to make sure that it is impossible for the corporation to act without the assent of the minority stockholders.

b. Unanimity may be required for both, although some courts seem to be reluctant to enforce such an extreme requirement. In many circumstances a lesser percentage is sufficient to give the desired veto power.

3. Legal Problems Created by Informal Management

In most small closely held corporations, corporate matters are likely to be resolved by unanimous consent with a minimum of formality and regard for statutory niceties. Meetings may be held infrequently, if at all, corporate records may be kept on an erratic basis, and decisions may be made without any recognition that the corporation theoretically consists of different layers with different rights and responsibilities. Failure to follow corporate formalities may create several legal issues. Ignoring corporate formalities may be grounds for piercing the corporate veil, with the result that the participants may be held personally liable on corporate obligations. Decisions that are made informally and without following the statutory norms may not be binding. The participants' control arrangements may be unenforceable.

C. ATTEMPTS TO VARY THE STATUTORY SCHEME

Attempts to reallocate the corporate powers in ways significantly different from the statutory scheme historically were viewed with suspicion and many were held to be against public policy and unenforceable.

1. Strict Common Law Approach

The strict common law approach was that agreements among stockholders to make decisions that are the responsibility of the board of directors were against public policy as expressed in the corporation statute and were unenforceable. *McQuade v. Stoneham*, 189 N.E. 234 (N.Y.1934). The traditional view was that all corporations should be governed by essentially the same rules set forth in the corporation statutes, and that no special rules could or should be developed for the closely held corporation. *See Kruger v. Gerth*, 263 N.Y.S.2d 1, 210 N.E.2d 355 (N.Y. 1965). The rationale for the strict common law approach is that corporation law is designed to protect minority stockholders who are not parties to the contract by assuring that they receive the protection of the unfettered best judgment of the board of directors.

2. Relaxation of Strict Common Law Approach

The strict common law rule sometimes leads to significant injustice because apparently reasonable and sensible contracts are invalidated even though they do not affect non parties. As a result, shortly after *McQuade* the New York court modified the strict common law approach by holding that contract among all stockholders that involves only minor infringement on statutory scheme was enforceable. *Clark v. Dodge,* 199 N.E. 641 (N.Y.1936). Some courts and statutes have relaxed even further the test for invalidating such agreements, and uphold substantially any stockholders agreement, so long as all stockholders agree to it. *Galler v. Galler,* 203 N.E.2d 577 (Ill.1964). *See also* MBCA 7.32 (authorizing broad ranging stockholder agreements even to the extent of management by the stockholders rather than a board of directors but only if authorized in the articles of incorporation and only for non publicly traded corporations).

D. STATUTES RELATING TO MANAGEMENT OF CLOSELY HELD CORPORATIONS

Many states have adopted statutes relating to management problems within the closely held corporation. These statutes may be traced to judicial dissatisfaction with the application of traditional corporation law principles to closely held corporations. They fall into three general categories: statutes of general applicability dealing with variations in management structure, special statutes applicable only to corporations making a formal election, and hybrid statutes such as MBCA 7.32. These statutes permit numerous kinds of control arrangements for closely held corporations.

1. General Statutes Permitting the Elimination of the Board of Directors

The statutes of many states permit any corporation to modify the traditional role of its board of directors by appropriate provision in its articles of incorporation. The provision may permit a corporation to dispense entirely with the board of directors and have the business and affairs managed directly by its stockholders or place restrictions on the discretion of directors. As a practical matter, this option is almost solely utilized by closely held corporations.

   a.   DGCL 141(a) provides The business and affairs of every corporation * * * shall be managed by or under the direction of a board of directors except as may be otherwise provided in this chapter or in its certificate of incorporation. If any such provision is made in the certificate of incorporation, the powers and duties conferred or imposed upon the board of directors by this chapter shall be exercised or performed to such extent and by such person or persons as shall be provided in the certificate of incorporation.

b.   MBCA 8.01(c) contained a provision similar to DGCL 141(a), but that provision was repealed in 1991 and a more general provision, MBCA 7.32, discussed below, was substituted.

2.   Statutes Applicable Only to Electing Close Corporations

a.   The statutes of several states contain special provisions applicable only to corporations that make a formal election. These statutes permit an electing close corporation, among other things, to dispense entirely with the board of directors, to restrict the discretion of directors, and to permit the business and affairs of the corporation to be conducted as though it were a partnership. *See* DGCL 341-355.

b.   The definition of an eligible corporation usually involves a limitation on the number of stockholders and a requirement that share transfer restrictions be imposed. Many such statues are limited to corporations with fewer than 35 stockholders or some other specified number. Some statutes, however, do not limit the corporations that may elect to become close corporations. A qualified corporation becomes a statutory close corporation by including in its articles of incorporation a statement to the effect that the corporation is a statutory close corporation.

c.   A statutory close corporation may adopt a variety of internal control arrangements, including restrictions on the discretion of directors and even dispensing with the board of directors entirely. If this option is elected, the liabilities otherwise imposed on directors are imposed on the stockholders as if they were directors. Where the board of directors has been eliminated the stockholders may be called *managing stockholders* and have the rights and duties of directors. *Graczykowski v. Ramppen*, 477 N.Y.S.2d 454 (App.Div. 1984). These statutes also permit an electing close corporation to eliminate bylaws, to broaden the power to create share transfer restrictions, to create mandatory buyouts upon the death of a stockholder, to require dissolution at the election of a minority interest, and so forth. These statutes contain special provisions to resolve dissension or deadlock such as the appointment of receivers, custodians or provisional directors.

d. Even though many states have adopted special close corporation statutes and this development has been widely praised, the actual experience in California, Delaware, Florida, Texas and other states indicates that this election is not widely used. It is probable that most attorneys are able to work out basic control relationships under the general corporation statutes and therefore do not feel it is necessary to use or experiment with these largely untried statutes. The complexity of some of these statutes may also have discouraged their widespread use.

e. Some lawyers may be concerned that the use of the close corporation election may have adverse tax consequences or may result in the possible loss of limited liability. Many of these statutes expressly attempt to negate this result.

f. Despite the broad remedial purposes underlying modern close corporation statutes, some courts have given them narrow and literalistic readings not consistent with the underlying purposes. *See Blount v. Taft*, 246 S.E.2d 763 (N.C.1978). Other courts have been more generous. *See Zion v. Kurtz*, 428 N.Y.S.2d 199, 405 N.E.2d 681 (N.Y. 1980). In *Nixon v. Blackwell*, 626 1366 (Del. 1993) the court held that special rules for close corporations in Delaware are applicable only to corporations making the election as required by the Delaware Close Corporation Statute. In an earlier case, *Zion v. Kurtz*, 428 N.Y.S.2d 199, 405 N.E.2d 681 (N.Y. 1980), the court upheld an agreement under Delaware law even though the corporation's certificate of incorporation did not contain the required language. The court ordered the certificate of incorporation reformed to include the mandatory language. It is doubtful that the Delaware courts would accept the *Zion* approach.

3. **Hybrid Statutes**

In 1991, the MBCA was amended by withdrawing a provision similar to DGCL 141 and adding the more general MBCA 7.32 (entitled *Stockholder Agreements*) and providing that an agreement that complies with that section is effective among stockholders and the corporation even though it is inconsistent with one or more specified provisions of the act.

a. Section 7.32 rejects the older line of cases relating to statutory norms and adds an element of predictability there to fore absent from the MBCA. It recognizes that many of the corporate norms contained in corporation statutes were designed with an eye towards public companies where management and share ownership are quite distinct.

b.   Section 7.32 validates virtually all stockholders' agreements relating to corporate governance and business arrangements, including agreements relating to: governance of the entity; allocation of the return from the business; and other aspects of relationships among stockholders, directors, and the corporation.

c.   MBCA 7.32 creates a broad but not universal mandate to customize the management of closely held corporations. Agreements that affect third parties and agreements that violate fundamental principles of public policy may not be validated.

d.   The agreement under MBCA 7.32 must be unanimously approved by the stockholders; it may appear in the articles of incorporation, the bylaws, or a stockholders' agreement.

e.   The existence of an agreement under MBCA 7.32 must appear on the share certificates or information statements reflecting shares. A purchaser of shares without notice of the existence of the agreement has the sole remedy of recission within 90 days after learning of the existence of the agreement.

f.   An agreement under MBCA 7.32 is valid for 10 years unless otherwise provided in the agreement. It automatically terminates if the shares of the corporation become publicly traded on a national securities exchange or public market for securities.

E. OPPRESSION AND DEADLOCK

It is common for disagreements to arise among stockholders in closely held corporations about business policies and practices. One of the more common problems arises when one group prefers reinvestment of available cash and growth of the company while another group prefers a generous payout policy. It is also common for personality conflicts to arise. In many cases, differences of opinion about business may evolve into personality conflicts so that it becomes difficult to determine the nature of the difficulty. If two stockholders or factions of stockholders have equal control or veto power, such conflicts may lead to deadlock. If one stockholder or faction has effective working control and the power to exclude other stockholders from meaningful participation in management or the economic benefits of the business, the faction with control may sometimes use its power inappropriately to infringe the legitimate interests of the minority. Advance planning may prevent such difficulties or reduce their severity. One common solution is to have a binding buy/sell agreement that is triggered by certain defined events, such as the failure to elect directors for a stated period.

1. **Oppression**

   a. The word *oppression* does not necessarily mean imminent disaster; it has been construed to mean lack of fair dealing or fair play, and in any event is a question for the trier of fact to resolve. *Mardikos v. Arger*, 457 N.Y.S.2d 371 (1982); *White v. Perkins*, 189 S.E.2d 315 (Va.1972); *Gidwitz v. Lanzit Corrugated Box Co.*, 170 N.E.2d 131 (Ill.1960).

   b. A recent development in closely held corporation law discussed below is that the term oppression is being defined by some courts in a broader fashion as meaning any action that is inconsistent with the expectations of the minority stockholders with respect to their roles in the corporation or that constitutes burdensome, harsh, or wrongful conduct.

   c. Where a corporation has been in existence for a generation or more, oppression should not be defined in terms of original expectations but in terms of whether conduct is inherently oppressive. *Gimpel v. Bolstein*, 477 N.Y.S.2d 1014 (Sup. 1984).

2. **Deadlock**

   a. Deadlock typically involves two stockholders (or two factions) in a control structure that does not permit either faction to have effective working control. It is also possible for a corporation with more than two factions to become deadlocked if each individual stockholder and/or director has a veto power but that is not common.

   b. A corporation is potentially subject to deadlock if two stockholders (or two stockholder factions) both own exactly fifty per cent of the outstanding shares, if there are an even number of directors and two factions each have the power to select the same number, or if a minority stockholder has retained a veto power.

c. A deadlock may occur either at the stockholders' level or at the directors' level. If the stockholders are deadlocked, the corporation may continue to operate under the guidance of the board of directors in office when the deadlock arose. The general rule is that directors serve until their successors are qualified; if the deadlock prevents a subsequent election, those in office remain in office indefinitely. A deadlock at the directoral level may prevent the corporation from functioning at all, though more commonly the president or general manager may continue to operate the business, often to the complete exclusion of the other faction.

3. Advance Planning to Avoid Oppression and Deadlock

Although it is always possible for the stockholders to agree to a fair business divorce after a dispute arises, it is preferable for the possibility of dissension, oppression, and deadlock to be addressed by the stockholders in advance in amity. It is ordinarily preferable to preserve a going corporation rather than to dissolve it. The business and assets of a corporation, including intangible good will, are ordinarily worth more as a unit than fragmented. Thus, the most sensible solution usually is a buyout agreement by which one faction buys out the other at a fair price in the event a serious disagreement arises. Such an agreement is usually called a buy/sell agreement. Such an arrangement must resolve several basic questions.

a. What events triggers the power to buy or sell? Some kind of objective standard as to what constitutes dissension or deadlock sufficient to trigger the buyout obligation is desirable, such as the failure to agree on a slate of directors for some specified period. But one must be careful not to create opportunities on the pretext of a minor dispute for stockholders who simply want to cash out.

b. Who is to buy out whom if both desire to continue the business? Often the senior stockholder retains the right to buy out the junior stockholder. But if the age discrepancy is large, it may be more sensible to reverse the order and have the junior buy out the senior. An agreement may provide that one stockholder sets a price at which she is willing to buy out the other stockholder or to sell her own shares, and the other stockholder has the election to buy or sell.

c. What pricing formula should be used? The formula chosen should not rely on an agreement to agree about the price. Presumably, the formula should yield as fair a price as possible rather than one that arguably creates a bargain for one faction or the other. On the other hand, some discount from full value may be appropriate to discourage opportunism.

d.   May the person who is bought out form a competing business, and if so, where and on what terms? A non-competition agreement is usually enforceable if it is reasonable under the circumstances.

F. SHARE TRANSFER RESTRICTIONS

In a corporation, transfer of shares conveys both financial and voting rights. Shares in a corporation are freely transferable unless there is an express restriction on the transferability of shares. In contrast, partnership interests may not be transferred without the consent of all the other partners, although a partner may always assign any financial benefits he may receive from the partnership. Although free transferability of shares is usually considered an advantage of the corporate form, there are many situations in which it is desirable to limit the transferability of shares, particularly in a closely held corporation.

1. Reasons for Imposing Share Transfer Restrictions

a.   Share transfer restrictions enable stockholders to decide who may participate in the venture. This is important in a closely held corporation in which there is substantial stockholder participation in management and where the shares carry the ability to elect one or more directors.

b.   Share transfer restrictions may protect against changes in the proportionate interests of stockholders, which may occur if one stockholder is able to purchase shares owned by other stockholders.

c.   Share transfer restrictions may simplify the estate tax problems of a deceased stockholder. If the corporation or other stockholders are obligated to purchase the shares owned by the deceased stockholder, the estate is assured that a large illiquid asset will be reduced to cash and that funds will be available to pay taxes.

d.   Share transfer restrictions may be imposed to maintain S Corporation status, for example, to ensure that the 100 stockholder maximum is not exceeded or that shares are not transferred to an ineligible stockholder.

e. Share transfer restrictions may be imposed where there are substantive limitations on who may be a stockholder or where governmental authorities wish to review, and possibly limit, who is participating in the ownership of the business.

f. Share transfer restrictions may be used to prevent violations of federal securities law where the corporation has issued shares pursuant to an exemption from registration requirements. In many cases, the exemption would be lost if the shares were transferred to ineligible persons, and the offering would be rendered illegal because it is unregistered. (i) In addition to placing a legend on certificates of restricted securities, the issuing corporation may require the purchase to execute a representation or agreement stating that the securities have been acquired for investment and not for redistribution and will not be transferred without the written permission of the issuer. Moreover, the issuing corporation typically instructs its transfer agent to refuse to accept restricted securities for transfer. (ii) Rule 144 under the Securities Act of 1933 is the principal rule establishing when restricted securities may be sold on the public market. Under Rule 144, limited quantities of restricted securities may be sold after they have been held for at least one year. In addition, Rule 144A permits the sale of restricted securities to qualified institutional buyers without significant restrictions. Finally, under SEC Regulation S, securities originally sold to non-US investors may be resold in the United States after specified waiting periods.

g. A temporary share transfer restriction (*lock-up*) may be imposed in connection with shares sold in an initial public offering (IPO) in order to ensure an orderly market for shares following the offering. For example, if shares are offered both to employees and outside investors, the employee shares may be frozen for trading purposes for some specified period of time, typically 180 days.

2. Permissible Restraints

Under the common law, the validity of a share transfer restriction depends on whether it unreasonably restrains transferability. Several states have adopted legislation broadening the types of restrictions that may be enforced.

a. DGCL 202(c) expressly validates restrictions that require consent by the corporation or the holders of a specified class of securities, that require the approval of the proposed transferee by the corporation, or that prohibit a transfer to designated persons or classes of persons if not manifestly unreasonable.

b. DGCL 202(d) provides that a restriction imposed to insure the continued availability of S Corporation status or any other tax advantage to the corporation is conclusively presumed to be for a reasonable purpose.

c. MBCA 6.27 follows the broad outline of the Delaware statute. It authorizes share transfer restrictions to maintain the legal status of the corporation, to preserve exemptions under securities laws, or for any other reasonable purpose.

d. Both the DGCL and the MBCA expressly authorize share transfer restrictions requiring the sale of shares to the corporation or other stockholders without limitation.

3. Forms of Transfer Restrictions

The power to transfer or dispose of corporate shares may be restricted by provisions in the articles of incorporation, the bylaws, or a stockholder agreement. MBCA 6.27(a). There are several different forms of transfer restrictions:

a. A *right of first refusal* gives the corporation or other stockholders an opportunity to meet the best price the stockholder has been able to obtain from a third party.

b. The corporation or other stockholders may retain an *option* to purchase shares at a designated or computable price shares owned by another stockholder upon the occurrence of a triggering event. *Allen v. Biltmore Tissue Corp.*, 161 N.Y.S.2d 418, 141 N.E.2d 812 (N.Y. 1957) (option at original purchase price enforceable upon death of stockholder despite fact that price was far below the market value of the shares).

c. A *consent restriction* requires approval of a proposed transfer by the board of directors, the stockholders, or in some cases a third party.

d. An outright prohibition on transfer is probably invalid unless a compelling need can be shown.

e. A *buy/sell agreement* by which a stockholder is obligated to sell and the corporation or other stockholders are obligated to buy shares at a

designated or computable price upon the occurrence of specified triggering events. A buy-sell agreement differs from an option in that the
buyer is required to buy the shares of the selling stockholder.

   f.   Many close corporation statutes also impose standard share transfer
        restrictions.

4. Terms

The option or obligation to purchase shares usually runs either to the
corporation or to some or all of the stockholders. MBCA 6.27(d) also
expressly permits the option or obligation to run to other persons.

   a.   There are several advantages of an option or obligation running first to
        the corporation. The corporation may be able to raise the necessary cash
        more easily than the stockholders individually. The proportionate inter-
        ests of the remaining stockholders are unaffected by a corporate acqui-
        sition of shares. If life insurance is to be used to provide funds to
        purchase shares on the death of a stockholder, it is usually simplest to
        have the corporation pay the premium and own the policies on the lives
        of each stockholder rather than having each stockholder attempt to
        insure the life of every other stockholder. Finally, purchase by the
        corporation may be more attractive from a tax standpoint.

   b.   The primary disadvantage of an option or obligation running to the
        corporation is that is that if the corporation lacks the necessary legal
        capital to lawfully repurchase the shares, the restriction may be unen-
        forceable. In this situation, it is usually possible to arrange for the
        corporation to repurchase the shares over time. MBCA 6.40. The agree-
        ment may also permit or require the stockholders or some of them to
        agree to buy the shares.

   c.   The primary disadvantage of having a share option run to other
        stockholders is that one or more of the stockholders may be unable or
        unwilling to purchase their allotment of shares. If so, the proportionate
        interests of the remaining stockholders will be affected if some purchase
        and some do not. The agreement may provide that shares not purchased
        should be offered proportionately to the remaining stockholders. In the
        absence of such a requirement, it is likely that unpurchased shares are
        thereafter considered free of all repurchase obligations. The agreement
        may also provide that the offer may be withdrawn if some decline to
        accept. *Helmly v. Schultz,* 131 S.E.2d 924 (Ga.1963).

5. Formalities and Notice

A restriction on transfer is enforceable against a transferee only if the transferee has actual knowledge of the restriction or notice in the form of a conspicuous statement (usually called a *legend*) on the share certificate or document. UCC 8–204; MBCA 6.27(b). Copies of restrictions appearing in contracts but not in the articles of incorporation or bylaws may be required to be filed with the corporation and be available for inspection under the statutes of some states.

6. Duration of Restraints

There is no absolute limit on the duration of share transfer restrictions. It is probable that a restriction remains enforceable without regard to the rule against perpetuities or similar limitations. Share transfer restrictions may terminate in several ways.

a. By express agreement of the stockholders involved.

b. By abandonment or disuse.

7. Strict Construction

Share transfer restrictions are restraints on alienation. Many courts have stated that they therefore should be strictly construed.

8. Price

The price provisions of buy-sell agreements raise difficult and important problems. Closely held shares have no easily determined market price. Thus, the usual goal is to establish a fair price defined as the price that would be agreed between a willing buyer and seller. The following methods are widely used to establish a purchase price:

- a stated price.

- book value.

- capitalization of earnings.

- best offer by an outsider.

- appraisal or arbitration.

- a percentage of profits.

- prior transactions in shares.

- sales of similar businesses.

a.   A price fixed in the agreement or by periodic negotiation is enforceable in the absence of fraud, overreaching, or breach of fiduciary duty. *Yeng Sue Chow v. Levi Strauss & Co.*, 122 Cal.Rptr. 816 (App. 1975); *In re Mather's Estate*, 189 A.2d 586 (Pa.1963).

b.   Book value is a popular method of valuation. This value is typically computed by a simple division of stockholder equity as shown on the balance sheet balance sheet by the number of outstanding shares. Book value tends to increase as the profitability of the business increases, assuming that earnings are retained in the business. But book value tends to decrease if the corporation pays liberal dividends. Thus, otherwise identical corporations may have radically different book values that may not accurately reflect the value of a business in terms of its ability to generate returns for its stockholders.

c.   The most widely accepted method of valuation in the finance industry is going concern value (GCV). GCV is the value of a business based on the returns it is likely to generate for investors into the future. Projected returns are discounted to present value to give a lump sum value expressed in current terms. GCV can be based on several different measures of return. Traditionally, it was based on income or earnings as calculated under generally accepted accounting principles (GAAP). It may also be based on projected dividend payments. The method preferred by most appraisers today, however is discounted cash flow (DCF).

d.   Cash flow is essentially the measure of how much cash a business could theoretically distribute to its owners without disrupting the business. Cash flow is calculated by adjusting GAAP earnings for various accounting conventions (such as depreciation) that cause earnings to vary from actual cash inflows and outflows. In most businesses, cash flow will differ from year to year. Thus, it is common to calculate individual present values for expected cash flows for the first five years and to calculate a lump sum residual value for cash flows after five years on the assumption that annual cash flow will level off at some average. On the other hand, if the business is relatively stable and can be expected to generate roughly the same return each year under normal circumstances, it may be acceptable to estimate its value based on a single calculation that assumes a consistent level of cash flows going forward. In such a case, the value of the business may be calculated by dividing the annual predicted cash flow by a rate of return (the capitalization rate) that would be required by a reasonable investor given the riskiness of the business:

$$\text{return/required rate of return} = \text{value}$$

The required rate of return is usually calculated by adding a premium to the prevailing riskless rate of return (usually the yield on a long term government bond).

e.   The reciprocal of the capitalization rate is often called the multiplier. For example, the reciprocal of 8 percent (.08) is 1/.08 or 12.5. In other words, one can figure the value of a company with an 8 percent capitalization rate by multiplying the periodic return by 12.5. In concept, the multiplier is the same thing as the price/earnings ratio (P/E) in a publicly traded company. Accordingly, appraisers often estimate the capitalization rate by comparison to the P/E of comparable publicly held businesses.

f.   Appraisers often consider various possible methods of valuation, including (i) book value, (ii) capitalized value, and (iii) liquidation value. if the assets were to be sold and (iv) sales prices of shares in isolated transactions in the past, and may take an average of these values. This is sometimes called the Delaware Block Method. This method is not favored today and has been abandoned by the Delaware courts.

g.   After the value of the overall business is obtained, a tentative per share value is usually obtained by a simple division by the number of outstanding shares.

h.   An appraiser may apply one or more discounts from the tentative per share value in order to reflect lack of marketability (if there is no ready market for the shares) or minority status (if the shares have no control value), and a variety of other factors that may affect the value of the shares. Where controlling stockholders dictate the terms of a transaction, courts are usually reluctant to accept discounts on the theory that all stockholders own shares that have the same value per share. On the other hand, a discount of some sort may be appropriate in a buy-sell agreement in which the exiting stockholder determines the timing of a transaction and receives a benefit that is not available to other stockholders. It may also be appropriate to apply a discount in connection with valuation for estate tax or in other situations in which non stockholders are involved.

G. INVOLUNTARY DISSOLUTION

In the absence of a buy/sell agreement, the traditional remedy for problems of oppression and deadlock is involuntary dissolution by judicial decree at the request of a stockholder. In order to obtain dissolution a petitioning stockholder must establish that statutory grounds for dissolution have been met. In addition, the court may withhold this remedy on equitable grounds.

1. Statutory Grounds

Generally, dissolution may not be available to a stockholder unless the stockholder can establish that the situation comes within the precise language of the statute.

a. There is no general common law right of involuntary dissolution and statutes authorizing this remedy are strictly construed. *Johnston v. Livingston Nursing Home, Inc.*, 211 So.2d 151 (Ala.1968); *Kruger v. Gerth*, 263 N.Y.S.2d 1, 210 N.E.2d 355 (N.Y. 1965); *Nelkin v. H. J. R. Realty Corp.*, 307 N.Y.S.2d 454, 255 N.E.2d 713 (N.Y. 1969).

b. Statutory grounds for involuntary dissolution vary to some extent from state to state. MBCA 14.30 provides that dissolution may be ordered by a court if (1) the acts of the directors or those in control of the corporation are illegal, oppressive, or fraudulent; (2) the directors are deadlocked in the management of the corporate affairs, the stockholders are unable to break the deadlock and irreparable injury to the corporation is threatened or being suffered, or the business and affairs of the corporation can no longer be conducted to the advantage of the stockholders generally, because of the deadlock; (3) the stockholders are deadlocked and have failed to elect successors to directors whose terms have expired during a period that includes at least two consecutive annual meeting dates; or (4) The corporate assets are being misapplied or wasted.

c. Even if statutory grounds for involuntary dissolution are established, the statute usually provides or is interpreted to provide that the court has discretion to grant dissolution upon finding that grounds exist. Discretion is necessary because dissolution may benefit one faction of stockholders at the expense of another. *Wollman v. Littman*, 316 N.Y.S.2d 526 (App.Div. 1970); *In re Radom & Neidorff, Inc.*, 119 N.E.2d 563 (N.Y. 1954).

d. Other remedies short of involuntary dissolution may sometimes be available and courts have declined to order dissolution until such other remedies have been tried. *Jackson v. Nicolai–Neppach Co.*, 348 P.2d 9 (Or. 1995); *Masinter v. WEBCO Co.*, 262 S.E.2d 433 (W.Va.1980).

H. JUDICIALLY ORDERED BUYOUTS

There is a significant trend toward recognition that courts may order a buyout of shares rather than involuntary dissolution in order to resolve problems of oppression or deadlock. Buyout orders are specifically authorized by statute in some states, and may be viewed as part of the inherent judicial power in states where they do not have express statutory sanction.

1. Judicial Recognition of the Buyout Remedy

In several cases, courts have ordered a buyout remedy in involuntary dissolution suits even when not expressly authorized by statute. *See Balvik v. Sylvester*, 411 N.W.2d 383 (N.D.1987); *Davis v. Sheerin*, 754 S.W.2d 375 (Tex.App.1988).

2. Statutory Provisions

In 1991, MBCA 14.34 was added expressly authorizing the buyout of shares owned by a stockholder who has filed a petition for involuntary dissolution. When a petition for involuntary dissolution is filed, the corporation or one or more stockholders may elect to purchase the shares of the petitioning stockholder. If one or more stockholders make this election, the remaining stockholders are entitled to purchase on a pro rata basis.

a. MBCA 14.34 is applicable to all corporations whose shares are not publicly traded whether or not the corporation has opted into the statute. There is no provision for opt out.

b. Once the election is made, the stockholder originally petitioning for dissolution may not withdraw the petition.

c. The price at which the shares are to be sold is the fair value of the shares. The parties are given an opportunity to reach a voluntary agreement as to the price, but if they fail to reach agreement on the price, the court determines the fair value of the shares. In determining fair value of shares under MBCA 14.34, neither minority status nor lack of marketability should be considered. *Charland v. Country View Golf Club, Inc.,* 588 A.2d 609 (R.I.1991).

d. If the court establishes the fair value of the shares, it may also establish terms for the purchase, including payment in installments and appropriate security.

e. If a judicially ordered purchase does not occur within ten days of the order, the corporation is deemed to be voluntarily dissolved.

f. MBCA 14.34 is one sided. Only the shares of the petitioning stockholder are subject to purchase.

g. In some states, the remedy of mandatory buyout is available only to corporations that have elected close corporation status.

h. Some courts have ordered remedies short of a mandatory buy/out. *Gimpel v. Bolstein,* 477 N.Y.S.2d 1014 (Sup. 1984) (corporation may elect to resume payment of substantial dividends in lieu of a buyout).

I. OTHER SOLUTIONS FOR OPPRESSION OR DEADLOCK

1. Minority Dissolution Provisions

Close corporation statutes of a few states authorize corporations to elect dissolution provisions that permit a minority stockholder to compel the dissolution of a corporation.

a. In the absence of specific statutory authorization, a minority dissolution right may be created through the use of a voting trust or other device that permits the minority stockholder to compel the majority stockholder to vote in favor of dissolution under specified circumstances.

b. A minority dissolution provision may permit a minority stockholder to use, or threaten to use, this power at an inconvenient time in order to opportunistically seek some additional benefit from the corporation.

2. Receivership

In some states, the courts may appoint a receiver for a deadlocked corporation. Some statutes contemplate the appointment of a receiver as an interim measure before dissolution is decreed.

a. If a corporation is placed in receivership, control passes from the hands of the stockholders to a court-appointed receiver; even if the business and assets are preserved during the receivership, it is unlikely that the causes of deadlock or dissension will be corrected and the business ever returned to its owners. In such situations, dissolution is usually the ultimate step in the receivership.

b. Receivership may encourage the warring stockholders to reach an agreement by which one agrees to buy out the other's interest; in such situations, the receivership may be terminated when sale is consummated. *Shaw v. Robison,* 537 P.2d 487 (Utah 1975).

3. Custodians

Some state statutes authorize courts to appoint custodians for corporations that are deadlocked or otherwise threatened with irreparable injury. DGCL 226. A custodian differs from a receiver in that the goal is to continue the business of the corporation and not to liquidate it or distribute its assets. If a custodian is appointed and the cause of the deadlock or irreparable injury is not eliminated, a custodianship may be converted into a receivership.

a. This provision is designed to provide a simpler, more flexible and less drastic solution for corporations than either the appointment of a receiver or dissolution. *In re Jamison Steel Corp.,* 322 P.2d 246 (Cal.App.1958); *Giuricich v. Emtrol Corp.,* 449 A.2d 232 (Del.1982).

b. The mere threat of the appointment of a custodian may encourage quarreling stockholders to make some kind of a mutual accommodation. But it is doubtful that the appointment of a custodian can cure deep-seated and fundamental differences of views among stockholders. Again, a buyout or involuntary dissolution may be the ultimate remedies.

4. Provisional Directors

A provisional director is an impartial person appointed by a court to serve on the board of directors of a corporation if the board itself is so divided that it cannot make decisions with the consequence that the business and affairs of the corporation can no longer be conducted to the advantage of the stockholders generally. DGCL 353.

a. Provisional directors are authorized in some states only in the case of corporations that have elected close corporation status.

b. A petition for the appointment of a provisional director may be made by one-half of the directors or by a specified fraction of the voting stockholders.

c. A provisional director may be removed by majority vote of the voting stockholders.

5. Additional Remedies

Close corporation statutes may expressly authorize a variety of additional remedies, including the performance, prohibition, alteration, or setting aside of any action of the corporation or of its stockholders, directors, or officers of or any other party to the proceeding; the cancellation or alteration of any provision in the corporation's articles of incorporation or bylaws; the removal of any individual as a director or officer; the appointment of any individual as a director or officer; an accounting with respect to any matter in dispute; the payment of dividends; the award of damages to any party.

J. FIDUCIARY DUTIES AMONG STOCKHOLDERS

The traditional view is that stockholders have no fiduciary duty to each other and that transactions that are unfair to minority stockholders cannot generally be attacked as a breach of a duty of loyalty or good faith by a majority stockholder. More recent decisions recognize that such duties exist and that many cases involving oppression or deadlock may be resolved by application of principles of fiduciary duty.

1. Strict Equal Treatment

The idea that there is a fiduciary duty running between stockholders was first adopted in *Donahue v. Rodd Electrotype Co.*, 328 N.E.2d 505 (Mass.1975). The court analogized the closely held corporation to a partnership and held that fiduciary duty required that where the controlling stockholder family caused the corporation to repurchase shares at an attractive price from a family member who had served as CEO, the same opportunity to sell shares back to the corporation should be afforded to minority stockholders.

a. Many cases support the result reached in *Donahue* on share buy backs at different prices. *See Estate of Meller v. Adolf Meller Co.,* 554 A.2d 648 (R.I.1989); *Sundberg v. Abbott,* 423 N.W.2d 686 (Minn.App.1988); *Balvik v. Sylvester,* 411 N.W.2d 383 (N.D.1987).

b. The *Donahue* doctrine has also been widely applied by courts in other situations as creating a basic fiduciary duty among stockholders and viewing freeze-out tactics as constituting a breach of that duty. *68th Street Apts., Inc. v. Lauricella,* 362 A.2d 78 (N.J.Super.Law Div.1976), *Knaebel v. Heiner,* 663 P.2d 551 (Alaska 1983), *Russell v. First York Savings Co.,* 352 N.W.2d 871 (Neb.1984), overruled on other grounds, *Van Pelt v. Greathouse,* 364 N.W.2d 14 (Neb.1985); *Muellenberg v. Bikon, Corp.,* 669 A.2d 1382 (N.J.1996); *Pedro v. Pedro,* 489 N.W.2d 798 (Minn.App.1992) (controlling stockholders breached fiduciary duty when they fired minority stockholder who had a legitimate expectation of lifetime employment and majority stockholders had engaged in misconduct).

2. Business Purpose Test

The rule of strict equal treatment has been somewhat modified by subsequent Massachusetts cases addressing other situations. For example, where a dispute arose over a business decision leading to extreme hostility among stockholders, three of four equal stockholders declined to reelect fourth stockholder to the board of directors and terminated him as salaried employee, the court held (1) that majority stockholders must show business purpose for actions and (2) that minority stockholder could show that less drastic alternative resolution was possible. *Wilkes v. Springside Nursing Home, Inc.,* 353 N.E.2d 657 (Mass.1976). Following *Wilkes,* the Massachusetts courts have continued to struggle to establish the line between appropriate majority action and breaches of the *Donahue* fiduciary duty.

a. In *Hallahan v. Haltom Corp.,* 385 N.E.2d 1033 (Mass.App.1979), the court ordered shares acquired by an equal co-owner of shares in an effort to change the balance of power to be returned to the seller at cost.

b. In *Smith v. Atlantic Properties, Inc.,* 422 N.E.2d 798 (Mass.App.1981), a minority stockholder had veto power over most decisions because of a unanimity requirement. The stockholder exercised the power arbitrarily to prevent the payment of all dividends, thereby causing the corporation to incur a penalty tax for unreasonable accumulation of surplus. The court held the minority stockholder liable has breached his duty to the other stockholders.

c. In *Leader v. Hycor, Inc.*, 479 N.E.2d 173 (Mass.1985) the court upheld a reverse stock split at the ratio of one new share for each 4,000 old shares, with fractional shares to be purchased for cash at a specified amount per share.

d. In *Goode v. Ryan*, 489 N.E.2d 1001 (Mass.1986), the court held that the Donahue duty did not permit the estate of a minority stockholder to compel the corporation to repurchase its shares in order to simplify the settlement of the estate. In this case, there was no prior contractual obligation to repurchase the shares.

e. In *Evangelista v. Holland*, 537 N.E.2d 589 (Mass.App.1989), the court held that a preexisting contract for the corporation to repurchase minority shares on the death of a stockholder at a set price should be enforced despite the argument that Donahue required the corporation to negotiate a price closer to the current value of the shares owned by the deceased stockholder. The court stated that there was a mutuality of risk and no violation of the Donahue duty.

f. In *Crowley v. Communications for Hospitals, Inc.*, 573 N.E.2d 996 (Mass.App.1991), controlling stockholders paid themselves excessive compensation while excluding the minority stockholders. Court should order the excessive compensation restored to the corporation but order a mandatory dividend to all stockholders only if creditors are adequately protected. It should not order a direct payment to the minority stockholders.

g. In *Merola v. Exergen Corp.*, 668 N.E.2d 351 (Mass. 1996), an employee who purchased stock in corporation was fired and later sold his stock back to the majority stockholder (at a profit) on terms apparently continuously available to all minority stockholders. The court held that stock ownership does not create entitlement to continued employment.

3. Other Approaches

In *Nixon v. Blackwell*, 626 A.2d 1366 (Del.1993), the Delaware Supreme Court rejected the *Donahue* approach, saying it would do violence to normal practice of corporation law to create a broad fiduciary duty among stockholders and noting that corporation had not elected statutory close corporation status. The case involved the claim of a non-employee minority stockholder that sellback option under employee stockownership plan should be available to all stockholders. Delaware nonetheless appears to recognize a somewhat enhance fiduciary duty to the corporation in the context of a closely held corporation.

a.   In *Toner v. Baltimore Envelope Co.*, 498 A.2d 642 (Md.1985), the court rejected a *per se* rule of strict equal treatment in connection with a stock buyback intended to resolve dispute between two stockholder factions and focusing on business purpose and feasibility, noting that corporation had not elected statutory close corporation status.

b.   New York recognizes a fiduciary duty within closely held corporations. *Alpert v. 28 Williams St. Corp.*, 473 N.E.2d 19 (N.Y. 1984). But the New York courts have held that a stockholder who is an at-will employee may be fired without cause. *Ingle v. Glamore Motor Sales, Inc.*, 535 N.E.2d 1311 (N.Y. 1989). The power to fire an at-will employee who is also a stockholder may be exercised in order to avoid the application of a new valuation formula for the purchase of the employee's shares. *Gallagher v. Lambert*, 549 N.E.2d 136 (N.Y. 1989).

c.   Cases from other jurisdictions recognize a fiduciary duty may exist but have not followed the implications of the strict *Donahue* duty. *Zidell v. Zidell, Inc.*, 560 P.2d 1091 (Or.1977), and *Masinter v. WEBCO Co.*, 262 S.E.2d 433 (W.Va.1980).

K.   ALTERNATIVE DISPUTE RESOLUTION (ADR)

Mandatory *arbitration* is sometimes used as a device to avoid a deadlock short of dissolution. The advantages of arbitration are speed, cheapness, informality (as contrasted with a court proceeding), and the prospect of a decision by a person with knowledge and experience in business affairs. Where the reason for deadlock is a question not involving basic personal or policy matters, arbitration may satisfactorily resolve a dispute and permit the corporation to continue. In addition, many courts today routinely require parties to business disputes to undertake *mediation*. The difference is that the decision of an arbitrator is binding whereas a mediator seeks only to facilitate a settlement between the parties.

a.   Arbitration is a matter of contract. The parties must agree to it. Thus, the parties must agree on the nature of disputes that an arbitrator may decide and the remedies that the arbitrator may order. Arbitration statutes contain virtually no restrictions on the types of disputes that may be resolved pursuant to arbitration.

b.   The agreement to arbitrate may be entered into at any time. Thus, it may be part of a stockholder agreement or the parties may agree to arbitration after a dispute has arisen. The courts will ordinarily enforce the decision of an arbitrator as long as the arbitrator has acted within the scope of the agreement to arbitrate.

c.   Traditionally, courts were reluctant to enforce agreements to arbitrate as an improper delegation of duty by the board of directors. Most courts today will enforce an agreement to arbitrate as long as all effected stockholders are party to the agreement. *Vogel v. Lewis*, 268 N.Y.S.2d 237 (App.Div.1966), *aff'd*, 224 N.E.2d 738 (N.Y.1967) (disagreement whether a corporation should exercise option to purchase is arbitrable); *Moskowitz v. Surrey Sleep Products, Inc.*, 292 N.Y.S.2d 748 (App.Div. 1968). On the other hand, a court might consider the corporation itself a necessary party to the dispute in some cases.

d.   Many disputes leading to deadlock in a closely held corporation involve personality conflicts or broad differences in policy. An arbitrator may have no criteria for resolving such disputes, and even if she does resolve a specific dispute, it is unlikely that the decision will cure the basic disagreement which led to the original deadlock. Nevertheless, the courts routinely order arbitration in closely held corporation disputes when provided for by contract without consideration of the probable success of the arbitration. Ultimately, if deep personal or policy conflicts continue, dissolution appears to be the only suitable remedy because arbitration cannot cure the root cause of the disagreement.

■ XII. PUBLICLY HELD CORPORATIONS

A. CONTROL IN THE PUBLICLY HELD CORPORATION

Corporate governance in a large publicly held corporation bears little relationship to the system contemplated by state corporation statutes or to the procedures followed by most closely held corporations. Who controls large publicly held corporations and for whose benefit are among the most controversial issues in corporation law.

1. Limited Role of Individual Stockholders

The number of voting shares in the large publicly held corporation is so large that the votes of any single investor are almost always irrelevant on any issue. With respect to the election of directors, the small stockholder is usually presented with a ballot and a list of candidates for the board of directors equal in number to the positions to be filled. The stockholder may vote for theses candidates or withhold a vote for some or all of them. But because the overwhelming majority of the stockholders almost always vote in favor of the proposed directors, it seldom makes a difference whether or not an individual stockholder exercises the right to vote.

2. The Board of Directors and the Chief Executive Officer (CEO)

In large publicly held corporations, professional managers run the business even though as a matter of statutory law the board of directors retains ultimate and complete authority to manage the business. In practice, the board of directors does not participate directly in management but serves a more limited role as a monitor of management. Rather, the chief executive officer (CEO) has the ultimate working responsibility for management of the enterprise. And in *very* large enterprises, even the CEO may have limited involvement with day-to-day operations. Instead, he or she may be primarily involved with financial matters, long term planning, the selection of operating personnel, and the like. Still, significant decisions are likely to be made by the CEO or in consultation with the CEO.

    a.   The board of directors in publicly held corporations is particularly important in the following areas:

- They provide general review and oversight of management.

- They select the CEO, set his compensation, and may replace him if overall performance is unsatisfactory.

- They assure that the corporation has in place working and effective auditing and accounting systems.

- They provide advice and counsel to management.

- They provide intellectual discipline for management (which must appear before the board and present views and defend proposals).

- They set dividend rates, approve significant financial transactions, approve stock option plans for managers and employees, and so forth.

- They act in crisis situations, where the CEO unexpectedly dies or is incapacitated, or where significant misconduct, fraud, or theft of corporate assets is discovered.

b. Although they do not establish objectives, strategies and policies of the corporation, many boards of directors are involved in strategic planning through participation on board committees dealing with specific problem areas. These committees may work closely with the CEO and management and may become directly involved in defining and establishing long term goals for the corporation.

c. Although it is clear that most boards of directors do not actually manage the company, neither do they act as adversaries or even a devil's advocate. Rather, most decisions are made by consensus. Indeed, caselaw effectively mandates that the board of directors reach a consensus. *See Smith v. Atlantic Properties, Inc.*, 422 N.E.2d 798 (Mass.App.1981). Corporation law presumes that board decisions are unanimous unless a director formally registers dissent. *See* MBCA 8.24. Moreover, corporation law generally prohibits action by the board without a meeting unless the decision is unanimous. *See* MBCA 8.21. It also effectively prohibits a director from voting by proxy. *See* MBCA 8.20.

3. Composition of the Board of Directors

Historically, the board of directors was viewed largely as a rubber stamp for management. Directors were viewed as having limited responsibilities.

Today, stock exchange rules mandated by the SEC require that the board of directors of listed companies be composed of a majority of independent members. Thus, most boards of directors consist partly of management representatives—*inside directors*—and partly of *outside directors* who are not officers or employees of the corporation

a. The Chief Executive Officer (CEO) is often also the chairman of the board of directors, though in an increasing number of corporations these positions are held by different people. If the CEO is also chairman of the board of directors he or she may control the agenda. However, it has also been recognized that it is often preferable for these two offices to be held by different persons. Where that is the case the chairman of the board rather than the CEO may largely develop the agenda.

b. Inside directors are high level executive officers employed by the corporation. Because they are subordinate to the CEO, they are generally assumed to largely reflect and support the CEO's policies.

c. Outside directors are often CEOs (or retired CEOs) of other corporations, though they may also include major investors, well known public figures, politicians, educators (such as university presidents and business school deans), and others. Experience with the management of complex bureaucratic structures and lack of prior economic involvement with the specific corporation are usually desirable characteristics for outside directors. Nevertheless an outside director is not likely to have detailed knowledge of company affairs. Thus, briefing books are distributed to directors in advance of a meeting so that they may become informed in connection with issues on the agenda. Most boards meet monthly as a board. Committees may meet more often. Special meetings may be held by conference call. As the role of outside directors has increased in importance, it has become recognized that they should raise significant issues for discussion at board or committee meetings. Many important questions are first raised informally with the CEO or at meetings of committees of boards prior to a discussion of them at a meeting of the board of directors. Recommendations with respect to these matters are usually discussed by management in advance of the meeting.

d. Under NYSE rules a director is not considered to be independent if:

   • The director is or has been within the last three years an employee of the listed company, or an immediate family member is or has been within the last three years an executive officer of the listed company.

- The director or an immediate family member has received more than $100,000 in compensation from the listed company during any twelve-month period within the last three years other than director and committee fees and pension or other forms of deferred compensation for prior service.

- The director or an immediate family member is a current partner of a firm that is the company's internal or external auditor; the director is a current employee of such a firm; the director has an immediate family member who is a current employee of such a firm and who participates in the firm's audit, assurance or tax compliance (but not tax planning) practice; or the director or an immediate family member was within the last three years a partner or employee of such a firm and personally worked on the listed company's audit within that time.

- The director or an immediate family member is or has been within the last three years employed as an executive officer of another company where any of the listed company's present executive officers at the same time serves or served on that company's compensation committee.

- The director is a current employee or an immediate family member is a current executive officer of a company that has made payments to or received payments from the listed company for property or services in an amount that exceeds the greater of $1 million or 2% of such other company's consolidated gross revenues in any of the last three fiscal years.

e. Under NYSE rules non-management directors must meet at regularly scheduled executive sessions without management.

f. A variety of factors has contributed to the emphasis on the role of independent directors. Officers and inside directors were blamed for corporate misconduct in the 1970s (particularly following Watergate) and even more significant criminal misconduct in 2000 and 2001, leading to federal legislation tightening internal financial controls at publicly traded corporations and requiring oversight by independent directors.

In addition, the courts have tended to respect decisions by disinterested directors in connection with stockholder derivative actions and takeover defenses.

4. Committees of the Board of Directors

In a publicly traded company, the board of directors must appoint several standing committees.

a. Under the Sarbanes Oxley Act, stock exchange rules must provide that all listed companies must have an audit committee that is directly responsible for the appointment, compensation, and oversight of the work of any registered public accounting firm employed by that issuer for the purpose of preparing or issuing an audit report or related work, and each such registered public accounting firm shall report directly to the audit committee. The audit committee must also establish procedures for the receipt, retention, and treatment of complaints received by the issuer regarding accounting, internal accounting controls, or auditing matters, the confidential, anonymous submission by employees of the issuer of concerns regarding questionable accounting or auditing matters. The audit committee must also have the authority to engage independent counsel and other advisers, as it determines necessary to carry out its duties.

b. Under NYSE rules, each listed company must have a nominating committee or corporate governance committee and a compensation committee. Both of these committees must be composed entirely of independent directors. Comparable rules apply to NASDAQ companies.

5. Statutory Duties of Officers Under Federal Law

Under the Sarbanes Oxley Act, the CEO and the chief financial officer (CFO) of each SEC registered company must certify in each annual or quarterly report filed with the SEC (1) that they have reviewed the report; (2) that based on the officer's knowledge, the report does not contain any untrue statement of a material fact or omit to state a material fact necessary in order to make the statements made, in light of the circumstances under which such statements were made, not misleading; (3) that based on such officer's knowledge, the financial statements, and other financial information included in the report, fairly present in all material respects the financial condition and results of operations of the issuer as of, and for, the periods presented in the report; (4) that the signing officers (A) are responsible for establishing and maintaining internal controls, (B) have designed such internal controls to ensure that material information relating to the issuer and its consolidated subsidiaries is made known to such officers by others within those entities, particularly during the period in which the periodic reports are being prepared, (C) have evaluated the effectiveness of the issuer's internal controls as of a date within 90 days prior to the report, and (D) have presented in the report their conclusions about the effectiveness of their internal controls based on their evaluation as of that date; (5) that the signing officers have disclosed to the issuer's auditors and the audit committee of the board of directors (or persons fulfilling the equivalent function) (A) all significant deficiencies in the design or operation of internal controls which could adversely affect the issuer's ability to record, process, summarize, and report financial data and have identified for the issuer's auditors any material weaknesses in internal controls, and (B) any fraud, whether or not material, that involves management or other employees who have a significant role in the issuer's internal controls; and (6) that the signing officers have indicated in the report whether or not there were significant changes in internal controls or in other factors that could significantly affect internal controls subsequent to the date of their evaluation, including any corrective actions with regard to significant deficiencies and material weaknesses.

6. **CEO Succession**

The ultimate power and duty to name the CEO rests with the board of directors. Traditionally, management of most publicly-held corporations has tended to be self-perpetuating. In most cases, the incumbent CEO, in consultation with the board of directors, recommends a successor and that recommendation is accepted by the board of directors. Major stockholders including institutional investors may have an important voice in the selection. With the requirement of an independent nominating/corporate governance committee, it is likely that boards of directors will exercise significant and increasing independence in reviewing recommendations by incumbent management and the outgoing CEO.

a. In many corporations, managers rise gradually through the ranks until one ultimately becomes CEO. But there are many examples of outsiders being named CEO.

b. The board of directors may also remove the CEO. Such actions, which may be based on dissatisfaction with profitability of the business, failure to eliminate corruption or misconduct, or unpopular actions by the CEO, have become more common since the 1980s. Studies indicate that CEO tenure has become shorter and shorter in recent years.

7. Nominees for the Board of Directors

Historically, candidates for the board of directors were identified by the CEO. This practice permitted the CEO to assure that the board of directors remained friendly. Today, most publicly held corporations must have an independent nominating committee to select new director candidates. As a result, the formal role of the CEO in selecting members of the board of directors has been significantly reduced, but the CEO may still have considerable voice in who is nominated to be a director on the management's slate.

a. Except in the case of a proxy fight, stockholders have no real choice in voting for alternative candidates. There is no requirement that management include competing candidates in its proxy materials even though the expense of the proxy solicitation is borne by the company. (A competing candidate (or slate of candidates) is free to solicit votes at his or her own expense and in compliance with SEC rules.) Thus, a stockholder may withhold her vote, vote for management's slate, or waste her vote on a write-in candidate. Accordingly, the role of stockholders when voting for directors is more to ratify the persons nominated by the corporation to serve as its directors.

b. Although institutional investors could in theory dictate the outcome of many board elections, most institutional investors support management nominees. In some cases, institutional investors have announced that they will not vote for one or more incumbent directors. Such an announcement is taken very seriously by current management, because it is likely that other institutional investors will withhold their votes also or demand changes in governance of the corporation.

c. In 2003, the SEC proposed to permit outside candidates to be nominated for election to the board of directors in the management proxy materials under specified circumstances including financial misconduct or the withholding of a 35 percent or more of stockholder votes from an individual candidate. As an alternative, it was proposed that Delaware corporation law might be amended to require election by a majority of votes cast for director. The SEC proposal was withdrawn and is not likely to be raised again in the near future.

B. STOCKHOLDERS IN PUBLICLY TRADED CORPORATIONS

A great deal of attention has been given to the place of stockholders in corporate governance, the role they should play, and the implications of the growth of institutional investors in the modern American economy. Scholars have several different views as to the appropriate role of stockholders.

1. Berle & Means View

In 1933, Adolph Berle and Gardiner Means, published *The Modern Corporation and Private Property,* a revolutionary book at the time, which pictured stockholders as scattered, isolated, and disorganized individuals who typically vote blindly in favor of management or as management recommends. Because management has total control of the enterprise in this view, the business is often operated as much for the benefit of the managers as it for the benefit of the stockholders—a model that is often called *managerialism.* This *separation of ownership from control* could be traced to several factors according to Berle and Means:

a. Management has control of the proxy machinery and the views of management are therefore routinely set forth before the stockholders as the institutional voice of the corporation. Challengers must locate and communicate with stockholders largely at their own expense and without the benefit of access to corporate information. Hence, it is expensive to challenge incumbent management, and the chances of success are slim.

b. The CEO not only controls who is nominated to serve as director but also dominates the meetings of the board by reason of being its chairman, by controlling its agenda, and by limiting the circulation of information to the directors.

c. There is a natural process of self-selection by stockholders. Most stockholders think first of their own financial interest. If they are dissatisfied with management, they sell their shares. Thus, dissatisfied stockholders tend to disappear by a process of self-elimination, and the remaining stockholders tend to be pro-management. This is often called the *Wall Street Rule* or the *Wall Street Option.*

d. On the other hand, it is always possible for stockholders to bring a derivative action challenging specific transactions or for an insurgent group to undertake a proxy fight seeking to oust management. These devices are usually seen as a last resort, because they are expensive and unlikely to succeed except in the most extreme cases.

e. Finally, several other forces may serve to discipline management. Perhaps most important, management is concerned with its own reputation in the company, the business world, and the community. There is almost always a better job to which even a CEO may aspire. In addition, poor management may cause large investors or even creditors to demand changes. Internal dissension or competition among senior officers may lead to a shake up of management.

2. The Market for Corporate Control

In the late 1970s, some scholars began to argue that the Berle and Means thesis ignored market forces that serve to discipline management. To be sure, it is only natural for a manager to work less hard to maximize the wealth of stockholders than it would be for him to maximize his own wealth. Moreover, a manager may be inclined to engage in a variety of tactics— ranging from exacting excessive salary and benefits to withholding dividends in order to grow the company through questionable acquisitions (*empire building*) to self-dealing to appropriation of corporate opportunities— designed to divert profits of the corporation to himself. Such shirking and opportunistic behaviors are often called *agency costs* because they reduce returns to stockholders. But if agency costs are too high, and stockholder return is too low, stock price will likely suffer and the company may become the target of a takeover attempt. In other words, if stock price falls because management is inefficient or self-serving, someone will likely emerge to make an offer to buy the company on the theory that the stock would be worth more if the company were better managed. In such a situation, the bidder may be able to afford to offer a premium over the market price to target stockholders and gain control of a company that will still be worth more than the price paid once better management is installed.

a. Stockholders can reduce agency costs by monitoring the performance of managers and by devising incentive systems that encourage managers to maximize the wealth of stockholders rather than their own personal wealth. Incentive devices such as bonuses, stock option and stock purchase plans, and long term incentive compensation, and even golden parachutes may link manager self interest to owner wealth maximization may limit agency costs by aligning the interests of the manager with the interests of owners. Outside directors can also serve as monitors particularly if they are required to own stock or are paid in stock rather than in cash, practices which became increasingly common in the 1990s. In addition, mandatory disclosure requirements under federal securities law facilitate monitoring, although some legal scholars have argued that publicly traded companies have adequate incentive to communicate with investors and the market in order to keep stock price as high as possible.

b. In the 1980s, cash tender offers for large publicly-held corporations became relatively common, because new sources of cash (such as junk bonds) became available and because shares has become relatively concentrated in the hands of institutional investors. In a significant number of cases, such takeover attempts proved successful and were followed by the replacement of the board of directors and management by presumably more competent managers.

c. Needless to say, the market for corporate control threatens managers who do not maximize stockholder wealth with the possibility of hostile takeover that may lead to their ouster from positions of control. This led to the development of a variety of takeover defenses and the adoption of state takeover legislation. Many legal scholars argued that such defenses were largely inappropriate because they were in fact designed to entrench incumbent management. Some argued that management should not be permitted to engage in any defensive tactics at all, because the fact that a bidder offers premium constitutes an increase in stockholder wealth and because the stockholders own the company the goal of management should be to increase stockholder wealth. These same scholars also argued that state takeover statutes and indeed federal tender offer law were unwise. The courts tended to take a middle view and to strike down defensive tactics that did not serve a business purpose but rather appeared to be motivated primarily by entrenchment. Generally, the courts did not impose a rule that management must seek to maximize stockholder wealth except in cases in which it was clear that the company would be sold to a new control group.

d. Cash tender offers became much less common after 1990 in part because market prices increased significantly (possibly because the market for corporate control had increased management solicitude for the interests of stockholders) and in part because takeover defenses became more sophisticated. In addition, companies appeared to be quite willing to divest operations if divestiture would likely lead to an increase in aggregate stockholder wealth. Thus, although many target managers had opposed takeover attempts on the grounds that bidders sought to break up the target company (and undo the corporate empire), would-be target managers came to undertake break-up voluntarily, possibly because a shift to compensation primarily in the form of stock options (which effectively aligned management interest with stockholder interest) and away from compensation based on aggregate earnings or other measures based on size. An increase in takeover activity beginning in the mid–1990s largely involved combinations of independent businesses. These transactions in some cases also may have led to the elimination of less effective managers and their replacement by more competent managers.

e. The collapse of the dotcom market as well as Enron, WorldCom, and other companies beginning in the year 2000, led to significant new regulation focused primarily on improving financial reporting as discussed above. It also led many scholars and commentators to question the use of stock options as compensation and to question market efficiency generally.

3. Stockholder Wealth Maximization as the Goal

The traditional view is that the objective of a corporation is to maximize the wealth of its stockholders. This view is expressed in early cases. *See Dodge v. Ford Motor Co.*, 170 N.W. 668, 684 (Mich.1919). It is also implicit in the Berle & Means thesis. And it is the basic premise on which the analysis of corporate governance by law and economics scholars.

a. Nevertheless, as a result of takeover activity in the 1980s, most states adopted *other constituency statutes* that permit (and in a few cases require) management to consider interests other than those of the stockholders in making decisions on behalf of the corporation. These other constituencies may include employees, customers, suppliers, creditors, and the communities in which the corporation has facilities. They are often called *stakeholders* to distinguish them from stockholders. These statutes were enacted by state legislatures without extensive consideration in response to fears that corporations incorporated in those states might become subject to unwanted takeover bids. Management of threatened companies believed that constituency statutes might permit them to reject a takeover bids at even above-market prices by relying expressly on the interests of stakeholders. There have been few reported instances of the actual application of these statutes. Delaware has not enacted such a statute.

b. These statutes have been widely criticized from various different perspectives. They have also had their defenders.

- Law and economics scholars have criticized these statutes on the grounds that stakeholders can protect themselves by contract and that aggregate wealth is maximized if managers are required to maximize the return to stockholders as residual claimants.

- The ABA's Committee on Corporate Laws and the Business Roundtable have criticized these statutes because they increase uncertainty and raise the specter of possible lawsuits brought by other stakeholders who are adversely affected by director or management decisions. In other words, by effectively giving management the choice of which constituency to serve in any given situation, management is in fact relieved of all effective responsibility.

- These statutes have been defended as being consistent with long term stockholder interests and as stating a more traditional view of corporate citizenship and social responsibility.

- Stockholder wealth maximization is easy to state as a goal but difficult to apply in light of stockholder diversification and the development of options and derivative securities that can affect share values.

c. Some legal scholars have suggested that an alternative model of the corporation as an organization focused on problems of *team production* may be more accurate than the traditional stockholder-owner model. The premise of the team production model is that in most corporations (1) it is necessary to commit goods and services to production and to forgo the right to withdraw those assets for a substantial period and (2) it is difficult to determine how much of the profits are attributable to individual contributions. Thus, the various contributors of inputs agree in effect to sell the profits to the stockholders and the board of directors serves as a largely disinterested mediator largely who determines the returns to be paid to the various contributors of inputs. Although the team production model has been offered as an explanation for why stockholders may not be the ultimate claimants on residual corporate returns, it does not address the fact that other constituencies all bargain for fixed returns. On the other hand, it suggests that management itself may well be seen as an important claimant, particularly where compensation is paid primarily in the form of gains from stock options.

C. INSTITUTIONAL INVESTORS

Institutional investors—including mutual funds and other investment companies, pension and retirement funds, insurance companies, bank trust departments, foundations, university endowments, and others—have grown tremendously in importance since the 1950s. Today, individual investors own only about one-third of all corporate equities. Moreover, in many listed companies, a relatively small number of institutional investors own a majority of all outstanding voting shares.

a. Traditionally, institutional investors have not been active in the control and management of publicly held corporations despite their potential voting power. Rather, they have tended to view themselves as passive investors and have not attempted to influence management decisions. On the other hand, institutional investors have generally been quite eager to sell at a gain in the event of a takeover, because such sales increase the returns to fund stockholders and enhance the competitive position of the fund compared to other funds. Moreover, in a struggle for control, shares held by institutional investors may be the critical swing votes and may effectively determine who will control the corporation. In addition, institutional investors have objected to management decisions to implement takeover defenses. As a result, some corporations have declined to adopt defenses such as the poison pill or have submitted proposed defenses to a stockholder vote.

b. The traditionally passive attitude of most funds may also be changing because of several other factors.

   • Changes to the SEC proxy regulations now permit institutional and other investors to communicate freely with each other with respect to corporate governance matters. Before 1992, communication among institutional investors was impeded by the worry that such efforts might be viewed as a proxy solicitation requiring filing with and approval by the SEC. In 1992, the SEC amended its proxy regulations to it make clear that institutional investors could freely communicate with each other without violating SEC regulations, so long as proxy appointments were not solicited.

- Some institutional shareholdings have become so large that it may no longer be possible to sell without an adverse effect on the market price.

- Legal scholars have suggested that institutional investors should consider increased activism on corporate governance matters.

- With the increasing number of independent directors, institutional investors may be able to raise issues with individual directors without approaching management directly.

c. Pension funds appear to be less reluctant to participate in corporate governance. Public employee retirement systems such as the California system (CALPers) in particular have been leaders in seeking to increase the voice of institutional stockholders in decisions relating to corporate governance.

d. Institutional investors have used a variety of tactics to express their views.

- Many institutional investors (particularly charitable organizations) have submitted stockholder proposals for inclusion in proxy statements under SEC Rule 14a–8. Some of these proposals have been approved and others have received substantial percentages of the vote, thereby calling management's attention to the dissatisfaction of large stockholders. In some cases, a corporation may negotiate with these organizations even before the proposal is disseminated in order to work out a mutually acceptable compromise that avoids the need for negative publicity.

- In several cases, institutional investors have announced their intention to withhold votes for some or all incumbent directors. These withhold vote campaigns prompted the SEC to propose a rule (as discussed above) that would have given large stockholders the ability to nominate candidates for the board of directors in certain circumstances. The rule was ultimately withdrawn and does not appear likely to be adopted in the near future.

- Federal securities law provides that in the case of a private securities fraud class action, the largest stockholder should be presumed to be the best representative of the class and thus should be deemed to be the lead plaintiff and privileged to direct the action including selecting counsel for the class. This provision was seldom invoked during the period up to 2004, but it appears that institutional investors have shown some interest recently in assuming a leadership role in such actions. On the other hand, several legal actions were filed against mutual funds in 2004 alleging that they had neglected to submit claims in some such actions even though entitled to participate in recovery.

e. In 2003, it was discovered that several mutual fund groups had permitted favored investors to engage in a variety of abusive trading strategies that had the effect of skimming returns away from ordinary investors. As a result, the SEC adopted a series of reforms designed to ensure the independence of mutual fund boards of directors from the investment advisers who manage the funds day to day. In addition, the SEC has independently adopted rules requiring enhanced disclosure of how mutual funds vote their shares.

f. Many institutional investors rely on third parties such as Institutional Stockholder Services (ISS) to advise them about the corporate governance practices of the companies in which they invest and even about how to vote their shares. This has raised the question whether such advisers may be in a position to dictate corporate governance policies and if so how they determine what position to take on the issues. In addition, such agencies issue scores for publicly traded companies in connection with their governance practices and advise companies about how to improve their scores. Some commentators have suggested that this dual role constitutes a serious conflict of interest and may give such agencies undue leverage.

■ XIII. SECURITIES FRAUD & INSIDER TRADING

This chapter deals generally with securities fraud. Although there are many forms of securities fraud, most cases involve either (1) trading by officers, directors, and other persons who have access to material non-public information about the corporation (referred to as insider trading), or (2) injuries to investors caused by reason of false or misleading information disseminated by the corporation.

A. STATE LAW REGULATING TRANSACTIONS IN SHARES

State law relating to trading in shares has been largely overshadowed by federal law. But the protection afforded by federal law to private plaintiffs has been scaled back significantly by a series of Supreme Court decisions dating from the 1970s and by several statutes enacted by Congress. As a result, state law has become somewhat more important in this regard in recent years.

1. Insider Trading

A director, officer or manager of a corporation may have material non-public information about corporate affairs that will likely affect the price of shares when it is disclosed. As a result, an insider may be tempted to purchase or sell shares (depending on the nature of the information) without publicly disclosing the information. Such trading is called insider trading.

a. State law generally permitted such trading in the absence of fraud on the assumption that the corporation itself was not harmed by insider trading. Moreover, in an anonymous public market, it was often difficult to determine precisely who took the other side of the trade in question. And, even if a particular outsider could be matched with the insider executing a trade, presumably the outsider had decided to enter into the transaction because he believed it was a desirable one in any event. He had simply made a poor decision. Hence, it seemed very doubtful that he should be viewed as having been injured at all. In other words, if the insider does nothing to induce the outsider to trade, it is difficult to see how that transaction can constitute common law fraud by the insider. The leading case for this position is *Goodwin v. Agassiz*, 186 N.E. 659 (Mass. 1933).

b. If an affirmative misrepresentation was made by an insider, however, normal fraud principles dictate that the defrauded person should be able to rescind the transaction or sue for damages.

c. Where certain facts are of critical importance and are within the sole knowledge of the insider because of his official capacity, some courts found an affirmative duty on the part of the insider to disclose these special facts before entering into a transaction with an uninformed investor. *Strong v. Repide*, 213 U.S. 419, 29 S.Ct. 521 (1909); *Taylor v. Wright*, 159 P.2d 980 (Cal.App.1945).

d. Kansas adopted a stricter rule of fiduciary duty designed to protect all outsiders in *Hotchkiss v. Fischer*, 16 P.2d 531 (Kan. 1932). However, the difference between cases involving the strict duty rule of *Hotchkiss* and those applying the special facts rule appeared to be one of degree.

e. This strict duty rule arose in cases involving closely held corporations and is apparently still the majority rule in such cases. See *Van Schaack Holdings, Ltd. v. Van Schaak*, 867 P.2d 892 (Colo. 1994).

f. Another principle is set forth in *Diamond v. Oreamuno*, 248 N.E.2d 910 (N.Y. 1969), where the court permitted the corporation to recover losses avoided by insiders who became aware of negative information and sold their shares before the negative information was disclosed. The court reasoned that inside information was corporate property and insiders should not be permitted to profit from the use of that property even though the corporation was not itself injured thereby.

2. Other Settings

a. State law may apply in cases where an insider competes with his corporation by buying or selling corporate shares when the corporation would have been financially benefited if it had directly entered into the same transactions. These cases are essentially corporate opportunity cases. Examples include: *Brophy v. Cities Service Co.*, 70 A.2d 5 (Del.Ch.1949) (purchase of shares when corporation was planning to make a repurchase); *Weissman v. Weissman*, 97 A.2d 870 (Pa. 1953) (purchase of creditor claims at a discount); *Manufacturers Trust Co. v. Becker*, 338 U.S. 304, 70 S.Ct. 127 (1949) (same, addressing treatment in bankruptcy); *People v. Floretino*, 456 N.Y.S.2d 638 (Crim.Ct. 1982) (criminal proceeding against bidder attorney who bought target shares ahead of client); *Perlman v. Feldmann*, 219 F.2d 173 (2d Cir. 1955). (sale of controlling shares at a premium to major customers when corporation was subject to price controls and could not raise prices.)

b. Under federal law only stockholders who actually buy or sell shares have standing to assert a claim for securities fraud against the offending corporation. But some state courts have held that stockholders who are misled and fail to buy or sell may sue as well. *Malone v. Brincat*, 722 A.2d 5 (Del. 1998); *Small v. Fritz Cos.*, 30 Cal.4th 167 (2003).

B. FEDERAL LAW AND RULE 10b–5

Rule 10b–5, promulgated by the SEC under § 10(b) of the Securities Exchange Act of 1934, is the source of most of the current principles relating to transactions in shares by insiders. The Rule provides:

It shall be unlawful for any person, directly or indirectly, by the use of any means or instrumentality of interstate commerce, or of the mails or of any facility of any national securities exchange, (a) To employ any device, scheme, or artifice to defraud, (b) To make any untrue statement of a material fact or to omit to state a material fact necessary in order to make the statements made, in light of the circumstances under which they were made, not misleading, or (c) To engage in any act, practice, or course of business which operates or would operate as a fraud or deceit upon any person, in connection with the purchase or sale of any security.

Rule 10b–5 is the broadest antifraud provision in the federal securities laws and is sometimes called a *catch-all* antifraud rule. It is thus common for the SEC, the DOJ, and indeed private plaintiffs to add a claim under Rule 10b–5 even though another provision of federal securities law is more on point.

1. Development of Rule 10b–5

Rule 10b–5 was originally promulgated because the express antifraud provisions of the federal securities laws applied only to sales of securities. But it is also quite possible for an insider to defraud an existing stockholder by purchasing the outsider's shares at a bargain price or by disseminating untrue bad news about the corporation before seeking to purchase the shares. Thus, the SEC promulgated Rule 10b–5 under its broad authority to adopt rules designed to prevent and remedy fraud, and to the extent possible, make a level playing field for transactions in shares. Prior to the mid–1970s courts generally interpreted Rule 10b–5 liberally in part because state law principles were seen as not providing adequate protection for stockholder interests. As a result, plaintiffs increasingly chose to file law suits in Federal courts under Rule 10b–5 rather than in state courts under state law. Beginning in 1975, however, the United States Supreme Court began to issue opinions that limited the scope of Rule 10b–5 and other provisions of federal securities law that had been interpreted as providing a general private cause of action for injured stockholders. When reading cases relating to Rule 10b–5 and related principles, it is important to consider the period in which the decision was issued. Nevertheless, today, Rule 10b–5 still is the single most important source of federal law in connection with trading in securities.

2. General Principles

Rule 10b–5 has the same force as a federal statute. Its violation may be made the basis of a criminal prosecution, an enforcement action brought by the SEC, or a private civil action by an injured stockholder. Although the Supreme Court has been reluctant since the mid–1970s to recognize implied private rights of action under the federal securities laws, it is clear that the private cause of action under Rule 10b–5 continues to exist. *Herman & MacLean v. Huddleston*, 459 U.S. 375, 103 S.Ct. 683 (1983). The Court also recognizes a private cause of action under Rule 14a–9. *J.I. Case v. Borak*, 377 U.S. 426, 432, 84 S.Ct. 1555 (1964).

a. Section 27 of the 1934 Act provides that all actions arising under that Act are subject to exclusive federal jurisdiction. Thus, state courts do not have jurisdiction to adjudicate Rule 10b–5 claims. While the doctrine of pendent jurisdiction permits the joinder of both state and federal claims arising from the same transaction in a Rule 10b–5 case, a Rule 10b–5 claim cannot be joined with a state cause of action in a state court.

b. There is worldwide service of process in Rule 10b–5 cases. There are also liberal venue provisions. State security for expenses statutes and other procedural rules are not applicable in suits brought under federal law. Procedure in federal court is generally simpler than in state court and discovery rights are broader.

c. Rule 10b–5 is applicable to any fraud in connection with the purchase or sale of any security, including those issued by closely held corporations. *Landreth Timber Co. v. Landreth*, 471 U.S. 681, 105 S.Ct. 2297 (1985) (fraudulent sale of stock in connection with sale of a small business).

d. *Blue Chip Stamps v. Manor Drug Stores*, 421 U.S. 723, 95 S.Ct. 1917 (1975) holds that only purchasers or sellers of securities may sue under Rule 10b–5. This doctrine is based on the early decision of *Birnbaum v. Newport Steel Corp.*, 193 F.2d 461 (2d Cir. 1952) and is sometimes referred to as the *Birnbaum rule*.

e. The plaintiff in a Rule 10b–5 action must allege and prove *scienter*, a term that is defined as a mental state embracing some level of intent to deceive, manipulate or defraud. Negligence is not sufficient. *Ernst & Ernst v. Hochfelder*, 425 U.S. 185, 96 S.Ct. 1375 (1976). *See also Aaron v. S.E.C.*, 446 U.S. 680, 100 S.Ct. 1945 (1980) (SEC enforcement action).

f. *Santa Fe Industries v. Green*, 430 U.S. 462 (1977), involved a short form merger at an allegedly unfair price. The case sets forth the basic principle that Rule 10b–5 applies only to situations involving deception. Unfair transactions that are adequately disclosed cannot be attacked under Rule 10b–5.

g. The statute of limitations for Rule 10b–5 cases was set as one year after discovery or three years after the transaction in question in *Lampf, Pleva, Lipkind, Prupis & Pettigrow v. Gilbertson*, 501 U.S. 350 (1991). Before this decision, lower federal courts had generally held that the applicable statute of limitations should be borrowed from state law. The Supreme Court ordered that the *Lampf* holding be applied retroactively. Congress then enacted a statute that sought to make this holding prospective only, but in *Plaut v. Spendthrift Farm, Inc.*, 514 U.S. 211, 115 S.Ct. 1447 (1995), the Court held that this statute was unconstitutional to the extent it sought to revive cases that had been finally dismissed pursuant to the *Lampf* holding. In 2002, section 804 of the Sarbanes Oxley Act extended the statute of limitations for private securities fraud claims to the earlier of two years after discovery of the facts constituting the violation or five years after the violation. This new statute of limitations applies to proceedings commenced after July 30, 2002.

h. Claims may be brought under Rule 10b–5 even though under the same factual situation a claim could also be brought under the more specific provisions of the Securities Act of 1933 or the Securities Exchange Act of 1934. *Herman & MacLean v. Huddleston*, 459 U.S. 375, 103 S.Ct. 683 (1983).

i. Rule 10b–5 proscribes not only affirmative misrepresentations and half-truths, but also a failure to disclose material facts that are necessary in order to make the statements made, in light of the circumstances under which they were made, not misleading. Rule 10b–5 does not itself impose a duty to disclose. Rather it affords a federal remedy in connection with misrepresentations and omissions that are otherwise in violation of a duty to speak the truth.

    • Courts agree that there is a clear duty to refrain from making affirmative misrepresentations. Thus, if a corporation chooses to issue a press release, it must tell the whole truth. For example, the financial analyst who touts a stock without disclosing that he has a financial interest in selling that stock violates Rule 10b–5. *Zweig v. Hearst Corp.*, 594 F.2d 1261 (9th Cir. 1979).

- A duty to disclose may arise as a result of a requirement to file a public document.

- A duty to disclose (or refrain from trading) may arise if a corporation or its agent possesses material non-public information about the corporation's business. The theory is that the corporation and its agents have a general fiduciary duty to use such information only for the benefit of all stockholders.

- Disclosure is required if undisclosed information renders previous public statements by the corporation misleading or if rumors can be traced to a source within the issuer. *In re Time Warner, Inc. Securities Litigation*, 9 F.3d 259 (2d Cir. 1993).

j. Rule 10b–5 applies only if there is failure to disclose a *material* fact. The test of what is material is whether a reasonable person would regard the information as important in deciding how to act. *TSC Industries v. Northway, Inc.*, 426 U.S. 438, 96 S.Ct. 2126 (1976). Disclosure of pending merger negotiations has been a particularly troublesome issue. Several courts held that disclosure was required only when an agreement in principle had been reached and that prior to that time a general denial was not misleading. *Greenfield v. Heublein, Inc.*, 742 F.2d 751 (3d Cir. 1984). The Supreme Court rejected this bright line test. *Basic Inc. v. Levinson*, 485 U.S. 224, 108 S.Ct. 978 (1988). Although the court agreed that it may sometimes serve the interests of stockholders for the company to deny that it is in negotiation in order to complete the deal on favorable terms, the Court nonetheless held that the general rule as stated in TSC applies. The practical effect may be to cause issuers to adopt a no comment policy with respect to all inquiries about negotiations.

k. In a case of failure to disclose a material fact, proof of reliance on the omission may be inferred and need not be separately established. *Affiliated Ute Citizens v. United States*, 406 U.S. 128 (1972). In the case of a misrepresentation relating to a publicly traded security, a purchaser or seller may be able to recover without establishing reliance on the misrepresentation under the principle of *Basic v. Levinson*. The theory is that investors rely on the efficiency of the securities markets in establishing an appropriate price for the shares. This principle is generally referred to as the fraud on the market theory. In *Basic*, the Court adopted this theory to the extent of creating a rebuttable presumption of reliance, thereby placing the burden of showing a lack of reliance upon the defendants.

l.   The SEC has adopted numerous safe harbor rules designed to permit corporations and insiders to engage in trading without fear of running afoul of Rule 10b–5. For example, it might be argued that a corporation's repurchase of its own shares is a per se violation because it indicates that the corporation likely has information indicating that the price should be higher. Thus, the SEC adopted Rule 10b–18 providing guidelines for such transactions.

3.   Securities Fraud Class Actions

A corporation may violate Rule 10b–5 if it makes a false statement in a filing or a press release or even in a conference call. Although *Blue Chip Stamps* requires that a *plaintiff* be a purchaser or seller of shares, there is no similar requirement for *defendants*. A person may violate Rule 10b–5 even though he neither purchases nor sells a security. For example, a publicly traded corporation that issues a press release knows that the market will react. By definition, such a press release is *in connection with* the purchase of sale of securities. It has long been clear that stockholders who buy or sell in actual reliance on a false press release may recover damages from the corporation. *See Mitchell v. Texas Gulf Sulphur Co.*, 446 F.2d 90, 91 (10th Cir. 1971). A class action on behalf of all who bought or sold during the fraud period under FRCP 23 is also possible. Indeed, the official commentary to FRCP 23 notes that the rule may be particularly useful for such cases. The problem is that questions of individual reliance may make a class action impractical. This issue was avoided in omission cases by *Affiliated Ute Citizens v. United States*, 406 U.S. 128, 92 S.Ct. 1456 (1972). As for cases based on an affirmative misrepresentation, class actions became practical with the 1988 decision by the United States Supreme Court in *Basic v. Levinson*, 485 U.S. 224, 108 S.Ct. 978 (1988) (upholding the fraud on the market theory presuming reliance on the integrity of market prices). *See also Blackie v. Barrack*, 524 F.2d 891 (9th Cir. 1975).

a.   Federal securities law requires corporations registered under § 12 of the 1934 Act periodically to file (and disseminate publicly) information about their business and finances. Prior to 1979, the SEC strongly discouraged the inclusion in such reports of *forward-looking information*, such as projections of future performance even though such information can be quite important to investors. In 1979, the SEC reversed its policy and adopted safe harbor rules for forward-looking information under both the 1933 Act (Rule 175) and the 1934 Act (Rule 3b–6). Under the safe harbor rules, a forward looking statement in a filed document is false and misleading only if it is made or reaffirmed without a reasonable basis or disclosed other than in good faith.

b. Nevertheless, many companies—particularly growth companies—became the target of class actions if they made optimistic projections and that failed to materialize. Defendants complained that plaintiff law firms often filed suit in order to extort settlements. Defendants also claimed that these law firms kept a stable of plaintiffs in whose name suit might be filed whenever a significant change in the price of a stock indicated that there may have been false information at work in the market. The courts generally permitted the plaintiff who was first to file to be the lead counsel, prompting a race to the courthouse in many cases. The filing of a suit was followed immediately by a demand for extensive discovery that many defendants saw as a fishing expedition to find a more solid basis for the action.

c. Federal courts faced with proliferating securities fraud class actions attempted to discourage them in several ways. They tightened the requirement for pleading by insisting that fraud be pleaded with particularity (as required by FRCP 9) and that the allegations give rise to a strong inference that the statements were made with scienter (fraudulent intent). They adopted the so-called *bespeaks caution doctrine* that precludes reliance on forward-looking statements if the document contains specific warnings that the investment is risky and that projections might not be fulfilled. *See In re Donald J. Trump Casino Securities Litigation–Taj Mahal Litigation*, 7 F.3d 357 (3d Cir. 1993).

d. In 1995 Congress enacted the Private Securities Litigation Reform Act of 1995 (PSLRA) to deal with the perceived evil of class action law suits brought against publicly held corporations for false or misleading statements or projections. This legislation was vetoed by President Clinton but the veto was overridden. PSLRA tightened the requirements for class action securities litigation and created a number of novel or experimental litigation devices.

- Plaintiffs must file a sworn statement they reviewed and authorized the filing and did not purchase securities at the direction of counsel or to qualify to act as plaintiff. A lead plaintiff may not serve as such more than three times in the previous five years. The lead plaintiff's compensation is limited to a proportionate share of any recovery.

- Courts are directed to select lead plaintiff and lead counsel based on a presumption that the plaintiff with the largest financial stake should be lead plaintiff.

- A statutory safe harbor for projections is created. A defendant is not liable for misrepresentations or omissions if a statement is (1) identified as a forward looking statement and (2) is accompanied by meaningful cautionary statements identifying factors that could cause results to differ materially from those protected in the statement. Alternatively, a defendant is protected by the statutory safe harbor unless the plaintiff can show that the person made the statement with actual knowledge that it was false or misleading.

- Courts must stay all discovery pending the disposition of a motion to dismiss. It is unlawful for any defendant to destroy relevant evidence during the stay.

- To avoid the naming of deep pockets as defendants (even though their involvement is slight), PSLRA provides for proportionate liability for parties who are found not to have committed knowing violations.

- Notice of proposed settlements must be given to all members of the class.

- PSLRA creates a presumption that sanctions should be imposed on plaintiff counsel for violations of FRCP 11. A similar presumption is not imposed on defendants' counsel.

- PSLRA mandates a strict standard that the facts be pleaded with particularity and must establish a strong inference that the misstatements were made with *scienter.*

- Independent public auditors must also report illegal conduct that they discover to the appropriate level of management, the board of directors, or the SEC. Auditors have no personal liability to third persons for failing to comply, but the SEC may impose civil penalties for failing to comply with these requirements.

- PSLRA contains a formula for limiting damages to the loss attributable to the fraud by determining the post fraud price on the basis of average price for 90 days following corrective disclosure.

- It provides that the SEC (but not private plaintiffs) may sue aiders and abettors, thus partially overruling *Central Bank.*

e. Although fewer securities fraud class actions were filed immediately after enactment of PSLRA, the number of actions has since increased and PSLRA seems to have had little lasting effect in terms of discouraging such actions.

f. In response to PSLRA, some securities fraud class actions were filed in state court, allegedly to avoid the limitations of PSLRA. As a result, Congress enacted the Securities Fraud Litigation Uniform Standards Act of 1998 (SLUSA) which preempts all state law securities fraud class actions based on failure of disclosure. SLUSA applies to state law actions based on the same facts and involving 50 or more plaintiffs whether or not the action (or actions) are formally styled as a class action (or even consolidated into a single action). SLUSA permits the defendant in a covered state law action to remove the action to federal court in order to have it dismissed. SLUSA contains an exception for state law actions— the so-called Delaware carve out—involving questions of internal affairs such as duty of care and duty of loyalty issues. Although such actions are almost always styled as derivative actions in which the corporation itself is the single nominal plaintiff, a derivative action may involve significant disclosure issues particularly if a stockholder vote is involved.

4. Mismanagement

Rule 10b–5 is potentially applicable when a corporation issues or acquires its own shares or the shares of another company because the phrase *purchase or sale* is broad enough to cover such transactions. If shares are issued or acquired by a corporation as a result of deception or a failure of someone (such as a director or officer or agent) to disclose material facts to the corporation, the corporation may have a claim under Rule 10b–5, and this claim may be asserted derivatively by a minority stockholder. *Drachman v. Harvey,* 453 F.2d 722 (2d Cir. 1971).

a. A rule 10b–5 violation also occurs if the corporation is fraudulently induced to issue shares for inadequate compensation even though such conduct also constitutes a violation of state-created fiduciary duties.

b. The potential use of Rule 10b–5 in connection with corporate level transactions is largely limited to mergers and other fundamental transactions because it is in such transactions that the corporation in effect purchases or sells shares (whether its own or those of another corporation). Although it appeared that the use of Rule 10b–5 in such settings was precluded by the Supreme Court in *Santa Fe Industries, Inc. v. Green,* 430 U.S. 462, 97 S.Ct. 1292 (1977) (short form merger in which plaintiff had no material use for the withheld information), a few such cases have since arisen. *See Goldberg v. Meridor,* 567 F.2d 209 (2d Cir. 1977). The dearth of such cases is attributable to several factors. First, such cases usually involve a proxy solicitation, triggering Rule 14a–9. These cases may also raise questions about whether the plaintiff has a material use for the undisclosed information. *See Virginia Bankshares, Inc. v. Sandberg,* 501 U.S. 1083 (1991). Second, state law has become much more responsive in such a setting. *See Weinberger v. UOP, Inc.,* 457 A.2d 701 (Del. 1983). In addition, if the case involves the issuance of securities by the defendant corporation, the 1933 Act may apply.

5. Other Applications

Rule 10b–5 has many applications outside the context of corporation law. For example, it provides a remedy for individual investors in connection with the mismanagement of an investment account. It may also apply to fraud in connection with the sale of a business where the sale is accomplished by a transfer of stock.

C. INSIDER TRADING

A director, officer, agent, or major stockholder of a corporation may have material non-public knowledge about corporate affairs that will likely affect the price of the shares when it is disclosed. As a result, such an insider may be tempted to buy or sell shares, depending on the nature of the information, without first disclosing the information. Such trading is called *insider trading.* Rule 10b–5 is applicable to trading by individuals and therefore constitutes a broad prohibition against trading on the basis of inside information by anyone who receives the information from the issuer in connection with a relationship to the issuer that gives rise to a duty not to use the information for personal gain (including accountants, lawyers, investment bankers, and other constructive insiders).

1. Early Cases—Disclose or Abstain

The basic principle that trading on inside information violates Rule 10b–5 was first established in *Cady, Roberts & Co.,* 40 S.E.C. 907 (1961), and *S.E.C. v. Texas Gulf Sulphur Co.,* 401 F.2d 833 (2d Cir. 1968).

a. *Cady Roberts* was an SEC enforcement proceeding arising from a broker's sales of stock in on non-public information that a corporation planned to cut its dividend. The information was obtained from a partner who sat on the board of directors of the issuing corporation. Cady Roberts seems to take the absolute position that trading while in possession of non-public information regardless of the source of the information or the traders relationship to the source is a violation.

b. *Texas Gulf Sulphur* was an appeal from an SEC enforcement proceeding arising from purchases by directors, officers, and employees of TGS on non-public information that TGS had discovered an unusually rich deposit of ore in Ontario. In addition, the corporation itself issued a false press release essentially denying the rumors about the ore strike. TGS holds that officers, directors, and employees of an issuer who know of a material favorable development as a result of their position with the corporation violate Rule 10b–5 if they purchase shares or options before the information is released. TGS also holds that insiders must wait until the information has been reasonably disseminated to the investing public through wire services and the like before they may trade and suggests that *tipees* (persons who obtain material information before it is publicly released) have an obligation not to trade on that information.

c. In *Shapiro v. Merrill Lynch, Pierce, Fenner & Smith, Inc.*, 495 F.2d 228 (2d Cir. 1974), a brokerage firm obtained information about a corporation in connection with a contemplated debt financing before the information was publicly available. The brokerage firm violated Rule 10b–5, because it traded before the information was released. To avoid violations of Rule 10b–5 in this situation, brokerage firms try to maintain separation (a Chinese Wall) between their investment banking (underwriting) operations and their brokerage (sales) operations. The failure to maintain such separation was also central many of the abuses that arose in connection with IPOs in the late 1990s.

2. Later Cases—The Misappropriation Theory

In the late 1970s, the Justice Department (largely under the direction of Rudolph Guiliani who was at the time the United States Attorney for the Southern District of New York) began a vigorous campaign to prosecute insider trading cases as crimes. These cases raised several difficult issues with the definition of what constitutes insider trading and with the scope of federal securities law generally.

a. *Chiarella v. United States*, 445 U.S. 222, 100 S.Ct. 1108 (1980), was the first insider trading case to reach the Supreme Court. It involved the criminal prosecution of a low level employee of a legal printing firm who regularly handled disclosure documents in connection with planned tender offers and who bought stock in the target companies before announcement of the offers. The Supreme Court reversed the conviction because the defendant owed no duty to the target or its stockholders (other than a general duty to refrain from affirmative misrepresentations). The court reasoned that the bidder was free to purchase shares before announcement of the offer and that therefore the printer and its employees violated no duty to the sellers of the shares, because the printer had been retained by the bidder. Chief Justice Burger dissented, arguing that the employee had a duty to his employer not to use information entrusted to the printer for business use only and thus could be held liable for having misappropriated the information for personal gain.

b. Following *Chiarella,* the SEC adopted Rule 14e–3 making it unlawful for any person who obtains advance information about a tender offer to use that information in connection with a securities transaction. This rule (together with the misappropriation theory advocated by Chief Justice Burger) was ultimately upheld in *United States v. O'Hagan,* 521 U.S. 642, 117 S.Ct. 2199 (1997), as a reasonable antifraud rule even though it might capture some instances of insider trading not involving a breach of fiduciary duty.

c. In *Dirks v. S.E.C.,* 463 U.S. 646, 103 S.Ct. 3255 (1983), the Supreme Court held that a tippee violates Rule 10b–5 only if the tipper breaches a fiduciary duty in disclosing the information to the tippee and the tippee is aware of the breach. Such a breach may be established for this purpose by showing that the insider-tipper disclosed the information for the purpose of obtaining an improper benefit. The tipper is also liable for unlawful insider trading by the tippee. In Dirks, the tipper was an employee of an insurance company that had fraudulently overstated its assets, and the employee was apparently motivated only by a desire to expose the fraud and not by the prospect of any monetary gain.

d. *Carpenter v. United States,* 484 U.S. 19, 108 S.Ct. 316 (1987) involved a criminal prosecution of Foster Winans, a Wall Street Journal writer who told friends that certain corporations would be favorably commented on in the *Heard on the Street* column. His friends traded on the information, and Winans shared in the profits. Winans was convicted on two theories: (1) insider trading under the misappropriation theory, and (2) mail and wire fraud. The Supreme Court split four to four on the insider trading theory, but agreed unanimously on the mail and wire fraud theory.

e. *United States v. Chestman*, 947 F.2d 551 (2d Cir. 1991), holds that disclosure of inside information by one family member to another, who in turn discloses the information to a broker, does not violate Rule 10b–5 because a mere family relationship does not give rise to a fiduciary duty.

f. In *United States v. O'Hagan*, 521 U.S. 642, 117 S.Ct. 2199 (1997), the Supreme Court upheld the misappropriation theory (as well as Rule 14e–3) in a case involving a lawyer who used information about a planned tender offer by a client for another company. But consistent with *Dirks*, the court based its holding on a duty not to use business information for personal profit.

3. Insider Trading Legislation and Rules

a. In 1984, Congress enacted the Insider Trading Sanctions Act (ITSA) which provides that the SEC may recover the profit made (or loss avoided) from insider trading plus an additional fine equal to three times that amount. In 1988, Congress enacted the Insider Trading and Securities Fraud Enforcement Act (ITSFEA) extending ITSA in a variety of ways. By the enactment of ITSA and ITSFEA, Congress has expressly approved the basic policy of enforcing sanctions against insider trading under Rule 10b–5.

b. ITSA and ITSFEA address a fundamental problem with respect to the remedies for insider trading. If the insider is liable only for the amount of the gain or loss avoided, there is little reason not to trade on inside information. If one is caught one simply gives back the gain. Thus, simple disgorgement of ill-gotten gains is not a significant deterrent. On the other hand, if an insider is liable for the losses of all who traded at or about the same time, the damages imposed would often far exceed the actual harm. ITSFEA also imposes for individuals a minimum fine of $100,000 and five years imprisonment and a maximum fine of up to $1,000,000 and 10 years imprisonment. For defendants other than natural persons fines may range up to $2,500,000. ITSFEA also adds a bounty provision that grants awards to informants of amounts not to exceed 10 percent of the penalties recovered as a result of the informant's efforts.

c. Under § 20A of the 1934 Act (added by ITSFEA) a person violating the insider trading prohibitions is liable to contemporaneous traders of the security even though there is no privity between the insider and the person trading. Liability under § 20A is limited to the total profit gained or loss avoided by the person violating the insider trading prohibitions, and is further reduced by any disgorgement of profits ordered by a court at the instance of the SEC.

d. Under ITSFEA the employer of an individual who engages in insider trading may also be liable as a controlling person. In order to recover from a controlling person, the SEC must establish either that the controlling person knew or recklessly disregarded the fact that such controlled person was likely to violate the Act or (for firms in the securities industry) knowingly or recklessly failed to establish, maintain or enforce policies or procedures designed to prevent insider trading.

e. The SEC has taken the position that trading while in mere possession of inside information may constitute insider trading, but the courts have ruled that a violation requires actual use of the information. *SEC v. Adler*, 137 F.3d 1325 (11th Cir. 1998). Thus, an insider who plans in advance to sell shares periodically pursuant to a plan may proceed with the plan despite coming into possession of new (adverse) information. In 2000, the SEC adopted a safe harbor rule (Rule 10b5–1) providing guidelines for such plans.

4. Criminal Prosecution and Civil Enforcement Actions

The Federal Government generally views insider trading as a serious offense that should be prosecuted vigorously, both civilly and criminally. This is true despite extensive academic commentary that suggests that insider trading in many instances harms no one and may be beneficial in several ways. The SEC has pursued individuals making relatively small profits on the basis of inside information.

a. Although the SEC has the authority to enforce the securities laws by means of civil action for an injunction or fine (an *enforcement action*), the Department of Justice (DOJ) has jurisdiction over criminal prosecution. It is quite common, especially in high profile cases, for both agencies to act. Moreover, many offenses may give rise to a private right of action and may also violate state law. Thus, a defendant may be subject to multiple actions for any given violation.

b. A violation of federal securities law must be *willful* in order to be prosecuted criminally. But given that a violation of Rule 10b–5 requires *scienter,* virtually every violation of Rule 10b–5 is also a crime.

c. The primary goal of many SEC enforcement actions is to impose an injunction on the defendant prohibiting future violations of the securities laws. Although an injunction that merely requires compliance with the law may seem to be a rather mild sanction, it has the effect of criminalizing any future violation and affording a summary remedy in the form of civil contempt.

D. SECTION 16 OF THE SECURITIES EXCHANGE ACT

Section 16 of the 1934 Act addresses trading by directors, officers, and ten percent stockholders of SEC registered companies. Section 16(a) requires reporting of all transactions in issuer stock by such persons and prohibits their engaging in any short sale of issuer stock. Section 16(b) provides that the gain (or loss avoided) from a purchase and sale (or sale and purchase) of equity securities within a six month period may be recovered by the issuer.

1. General Principles

a. Section 16(a) requires all persons subject to Section 16 to file reports with the SEC. The first report must be filed within ten days of the date one becomes subject to the requirement and must describe the person's initial ownership of the issuer's shares. Subsequent reports must be filed within two days of any purchase or sale thereafter. The SEC publishes this information so that it is possible to identify violations from the public record. Registered companies are required to disclose failures to comply with § 16(a). In 1991 and 1996, the SEC adopted rules identifying which officers are subject to § 16(a). Officers covered by § 16 include officers referred to in the corporation's 10-K and officers designated by the corporation as having significant policy making roles. Effectively these regulations determine the scope of § 16(b) as well as § 16(a) because persons exempt from the reporting requirements of § 16(a) are also exempt from § 16(b).

b. Section 16(b) is applicable only to directors, officers, and ten percent stockholders of companies registered under § 12 of the Securities Exchange Act. In contrast, Rule 10b–5 covers all persons and all companies. Section 16(b) is a bright line rule that creates automatic liability. It is unnecessary to show actual use of inside information. A sale for entirely justifiable reasons (such as to cover unexpected medical expenses) triggers § 16(b) if there has been any offsetting purchase within the previous six months or there is a subsequent purchase within the following six months. In contrast, Rule 10b–5 requires proof of *scienter*. A recovery under § 16(b) is payable only to the corporation. In contrast, Rule 10b–5 authorizes private damage recovery in many situations by buyers or sellers.

c. Attribution rules apply to § 16(b) so that transactions in the name of spouses, relatives, or nominees may be attributed to an officer, director, or ten percent stockholder. In *Blau v. Lehman*, 368 U.S. 403, 82 S.Ct. 451 (1962), a partner in Lehman Brothers was a director of the issuer. Unknown to him, Lehman Brothers engaged in purchases and sales of the issuer's stock (but never became a ten per cent holder). The Court held that the partnership might be considered a director only if the partnership deputized the partner to represent the partnership on issuer's board of directors. *See also Feder v. Martin Marietta Corp.*, 406 F.2d 260 (2d Cir. 1969).

d. Section 16(b) is applicable to offsetting paired purchases and sales (or sales and purchases) of an equity security of the issuer within any six-month period. But a sale made six months plus one day after the purchase does not trigger section 16(b). Section 16(b) differs from Rule 10b–5 in that Rule 10b–5 may be violated by a single transaction or a single sale without any off-setting requirements.

e. The words *purchase* and *sale* are construed broadly. A transaction is considered to be a purchase or a sale for purposes of § 16(b) if it is of a kind that can lend itself to the abuse through short swing trading. Under some circumstances a sale may occur as a result of a gift, redemption, conversion or exchange pursuant to a merger. In 1991, the SEC adopted regulations addressing derivative securities under § 16(b). The acquisition of a warrant to acquire a security may be treated as a purchase of the underlying security. The purchase of a derivative security, such as a call or put, may also be the purchase or sale of the underlying security. Section 16(a) does not prohibit a *covered* short sale—also called a *short sale against the box*—as a way of *hedging* against the decline in price of issuer stock. The SEC has authority to exempt classes of transactions from § 16(b). It has exercised this authority in a number of circumstances. The most important is rule 16b–3, relating to stock option plans, stock purchase plans, and compensation plans of various types that are based on stock prices.

f. A purchase and sale matched under § 16(b) must generally be of the same class of stock. But if preferred is convertible into common and is trading at or close to the conversion price, matching may be permitted because the two securities then are essentially trading as economic equivalents.

g. Purchases and sales are matched so as to squeeze out all possible profit by matching the highest sale price with the lowest purchase price, the next highest sale price with the next lowest purchase price, and so forth.

h. Even though profits are recoverable by the corporation, corporations may be reluctant to enforce § 16(b) against its own directors, officers, and substantial stockholders. But, § 16(b) expressly recognizes that enforcement by a derivative action brought by a single stockholder is permissible. Like Rule 10b–5, the jurisdiction of § 16(b) is exclusively federal.

2. Application of Section 16(b) in Takeover Situations

During the 1970s, the United States Supreme Court struggled with the application of § 16(b) to takeover situations where an unsuccessful bidder acquires more than ten percent of the target's shares and then sells that interest (or has it merged out) within six months thereafter.

a. *Reliance Elec. Co. v. Emerson Elec. Co.*, 404 U.S. 418, 92 S.Ct. 596 (1972), holds that a 13.2 per cent stockholder could dispose of its holdings by first selling just over 3.2 per cent of the target's shares subject to § 16(b) and then disposing of the remainder free of § 16(b) requirements because it was no longer a ten percent stockholder.

b. *Kern County Land Co. v. Occidental Petroleum Corp.*, 411 U.S. 582, 93 S.Ct. 1736 (1973) holds that a forced sale pursuant to a merger is not covered by § 16(b).

c. *Foremost–McKesson, Inc. v. Provident Securities Co.*, 423 U.S. 232, 96 S.Ct. 508 (1976), holds that the purchase by which a bidder exceeds the ten percent threshold is not a § 16(b) purchase. The rationale is that a ten percent stockholder is covered by § 16(b) because a ten percent stockholder is presumed to have access to inside information. Thus, a purchase by which one *becomes* a ten percent stockholder is presumed to be made without the benefit of inside information.

3. Section 16(b) in Perspective

People do not knowingly violate § 16(b). The penalties are simply too great and the chance of discovery almost certain. Most violations appear to be a result of mistake or ignorance rather than actual misuse of inside information.

a. Most inadvertent violations probably are a result of a failure to keep track of precisely when the six month period ends. Other causes of inadvertent violations include a failure to appreciate how broadly the words purchase and sale are construed in the case of unusual transactions, uncertainty as to whether a specific person is covered by § 16(b), the failure to recognize that attribution rules may apply. For example, it is not clear whether if a director who resigns from a board and then immediately sells his shares should be viewed as within § 16(b).

b. Despite its shortcomings, § 16(b) has effectively eliminated the evil of in-and-out trading that existed prior to 1934. In the 1990s, proposals have been made to repeal this section because its application is erratic and insider trading is now more broadly delineated and policed under Rule 10b–5.

c. Reports under § 16(a) are often published in the financial press and have been used by some to attempt to devise trading strategies on the theory that reported insider trades contain implicit information about company prospects. Generally, these strategies have not led to gains.

■ XIV. SALES OF CONTROL & TENDER OFFERS

This chapter addresses the variety of ways by which control of a corporation may be transferred from one party to another, including sales of control and tender offers. Such a transaction may be friendly or hostile. Friendly transfers of control may also be affected by a merger or sale of assets. Such *fundamental transactions* or *organic changes* are addressed in another chapter. If the transaction is hostile, it will almost certainly be accomplished by one of the methods discussed here. But it is quite common following a hostile takeover for a corporation to engage in some sort of merger or sale of assets to complete the transaction. A hostile takeover may also be affected by means of a proxy fight. An insurgent group may undertake a proxy fight without acquiring a significant number of shares, though it is uncommon. Nevertheless, because proxy fights are ultimately about stockholder voting, they are addressed in that chapter and not here.

A. SALES OF CONTROL

The general rule in the United States is that a controlling shareholder may sell a controlling block of shares to a purchaser thereby transferring working control of the corporation to the purchaser. A sale of controlling shares is almost always at a premium over the market price (or the price a minority stockholder would be able to command). Although a controlling stockholder owes a fiduciary duty to the minority not to use control to exact an improper benefit from the corporation, there is no general requirement that a controlling stockholder seek a buyer who is willing to buy all the shares from all the stockholders or that the controlling stockholder share the control premium with the minority or the corporation.

1. Control Premiums

Shares owned by a controlling shareholder command a premium over other shares because they represent the power to control the business. A controlling stockholder typically has the power to elect the entire board of directors, which in turn carries the power to establish business policies, including those with regard to the payment (or not) of dividends, reinvestment of available cash, as well as overall business strategy. A controlling stockholder may also effectively designate the officers of the corporation as well as their compensation.

a. This premium is usually referred to as the *control premium* and may be expressed as a per share differential or as an additional lump sum payment for the controlling shares. Shares which carry with them control of the corporation are often called *control shares*.

b. A controlling stockholder may not use control to extract improper benefits to the exclusion of minority stockholders. *See Sinclair Oil Corp. v. Levien*, 280 A.2d 717 (Del.1971). But control is valuable for several other reasons:

- the controlling stockholder avoids the risk inherent in management by others.

- the controlling stockholder may change business policies in such a way as to increase the value of the business.

- the seller of control will insist on some premium if only because it is presumable that the buyer perceives a gain from the transaction whatever the source.

c. It is nevertheless possible for a controlling stockholder to use control in such a way as to extract benefits to the exclusion and detriment of minority stockholders. Such tactics are usually referred to as *looting* the corporation.

d. In the case of a publicly traded company, the market price of company stock will presumably reflect the danger of looting. If the market perceives that the buyer of control is likely to engage in some form of looting, presumably stock price will fall. If stock price rises, presumably the market thinks that the buyer of control is likely to make the company more profitable.

2. Looting

The US rule is generally based on idea that looting can be addressed when it happens. Eliminating private sales of control would make acquisitions more difficult and expensive than necessary. If looting is suspected, the looter is primarily liable, but the seller of control may be liable on various theories ranging from breach of fiduciary duty, to aiding and abetting, to conspiracy. Generally a controlling shareholder may sell controlling shares for whatever price he or she can obtain.

a. The virtually unanimous position of courts is that there is nothing inherently wrong in receiving a premium for control shares. *Zetlin v. Hanson Holdings*, Inc., 397 N.E.2d 387 (N.Y. 1979); *Tryon v. Smith*, 229 P.2d 251 (Ore.1951); *McDaniel v. Painter*, 418 F.2d 545 (10th Cir.1969). But some courts have imposed duties on the selling shareholder with respect to investigating the honesty of the purchaser.

b. A controlling shareholder who sells his shares to a buyer who thereafter loots the corporation may be liable for any loss suffered by the corporation. Some cases take the position that the controlling share-holder has a duty to make a reasonable investigation of potential purchasers. *Gerdes v. Reynolds*, 28 N.Y.S.2d 622 (N.Y. 1941); *DeBaun v. First Western Bank and Trust Co.*, 120 Cal.Rptr. 354 (Cal.App.1975). Other cases take the position that the controlling shareholder has a duty to investigate potential purchasers only if there is reason to believe that the purchaser may loot the corporation. *Clagett v. Hutchison*, 583 F.2d 1259 (4th Cir.1978); *Swinney v. Keebler Co.*, 480 F.2d 573 (4th Cir.1973). PCG 5.16(b) states that investigation is required when it is apparent from the circumstances that the purchaser is likely to violate a duty of fair dealing. Danger signs include, (1) an obviously excessive price for the shares willingly paid, (2) an unusual interest in the liquid and readily salable assets owned by the corporation, (3) insistence by the buyers on an immediate transfer of control, (4) insistence by the buyers that the liquid assets be made available immediately, (5) little interest by the purchasers in the operation of the corporation's business. *Swinney v. Keebler Co.*, 480 F.2d 573 (4th Cir.1973) holds that on the facts of that case no duty to investigate arose even though with hindsight several of these factors existed. Investment companies that have liquid and readily salable assets are a likely target for looting but many looting cases involve regular business corporations.

c.   If the duty of reasonable investigation is not met, liability may be imposed on the seller based on negligence. Recovery is based on the damage suffered—the amount looted by the purchasers—rather than by the purchase price paid or the amount of the control premium. *DeBaun v. First Western Bank & Trust Co.*, 120 Cal.Rptr. 354 (Cal.App.1975); *Harris v. Carter*, 582 A.2d 222 (Del.Ch.1990).

3.   Other Theories

In addition to arguments based on possible looting, courts have considered other theories that might be used to hold a controlling shareholder liable to return a premium received for a sale of control. Again, most cases hold that a controlling shareholder may retain any control premium paid, but a few cases have compelled the controlling shareholder to share the control premium with minority shareholders.

a.   Some cases contain broad statements to the effect that a director owes a fiduciary duty to the corporation and to the minority shareholders, but they do not explain when the premium may be recovered and when it may not. *See Perlman v. Feldmann,* 219 F.2d 173 (2d Cir.1955).

b. Some cases have permitted the recovery of a control premium on a theory of usurpation of corporate opportunity. For example, if the purchaser first offers to buy the assets of the corporation at an attractive price and the controlling shareholder suggests that the transaction be recast in the form of a purchase of the controlling shares, the opportunity to sell the assets may be a corporate opportunity belonging to all the shareholders, rather than to the majority shareholder. *Perlman v. Feldmann* may be explained on this basis. *See also Birnbaum v. Newport Steel Corp.,* 193 F.2d 461 (2d Cir. 1952) (same case under federal securities law). In addition, the subject company in *Perlman v. Feldmann* was precluded from raising the price of steel because of wartime price controls. Thus, the sale of control to steel users at a premium may be seen as a way for the controlling stockholder to gain the benefit of customers' willingness to pay higher prices without sharing what would have been higher profits with minority shareholders.

c. Some cases have viewed the payment of a control premium as a sale of corporate office rather than a sale of shares. A shareholder owning or controlling less than a majority of the shares may have effective working control of the corporation when other shareholders are numerous and disorganized. If the shareholder's interest is very small, the sale of that interest at a premium is more likely to be viewed as a sale of office rather than a sale of shares. Because sale of office is against public policy, the excess payment may be recovered by the corporation for the benefit of the minority shareholders.

d. Some cases have imposed liability for a control premium on a theory of nondisclosure or misrepresentation.

e. Some cases have imposed liability for the control premium on the basis of the extreme unfairness of the transaction.

f. Where a control premium is recoverable, courts have permitted either the corporation or the minority shareholders to recover, depending on the theory adopted. If the theory of recovery is looting, corporate opportunity, corporate action, or the sale of corporate office, logically only the corporation should recover and a suit by a shareholder should be considered exclusively derivative in nature. If the theory is misrepresentation or violation of rule 10b–5, the minority shareholders should recover in their own right.

g. Delaware courts have tended recently to scrutinize sale of control transactions closely. *Hollinger International, Inc. v. Black*, 844 A.2d 1022 (Del. Ch. 2004) (sale of control enjoined where controlling shareholder had agreed in writing to assist company in divestiture of assets); *Omnicare, Inc. v. NCS Healthcare, Inc.*, 818 A.2d 914 (Del. 2003) (merger in which controlling shareholders agreed unconditionally to vote in favor was breach of fiduciary duty where merger at higher price was proposed). *See also McMullin v. Beran*, 765 A.2d 910 (Del. 2000) (board of directors owed minority fiduciary duty in recommending sale of company even though 80 percent shareholder could dictate terms and should have disclosed material information to allow minority shareholders to decide whether to accept the tender offer or seek appraisal).

B. TENDER OFFERS

In a *tender offer* the prospective *acquirer* (often called the *bidder* or *offeror*) of a *target* corporation makes a public offer to purchase shares directly from shareholders, bypassing the board of directors. The company to be acquired is usually called the *target* company. A tender offer is so called because technically it is an offer for target stockholders to tender their shares for purchase by the bidder if the conditions of the offer are met. In other words, the shares tendered are not usually purchased immediately by the bidder. Indeed, federal law effectively prohibits the immediate purchase of tendered shares. The price is set at a premium over current market price so as to attract tenders. In many tender offers during the latter part of the 1980s, the premium was set at 50 per cent or more over the current market price of the shares. In other periods smaller premiums were offered, but the historical average is about 50 percent.

a. Such an offer is usually made in exchange for cash and thus is often called a *cash tender offer*. An *exchange offer* differs from a cash tender offer in that the bidder offers a package of its own securities—often a combination of cash, debt, and equity securities—for the securities of the target corporation. Such an offer is subject to registration and disclosure requirements of the Securities Act of 1933 because it involves a public offer of new securities. As a result target and target stockholders are given advance notice of the offer. A cash tender offer does not require registration, because cash is not a security. Prior to 1968 it was therefore possible to mount a tender offer without advance notice and to give target stockholders minimal time to respond. In 1968, Congress passed the Williams Act, amending the 1934 Act, to regulate tender offers. A number of substantive rules have been established by the Williams Act and SEC regulation with respect to tender offers. For example, tender offers must remain open for specified periods, shares previously tendered may be withdrawn during specified periods, if the price is increased during an outstanding tender offer, the higher price must be paid for all shares previously tendered, a person making a tender offer must purchase only through the offer and may not make private purchases while the offer is outstanding, oversubscribed cash tender offers must be accepted pro rata rather than on a first-come-first-bought basis, and so forth.

b. The type of consideration offered in a tender offer (and in mergers generally) tends to depend on whether the stock market is generally high or low. When stocks are trading at high prices, target stockholders are more willing to accept stock as consideration. When the market is low, cash is relatively more attractive.

c. Although the bidder may seek just enough shares to ensure voting control, in many instances the bidder seeks to acquire all the outstanding shares. Such an offer is called an *any or all* tender offer and is usually conditioned on some minimum number of shares being tendered (typically enough to assure control of the target). If the ultimate goal is to obtain all of the shares of the target corporation, a second transaction to acquire the balance of the outstanding shares shortly follows a successful acquisition of sufficient shares for control.

d. No tender offer ever obtains all of the outstanding shares of a target. If the bidder desires to acquire all of the outstanding shares they may be acquired in a cash out merger that compels minority shareholders to accept the proffered terms (or follow the statutory dissent and appraisal procedure). Such a second step merger is also called a *mop up* merger or *freeze out* merger.

e. Many tender offers in the 1980s were financed by the bidder's borrowing of large sums of cash from banks or by issuing *junk bonds*. A junk bond is a bond of less than investment grade. Bonds issued to finance a takeover were low rated because there was no assured source of repayment if the takeover did not succeed. And if the takeover did succeed, the bonds would typically be assumed by the target company and subordinated to outstanding bonds. Before the 1980s such bonds were thought to be unmarketable because of their low rating, but the investment bank Drexel Burnham Lambert developed a market for such bonds through cooperation with successful takeover firms such as Kohlberg Kravis & Roberts (KKR).

f.   In some cases, a bidder will offer a premium for enough shares to establish control over the company and announce in advance that remaining shares will be bought at a lower price in a back end merger—possibly even at the market price for target shares before the offer. Such an offer is usually called a front end loaded two tiered tender offer. Such offers are generally seen as coercive in that they may induce target stockholders to tender their shares for less than their true *reservation price* (price at which they would willingly sell). A partial offer in which the bidder makes no announcement about the fate of minority shares after the transfer of control is arguably even more coercive. Several states have enacted fair price statutes requiring that any mop up merger be done at the same price paid in the front end. But these statutes do not generally *require* a back end merger.

g.   Target managers often argue that coercive tactics used by bidders justify defensive tactics designed to thwart a hostile bid and preserve incumbent control. Target shareholders often object to such tactics because they almost always prefer the opportunity to sell their shares at a premium.

h.   A tender offer may also be used in a friendly negotiated deal as a way of permitting target stockholders to sell voluntarily and avoiding issues of fiduciary duty as well as appraisal rights for those stockholders who accept the offer. In some cases, a deal may start out friendly and turn hostile or vice versa.

i.   Tender offers provide an important source of discipline for corporate managers in that those who fail to maximize stockholder value may find that their company becomes the target of a hostile offer. In such a case, a bidder may seek to take over the target by offering target stockholders a premium over the market price and after gaining control impose new management policies to increase target value, thus recouping the purchase price and then some. In many cases, a successful bidder will sell off parts of the target business, particularly if the tender offer has been financed by borrowing. (Indeed, buyers for pieces of the business may have been lined up even before the offer is announced.) Such a transaction is sometimes called a *bust up takeover*.

j.   A tender offer may also be used by an issuer that seeks to buy back a large number of its own shares—often called a *self tender* offer.

k.   When a cash tender offer is made, the open market price for the shares increases dramatically. Target shareholders thus have the choice of selling their shares in the open market (usually at a discount from the tender offer price) or tendering their shares. (When a competing bid seems likely, the market price for target shares may exceed the price offered in the tender offer.) Most shares sold on the open market are ultimately tendered because of the activities of arbitrageurs.

l.   Arbitrageurs are speculators who purchase shares in the open market at prices below the tender offer price in order to tender them and profit by the difference between the two prices. Arbitrageurs are the natural allies of bidders since they profit only if the transaction is consummated. As a result of activities of arbitrageurs a corporation that is put *into play* (made the subject of a cash tender offer) is likely to be purchased by someone and not to remain independent.

C. ECONOMIC ANALYSIS OF TAKEOVERS

Generally speaking, target stockholders favor takeover bids because they afford an opportunity to sell shares at a substantial premium. On the average, bidders offer about 50 percent more than the pre-bid market price. Thus, target stockholders generally oppose efforts by target management to resist takeover, although sometimes resistance may lead to the emergence of a competing bidder who is willing to pay even more. Although resistance may lead to a higher price in a given deal, it may reduce the number of deals proposed overall and thus may reduce overall stockholder wealth. It is not entirely clear why bidders are willing to pay premiums to acquire target companies. Several theories have been suggested.

1. Inefficient Management

Many commentators views takeover bids as part of the market for corporate control and an important mechanism for improving the quality of management by weeding out inefficient managers and assuring that assets are devoted to their highest most profitable use. Some have even suggested that management should never attempt to defeat a hostile offer, but should simply stand aside and let the shareholders determine what is in their best interest. Moreover, some suggested that efforts to regulate takeovers, including the Williams Act ultimately had the effect of making takeovers more difficult to do and thus reducing stockholder wealth. These arguments are ultimately based on the assumption that the stock market is efficient and accordingly that market price accurately reflects the value of the target company as currently managed. Thus, a bidder would be willing to offer a premium over market only if the bidder has a better idea about how to manage the company or if the currently management is inefficient (which is really the same thing).

2. Synergy

Some commentators have suggested that takeovers may provide synergistic benefits by combining complementary businesses that are worth more as a single unit, for example, because of economies of scale.

3. Other Motivations

It is possible that the gains to shareholders are largely due to tax savings caused by the substitution of debt for equity capital. Many takeovers were financed by issuing so-called junk bonds and using the proceeds to purchase target stock, with the target company assuming the obligation to pay off the bonds after takeover. This tactic had the effect of increasing the leverage of the target company and increasing the rate of return to remaining stockholders following the takeover. It also had the effect of requiring the target company to distribute available cash in the form of interest payments to bondholders, albeit at the cost of increasing the chances of bankruptcy. Nevertheless, one common justification for takeovers in the 1980s was that target companies had failed to pay dividends and had used available cash to invest in uneconomic expansion. Thus, in addition to their tax effect, junk bonds may also be seen as a remedy for a form of mismanagement.

D. THE WILLIAMS ACT

The Williams Act was passed by Congress in 1968 in response to perceived abuses in the conduct of tender offers. The Williams Act consists in a series of amendments to the 1934 Act, codified in §§ 13(d), 13(e), 14(d), and 14(e). The Williams Act applies to tender offers *for equity securities* of companies registered under Section 12 of the 1934 Act. The general goal of the Williams Act is not to favor or disfavor takeovers but to assure full disclosure of proposed transactions and provide a fair set of rules for the struggle for control of the corporation. Nevertheless, it is clear that the Williams Act was intended to reduce the perceived advantages enjoyed by bidders in connection with unregulated offers. Some legal scholars have argued that the Williams Act thus reduces the number of offers made and ultimately reduces aggregate stockholder wealth.

a. Any person who makes a cash tender offer for a registered corporation must disclose the source of funds used in the offer, the background of persons involved in the offer, the purpose for which the offer is made, plans for the target if successful, and any contracts or understandings it has with, or with respect to, the target corporation. SEA 14(d). This information must be filed on Form 14D and distributed to target shareholders when the offer begins. In other words, the Williams Act differs from a 1933 Act registration statement in that it does not require advance notice of an offer.

b. Disclosure of similar information is required by any person or group who acquires more than 5 per cent of the outstanding shares of any class of stock of a registered company, whether or not a tender offer is in progress or is contemplated. SEA 13(d). This information must be filed on Form 13D and furnished to the issuer within ten days. A new Form 13D must be filed and furnished within ten day of any further purchase or sale. This rule provides potential target companies with advance information about potential offers.

c. Similar information must be disclosed by issuers making an offer for their own shares, or issuers in which a change of control is proposed. SEA 13(e).

d. Aside from requiring disclosure, the Williams Act and the rules adopted by the SEC there under contain a series of substantive rules about the terms of an offer:

  • the offer must remain open for 20 business days.

  • tendered shares must be purchased no later than 60 business days after the beginning of the offer.

- the offer must be made to all holders of the class of securities for which the offer is made.

- if the offer is for fewer than the number of shares tendered, the bidder must purchase an equal proportion of shares from each tendering stockholder.

- a tendering stockholder has the right to withdraw tendered shares at any time during the course of the offer.

- if the offer price is increased or decreased during the offer the highest price paid to a tendering shareholder must be paid to all tendering shareholders.

- during an offer, the bidder may not purchase any shares outside the offer.

- a stockholder must own all shares tendered.

e. Section 14(e) imposes a broad prohibition against the use of false, misleading or incomplete statements in connection with a tender offer. Section 14(e) adopts the standards of materiality, *scienter*, and disclosure of Rule 10b–5. The Supreme Court has held that § 14(e), like Rule 10b–5, relates only to nondisclosure or deception and does not reach unfair practices generally. *Schreiber v. Burlington Northern*, Inc., 472 U.S. 1, 105 S.Ct. 2458 (1985).

f. In *Piper v. Chris–Craft Industries, Inc.*, 430 U.S. 1, 97 S.Ct. 926 (1977), the Court held that a defeated tender offeror does not have standing to sue for damages, but injunctive relief may be available. An issuer has standing to enjoin violations of section 14(e), acting on behalf of shareholders. *Polaroid Corp. v. Disney*, 862 F.2d 987 (3d Cir.1988).

g. Tendering shareholders have standing to seek injunctive relief and, probably, damages. *Lowenschuss v. Kane*, 520 F.2d 255 (2d Cir.1975). The Supreme Court in *Chris-Craft* specifically left open the question whether a nontendering shareholder might have standing to sue a bidder. Some cases hold that such a shareholder does have standing. *See Plaine v. McCabe*, 797 F.2d 713 (9th Cir.1986).

h. The Williams Act does not contain a definition of what constitutes a tender offer. A variety of techniques have been devised to acquire control of a target corporation without triggering the Williams Act. The principal legal issue involved in such transactions is whether the transaction should be viewed as a tender offer subject to the requirements of the Williams Act.

E. STATE TAKEOVER STATUTES

Most states have enacted statutes dealing with of takeovers. Unlike the Williams Act, these statutes were openly designed to protect corporations against bidders.

a. State statutes enacted before 1982 generally imposed hearing requirements and fairness standards on tender offers made with respect to corporations with significant contacts with the state. The Illinois statute of this type was held unconstitutional in *Edgar v. MITE Corporation*, 457 U.S. 624, 102 S.Ct. 2629 (1982) on the grounds it was an unreasonable burden on interstate commerce.

b. New attempts by states to impose restrictions on tender offers began promptly after the decision in *MITE*. These statutes are often called accord generation takeover statutes and they apply only to corporations incorporated in the state in question. They all build on the established power of states to regulate the internal affairs of domestic corporations.

c. The most important of these statutes is DGCL 203. This statute provides that if a person acquires 15 per cent or more of a corporation's voting stock, that person may not enter into mergers or other specified transactions with the corporation unless (a) the person acquires 85 per cent or more of the corporation's stock, or (b) the transaction is approved by the board of directors and at least two-thirds of the shares other than the shares held by the person acquiring the stock. Section 203 is important because so many publicly held corporations are incorporated in Delaware. More than twenty-five other states, including New York, have adopted similar business combination statutes. The Wisconsin statute modeled on the Delaware statute was upheld in *Amanda Acquisition Corp. v. Universal Foods Corp.*, 877 F.2d 496 (7th Cir. 1989).

d. Ohio and Indiana pioneered the *control share acquisition statute*. The Indiana statute was upheld by the Supreme Court in *CTS Corporation v. Dynamics Corp. of America*, 481 U.S. 69, 107 S.Ct. 1637 (1987). In this type of statute, shareholder approval must be obtained for purchases by an individual or group that crosses the 20 percent, the one-third, and the 50 percent thresholds. If a shareholder fails to obtain approval, the acquired shares lose the right to vote and may be reacquired by the corporation on terms set forth in the statute. The net effect of a control share acquisition statute may be to reward holdout stockholders by necessitating a back end premium. In other words, these statutes may lead to the transfer of a front end premium to the back end. Arguably, this is a good result because holdout stockholders presumably attach a higher value to their shares than do stockholders who sell quickly.

e. Pennsylvania provides that if a shareholder acquires more than 20 per cent of the voting shares of a corporation, other shareholders have the right to compel that shareholder to acquire their shares at fair value. This statute is similar to the rule in the UK and many other countries.

f. More than 30 states have adopted statutes authorizing boards of directors to consider constituencies other than shareholders when making decisions. These are generally viewed as being motivated by a desire to make takeovers more difficult.

F. DEFENSIVE TACTICS

Numerous defensive tactics have been devised in order to defeat or deter takeover bids. These tactics increased in sophistication during the 1980s. By 1990, more than 90 per cent of all publicly held corporations had adopted various standings defenses against unwanted takeover attempts. The most successful defense is the poison pill discussed below.

1. Creating Legal Obstacles

A target corporation may seek to create legal obstacles to the takeover. A target might buy a business that increases the chances that the threatened takeover will give rise to anti-trust problems. *See Panter v. Marshall Field & Co.*, 646 F.2d 271 (7th Cir.1981); *Marathon Oil Co. v. Mobil Corp.*, 669 F.2d 378 (6th Cir. 1981). A target might acquire and hold a business that requires governmental approval for its transfer, e.g. a parent corporation owning an insurance subsidiary. A target might institute suit to enjoin the offer for violations of the Williams Act, the antitrust laws or on other grounds. *See Corenco Corp. v. Schiavone & Sons, Inc.*, 488 F.2d 207 (2d Cir.1973).

2. Porcupine Provisions

Amendments may be made in the articles of incorporation or bylaws that make it difficult for a bidder who acquires a majority of the voting shares to obtain control of the board of directors. These are sometimes referred to as *porcupine provisions*. Common devices included limiting removal of directors for cause the articles of incorporation or, staggering the election of directors, and requiring a supermajority vote to amend only bylaws or to take other specified actions.

3. Supervoting Stock

The articles of incorporation may be amended to provide for supervoting stock (stock with multiple votes per share) and placing that stock in the hands of members of the founding families or other persons friendly to the incumbent management. Supervoting stock is generally made non-transferable but convertible into ordinary voting stock that is transferable. A person holding supervoting stock is thus unable to convey the supervoting privilege but may sell the shares after they are converted into ordinary voting stock. Supervoting stock permits a target corporation to make itself completely takeover-proof.

a. Supervoting stock may be created at the time the stock is issued or at some later time by offering to exchange the shares of non controlling stockholders for lesser voting shares with the same financial rights as ordinary shares. Typically, the company offers additional lesser voting shares to as an inducement to take the exchange. Thus, a stockholder who accepts the exchange offer typically receives enhanced financial rights in exchange for giving up a vote that probably has little value to the stockholder.

b. A variation of supervoting stock is tenure voting. For example, as of a specified date a reclassification is effected by which each share of stock is entitled to 10 votes. If any shares are transferred, the voting power of the shares is reduced to one vote per share. If the shares are held for a stated period, (say) 36 or 48 months, they again obtain the power to cast 10 votes. A tenure voting plan was upheld In *Williams v. Geier*, 671 A.2d 1368 (Del. 1996).

4. White Knight

A corporation facing an undesired takeover attempt may seek to find a more congenial suitor, a *white knight*. In order to assure the white knight's success, the target may seek to negotiate exclusively with the white knight and in addition may grant the white knight a lockup.

5. Lockups

Lockups involve entering into transactions with friendly party on favorable terms to make takeover by others difficult or unattractive. A lockup may involve the sale of shares at a bargain price or the grant of options to purchase shares.

a. A corporation faced with an unwanted tender offer may create employee stock ownership plan (ESOP) with a trustee friendly to incumbent management and distribute a significant number of shares to that trustee. *NCR Corp. v. American Tel. & Tel. Co.*, 761 F.Supp. 475 (S.D.Ohio 1991); *Shamrock Holdings, Inc. v. Polaroid Corp.*, 559 A.2d 278, 290 (Del.Ch.1989).

b. A corporation may find a white knight and grant it options to purchase shares at current market prices. *Smith v. Van Gorkom*, 488 A.2d 858 (Del.1985). The options give the white knight a *leg up* on any competing bidder and also protect the white knight if the competing bidder appears and acquires the target at a higher price because the white knight may tender the acquired shares for purchase under the competing bid.

c. A corporation facing an unwanted tender offer may sell or grant options to purchase a desirable asset or line of business (crown jewels) to a favored bidder at a bargain price. *See Hanson Trust PLC v. ML SCM Acquisition, Inc.*, 781 F.2d 264 (2d Cir.1986); *Mobil Corp. v. Marathon Oil Co.*, 669 F.2d 366 (6th Cir. 1981). This type of lockup is designed to discourage the competing bidder by making the target less attractive, and may be enjoined if it the transaction is unreasonable.

6. Greenmail

A target corporation facing an unwanted tender offer may seek in effect to bribe a bidder by repurchasing bidder shares at a premium. This is usually called greenmail. *See Heckmann v. Ahmanson*, 214 Cal.Rptr. 177 (1985); *Cheff v. Mathes*, 199 A.2d 548 (Del.1964).

a. In 1987, the Internal Revenue Code was amended to impose a 50 percent nondeductible excise tax on greenmail payments (in addition to the normal income tax payable on sales of shares). IRC 5881.

b.   Some states (notably Pennsylvania) have statutes that prohibit greenmail or require that any premium be returned to the company.

7. Manipulation of Target Share Price

A corporation facing an unwanted tender offer may seek to defeat it by driving up the price of its shares to make the takeover price unattractive.

a.   The target may buy back its own shares in the open market for ostensibly proper reasons. Such transactions drive up the price and make a purchased takeover more difficult. *Bennett v. Propp*, 187 A.2d 405 (Del.1962); *Herald Co. v. Seawell*, 472 F.2d 1081 (10th Cir.1972).

b.   A target may make an offer to repurchase its own shares but limit the offer by excluding shares acquired by the bidder. In *Unocal Corp. v. Mesa Petroleum Co.*, 493 A.2d 946 (Del.1985), the Delaware Supreme Court upheld this type of transaction on the basis of an expanded business judgment rule, discussed below. Shortly thereafter, the SEC adopted Rule 14d–10, the *all holders* rule requiring equal treatment of all shareholders of the same class.

c.   The target may declare an extraordinary dividend or announce an increase in its regular dividends. In some cases, the target may borrow large amounts of money to pay a dividend, thereby effecting a *leveraged recapitalization*. Or the target may distribute debt obligations directly to its own stockholders. Although these tactics will usually have the effect of lowering stock price, they also drain the company of cash and borrowing power and make it less attractive as a target. In addition, the target may include a provision in its debt instruments that requires payoff in the event of a takeover. Such debt is usually called *poison pill debt*.

8. Poison Pills

A poison pill is a new issue of stock that increases in rights if any person makes a cash tender offer or acquires more than a specified percentage of shares.

a.   A poison pill is technically a new series of preferred shares distributed to common shareholders in the form of a dividend. The new series is usually created by the board of directors without shareholder action under blank check authority in the articles of incorporation.

b. The increased rights of the holders of the poison pill preferred may consist of *flip in* or *flip over* rights or both. Flip in rights permit the holder to purchase additional shares or debt securities of the target at a bargain price, to sell shares back to the target at high prices, or to exchange the poison pill preferred for valuable packages of debt and securities issued by the target. Flip over rights permit the holder to purchase shares of the bidder at a bargain price if there is a subsequent merger or other defined transaction between the target and the bidder. Most poison pills contain both flip in and flip over provisions, both of which alone would result in unacceptable dilution of the bidder's interest if triggered.

c. Before a triggering event occurs, the board of directors may redeem the poison pill preferred at a nominal cost. After a triggering event occurs, the preferred is generally not redeemable. Thus, a poison pill compels the bidder to negotiate with the board of directors to neutralize the pill through redemption of the poison pill rights.

d. The principal case approving the issuance of poison pill preferred is *Moran v. Household International, Inc.*, 500 A.2d 1346 (Del.1985).

e. Two courts have applied New Jersey law to conclude that the board of directors may not adopt "poison pill" preferred stock that materially changes the voting rights of shareholders without approval of the shareholders. *Asarco, Incorporated v. Court*, 611 F.Supp. 468 (D.N.J.1985); *Minstar Acq. Corp. v. AMF, Inc.*, 621 F.Supp. 1252 (S.D.N.Y.1985). The second case also invalidates a "scorched earth" plan under which the target corporation granted excessive amounts of compensation to high-level employees. As a result of these two decisions, most corporations have not attempted to create poison pills in which voting rights change upon the occurrence of a triggering event.

G. JUDICIAL REVIEW OF DEFENSIVE TACTICS

A large number of cases have considered the validity of defensive tactics in different contexts. No general theory has developed. The lawfulness of defensive tactics is largely governed by state law. Attempts to attack these tactics under Rule 10b–5 was foreclosed by the United States Supreme Court decisions in *Santa Fe Industries, Inc. v. Green*, 430 U.S. 462, 97 S.Ct. 1292 (1977) (limiting Rule 10b–5 to cases of deception rather than unfairness or breach of fiduciary duty), and *Schreiber v. Burlington Northern, Inc.,* 472 U.S. 1, 105 S.Ct. 2458 (1985) (extending the same limitation to suits under § 14(e) of the Williams Act). On the other hand, some of the actions described below have been successfully attacked by regulations promulgated under the Williams Act.

1. Early Tests

The early test of the propriety of defensive tactics was one of underlying purpose. If the action of the board of directors was motivated by a business purpose (such as preserving existing business policies or strategies), the action was protected by the business judgment rule. On the other hand if the board or management acted primarily because of the personal desire to perpetuate or *entrench* itself in office, the defensive tactic may be invalidated. *Cheff v. Mathes,* 199 A.2d 548 (Del.1964). This early test may be criticized on the ground that it is possible to dress up virtually every transaction with a proper business purpose even through the real motive is entrenchment. Nevertheless, entrenchment remains an important basis for invalidation defenses.

2. Business Judgment Rule

In the early 1980s, the most courts took the position that defensive tactics were simply a matter of the exercise of the business judgment of the directors and such decisions were immune from judicial review under the business judgment rule. *See Panter v. Marshall Field & Co.,* 646 F.2d 271 (7th Cir.1981); *Gearhart Industries, Inc. v. Smith International, Inc.,* 741 F.2d 707 (5th Cir.1984). *See also Hilton Hotels Corp. v. ITT Corp.,* 962 F. Supp. 1309 (D. Nev. 1997).

3. Intermediate Scrutiny

Beginning in the mid 1980s, the Delaware Supreme Court developed a balancing test that seems to fall somewhere between the business judgment rule applied in connection with the duty of care and the fairness test applied in connection with the duty of loyalty.

a. In *Unocal Corp. v. Mesa Petroleum Co.,* 493 A.2d 946 (Del.1985), the court upheld a self tender offer of debt for stock that excluded the bidder from participation, stating that "If a defensive measure is to come within the ambit of the business judgment rule, it must be reasonable in relation to the threat posed. This entails an analysis by the directors of the nature of the takeover bid and its effect on the corporate enterprise."

b. In *Moran v. Household International, Inc.,* 500 A.2d 1346 (Del.1985), the court upheld the adoption of a poison pill as a defensive tactic in advance of a specific takeover attempt, reasoning that the poison pill did not prevent all takeover attempts, and that the management's invocation of the poison pill in response to a specific takeover attempt could be considered when the occasion arose.

c. In *Revlon, Inc. v. MacAndrews & Forbes Holdings, Inc.,* 506 A.2d 173 (Del.1985), the court held that a lock up agreement that favored one contestant in a takeover attempt over another was invalid and should be enjoined because the board of directors had resolved to sell the corporation and that upon making that decision, the board had an obligation to get the best possible price for shareholders and could not arbitrarily favor one contestant over another. In other words, *Revlon* holds that once it is clear that the company will either be sold or broken up, the board of directors must conduct an auction to insure that shareholders receive the best possible price. *See also Ivanhoe Partners v. Newmont Mining Corp.,* 535 A.2d 1334 (Del. 1987) (same rule if board initially resists takeover); *Mills Acquisition Co. v. MacMillan, Inc.,* 559 A.2d 1261 (Del. 1989) (addressing conduct of auction); *Cottle v. Storer Communication, Inc.,* 849 F.2d 570 (11th Cir. 1988) (addressing end of auction); *Barkan v. Amsted Industries, Inc.,* 567 A.2d 1279 (Del. 1988) (addressing use of market test).

d. In *Paramount Communications, Inc. v. Time, Inc.,* 571 A.2d 1140 (Del.1989), the court held that in a true merger in which two companies seek to combine rather than a takeover in which control of the target company is transferred, the auction requirement is not triggered and the offer of a competing bidder need not be considered. This decision has given rise to the *just say no* defense by which a company may refuse to consider an offer on the grounds that the company is not for sale even if the offer clearly increases stockholder wealth.

e. In *Unitrin, Inc. v. American General Corp.,* 651 A.2d 1361 (Del.1995) the court refined the rule of *Unocal* holding that to be proportional to the perceived threat a defensive tactic may not be *coercive* or *preclusive.* In other words, the tactic may not be designed to force target stockholders to reject the bid or to prevent the bid from going forward. Presumably, this means that the target board may take steps to level the playing field or even to favor itself, but may not dictate a result in its own favor. The *Unitrin* court also made it clear that this intermediate level of scrutiny is in addition to scrutiny if any under the business judgment rule. If management shows that its response is proportional, the plaintiff may nonetheless seek to show that management tactics were not based on an valid exercise of business judgment, but, for example, that they were motivated primarily by a personal desire to remain in office (entrenchment). In other words, the action may not be dismissed solely on the ground that that the target board has met the intermediate standard of care.

f.   *Quickturn Design Systems, Inc. v. Shapiro,* 721 A.2d 1281 (Del. 1998), held that a provision limiting the ability of the board of directors to redeem poison pill rights for a period of six months was an undue limitation on the power of the board of directors. *But see Int'l Bhd. of Teamsters Gen. Fund v. Fleming Cos., Inc.,* 975 P.2d 907 (Okla. 1999) (stockholders may adopt a bylaw requiring board to obtain stockholder approval in connection with issuing poison pill).

g.   In *Omnicare, Inc. v. NCS Healthcare, Inc.,* 818 A.2d 914 (Del. 2003), the court held that an unconditional agreement by controlling shareholders to vote in favor of a proposed merger was preclusive and coercive where a merger at higher price was subsequently proposed by a competing bidder.

H.   LEVERAGED BUYOUTS

A leveraged buyout (LBO) is an acquisition of a target usually by a group including existing management and additional private investors, using borrowed funds which are to be repaid out of the earnings and assets of the target. If incumbent management forms a part of the group that makes the cash tender offer, the transaction may be called a management buyout (MBO). Such deals are often also called *going private.* The spectacular collapse of some leveraged buyout transactions contributed to the cessation of takeovers at the end of the 1980s.

a.   In a leveraged buyout, the bidder creates a new corporation (NEWCO) to acquire the shares of the target (OLDCO). NEWCO receives minimal equity capital from the bidder group and borrows the balance of the purchase price for the publicly held shares of OLDCO. Typically,

NEWCO makes a tender offer for any and all of the shares of OLDCO held by stockholders other than the bidder group so that the target becomes a subsidiary of NEWCO.

b. Following the acquisition of the shares of the target (and the subsequent mop up merger) the target and NEWCO are merged so that the target's assets become available to service the takeover debt of NEWCO. Alternatively, the separate existence of the target as a subsidiary of NEWCO may be retained, but the target may formally guarantee the payment of the debt of NEWCO (an *upstream guarantee*). The acquisition debt may be paid down by the sale of assets by the recapitalized target or out of its cash flow.

c. In effect a leveraged buyout results in recapitalization of the target by the massive substitution of debt for equity capital. An important factor in the economics of LBO transactions is that an LBO sharply reduces or eliminates income tax liability of the acquired business through the substitution of deductible interest payments for taxable dividend payments.

d. After a leveraged buyout, the surviving company typically has too few stockholders to be required to report under section 12 of the Securities Exchange Act of 1934. Thus, the company may reduce costs (and increase profits) by eliminating various regulatory requirements that follow from registration.

e. An LBO differs from a sale of control or a takeover in that the existing controlling stockholders usually remain in control and effectively buy out the interests of the minority, albeit using the assets of the corporation. A sale of control usually involves the payment of a premium to the controlling stockholder and leaves the minority in place, whereas a hostile takeover may involve the payment of a premium to public stockholders leaving management in a minority position.

f. An LBO may also be seen as a preemptive defensive tactic designed to prevent takeover or may be proposed following the announcement of a hostile takeover as an alternative to the hostile takeover. In some cases, the proposal of an LBO will prompt a third party offer if the proposed LBO price appears to be attractive.

g. An LBO is similar to a transaction in which a parent company eliminates the minority stockholders in a subsidiary by means of a freeze out merger. *See Weinberger v. UOP, Inc.*, 457 A2d 701 (Del. 1983).

h. Several private investment firms specialize in arranging LBOs. The most prominent of these firms is Kohlberg Kravis Roberts (KKR) which arranged the $25 billion buyout of RJR Nabisco in 1989. *See Metropolitan Life Ins. Co. v. RJR Nabisco, Inc.*, 906 F.2d 884 (2d Cir. 1990).

i. LBOs have been criticized as involving an inherent duty of loyalty problem in that the controlling stockholders are privy to more and better information regarding the value of the company. Thus, the SEC has adopted Rule 13e–3 specifically addressing tender offers in connection with going private transactions.

j. Delaware law appears to favor LBOs and other going private transactions. *See In re Siliconix Inc. Shareholders Litigation*, 2001 WL 716787 (Del.Ch.) (in the absence of coercion, a self tender offer by a majority stockholder will not be reviewed for entire fairness but only for full disclosure). Moreover, the Delaware courts have held that where the acquiring company owns 90 percent or more of the target and thus may use a short form merger in the back end mop up, the business judgment rule applies. *Glassman v. Unocal Exploration Corp.*, 777 A.2d 242, 248 (Del. 2001) (appraisal is the sole remedy available to a minority stockholder in a short form merger). *But see Smith v. VanGorkom*, 488 A.2d 858 (Del.1985) (proposed third party buyout by merger violated business judgment rule).

k. A similar transaction is often used to effect the divestiture of a division to a subgroup of management. Such a transaction is often called a *split off*. In some cases, a company may choose to *spin off* a division, by forming a NEWCO to hold the assets and then distributing shares of NEWCO to existing stockholders as a dividend. In other cases, a company may split off a division and sell or spin off a small amount of stock in NEWCO in order to create a public market for the shares as a prelude to a public offering of NEWCO. Such a transaction is often called an equity carve out. As with LBOs, such divestitures may be seen as a defensive tactic designed to preempt a hostile bid financed with borrowed money to be paid back through the break up and piecemeal sale of the target company.

I. TAKEOVERS AND MERGERS AFTER 1990

Takeover activity (as well as merger activity generally) largely ceased around 1990, because of state takeover laws, more powerful defenses, and lack of funding. The merger market resumed in the mid 1990s albeit in a very different form. Because of high stock market prices, most mergers and takeovers involved stock rather than cash as consideration. In addition, a general relaxation of the antitrust laws together with globalization led to horizontal consolidation in larger companies. Finally, as a result of the takeovers of the 1980s, managers began to focus on maximizing share value as the best defense against takeover. Indeed, by the year 2000, the CEOs of the largest companies received 90 percent of their compensation in some form of equity, primarily stock options. Accordingly, management was induced to undertake value maximizing transactions such as divestitures of underperforming divisions even if it meant shrinking the size of the company, whereas during the 1980s such transactions could only be forced by hostile takeover.

■ XV. MERGERS & ACQUISITIONS

Corporation statutes typically provide for certain kinds of corporate combinations, including (1) *merger* of one corporation into another corporation, (2) *consolidation* of two corporations into a new corporation, (3) merger of a subsidiary of a corporation into the parent corporation, and (4) in some states a compulsory share exchange. Although the word *merger* may connote that stockholders in the non surviving corporation receive shares in the surviving corporation, most merger transactions today do not involve the simple amalgamation of two businesses as the term appears to contemplate. A nonstatutory transaction such as a share purchase (possibly through a tender offer) or an asset purchase may achieve the same economic result as a statutory transaction but with different legal consequences. For example, if an acquiring corporation purchases of the assets of a target corporation in exchange for shares of the acquiring corporation, and the target corporation then dissolves and distributes the shares to its stockholders, the transaction is economically equivalent to a merger. But under Delaware law, for example, the stockholders of the acquiring corporation do not have a vote or appraisal rights and the stockholders of the target corporation have do not have appraisal rights. In a few cases (though not in Delaware), the courts have recharacterized such a transaction as a merger under the *de facto merger doctrine* in order afford stockholders the rights they would have in a statutory merger.

A. STATUTORY MERGERS & SHARE EXCHANGES

1. Mergers, Consolidations, and Share Exchanges

a.   A *merger* of corporation A into corporation B means that the two corporations are combined and corporation B survives while corporation A disappears. On the effective date of a merger, the assets and liabilities of the non surviving corporation become assets and liabilities of the surviving corporation automatically by operation of law and are not deemed to be transfers of assets or liabilities. See MBCA 11.07. This may be of importance when a corporation has assets that may not be transferred without the prior consent of a governmental agency or third person.

b.   A *consolidation* of corporation A and corporation B means that the two corporations are combined but both corporation A and corporation B disappear and a new corporation C is created. The MBCA has eliminated the concept of consolidation. It is seldom used, because it is almost always advantageous for one of the entities involved in a transaction to survive corporation, and because a new entity may always be created and the other entities merged into it.

c.   In a *share exchange* all stockholders of a class of shares are obligated to exchange their shares for the consideration specified in the plan of share exchange when that plan is approved by a majority of the shares of that class following essentially the same procedure that is applicable to the approval of a merger. The exchange is mandatory. A share exchange is similar in effect to a reverse triangular merger (described below) in that the target corporation survives and becomes a subsidiary of the acquiring corporation.

2. Basic Procedures

A statutory merger must be approved by the board of directors and by a specific percentage of the stockholders of one or both corporations.

a.   A plan of merger must be approved by the board of directors and recommended to the stockholders. MBCA 11.04. The board of directors may condition the plan on such terms as it deems desirable. For example, the plan may require that the merger be approved by one or more classes of shares voting as separate voting groups or that no more than a specified number of stockholders elect the right of dissent and appraisal (described below). Following approval, articles of merger must be filed with the state.

b.   The vote of stockholders required for approval of a merger varies from state to state. Under the MBCA, most mergers require a vote of the stockholders of the non surviving corporation only. The stockholders of the surviving corporation need not vote on the merger if the articles of incorporation of the surviving corporation will not be changed in a way that requires a stockholder vote, each stockholder of the surviving corporation will hold the same number of shares rights, and the issuance in the merger of shares does not require a vote under MBCA 6.21(f), which requires a stockholder vote if the aggregate voting power of the corporation will increase by 20 percent or more as a result of the issuance of new shares. MBCA 11.04. Voting by voting group is required if a class or series would be entitled to vote as a separate group on a provision in the plan that, if contained in a proposed amendment to articles of incorporation, would require action by separate voting groups under MBCA 10.04.

c.   Most states follow similar rules except that the 20 percent trigger relates to shares to be issued in the merger by the surviving corporation, whereas under the MBCA it relates to any 20 percent increase in voting power whether or not the shares are issued in the context of a merger. In other words, the MBCA provision relates to *all* new issues of a substantial number of voting shares, including rights to purchase such shares. Thus, in most states, the stockholder vote by the surviving corporation may be avoided even if the number of shares is increased by more than 20 per cent by casting the transaction as a triangular merger rather than a direct merger. (Triangular mergers are discussed below.) As a practical matter, however, because stock exchange rules require stockholder approval of any new issue of shares in excess of about 20 percent of the outstanding number, a stockholder vote will be required, though technically not in connection with the merger.

d.   Under the MBCA, the required vote is a simple majority of shares present and voting at meeting at which there is a quorum of at least a majority of shares eligible to vote. Many states require a majority vote of all outstanding voting shares (as did the MBCA prior to 1999). Older statutes require the affirmative vote of two-thirds of outstanding shares, which may include both voting and nonvoting shares.

    e.   Stockholders have a right of dissent and appraisal if the plan of merger must be approved by the stockholders and the stockholder in question has the right to vote on the merger. MBCA 13.02. The rules about voting and the right of dissent and appraisal are technical and vary significantly from state to state. The requirements may sometimes be avoided by casting the transaction in a non-statutory form.

    f.   If the directors of the two corporations are not acting at arms length, as where one corporation owns enough shares of the other to name a majority or all of the board of directors of the other, the merger is a form of self-dealing and is judicially reviewed for fairness. *See Weinberger v. UOP, Inc.*, 457 A.2d 701 (Del.1983); *Singer v. Magnavox Co.*, 380 A.2d 969 (Del.1977); *Sterling v. Mayflower Hotel Corp.*, 93 A.2d 107 (Del.1952). Approval of the merger by disinterested directors or by a vote of disinterested stockholders may avoid the full scale fairness review.

3.   Short Form Mergers, Cash Mergers, and Triangular Mergers

Although it is common to think of a merger as a deal by which two corporations become one and the two groups of stockholders become stockholders in the surviving corporation, most transactions are otherwise. The merger statutes of most states provide expressly that the shares of a party to a merger may be converted into shares, obligations or other securities of the surviving or any other corporation or into cash or other property. MBCA 11.02.

    a.   Most states permit a parent corporation that owns 90 percent or more of the outstanding shares of a subsidiary corporation to merge the subsidiary into the parent without a stockholder vote of either corporation. This procedure is usually called a *short form merger*. MBCA 11.05 Although they do not have a vote, the stockholders of the subsidiary have the statutory right to dissent and receive the appraised value of their shares. MBCA 13.02(a). The short form merger procedure creates no appraisal rights on the part of stockholders of the parent corporation since those stockholders are not entitled to vote on the transaction.

    b.   A cash merger is a merger in which some stockholders who are parties to the merger are required to accept cash or property (other than shares) for their shares. A cash merger permits the statutory merger procedure to be used to squeeze out one or more stockholders. It is in effect a compulsory buy out of the shares of certain stockholders. A cash merger may be used as the second part of a two-step acquisition of all the outstanding shares of a target corporation. Such a merger is usually called a *back end* or *mop up merger.*

c.   Cash mergers are a relatively recent phenomenon. Before the 1960s, many states limited the consideration payable in connection with a merger to shares of the surviving company. Nevertheless, it was possible to effect something like a cash merger by paying target stockholders in redeemable preferred stock. *See Matteson v. Ziebarth,* 242 P.2d 1025 (Wash.1952).

d.   In a *triangular merger,* the acquiring corporation forms a wholly-owned subsidiary with nominal assets—sometimes called a *shell corporation* or *acquisition vehicle*—which then merges with the corporation to be acquired. In most cases, the stockholders of the acquired corporation receive shares or other securities of the acquiring corporation or cash. The acquired corporation becomes a wholly-owned subsidiary of the acquiring corporation. One distinct advantage of a triangular merger is that the acquiring corporation does not assume liabilities of the acquired corporation.

e.   In effect, a cash merger involves the payment of cash to minority stockholders while the controlling stockholder effectively receives stock because the controlling stockholder remains in control of the combined entity. Formally, the controlling stockholder corporation might also receive cash for its shares in the subsidiary, but that would only be to take the cash out of one pocket and to put it in another. Thus, many state statutes provide that the plan of merger may specify differing forms of consideration for different stockholders.

f.   These devices are often used in combination to avoid a vote by the stockholders of the acquiring corporation. For example, an acquiring corporation may form a shell corporation to merge with the target and then merger the shell into the parent by means of a short form merger. Given that the parent is the sole stockholder of the subsidiary corporation, it is the board of directors of the parent corporation that technically votes the shares of the subsidiary. Similarly, it is the parent corporation that would have appraisal rights if any. Whereas, individual stockholders of the parent corporation might vote against the deal or even use it as an opportunity to cash out by exercising appraisal rights, presumably the board of directors that negotiated the deal will have no objections to it!

4. Reverse Triangular Mergers & Share Exchanges

In some transactions, it is important that the acquired corporation survive. Such a result may be achieved through a *reverse triangular merger.*

a.   Survival of the target corporation may be important where that corporation is organized under a special statute under which incorporation is difficult (, banks, insurance companies) or where the corporation has government licenses or other contracts that do not permit assignment.

b.   In a reverse triangular merger, the acquiring or holding company creates a new subsidiary and contributes assets to that subsidiary to be used to acquire the shares of the target corporation. (The contribution of assets, which may be cash or parent stock or anything else of value, is often called a *drop down*. It does not require any special approval, because both the creation of the subsidiary and the drop down of assets transactions in the normal course of business.) The subsidiary is then merged into the target corporation and the assets of the subsidiary corporation are exchanged for the shares of the target corporation. The result is that the target corporation becomes a wholly owned subsidiary of the parent and stockholders of the target receive stock or cash or other consideration for their shares.

c.   A compulsory *share exchange* accomplishes the same end as a reverse triangular merger. MBCA 11.03 This procedure permits the mandatory acquisition of all shares of a target corporation upon the affirmative vote of a majority of the shares to be acquired. The consideration for the shares being acquired may consist of cash, property, or shares in another corporation. As with a merger, a compulsory share exchange requires approval of the board of directors and submission of the proposed share exchange to the stockholders of the target corporation. If a majority of the shares being exchanged approve the transaction, it is binding on all holders. Stockholders who object to the share exchange have the statutory right of dissent and appraisal. MBCA 13.02(a).

5. Fairness Standards

In a merger between a parent and subsidiary, the parent as the controlling stockholder has the power to force terms on the subsidiary and may thus be tempted to take advantage of its controlling position to effect the transaction on terms unduly favorable to the parent. In theory, minority stockholders are protected by their right of dissent and appraisal. But the appraisal remedy is widely viewed as inadequate protection.

    a.   Caselaw holds that such transactions should be seen as self dealing so that a test of *entire fairness* is applicable and that compliance with statutory formalities alone is not sufficient. *Weinberger v. UOP, Inc.*, 457 A.2d 701 (Del.1983). But the courts have struggled with the precise test to be applied to such transactions.

    b.   *Singer v. Magnavox Co.*, 380 A.2d 969 (Del.1977), combined a business purpose test with the test of entire fairness. In essence, the court recognized a residual right of a stockholder to continue to be a stockholder rather than an absolute right of the parent to cash out the minority at any time. Several non-Delaware cases accept this standard. *Gabhart v. Gabhart*, 370 N.E.2d 345 (Ind.1977); *Coggins v. New England Patriots Football Club*, 492 N.E.2d 1112 (Mass.1986); *Alpert v. 28 Williams St. Corp.*, 483 N.Y.S.2d 667, 473 N.E.2d 19 (N.Y. 1984). In *Tanzer v. International Gen. Indus., Inc.*, 379 A.2d 1121 (Del.1977), the court held that the business purpose requirement may be satisfied by considering the interests of the majority stockholder. As so construed, the business purpose test has little force in preventing abusive transactions. Nevertheless, the court extended the business purpose test to short form mergers. *Roland Intern. Corp. v. Najjar*, 407 A.2d 1032 (Del.1979).

    c.   In *Weinberger v. UOP, Inc.*, 457 A.2d 701 (Del.1983), the court rejected the business purpose test and substituted an increased emphasis on the entire fairness of the transaction. *Weinberger* states that entire fairness has two elements: fair dealing and fair price. Fair dealing includes full disclosure of all information relating to fairness. *Weinberger* also holds that the statutory right of dissent and appraisal is normally the sole remedy for minority stockholders complaining about the price in freeze-out mergers. The court, however, significantly liberalized that remedy.

    d.   The burden of proving entire fairness is on the corporation proposing the cash transaction. *Kahn v. Lynch Communication Systems*, 638 A.2d 1110

(Del.1994). *Weinberger* suggests, however, that strong evidence of fairness of a transaction may be derived from (a) approval by independent directors of the acquired corporation and (b) approval of the transaction by a *majority of the minority* of shares being cashed out. If these steps are taken, the burden of proof shifts from the parent corporation to the complaining stockholders.

e.   Federal law provides virtually no protection against unfair cash out merger transactions unless the merger is accomplished by means of deception. *See Santa Fe Indus., Inc. v. Green,* 430 U.S. 462 (1977); *Cole v. Schenley Indus., Inc.,* 563 F.2d 35 (2d Cir.1977). *But see Virginia Bankshares, Inc. v. Sandberg,* 501 U.S. 1083 (1991) (considering possibility that deception in connection with majority of minority vote could give rise to federal cause of action if vote insulates transaction from challenge and there is no remedy under state law). *See also Goldberg v. Meridor,* 567 F.2d 209 (2d Cir.1977); *Healey v. Catalyst Recovery of Pennsylvania, Inc.,* 616 F.2d 641 (3d Cir.1980).

B.   SALE OF ASSETS

In most states, a sale, lease, exchange, or other disposition of *all or substantially all* of the assets of a corporation (other than in the usual and regular course of business) must be approved by the stockholders. The MBCA followed this pattern until 1999. MBCA 12.02 now provides that stockholder approval is required only if the disposition would leave the corporation without a significant continuing business activity. More specifically, MBCA 12.02 provides that if a corporation retains a business activity that represents at least 25 percent of total assets *and* 25 percent of *either* income from continuing operations before taxes or revenues from continuing operations, the corporation will be deemed conclusively to have retained a significant continuing business activity. These tests are applied on the basis of financial information as of the end of the most recently completed fiscal year and on a consolidated basis including the corporation and its subsidiaries.

1.   Sales in Ordinary Course of Business

A sale of all, or substantially all, the property and assets of a corporation in the ordinary course of business (which is not common), does not require stockholder approval. MBCA 12.01(a)(1).

a. Many state statutes provide that a pledge, mortgage, or deed of trust covering all the assets of the corporation to secure a debt is in the ordinary course of business. MBCA 12.01(a)(2).

b. MBCA 12.01(a)(3) provides that stockholder approval is not required where a corporation drops down substantially all of its assets to a wholly owned subsidiary. *See Campbell v. Vose*, 515 F.2d 256 (10th Cir.1975) (invalidating such a transaction in the absence of stockholder approval). The MBCA Official Comment notes that this provision should not be permitted to be used as a device to avoid a vote of stockholders.

2. All or Substantially All

The scope of the phrase *all or substantially all* is a matter of dispute.

a. All or substantially all of the assets of a corporation are sold even if the corporation retains some small amount of property as a pretext. *Stiles v. Aluminum Products Co.*, 86 N.E.2d 887 (Ill.App.1949). For example, a sale of all the corporate assets other than cash or cash equivalents is the sale of all or substantially all of the corporation's property. A sale of several distinct manufacturing lines while retaining one or more lines is normally not a sale of all or substantially all even though the lines being sold are substantial and include a significant fraction of the corporation's former business, unless the lines are retained only as a temporary operation or as a pretext to avoid the statutory requirements. A sale of a plant but retention of operating assets (machinery and equipment), accounts receivable, good will, and the like, which permits the operation of the same business at another location is not the sale of all or substantially all of the corporation's property.

b. Until 1999, the MBCA Official Comment stated that the phrase *all or substantially all* should be read to mean what it literally says and noted that the phrase substantially all was added merely to make it clear that the statutory requirements could not be avoided by retention of some minimal or nominal residue of the original assets.

c. Judicial decisions adopt a much broader view of the phrase *all or substantially all*. These cases view the test as whether the change of business activity implicit in the sale is sufficiently important that it should be submitted to the stockholders for approval. *See Gimbel v. Signal Companies, Inc.*, 316 A.2d 599 (Del.Ch.1974), *aff'd per curiam*, 316 A.2d 619 (Del.1974). *But see Murphy v. Washington American League Base Ball Club, Inc.*, 293 F.2d 522 (D.C.Cir.1961).

3. Procedural Requirements

As with a merger or share exchange, a sale of assets must be approved by the board of directors and recommended to the stockholders for approval. The transaction must be approved by a majority of the shares voting at a meeting at which a majority quorum of shares entitled to vote is present. Voting by voting groups is not required, because the proceeds of the sale are payable to the corporation and not to the stockholders directly. Under the MBCA and the laws of most states, stockholders who are entitled to vote and who oppose the transaction have a right of dissent and appraisal. MBCA 12.02. Some states, including Delaware, do not grant the right of dissent and appraisal in connection with sales of asset transactions.

C. NONSTATUTORY COMBINATIONS

A statutory merger or share exchange is only one of several ways of effecting a corporate acquisition or combining or amalgamating two or more corporations into a single operation.

1. Types of Transactions

There are basically two types of nonstatutory combinations: a stock purchase and an asset purchase.

a. A stock purchase transaction is one in which one corporation purchases all or most of the outstanding shares of the other corporation in one or more voluntary transactions (such as a negotiated purchase, an open market purchases, or a tender offer). As a result, the target corporation becomes a subsidiary of the acquiring corporation. Thereafter, the parent may liquidate or merge the acquired corporation into itself using one of the devices discussed above.

b. An asset purchase or asset acquisition is a transaction in which one corporation purchases substantially all the assets of another corporation. The purchase may include all or virtually all of the assets of the acquired corporation, or it may include only the assets used in one line of business. The liabilities assumed by the asset purchaser are a matter of negotiation. Often, all liabilities remain with the seller, though it is common for the purchaser to assume liabilities to trade creditors. In any event,claims not assumed remain the responsibility of the seller. The ability to avoid assuming certain types of liabilities is one of the most important advantages of an asset acquisition.

c. After the transaction is completed, the seller corporation retains its separate existence as an independent corporation but its assets consist only of the proceeds of the sale, usually cash or stock, and whatever assets were not purchased. Such a corporation may continue in existence operating thereafter essentially as an investment company. The selling corporation may liquidate after making provision for liabilities not assumed by the purchaser and distribute the remaining proceeds of the sale to its stockholders. But it is common for the purchasing corporation to require that the selling corporation remain in existence for a number of years to avoid the possibility that the transaction will be recharacterized as a merger.

d. There is no right of dissent and appraisal for stockholders of the purchasing corporation even though stockholder approval would be required if the transaction were cast as a statutory merger.

2. Selection of Form of Transaction

Nonstatutory transactions may have the same economic effect as a statutory merger or share exchange. For example, a sale of assets in exchange for stock of the buyer corporation followed by dissolution of the seller and distribution of the buyer stock to seller stockholders amounts to the same thing as a merger of the two corporations.

a. The choice of form for a particular transaction involves a variety of business and tax considerations. The parties to a specific transaction may have different views on this question, one preferring an asset purchase, the other a stock purchase or statutory merger, often depending on the tax consequences. Generally the controlling stockholder may structure the transaction according to its own interests. *Grace v. Grace Nat. Bank of New York*, 465 F.2d 1068 (2d Cir.1972).

b. It is perfectly legal to structure a transaction in one form rather than another in order to simplify the procedures to be followed or to avoid granting dissenting stockholders the right of dissent and appraisal. *Hariton v. Arco Electronics, Inc.*, 188 A.2d 123 (Del.1963). On the other hand, because the transactions may be economically equivalent, some courts have held that a sale of assets may be treated as a merger in some circumstances under the *de facto merger doctrine*. *See Farris v. Glen Alden Corp.*, 143 A.2d 25 (Pa. 1958) (purchase of assets for stock by small Pennsylvania corporation from larger Delaware corporation recast as merger where structure of deal avoided appraisal rights for Pennsylvania corporation stockholders as well as real estate transfer taxes and stockholders of Delaware corporation constituted large majority of stockholders following transaction). *See also Applestein v. United Bd. & Carton Corp.*, 159 A.2d 146 (N.J.Super.Ch.Div.1960). The Pennsylvania statutes were later amended to reverse the result in *Farris*. *See Terry v. Penn Central Corp.*, 668 F.2d 188 (3d Cir.1981) (challenging series of triangular mergers designed to avoid vote of preferred stockholders). *See also Orzeck v. Englehart*, 195 A.2d 375 (Del.1963).

c. The de facto merger doctrine has been applied more recently in connection with cases involving products liability claims and environmental harms in order to hold the purchasing corporation liable as it would be if the transaction had taken the form of a statutory merger. Some courts reach the same result under a variety of theories: (1) there is an express or implied agreement to assume the liabilities; (2) the transaction amounts to a consolidation or merger; (3) the successor entity is a mere continuation or reincarnation of the predecessor entity; or (4) the transaction was fraudulent, not made in good faith, or made without sufficient consideration; or (5) continuity of enterprise. *See North Shore Gas Co. v. Salomon, Inc.*, 152 F.3d 642, 651 (7th Cir. 1998); *Nissen Corp. v. Miller*, 323 Md. 613, 594 A.2d 564, 565–66 (Md. 1991). In addition, under some circumstances it may be possible to argue that the two corporations have entered into a partnership with each other. *See Good v. Lackawanna Leather Co.*, 233 A.2d 201 (N.J.Super.Ch.Div.1967).

d. Under most state statutes, suit against a dissolved corporation must be brought within three years of public notice of dissolution. MBCA 14.07. And the stockholders may be held liable to the extent that assets of the dissolved corporation have been distributed to them.

3. **Divisive Transactions**

A few states have adopted statutes permitting corporations to divide into two or more corporations. The ABA and NCCUSL have undertaken jointly to draft model legislation in this area.

a. Such transactions constitute about half of all corporate deals but have not traditionally been addressed by statute. Rather, in most cases such a division is accomplished by a transfer of assets to a newly formed subsidiary corporation (or an existing subsidiary) followed by a distribution of subsidiary shares.

b. If the distribution of subsidiary stock is made to all stockholders of the parent (a spinoff), the distribution will likely be treated as a distribution of property (such as a cash dividend). Such a distribution of stock is not a stock dividend because the stock distributed is stock of another corporation (the subsidiary). It is property of the distributing corporation. If the distribution of subsidiary stock is made to some stockholders but not others and the distributee stockholders give up their stock in the distributing corporation (a split off), then the transaction will likely be treated as a repurchase of stock. In many states, the same basic rules apply to both types of transactions, but there may be subtle variations even in those states. In other states, the rules may vary considerably between the two. In some cases, if the operations to be shed are quite significant in comparison to those remaining with the distributing corporation, the transaction may arguably qualify as a sale of assets, triggering the rules relating to such transactions.

c. One important issue in such deals is the division of liabilities between successor entities. In most cases, the offshoot corporation will assume minimal current liabilities, while the distributing corporation will retain most long term liabilities. (The corporation cannot shed its own liabilities even if another corporation assumes them, but a new corporation is not obligated to creditors except to the extent that it assumes such obligations.) Thus, the creditors will have a strong interest in the deal. In extreme cases, the deal may be unwound by means of piercing the corporate veil or theories of successor liability.

D. GOING PRIVATE & LEVERAGED BUYOUTS

The term *going private* refers to a transaction by which a publicly held corporation cashes out its public stockholders and becomes privately held. The transaction permits deregistration of the corporation under the Securities Exchange Act of 1934, thereby eliminating expensive reporting and disclosure requirements. Most corporations considering a traditional going private transaction went public by selling shares publicly at a time when market conditions were favorable. Typically only a minority interest was sold to the public. The going private transaction is likely to occur some years later when the stock prices are depressed.

1. Form of Going Private Transactions

A going private transaction may take the form of a cash merger of the publicly held corporation into a corporation wholly owned by the control group, by a cash tender offer followed by a mop up merger, by a reverse stock split, or by an amendment to articles of incorporation changing the rights of stockholders. If the transaction is accomplished by reverse stock split, the ratio between outstanding shares and post transaction shares is set at a level that makes the holdings of the largest public stockholder into a fractional share. The corporation purchases all fractional shares at a specified price, as is permitted by most corporation statutes. *See* MBCA 6.04.

2. Leveraged Buyouts

A leveraged buyout (LBO) is essentially a going private transaction involving outside investors. In an LBO, a private corporation acquires all of the outstanding shares of a publicly held corporation. The acquiring corporation may be financed by investors who specialize in such transactions often using borrowed money and often by issuing junk bonds. After the LBO is completed, the corporation is no longer publicly owned. Typically, the corporation assumes the obligation to repay the loans required to accomplish the transaction. Pieces of the acquired company are often sold off to help pay down this debt. Thus, such a transaction is often called a bust up takeover, though that term may be used in the context of both friendly and hostile deals.

a. An LBO differs from a going private transaction primarily in that outside investors rather than incumbent managers acquire the predominant equity ownership of the company. Incumbent management may participate in an LBO, usually with a minority stake. Such a transaction may be called a management buy out (MBO). Still, the economic interest of management in the corporation is usually increased significantly as a result of the transaction.

b. As much as possible of the purchase price is borrowed. The interest payable on LBO debt is tax deductible by the acquired company, subject to limitations imposed by FRB rules. Income taxes may thus be reduced to zero by the LBO and cash flow formerly used to pay taxes may be used to pay interest.

c. Often the hope of the investors in the LBO is that the company will be able to pay down the debt with cash flow and possibly even again become a publicly owned company.

3. Regulation

Going private transactions are similar in form to a parent-subsidiary merger and thus are subject to entire fairness review under *Weinberger*. Some states also grant stockholders cashed out by a reverse stock split the right of dissent and appraisal. MBCA 13.02(a). In addition, in 1979 the SEC adopted Rules 13e-3 and 13e-4 to assure full disclosure in connection with going private transactions, including a statement as to the belief of the issuer whether the transaction is fair or unfair to the public stockholders and a discussion in reasonable detail of the material factors upon which the belief is based.

E. RIGHT OF DISSENT & APPRAISAL

State statutes give stockholders the right to dissent from certain types of transactions and to obtain the appraised value of their shares in cash through a judicial proceeding. MBCA 13.01–13.31.

1. Scope of the Appraisal Right

The appraisal right is a creature of statute and is available only when the statute specifically so provides. State statutes vary considerably in terms of the transactions that give rise to appraisal rights.

   a.   MBCA 13.02 extends appraisal rights to (1) a merger in which the stockholder has the right to vote, (2) a short form merger of subsidiary into parent as to stockholders of the subsidiary only, (3) a share exchange if the stockholder has the right to vote as to stockholders of the target only, and (4) a sale of assets if the stockholder has the right to vote on the sale, (5) a reverse stock split as to stockholders who will have their shares repurchased, (6) domestication if the stockholder does not receive shares in the foreign corporation resulting from the domestication that have terms as favorable to the stockholder in all material respects, and represent at least the same percentage interest of the total voting rights of the outstanding shares of the corporation, as the shares held by the stockholder before the domestication; (7) consummation of a conversion of the corporation to nonprofit status; (8) consummation of a conversion of the corporation to an unincorporated entity, or (9) transactions as to which the articles of incorporation, bylaws, or a resolution of the board of directors specifies that dissenters' rights shall be provided.

   b.   Prior to the 1999 amendments, the MBCA also provided for appraisal rights in the case of an amendment to the articles of incorporation that materially and adversely affects stockholder rights in specified ways–roughly similar to the situations in which a stockholder vote is triggered for non voting shares though somewhat narrower.

c. The law of many states includes an exception for publicly traded companies on the theory that if there is a liquid market for the shares of the subject company, market price is a reliable measure of value. In other words, stockholders of a publicly traded company do not have appraisal rights even though the transaction is one that would ordinarily trigger such rights. As of 1999, the MBCA also includes such an exception. (The MBCA also included a similar exception prior to 1984.) Specifically, the MBCA exempts companies that are listed on the NYSE, AMEX, or NASDAQ NMS or that have 2000 or more stockholders and a public float of $20 million or more. MBCA 13.02(b). Delaware law also includes a market exception but only for mergers in which the consideration to be paid is stock of a publicly traded company. Delaware law also grants appraisal rights to the stockholders of the *surviving* corporation unless it is listed or widely held *and* no stockholder vote is required. DGCL 262.

d. Under the MBCA There is an exception to the exception for (1) transactions in which the stockholders will be paid in anything other than cash or shares of a publicly traded company, and (2) transactions in which an insider or insider affiliate acquires the subject company. MBCA 13.02(b). For these purposes, an insider is defined as anyone who (before the transaction) owns 20 percent or more of the subject company stock (excluding shares acquired in an any-or-all offer within the preceding 12 months at an equal or lesser price), or anyone who had the power to elect or appoint one-fourth or more of the company's directors, or anyone who will receive a financial benefit not generally available to other stockholders (other than employment by or a seat on the board of directors of the surviving company). In other words, appraisal is available notwithstanding the market exception in the context of an interested transaction.

2. Exclusiveness of Appraisal Right

The statutes of some states provide that appraisal is the exclusive remedy for dissenting stockholders. MBCA 13.02(d) provides that appraisal is the exclusive remedy unless the action is unlawful or was procured as a result of fraud or material misrepresentation. In some states, caselaw holds that appraisal is the exclusive remedy. *Weinberger v. UOP, Inc.*, 457 A.2d 701

(Del.1983); *Glassman v. Unocal Exploration Corp.*, 777 A.2d 242, 248 (Del. 2001) (short form merger). Other states hold that the right of dissent and appraisal is exclusive when the stockholders' only complaint is the inadequacy of the price. *Stringer v. Car Data Systems*, 841 P.2d 1183 (Ore.1992). Several states appear to permit stockholder actions challenging the fairness of terms on a variety of grounds including lack of business purpose even though the statute states that the appraisal remedy is exclusive. *See Alpert v. 28 Williams St. Corp.*, 483 N.Y.S.2d 667, 473 N.E.2d 19 (N.Y. 1984); *Matteson v. Ziebarth*, 242 P.2d 1025 (Wash.1952). It is not entirely clear what it means for the appraisal statute to be the exclusive remedy given that the notion of fraud is broadly construed in the context of corporation law as essentially equivalent to a breach of fiduciary duty.

3. Procedure

State statutes provide elaborate procedures for establishing the right to an appraisal and fixing the price.

a. The corporation has a duty to provide correct information as to the procedures to be followed. *Gibbons v. Schenley Indus., Inc.*, 339 A.2d 460 (Del.Ch.1975). The statutory right may be lost if the statutory procedures are not precisely followed. *Gibson v. Strong, Inc.*, 708 S.W.2d 603 (Ark.1986). If the right is lost, the dissenting stockholder must go along with the transaction.

b. The notice of meeting to stockholders at which the transaction is considered must state that dissenters' rights may arise from the transaction. MBCA 13.20. A written notice of intent to demand payment must be filed by each dissenting stockholder before the vote of stockholders is taken on the proposed action. MBCA 13.21. Following approval of the transaction, the corporation must send a notice to each dissenter. MBCA 13.22. Each dissenting stockholder must then file a demand for payment. MBCA 13.23. A stockholder must dissent with respect to all shares, but record owners who hold shares for more than one beneficial owner may dissent owner by owner. MBCA 13.03. The MBCA permits either the record owner or the beneficial owner to commence an appraisal proceeding. MBCA 13.03. Under Delaware law, only a record owner may do so.

c. In most states, no money is paid by the corporation until the judicial proceeding is concluded. Under the MBCA, the corporation must estimate the fair value of the shares and pay to each dissenter that amount immediately. MBCA 13.24. If the dissenting stockholder is dissatisfied with this payment, he must submit an estimate of the fair value of his shares. MBCA 13.26. If the stockholder and the corporation cannot agree as to an additional amount to be paid, the stockholder or the corporation may obtain a judicial appraisal of the value of the shares. MBCA 13.30. To avoid possible speculation on the outcome of an appraisal proceeding, the MBCA provides that a corporation may refuse to make immediate payment to a stockholder who acquires shares after announcement of the transaction. MBCA 13.27. Such a stockholder is entitled to payment only upon the completion of the appraisal proceeding.

d. The fair value of shares is to be fixed as of a time immediately before the transaction and without consideration of the effect of the transaction on the value of the shares. MBCA 13.01. Some statutes specify that value should be determined as of the day before the announcement of the deal, while other statutes specify the day before the stockholder. The MBCA permits consideration of appreciation or depreciation in anticipation of the transaction if equitable. MBCA 13.01. Caselaw addresses a variety of factors to be considered in this regard. *See Weinberger v. UOP, Inc.,* 457 A.2d 701 (Del.1983) (court may consider premiums in comparable transactions); *Rapid-American Corp. v. Harris,* 603 A.2d 796 (Del.1992) (court should consider control premium that could be commanded by parent in connection with sale of subsidiary); Cede (going concern value should be calculated based on lower capitalization rate calculated before announcement affected volatility of stock).

e. The traditional manner of establishing fair value is the Delaware Block Method. In this manner of valuation, the court calculated a weighted average of asset value, market value, and earnings value. Weights are assigned according to the reliability of each factor. *See Gibbons v. Schenley Indus., Inc.,* 339 A.2d 460 (Del.Ch.1975). In a case in which the market value for the stock is based on only a few transactions, market value is given a relatively low weight. *Piemonte v. New Boston Garden Corp.,* 387 N.E.2d 1145 (Mass.1979) (ten percent); *Brown v. Hedahl's-Q B & R, Inc.,* 185 N.W.2d 249 (N.D.1971); *Application of Delaware Racing Ass'n,* 213 A.2d 203 (Del.1965). Earnings value is usually based on the capitalized value for average earnings over the most recent five years. *Francis I. duPont & Co. v. Universal City Studios, Inc.,* 312 A.2d 344 (Del.Ch.1973). There is no assurance under these tests that the court-determined price will be equal to or more than the merger price. See *Gibbons v. Schenley Indus., Inc.,* (merger price $53.33 was per share and appraised value was $33.86 per share).

f. In *Weinberger v. UOP, Inc.,* 457 A.2d 701 (Del.1983), the Delaware Supreme Court abandoned the Delaware Block Method and adopted a more flexible approach that permits use of valuation techniques acceptable in the financial community. The trial court has broad discretion in the process. The most common method followed by courts today is valuation by means of discounted cash flow (DCF) using the capital asset pricing model (CAPM) to determine the capitalization rate based on the risk inherent in the stock as measured by its beta coefficient (the volatility of the stock compared to the market as a whole).

g. The MBCA provides that the costs of an appraisal proceeding including the fees of a court appointed appraiser shall be borne by the corporation. Attorney fees may be assessed against the corporation if it did not substantially comply with the requirements of the statute or against the dissenting stockholders if they acted arbitrarily, vexatiously, or not in good faith. The court may also order attorney fees paid out of the award to the dissenters. MBCA 13.31. The court also has broad discretion with respect to an award of prejudgment interest.

4. Evaluation of the Appraisal Remedy

The appraisal remedy has a superficial appeal, but from the stockholder's point of view it is not an attractive remedy. Accordingly, stockholders and their lawyers typically look for some way to maintain an action against the corporation based on breach of fiduciary duty or some other broad claim.

a. Appraisal involves potentially long delays while the price is established. In most states there is no requirement that the corporation make immediate payment of the amount it estimates to be the fair value of the shares. All payments are deferred until completion of the appraisal proceeding. Accordingly, the stockholder may lose the returns that would have been available if the merger price had been taken and the funds reinvested. Although the courts have broad discretion in the award of prejudgment interest, they seldom award it at a rate that would compensate the investor for investment returns in the interim. The MBCA has sought to alleviate some of these problems, but it has not been widely followed in this regard.

b.   Litigation over the value of shares is complicated, expensive and risky. The corporation is an active participant in the judicial proceeding and seeks to establish the lowest possible valuation. The corporation has extensive knowledge about its own affairs and virtually unlimited resources to litigate the issue. There is always a risk that the court will find the appraised value to be less than the price offered in the merger. Practically speaking, a lawyer is likely to prefer to pursue a class action on behalf of all stockholders because if the action is successful, attorney fees will likely be a percentage of a much larger pot and are assured to be paid out of that pot. Thus, it is much more likely that a stockholder will be able to retain effective counsel for a class action than for an appraisal proceeding.

c.   Because appraisal rights may constitute a serious cash drain for the corporation, it is common in a merger agreement to provide an escape clause for the parties the parties to a merger if an excessive number of dissents are filed. Arguably, the elaborate procedures to be followed in a appraisal proceeding were developed to permit the corporation to withdraw from a transaction once it learns that a large number of dissents will be filed. But the complex procedural requirements may also create injustice if a relatively minor failure to follow the prescribed procedures results in a loss of the right to dissent.

d.   On the other hand, a stockholder has a right to appraisal that cannot be dismissed for failure to state a cause of action or as a result of summary judgment. Moreover, the existence of the appraisal remedy may cause acquiring corporations to offer a fair price in the first place.

F.   VOLUNTARY DISSOLUTION

Generally, a corporation may dissolve if the board of directors so proposes and a majority of stockholders (or some other specified percentage) approves. MBCA 14.02. In this regard, dissolution is similar to other organic changes such as a merger or sale of assets. There are special rules that permit dissolution before commencement of business by the incorporators or initial directors by filing a simple notice of dissolution. MBCA 14.01. Dissolution is permitted in many states at any time with the unanimous consent of the stockholders if suitable provision is made for creditors. This provision is widely used by closely held corporations. The MBCA does not contain a provision to this effect. Even though stockholders may act by unanimous consent under the MBCA, action by the board of directors is also required for dissolution.

1. **Procedure**

    Some states require the filing of a notice of intent to dissolve, followed by a period in which the business and affairs of the corporation are wound up, followed by the filing of final articles of dissolution. The MBCA (1969) followed this multiple step procedure. MBCA 14.03 permits articles of dissolution to be filed at any time during the dissolution process.

    a. The corporation must give written notice of the dissolution to known creditors and claimants. MBCA 14.06. The notice must state a deadline for filing claims no fewer than 120 days from the effective date of the notice. If the corporation rejects a claim, the claimant has 90 days from the date of the rejection notice to begin a judicial proceeding to enforce the claim. If a claimant who receives notice fails to make a claim or fails to commence an enforcement proceeding within the specified periods, the claim is barred.

    b. As for possible unknown claimants, the corporation may publish a notice of dissolution in a newspaper of general circulation in the county of its principal office or, if it has no office in the state, the county of its registered agent. The notice must specify a procedure for filing claims and state that claims not filed within three years are barred. MBCA 14.07.

    c. State statutes usually provide that the existence of a corporation continues after dissolution for a stated period so that the corporation may be sued on pre-dissolution claims. MBCA 14.07 states simply that the corporation's existence continues (indefinitely) after dissolution, but bars claims that are not timely filed.

    d. A claim that is not barred may be enforced (1) against the dissolved corporation to the extent of its undistributed assets or (2) against a stockholder of the dissolved corporation to the extent of the stockholder's pro rata share of the claim or the corporate assets distributed to the stockholder in liquidation, whichever is less, but a stockholder's total liability for all claims under this section may not exceed the total amount of assets distributed to the stockholder. MBCA 14.07.

    e. MBCA 14.08 provides a procedure by which a corporation may commence a judicial proceeding to determine the necessary security for claims that have not been filed or that may arise after the effective date of dissolution. If the corporation provides such security, then unknown claimants may not enforce their claims against the stockholders.

f.   There is no statutory right of appraisal in connection with a voluntary dissolution.

2.   Equitable Limitations

Equitable limitations on the power to dissolve have sometimes been imposed in situations where a voluntary dissolution is unfair to minority stockholders or is used as a way to freeze out of such stockholders.

a.   If the business is losing money dissolution may be reasonable, because the majority should not be required to wait until the corporation is insolvent and their investment is lost. On the other hand, dissolution may involve the sale of assets at inadequate prices.

b.   Cases have arisen where dissolution is part of a broader scheme to eliminate some stockholders from sharing in the future profits of a profitable business. For example, the business may be sold as a going concern to a new corporation which is owned by some but not all of the original owners. *Lebold v. Inland Steel Co.*, 125 F.2d 369 (7th Cir.1941).

c.   In some early cases, dissolution and reincorporation was used to eject a minority from a successful venture. Today, such a transaction is normally cast as a cash out merger. The tests developed in the cash merger cases may have potential applicability in dissolutions that are designed to eliminate unwanted minority stockholders.

Perspective

Corporation law is primarily about the *internal affairs* of the business corporation. It focuses on the control rights and financial rights of stockholders, directors, and officers. Thus, corporation law is rather like constitutional law for individual businesses. As for the relationship of the corporation to the outside world, a corporation is for the most part just another legal person to whom other law applies with minor adjustments. Nevertheless, there are a few issue areas relating to outsiders that are traditionally considered part of corporation law, such as the law relating to piercing the corporate veil, to preincorporation transactions, and to successor liability to some extent. These areas may also be considered to be matters of agency law and the law of creditor rights. (And as one might suspect, the analysis of a controversy may differ in interesting ways depending on the law applied.)

Since the late 1800s and through the mid 1990s, most US businesses of any significant size were conducted in the form of the business corporation. It is still the case that large publicly held businesses are almost invariably conducted in corporate form. The economic importance of these businesses alone justifies a careful examination of corporation law. Traditionally, the corporate form was also widely used for smaller closely held businesses–rather than the partnership– because the corporation offered limited liability for owners and investors. The major exception was professional practices (such as law firms) which were prohibited from using the corporate form until the advent of the professional corporation in the 1970s.

As late as 1990 these patterns appeared to be settled and unchanging. But in the meantime, several new business forms have emerged, including the limited liability company (LLC), which appears likely to become the business form of choice for closely held businesses. The LLC combines limited liability for members with the management flexibility of a partnership. And it is taxed under the Internal Revenue Code (IRC) as a partnership rather than as a corporation. That is, the entity itself pays no income tax. Rather the income passes through to investors (in whatever proportions they may reasonably specify), and tax is paid at the individual level. (Generally speaking, one level of tax is preferable to two, but it must be kept in mind that with pass through taxation, the investor pays tax on his or her share of the income whether or not the business distributes cash.)

This does not mean that the corporate form will wither away for closely held businesses. For one thing, the LLC may be attractive for new businesses, but it is not realistically available for established businesses that have already elected the corporate form. The tax cost of shifting from a corporation to an LLC is usually prohibitive. In addition, if a business is publicly traded (even if the market is quite thin), the business will be treated as a corporation for tax purposes no matter how it is organized. Thus, if a business plans to go public in the near future, it should probably elect the corporate form from the outset. Indeed, if a business seeks capital from outside investors such as a venture capital fund, it is likely that the investor will insist that the business be conducted in the corporate form, in part because the investor may ultimately want to cash out through a public offering, and in part because the law relating to corporations is more settled than the law relating to LLCs and other forms. Finally, in 2003, the IRC was amended to reduce dramatically the tax rate applicable to dividends and capital gains, so that the financial advantages of partnership taxation have become much less significant. Indeed, in many cases the corporate form may offer a distinct advantage in that income may be accumulated in the corporation which may be in a lower tax bracket than the individual investor. (The investor pays tax only if the corporation distributes cash or other property.) In effect, the investor can choose when to pay the individual level tax–at the new lower rates–by selling some stock at a gain or–in the case of a controlling stockholder–causing the corporation to declare a dividend.

Aside from the foregoing, and probably more important, the issues that arise in connection with other forms of organization are the same issues that arise in connection with corporation law. The difference is the statute or case law under which the issue is analyzed. For example, with both the partnership and the LLC, the parties are largely free to structure their relationship by private contract. There are very few mandatory provisions in the statutes. Nevertheless, the parties must address the same issues that are addressed under corporation law. They must specify the financial interests of various investors. And they must determine who has the power to make business decisions and how that power may be exercised. Ironically, it is quite common to incorporate by reference the law of corporations rather than to reinvent the wheel with an elaborate private contract. Moreover, corporation law has become increasingly flexible in recent years. Many provisions once considered mandatory may now be modified in the articles of incorporation, or the bylaws, or by stockholder agreement. To be sure, default rules matter when the parties fail to specify another arrangement. And default rules differ for different forms of organization. But these rules are relatively simple to find in the statutes. For example, in a corporation the rule is one share one vote, whereas in a partnership the rule is one partner one vote.

Finally, it is difficult to appreciate some of the nuances of the law relating to closely held businesses without a firm grounding in the law relating to corporations in general. For example, much of the law relating to closely held corporations has developed in reaction to less flexible rules governing publicly traded corporations. Thus, although it might seem sensible to think about the law of corporations (and other forms of organization) by thinking first about very small businesses and then about larger and larger businesses, the law has in fact evolved in the other direction from the top down. Thus, the law of corporations is therefore the foundation of business law curriculum.

Nevertheless, the development of the LLC is a problem for any work that seeks to summarize the law of corporations and for law school courses addressing the law relating to business organizations. In some schools, there are two basic courses dealing with business associations. One covers closely held business forms (partnerships, limited partnerships, LLCs, closely held corporations), and the other deals with publicly held corporations (often including some coverage of securities law).

This book focuses on corporations, both closely held and publicly held. It does not cover LLCs, partnerships or limited partnerships, except in passing or by way of obvious contrast. Neither does this book address in detail specialized areas of law relating to corporations that are usually the subject of advanced law school courses, such as securities regulation and corporate tax. Nevertheless, it is important to have a basic understanding of the relationship between corporation law and these other bodies of law.

As previously noted, many of the problems addressed by corporation law involve agency principles. For example, fiduciary duty, including both the duty of care and the duty of loyalty (or fairness) are derived from the common law of agency (as well as the law of trusts.) Indeed, these issues often command more class time than any others in a law school course on corporation law. Some schools offer a separate course in agency (or agency and partnership), but these courses tend to be taken by many students after they have taken a basic course in business associations or corporations. Nevertheless, instructors in corporation law generally seem to assume that students have received a grounding in common law agency concepts in courses relating to contracts and torts at least in passing. Some casebooks on business associations also contain brief discussions of agency. Although it may be helpful in some cases to have had more formal instruction in the law of agency, the concepts and rules are usually clear enough from the context of corporation law cases. The approach here is to point out the connections between corporation law and agency law when they arise and to explain any differences in approach as between the common law and corporation law which is primarily statutory.

The relationship between corporation law and the law relating to federal income taxation is a bit like the relationship between the chicken and the egg. Many areas discussed in the law of corporations are shaped to some degree by federal tax concepts. On the other hand, many issues discussed in a corporate tax course presuppose a working knowledge of corporation law. While there is no rigid rule about which course should be taken first, or whether it is desirable to take the two courses simultaneously, the most common pattern is for law students to take corporations without previously having had a course in federal income taxation. As a result, many instructors of corporation law do not emphasize tax concepts. Fortunately, even where tax-related concepts are discussed, they can almost always be understood without a broader knowledge of federal income tax law. On the other hand, a basic working knowledge of corporations is usually assumed without discussion in federal income taxation courses and certainly in advanced courses on corporate tax. Indeed, to a large extent, corporate tax law is built on a somewhat idealized (and dated) notion of state corporation law. Thus, although it is probably a good idea for a student who is focused on business law to take the basic courses on both corporation law and income tax law as early as possible, one should wait to take a course on corporate tax or partnership tax (or any more advanced business tax course such as reorganizations) until after one has completed a basic course focused on corporation law.

Although law schools offer an advanced course in securities regulation which focuses primarily on the federal Securities Act of 1933 and the Securities Exchange Act of 1934, most courses on corporation law also address certain issues arising under these statutes. In particular, most corporation law courses include an introduction to the law relating to public offerings (and exemptions therefrom for small or private offerings) as well as often more substantial treatment of the law relating to proxy solicitations, securities fraud (including insider trading), and the federal regulation of tender offers. These topics will likely also be addressed in a course on securities regulation albeit in more detail. They come up in the basic corporation law course because they involve issues that may also give rise to questions of state law. This book addresses these overlapping issues of federal securities law in some detail, but it does not seek to serve as an outline that would be adequate for a law school course in securities regulation.

As for how to prepare for an examination, the law of corporations is derived partially from state and federal statutory provisions and partly from common law sources. Some teachers use the corporations course largely as an exercise in statutory construction and analysis of the law (sometimes of a particular state) while others emphasize the broader common law or general issues. In either event, some attention is normally paid to federal law dealing with corporate issues as well as state law. In preparing for an examination a student must recognize the emphasis the instructor has placed on these areas and concentrate preparation time accordingly. One must also consider the nature of the examination. A short answer or multiple choice examination in a course that has heavily emphasized the statutes and case law of a particular state, calls for quite different preparation from an essay examination in a course that has focused on general principles.

The practice questions included in this outline are designed to give students experience with both short answer and essay questions. Needless to say, questions based on specific state statutory provisions can be answered correctly only by reference to the specific language of the statute.

When answering essay questions, a student should usually follow the same method of analysis of that is applicable to other law school essay exams. But the student should take into account the possibility that the question raises issues of statutory construction or application of federal law as well as traditional common law principles. A low grade is virtually certain if one answers a question that centers on the construction of a specific statutory provision by reference to general equitable principles. The same unfortunate result follows if a student applies principles of federal law to a situation in which no federal jurisdiction exists. The following suggestions may help to avoid these common errors.

The first step in any examination is to read the question very carefully and to identify the issues and questions raised. While this may seem self-evident, a low grade is more often the result of inadequate analysis of the question than any other single cause. It may be helpful to ask yourself why is the instructor asking about this factual situation and what areas of the course are involved.

The second step is to isolate the legal principles that are applicable to the issues and questions raised. In corporations, the legal principles may be found (a) in a corporation statute of a specific state (often Delaware) or of the Model Business Corporation Act; (b) in the general case law dealing with corporations; or (c) in the federal Securities Act of 1933 or the Securities Exchange Act of 1934. It is possible that a single question may implicate several sources of law.

Having isolated the issues and the sources of legal principles, one should organize one's answer and respond to the issues raised in the same manner as in any other law school examination. Conclusions should be clearly stated and supported by reasons. If you have rejected an argument that appears to be plausible, it is usually desirable to say so and give a reason. Make sure that your answer responds to all the issues raised by the question.

Be careful about just throwing things in because you know about them. A canned essay on an irrelevant topic almost certainly will not help you, and may well detract from the overall evaluation of your answer. Also, some exam questions in corporations (and in other subjects as well) may be designed to test whether you know that some principle is not applicable. For this reason you should concentrate on why the principle is not applicable, not on what would happen if the inapplicable principle were applicable.

Finally, it seldom matters what position you take on a given issue.

I

Corporation Law in General

A corporation is a form of organization that provides (1) limited liability for its owners, (2) perpetual existence independent of its owners, (3) centralization of management in persons who need not be owners (directors and officers), and (4) free transferability of ownership interests (shares). The owners of a corporation are the *shareholders* or *stockholders*. The stockholders elect the board of directors which in turn sets general policies for the corporation and elects the officers who carry out those policies day to day and generally manage the corporation.

Caveat: These characteristics may be modified to a significant extent by agreements among the participants. Moreover, many states also have statutes providing for the formation of close corporations that have characteristics more akin to partnerships. For example, a statutory close corporation may be managed by the stockholders rather than a board of directors and shares may not be transferable without the approval of other stockholders.

A. THEORETICAL FOUNDATION

Several different theories have been proposed to describe the corporation. Each is to some degree a useful picture of what a corporation is.

1. Entity Theory

A corporation may be most readily envisioned as an entity created for the purpose of conducting a business. The basic elements are:

a. The entity has the power to conduct its business in its own name, including entering into contracts, buying or selling land, bringing suits or being sued, filing tax returns, paying taxes, and the like.

b. The entity is formed by a grant of authority from a government agency, in most states, the secretary of state. A basic governing document usually called the *articles of incorporation* must be filed with the state and a filing fee paid. The grant of authority may be evidenced by a *certificate of incorporation* or other document issued by the government agency. Subsequent formal steps may also be required to complete formation.

    Caveat: The terminology varies from state to state. For example, in Delaware the term *certificate* is generally used to refer to the basic governing document of a corporation. In some jurisdictions the word *charter* is used.

c. The entity is generally recognized as separate from its owners by the states, the federal government, and those who deal with it.

    Caveat: The artificial entity is ultimately a fiction. In reality, real people conduct a business, whether or not it is in corporate form, and real people enjoy the profit or suffer the loss from the business.

d. In some limited situations courts may refuse to follow the artificial entity analysis to its logical conclusions if it leads to fraudulent or significantly unfair consequences, frustration of clearly defined statutory policies, or other undesirable results. These situations are discussed in somewhat greater detail below under the doctrine of *piercing the corporate veil*.

2. Concession Theory

A second theory is that a corporation is a grant or concession from the state. Cf. *Association for the Preservation of Freedom of Choice, Inc. v. Shapiro*, 214 N.Y.S.2d 388, 174 N.E.2d 487 (N.Y. 1961). This theory is based on the role of the state in the formation of a corporation.

a. This theory was more accurate at an earlier time when corporate charters were granted only by act of the state legislature for a specified purpose and were subject to significant restrictions or limitations.

b. This theory is sometimes referred to today in the debate over the social responsibility of corporations. The argument is that because a corporation is a grant or concession by the state, the grant may be qualified by the state as it sees fit. The theory is that the state may therefore validly impose restrictions on corporate behavior and withdraw the corporate privilege completely if the restrictions are not obeyed.

> *Caveat:* The concept that a corporation is based on a grant of authority or concession from the state is largely a fiction. The process of incorporation today involves only ministerial acts and no significant substantive decisions are made in this process by the state or agency that issues charters to corporations.

3. Contract Theory

A third theory is that the charter of a corporation represents a contract (a) between the state and the corporation, or (b) between the corporation and its stockholders, or (c) among the stockholders.

a. The argument that a corporate charter represents a contract between the state and the corporation was relied upon by the United States Supreme Court in *Trustees of Dartmouth College v. Woodward*, 17 U.S. (4 Wheat) 518 (1819) to prevent the state of New Hampshire from enacting a statute amending the charter of the College. The case is primarily of historical interest today, because following a suggestion in an opinion in that case, all modern state statutes specifically reserve the power to subject outstanding charters to subsequent statutory amendments.

> **Example:** MBCA 1.02 provides: The [name of state legislature] has power to amend or repeal, all or part of this Act at any time and all domestic and foreign corporations subject to this Act are governed by the amendment or repeal.

b. The argument that a corporate charter represents a contract among the stockholders or between the corporation and the stockholders often surfaces in the context of disputes between different classes of stockholders. Rights of senior classes of securities (preferred shares) are defined and limited by the basic corporate documents. The provisions in these documents relating to the rights of the senior securities are described as the contract between the senior securities holders and the sometimes corporation.

> **Example:** Articles of incorporation provide that preferred shares are entitled to receive, when and as declared by the board of

directors, dividends equal to but not exceeding two dollars per share per year before any dividend is declared or paid on common shares. The corporation has an exceptional year and the directors are considering paying dividends in excess of $20.00 per share. The preferred shares are nevertheless only entitled to receive two dollars per share; if the directors attempt to declare a discretionary dividend of, say, ten dollars per share on the preferred, that is a breach of the common stockholders' contract which entitles them to enjoin any dividend on the preferred in excess of two dollars per share.

4. Nexus of Contracts

Economists have developed a theory of corporateness that permits analysis of the corporation as an economic phenomenon. This theory rejects the notion that the stockholders are the ultimate owners of the enterprise but treats them, along with bondholders and other creditors, as providers of capital in anticipation of receiving a desired return. The *nexus of contracts* theory assumes that corporate managers obtain the requirements of the corporation for capital, labor, materials, and services through a series of contractual relationships.

Caveat: Many arrangements made by corporations are contractual in a free will sense. For example, employment contracts are entered into by corporate officers and employees. Many arrangements, however, are not. For example, stockholders who buy shares of stock on a public market do not enter into a contract with the corporation in the normal sense of the word. Tort creditors and other persons affected by corporate actions typically also have claims or rights that are not truly contractual in nature.

Caveat: The nexus of contracts theory uses the word contract in the sense used by many economists as including non-consensual rational economic relationships. Arrangements not the subject of actual contracts are seen as implicit contracts, i.e. contracts that might reasonably have been entered into had there been actual negotiation. The terms of those implicit contracts are the terms economists believe would reasonably be entered into by investors under similar circumstances.

Caveat: So far as stockholders are concerned, the initial subscribers to shares when the corporation is formed do typically enter into contracts with the corporation. But in the case of large, publicly held corporations, few shares are held by persons who are initial subscribers.

Caveat: The nexus of contracts approach is an economic model of the corporation. Economic models are useful because they permit study of economic phenomena in a simplified environment where inferences and conclusions may be drawn in a logical fashion. One must always remember, however, that a model is not necessarily a reflection of the real world, and conclusions drawn from economic models may be applied to real world phenomena with confidence only if one is satisfied that the model itself incorporates the critical variables affecting the real world phenomena.

a.   According to the nexus of contracts model, it follows that the state should not—and indeed possibly may not—prescribe mandatory rules for corporations by statute that are inconsistent with the express or implicit contracts. The role of corporation statutes, according to this theory, is to provide standardized rules that most corporations will adopt, thereby providing savings for corporations that do not need to incur the cost of independently drafting such provisions.

Caveat: Many scholars reject the implication of the nexus of contracts theory that all statutory protections for stockholders should be viewed as permissive and subject to modification by provision in the articles of incorporation. Mandatory minimum voting rules for fundamental changes in the corporate structure and the right of dissent and appraisal are often cited as examples of provisions that should not be subject to modification.

Caveat: Economists tend to view the nexus of contracts as a normative model, incorporating what ought to be rather than what is. The problem with this analysis is that economic models are based on certain fundamental assumptions that all persons have adequate knowledge about transactions and that they act rationally to maximize their wealth. In the real world many people do not meet this economic ideal.

b. Some scholars have extended the nexus of contracts theory to argue that attempts by states to impose restrictions on takeovers are prohibited by the United States Constitution in that they impair contractual obligations.

> *Caveat:* This argument has been criticized as an attempted end run around United States Supreme Court decisions reserving to the states the power to establish rules regulating corporations formed under their laws. *See CTS Corporation v. Dynamics Corp. of America,* 481 U.S. 69, 107 S.Ct. 1637 (1987); *Kamen v. Kemper Financial Services, Inc.,* 500 U.S. 90, 111 S.Ct. 1711 (1991). There is no modern legal authority that supports the argument that the clause of the federal constitution prohibiting states from impairing contracts limits or prohibits amendments to state corporation statutes. All state corporation statutes reserve that power.

c. A few scholars have argued that the nexus of contracts theory requires corporations to make provision for creditors or displaced employees on the theory that the terms of implicit or express contracts require directors to take steps to protect the interests of those groups.

d. Under the nexus of contracts theory, the concept that stockholders own the corporation is rejected. Rather, stockholders are viewed as contributors of capital in return for the right to receive the residual return produced by the corporation. Under this theory, stockholders and creditors share the risk that total revenues will be less than total costs during an accounting period.

e. The central figure in the corporation under the nexus of contracts theory is the manager who assembles the contractual components into a successful enterprise.

5. Process Theories

Scholars have also suggested that a corporation may be viewed as a process by which various inputs of capital, services, and raw materials are combined to produce desirable products. It may also be viewed as a form of private governance for persons involved in a business.

B. CONSTITUTIONAL INCIDENTS OF THE CORPORATE PERSONALITY

A corporation is viewed as a legal person entitled to some but not all of the constitutional protections available to individuals. Which constitutional protections are available to corporations and which are not is a matter of constitutional construction. The usual test is "whether the protection is a purely personal guarantee . . . whose historic function has been limited to the protection of individuals." *First National Bank of Boston v. Bellotti*, 435 U.S. 765, 779, 98 S.Ct. 1407, 1417 (1978).

1. Privileges and Immunities

A corporation is not a citizen of a state or of the United States for purposes of the privileges and immunities clause. *Paul v. Virginia*, 75 U.S. (8 Wall.) 168 (1868). Therefore states may validly impose restrictions on a foreign corporation's activities within the state, *Eli Lilly & Co. v. Sav–On–Drugs, Inc.*, 366 U.S. 276, 81 S.Ct. 1316 (1961), though such restrictions may relate only to *intrastate* activities and may not burden interstate commerce. *Allenberg Cotton Co., Inc. v. Pittman*, 419 U.S. 20, 95 S.Ct. 260 (1974).

2. Free Speech

A corporation has rights of free speech which may not be restricted as such by state statute. *Pacific Gas & Elec. Co. v. P.U.C. of California*, 475 U.S. 1, 106 S.Ct. 903 (1986); *First Nat. Bank of Boston v. Bellotti*, 435 U.S. 765, 98 S.Ct. 1407 (1978); *Consolidated Edison Co. v. Public Service Commission*, 447 U.S. 530, 100 S.Ct. 2326 (1980). In *Austin v. Michigan Chamber of Commerce*, 494 U.S. 652, 110 S.Ct. 1391 (1990), however, the Court upheld a Michigan statute that prohibited corporations from using general corporate funds in support of or in opposition to candidates for state office.

3. Self Incrimination and Privacy

A corporation has no privilege against self incrimination. *Wilson v. United States*, 221 U.S. 361, 31 S.Ct. 538 (1911); *Wild v. Brewer*, 329 F.2d 924 (9th Cir.1964). Nor does it have a right to privacy. *United States v. Morton Salt Co.*, 338 U.S. 632, 70 S.Ct. 357 (1950).

4. Due Process and Equal Protection

A corporation may not be deprived of property without just compensation. *Penn Central Transportation Co. v. City of New York*, 438 U.S. 104, 98 S.Ct. 2646 (1978). A corporation is also entitled to due process and equal protection of the law. *Helicopteros Nacionales de Colombia v. Hall*, 466 U.S. 408, 104 S.Ct. 1868 (1984); *Oklahoma Press Pub. Co. v. Walling*, 327 U.S. 186, 66 S.Ct. 494 (1946); *Metropolitan Life Ins. Co. v. Ward*, 470 U.S. 869, 105 S.Ct. 1676 (1985); *Munn v. Illinois*, 94 U.S. (4 Otto) 113 (1876); *Wheeling Steel Corp. v. Glander*, 337 U.S. 562, 69 S.Ct. 1291 (1949).

5. Former Jeopardy and Unreasonable Searches

A corporation is protected from unreasonable searches and seizures, *Marshall v. Barlow's, Inc.*, 436 U.S. 307, 98 S.Ct. 1816 (1978), and can plead former jeopardy as a bar to prosecution, *United States v. Martin Linen Supply Co.*, 430 U.S. 564, 97 S.Ct. 1349 (1977).

C. SOURCES OF LAW

The law of corporations is derived from several sources.

1. State Corporation Statutes

Every state has a general corporation statute that describes the incorporation process, defines generally the rights and duties of stockholders, directors, and officers and provides rules about fundamental corporate changes. While these statutes vary from state to state, there is a substantial trend toward liberalization with the result that variations from state to state are declining in importance. Three sources of statutes have been particularly influential:

a. The Model Business Corporation Act (MBCA) is published by the Committee on Corporate Laws of the ABA Section of Business Law. The original version of this statute was published in 1950 and was substantially revised in 1969. The MBCA has been quite influential and has been followed substantially by many states (sometimes called *model act states*). Another major revision was completed in 1984 and was for a time called the Revised Model Business Corporation Act (RMBCA). Today it is now called simply the Model Business Corporation Act and it is more or less continually under revision. Most references here are to the MBCA as revised through 2002. References to earlier versions of the MBCA are identified as MBCA (1969) or MBCA (1984).

b. Most large publicly traded corporations are incorporated in Delaware and are therefore subject to the Delaware General Corporation Law (DGCL) with regard to their internal affairs such as governance and finance. The reasons for the peculiar concentration of the largest corporations in one small state can be traced to an accident of history. But for a variety of reasons, Delaware is and is likely to remain the most influential jurisdiction in the area of corporation law. And because of its stature in corporation law, Delaware law is also widely followed for some other forms of organization such as limited liability companies (LLCs).

c.   The statutes of New York, California, and other important commercial states have been influential in the enactment or amendment of statutes in a number of different states.

d.   Because of the importance of statutory provisions in the law of corporations, the common law has become less important. Many judicial decisions are interstitial in nature, either supplying supplementary principles when the statutes are silent or construing statutory provisions. Nevertheless, in some areas broad common law principles are still generally applied because they define basic rights and duties within a corporation and have not been affected by statutory enactments. One important area that common law principles continue to have relevance is the articulation of duties of directors and officers. One of the most important principles is the business judgment rule, which creates a presumption of propriety for decisions of the board of directors made in the absence of a conflict of interest.

2.   Federal Statutes

The Securities Act of 1933 and the Securities Exchange Act of 1934 are major federal statutes applicable to broad categories of corporations. The 1933 Act regulates the public offer and sale of securities, while the 1934 Act generally regulates securities markets, securities trading, and the public dissemination of information by publicly held corporations. The Securities and Exchange Commission (SEC) has broad rule making power under these statutes. A significant portion of the law applicable to publicly held corporations is based on these statutes, and rules promulgated thereunder. Other federal statutes relating to securities law are the Investment Advisers Act of 1940, the Investment Company Act of 1940, and the Trust Indenture Act of 1939.

a.   There is no general federal common law of corporations. See *Kamen v. Kemper Financial Services, Inc.,* 500 U.S. 90, 111 S.Ct. 1711 (1991). Prior to 1975 some federal cases and law review commentaries suggested that a federal law of corporations was developing under the federal securities acts. In particular, Rule 10b–5, the catch-all antifraud rule adopted in 1943 by the SEC under the Exchange Act has been applied in a wide variety of circumstances ranging from insider trading to corporate level mismanagement. But as a result of a series of restrictive decisions by the United States Supreme Court the trend has reversed. In the 1980s, many commentators argued that a market for corporate control existed that was interstate in character and beyond the power of states to limit or control. *CTS Corporation v. Dynamics Corp. of America,* 481 U.S. 69, 107

S.Ct. 1637 (1987), rejected this argument and held that state law controlled corporations formed under the laws of that state. As *CTS* makes clear, federal securities law is focused primarily on disclosure of material information to the market and investors, whereas state corporation law provides the substantive rights and duties of stockholders, directors, and officers.

b.   There have been several important amendments to federal securities law over the years.

- The Williams Act (1968) (relating to tender offers) is a part of the Securities Exchange Act.

- The Insider Trading Sanctions Act (ITSA)(1984) and the Insider Trading and Securities Fraud Enforcement Act (ITSFEA)(1988), both setting forth penalties for insider trading, are also part of the Securities Exchange Act.

- The Private Securities Litigation Reform Act (PSLRA) regulates class actions under federal securities law. PSLRA amended both the 1933 Act and the 1934 Act to make it more difficult for private plaintiffs to file a class action based on federal securities law. It was adopted in response to the perception that numerous frivolous actions had been filed primarily to generate legal fees for plaintiff attorneys.

- The Securities Litigation Uniform Standards Act (SLUSA) was enacted in 1998 to plug a loophole in PSLRA and to require that all class actions based on theories of misrepresentation or nondisclosure be brought in federal court.

- The Sarbanes Oxley Act is the most significant general regulatory statute adopted since the 1933 Act and the 1934 Act. Formally titled the Public Company Accounting Reform and Investor Protection Act of 2002, the Act is usually called simply the Sarbanes Oxley Act. The Sarbanes Oxley Act was adopted in response to the collapse of Enron, WorldCom, and several other major corporations. It focuses primarily on the accounting profession, which sets the rules by which financial reports are prepared, and which is responsible for auditing the reports of publicly traded companies to assure their accuracy. But the Sarbanes Oxley Act also contains many provisions that directly govern public companies and the stock exchanges.

3. Stock Exchange Listing Standards

In addition to state and federal law, a publicly traded company must comply with elaborate rules adopted by stock exchanges as a condition of being listed for trading. Stock exchange listing standards often impose requirements beyond those of state and federal law. For example, they typically require a stockholder vote in connection with the issuance of a significant number of new shares even though such a vote is not required by state law. Moreover, stock exchange rules require that the board of directors of all listed companies have an audit committee composed of independent (non–officer) directors. The SEC has general regulatory authority over the stock exchanges and must approve any rule changes. Many of the reforms imposed by the Sarbanes Oxley Act take the form of instructions to the SEC to require the stock exchanges to adopt new rules in areas related to corporate governance, for example, the composition of the audit committee of the board of directors. Thus, although state law is the primary source of substantive corporation law, federal law has become increasingly significant in connection with the regulation of publicly traded companies.

4. State Securities Laws (Blue Sky Laws)

Every state has enacted a statute that regulates the public distribution of securities within that state. Many of these statutes are similar to, and overlap, the federal Securities Act of 1933. In 1996, Congress significantly reduced the overlap that traditionally existed between federal securities acts and state blue sky laws by the passage of the National Securities Markets Improvement Act (NSMIA) which in essence preempts state securities laws to the extent that they impose duplicative regulation of securities offerings. State law continues to apply to wholly intrastate offerings.

D. FUNCTIONAL CLASSIFICATION OF CORPORATIONS

The basic distinction underlying much of the law of corporations is between the *closely held corporation* and the *publicly held corporation*. While the same general corporation statutes are applicable to both types of corporations, the issues are usually quite different.

1. Closely Held Corporations

A closely held corporation is a corporation with most of the following attributes:

- It has a few stockholders, all or most of whom are usually active in the management of the business;

- There is no public market for its shares;

- Its shares are subject to one or more contractual restrictions on transfer.

2. Publicly Held Corporations

A publicly held corporation is a corporation with most of the following attributes:

- Its shares are widely held by members of the general public and the overall number of stockholders is large;

- There is a public market for its shares;

- The corporation is subject to reporting and disclosure requirements under federal law.

3. Significance of the Distinction

While many publicly held corporations are relatively large and many closely held corporations are relatively small in terms of assets, the importance of the distinction is not size as much as the number of stockholders and the marketability of shares.

a. The presence or absence of a public market for the corporation's shares is the most important difference between the two types of corporations.

- A stockholder in a publicly held corporation who is dissatisfied with management may sell in the public market. A stockholder in a closely held corporation may have no place to sell except to other stockholders who may be willing to buy only at relatively low prices.

- In the publicly held corporation, the value of shares may be readily estimated, because the public market for shares provides a benchmark as to what numerous buyers and sellers believe the shares to be worth. In contrast, in a closely held corporation, there may be no easy and objective way to estimate the value of corporate shares.

- Because there is no market for shares in a closely held corporation, a minority stockholder may be locked in to an unsalable asset and be subject to freeze-out or squeeze-out tactics.

- A stockholder's agreement may require a closely held corporation or its other stockholders to purchase shares of a minority stockholder at a fixed or determinable price and thereby avoid some of the concerns about the lack of marketability.

b. A second major difference is that in a closely held corporation, most of the stockholders are likely to be employed by the corporation while in a publicly held corporation, most of the stockholders are not connected with management and have only a limited say in the policies adopted by the corporation. As a result, ownership and control are likely to be separated in a publicly held corporation but closely interconnected in a closely held corporation.

c. A third difference is that the presence of public stockholders unconnected with the business of a publicly held corporation is thought to present a strong case for governmental regulation of internal affairs, while in a closely held corporation there is usually thought to be only a relatively weak (or nonexistent) case for governmental regulation of the internal affairs of the corporation.

Caveat: Corporations form a continuum from private to public. At the margin it may be unclear whether a specific corporation has more of the attributes of a publicly held or a closely held corporation.

Example: Y Corporation is owned by six persons, three of whom participate full-time in the management of the business. Shares were originally sold to four persons. When one withdrew, he sold his shares to three other investors. Thereafter share transfer restrictions on the shares were imposed by unanimous agreement. Y corporation will probably be treated as a closely held corporation.

Example: AB Corporation was wholly owned by two brothers in 1969, when they decided to go public by selling shares through a registered public offering. At the present time, A and B own 87 per cent of the stock; the balance of the shares are owned by several hundred members of the general public. A and B continue to operate the business, electing themselves as directors. One brokerage firm makes a market in AB Corporation stock by quoting bid and asked prices for shares. But trading is infrequent. AB Corporation is a publicly held corporation; if the number of stockholders is over 500 and corporate assets exceed $10 million, ABC Corporation must register under the Securities Exchange Act of 1934 and file annual and quarterly reports covering its finances and operations. In addition, registration under the 1934 Act triggers a variety of other federal regulations relating to proxy solicitations, tender offers, and restrictions on purchases and sales of shares by insiders.

Example: X Corporation was originally wholly owned by two brothers who died in 1936 and 1938. They left the bulk of their shares to their fourteen children, though one brother made several gifts of shares to trusted employees. Of the fourteen children and employees owning shares, several have died leaving shares to children, nephews, nieces, spouses, etc. By 1980, there are a total of 123 stockholders and no stockholder owns more than 20 per cent of the outstanding shares. There has never been a public offering of the shares and there is no organized trading in X Corporation shares, although a few isolated sales have occurred from time to time. Despite the large number of stockholders, X Corporation has more of the characteristics of a closely held corporation than a publicly held corporation.

E. EFFICIENT MARKET THEORY

The *efficient capital market hypothesis (ECMH)* posits that prices move rapidly—indeed almost instantaneously—to reflect information about publicly traded securities. In an efficient market, there are many purchasers and sellers all seeking to make a profit. Traders seek to take advantage of information, using increasingly sophisticated analysis. The most commonly cited version of the ECMH is the semi-strong form, which posits that all public information is quickly incorporated into security prices. The strong form of the ECMH posits that even nonpublic (inside) information is reflected quickly in security prices. The weak form of the ECMH posits only that it is impossible to predict the next change in price for a security on the basis of previous changes.

Caveat: Although the evidence in favor of the semi-strong version of the ECMH is viewed by many as persuasive, increasing doubt about the ECMH has arisen as a result of the 1987 market crash, the collapse of internet stocks beginning in 2001, the large premiums over market price often paid for targets in mergers and takeovers and other similar events. On the other hand, commentators often distinguish between informational efficiency (the idea that one cannot beat the market solely by analysis of public information) and allocative efficiency (the idea that market prices are essentially accurate and tend to lead to the optimum allocation of capital).

Caveat: Empirical evidence supporting the validity of the ECMH is largely based on studies of the broadest securities markets, including the New York Stock Exchange. The market for many other publicly held securities is much thinner and less active and there is little empirical evidence as to whether these thinner markets are also efficient. Like the distinction between publicly held and closely held corporations, the efficiency of markets may be a matter of degree, and one can not assume that merely because a corporation is classified as publicly held an efficient and broad market necessarily exists for its shares.

1. Implications of the ECMH

A number of inferences, some of which are counter-intuitive, may be drawn from the ECMH:

a. Price movements are random in the absence of new market information. It is not possible to predict from a previous transaction whether the next transaction will be higher or lower.

b. Those who analyze historical changes in prices (technical analysts or chartists), are engaged in a futile and irrelevant exercise, because market price already incorporates that information. Moreover, because all public information is incorporated in the current price of the shares, one cannot systematically improve one's investment success by studying publicly available information about investment alternatives.

c. It is not possible to develop and apply a trading strategy that consistently outperforms the market.

d. Large institutional investors cannot hope in the long run to perform better than broad-based market indexes.

2. Judicial Recognition of the ECMH

The ECMH was accepted by the United States Supreme Court as creating a rebuttable presumption that investors relied on a false press release in *Basic Inc. v. Levinson*, 485 U.S. 224, 108 S.Ct. 978 (1988) by virtue of the fact that the false press release affected the market price and investors in turn relied on the fairness of that price. This doctrine is usually referred to as the fraud on the market theory. The ECMH has also been cited and relied upon by the Securities & Exchange Commission and lower federal courts.

F. STATE COMPETITION FOR CORPORATIONS

Since the late 1800s, individual states have competed to attract businesses to incorporate under their statutes. The undisputed winner of this competition is the state of Delaware. The incorporation business provides filing fees and tax revenues for the state, fees for members of the local bar, and other economic benefits. More than half of the Fortune 500 corporations are incorporated in Delaware. Over one-third of all the corporations listed on the New York Stock Exchange are incorporated in Delaware. Every year several publicly held corporations incorporated in other states reincorporate in Delaware. There are few (if any) examples of movement in the opposite direction. The Delaware Legislature and the Delaware Supreme Court are therefore important sources of corporation law.

1. Race to the Bottom

The earliest explanation of Delaware's success was that the Delaware General Corporation Law (DGCL) was permissive and permitted management the freedom to operate without constraint. It was also suggested that the Delaware judiciary made decisions favorable to management in order to preserve the economic benefits of the incorporation business. In this view, put forth by Professor Cary in 1974, Delaware was leading a race for the bottom.

a. Economists have pointed out that if this explanation is accurate, corporations that reincorporate in Delaware should suffer a loss in the value of their shares. But studies indicate that when a corporation moves its charter to Delaware from another state, its stock price usually rises.

b. The Delaware statute and the Delaware judiciary do not appear to be more management-oriented and permissive than the laws and courts of other states. A comparison of the provisions of the DGCL with the MBCA (1984) and other modern corporation statutes does not reveal significant substantive differences that can be identified as systematically pro-management. Recent Delaware court opinions stress protection of minority stockholders and hold management responsible for abuses of their position.

2. Race to the Top

The popularity and primacy of the state of Delaware may be explained partially by history, partially by the continued efforts by the bar of that state to provide an efficient body of corporate law, and partially by the familiarity of corporate lawyers generally with the DCL. Also contributing to Delaware's primacy is its sophisticated judiciary and efficient filing office that assures reasonable and knowledgeable decision making.

a.   The DCL is flexible and simplifies the problems faced by corporations in conducting routine internal business under that statute.

b.   There is more corporation law in Delaware than in any other state. As a result, there are fewer areas of uncertainty in Delaware corporation law than in the law of other states, and Delaware corporation lawyers may plan transactions with a relatively high degree of certainty.

c.   The sophisticated judiciary, corporate bar, and filing authorities in Delaware are familiar with the issues, particularly in the areas of contests for corporate control and derivative litigation. This sophistication tends to assure that corporate problems are handled fairly and efficiently.

d.   Procedures exist in Delaware that permits unexpected problems to be dealt with expeditiously by amendment to the DCL. Examples include the enactment of provisions protecting directors from personal liability in certain circumstances and the enactment of a complex provision dealing with business combinations following takeovers.

e.   Delaware case law generally permits corporations to adopt defensive tactics to combat unwanted takeovers.

   Caveat: It may be argued that these factors tend to favor management interests and therefore may not be in the best interest of stockholders generally.

G.   ALTERNATIVES TO THE CORPORATION

Publicly held businesses are almost always corporations. Traditional alternative business forms for closely held businesses are the partnership and the limited partnership. A major disadvantage of these forms was that they did not provide limited liability for all participants. Since the 1980s, a new business form, the limited liability company, (the "LLC") has achieved wide acceptance. The LLC provides limited liability for all members, flexibility in internal operation similar to that provided by partnerships, and, of paramount importance, partnership tax treatment. The LLC has become the predominant business form for newly created closely held businesses. Since there is usually a tax cost for converting from corporations to LLCs, it is likely that many closely held corporations will continue in existence indefinitely. Because the LLC provides limited liability for all members, many principles of corporation law, such as the doctrine relating to "piercing the corporate veil," have become applicable to LLCs. Similarly, in a manager managed LLC, principles applicable to directors of corporations may be applied by analogy. The extent to which principles of closely held corporations will be applied to this new business form is uncertain.

> **Example:** A court has held that an LLC may appear in court only through an attorney and cannot be represented by an officer, agent, manager of member. A partnership may be so represented, but a corporation may appear only through an attorney. Poore v. Fox Hollow Enterprises, 1994 WL 150872.

REVIEW QUESTIONS

1.1. True or False: Corporate problems are easy. One should simply visualize the corporation as a separate person and answer the question.

1.2. True or False: Corporate problems are easy. One should simply view the corporation as a contract among the various participants.

1.3. True or False: Corporate problems are easy. One should simply assess the situation and decide what is reasonable or fair.

1.4. True or False: If one person owns all of the stock of a corporation he is that corporation, and all the fictions in this world cannot dispute that fact.

1.5. True or False: The state grants the corporation its charter and may impose any restrictions it wishes. A corporation therefore has only whatever rights the state chooses to give it.

1.6. True or False: The rights of preferred stockholders are set forth in articles of incorporation and common stockholders may limit the rights of the preferred stockholders to whatever is set forth in the articles.

1.7. True or False: The state grants the corporation its charter and its law therefore controls all aspects of the corporation's conduct.

1.8. How does a closely held corporation differ from a publicly held corporation?

1.9. Why is it to the advantage of the state in which you live to have a corporation statute that is modern, up-to-date, and reasonably fair to all interests within a corporation?

1.10. Professor Cary argued that Delaware is successful in attracting corporations to that state because it has won the "race to the bottom." Comment on that argument.

1.11. When creating a new business today, should the corporate form be preferred over a limited liability company, a partnership, or a limited partnership?

*

II

Forming A Corporation

A. STATE OF INCORPORATION

The first question that must be resolved in forming a new corporation is what state should be the state of incorporation. For small enterprises planning to transact business primarily in one state, the corporation should usually be incorporated in that state. For larger enterprises transacting business in many states, incorporation in any one of several states is usually feasible; incorporation in Delaware is attractive for these businesses, though many remain incorporated in the state in which they originated.

1. Factors in Selection

There are several factors that enter into the selection of the state of incorporation.

a. If a corporation plans to conduct business in state X, the costs of incorporating in Delaware and qualifying to transact business as a foreign corporation in state X are higher than incorporating in state X to begin with.

b. With the modernization of state statutes and the elimination of onerous requirements, the disadvantages of local incorporation have tended to diminish or disappear. But, variations do exist in state law, and in some instances restrictive state rules about internal governance may dictate incorporation in a more liberal state.

c. Incorporation in Delaware or another state may create later problems; for example, the corporation or its directors may be subject to suit in Delaware or elsewhere even though little or no business is conducted there and none of the directors are present in that state. In addition, state taxation statutes vary widely and may change over time, thereby unexpectedly increasing the cost of operation of a multi-state corporation.

d. Advantages of incorporating in Delaware are that there is a lot of law available in that state (so that many questions can be firmly resolved under Delaware law) and one will deal with filing authorities and courts that are experts on all aspects of corporation law and practice. The same may not be true in many smaller states.

2. Mechanics of Forming Corporation in an Unfamiliar State

Where a decision has been made to form a corporation in an unfamiliar state, the easiest way for a lawyer to do so is to use a corporation service company. These companies routinely prepare and file the necessary documents to form a corporation in any jurisdiction, and may provide additional services (such as obtaining minute books or seals, and preparing and filing tax and other forms required by state law) if requested to do so.

B. VARIATIONS IN STATUTORY REQUIREMENTS AND NOMENCLATURE

1. Statutory Requirements

It is essential to comply with the specific statutory requirements of the state chosen for the state of incorporation.

a. While numerous variations exist from state to state, there is a surprising degree of uniformity and consistency in most modern statutes. Virtually all onerous substantive requirements have been eliminated in most states.

b. Procedural variations in the incorporation process may still exist in some states. Most states simply require a filing with a state official, but Delaware and several other states also require a local filing in the county in which the registered office is located. Arizona and several other states require a public advertisement in a newspaper of general circulation of the fact of incorporation. Some states also continue to require the filing of additional documents to establish compliance with various statutory requirements.

Caveat: The consequences of failing to meet these additional requirements may be set forth in the statute itself. For example, Delaware provides that a failure to file locally within the specified period increases the filing fee but does not affect the existence of the corporation. DGCL 103(d). In some states, failure to meet these requirements may mean that no corporation has been validly formed though the doctrine of *de facto* incorporation may be applicable.

c. Variations may also exist with respect to filing fees, franchise taxes, stock issuance or transfer taxes, and similar items.

2. Nomenclature

MBCA nomenclature is followed in most states. The document filed with the secretary of state is called the articles of incorporation. Under earlier versions of the Model Act (and the statutes of many states), the secretary of state issued a document called a certificate of incorporation after accepting the articles of incorporation for filing. Under the MBCA (1984) (and the statutes of an increasing number of states), the paperwork is simplified by requiring the Secretary of State simply to issue a fee receipt as indicating acceptance of the filing.

a. In Delaware and several other states the document filed with the secretary of state is called a *certificate of incorporation*.

b. In some states, the document issued by the secretary of state is called a *charter.*

C. DOCUMENTS FILED IN THE OFFICE OF THE SECRETARY OF STATE

The basic requirement is that articles of incorporation conforming to the statutory requirements of the specific state be filed in a specified government office and be accompanied by the appropriate filing fee. The state official charged with accepting corporate filings is usually the Secretary of State, but some states use a different designation for the filing officer.

1. Filing Procedure

Under older state statutes, duplicate originals (both manually signed and acknowledged before a notary public) or an original and a copy of the articles of incorporation, must be filed with the secretary of state. If the articles of incorporation conform to the statute, the office of the secretary of state attaches the certificate of incorporation to the copy or duplicate original and returns them to the incorporators or their representative. Many states have simplified this process to reduce the handling of many pieces of paper.

a. A certified copy of the original articles on file with the secretary of state may be obtained for a nominal fee.

b. Many states permit articles of incorporation to be transmitted by fax. Electronic filing is also permitted in some states.

2. Discretion of Filing Authority

Many state statutes grant the filing authority discretion to refuse to file documents unless they conform with law and may also grant that office the power to prescribe forms or to issue regulations relating to the documents being filed.

a. In some states, the filing authority has been criticized for rules that are unduly technical and for substantive review of portions of articles of incorporation, such as complex provisions creating classes of preferred stock, that is unnecessary and disruptive of carefully negotiated financial arrangements.

b. MBCA 1.25 limits the discretion of the secretary of state in reviewing documents submitted for filing to a ministerial role and limits his power to establish mandatory forms.

Caveat: Some states have not adopted provisions limiting the discretion of the filing authority.

D. INCORPORATORS

Articles of incorporation are executed by one or more persons called *incorporators*. Historically, three incorporators who were natural persons were required and many states imposed special residency or other requirements for incorporators. The signatures of incorporators usually were required to be verified or acknowledged under oath before a notary public.

1. Role of Incorporators

The principal function of incorporators is to execute the articles of incorporation and receive back the certificate of incorporation or receipt for the filing fee. They generally serve no other function, although in some states, the incorporators may also meet to complete the formation of the corporation.

a. In most states, only a single incorporator is required, who may be a corporation, trust, estate or partnership. There are usually no residency requirements for incorporators who are individuals. A secretary or employee of the law firm creating the corporation, a low level employee of a corporation service company, or any other person unconnected with the future business may serve as an incorporator.

b. Requirements of oaths, verifications, and seals have been eliminated in most states by statute or judicial decision.

c. In some states the incorporators meet to complete the formation of the corporation. In other states, initial directors named in the articles of incorporation complete the formation of the corporation. MBCA 2.02(b) (1) and 2.05(a) give each corporation the option of having the formation completed by the incorporators or by initial directors named in the articles of incorporation. Initial directors may be used if they will be the permanent board of directors and there is no objection to the public disclosure of their identity.

> *Caveat:* Some states may continue to require the contribution of a specified minimum amount of capital in order to complete the formation of a corporation. If so, where incorporators complete the organization of the corporation, there is a potential risk of personal liability if required funds are not actually received by the corporation.

E. ARTICLES OF INCORPORATION

1. Mandatory Requirements

There is a trend toward simplifying the mandatory disclosure requirements for articles of incorporation. In many states the required information comfortably fits on a post card.

a. Older state statutes generally require the following minimum information to appear in the articles of incorporation:

- The name of the corporation.

- Its duration, which may be perpetual.

- Its purpose or purposes which may be, or include, the conduct of any lawful business.

- The stock it is authorized to issue.

- The name of its registered agent and the street address of its registered office.

- The names and addresses of its initial board of directors.

- The name and address of the incorporator or incorporators.

b. Virtually all corporations elect the duration to be perpetual and their purposes to be the conduct of any lawful business. As a result, many states provide that every corporation has perpetual duration unless a shorter period is chosen and a purpose of engaging in any lawful business unless a more limited purpose is set forth in the articles of incorporation.

2. Discretionary Provisions

In addition to the required minimum provisions, state statutes permit additional provisions to be included in the articles of incorporation at the election of the corporation.

a. State statutes typically provide that specified rules of corporate governance are automatically applicable unless the corporation elects to eliminate or modify them by specific provision in the articles of incorporation. These are called opt-out provisions.

   Example: In many states each stockholder has preemptive rights and a right to vote cumulatively unless these rights are specifically limited or excluded by provisions in the articles of incorporation.

b. State statutes also may provide that a corporation may elect to make specific rules of corporate governance applicable by making specific provision in the articles of incorporation for the application of those rules. These are called opt-in provisions.

   Example: Under the MBCA, both preemptive rights and cumulative voting are opt-in provisions. MBCA 6.30(a); MBCA 7.28(b). A corporation has these rules only if an express election to have them is made. This change was made because automatic application of these provisions often constituted traps for the unwary stockholder. Most publicly held corporations elect to eliminate both preemptive rights and cumulative voting on the theory that they complicate raising capital and voting for directors and are of little benefit.

Example: A publicly held corporation wants a provision stating that a quorum of stockholders may consist of one-third or more of the shares instead of a majority. The statutes of many states provide that a quorum consists of a majority of the outstanding shares but permit the requirement to be reduced to one-third by specific provision in the articles of incorporation. In most states, a similar provision placed only in the bylaws would be ineffective.

c. State statutes authorize additional discretionary provisions to be placed either in the articles of incorporation or the bylaws. Typically bylaws may be amended either by the board of directors or by the stockholders, but many jurisdictions limit the power of the board of directors to amend bylaws adopted by the stockholders. The decision to place a given provision in the articles of incorporation or in the bylaws thus affects the ease with which amendments may be made.

Caveat: It is usually more difficult to amend the articles of incorporation than the bylaws. Ordinarily, an amendment to the articles of incorporation requires both a resolution adopted by the board of directors and an affirmative vote by a majority of the stockholders at a meeting called for the express purpose of approving the amendment. The bylaws may be amended by the board of directors acting alone or by the stockholders acting alone but many jurisdictions limit the power of the board of directors to amend bylaws that have been adopted by the stockholders. The decision whether to place a given provision in the articles of incorporation or the bylaws may depend on how difficult it should be to amend the provision. Moreover, it is important to keep a record as to the procedures followed in adopting bylaws. It is also desirable to state in the bylaws themselves the conditions under which they were adopted and how they may be amended. Of course, the procedures to be followed in amending, adopting, or repealing bylaws may be changed by statute.

Caveat: Corporate officers and directors are generally more familiar with the bylaws than with the articles of incorporation. It is a common practice to place important provisions in both the articles of incorporation and the bylaws for the convenience of corporate officers, directors, and stockholders. Where amendments are made to these common provisions, it is important that both provisions be amended in exactly the same way. The articles of incorporation trump the bylaws. If a provision in the articles of incorporation is repeated in the bylaws, the version in the articles of incorporation rules if there are any inconsistencies. Amendment of the version in the bylaws does not change the provision amending the articles of incorporation.

Example: A corporation desires to limit the right of directors to obtain indemnification of litigation costs from the corporation. Under the statute of the state of incorporation, the right of indemnification may be limited or excluded by an appropriate provision either in the articles of incorporation or the bylaws. A provision of this nature would normally appear in the bylaws rather than in the articles of incorporation.

Example: A corporation proposes that the board of directors may act only by unanimous vote. Even though such a clause is effective if placed in either the bylaws or the articles of incorporation under the state statute in question, an attorney may recommend that the provision be included both in the articles of incorporation and the bylaws because it is unusual and has the potential of creating a deadlock.

Example: A closely held corporation plans to create share transfer restrictions that require all stockholders to sell their shares to the corporation upon death or retirement at book value less 25 per cent, a price that is recognized as being artificially low. All stockholders are willing to enter into these restrictions. Such a restriction is valid if placed in the bylaws, but the attorney also recommends that the articles of incorporation be amended to include the provision because she wishes to maximize the probability that the restrictions will be enforced in accordance with their terms.

d. State statutes generally authorize corporations to include in the articles of incorporation provisions relating to corporate powers. Though it is unnecessary (and often undesirable) to refer to powers specifically and unambiguously granted to corporations by statute, references to specific powers may be helpful where the state statute is silent or it is unclear whether corporations generally possess the specific power.

Example: Old case law in State X makes it clear that corporations generally do not have power to act as general partners in general or limited partnerships. The present state incorporation statute contains an oblique reference to investing in partnerships but does not specifically authorize a corporation to act as a general partner. A specific grant of power to act as a general partner in a general or limited partnership should be routinely included in the articles of incorporation of every corporation in State X. Such a clause effectively broadens the power of the corporation, reduces the likelihood that later transactions may be questioned, and avoids future litigation.

e. Special clauses relating to the purposes of a corporation are sometimes included in articles of incorporation even in states where the statute, like MBCA 3.01, automatically grants every corporation the power to engage in any lawful business.

3. Name

Under most state statutes, a corporate name (i) must contain a reference to the corporate nature of the entity (using the words Corporation, Incorporated, Inc. or a similar word or abbreviation), (ii) must not be the same as or deceptively similar to a name already in use or reserved for use, and (iii) must not imply that a corporation is engaged in a business in which corporations may not lawfully engage. The MBCA substitutes the test of distinguishable upon the records of the Secretary of State for the same or deceptively similar test. Filing authorities maintain lists of names that are reserved or currently in use (and hence unavailable) and may have internal rules about name availability. As a result, it is always desirable to check whether a specific name is available with the filing authority before it is used.

Example: Articles of incorporation are filed under the corporate name *Chicago Allied Steel Company*. The name is rejected because an existing corporation is using the name *Allied Steel Company* and the internal rules of the secretary of state's office require that geographical names be ignored in determining whether names are identical. (Whether or not the secretary of state is correct is usually irrelevant in such situations. It is easier to choose another name than to litigate. Hence, even the most arbitrary rules are unlikely to be tested.)

Example: Transamerica Airlines, Inc. is distinguishable upon the records of the secretary of state from Transamerica, Inc. and Trans International Airlines, Inc. *Trans-Americas Airlines, Inc. v. Kenton*, 491 A.2d 1139 (Del.1985).

Caveat: The word *company* and its various abbreviations do not necessarily connote that the business is a corporation. It is common for a partnership to use the word *company*. Thus, in some jurisdictions, the word *company* and its abbreviations may not suffice because they do not unambiguously signal that the company has been incorporated and therefore has limited liability. Some states permit the use of the word *company* but not the construction *and company*. Some states also permit the use of the word *limited* and its various abbreviations. Thus, it may be necessary to identify an incorporated entity as *ABC Company, Inc.* and not merely *ABC Company.*

a. The requirement that each corporation have a unique name is designed primarily to avoid confusion in such matters as sending tax notices and naming defendants in law suits.

b. In many states, the name requirements are also designed to prevent unfair competition. These statutes prohibit the use of names that are the same or deceptively similar. Some states distinguish further between names that are the same or deceptively similar, or merely similar. Same or deceptively similar names may not be used under any circumstances while a similar name may be used if the proposed corporation obtains a letter of consent from the other corporation. These rules seem to be based on unfair competition considerations.

c. Delaware and a few other states have changed the *same or deceptively similar* test to one requiring that names "be distinguishable upon the records of the secretary of state." MBCA 4.01 adopts this standard on the theory that the secretary of state does not generally police the unfair competitive use of names and indeed, usually has no resources to do so.

d. Persons planning to form a corporation may reserve an available name for a limited period of time (usually 120 days) for a small fee. MBCA

4.02. The reservation of a name permits the preparation of corporate documents, ordering of stationery, etc., with assurance that the proposed name will be available if the articles of incorporation are filed within the period the name is reserved. Reservations of name may not be renewable in some states.

e. A foreign corporation not transacting business in a state may register its name with the secretary of state to assure that no local business will obtain the right to use its name. MBCA 4.03. Registration of a name thus protects the foreign corporation's good will reflected in its name and preserves its option to later expand its operations into the state under its current name. In most states, registration is on an annual basis and may be renewed indefinitely. Some states do not authorize the registration of names of foreign corporations.

f. Business corporation statutes generally do not require a corporation to conduct business in its corporate name. A corporation has the same right as an individual to conduct business under an assumed name so long as the use of the name is not fraudulent and does not constitute unfair competition with some other person already using the same or a similar name.

g. Many states have *assumed name statutes* that require individuals or corporations using assumed names to file an assumed name certificate. A corporation that uses its own corporate name is not considered to be using an assumed name and therefore is not subject to the filing requirement. A corporation that elects to transact business under a name other than its corporate name usually must comply with such a statute in the same way as an individual. In some cases, a business using an assumed name will identify itself as such by using the phrase *doing business as (DBA)* or rarely *trading as (TA)*.

h. A foreign corporation that has not previously registered its name may discover that its own name is not available when it seeks to qualify to transact business in a new state. In this situation, the statutes of many states require the foreign corporation to qualify to transact business under an assumed name in the new state and file an assumed name certificate with the secretary of state.

   Caveat: In many states, partnerships must file an assumed name certificate. Section 201(a) of UPA (1997) provides that a partnership is an entity distinct from its partners. This provision should be contrasted with § 6(1) of UPA (1914) which provides that a partnership is an association of two or more persons to carry on as co-owners a business for profit. In many states, partnerships must file an assumed name certificate because no filing is required to form a partnership, which traditionally has been viewed merely as a collection of individuals. Under the UPA (1997), a partnership is viewed as an entity independent of the individuals who compose it.

4. Duration

Most statutes authorize a corporation to have perpetual existence. Although it is possible to specify a shorter period of existence, it is almost never desirable to do so. A shorter period of existence creates the risk that the corporate existence may expire without renewal with uncertain rights and liabilities of participants thereafter.

5. Purpose

Most statutes authorize very general purposes clauses, e.g., "the purpose of the corporation is to engage in any lawful business or businesses." The use of such clauses is a recent phenomenon. The MBCA and the statutes of several states go even further and provide that every corporation automatically has a broad purpose to engage in any lawful business unless a narrower purpose is specified in the articles of incorporation.

a.   The nature of purposes clauses has evolved over a long period of time, reflecting varying attitudes of mistrust toward the corporation. They were formerly of much greater importance than they are today. Before 1875, most corporations were formed by special legislative enactment. Each purposes clause was separately developed in the legislative process.

b.   Under early general incorporation statutes a corporation could be formed only for a limited and specific purpose, e.g., to operate a mill for the grinding of wheat, corn, and other grain. Corporations were usually limited to a single specific purpose, though ancillary powers might be implied from such a purposes clause.

   Example: A railroad corporation was authorized to purchase, hold, and use real estate and other property as may be necessary for the construction and maintenance of its road and canal and the stations and other accommodations necessary to accomplish the objects of its incorporation. The lease of a seaside hotel by the corporation was within this purpose clause and was therefore not *ultra vires*. *Jacksonville, M., P. Ry. & Nav. Co. v. Hooper,* 160 U.S. 514, 16 S.Ct. 379 (1896).

c. Many early statutes restricted the power of corporations to amend articles of incorporation to broaden purposes clauses. Over time, state statutes were amended to permit corporations to include an unlimited number of specific purposes. This quickly eliminated any significance that purpose clauses might have had, and restrictions on amendments were gradually eliminated as the practice of using multiple purposes clauses grew. Now corporations with limited purposes clauses may freely amend them to include whatever purposes are permitted under the applicable state statute.

d. Today, there is usually no reason to have a purpose clause at all, and doctrines based on the premise that a corporation is formed for a specific purpose, such as *ultra vires* or implied powers, have little relevance. Nevertheless, purposes clauses may be necessary or desirable in some situations. A recitation of the purpose of a corporation may be required by a regulatory statute or agency if the corporation is to engage in a specific business. Some business people and investors may prefer that articles of incorporation provide information about the purpose of the corporation. A purposes clause that describes in general terms the business in which the corporation plans to engage may be coupled with a clause such as "and any other lawful business" in order to assure that the corporation may enter into new lines of business without going to the expense of amending its purposes clause.

> *Example:* Professional corporation statutes require that a corporation specify in its articles of incorporation the profession in which it proposes to engage and permits the corporation to engage only in that profession.

> *Example:* A corporation planning to go into the beer production business might have a purposes clause that states that the purpose of the corporation is to engage in the business of manufacturing and selling beer, alcoholic and non-alcoholic beverages, and any other lawful business.

e. A limited purposes clause may be used today (despite broader statutory authorization) as a planning device or to limit corporate activities as a protection for investors. A corporation that pursues a business that exceeds such a limited purposes clause is acting *ultra vires*.

Example: The statute of State *X* provides that every corporation has the power to engage in any lawful business unless a narrower purpose is specified in the articles of incorporation. *A* is an investor in a new corporation which is to be operated by *B* and *C* who are each making much smaller investments. *A* wants to ensure that the corporation will only engage in the retail drug business. He insists that a clause restricting the purposes of the corporation be included in the articles of incorporation. *A* can thereafter enjoin *B* and *C* from engaging in a broader business if the rights of third persons have not intervened.

Caveat: Because of modern rules relating to *ultra vires*, it is doubtful that the narrow purposes clause requested by A will effectively limit the activities of the corporation. For example, if A, B, and C comprise the board of directors, and B and C vote to expand the business into another line, A would have no power to stop the expansion other than by seeking an injunction in court. A should establish more effective voting or control devices if he wishes to assure himself that his capital will be invested only in the retail drug business.

6. Authorized Shares

The articles of incorporation must state the number of shares that the corporation is authorized to issue. If shares with special rights are to be issued (such as shares that carry a fixed dividend), those special rights must be described in detail. If no special rights are specified, each share is entitled to one vote per share on each matter put up to a stockholder vote and to a pro rata share of each distribution made to the stockholders generally. Such shares are called *common shares* or *common stock*.

a. MBCA 2.02(a)(2) requires only that the corporation set forth the number of shares the corporation is authorized to issue. But MBCA 6.01(a) provides that if a corporation plans to issue more than one class of shares, the articles of incorporation must prescribe the classes of shares and the number of shares of each class that the corporation is authorized to issue.

b. The number of authorized shares is a ceiling not a floor. The corporation is under no obligation to issue the entire number of authorized shares, but it may not exceed that number unless it first amends the articles of incorporation to increase the number of authorized shares. Thus, it is standard practice to authorize significantly more shares than it is planned to issue immediately in order to assure the corporation flexibility in future financing. In some states, the annual fee paid to maintain a corporation (sometimes called a *franchise tax*) increases as the number of authorized shares increases.

c. The statutes of about half of the states also require that the articles of incorporation set forth the par value of the authorized shares or a statement that the shares are issued without par value. Par value refers to the minimum price for which shares may be sold and is typically set very low. One cent per share is common but even lower amounts are often used. No par shares may usually be sold for any amount. Par value is a floor not a ceiling. A corporation may sell its shares for the highest price it can get, and the board of directors may be held liable for issuing shares for inadequate consideration. Par value has other implications in connection with dividends and distributions. Some states that continue to require that par value be specified in the articles of incorporation have eliminated most of the restrictions that flow from it. For example, in some jurisdictions shares may be sold for any amount even if the amount is less than par value.

d. Most states do not require any provision in the articles of incorporation authorizing the corporation to issue debt securities except to the extent that such securities may be convertible into shares.

7. Registered Office and Agent

The registered office and registered agent must be specified in the articles of incorporation. They serve the purposes of providing a location where the corporation may be found for service of process, tax notices, and the like and a person on whom process may be served. State statutes require filings to reflect changes in the registered office or registered agent. Corporation service companies serve as registered agents for many corporations. MBCA 5.03 addresses how a registered agent may resign. MBCA 5.02(b) also sets forth a simplified procedure dealing with the possibility that the corporation service company moves its office to another location. This procedure avoids the need for each of the company's clients to file a change of registered address.

F. COMPLETING FORMATION

The filing of articles of incorporation is only the first step in forming a corporation. In most jurisdictions the existence of the corporation begins at the moment of the filing of the articles of incorporation. A filed copy of the articles of incorporation is conclusive proof of corporate existence against any challenge to corporate existence (other than by the attorney general of the state of incorporation). Nevertheless, the law of most states provides that an organizational meeting *shall* be held following the filing of the articles of incorporation. For example, MBCA 2.05 provides that after incorporation: (1) if initial directors are named in the articles of incorporation, the initial directors shall hold an organizational meeting, at the call of a majority of the directors, to complete the organization of the corporation by appointing officers, adopting bylaws, and carrying on any other business brought before the meeting; (2) if initial directors are not named in the articles, the incorporator or incorporators shall hold an organizational meeting at the call of a majority of the incorporators: (i) to elect directors and complete the organization of the corporation; or (ii) to elect a board of directors who shall complete the organization of the corporation. These actions may be taken without a meeting in most states if all of the directors or incorporators sign written consents describing the actions taken. If a meeting is held, it is common for the lawyer handling the formation of the corporation to prepare minutes of the meeting in advance and to use them as a script for the actual meeting.

1. Additional Steps

Lawyers generally are expected to complete the formation of a corporation on behalf of a client. The following additional steps may be necessary to complete the formation of a corporation:

- Prepare bylaws.

- Prepare minutes of the various organizational meetings, including waivers of notice or consents to action without formal meetings.

- Obtain a minute book and seal.

- Obtain blank share certificates and make sure they are properly prepared and issued for the consideration specified for those shares.

- Prepare stockholders' agreement, if any.

- Obtain necessary tax identification numbers and comply with other state and federal legal requirements.

- Determine whether the S corporation tax election should be made, and, if so, make that election.

- Make sure the directors and officers understand the nature of their duties and responsibilities.

These steps may require additional meetings or signatures of the incorporators, the board of directors, or the stockholders. It is customary to act by written consent rather than by actually conducting meetings.

2. Consequences of Failure to Complete Formation

The consequences of a partial formation of a corporation usually arise in the context of a suit against officers, directors, or stockholders seeking to hold them personally liable for obligations incurred in the name of the corporation. Although the organizational meeting is mandatory under a literal reading of the statutes of many states, failure to hold the meeting does not affect the existence of the corporation, which begins with the filing of the articles of incorporation. Thus, it is unlikely that failure to hold an organizational meeting carries any negative consequences. *See In re Whatley*, 874 F.2d 997 (5th Cir. 1989). Several cases hold that no personal liability is created so long as articles of incorporation were properly filed. *See Moe v. Harris*, 172 N.W. 494 (Minn.1919). If personal liability is imposed after the filing of articles of incorporation, it is likely to be based either on a contract or other action for the benefit of the corporation that occurred before the filing of the articles of incorporation (promoter liability), or as a result of piercing the corporate veil. Both are discussed in detail in subsequent chapters. On the other hand, failure to hold the organization meeting may be viewed as a breach of duty on the part of the directors or cited for the proposition that an officer or other agent of the corporation was not authorized to act on behalf of the corporation.

G. INITIAL CAPITALIZATION

Prior to 1970, many states required that a corporation have a minimum amount of capital (often $1,000 in cash or property) before it could commence doing business.

1. Current Trend

The trend is clearly in the direction of eliminating capital requirements. Most states today have eliminated all minimum capitalization requirements. The theory is that minimum capitalization requirements are arbitrary and unrelated to the true capital needs of the corporation, and therefore do not provide meaningful protection to creditors.

2. Failure to Meet Minimum Initial Capital Requirements

In states that retain minimum capitalization requirements, directors are usually personally liable if business is commenced without the required minimum capital. This liability is limited to the difference between the minimum required capitalization and the amount of capital actually contributed.

> *Example:* In a state with a minimum $1,000 capital requirement, a corporation commences business with $700 in capital. The directors are liable for $300. This liability disappears if the corporation thereafter obtains additional capital of $300 or more.

a. A few early state statutes were construed to impose unlimited liability on directors for all debts incurred before the minimum capitalization was paid in.

> *Example:* In a state with a minimum $1,000 capital requirement, a corporation commences business with capital of $700. In the course of its business, the corporation incurs liabilities of $10,000 before any further capital is paid in. The directors are liable for $10,000 and this liability is not eliminated even though thereafter capital contributions of $300 or more are received. *See Sulphur Export Corp. v. Carribean Clipper Lines, Inc.*, 277 F.Supp. 632 (E.D.La.1968). *Tri-State Developers, Inc. v. Moore*, 343 S.W.2d 812 (Ky.1961).

b. There is no requirement that a corporation *maintain* any specified minimum capital after incorporation.

H. BYLAWS

The bylaws of a corporation are a set of rules for governing the internal affairs of the corporation. They are typically adopted as part of the formation of a new corporation, and generally may be modified thereafter either by the board of directors or by the stockholders subject to (1) limitations on the ability of the directors to amend bylaws adopted by the stockholders and (2) supermajority requirements that may be imposed in the case of bylaws that themselves require a supermajority for certain actions. See MBCA 10.20–10.22.

1. Legal Effect of Bylaws

Bylaws are binding on intra-corporate matters. They may be viewed as a contract between the corporation and its members, or as a set of binding internal rules of governance. Amendments to the bylaws that have the effect of changing the rules in the middle of a controversy may be found to be invalid even if appropriate procedures have been followed. For example, if the board of directors attempts to change a bylaw that permits 10% of the stockholders to call a special meeting to increase the requirement to 20% (having already received a proper demand signed by 10% of the stockholders), the amendment is probably ineffective even if duly adopted. *See Schnell v. Chris–Craft Industries, Inc.*, 285 A.2d 437 (Del., 1971); *Blasius Industries, Inc. v. Atlas Corporation*, 564 A.2d 651 (Del. Ch. 1988). In addition, bylaws that restrict the discretion of the board of directors to manage the corporation may be held to be invalid. *See Quickturn Design Systems, Inc. v. Shapiro*, 721 A.2d 1281 (Del. 1998).

2. Practical Effect of Bylaws

Bylaws essentially are an operating manual of basic rules for the conduct of the ordinary business of the corporation. They may be relied upon by the corporate officers as a checklist in administering the affairs of the corporation.

a. Corporate officers and directors are likely to be more conversant with the bylaws than the articles of incorporation.

b. Procedural matters and mandatory provisions that appear in the articles of incorporation relating to corporate governance should normally also appear in the bylaws.

> *Caveat:* Provisions in the articles of incorporation trump any conflicting provision in the bylaws. Thus, if for convenience a bylaw is adopted that is identical to the language of the articles of incorporation, a change in the bylaw will not be effective unless the provision in the articles of incorporation is also amended.

I. CORPORATE POWERS

MBCA 3.02 provides that every corporation has the same powers as an individual to do all things necessary or convenient to carry out its business and affairs, including without limitation a list of specific powers. Most states have an enumeration of specific powers but without the broadening language of MBCA

3.02, (which was drawn from the California statute).

1. Enumerated Powers

Every state statute enumerates general powers that every corporation possesses. Generally, it is unnecessary (and undesirable) also to list these powers in the articles of incorporation. The traditional enumerated powers possessed by corporations under modern statutes include the power:

- To sue and be sued.

- To have a corporate seal.

- To purchase, receive, lend, sell, invest, convey and mortgage personal and real property.

- To make contracts, borrow and lend money, and guarantee the indebtedness of third persons.

- To conduct its business within or without the state.

- To elect or appoint officers or agents, define their duties, and fix their compensation

- To purchase shares or interests in, or obligations of, any other entity.

- To make charitable, scientific or education contributions or donations for the public welfare.

- To be a partner or manager of a partnership or other venture.

- To make and alter bylaws for the administration and regulation of its internal affairs.

- To indemnify directors and officers against liabilities imposed on them while acting on behalf of the corporation, and to provide liability insurance for them.

MBCA 3.02(15) also permits a corporation to make payments or donations, or do any other act, not inconsistent with law, that furthers the business and affairs of the corporation. This power permits corporations to make political donations or contributions to influence elections to the extent permitted by state law.

2. Acts in Excess of Powers

If a corporation does an act which it does not have power to do, it is acting *ultra vires*.

3. Partial Enumeration of Powers

The danger of a partial enumeration of statutory powers in the articles of incorporation is that a negative inference may be drawn that the inclusion of some enumerated powers implies the exclusion of unenumerated ones.

J. ULTRA VIRES

The phrase *ultra vires* means beyond the power. It is used to describe acts that exceed the stated purposes of the corporation or restrictions on the power of the board of directors. See California Public Employees' Retirement System v. Coulter, 2002 WL 31888343 (Del.Ch.2002).

Example: A corporation is formed for the purpose of selling or lending all kinds of railway plant, carrying on the business of mechanical engineers, etc. The corporation contracts to build a railroad in a foreign country. The contract was held to be *ultra vires. Ashbury Railway Carriage & Iron Co. v. Riche,* 7 N.S. Law Times Rep. 450 (1875).

1. Common Law

The early common law view was that an *ultra vires* transaction was void, because the corporation lacked the power to enter into the transaction. This doctrine led to potentially undesirable results and gradually has been modified.

a. A transaction that was purely executory might be enjoined if it was *ultra vires* with respect to either party.

b. If the transaction was wholly executed by both parties, the transaction could not be attacked on the ground of *ultra vires. Herbert v. Sullivan,* 123 F.2d 477 (1st Cir.1941).

c. If the transaction was partially executed, *ultra vires* might be raised, but doctrines of estoppel, unjust enrichment, or fairness might mitigate the strict common law view. *Goodman v. Ladd Estate Co.,* 427 P.2d 102 (Ore.1967).

d. An *ultra vires* transaction might be ratified by all the stockholders. See *Lurie v. Arizona Fertilizer & Chemical Co.,* 421 P.2d 330 (Ariz.1966) (corporation entering partnership).

e. Generally, the defense of *ultra vires* is not available to a corporation in a suit based on tort or in a prosecution for criminal conduct.

f.   Directors and officers causing the corporation to enter into *ultra vires* transactions were not automatically liable for losses suffered thereby, although the fact that the conduct was *ultra vires* might cause courts to be more willing to pierce the corporate veil or otherwise impose personal liability on the stockholders. *See Lurie v. Arizona Fertilizer & Chemical Co.,* 421 P.2d 330 (Ariz.1966).

g.   The attorney general of the state may enjoin corporations engaging in *ultra vires* transactions, seek a writ of *quo warranto,* or bring a suit to dissolve the corporation. As a practical matter, such actions are extremely rare.

2. Statutory Law

The *ultra vires* doctrine has been narrowly confined by statute. For example, MBCA 3.04 provides that the validity of a corporate action may not be challenged on the ground that the corporation lacks the authority to act, except (1) in a proceeding by a stockholder against the corporation to enjoin the act, (2) in a proceeding by the corporation, directly, derivatively, or through a receiver, trustee, or other legal representative, against an incumbent or former director, officer, employee, or agent of the corporation, or (3) in a proceeding by the attorney general.

Example: A corporation formed for the purpose of doing ship repairs signs a lease to rent a motion picture theater. The landlord regrets entering the lease and seeks to cancel it on the ground it is *ultra vires* from the standpoint of the tenant. The landlord loses under the above statute even though the tenant has not amended its articles of incorporation to broaden its purpose. *711 Kings Highway Corp. v. F. I. M.'s Marine Repair Serv., Inc.,* 273 N.Y.S.2d 299 (1966).

Example: A corporation is sued on a guarantee of indebtedness which it made to secure a loan to a customer. Such a guarantee is *ultra vires* under the law of the state in question. The corporation nevertheless may not defend on the ground that the guarantee is *ultra vires* because the statute precludes raising *ultra vires* as a defense. But a stockholder may intervene and raise the *ultra vires* issue in a suit to enjoin the making of such a guarantee. If a stockholder does so, the court has discretion whether or not to enforce the *ultra vires* contract on the ground of equity or fairness. The plaintiff may also seek to avoid the claim of the intervening stockholder on the ground that the stockholder is acting for the corporation and therefore is not entitled to seek to enjoin the action. *See Goodman v. Ladd Estate Co.,* 427 P.2d 102 (Or.1967); *Inter-Continental Corp. v. Moody,* 411 S.W.2d 578 (Tex.Civ.App.1966).

3. Other Factors

Three other factors minimize the significance of the *ultra vires* doctrine today:

a. The use of multiple purposes clauses, and more recently, the use of general purposes clauses.

b. The broadening of the general powers that every corporation possesses by statute.

c. The power of a corporation to amend its articles of incorporation to broaden its purposes and to accommodate desirable transactions.

4. Areas of Continuing Concern

The doctrine of *ultra vires* may continue to apply in connection with controversial corporate acts:

a. Making political contributions or engaging in activities designed to influence legislation.

b. Granting employee fringe benefits that appear to be unrelated to the value of the services rendered.

c. Making large charitable donations that appear to provide no benefit to the corporation.

d. Guaranteeing indebtedness of others that provide no apparent benefit to the corporation.

e. Making loans to officers or directors.

> *Caveat:* Even when not expressly enumerated, a court may conclude that a corporation implicitly has power to engage in a particular act. *See Union Pac. Railroad Co. v. Trustees, Inc.,* 329 P.2d 398 (Utah 1958) (charitable contribution).

> *Caveat:* Even where state statutes grant the power to enter into transactions in broad terms, courts may impose a limitation of reasonableness based on public policy or common sense.

Example: A state statute authorizes a corporation to make donations for the public welfare or for charitable, scientific or educational purposes. A closely held corporation with income in excess of $19,000,000 per year proposes to make a gift of over $500,000 to a charitable corporation controlled by the majority stockholder. The gift is valid. The statute should be construed to permit reasonable charitable gifts, and the proposed contribution is reasonable under the circumstances. *Theodora Holding Corp. v. Henderson,* 257 A.2d 398 (Del.Ch.1969). In concluding that a $500,000 gift was reasonable, some reliance may be placed on the federal income tax law that permits the deduction of up to ten percent of taxable income as charitable donations.

Example: After the death of two corporate officers, the board of directors of the corporation votes to pay certain bonuses to their widows. Such payments are *ultra vires* because they are not charitable and, under the specific circumstances, not supported by consideration or justifiable as executive compensation. *Adams v. Smith,* 153 So.2d 221 (Ala.1963). Some courts have disagreed. *Chambers v. Beaver–Advance Corp.,* 140 A.2d 808 (Pa.1958). If a program by which stipends are to be paid to widows or widowers of employees is announced in advance, that plan should be valid as a type of employment compensation.

Example: X, an 80 per cent stockholder of corporation Y, causes Y corporation to place a second mortgage on its property to secure a loan made to a corporation that is wholly owned by X. Such a mortgage is *ultra vires* and may be set aside at the suit of the 20 per cent stockholder of Y. *Real Estate Capital Corp. v. Thunder Corp.,* 287 N.E.2d 838 (Ohio Com.Pleas 1972). It is unclear whether the holder of the mortgage had reason to know that Y received no benefit from the mortgage. This transaction may also constitute a breach of fiduciary duty by X.

Example: In order to secure passage of legislation, a corporation agrees to make certain payments to local taxing authorities in lieu of taxes. As a result of that agreement, the local taxing authorities withdraw their opposition to the legislation.

Such payments are not *ultra vires*. They are donations to local taxing authorities though not contributions and not lobbying expenditures. *Kelly v. Bell*, 254 A.2d 62 (Del.Ch.1969). The Supreme Court of Delaware affirmed, commenting that personal liability should not be imposed on the directors for such a payment because they exercised a reasonable business judgment in agreeing to make the payment.

K. FOREIGN CORPORATIONS

Corporations that do business in one state but that are formed under the laws of another state are called *foreign corporations*. Corporations formed under the law of foreign countries are also called foreign corporations, but the discussion here focuses primarily on issues of interstate commerce. The various states are required to recognize each other's corporations under the full faith and credit clause of the Constitution. But a host state also has the constitutional right to regulate foreign corporations doing business within its borders. Thus, every state has a procedure by which a foreign corporation may qualify to do business in that state. But a state may not exclude foreign corporations from entering into transactions with its citizens in interstate commerce. Thus, the question of what constitutes doing business may be an important one.

Caveat: The phrase *doing business* is used here in a different sense from its use in connection with (say) long arm jurisdiction. A foreign corporation may be subject to long arm jurisdiction by virtue of doing business in the host state even though it is not doing business to an extent that requires it to qualify as a foreign corporation in that state.

1. Qualification to Transact Business

A foreign corporation qualifies to transact business by obtaining a certificate of authority to transact business from the host state.

a. An application for a certificate of authority must contain information required by statute. MBCA 15.03(a). A certified copy of the foreign corporation's articles of incorporation must accompany the application. It must also be accompanied by the required filing fee.

b. The foreign corporation's name must meet the statutory standards for names. If the foreign corporation's name is unavailable, the foreign corporation must designate a different name under which it will transaction business in the host state. MBCA 15.06.

c. A foreign corporation qualifying to transact business in the host state must designate a registered office and registered agent. MBCA 15.07.

d. A qualified corporation may withdraw from a host state by following mandated statutory procedures. MBCA 15.20.

2. Qualification Requirement

Qualification is required when the foreign corporation's local business activities are such that it is deemed to be transacting business in the host state. Transactions involving interstate commerce are not considered in this determination.

a. Statutes contain a list of activities that do not constitute the transaction of business within the host state. MBCA 15.01(b). This list includes a variety of business and legal relationships.

Example: A foreign corporation opens a local office to sell the products it manufactures in a state in which it is not qualified to transact business. It must thereafter qualify to transact business in that state.

Example: A foreign corporation solicits purchasers of its product by mail. It opens a warehouse in a state in which it is not qualified to transact business and fills orders from that warehouse in an eight state region, including the state in which the warehouse is located. The corporation must qualify to transact business in the state in which its warehouse is located.

b. Most large publicly held corporations qualify to transact business in all states.

3. Effect of Qualification

A foreign corporation that qualifies to transact business in a host state generally obtains the rights and privileges of domestic corporations formed within that state. MBCA 15.05(b).

a. A qualified foreign corporation also becomes subject to suit in the host state not only on transactions occurring within the state but on other transactions as well, subject to principles of *forum non conveniens*.

b. A qualified foreign corporation may becomes subject to state taxes on the proportion of income earned from business within the host state. Allocation of income and expense is an important aspect of state taxation of multistate corporations.

4. Failure to Qualify

State statutes provide sanctions applicable to corporations that are required to qualify to transact business in the state but fail to do so.

a. The corporation may be disqualified from suing in the courts of that state or from interposing the statute of limitations as a defense in litigation brought against it within the state. MBCA 15.02(a) (courts of state are closed to proceedings brought by unqualified foreign corporations). State statutes usually prohibit a successor to an unqualified foreign corporation, or an assignee, to maintain a suit that would be barred if brought directly by the predecessor or assignor. MBCA 15.02(b). The MBCA (1984) and the statutes of many states provide that qualification after suit is filed permits the suit to be maintained. In other words, the closure of the courts is designed to assure qualification rather than being a sanction for failing to qualify.

b. The statutes of some states make unenforceable contracts entered into by a nonqualified corporation that should have qualified to transact business. This is a true sanction for failing to qualify. The MBCA does not include this sanction.

c. Most states impose a monetary penalty on the corporation for each year that it should have qualified to transact business but did not. MBCA 15.02(d). Some states also impose penalties on officers or directors of the corporation who are within the state.

5. Amenability of Nonqualified Corporation to Suit

A corporation that is not required to qualify to transact business in the state may nevertheless have sufficient contacts with that state to be subject to service of process within that state on suits arising out of those contacts. *International Shoe Co. v. Washington,* 326 U.S. 310, 66 St.Ct. 154 (1945); *Helicopteros Nacionales de Colombia, S.A. v. Hall,* 466 U.S. 408, 104 S.Ct. 1868 (1984).

6. Liability of Nonqualified Corporation to State Taxation

A corporation that is not required to qualify to transact business in the state may be subject to taxation in that state but the tax must be commensurate with the corporation's activities in that state. Requirements include sufficient nexus with the taxing state, fair relationship of tax to benefits received, nondiscrimination against interstate commerce, and fair apportionment. *Mobil Oil Corp. v. Commissioner* 445 U.S. 425, 100 S.Ct. 1223 (1980). A federal statute, the Federal Interstate Income Act of 1959, 15 U.S.C.A. § 381, et seq., limits the application of state income tax laws to foreign corporations where the only contact with the host state is solicitation of orders in interstate commerce.

7. Internal Affairs Rule

Litigation involving corporate issues may be filed in states other than the state of incorporation. The general rule is that the internal affairs of a corporation are governed by the laws of the state of incorporation. This rule is statutory in many states. MBCA 15.05(c).

> *Example:* A corporation planning a cash-out merger is sued in a state other than its state of incorporation by stockholders resident in that state seeking to enjoin the merger. The merger is not permitted under the laws of the state in which suit is brought but is permitted under the laws of the state of incorporation. The internal affairs rule requires the court to apply the law of the state of incorporation in determining the validity of the cash-out merger, the procedures that must be followed to approve it, and the rights of dissenting stockholders.

a. The internal affairs rule means that many issues of Delaware law are resolved in federal or state courts other than in Delaware.

b. New York and California have adopted statutes that require courts to apply domestic principles to a limited number of issues to corporations that are incorporated in other states but have dominant economic contacts with New York of California.

c. New York requires corporations doing business in New York to be subject to New York statutory provisions imposing liability on directors for cash or property distributions to stockholders that are unlawful under New York law. NYBCL 1315–1319.

d. California requires corporations incorporated in other states that have their predominant business activities in California and more than half of their outstanding shares held by persons resident in California to provide procedural protections to stockholders, including cumulative voting, permitting removal of directors without cause, defining the directors' duty of care, and providing for dissenters' rights in specified situations. Corporations subject to these provisions are sometimes called pseudo-foreign corporations. CCC 2115.

e. The constitutionality of these statutes has never been definitively resolved. Recent decisions by the Supreme Court cast the power of the state of incorporation to regulate the affairs of domestic corporations in near constitutional terms.

8. Domestication and Conversion

The MBCA was amended in 2002 to permit *domestication* and *conversion* into other entities without merger. *Domestication* refers to a change in the state of incorporation. (It is so-called because from the point of view of the new state of incorporation the corporation is converted from a foreign corporation to a domestic corporation.) In the absence of a statute providing for domestication, the usual practice is for the foreign corporation to merge with a newly formed domestic corporation which survives the merger. The amendments eliminate the need for a merger and accomplish domestication by means of a simple filing, thus avoiding the dangers that may be associated with using the merger statute (such as triggering appraisal rights). Similarly, provisions relating to conversion permit a corporation to convert into a partnership or LLC (or other non-corporate form) or into a non-profit corporation, without the need for a merger. Conversion may also be accomplished by merger, although the possibility of a merger between different forms of organization is a relatively recent development. As with domestication, provisions relating to conversion provide a simpler alternative than merger for internal changes in corporate governance.

REVIEW QUESTIONS

2.1. True or False: Delaware is the best state in which to incorporate a new business.

2.2. True or False: Incorporation is an expensive process not suitable for small businesses.

2.3. True or False: When forming a corporation, it makes no difference who serves as an incorporator.

2.4. True or False: Articles of incorporation may contain only provisions authorized by statute.

2.5. Why would provisions relating to internal governance that may be included in either articles of incorporation or bylaws ever be included in the articles of incorporation?

2.6. True or False: A corporation must do business under its official name and may not use a fictitious name.

2.7. What is the difference between a reserved and a registered name?

2.8. When should a period of duration less than perpetual be elected?

2.9. True or False: Corporations must specify the purposes for which they are formed and limit their activities to those purposes.

2.10. True or False: Corporations should always use the broadest possible purposes clause permitted by the state statute.

2.11. Why does a corporation need a registered agent and registered office?

2.12. Should corporate powers ever be listed in articles of incorporation?

2.13. What does *ultra vires* mean?

2.14. Why do modern statutes restrict or eliminate the doctrine of *ultra vires?*

2.15. What factors have led to the decline of *ultra vires?*

2.16. What steps are required to complete the formation of a corporation after articles of incorporation have been filed?

2.17. What is the consequence of filing articles of incorporation and commencing business without completing the organization of the corporation?

2.18. Two lawyers, one practicing real property and estates law and the other specializing in the trial of negligence cases, share an office. Each pays half the rent, the salaries of the employees, the cost of office equipment, supplies, utilities, and the upkeep of the library. They each have their own clients and receive their respective fees. Would they enjoy any advantages by incorporating, including minimizing their taxes and maximizing their tax benefits? To what extent would they have to change their manner of operations?

2.19. What factors enter into the decision to place optional provisions in the articles of incorporation rather than the bylaws?

2.20. True or False: If provisions appear in the articles of incorporation it is unnecessary to repeat them in the bylaws.

*

III

Preincorporation Transactions

A. PROMOTERS

A *promoter* is someone who undertakes to form a new business. Although the term *promoter* may have a pejorative connotation, promoters are often shrewd, visionary individuals who serve important social and economic functions. In promoting a new venture, a promoter may arrange for the necessary business assets and personnel so that the new business may function effectively. This may include obtaining or renting a plant, assembling work and sales forces, finding sources of raw materials and supplies, finding retail outlets, making long term commitments of various types, and so forth. A promoter may also obtain the necessary capital to finance the venture. The sources of initial capital include (i) equity capital contributed by investors, (ii) loans from third parties, either secured or unsecured, and (iii) loans from the investors supplying the equity capital.

B. PROMOTER CONTRACTS

Promoters may enter into contracts on behalf of the venture being promoted either before or after articles of incorporation have been filed. Most problems are created by preincorporation contracts because under modern statutes the corporate existence begins when articles of incorporation are accepted for filing, and contracts entered into by the promoter in the corporate name after that date normally bind only the corporation. The legal consequences of preincorporation contracts entered into by promoters vary, depending in part on the form of the contract itself.

1. Contracts in the Name of a Corporation to Be Formed

In contracts of this type, the promoter enters into a preincorporation contract which on its face shows that the corporation has not yet been formed. A typical form of execution of a contract of this type is: ABC Corporation, a corporation to be formed, By _____. Such a contract may be analyzed in several different ways, depending on the facts and the context, which may lead to widely different legal consequences.

a. The traditional analysis is that the promoter is personally liable on the contract and is not relieved of liability if the corporation is later formed and adopts the contract. Assuming that the corporation is formed and adopts the contract, both the promoter and the corporation are liable on the contract. Presumably the promoter may look to the newly formed corporation for indemnification if the contract benefits the corporation but the promoter remains personally liable.

b. A related analysis is that the promoter is personally liable on the contract, but is thereafter relieved of liability if the corporation is later formed and adopts the contract. This is a *novation*.

c. Another analysis that leads to a diametrically different result is that the promoter is not personally liable on the contract because the third party intended to deal only with the corporation. While the corporation may become liable if it is later formed and enters into the contract, no one is liable under this analysis until that event occurs.

    Caveat: Under this analysis the third party has made only an offer to the corporation which may be revoked by the third party before the corporation accepts the contract (unless the offer is an option supported by consideration or is otherwise made irrevocable by law).

d. Another analysis is that the promoter is not personally liable on the contract but has agreed to use best efforts to cause the corporation to be formed and to adopt the contract. The promoter's best efforts promise may be consideration for the third party's promise under the contract. This differs from (c) in that both parties have incurred liability: the promoter is liable on the promise if no steps are taken to form the corporation even though the promoter is not liable on the contract itself.

e. The question of which of these four alternatives is the appropriate one to apply in a specific case depends on the intention of the parties. Where the intention is not clearly expressed uncertainty may exist as to the appropriate legal analysis. Most cases find the promoter personally liable on one theory or another.

Example: Ralph O'Rorke enters into a contract to build a bridge with D. J. Geary on behalf of a bridge company to be organized and incorporated. O'Rorke is to commence work within 10 days and payments are to be made to him by Geary periodically after work is commenced. Geary, as the promoter, is personally liable on the obligation: the fact that payments are required to be made (by Geary) before the bridge company is formed indicates an intent that Geary be personally liable. *O'Rorke v. Geary*, 56 A. 541 (Pa.1903). Accord: *Coopers & Lybrand v. Fox*, 758 P.2d 683 (Colo.App.1988); *Goodman v. Darden, Doman & Stafford Assoc.*, 670 P.2d 648 (Wash.1983); *Stanley J. How & Associates, Inc. v. Boss*, 222 F.Supp. 936 (S.D.Iowa 1963).

Example: Quaker Hill, Inc. sells nursery stock to a corporation to be formed by Parr and Presba. At the urging of Quaker Hill's representative, the contract is entered into in the name of Mountain View Nurseries, Inc. by Parr, President even though Quaker Hill's representative knows that no corporation has been formed. Parr and Presba are not personally liable to Quaker Hill because Quaker Hill, by its conduct, clearly indicated that it intended to look for payment only to the newly formed corporation. *Quaker Hill, Inc. v. Parr*, 364 P.2d 1056 (Colo.1961). Accord: *Tin Cup Pass Ltd. Partnership v. Daniels*, 553 N.E.2d 82 (Ill.App.1990); *Sherwood & Roberts–Oregon, Inc. v. Alexander*, 525 P.2d 135 (Or.1974); *Stewart Realty Co. v. Keller*, 193 N.E.2d 179 (Ohio App.1962).

Example: In the previous example, before the corporation is formed, Quaker Hill changes its mind and refuses to ship the nursery stock. Quaker Hill is not liable for breach of contract because no contract exists. Because Parr and Presba are not personally liable on the contract, and no corporation has been formed, no one is bound to purchase the nursery stock, and Quaker Hill has effectively revoked its offer to ship the nursery stock.

2. Contracts in the Corporate Name

In these cases, a contract is entered into in the name of a corporation even though a corporation has not been formed. One or both of the parties to the transaction erroneously believe the corporation has been formed. The factual patterns under this heading may vary because the contract may be entered into at various times during the incorporation process. For example, the contract may be entered into when no steps at all toward incorporation have been taken, or it may be entered into after articles of incorporation have been prepared but not filed, or after the articles of incorporation have been mailed to the secretary of state but before the certificate of incorporation has been issued.

a. If a promoter represents that she is acting on behalf of a corporation when she knows no steps to form a corporation have been taken, she is usually personally liable on the contract. This result may be justified because a person who purports to act as an agent for a nonexistent principal is personally liable on the contract, or because a person who purports to act as an agent for a principal warrants that she has authority to act.

Example: A promoter reserves the name of a proposed corporation but takes no further steps to incorporate. The promoter then purchases hot dogs from a wholesaler on open account, using the corporate name exclusively. The promoter is personally liable for the purchases. *Echols v. Vienna Sausage Mfg. Co.,* 290 S.E.2d 484 (Ga.App.1982).

b. The common law developed concepts of *de facto* corporations and *de jure* corporation to deal with preincorporation problems. In a suit brought by a private plaintiff against a promoter, the conclusion that either a *de facto* or a *de jure* corporation existed effectively absolves the promoter.

c. A *de jure* corporation is one that has sufficiently complied with applicable incorporation requirements so that a corporation is legally in existence for all purposes. A *de jure* corporation exists if there is compliance with all mandatory statutory requirements; failure to comply with less important requirements (called directory requirements) do not affect the *de jure* status of a corporation. The distinction between mandatory and directory requirements is a matter of degree. *People v. Ford,* 128 N.E. 479 (Ill.1920) holds (over one dissent) that the statutory requirement that a corporation have a seal is a directory requirement.

However, in evaluating this case it should be noted that the contrary conclusion would have called into question the validity of over 4,300 corporations.

Example Articles of incorporation fail to comply with the statutory requirement that addresses be stated because two addresses of directors or incorporators are incorrect. All other statutory requirements are observed. The corporation is a *de jure* corporation.

Example: Under the applicable state statute, articles of incorporation must be filed with the secretary of state and recorded with the county recorder of the county in which the registered office is located. The statute does not set forth the consequences of failure to file with the county. A corporation files articles of incorporation with the secretary of state but fails to file locally. Such a corporation is probably not a *de jure* corporation, but it may be a *de facto* corporation (defined below).

d. A *de facto* corporation is a corporation that is partially but defectively or incompletely formed. It is sufficiently formed, however, to be immune from attack by everyone but the state. Because virtually all litigation in this area involves private plaintiffs rather than the state, a holding that a corporation is *de facto* is virtually as good as a holding that it is *de jure*. The traditional test of *de facto* existence is threefold: (1) there must be a valid statute under which the corporation might incorporate; (2) there must be a good faith or colorable attempt to comply with the statute; and (3) there must have been actual use of the corporate privilege.

Example: A corporation files articles of incorporation with the secretary of state but does not file the articles locally as required by statute. In most states the corporation is a *de facto* corporation not a *de jure* corporation.

Example: A corporation prepares articles of incorporation but because of a clerical mistake by the attorney no filing is ever made with the secretary of state. The company is neither a *de facto* nor a *de jure* corporation. *Conway v. Samet*, 300 N.Y.S.2d 243 (1969).

Caveat: In practice the de facto doctrine tends to be result oriented rather than objective.

Example: In a tort case, a defect in formation might be sufficient to prevent the formation of a de facto corporation. In a contract case where a third person clearly has relied only on the credit of the corporation, a court might hold on essentially the same facts that a de facto corporation existed.

Example: A corporation commences business with less than $1000 in capital, the minimum requirement in the state statute. The statute also provides that directors who permit the corporation to commence business with less than the minimum capital are jointly and severally liable only for the difference. The statutory liability should be deemed exclusive. In a suit to impose personal liability on stockholders (other than the directors liable under the statute) an argument that the failure to provide the minimum capital prevents the creation of a de facto corporation should be rejected.

Example: The foregoing transaction occurs in a state that does not expressly limit the liability of the directors to the unpaid portion of the minimum capital. No *de facto* corporation was formed and the directors and officers may be held personally liable for all debts or liabilities incurred before the minimum capital is paid in. *Sulphur Export Corp. v. Carribean Clipper Lines,* Inc., 277 F.Supp. 632 (E.D.La.1968).

Caveat: State statutes may set forth the legal consequences of a failure to comply with some statutory filing requirements. Such statutes are a substitute for the *de facto* doctrine.

e.   Most states now have statutes that provide an objective test that upon the issuance of the certificate of incorporation the corporate existence begins. MBCA (1969) § 50. MBCA 2.03(a). The statutes also provide that a delayed effective date may be specified and the corporate existence begins when the articles of incorporation are filed. Under these provisions all transactions entered into in the corporate name after the certificate of incorporation has been issued or the articles of incorporation filed should be corporate obligations.

Example: Articles of incorporation are filed and accepted, and a certificate of incorporation issued. The following day a lease is entered into in the corporate name. No further steps are taken to complete the formation of the corporation. No meetings are held. No shares are issued. The lease is a corporate obligation, because the certificate of incorporation conclusively establishes the existence of the corporation. *Cardellino v. Comptroller of Treasury*, 511 A.2d 573 (Md.App.1986). It may still be argued however that the person who signed the lease is personally liable based on the concept of piercing the corporate veil, or lack of authority.

Caveat: These provisions stating when the corporate existence begins do not specifically address the question of the status of obligations entered into in the corporate name before the issuance or the filing of articles of incorporation. Statutes addressing this question are discussed below.

Caveat: One court has declined to rely on the principle that the issuance of the certificate of incorporation establishes the existence of a corporation and applied common law *de facto* principles even though a certificate of incorporation had been issued. *Matter of Whatley*, 874 F.2d 997 (5th Cir.1989) (competing priorities of security interests.)

f. Several state statutes contain a provision based on MBCA (1969) § 139 that addresses the status of preincorporation obligations: "All persons who assume to act as a corporation without authority so to do shall be jointly and severally liable for all debts and liabilities incurred or arising as a result thereof." Some courts have read § 139 literally to provide that the issuance of the certificate of incorporation is the bright line that distinguishes the corporation from the noncorporation. Under this reasoning, personal liability automatically exists on all obligations that antedate the time the secretary of state issues the certificate of incorporation.

Example: A person mails articles of incorporation to the secretary of state and on the following day executes a note in the corporate name on behalf of the corporation. On the day after the note is executed, the secretary of state receives the articles of incorporation, reviews them, rejects them, and returns them for correction. Corrections are made and the articles later accepted and the certificate of incorporation issued. In many states the person signing the note is personally liable. *Robertson v. Levy*, 197 A.2d 443 (D.C.App.1964). *Accord Booker Custom Packing Co., Inc. v. Sallomi*, 716 P.2d

1061 (Ariz.App.1986); *Thompson & Green Machinery Co., Inc. v. Music City Lumber Co., Inc.,* 683 S.W.2d 340 (Tenn.App.1984); *Bowers Building Co. v. Altura Glass Co., Inc.* 694 P.2d 876 (Colo.App.1984); *Cahoon v. Ward,* 204 S.E.2d 622 (Ga.1974); *Timberline Equipment Co. Inc. v. Davenport,* 514 P.2d 1109 (Or.1973).

Caveat: Secretaries of state usually backdate certificates of incorporation or fee receipts to the date the articles of incorporation are received, in effect ignoring processing time. This practice, which is not universal, may eliminate some time-of-issuance questions.

Example: The articles of incorporation are filed on May 1, and the corporation executes a promissory note on May 3. On May 4, the secretary of state issues the certificate of incorporation but follows the standard practice of dating it May 1, the date of filing. The corporate existence began on May 1 and the promissory note is solely a corporate obligation.

Example: The articles of incorporation are filed on May 1, but are returned to the incorporators because of the absence of a notarial certificate. The certificate is added, and the same articles are refiled on May 3. If the articles are reexecuted on May 3 so that the notarial certificate bears that date, it is unlikely that a secretary of state would date the certificate earlier than May 3.

g.   Under MBCA (1969) § 139, some courts have distinguished between active participants and passive investors with the usual result that; the latter are not personally liable on transactions entered into before the certificate of incorporation is issued. This view is based on the statutory language referring only "to persons who assume to act on behalf of the corporation." *Timberline Equipment Co., Inc. v. Davenport,* 514 P.2d 1109 (Or. 1973).

h.   Some statutes contain provisions making the issuance of the certificate of incorporation conclusive of the existence of the corporation but do not contain language similar to that appearing in MBCA (1969) § 139, referring to persons who assume to act on behalf of the corporation. In these states, an argument may be made that the traditional common law concept of the *de facto* corporation continues to exist because the statute does not purport to deal explicitly with precorporation transactions.

Example: In a state that does not follow the practice of backdating articles of incorporation, an incorporator prepares articles of incorporation on April 1 and mails them to the secretary of state. Because of a delay in the mails the articles are not received until April 5, and a certificate of incorporation is issued on April 7, showing that date as the date of issuance. The corporation enters into a contract on April 4. Even though the *de jure* existence of the corporation did not begin until April 7, a corporation *de facto* exists from April 1, and only the corporation is liable on the April 4 obligation. *Cantor v. Sunshine Greenery, Inc.*, 398 A.2d 571 (N.J.Super. App.Div. 1979).

i. MBCA 2.04 provides that all persons purporting to act as or on behalf of a corporation, knowing there was no incorporation under this Act, are jointly and severally liable for all liabilities created while so acting. This provision is consistent with the results reached in most of the above cases.

Caveat: The requirement that a person must *know* that there has been no incorporation in order to be held liable arguably restores an even broader *de facto* corporation doctrine than existed under the common law.

j. Some cases have applied a concept of *corporation by estoppel* that appears to be independent of both statutes and the common law *de facto* corporation concept.

Example: X executes articles of incorporation and reasonably but erroneously believes that they have been filed with the secretary of state by his attorney. X negotiates the purchase of typewriters in the corporate name and executes notes in the corporate name to pay for them. The seller relies solely on the corporation's credit but later discovers that the articles of incorporation were never filed and brings suit against X personally. The seller is estopped to deny the existence of the corporation under these circumstances. *Cranson v. IBM*, 200 A.2d 33 (Md.1964). *Cf. Harry Rich Corp. v. Feinberg*, 518 So.2d 377 (Fla.App.1987) (on similar facts, officer held not liable under 1969 MBCA § 139). X may have a claim over against the attorney for malpractice if held liable on the underlying contract. *Conway v. Samet*, 300 N.Y.S.2d 243 (1969). If the defendant seeks to avoid liability on the ground that the plaintiff may not sue because it is not a lawful corporate entity, the doctrine of corporation by estoppel is usually applied. *Timberline Equipment Co., Inc. v. Davenport*, 514 P.2d 1109 (Ore.1973).

Caveat: Because estoppel depends on reliance, it is effective only as to creditors who can show reliance. Thus, estoppel does not apply at all in tort cases. In contrast, a finding that a *de facto* corporation exists is presumably effective against all claimants and may be established as a procedural matter by collateral estoppel.

k.   If carried to its logical conclusion, the concept of corporation by estoppel would permit stockholders to obtain the benefits of limited liability simply by consistently representing the corporation's existence. Notions of public policy and the need to preserve the incorporation process therefore dictate that only persons who honestly but erroneously believe that articles have been filed should be able to take advantage of the corporation by estoppel concept. MBCA 2.04 accepts this view.

l.   The failure to complete the formation of the corporation usually is discovered long after the transaction in question. Discovery following the commencement of litigation usually leads to information that reveals that the corporation was not fully formed when the transaction was entered into. Some courts have accepted the windfall argument and have refused to impose personal liability even in circumstances where no steps toward incorporation have been taken. *Frontier Refining Co. v. Kunkel's Inc.*, 407 P.2d 880 (Wyo.1965).

m.   This area of the law of corporations reflects the interplay of conflicting general principles. In such situations, unpredictability of result and irreconcilable precedents often result. The statutes and common sense say no certificate of incorporation, no corporation. Under this approach there should be unlimited personal liability for all obligations entered into in the corporate name before the corporation is formed. But where third persons deal with an apparent corporation, they receive a windfall if they may subsequently hold promoters or investors liable.

3. Liability of Corporation on Promoter's Contracts

The corporation is not automatically liable on contracts made for its benefit before it came into existence. Rather, a newly formed corporation may accept or reject preincorporation contracts.

a. Technically, an acceptance of a preincorporation contract by a corporation is an *adoption* not a *ratification*. *Ratification* assumes that the principal was in existence when the agent entered into the unauthorized contract. When a principal ratifies a contract, the principal is bound on the contract from the time the contract was formed. Because a corporation is not in existence when a preincorporation contract is formed, ratification is not the proper concept. Some courts, however, loosely use the word ratification to describe the corporate adoption of a preincorporation contract.

b. This rule allows subsequent investors in some cases to review promoters' contracts and reject those that seem improvident. The rule works unevenly however, because the time for adoption may occur before the outside investors appear or while the promoter is the dominant force in the newly formed corporation.

c. *Adoption* may be express or implied and presupposes knowledge of the terms of the contract. A recovery in *quasi contract* is normally available where benefits are accepted even if the contract has not been adopted.

> *Example:* Z is given a one-year employment contract involving a salary of $5000 per month by a promoter in the name of a corporation. With knowledge of the terms, the directors of the newly formed corporation accept the benefits of the employment contract for four months. Z is then fired. Whether or not the contract was formally adopted by the board of directors, the corporation has adopted the contract and is bound by it. It is therefore liable to Z for breach of the employment contract. This is an implied adoption. *McArthur v. Times Printing Co.*, 51 N.W. 216 (Minn.1892). Accord: *Stolmeier v. Beck*, 441 N.W.2d 888 (Neb.1989); *Kridelbaugh v. Aldrehn Theatres Co.*, 191 N.W. 803 (Iowa 1923).

> *Example:* In the foregoing illustration, the promoter also secretly promises Z a year-end bonus of $6,000 as part of his employment contract. The directors of the corporation are unaware of this promise and the circumstances are such as

to give the directors no reason to believe that additional compensation was promised. The corporation has not adopted the contract with Z and is not bound by the promise to pay the bonus because adoption requires knowledge of the terms of the contract. Z has a quasi-contractual claim for the fair market value of his services, which may be greater or less than $5000 per month.

d. Where the contract relates to services leading to the formation of the corporation (for example, lawyer's services in connection with forming the corporation), mere existence of the corporation does not constitute adoption of the contract. However, the lawyer may recover in *quasi contract* for the reasonable value of his services.

4. Relationship Between Promoter's Liability and Corporate Adoption

Generally, corporate adoption of a contract releases the promoter from further liability if the parties expressly agree that a novation will occur.

Example: The promoter executes a contract with a third party which contains the following clause: It is understood by the parties hereto that it is the intention of the Purchaser to incorporate. If such incorporation is completed by closing, all agreements, covenants, and warranties contained herein shall be construed to have been made between Seller and the resultant corporation and all documents shall reflect same. The corporation is duly formed and thereafter adopts the contract. Since this clause does not expressly release the promoters from liability upon the adoption of the contract by the corporation, the promoter remains liable as a co-obligor with the corporation. *RKO-Stanley Warner Theatres, Inc. v. Graziano*, 355 A.2d 830 (Pa.1976). It is possible, however, that some courts might construe the last quoted sentence as an indication that the third person intended to look solely to the corporation after its formation and conclude that a novation was intended.

Example: In the foregoing example the corporation is formed but does not adopt the contract. The corporation is not bound despite the language of the agreement. The promoter remains personally liable on the theory that the third person intended someone always to be liable.

a. Williston argued that a novation is almost always contemplated on the theory that the third person usually intends to look solely to the corporation after it is formed.

b. This complete novation theory may lead to promoters deciding to form shell corporations solely to escape personal liability even after it is clear that the promotion will fail. In other words, the complete novation theory permits a promoter to obtain an option at no cost, a deal to which the contracting party would not likely agree.

> *Example:*   A plaintiff testifies, "I understood that I was working for Mr. Jones personally until the railroad was organized; and after the railroad was organized, I was working for the railroad, of course." This testimony indicates that a novation was intended and the railroad but not the promoter is personally liable on the employment contract after the formation of the railroad. *Bradshaw v. Jones,* 152 S.W. 695 (Tex.Civ.App. 1912).

> *Caveat:*   Courts have generally refused to accept Williston's argument and find novations only where there is some indication that a novation was actually intended. *Frazier v. Ash,* 234 F.2d 320 (5th Cir.1956).

C. FIDUCIARY DUTIES

Promoters of a venture owe fiduciary duties to each other and to the corporation. The duty is essentially the same as the duties owed by a partner to a partnership or partners. A duty of full disclosure is owed to subsequent investors.

1. To Corporation

After the corporation is formed it may obtain from the promoter any benefits or rights the promoter obtained on its behalf.

> *Example:*   A promoter, secretly buys land needed by the corporation and sells it to the corporation after it is formed at a profit. The transaction constitutes a breach of fiduciary duty and the corporation may recover the secret profit.

2. To Fellow Promoters

Promoters are essentially partners in the promotion of the venture, and any benefits or rights one promoter obtains must be shared with co-promoters.

> *Example:*   A, a co-promoter, secretly buys land needed by the corporation, planning to resell it to the corporation. The promo-

tion fails, no corporation is ever formed, and A later resells the land to a third person at a profit. Co-promoters may recover their share of the secret profit.

3. To Subsequent Investors

A major issue relating to promoters' fiduciary duties is the extent to which *subsequent* stockholders or investors are protected by fiduciary duties.

a. Under the Massachusetts rule, a corporation may attack an earlier transaction if the subsequent sale to public investors was contemplated at the time of the earlier transaction. *Old Dominion Copper Mining & Smelting Co. v. Bigelow*, 89 N.E. 193 (Mass.1909).

b. Under the federal rule, the corporation may not attack an earlier transaction because all the stockholders at the time consented to the transaction. *Old Dominion Copper Mining & Smelting Co. v. Lewisohn*, 210 U.S. 206, 28 S.Ct. 634 (1908).

> *Example:* At a time when only A and B are stockholders of a corporation, A and B enter into employment contracts with the corporation. Thereafter shares are sold to public investors who are unaware of the employment contracts. When they learn of the employment contracts, they object on the ground that the compensation to A and B is excessive. Under the Massachusetts rule, the corporation or the subsequent investors may attack the earlier transaction if the subsequent sale to investors was contemplated at the time the employment contracts were executed. Under the federal rule neither can do so.

c. These rules were both established in the early 1900s. The Massachusetts rule has been followed more widely than the Federal rule.

d. Arguably, the real issue in these cases is whether there was full disclosure of the transaction at the time the public investors decided to make their investments. If there was full disclosure, the public investors should have reduced the price they agreed to pay for the shares to reflect the transactions in question.

e. Cases of this nature usually are litigated today as disclosure or securities fraud cases rather than as promoters fraud cases. Cases such as these, together with the market crash of 1929 and the Great Depression, provided much of the original impetus for the passage of federal Securities Act of 1933.

4. To Creditors

Fiduciary concepts may also protect creditors against unfair or fraudulent transactions by promoters. *Frick v. Howard,* 126 N.W.2d 619 (Wis.1964). Most of these transactions also may be attacked on the ground they constitute fraud on creditors.

D. AGREEMENTS TO FORM CORPORATIONS

A preincorporation agreement to create a corporation is enforceable to the same extent as any other contract. Today promotions are usually cast in the form of such a contract.

1. Form of Contract

A preincorporation agreement normally sets forth all the basic terms of the business arrangement among the parties. Attachments to the contract may include the proposed articles of incorporation, bylaws, stockholder agreements, and minutes of proposed meetings.

2. Survivability of Agreement

One issue relating to preincorporation contracts is whether provisions of the agreement that are not incorporated into the governing documents of the corporation survive the formation of the corporation. Because the articles of incorporation, bylaws, stockholder agreements, and minutes of meetings on their face appear to provide a complete set of rules of governance, the contract will normally not survive the formation of the corporation unless specific and precise provisions to that effect are included. Where such provisions are included, they may be enforced so long as they do not violate public policy.

> *Caveat:* To assure that the terms of the preincorporation contract are fully enforceable after the formation of the corporation, it may be appropriate to have the corporation expressly assume the preincorporation contract or enter into individual contracts with the stockholders to cover matters that appear in the preincorporation contract.

E. PREINCORPORATION SUBSCRIPTIONS

A preincorporation subscription is a written promise by a person prior to the formation of a corporation to purchase a specific number of shares of the corporation at a specific price after the corporation is formed. Such promises may be obtained by promoters as part of their capital-raising efforts.

1. Use of Preincorporation Subscriptions

Historically most capital for new ventures was raised through preincorporation subscriptions. Their public use was made impractical by the enactment of the Federal Securities Act of 1933, which imposes registration requirements on both the subscription itself and on the subsequent sale of shares. A subscription agreement may still be used in connection with the formation of a closely held corporation, though simple contractual agreements are now more common.

2. Enforceability in Absence of Statute

Preincorporation subscriptions may be obtained independently from several individuals. If so, promises of individual subscribers are not likely to be viewed as made in consideration of the promises of other subscribers, and, because the corporation has not yet been formed, such subscriptions may not be enforceable as contracts. As a result, in the absence of statute, a subscriber may withdraw a subscription at any time before it is accepted by the corporation.

   a.   In some instances subscriptions may be made in a form that indicates that the promises of various investors are made in exchange for each other. In these instances, preincorporation subscriptions become contractual and therefore irrevocable.

   b.   A subscription may be conditioned on the occurrence of a specified event, and such a subscription is normally not enforceable until the condition occurs.

   c.   A subscription obtained through fraud may be rescinded in the same manner as a contract.

3. Statutory Treatment of Preincorporation Subscriptions

The statutes of most states provide that preincorporation subscriptions are irrevocable for a stated period, often six months, without regard to whether they are supported by consideration. MBCA 6.20(a). The six month period may be extended or shortened by specific provision in the subscription itself.

   a.   These statutes also generally provide that calls for payments on subscriptions that have been accepted by the corporation must be uniform. MBCA 6.20(b).

b. Subscription statutes generally provide for forfeiture of partial payments on subscriptions in the event later installments are not paid. Notice generally must be given to a subscriber before a subscription may be forfeited. MBCA 6.20(d).

c. All other subscribers may release a subscriber from his or her subscription.

> *Caveat:* These statutory provisions apply only to subscriptions entered into before the corporation is formed. After incorporation, a promise by an investor to subscribe for shares of the corporation is a contract between that investor and the corporation and is enforceable to the same extent as any other contract.

> *Caveat:* A subscriber becomes a stockholder only upon the payment of the subscription price, though some statutes permit a subscription to be paid with a promissory note, with the shares held in escrow until the promissory note is paid.

REVIEW QUESTIONS

3.1. True or False: A promoter and an incorporator perform the same functions.

3.2. True or False: A promoter enters into a contract in the form: "ABC Corporation, a corporation to be formed. By _____." The promoter is not personally liable on this transaction because it shows on its face that the corporation is a party.

3.3. True or False: A promoter who enters into a contract in the form described in question 3.2, even if liable originally on the contract, will certainly be released from liability if the corporation is formed and takes over the contract.

3.4. How do cases involving corporations de facto differ from cases involving promoters?

3.5. True or False: The Model Business Corporation Act abolishes the concept of de facto corporation.

3.6. What is a corporation by estoppel?

3.7. True or False: The corporation after it is formed automatically assumes all promoters' contracts.

3.8. A and B are promoters. B purchases an inventory of furniture for $60,000 which she represents to A cost $75,000. A agrees to the $75,000 figure. Has B breached a duty to A?

3.9. True or False: A corporation after it is formed can sue promoters for unfair or fraudulent transactions.

3.10. True or False: Preincorporation subscriptions for shares are contracts.

3.11. D entered into a contract with P for the building of a bridge across the Allegheny River. The contract recited that it was between P and D for a bridge company to be incorporated. The bridge was built and subsequently the corporation was formed. P sues D personally to recover on the contract contending that D is personally liable inasmuch as the corporation was not in existence at the time the contract was entered into. D contends that in executing the contract he acted for a corporation to be formed and that the corporation, and not D, is liable on the contract. Is D personally liable to P? Explain your answer.

3.12. A, a promoter of XYZ Publishing Co., engaged M to solicit advertisements for XYZ Publishing Co. prior to its incorporation. M's contract was for one year beginning October first. M started work on October first. XYZ was incorporated on October 16. M worked six months and then was discharged by XYZ. XYZ never took formal action through its board of directors to adopt the contract with M but its stockholders, officers and directors knew of the contract and M was paid by the corporation until the time of his discharge. M sues XYZ for breach of contract. XYZ defends on the basis that it was not in existence at the time the contract was made and cannot be bound by acts of its promoters without adoption by the board of directors. Is XYZ liable on the contract?

IV

Piercing the Corporate Veil

When a court refuses to recognize the separate existence of a valid corporation and holds the stockholders personally liable for the obligations of the corporation, it is said to *pierce the corporate veil*. The phrase is often abbreviated PCV. Piercing is a remedy that is asserted by *creditors* of the corporation—usually against stockholders—when the corporation is unable or unwilling to make good on its obligations whether arising in contract or tort. An aggrieved stockholder has other remedies available against fellow stockholders who may have extracted excessive benefits from the corporation. A stockholder may sue derivatively for the benefit of the corporation for the return of an improper distribution or may sue directly on the theory that the distribution should have been *pro rata* to all stockholders. On the other hand, a stockholder may also be a creditor of the corporation.

Caveat: Piercing may be seen as a matter of agency law or creditor rights as well as a matter of corporation law. There is typically no general statute included in state corporation law that sets forth piercing doctrine. Thus, a piercing case may give rise to difficult choice of law issues. There may be scattered statutes that address piercing in particular situations, such as in connection with tax and environmental matters.

Caveat: With the advent of many new forms of organization with limited liability, such as LLCs and LLPs, the question has also arisen as to when the members or partners in such organizations may be held personally liable. Thus, the idea of piercing the corporate veil has given way to some extent to a more general notion of *veil piercing*. It is likely that the law of piercing will apply in most cases to these other forms of organization. But some concepts developed in the context of the corporation do not fit well in the context of other forms. For example, a partnership is sometimes viewed as a collection of individuals with no separate existence. It thus makes little sense to ask whether the separate identity of the partnership has been respected or whether it is the alter ego or a mere instrumentality of the partners.

A. GENERAL CONSIDERATIONS

Many courts state that the general rule is that the corporation is separate and independent from its stockholders and that its separate existence should be recognized. *Billy v. Consolidated Machine Tool Corp.,* 412 N.E.2d 934 (N.Y. 1980); *Port Chester Elec. Corp. v. Atlas,* 357 N.E.2d 983 (N.Y. 1976). Courts also state that one should be reluctant to pierce, *Eagle v. Benefield–Chappell, Inc.,* 476 So.2d 716 (Fla.App.1985), or that piercing should be applied only with great caution and in extreme circumstances. *Amason v. Whitehead,* 367 S.E.2d 107 (Ga.App.1988); *Farmers Warehouse v. Collins,* 137 S.E.2d 619 (Ga.1964).

1. Nature of Liability

Although it is often assumed that piercing is more common in nonconsensual tort cases in which the plaintiff has had little or no practical ability to conduct a credit check of the defendant in advance, empirical studies of judicial opinions have found that it is in fact somewhat more common for piercing to be ordered in cases based on contractual relationships. On the other hand, most litigated cases involve only the sufficiency of a complaint to withstand a motion to dismiss rather than review of a judgment on the merits. Settlement statistics may reflect that tort cases are settled more often than contract cases.

2. Publicly Held and Closely Held Corporations

Piercing is exclusively a doctrine applicable to closely held corporations. But piercing may be applied to subsidiary corporations owned by a publicly held parent corporation. But in these cases, the separate existence of the subsidiary and not the parent is ignored. A one-person corporation is treated no differently than other corporations in piercing cases. While piercing is probably more likely to occur in small corporations with one or two stockholders than in corporations with more stockholders, essentially the same tests are applied.

3. Sibling Corporations

Piercing cases are not limited to the liability of individual or corporate stockholders for corporate obligations. In appropriate cases, the separate existence of related corporations—corporations with common stockholders—may be ignored so that the two corporations are treated as a single entity. This may occur even though the common stockholders are not found to be personally liable for corporate obligations under a piercing theory. These cases are discussed in more detail below.

4. Motive for Incorporation

Motive is unimportant in the sense that the separate corporate existence may be recognized even though the corporation was formed solely for the purpose of avoiding unlimited liability.

> *Example:* X is the sole owner of a retail drug business which includes home deliveries. X decides to incorporate solely because she fears potential liability for (1) accidents by her delivery trucks and (2) adverse drug reactions from the products she sells. If the corporation is formed and operated consistently with the principles set forth below, its separate corporate existence should be recognized despite the liability-avoiding motive of the sole stockholder.

5. Inactive Stockholders

Piercing is not an all-or-nothing principle. In appropriate cases, active stockholders may be held liable for corporate debts on a piercing theory, but inactive stockholders may be found not to be personally liable on such obligations.

6. Estoppel

Piercing is basically an equitable doctrine available to creditors of the corporation. It generally is not available to the corporation itself or its stockholders. Similarly, piercing may not be available to a bankruptcy trustee who stands in the shoes of the corporation and may assert claims on the name of the corporation. But individual creditors may be able to assert a claim under piercing doctrine even through a bankruptcy trustee cannot do so. *Stodd v. Goldberger,* 141 Cal.Rptr. 67 (Cal.App.1977).

> *Caveat:* A few cases have permitted stockholders to *reverse pierce* and successfully argue that the separate existence of a corporation should be ignored. *See Roepke v. Western National Mutual*

Insurance, 302 N.W.2d 350 (Minn.1981); *Cargill, Inc. v. Hedge*, 375 N.W.2d 477 (Minn.1985). These cases generally involve attempts to extend statutory protections available to individuals, such as the protection of farm homesteads, to property owned by a wholly owned corporation.

B. LEGAL TESTS

The law relating to piercing is quite confused. There is no generally agreed test. Rather the courts tend to refer to broad goals such as to prevent fraud or oppression, to avoid illegality, or to achieve equity. These tests are result-oriented and give little indication of the circumstances in which a court will refuse to recognize the separate existence of a corporation. There are several factors that tend to be cited in piercing cases.

1. Alter Ego and Instrumentality

The phrase *alter ego* literally means *other self*. Courts hold that piercing is proper under the alter ego doctrine where (a) such unity of ownership and interest exists between corporation and stockholder that the corporation has ceased to have separate existence, and (b) recognition of the separate existence of the corporation sanctions fraud or leads to an inequitable result. A corporation becomes the *instrumentality* of a stockholder where there has been an excessive exercise of control by the stockholder that leads to wrongful or inequitable conduct that in turn causes the plaintiff a loss.

a. It is unclear whether alter ego and instrumentality are subdivisions of piercing or whether they are grounds for holding stockholders liable independent of the general tests of preventing fraud or achieving equity. Many courts and commentators view these various doctrines as interchangeable with and essentially the same as the general concept of piercing.

b. These tests are particularly unrealistic in a one-person corporation, because a sole stockholder always dominates the corporation, and the corporation in the same sense is always an instrumentality of the stockholder, as well as the alter ego of the stockholder, because there is no one else with an ownership interest in the corporation.

Caveat: In *Castleberry v. Branscum*, 721 S.W.2d 270, 273 (Tex.1986), the Court stated that alter ego is separate from other grounds for piercing and applies where there is such unity between corporation and individual that the separateness of the corporation has ceased and holding only the corporation liable would result in injustice. The court described other grounds for piercing as involving situations in which even though corporate formalities have been observed and corporate and individual property has been kept separate, the corporate form has been used as an unfair device to achieve an inequitable result. The Texas legislature has twice enacted legislation to narrow or reverse the holding in *Castleberry*, but Texas courts continue to quote the broad dicta of that case.

2. Misrepresentation and Fraud

Piercing may be ordered if information about the corporation is misrepresented or if a third party is in some way misled or tricked into dealing with the corporation. An affirmative misrepresentation by a stockholder may also constitute actionable fraud independent of the piercing doctrine.

Example: A creditor considering an extension of credit to AB Corporation requests financial information. A two-week old balance sheet is supplied showing substantial liquid assets and relatively few current liabilities. The balance sheet was accurate as of the time it was prepared, but in the intervening two weeks the stockholders have caused the corporation to make a substantial distribution to themselves as dividends. It is likely that the stockholders would be held personally responsible to the creditor. The theory may be piercing, fraudulent misrepresentation, or fraud on creditors.

Caveat: The distribution of the dividend was probably illegal because it rendered the corporation insolvent in the equity sense (unable to pay its bills as they become due). Directors are liable to the corporation to the extent a distribution is illegal, and stockholders must indemnify the directors for any illegal distribution they knowingly receive. MBCA 8.33. The problem is that in most states creditors do not have standing to assert a claim belonging to the corporation, and thus may not seek the return of the illegal distribution directly. On the other hand, if the corporation is bankrupt, a bankruptcy trustee may assert claims of the corporation for the ultimate benefit of the creditors.

Example: X negotiates a contract directly with Y, believing that he is dealing with Y on an individual basis. After the deal is concluded in principle, Y presents a contract in which his wholly owned corporation is the sole obligor on the contract. X does not notice this change. If the change is not conspicuous or X is misled in some way, X may hold Y personally on the contract. But if the change is conspicuous and there is no deception, it is likely that X must look solely to the corporation on the theory that a person who signs a contract without reading it is bound by its contents.

3. Personal Guaranty

Piercing may also be ordered if the stockholder orally promises to be personally responsible for corporate obligations under circumstances where it is inequitable to permit the stockholder to rely on the statute of frauds. Except for the possible applicability of the statute of frauds, enforcement of a personal guaranty is not really an example of piercing. Indeed, it is quite common for creditors such as banks to require a personal guaranty when dealing with a small corporation.

> *Example:* A supplier to the corporation refuses to make further shipments unless paid in cash on delivery. The stockholder orally promises to pay for the goods personally if the corporation does not as an inducement to encourage the supplier to ship the goods immediately. The supplier ships the goods in reliance on the stockholder's promise. In most jurisdictions, the supplier may enforce the stockholder's promise even though not in writing. This may be based on a piercing analysis, on the main object exception to the statute of frauds, on a reliance exception to the statute of frauds, or conceivably on other theories as well. *DeWitt Truck Brokers, Inc. v. W. Ray Flemming Fruit Co.,* 540 F.2d 681 (4th Cir.1976).

4. Undercapitalization

Lack of adequate capitalization is a major factor in tort cases, but in most cases there is also some additional justification for piercing. If capital was originally adequate but has been reduced by business reverses, a piercing argument is likely to be rejected. A piercing argument is more likely to be accepted if the original capital is nominal or clearly inadequate in light of contemplated business risks.

a. Piercing is more likely to be ordered if a corporation is formed with minimal capital to engage in hazardous activities. To recognize the separate corporate existence of a nominally capitalized (judgment proof) corporation engaged in a hazardous activity in effect shifts the risk of loss or injury to random members of the general public who happen to be injured by the activity.

b. Liability insurance should be viewed as the equivalent of capital for purposes of piercing in torts cases because such insurance provides readily available funds to tort victims. *Radaszewski v. Telecom Corp.*, 981 F.2d 305 (8th Cir.1992).

c. Inadequate or nominal capitalization should not usually be a factor in contract cases. Absent unusual circumstances, a contract creditor assumes the risk that the corporation will be unable to meet its obligations when dealing voluntarily with the corporation and in the absence of a personal guarantee from the stockholder. Indeed, the formation of a nominally capitalized corporation may be an integral part of a carefully devised plan by the parties to allocate the risk of loss. The courts should not change allocations of risks that are worked out by the parties in the absence of fraud or other abuse. In cases involving nonconsensual transactions (torts) there is usually no element of voluntary dealing. As a result, one cannot usually argue that the third person assumed the risk by dealing with a nominally capitalized corporation. *See Consumer's Co-op. of Walworth Co. v. Olsen*, 419 N.W.2d 211 (Wis.1988).

> ***Example:*** A corporation is formed to lease and operate a swimming pool. No capital is paid in by the stockholders. A child drowns at the pool due to the negligence of an employee. An attorney who is an officer and may have been an investor was responsible for forming the corporation and was personally involved in the operation of the corporation. He may be held personally liable for the damages. *Minton v. Cavaney*, 364 P.2d 473 (Cal. 1961). Again, aggravating circumstances were involved, including the failure to complete the formation of the corporation and failure to observe corporate formalities.

> ***Example:*** A corporation is formed to do blasting pursuant to a contract. As a result of the blasting operations damage occurs to adjoining property. The stockholders are indirectly involved in decisions as to the conduct of the business. The corporation is nominally capitalized with the bulk of the assets lent to the corporation by the stockholders. The

stockholders are personally liable for the damages caused by the blasting operations. *Western Rock Co. v. Davis*, 432 S.W.2d 555 (Tex.Civ.App.1968).

Example: X creates X Corporation (of which he is sole stockholder) with capital of one dollar. Y sells $50,000 worth of goods to X Corporation on credit without conducting any credit check and without being misled in any way. Y may not recover from X on a piercing theory and is limited to suit against X Corporation. *See Brunswick Corp. v. Waxman*, 599 F.2d 34 (2d Cir.1979); *Texas Industries, Inc. v. Dupuy & Dupuy Developers, Inc.*, 227 So.2d 265 (La.App.1969).

Example: Polan forms a corporation to enter into a lease. The organization of the corporation is never completed and the corporation has no assets or bank account. One payment is made on the lease from Polan's personal funds. No further payments are ever made. The court holds that when nothing is invested in the corporation, the corporation provides no protection to its owner. If Polan wishes the protection of a corporation to limit his liability, he must follow the simple formalities of maintaining the corporation. *Kinney Shoe Corp. v. Polan*, 939 F.2d 209 (4th Cir.1991).

Example: A agrees to supply widgets to B at a specified price for resale. The understanding is that A will be paid only out of the proceeds of the resale of the widgets and B will not be personally responsible for any deficit or for any unsold widgets. To effectuate this understanding, B forms a wholly owned corporation with a capital of one dollar and all sales of widgets are made to or by the corporation. Sales are unprofitable and some widgets are unsalable. B is not liable to A. The application of any such theory would change the allocation of loss agreed to by the parties in an arms-length negotiation.

Example: A agrees to supply widgets to B's wholly owned corporation at a specified price for resale. Concerned that B's corporation may lack sufficient assets to pay for the widgets, A requests B personally to guarantee the payments due from B's corporation. B refuses. A decides to deal directly with B's corporation anyway. B is not liable to A.

5. Operation on the Edge of Insolvency

Piercing may be ordered if the corporation is operated so that it can never make a profit, or available funds are siphoned off to the stockholder without regard to the needs of the corporation, or it is operated so that it is always insolvent. *Iron City Sand & Gravel Div. v. West Fork Towing Corp.*, 298 F.Supp. 1091 (N.D.W.Va.1969); *DeWitt Truck Brokers, Inc. v. W Ray Flemming Fruit Co.*, 540 F.2d 681 (4th Cir.1976).

Example: A corporation is formed by a group of persons to build houses to be sold to the stockholders. The corporation prices each home at less than cost so that the corporation must ultimately fail. Creditors who are unaware of the pricing practice probably can hold the stockholders individually liable, *Yacker v. Weiner*, 263 A.2d 188 (N.J. Super.Ch.Div. 1970), though there is some case law to the contrary, *Bartle v. Home Owners Cooperative*, 127 N.E.2d 832 (N.Y.1955).

Example: X forms two corporations, one to manufacture a product and the other to sell it. The price at which the manufacturing corporation sells the products to the selling corporation determines in which corporation the profits will accumulate. X conducts the business so that liabilities end up in the selling corporation and assets in the manufacturing corporation. If the distinction between the two corporations is not sharply maintained and creditors believe they are dealing with a single enterprise, both corporations are liable for all corporate obligations. *Holland v. Joy Candy Mfg. Co.*, 145 N.E.2d 101 (Ill.App. 1957); accord, *Ampex Corp. v. Office Electronics, Inc.*, 320 N.E.2d 486 (Ill.App.1974).

Caveat: It is probable that transactions of this type that injure creditors may be attacked directly on the theory that they constitute usurpation of corporate opportunities, fraudulent transfers, or voidable preferences independently of the piercing doctrine. Nevertheless, the piercing doctrine is regularly applied to transactions of this type.

6. Commingling and Confusion

Piercing may be ordered if the stockholder conducts business in such a way as to cause confusion between individual and corporate finances. *See Zaist v. Olson*, 227 A.2d 552 (Conn.1967).

Example: For convenience, X pays all bills of his corporation by his personal checks and reimburses himself at the end of each week by a single corporate check. X may be personally liable on corporate obligations to persons who have been paid from personal funds.

Example: The sole stockholder of a corporation lists certain corporate assets on his personal financial statements on the theory that the assets belong to him because he owns all the stock of the corporation. In addition, personal expenditures are paid from corporate accounts and he intermingles business and personal transactions. The stockholder is liable to an employee familiar with these transactions for promised bonuses, vacation pay, and pension and profit sharing benefits. *Anderson v. Chatham,* 379 S.E.2d 793 (Ga.App.1989).

Caveat: In both of these examples, the plaintiff was personally familiar with the intermingled transactions and may have relied on them. A creditor who was not directly aware of them may also be able to hold the stockholder liable under piercing principles in many states, though such a claim is more difficult in the absence of detrimental reliance.

7. Artificial Division of Business Entity

In many PCV cases, an important factor is whether a single business is artificially divided into several different corporations to reduce exposure of assets to liabilities. The normal response to an artificial division of a single business entity should be to hold the entire entity responsible for the debts of the business rather than to hold the stockholders personally liable for such debts. One might also argue in such cases that the various related corporations are in partnership with each other and thus liable for the business debts of each other. Two or more corporations owned by a single stockholder or owned more or less proportionally by several stockholders are often referred to as *sibling corporations.* Such a relationship may be analyzed in a similar fashion as *parent and subsidiary* corporations discussed below.

Example: Ace is the owner of a fleet of taxicabs and forms a separate corporation for each taxicab, a separate corporation for the garage that services the cabs, and a separate corporation for dispatching. The business is operated as a single unit. Each corporation is liable for the debts of each other corporation.

Mangan v. Terminal Transp. System, 284 N.Y.S. 183 (App.Div. 1935), *aff'd per curiam*, 286 N.Y.S. 666 (1936).

Example: In the previous example, assume that the various corporations are operated with minimum capitalization and minimum insurance required by law and that the policy of the corporation is to distribute all excess cash to the stockholder as promptly as possible. One of the cabs seriously injures a pedestrian. Some courts would apply a piercing analysis to hold the controlling stockholder liable. Other courts would respect the separate existence of the corporation because it complied with legislatively mandated minimum insurance requirements. *Walkovszky v. Carlton*, 223 N.E.2d 6 (N.Y. 1966). Most cases finding liability involve some aggravating circumstances.

8. Mere Continuation

A situation that is closely related to artificial division may arise if a stockholder conducts a single business under a succession of corporations, abandoning one and forming the next whenever he needs a fresh start. Again, the logical result should be to hold the successor corporation liable for the debts of the predecessor corporation(s). But in some cases, the courts hold the stockholder personally liable, possibly on a theory of abuse or misuse of the corporate form. *See K.C. Roofing Center v. On Top Roofing, Inc.*, 807 S.W.2d 545 (Mo.App.1991).

9. Failure to Follow Corporate Formalities

A piercing argument is somewhat more likely to be accepted if the plaintiff can show (in addition to other factors) failure to follow corporate formalities. Many cases rely to some extent on the failure of the corporation and the stockholder to follow corporate formalities (such as holding an annual meeting or keeping proper minutes) as a basis for piercing. But it is unlikely that failure to follow corporate formalities alone will suffice as grounds for piercing unless failure to follow formalities (such as statutory restrictions on distributions) caused or contributed to the loss.

a. Formalities that are often cited include failure to complete the formation of the corporation; failure to contribute capital or to issue shares; failure to hold elections or meetings; a pattern of decision-making in which stockholders make business decisions much as though they were partners; failure to designate clearly the capacity of persons who are acting on behalf of the corporation; and a pattern involving the mixing of personal and corporate activities, such as informal loans, use of corporate funds for personal purposes or vice versa. *See generally Zaist v. Olson,* 227 A.2d 552 (Conn.1967).

b.   While a failure to follow corporate formalities may lead to confusion or deception in some cases, liability does not appear to be dependent on a showing that third persons were misled or confused. Reliance on failure to follow formalities to establish piercing may be justified on at two least two different grounds. The failure to follow formalities may indicate that the stockholders treat the corporation as an alter ego or instrumentality by not maintaining the separate existence of the corporation. Piercing may also be viewed as a sanction to assure that corporate formalities are in fact followed as contemplated by statute.

> *Caveat:*   Few cases (if any) impose liability merely because of failure to follow corporate formalities. *See Zubik v. Zubik,* 384 F.2d 267 (3d Cir.1967).

> *Caveat:*   Failure to follow corporate formalities may be avoided by (1) maintaining proper written records using the unanimous consent procedure provided by statutes, and (2) taking steps to assure that the capacity of persons acting on behalf of the corporation is always properly identified.

> *Example:*   Articles of incorporation are filed but no further steps are taken to complete the corporation. The corporation commences business. The active stockholders may be held personally liable for corporate debts in some states.

> *Example:*   The corporation is properly formed in the sense that articles of incorporation are filed, bylaws adopted, shares issued, and minutes of the organizational meetings are prepared. But thereafter no stockholders' or directors' meetings are held. All decisions are made in the corporate name by the stockholders after talking among themselves. Even though no third party is harmed by such informal conduct and decision-making, active stockholders may be held personally liable for corporate debts in some states.

10. Other Theories

In recent years, the courts have begun to recognize that when a corporation is operating on the edge of insolvency, the board of directors assumes a fiduciary duty to protect the interests of creditors. It is not completely clear what the duty to creditors entails or when it is triggered. It might be argued that the duty is one primarily to preserve assets for the benefit of creditors. Or it might be argued that the board of directors remains free to pursue risky strategies that may entail losses for creditors, but should not undertake transactions for the benefit of the stockholders at the expense of creditors. Thus, some courts have limited the duty to creditors. One court, in applying Delaware law, has limited the duty to situations where directors of an insolvent corporation diverted corporate assets for the benefit of insiders or preferred creditors.

a.   It is not clear exactly when the duty to creditors is triggered. One court has stated that in determining when this duty attaches, Delaware law is concerned with insolvency in fact, rather than insolvency as defined by a statutory filing. Thus, the better view appears to be that the duty may be triggered somewhat before the appointment of a receiver or trustee. The appointment of a receiver is an extraordinary event because management is removed and replaced with an independent third party either to operate or to liquidate the company. As a result, this test arguably permits a corporation to avoid insolvency until it essentially can no longer pay its debts by any means, including borrowing money on its assets. By the time a corporation cannot pay its current maturing debts—or is in the vicinity of not being able to pay its current maturing debts—it would be too late to protect a creditor's interest in such a way as to give the fiduciary duty any meaning.

b.   The courts appear to view the trigger for this duty to be similar to the statutory test for distributions, employing (1) a balance sheet test (a comparison of a company's debts to the fair value of its assets) and (2) the inability to pay debts as they become due approach (a determination whether the company is unable to meet its current maturing obligations in the ordinary course of business).

c.   There are at least two interpretations of the latter standard. One interpretation focuses on the immediate ability to pay debts. Another looks to future ability to pay debts.

d.   In support of the first interpretation, it has been argued that inability to pay should be tested by the same standard that would be applied in connection with the appointment of a receiver. Under that case law, insolvency exists when (1) the corporation's liabilities exceed its assets or (2) the corporation is unable to meet its current maturing obligations in the ordinary course of business.

e. In support of the second interpretation, it has been argued that in ability to pay should be tested by a standard similar to that found in fraudulent transfer law. One court has held that in light of the policy reasons underlying the creation of a fiduciary duty when a corporation enters the vicinity of insolvency, the stricter test is more appropriate and that the ability to pay is measured by a corporation's ability to obtain enough cash to pay for its projected obligations and fund its requirements for working capital and capital expenditures with a reasonable cushion to cover the variability of its business needs over time.

C. LIABILITY OF PARENT FOR OBLIGATIONS OF SUBSIDIARY

Many piercing cases involve corporations as stockholders. In other words, the issue involves the responsibility of a parent corporation for the actions of a subsidiary (or vice versa). Most publicly held corporations have numerous subsidiaries engaged in a variety of businesses. Subsidiaries are usually wholly owned by the parent corporation but they may also be partially owned. It is often stated that courts are more likely to pierce when the stockholder is itself a corporation than when the stockholder is an individual, but there is little empirical evidence supporting this assertion. Most courts appear to apply the same piercing principles to parent-subsidiary relationships as are applied to stockholders who are individuals. Still, with the continued growth of corporate groups in the future and the increased number of regulatory and environmental laws, it is possible that a unique set of principles for piercing in corporate groups will evolve.

1. Issues That May Arise

Piercing in the parent-subsidiary context may arise in several ways. The issue may be whether transactions between parent and subsidiary or between two subsidiaries must be recognized by third persons who are affected by the transaction.

a. The issue may involve a question of statutory or contract construction. For example, does the relevant statute or contract refer to the corporation or to the owner or operator of the business? Depending on the precise language of the statute or contract it may apply only narrowly to a single corporation or it may apply broadly to affiliated corporations.

b. It is common for a single corporation with several lines of business to separate the businesses by *dropping* the assets and liabilities of a particular business into a newly formed subsidiary. In some cases, shares in the newly formed corporation are then distributed (*spun off*) to the stockholders of the parent corporation with the result that there are now two separate corporations that over time may become wholly unrelated as a result of decisions by various stockholders to hold or sell parent or subsidiary stock. Often such *spin-offs* result in an increase in total stockholder wealth because the two corporations may have more focused competitive businesses. But such transactions may raise questions if one of the corporations is left with a greater share of the liabilities. *See HB Korenvaes Inv., L.P. v. Marriott Corp.*, 1993 WL 205040; 1993 WL 257422 (Del.Ch.1993). And if one of the corporations fails after the spin-off, creditors may argue that the other corporation should remain responsible for excess liabilities of the failed corporation.

> *Example:* Subsidiary A, a gas pipeline company, is obligated to pay X a royalty based on the sales price of natural gas taken under a mineral lease. Because of changes in methods of marketing gas, the parent corporation creates Subsidiary B, a gas marketing company, to locate retail buyers. Subsidiary B buys natural gas from Subsidiary A (and also from other suppliers) at a price (essentially a wholesale price) that is less than the price Subsidiary B receives on resale of the gas to end users (essentially a retail price). X claims that his royalty should be based on the price Subsidiary B receives for gas, not the amount Subsidiary A receives from Subsidiary B. The test in such cases is whether the price paid by Subsidiary B to Subsidiary A for gas is reasonable, that is, closely related to the prices being paid by unrelated companies.

2. Confusion of Affairs

A parent corporation may be held liable for its subsidiary's obligations if it fails to maintain a clear separation between parent and subsidiary affairs. A failure to maintain a clear separation between affairs of different subsidiary corporations may result in the separate existence of those corporations being ignored as well. Conduct that may lead to parental liability includes: referring to the subsidiary as a department or division of the parent; mixing business affairs, such as using parent stationery to respond to inquiries addressed to the subsidiary; having common officers who do not clearly delineate the capacity in which they act; mixing assets, such as having the subsidiary sign a pledge of assets to secure parent indebtedness, transferring funds informally from one entity to the other without the formalities normally involved in a loan, or having a common bank account. *See Bernardin, Inc. v. Midland Oil Corp.*, 520 F.2d 771 (7th Cir.1975).

3. Permissible Activities

As long as affiliated corporations avoid commingling of affairs, a piercing argument should be rejected even though one corporation owns all the shares of the other corporation; the corporations have common officers or directors; the corporations file a consolidated tax return or report their earnings to their stockholders on a consolidated basis; the parent corporation maintains a cash management function by which all cash accounts are centralized to obtain the most favorable interest rates and minimize borrowing costs, so long as records are carefully kept and each subsidiary has immediate access to its funds as needed for its operations; the parent corporation provides centralized accounting and legal services for all subsidiaries, charging for such services on an even-handed and reasonable basis; the parent and subsidiary have a common office or share common office space, so long as the terms of the arrangement are reasonable and the separate identities are maintained by appropriate signs, telephone listings, and the like; the board of directors of the subsidiary consists of employees of the parent; actions by employees of the subsidiary are reviewed by employees of the parent; and the organizational chart of the parent includes the subsidiary. *See Berger v. Columbia Broadcasting System, Inc.*, 453 F.2d 991 (5th Cir.1972).

> *Caveat:* Parent and subsidiary corporations have common economic interests and some degree of interaction and oversight is permitted. But, if the separate existence of the subsidiary is to be recognized it is essential that the subsidiary have some independence and discretion with respect to business matters.

4. Fraud or Injustice

Some cases have concluded that in a contract case a parent is liable for its subsidiary's liabilities only upon a showing of fraud or injustice. *Edwards Co., Inc. v. Monogram Industries, Inc.*, 730 F.2d 977 (5th Cir.1984).

D. ALTERNATIVES TO PIERCING

There are many ways other than piercing doctrine to hold individual stockholders liable for unsatisfied claims against a corporation.

a. As a matter of corporation law, a stockholder may be held liable to the corporation for failure to contribute capital as agreed or for knowing receipt of an illegal dividend (including an illegal liquidating dividend following dissolution). A stockholder may also be held liable for mismanagement or misappropriation as a matter of fiduciary duty. Although these claims may ordinarily be asserted only by the corporation itself or a stockholder suing derivatively, a corporation that has failed to pay a valid obligation to a creditor is presumably bankrupt, and these claims of the corporation may be asserted by a bankruptcy trustee for the ultimate benefit of creditors.

In addition, recent case law suggests that the benefits of fiduciary duty may extend to creditors of a corporation on the edge of insolvency.

b. Or it may be possible to argue that benefits extracted by a stockholder from a corporation constituted a fraudulent conveyance or transfer or a voidable preference under bankruptcy law.

c. There is also a growing body of case law in which buyers of assets and even lenders have been held liable for the unsatisfied obligations of the seller or borrower corporation, as discussed in more detail below.

d. The individual tortfeasor who actually caused the injury is personally liable whether or not he was acting as an agent of the corporation. If he was acting as a corporate agent, the corporation is also liable for the tort under the theory of *respondeat superior*. If the tortfeasor is also a corporate stockholder, officer or agent, he is liable because he is a tortfeasor and it is unnecessary to argue for piercing.

e. It may also be possible to argue in many cases that a stockholder exerted such control over a corporation as to make the corporation an agent under principles of agency law. If the corporation may be viewed as the agent of a stockholder, the stockholder may be liable for corporate torts on a *respondeat superior* theory. In a typical case, however, the tortfeasor is a judgment proof employee, the corporation is also unable to satisfy the claim, and attempts are made to hold stockholders personally liable on a piercing theory.

f. In some cases, actual domination and control of a subsidiary's affairs may be sufficient to justify piercing and hold the parent liable. *See Craig v. Lake Asbestos of Quebec, Ltd.*, 843 F.2d 145 (3d Cir.1988) (control found insufficient to hold parent liable for asbestos injury to employee of subsidiary.)

E. SUCCESSOR LIABILITY

Piercing of a sort may arise if a business is transferred from one corporation to another particularly by means of a sale of assets in which the seller corporation retains the long term liabilities of the business and where the selling stockholder then distributes the proceeds to himself.

Example: ABC Corporation is in the business of manufacturing road repair tools. Jack Hammer is the sole stockholder of ABC. He wants to retire. XYZ Corporation has agreed in principle to buy the business. There are several ways that the transaction may proceed. First, XYZ may agree to buy the stock from Hammer. If so ABC becomes a subsidiary of XYZ and XYZ continues to be responsible for its corporate obligations. Second, XYZ may agree to merge with ABC with XYZ presumably to be the surviving company. If so, XYZ assumes the assets and liabilities of ABC by operation of law. In effect, the two companies become one. Third, XYZ may agree to buy the assets of ABC, in which case XYZ may or may not also agree to assume some or all of the liabilities of ABC. It may be, for example, that XYZ is worried that there are unknown products liability claims that may arise against ABC. The proper way to handle this uncertainty is for ABC to retain part of the proceeds from the sale for some period of time or to use part of the proceeds to purchase an insurance policy to cover any later claims. The proceeds that remain may then be invested or distributed to Hammer. In the latter case, ABC may then choose to dissolve. But suppose that Hammer distributes all of the proceeds to himself leaving ABC with no assets and no way to satisfy later-filed claims. This may constitute an illegal dividend or may run afoul of rules relating to dissolution (discussed later). But because ABC is no longer actively in business, it may be difficult for creditors to find Hammer or to gain jurisdiction over him. And Hammer may have taken steps to hide or protect the money. It is also possible that XYZ Corporation knew or suspected that ABC was likely to be the target of future claims and that Hammer would therefore accept a lower price for the assets of the business that might become worthless if he were unable to sell soon. For example, suppose that the unencumbered assets are worth $10 million but are likely to be depleted to $2 million by future claims. Hammer agrees to sell to XYZ for $5 million. In such a case, the courts may hold XYZ liable for the obligations of ABC.

1. Tests for Successor Liability

The courts generally recognize four situations in which a successor business may be held liable for the obligations of the transferor business:

a.   Contract: The successor corporation agrees to assume the liabilities of the transferor.

b. Merger: The successor corporation assumes the liabilities of the transferor by operation of law.

c. Mere Continuation: The successor corporation is so similar to the old business (in terms of stock ownership, control, employees, etc.) that it is deemed to be the same business and is therefore liable for the obligations of the old business. (In such cases, there will not likely have been a formal transfer and the original business may remain in existence as a formal matter in order to bolster the argument that the two businesses are separate.)

d. Fraud: Fraud comes in many forms, but one example is the scenario above where the parties agree to transfer the business for what appears to be a bargain price. In effect, the parties conspire with each other to the detriment of future creditors. In a good faith transaction, the buyer will presumably seek some form of assurance from the seller that the proceeds will be held in escrow or insurance obtained so as to guard against subsequent allegations of fraud. Thus, the absence of any such assurance or efforts to enforce such provisions may be evidence of fraud or conspiracy.

2. De Facto Merger

In some cases, the courts have resorted to a theory known as the *de facto merger doctrine* and hold that the two companies in fact engaged in a merger even though the transaction was structured as a sale of assets. If the transaction is ruled to be a merger *de facto* the successor corporation is liable for the debts of the transferor. These issues have arisen with some frequency in recent years in products liability cases and in cases involving environmental harms. *See Patin v. Thoroughbred Power Boats, Inc.,* 294 F.3d 640 (5th Cir. 2002) (products liability); *Nettis v. Levitt,* 241 F.3d 186 (2d Cir. 2001) (wrongful discharge of employee); Knapp v. North American Rockwell Corporation, 506 F.2d 361 (3d Cir. 1974) (products liability). In cases involving environmental harms, a common pattern is for a company engaged in several lines of business to sell off clean businesses leaving dirty businesses behind. *See North Shore Gas Company v. Salomon Inc.,* 152 F.3d 642 (7th Cir. 1998) (CERCLA).

> *Caveat:*   The fact that grounds exist for piercing between corporations does not imply that a court should pierce the corporate veil in order to hold individual stockholders personally liable.

F. USE OF CORPORATION TO DEFEAT PUBLIC POLICY

The flexibility of the corporate fiction often permits it to be used in a way that arguably tends to defeat or undercut statutory policies. The issue generally revolves more around the strength and purpose of the statutory policy than any abuse of the corporate form. Piercing analysis may also be used to determine whether a parent corporation is bound by a subsidiary's union contract. *United Paperworkers Intl. Union v. Penntech Papers, Inc.*, 439 F.Supp. 610 (D.Me.1977), aff'd, 583 F.2d 33 (1st Cir.1978).

Example: X is a 63 year old farmer who learns that his social security benefits will be increased if he establishes a favorable employment record during the last two years before his retirement. Accordingly, he incorporates his farm, becoming the sole stockholder and hiring himself as an employee of the corporation to improve his earnings record. The establishment of the corporation to improve a person's social security entitlement is not an improper use of a corporation in light of the purpose of the social security system to assure persons an adequate retirement income. *Stark v. Flemming*, 283 F.2d 410 (9th Cir.1960). But a court may revise the salary downward to a reasonable amount to prevent an artificially high entitlement.

Example: A farmer incorporates his business in order to obtain unemployment benefits during the winter months when little farm work is done. He lays himself off during these slow periods, and files for unemployment compensation. This claim should be rejected because the unemployment benefit system was not intended to cover employers or owners of a business. *Roccograndi v. Unemployment Compensation Board of Review*, 178 A.2d 786 (Pa.Super.1962).

Example: A statute prohibits bank directors from borrowing from their bank. A corporation that is wholly owned by a bank director seeks to obtain a loan from the bank. The argument that the corporate borrower has a separate identity from the stockholder and that therefore the loan may be validly made would defeat a clearly defined public policy expressed in the statute. The loan should therefore be held to violate the statute. This result also might be rationalized on the ground that the corporation is the *alter ego* of its stockholder and that a loan to the corporation is therefore a loan to the stockholder.

G. CHOICE OF LAW IN PIERCING THE CORPORATE VEIL

Some states are more liberal than others in permitting piercing. A question may arise in the case of a foreign corporation whether the law of the state of incorporation or the law of the state in which the transaction occurred should apply in determining whether the court should pierce.

1. Historical Development

Until about 1980 no attention was paid to the choice of law issue because there did not seem to be significant variations in the law of piercing from state to state. The few cases in which the choice of law issue was raised generally concluded that the law in various states was essentially the same and it was unnecessary to determine which law was applicable. In most cases arising during this period, the court simply applied the case law of the forum state without discussing the choice of law issue at all.

2. General Principles

The rule generally followed in the few cases that have addressed the issue is that the liability of a stockholder for the debts of the corporation is a matter of the internal affairs of a corporation, to be governed by the law of the state of incorporation.

a. This rule is likely to be followed where the corporation has significant economic ties to the state of incorporation, particularly if the stockholders are themselves residents of the state of incorporation.

b. A Texas statute mandates the application of the internal affairs rule to piercing in the case of foreign corporations authorized to transact business in Texas.

Caveat: Under general conflict of laws principles applicable to torts, a court sitting in the state where the accident or event occurred may determine to apply local law to the piercing issue if the contacts of the corporation with the state of incorporation are minimal, and all significant contacts are with the forum state. Such a corporation is often called a *pseudo foreign corporation.*

Example: A Delaware corporation operates only in Missouri. All the officers, directors, and stockholders of the corporation are residents of Missouri, the person injured is a resident of Missouri, the accident occurred in Missouri, and the corporation's principal business office and all business activities occur in Missouri. A Missouri court might reasonably conclude that the Missouri law of piercing should apply rather than Delaware law.

H. THE FEDERAL LAW OF PIERCING THE CORPORATE VEIL

Federal courts have held that where the enforcement of a federal statute is involved, and a uniform federal policy of piercing will further federal policies, the federal courts should apply federal law of piercing.

Example: The United States brings suit to recover funds from a provider of services under the Medicare program. The provider is a corporation, but the United States seeks recovery from the stockholders of the provider on a piercing theory. The piercing issue should be determined by application of a uniform federal rule under the doctrine enunciated in *Clearfield Trust Co. v. United States,* 318 U.S. 363, 63 S.Ct. 573 (1943). In determining what this federal rule should be, the court may consider not only the federal policy involved, but also the federal decisions applying state piercing principles in diversity cases. *United States v. Pisani,* 646 F.2d 83 (3d Cir.1981).

1. CERCLA

The Comprehensive Environmental Response Compensation and Liability Act (CERCLA) imposes responsibility for clean-up and response costs on all owners and operators of hazardous waste disposal sites. In *United States v. Bestfoods,* 524 U.S. 51, 118 S.Ct. 1876 (1998), the Supreme Court held that CERCLA did not change the settled law of piercing the corporate veil. A parent-subsidiary relationship standing alone is not enough to hold the parent liable for the acts of the subsidiary even though (1) the parent controls the subsidiary through stock ownership, (2) the parent places its representatives on the board of directors of the subsidiary, and (3) some individuals are actively involved in the management of both corporations. In other words, the parent is liable under a piercing theory only if there is some *misuse* of the corporate form to accomplish a wrongful purpose. A parent corporation may be held liable, however, for its own actions as an owner-operator if its agents participate directly in the operation of the subsidiary's facility. In such a case, the parent corporation may be seen as a joint venturer with the subsidiary. In addition, a court may pierce if agents of the parent corporation become directly involved in the operation and management of the subsidiary without regard to the customary norms of corporate behavior applicable to parent and subsidiary as separate corporations. *See also North Shore Gas Company v. Salomon Inc.,* 152 F.3d 642 (7th Cir. 1998).

2. Fair Housing Act

In *Meyer v. Holley,* 537 U.S. 280, 123 S.Ct. 824 (2003), the Supreme Court addressed an important issue arising under the Fair Housing Act which forbids racial discrimination with respect to the sale or rental of a dwelling. In that case, a salesperson for the defendant real estate brokerage company was alleged to have prevented the plaintiffs from buying a house for racially discriminatory reasons. The plaintiffs sued the president, sole stockholder, and licensed officer/broker of the brokerage company claiming that he was vicariously liable individually in one or more of these capacities for the salesman's unlawful actions. The Ninth Circuit held that the strong public policy behind the Fair Housing Act requires the imposition of strict liability principles beyond those traditionally associated with principal-agent or employer-employee relationships. The Supreme Court reversed, holding that the Fair Housing Act imposes liability without fault upon the employer corporation in accord with traditional agency principles but not on its individual officers or owners. Consistent with its holding in *Bestfoods*, the Court expressly rejected the idea that corporate owners and officers may be held liable for an employee's unlawful act simply because they control or have the power to control the employee's actions. In addition, the Court rejected the argument that the act creates a nondelegable duty not to discriminate that is so strong that an officer may be held liable even if he acts reasonably and within his actual authority. The Court did not, however, reject the idea that a corporate officer may be held liable for failure to supervise or negligent hiring, although it is unclear whether a third party would have standing to assert such a claim.

3. Choice of Law

In *Bestfoods*, the Court declined to rule on the question whether state or federal law of piercing should apply, stating (in footnote 9): "There is significant disagreement among courts and commentators over whether, in enforcing CERCLA's indirect liability, courts should borrow state law, or instead apply a federal common law of veil piercing. *Compare, e.g.,* [Bestfoods], 113 F.3d at 584–585 (Merritt, J., concurring in part and dissenting in part) (arguing that federal common law should apply), Lansford–Coaldale Joint Water Auth. v. Tonolli Corp., 4 F.3d at 1225 (given the federal interest in uniformity in the application of CERCLA, it is federal common law, and not state law, which governs when corporate veil-piercing is justified under CERCLA), and Aronovsky & Fuller, Liability of Parent Corporations for Hazardous Substance Releases under CERCLA, 24 U.S. F. L. Rev. 421, 455 (1990) (CERCLA enforcement should not be hampered by subordination of its goals to varying state law rules of alter ego theory), with, *e.g.*, 113 F.3d at 580 (Whether the circumstances in this case warrant a piercing of the corporate veil will be determined by state law), and Dennis, *Liability of Officers, Directors and Stockholders under CERCLA: The Case for Adopting State*

Law, 36 Vill. L. Rev. 1367 (1991) (arguing that state law should apply). *Cf.* In re Acushnet River & New Bedford Harbor Proceedings, 675 F. Supp. 22, 33 (Mass. 1987) (noting that, because federal common law draws upon state law for guidance, . . . the choice between state and federal [veil-piercing law] may in many cases present questions of academic interest, but little practical significance). *But cf.* Note, *Piercing the Corporate Law Veil: The Alter Ego Doctrine Under Federal Common Law,* 95 Harv. L. Rev. 853 (1982) (arguing that federal common law need not mirror state law, because federal common law should look to federal statutory policy rather than to state corporate law when deciding whether to pierce the corporate veil). Because none of the parties challenges the Sixth Circuit's holding that [the parents] incurred no derivative liability, the question is not presented in this case, and we do not address it further."

I. PIERCING IN TAX CASES

Under the Internal Revenue Code the government has broad power to ignore or restructure transactions that have as their sole or principal purpose the avoidance or minimization of taxes.

1. Recognition of Corporation in General

Generally, the separate existence of a corporation is recognized for tax purposes if it is carrying on a bona fide business and is not merely a device to avoid taxes.

a. In some cases, high tax bracket individuals may seek to use a corporation as a repository for income primarily to avoid paying tax at the individual level. Several sections of the IRC address such practices. *See* IRC §§ 531–537 (accumulated earnings tax on corporations); IRC §§ 541–547 (personal holding companies).

b. Similarly, if a single business is conducted by a series of related corporations as a way of splitting income in order to keep each corporation in a low tax bracket, the IRS may treat the business as a single corporation for tax purposes. *See United States v. Vogel Fertilizer Co.,* 455 U.S. 16, 102 S.Ct. 821 (1982).

c. In addition, stockholders may sometimes seek to avoid tax at the corporate level by attempting to zero out corporate income by paying themselves large salaries and bonuses. In such cases, the IRS may recharacterize corporate expenses as distributions from corporate income that should have been taxed at the corporate level. *See Hatt v. CIR,* 457 F.2d 499 (7th Cir. 1972). In effect this amounts to a reverse piercing.

2. Estoppel Against Taxpayer

If a taxpayer selects the corporate form of business, the taxpayer is generally bound by that selection and cannot argue that the separate existence of the corporation should be ignored. Prior to 1995, the IRS often scrutinized unincorporated businesses to determine if they had the characteristics of corporations and should be taxed as such. (Under tax law the word *association* is used to denote such a business). In 1995, the IRS adopted the *check the box* rules that allow unincorporated business to choose whether to be taxed as a corporation (association) or as a partnership. (An unincorporated business with a single owner is ignored for tax purposes, and its income is treated as income of the owner.) The check the box rules apply only to unincorporated businesses. A corporation may not elect to be taxed other than as a corporation. Moreover, under IRC § 7704 a business whose ownership interests are publicly traded must be taxed as a corporation no matter what formal structure it has adopted.

J. PIERCING IN BANKRUPTCY

Under the Federal Bankruptcy Code, courts have considerable flexibility in dealing with corporations and stockholders for the purpose of protecting and preserving the rights of creditors.

1. Complete Piercing

The court may ignore the separate corporate existence and hold the stockholders liable for all corporate obligations.

2. Reclassification of Transaction

The court may refuse to recognize, may reclassify, may change the form of a transaction between stockholder and corporation if it is equitable or reasonable to do so.

Example: A loan by a stockholder to a corporation which is essentially part of the initial capital needed by the corporation to conduct business may be treated as a contribution of equity capital and subordinated. *Costello v. Fazio*, 256 F.2d 903 (9th Cir.1958). On the other hand, where the initial capital is more than nominal and the corporation was organized in good faith, subsequent loans to cover losses should not be subordinated. *In re Mader's Store for Men, Inc.*, 254 N.W.2d 171 (Wis.1977).

Example: In the previous example, essentially the same result may be reached by rejecting the stockholder's claim in its entirety rather than subordinating it to third party claims.

3. Subordination

The court may subordinate claims of stockholders to claims of other creditors where the claim of the stockholder is inequitable. This power was viewed by the Supreme Court as inherent in the bankruptcy jurisdiction of federal courts. *Pepper v. Litton*, 308 U.S. 295, 60 S.Ct. 238 (1939). It is now codified in § 510(c)(1) of the Bankruptcy Reform Act of 1978.

a. The power to subordinate inequitable claims is known as the Deep Rock doctrine from the name of the subsidiary in the leading case applying the doctrine. *Taylor v. Standard Gas & Electric Co.*, 306 U.S. 307, 59 S.Ct. 543 (1939).

> *Example:* A sole stockholder transfers funds to her corporation in the form of loans and backdated deeds of trusts, at a time when the corporation is insolvent. The original capital was about $5,000 while the loans aggregated $77,500. The loans are in fact capital contributions, the deeds of trust are a fraud on creditors, and the stockholder's claims should be subordinated to all other creditors. *In re Fett Roofing & Sheet Metal Co., Inc.*, 438 F.Supp. 726 (E.D.Va.1977), *aff'd without opinion* 605 F.2d 1201 (4th Cir. 1979).

b. Subordination theoretically simply changes the order of payment so that the stockholder's claim may be paid after other creditors are satisfied in full. As a practical matter, however, the claims of other creditors usually exhaust the estate so that if a claim is subordinated under the Deep Rock doctrine, it is seldom paid evening part.

c. Where both the parent and subsidiary are bankrupt, proceedings may be consolidated and priorities between the parent's and subsidiary's creditors determined on an equitable basis. *Stone v. Eacho*, 127 F.2d 284 (4th Cir.1942).

d. It may be important whether a claim is merely subordinated or the supposed debt obligation is deemed to be equity. In the latter case, an otherwise valid security interest in connection with the obligation will presumably be cancelled. It is also possible for a court to invalidate a security interest without expressly subordinating the underlying obligation.

e. In many cases, a bona fide creditor may assume a large degree of control over a debtor in an effort to rehabilitate the debtor pursuant to a workout plan. If the creditor assumes too much control, however, there is a risk that the creditor's claim will be subordinated to the claims of other creditors or in extreme cases that the creditor will be held liable for the claims of other creditors on the theory that the controlling creditor assumed the status of principal and the debtor corporation the status of agent. *See A. Gay Jenson Farms Co. v. Cargill, Inc.*, 309 N.W.2d 285 (Minn. 1981). *Cf. Martin v. Peyton*, 246 N.Y. 213 (1927) (question whether lender became partner).

K. OTHER USES OF PIERCING DOCTRINE

While piercing is usually limited to the liability of a stockholder for corporate obligations, the same issue arises in other contexts. The principles applied in these other contexts appear to be the same as those applied in traditional piercing cases, but the nature of the issue involved dictates whether the doctrine should be narrowly or broadly applied.

Example: S is a wholly owned subsidiary of P and transacts extensive business in Louisiana. P does not transact business in Louisiana and is not qualified to transact business in that state. A Louisiana resident attempts to obtain jurisdiction over, and service of process on, P by serving S in a lawsuit involving a transaction between the Louisiana resident and P that occurred in New York. On a motion to dismiss for want of jurisdiction the plaintiff seeks to apply piercing principles and further argues that S's activities in Louisiana directly benefit P, so that S's contacts with Louisiana should be attributed to P. This effort should fail. *Cannon Mfg. Co. v. Cudahy Packing Co.*, 267 U.S. 333, 45 S.Ct. 250 (1925). P is subject to suit in Louisiana only if the control exercised over S is such that day-to-day decisions are in fact made by P rather than S. *Quarles v. Fuqua Industries, Inc.*, 504 F.2d 1358 (10th Cir.1974). While this test may be referred to as an application of piercing doctrine, it is more stringent than the test usually applied in stockholder liability cases.

Example: In community property states, the general rule is that shares in a corporation and any increase in their value are the separate property of a spouse who owns them at the time of marriage, whereas dividends received on those shares are community property. In the case of a one-stockholder corporation, the stockholder can dictate the dividend policy of the corporation and can cause the corporation to retain cash so as to increase the value of shares and deprive the community estate of income. Thus, in divorce cases it is common for the non-stockholder spouse to argue that the assets of the corporation (or at least their increase in value attributable to retained cash) be treated as assets of the community. Such a recharacterization of corporate assets as personal assets is more akin to reverse piercing but it is nonetheless frequently called piercing. It may also be thought of as a constructive compulsory dividend.

REVIEW QUESTIONS

4.1. How does the piercing the corporate veil concept differ from promoters' transactions, corporations de facto, and similar concepts?

4.2. True or False: X forms a corporation for a risky business solely because of fear of unlimited liability. The corporate veil of X's corporation may be pierced for this reason.

4.3. True or False: X forms a corporation with one dollar of capital as permitted by the statutes of his state. The corporation enters into a lease but defaults after six months because of business losses. X is personally liable on the lease.

4.4. True or False: In the same situation as question 4.3, the corporation is found liable for a tort committed by an employee in which X did not participate. The corporate form protects X against this liability.

4.5. True or False: In the same situation as question 4.3, X commingles business and personal finances and does not keep separate corporate records. X is liable for both liabilities described in questions 4.3 and 4.4.

4.6. True or False: X Corporation creates a subsidiary, Y Corporation, with the same officers and directors as X. Because of this confusion of personnel, X Corporation is liable for Y Corporation's debts.

4.7. True or False: In question 4.6, X Corporation often refers to Y Corporation as a division and transfers money to assist Y Corporation simply by check without formally entering the transaction as a loan in the books of X and Y. X Corporation is liable for Y Corporation's debts.

4.8. True or False: X, an individual aged 60, decides to incorporate her own business and employ herself to establish the necessary earnings record for social security purposes. This is a fraud on the Federal Government and X is ineligible for social security benefits.

4.9. P sued A Corporation for damages on the ground that P had been fraudulently induced to enter into a training course contract. P served A Corporation under a state long-arm statute allowing service on any person who transacts any business in the state. A Corporation is incorporated in another state and directly transacted no business in the state. P contended that A Corporation was doing business because it was a holding company for S Corp. which was doing business in the state. The trial court found that A Corporation owned 100 per cent of the stock of S but allowed S's management autonomy as to achievement of goals set in conjunction with A's management; A Corporation provided S with a general financial, legal, tax and administrative services, and acted as its banker but S kept separate books and records, S and A had separate auditors, officers and office staffs. Should the court hold that A was transacting business in the state?

4.10. D purchased Blackacre for the purpose of mining coal. He formed A Corporation and posted a sign identifying the property as "A Corporation Mines." There was issued to D all of the shares of the corporation except one share which was issued to D's wife. Neither D nor his wife paid any money for these shares. There was no meeting of stockholders, no directors were elected, no corporate control was exercised and no corporate books were kept. The mine was operated as though it were the private business of D: the expenses of the mine were paid by D from his private bank account and the income was deposited in D's private account. One of the employees in the mine is killed as a result of negligence in the mining operations. His executor sues D. Is D liable?

*

V

Corporation Finance

Capital is the money or property that must be invested more or less permanently in a business in order for the business to start up and continue to operate. Capital may take the form of either equity or debt. Capital that is contributed by stockholders in exchange for shares of stock is *equity capital*. Capital that is borrowed is *debt capital*. Equity holders are generally thought of as the owners of the business, whereas debtholders have no ownership interest in the business but rather are viewed as third party creditors. Roughly speaking, the difference between equity and debt is that there is no maturity date for equity, and return is dependent on the profitability of the business. Moreover, the board of directors retains the discretion to make distributions subject to statutory limitations. In contrast, debt must be repaid at some point and the periodic return is fixed. Payment of interest is mandatory and not subject to limitations under corporation law. Default may trigger bankruptcy. Because the return on equity fluctuates with the fortunes of the business, equity may enjoy increasing returns (growth) if the business does well. Thus, stockholders (equity holders) are said to have a residual claim. But because equity is paid a return only if debt is paid first, equity is naturally riskier than debt. Thus, equity holders generally require a higher rate of return. In addition to borrowed funds and funds contributed by stockholders, a corporation may use internally generated funds (retained earnings) as a third source of capital. But these funds also constitute stockholder equity and may therefore be seen as contributed by the stockholders in the form of forgone dividends. The mix of debt and equity (including both common stock and preferred stock) is sometimes called the *capital structure* of the business.

A. SHARES AND STOCK

Shares and *stock* are synonyms for the basic units of ownership of a corporation. If the corporation is authorized to issue more than one class of shares, the number of shares of each class and a detailed description of each class, (other than common shares) must be set forth in the articles of incorporation (or equivalent governing document).

1. Common Shares or Common Stock

When shares are authorized in the articles of incorporation without any specified rights, such shares are common shares. Such shares are entitled to (1) one vote per share on any matter submitted to a vote of the stockholders and (2) a pro rata share of any distribution of cash or property to the stockholders generally. These rights are automatic and need not be described in the articles of incorporation.

2. Preferred Shares or Preferred Stock

Preferred shares or *preferred stock* are shares that have preference over common shares either as to dividends or on liquidation or both. A *preference* simply means that the preferred shares are entitled to a payment of a specified amount before the common shares are entitled to anything. Most preferred shares have both dividend and liquidation preferences. The MBCA does not use the terms *common shares* and *preferred shares* but these terms are widely used in practice and in many state statutes.

3. Authorized Shares

The articles of incorporation define the *authorized shares* the corporation may issue. MBCA 2.02(a)(2) provides that the articles of incorporation must set forth the number of shares the corporation is authorized to issue. MBCA 6.01(a) provides that the articles of incorporation must prescribe the classes of shares and the number of shares of each class that the corporation is authorized to issue. In addition, if more than one class of shares is authorized, the articles of incorporation must prescribe a distinguishing designation for each class, and, prior to the issuance of shares of a class, the preferences, limitations, and relative rights of that class must be described in the articles of incorporation.

4. Issued Shares

Issued shares are the shares of one or more classes actually held by stockholders as distinct from merely being authorized but unissued. Under the MBCA the terms *issued* and *outstanding* are synonymous. It is customary in modern corporate practice to authorize more shares than the number planned to be issued initially. Additional capital may be needed at a later date, and authorized shares may be issued to raise that capital without amending the articles of incorporation. Shares authorized but not issued may be issued at a later date by the board of directors acting alone without approval of the stockholders.

5. Treasury Shares

Treasury shares are shares of the corporation that have been issued and reacquired by the corporation. Under traditional statutes, treasury shares have an intermediate status. They are not *outstanding* for purposes of voting or dividend payments but are viewed as *issued* for some purposes as discussed further below. MBCA 6.31(a) provides that when a corporation acquires its own shares, they automatically become *authorized but unissued* shares. This change was made in recognition of the fact that with the elimination of restrictions on the issuance of shares, there is no reason to retain the concept of treasury shares.

6. Par Value and Stated Capital

In some jurisdictions, a corporation must specify a *par value* for its shares in the articles of incorporation. Par value is the minimum price for which shares may be issued by the corporation. It is an arbitrary number. Shares may always be sold for more than par value. Par value rules apply only to the original issue of shares by the corporation. A stockholder may resell for any amount, whether more or less than par value. After shares are issued, the aggregate par value of the outstanding shares constitutes the *stated capital* or *legal capital* of the corporation. As a general rule, the corporation may not invade stated capital to make a distribution to stockholders. In other words, assets must be at least equal to liabilities plus stated capital after giving effect to the dividend. In effect, the capital accounts created from the par value concept control the extent to which distributions of capital may be made in these states. Most of these rules have been abolished under the MBCA.

B. COMMON STOCK

Common stock reflects the ownership of the residual interest in the corporation. The two basic rights of common shares are: (1) entitlement to vote for directors and on basic corporate matters, and (2) entitlement to the net assets of the corporation when distributions are made or upon dissolution. Common shares reflect the residual ownership of the corporation. All corporations must have at least one share outstanding with such rights. MBCA 6.03(b) also requires that at least one share with each of these basic attributes must always be outstanding. Common stock may be issued in different classes. There are virtually no restrictions or limitations on the rights that may be varied from class to class. Because of this flexibility, classes of common shares are widely used as planning devices in closely held corporations.

a.   A class of nonvoting common shares may be created under the statutes of most states. Historically, some states have prohibited nonvoting shares (in some cases in the state constitution).

b.   In many states, classes may be created with identical financial rights but with multiple or fractional votes per share. Traditionally, the NYSE refused to list the shares of any such company, but those rules were relaxed in the 1990s, and variable voting shares have become common even among publicly traded companies.

c.   It is also possible to create a class of shares with full voting power but with little or no financial interest in the corporation. *Stroh v. Blackhawk Holding Corp.*, 272 N.E.2d 1 (Ill. 1971); *Lehrman v. Cohen*, 222 A.2d 800 (Del.1966). *But see Telvest, Inc. v. Olson*, 1979 WL 1759 (enjoining issue of piggyback preferred stock solely with supermajority voting right in connection with mergers). *See also Moran v. Household International, Inc.*, 500 A.2d 1346 (Del. 1985) (suggesting that poison pill rights must have economic substance).

d.   Different classes of common shares are often designated by alphabetical notation: Class A, Class B, Class C, etc. When used as a planning device, all Class A shares might be issued to one stockholder, all Class B shares to another stockholder, and so forth. Class A shares may have the right to elect two directors, whereas Class B and Class C shares may have the right to elect one director each. This arrangement would permit Class A to elect half of a four person board even though Class A shares might represent only one-third of the financial interest in the company. Or Class A may have twice the dividend right per share of Class B. This arrangement would permit two stockholders to share equal voting control but unequal dividend rights by issuing the same number of class A and class B shares.

Caveat: If the size of the board is increased to five (as it could be by vote of the stockholders), presumably the fifth director would be elected by all of the stockholders, each casting one-vote per share. Thus, as a planning matter, one must be careful to include protective provisions in the articles of incorporation or bylaws to prevent inadvertent changes in control of the corporation.

e. In most jurisdictions, all shares of a class or series must have identical rights with those of other shares of the same class or series. *See Asarco Incorporated v. M.R.H. Holmes A Court*, 611 F. Supp. 468 (D.N.J. 1985).

> *Caveat:* Classes or series of shares may be created that have rights that distinguish between holders of the same class of shares on the basis of a formula or outside event. *See Providence & Worcester Co. v. Baker*, 378 A.2d 121 (Del. 1977) (upholding provision specifying one vote per share up to 50 shares and one vote per 20 shares thereafter, and prohibiting any stockholder from voting more than 25 percent of the stock issued and outstanding other than by proxy). These classes or series are often designed to treat a hostile bidder differently from other stockholders in order to defend against takeover. *See Moran v. Household International, Inc.*, 500 A.2d 1346 (Del. 1985) (upholding poison pill rights generally but without addressing differential effect on bidder).

C. PREFERRED STOCK

Common shares are the residual ownership interests in the corporation. Corporations may also issue classes of shares that have rights that must be satisfied before the common shares are entitled to distributions. These shares are called *preferred* (or *preference*) shares or stock. Preferred stock and debt securities have many similar characteristics and may be used to achieve similar results. Thus, the term *senior securities* is sometimes used to refer to preferred stock and debt securities collectively. With minor exceptions the MBCA (1984) does not use these terms because it is possible to create classes of shares that have some characteristics of both types of shares and there is no precise dividing line. These terms, however, are widely used in corporate practice and have well understood meanings.

1. Distributions

Preferred shares typically have a preference over common shares either as to dividends, or on liquidation, or both. That is, preferred shares are entitled to a payment of a specified amount before the common shares may be paid anything. Most preferred shares have both dividend and liquidation preferences. Most traditional preferred shares are nonvoting shares that are limited to a right to receive a specified amount and no more, no matter how profitable the corporation may be.

a. Preferential rights must be defined in the articles of incorporation, and the attributes of preferred shares may include some rights normally associated with common shares.

Example:　A class of $3.50 preferred means that each preferred share is entitled to a dividend of $3.50 per share before any dividend may be paid on the common shares. Such a share is not entitled to more than $3.50 per share no matter how much is available for distribution. The $3.50 payment is a dividend, however, and is discretionary with the board of directors. Unlike interest, it is not based on a debt owed by the corporation and it may not be deducted as a business expense for tax purposes.

Example:　In the prior example the preferred shares may also be entitled to a preferential liquidating payment of $75.00. On liquidation, nothing may be paid on the common until the $75.00 per share is paid to the holders of the preferred. On the other hand, once the preferred receives $75.00 it is not entitled to anything more no matter how much is available for distribution. The question whether unpaid preferential dividends must also be satisfied in liquidation depends on the language of the articles of incorporation. *Matter of Chandler & Co.*, 230 N.Y.S.2d 1012 (1962).

Example:　Preferred shares may be entitled to vote generally on all matters on which common stockholders vote. Or they may be entitled to vote only upon the occurrence of a specified event such as the omission of preferred dividends for a specified period. Preferred shares may also be entitled to additional distributions of dividends or liquidation payments by specific provision in the articles of incorporation. Sometimes preferred shares carry the right to a preferred dividend and in addition the right to some share of a distribution if any is made to the common shares. Such shares are called *participating preferred* or sometimes *Class A* stock.

Example:　In *Zahn v. Transamerica Corp.*, 162 F.2d 36 (3d Cir.1947), a corporation created a class of preferred stock called Class A stock. These shares were entitled to a dividend of $3.20 per year plus the right to share equally with common shares in all declarations of dividends in excess of $4.80 per share. In effect, $3.20 was first to be paid to the Class A shares, then $1.60 to the common, and excess distributions were to be shared equally on a per share basis. In the absence of specific provision, it is unlikely that a dividend participation right of this nature would be construed to include an implied liquidation-preference on the same terms. *Squires v. Balbach Co.*, 129 N.W.2d 462 (Neb.1964).

b. A dividend preference may be *cumulative*, or *non-cumulative*, or *partially cumulative*, or *cumulative-to-the-extent-earned* or cumulative as otherwise specified in the articles of incorporation. If no such rights are set forth in the articles of incorporation, then the shares are presumed to be non-cumulative except in jurisdictions that follow the New Jersey dividend credit rule described below. A cumulative dividend that is not paid in one year carries over to the next year and following years and must be satisfied in addition to the following years' preferred dividends before any dividend can be paid on the common stock. A non-cumulative dividend not declared for a given period is gone. A cumulative-to-the-extent-earned dividend is cumulative only to the extent of earnings in a specified period. If earnings fail to cover the preferred dividend, the portion of the dividend that is not covered does not cumulate and is gone.

Example: A preferred carries a $5 cumulative dividend. The directors fail to declare the dividend for three years. In the fourth year, a dividend is declared. Because the preferred dividend is cumulative, $20 must be paid to the holders of the preferred before any common dividend may be paid.

Example: If the foregoing preferred were non-cumulative, the directors could pay a dividend on the common in the fourth year after paying only the $5.00 current dividend on the preferred. An attempt to pay past non-cumulative dividends could probably be enjoined by the common stockholders as a violation of their rights.

Caveat: In New Jersey and a few other states, equitable principles have been developed that limit the power of the corporation to omit the payment of non-cumulative dividends when earnings are sufficient to cover the dividend.

Example: A New Jersey corporation omits a non-cumulative dividend of $1.00 per share in 1990 even though earnings of the corporation that year exceed $1.00 per share. A dividend credit is attached to these earnings, and in 1992 the corporation may not pay a dividend on common shares without satisfying the non-cumulative dividend for 1992 <u>and</u> the unpaid dividend for 1990. *See Sanders v. Cuba R. Co.,* 120 A.2d 849 (N.J.1956); *Lich v. United States Rubber Co.,* 39 F.Supp. 675 (D.N.J.1941); compare *Guttmann v. Illinois Central R. Co.,* 189 F.2d 927 (2d Cir.1951).

Example: The New Jersey dividend credit rule is essentially a cumulative-to-the-extent-earned dividend. In other states a cumulative-to-the-extent-earned dividend exists only if specific provision is made for such a dividend in the articles of incorporation.

2. Redemption and Conversion

Preferred shares may be made *redeemable* at a price set forth in the articles of incorporation. Upon redemption, the holder of redeemable shares is entitled only to the redemption price set forth in the articles of incorporation. Preferred shares also may be made *convertible* at the option of the holder into common shares and sometimes other classes of securities (*conversion securities*) at a ratio set forth in the articles of incorporation.

Example: Preferred shares sold for $50.00 per share may be made redeemable at the option of the corporation at $60.00 per share plus unpaid cumulative dividends. The corporation may at any time thereafter at its option elect to redeem those shares at $60 per share plus unpaid dividends if any. The difference between the $50 issue price of the preferred stock and the $60 redemption price is usually called the *redemption premium*. A redemption premium (if any) may be provided as a way of compensating the investor for the loss of an attractive investment.

Example: Under most state statutes, it is permissible to make shares redeemable at the option of the holder. Such shares are similar to a demand note. They may be used instead of a debt instrument when the investor is a corporation. Corporations pay little or no income tax on dividends received, whereas interest income is fully taxed at the applicable corporate tax rate. The SEC requires preferred shares redeemable at the option of the holder to be shown on the balance sheet in a separate category that is neither debt nor equity.

Caveat: The word redemption is generally used in corporation law to refer to the right of the corporation to buy back shares (or the right of the stockholder to sell shares back to the corporation). Redemption rights are thus similar to options: a *call* option in the case of the corporation, a *put* option in the case of the stockholder. A redemption should thus be distinguished from a repurchase which is usually pursuant to an agreement of some sort between the corporation and the stockholder. The IRC uses the word *redemption* to refer to all transactions by which a corporation reacquires its own shares.

Caveat: Corporation law generally prohibits the repurchase of redeemable shares at a price higher than the redemption price.

Caveat: Both repurchases and redemptions are governed by elaborate rules similar to those that govern when a corporation may pay dividends.

Example: A corporation issues preferred shares that are convertible into two shares of common for each share of preferred. The conversion ratio is therefore 2 for 1.

a. The *conversion ratio* is usually subject to adjustment for *dilution* that may occur if the number of outstanding conversion securities is increased through share split, share dividend, or recapitalization prior to conversion.

Example: In the example, the conversion security is split 3 for 1. If the preferred conversion right is protected against dilution, the conversion ratio is changed to 6 for 1. *See Merritt–Chapman & Scott Corp. v. New York Trust Co.,* 184 F.2d 954 (2d Cir.1950).

Example: In the prior example, if the preferred's conversion right is not protected against dilution, the preferred share's conversion ratio remains at 2 for 1, and as a result of the stock split, the value of the conversion right has been reduced by 2/3ds.

Caveat: Many state statutes prohibit *upstream conversion,* that is the creation of a right of common to convert to preferred, or either common or preferred to convert to debt. The MBCA permits upstream conversions on the theory that they are potentially less damaging to creditors and other senior security holders than the redemption of shares for cash.

b. In some cases, conversion rights arise only upon a call for redemption. If so, the conversion right typically continues to exist for a limited period after the call for redemption is announced. In such cases, the corporation may induce conversion by calling the preferred for redemption at a time when the market value of the conversion security is greater than the redemption value of the convertible security.

> *Example:* A preferred share is redeemable at $70 per share and convertible into common on a two for one basis. When the market price of the common is $45 per share the shares are called for redemption. The stockholder almost certainly will choose to convert because the value of the conversion security ($90) exceeds the redemption value ($70).

> *Caveat:* In practice, some convertible shares may not be converted because of inadvertence. Holders of unconverted shares will receive the lower redemption value rather than the higher conversion value.

> *Example:* In *Zahn v. Transamerica Corp.*, 162 F.2d 36 (3d Cir.1947), convertible shares were redeemed by the corporation without disclosing that it would be advantageous for minority stockholders to elect to convert shares. The corporation was held to have violated a duty to the stockholders to advise them of their rights. See *Speed v. Transamerica Corp.*, 235 F.2d 369 (3d Cir.1956). The courts have not generally found that a similar duty is owed to holders of convertible debt securities.

3. Other Features

a. In states with par value statutes, preferred shares are assigned a par value (or are issued without par value) in the same way as common shares and are subject to the same rules as common shares.

> *Caveat:* It is arguable under some statutes that the par value of preferred shares must be at least equal to the liquidation preference.

b. A corporation may issue several classes of preferred shares, each having varying dividend and other rights specified in the articles of incorporation. While a class of preferred shares may be junior to other classes of preferred, it is nevertheless a preferred stock, because it is preferred in comparison to common stock.

> *Caveat:* Names of classes of preferred shares give little information as to their relative priorities. A class of shares with only nominal or unimportant preferential rights may be given a formal designation such as senior preferred shares which may give the impression that its preferential rights are greater than they actually are.

> *Caveat:* A class of shares with preferential rights may be called Class A common or be given some other designation that does not use the word preferred and does not indicate that it has preferential rights.

c. The 1980s saw the development of novel classes of preferred shares. Most of these were designed to give corporate holders the benefit of the tax credit for intercorporate dividends while providing economic terms similar to debt instruments.

> *Example:* Corporations may create classes of preferred shares with floating or adjustable dividend rates that vary with market interest rates, the prime rate, or some similar measure.

> *Example:* Corporations may create classes of preferred shares that require the corporation to reset the dividend rate and other rights of the preferred if its market price declines below a set value to restore the market price of the preferred to that value.

4. Preferred Issued in Series

Most state statutes authorize the creation of preferred shares *in series*, with terms that may vary from series to series. Specific authorization to create one or more series of preferred shares out of a larger class of preferred shares must appear in the articles of incorporation. (The term *series* refers in effect to a subset of the class of stock specifically authorized in the articles of incorporation.) If series issue is authorized, the board of directors has the authority to set the terms of each series from time to time by resolution. Some statutes limit the discretion of the board in certain respects. Preferred shares that may be issued in series are often called *blank check stock* because the board may fill in the terms.

a. The rationale for the use of series is that the board of directors may set the financial terms of the series just before the shares are marketed in order to obtain the best price for the shares. In a publicly held corporation, it is not practical to create a new class of preferred shares by amendment to the articles of incorporation because of the need for a stockholders' meeting to approve the amendment. Typically, a meeting of the stockholders requires several days notice and, in the case of a publicly traded corporation, the filing of proxy materials with the SEC. During this period, market conditions may change, requiring a change in the terms of the preferred shares to be issued. For example, interest rates may rise or fall, and because preferred stock is usually a fixed income security, the dividend rate must usually be adjusted accordingly. Although the corporation could in theory sell the stock at a different price—for example, at a lower price if interest rates have risen—preferred stock also typically carries a liquidation preference so that investors who paid the lower price would become entitled to a liquidation preference in excess of the price paid. In other words, the various terms of preferred stock are quite precisely coordinated with each other. These problems do not arise with respect to common stock because common stock generally has no terms that are specified in the articles of incorporation.

Caveat: Although authority for series issue is, usually justified by potential timing problems, series may be used for purposes other than financing. For example, anti-takeover devices known as *poison pills* can be created by the board of directors pursuant to the power to create series shares.

b. A formal certificate describing the terms of the series must be filed with the secretary of state after the series has been created. This certificate becomes a formal amendment of the articles of incorporation even though it does not require action by the stockholders. This amendment is often called the *certificate of designation.*

c. There is no difference between *classes* and *series* of shares except in method of creation. MBCA 6.02 permits the board of directors to fix the terms of <u>classes</u> as well as series of shares if that power is granted to the board of directors by the articles of incorporation.

5. Alteration of Rights

At one time, the rights attaching to shares were viewed as vested and unchangeable except possibly by unanimous consent of the affected stockholders. Today, it is clear in most jurisdictions that the rights attaching to preferred shares (or any class or series of shares) may be changed by amendment to the articles of incorporation. Such an alteration of rights is sometimes called a *recapitalization* because in effect it constitutes a change in the capital structure of the business.

> *Example:* It is not unusual for a corporation with cumulative preferred stock outstanding to fall behind in paying dividends on that stock as a result of a downturn in business. When the business revives, the board of directors, which is elected by the common stockholders, may be unwilling to exhaust cash resources of the corporation by paying off the arrearages. As a result common stockholders cannot receive dividends. No one is willing to invest fresh capital in the form of new common stock so long as the arrearages remain as a restriction on future distributions. The board of directors may thus decline to pay even current preferred dividends in order to pressure the preferred stockholders into accepting a recapitalization. In such a situation, the preferred stockholders may be willing to exchange their preferred for common, giving up the arrearages, because they are currently not receiving dividends and the corporation is unlikely to pay them anything unless the recapitalization is approved.

a. A recapitalization usually takes one of two forms: either an amendment to the articles of incorporation or a merger into a wholly owned subsidiary that has the same economic effect. There may be different procedural rules applicable to these transactions, depending on how they are structured and the precise language of the applicable state statute. *Bove v. Community Hotel Corp. of Newport, R.I.*, 249 A.2d 89 (R.I. 1969).

b. These transactions are not subject to attack on the ground they impair vested rights. *McNulty v. W. & J. Sloane*, 54 N.Y.S.2d 253 (1945). Some courts have narrowly construed the amendment and reservation power to invalidate transactions deemed by the court to be of questionable fairness. *Bowman v. Armour & Co.*, 160 N.E.2d 753 (Ill.1959). But most courts have rejected arguments that in effect would restore the vested rights theory. *Langfelder v. Universal Laboratories, Inc.*, 163 F.2d 804 (3d Cir.1947).

c. One protection to stockholders often applicable in such transactions is the right to vote by separate voting groups. A stockholder objecting to the recapitalization also may have the statutory right of dissent and appraisal. Some courts have reviewed such transactions for fraud or unfairness so great as to constitute fraud, *Porges v. Vadsco Sales Corp.*, 32 A.2d 148 (Del.Ch.1943); *Barrett v. Denver Tramway Corp.*, 53 F.Supp. 198 (D.Del.1943).

D. ISSUING SHARES UNDER THE MBCA

MBCA 6.21(b) authorizes shares to be issued for consideration consisting of any tangible or intangible property or benefit to the corporation, including cash, promissory notes, services performed, contracts for services to be performed, or other securities of the corporation. MBCA 6.21(c) provides that before the corporation issues shares, the board of directors must determine that the consideration received or to be received for shares to be issued is adequate. That determination by the board of directors is conclusive insofar as the adequacy of consideration for the issuance of shares relates to whether the shares are validly issued, fully paid, and non-assessable. MBCA 6.21(d) provides that when the corporation receives the consideration for which the board of directors authorized the issuance of shares, the shares issued therefor are fully paid and non-assessable.

1. Amount of Consideration

The traditional par value requirement has been eliminated in the MBCA. There is no minimum issue price for shares. The price at which shares are issued is set by the board of directors. Shares may be issued for any tangible or intangible property or benefit to the corporation. MBCA 6.21(b).

> *Example:* A and B plan to contribute $10,000 each for fifty per cent of the stock of a new corporation. The state has enacted MBCA (1984). The attorney forming the corporation recommends that 500 shares of common stock be authorized and that 100 shares be issued each to A and to B for $100 per share. Three hundred shares have the status of "authorized but unissued shares." The same economic result may be achieved by issuing 10 shares each to A and to B for $1000 per share or 1 share to each for $10,000. The only difference is that the number of authorized but unissued shares of the corporation will be 480 instead of 300 or 498 rather than 300. Authorized but unissued shares may be issued later by the

board of directors at a price then decided upon by the board of directors. Shares may be issued at more or less than the original issue price.

2. Optional Par Value

Par value may be used on an optional basis at the election of the corporation. MBCA 2.02(b). The Official Comment explains that such provisions may be of use to corporations which are to be qualified in foreign jurisdictions if franchise or other taxes are computed upon the basis of par value. Optional par value may also be given effect or meaning essentially as a matter of contract between the parties. In other words, the par value rules described below may be elected by a corporation.

3. Conclusive Valuation

The MBCA and most state statutes provide that in the absence of fraud, the judgment of the board of directors as to the value of the consideration received for shares shall be conclusive and that when that value is received by the corporation in exchange for shares the shares are validly issued. This rule is designed to protect the stockholder any from challenge that the price paid is inadequate and that the shares have not been validly issued. It does not protect the board of directors from a challenge (for example) that it failed to exercise its business judgment in connection with setting the price.

Caveat: This rule does not protect the stockholder against a challenge based on failure to pay at least par value in states that continue to follow the par value system.

Caveat: Whether or not the par value rules apply, shares issued for no consideration may be canceled. *Triplex Shoe Co. v. Rice & Hutchins,* 152 A. 342 (Del.1930). Votes cast by such shares may be nullified, and the stockholder may be required to return any distributions.

4. Permissible Consideration

Traditional rules in most par value jurisdictions prohibited payment for shares by a promise to pay in the future or to render future services or a future benefit. These rules create anomalous results and have been eliminated in the MBCA. On the other hand, a corporation may escrow shares issued for such consideration until the consideration is received. MBCA 6.21(e).

Example: A famous actress agrees to make a film in exchange for a twenty-five percent interest in the film. Under traditional rules she could not be issued shares upon the execution of her contract. On the other hand, a bank might lend the new corporation $10,000,000 solely on the basis of the contract. Under MBCA § 6.21, shares may be issued to the actress in exchange for her contract to perform services.

Example: Under traditional rules, a wealthy financier may not give his promissory note for shares even though his note is as good as gold. On the other hand, a third party who holds the note could acquire shares in exchange for the note. Under § 6.21, the note may serve as consideration for the issuance of shares to the maker.

5. Tax Implications

a. The contribution of property to a corporation in exchange for its shares is not a taxable disposition of the property contributed, if immediately after the exchange the persons contributing the property own at least 80 per cent of the voting and nonvoting shares of the corporation. This nonrecognition of gain is limited to shares received by the contributor and only to the extent that the liabilities assumed by the corporation do not exceed the basis of the property in the hands of the contributor. IRC 351, IRC 357. No gain or loss is recognized by the corporation by the issuance of shares. IRC 1032.

Caveat: If IRC 351 is not applicable, a stockholder who contributes appreciated property to the corporation is taxed on the appreciation in the same manner as though he had sold the appreciated property to an unrelated person.

b. If shares are issued for services already performed or to be performed, the fair value of the shares so received is subject to federal income tax at ordinary income tax rates. This tax liability may create problems for the stockholder who must find the cash to pay the tax if shares cannot be sold. IRC 83.

E. ISSUING SHARES IN PAR VALUE STATES

Several states retain the concept of par value to some extent. In these states, the articles of incorporation must state the par value of the shares of each class (or state that the shares are issued *"with no par value"* or *"without par value"*). The current trend is toward the elimination of the concept of par value as an historical anomaly.

1. Par Value

Par value is an arbitrary value associated with shares. The par value of shares is set forth in the articles of incorporation and appears on the face of certificates for shares. In states with par value statutes, the board of directors may set the price at which shares are issued, but shares may not be issued for less than par value. Shares may always be issued for more than par value.

a. If par value shares are issued for consideration worth less than par, the recipient remains obligated to pay to the corporation the difference between par value and the amount actually paid. Shares so issued are usually called *watered shares* or *watered stock*.

   Example: H and W form a corporation with authorized capital of 100 shares of common stock with a par value of $1,000 per share. H and W each receive 50 shares of common stock without paying anything for them. They lend $10,000 to the corporation and the corporation then executes a promissory note for $45,000 to S in connection with the purchase of a retail store. The corporation becomes insolvent without paying the note. H and W are personally liable to the corporation for $50,000 each. *Hanewald v. Bryan's Inc.*, 429 N.W.2d 414 (1988).

   Caveat: Although some courts have held that creditors may sue the nonpaying stockholder directly, in most cases the statutes specify that the obligation to pay at least par runs to the corporation, which presumably must sue to enforce it. Nevertheless, creditors may recover indirectly if the obligation is enforced through action by a bankruptcy trustee.

   Example: In *Hanewald*, the corporation was created with common shares of $1 par value. The corporation issued 50 shares each to H and to W for $10,000 in cash, and then executed the $45,000 promissory note to Hanewald. The corporation became insolvent without paying this note. H and W have no liability because they paid more than par value for their shares.

b. It is customary to use *low par* shares rather than *high par* shares. High par value leads to undesirable consequences: (i) no shares of the corporation can be issued by the corporation at less than par even if the fair market value is less than par, (ii) some state taxes are computed on the basis of par value so that a high par value simply increases tax liabilities with no offsetting benefits; and (iii) the transaction is reflected in the capital accounts of the corporation in a way that is less advantageous to the corporation than if nominal par shares are used.

c. Par value, once set in the articles of incorporation, cannot be thereafter changed except by formal amendment to the articles of incorporation.

>   *Example:* A corporation originally issues shares with a par value of $100 per share at a sales price of $100. The corporation suffers financial reverses so that its outstanding shares are now worth less than $100 per share. The corporation decides to issue additional authorized shares to raise much needed capital. These shares can only be sold at the current market price of $60 per share. Because they are $100 par value shares, any person who purchases the new shares at $60 per share may also incur a potential watered stock liability of $40 per share. The corporation may amend its articles of incorporation to reduce the par value of the authorized shares to $1 per share or may create a new class of low par value shares.

>   *Caveat:* Some older cases suggest that there may be an exception to the general common law rule for cases in which a troubled corporation needs to raise capital. *See Handley v. Stutz,* 139 U.S. 417 (1891).

d. There is no benefit to the corporation from using high par shares in dealing with creditors because lenders do not rely on par value in deciding whether or not to extend credit.

e. The requirement to pay at least par value for shares generally applies only to the purchase of newly issued shares directly from the corporation. It does not apply to a purchase of shares from an existing stockholder, unless the purchaser knows that the shares are not fully paid. When the full agreed consideration (equal to or greater than par value) is paid to the corporation, the shares are said to be *fully paid and non assessable.*

f. In most jurisdictions the requirement that shares be sold for at least par value does not apply to the resale of treasury shares by the corporation. It is not clear that this latter exception has been accepted in Delaware. *See*

Byrne v. Lord, 1996 WL 361503 (Del.Ch.). A stockholder who purchases shares for less than par value remains liable for the difference between the price paid and the par value even if the stockholder sells the shares.

2. Par Value and Capital Accounts

Corporation statutes that retain the concept of par value provide that the aggregate par value of issued shares constitutes the *stated capital* of the corporation and that any excess received for the issuance of shares over par value is *capital surplus.*

> *Caveat:* The names of the capital accounts used here are those that appear in the MBCA (1969). Some state statutes adopt different terms for these accounts. The names of the capital accounts used in corporation statutes often differ from the names assigned to accounts by the accounting profession or under tax law. The concepts set forth here are applicable only to states with par value statutes. Under the MBCA there are no rules as to how the capital accounts of a corporation should be structured.

> *Example:* If 100 shares of $1 par value shares are issued to each of A and B for $100 per share (or an aggregate of $10,000 each), the balance sheet of the corporation immediately after its formation will be as follows:

Assets		Liabilities	–0–
Cash	$20,000		
		Equity	
		Capital Surplus	$19,800
		Stated Capital	200
Total	$20,000	Total	$20,000

a. Capital accounts are based on *issued* shares, not *authorized* shares.

> *Example:* If a par value of $100 per share is assigned, the balance sheet will be as follows:

Assets		Liabilities	–0–
Cash	$20,000		
		Equity	
		Capital Surplus	
		Stated Capital	20,000
Total	$20,000	Total	$20,000

b. A major advantage of reflecting the bulk of the capital contributions as capital surplus is that under most state statutes stated capital is locked in while capital surplus may be distributed to the stockholders or used to reacquire outstanding shares.

Example: In the preceding example, *B* would like to withdraw half of his $10,000 contribution. *A* agrees to this so long as *B*'s shares are reduced correspondingly by the corporation repurchasing 50 of *B*'s shares. Under most state statutes, capital surplus may be used to reacquire outstanding shares but stated capital may not. As a result, a corporation with low par could reacquire one half of *B*'s shares for $5,000, but a corporation with high par could not because it does not have $5,000 of capital surplus. The balance sheet of the low par corporation might look like this after reacquiring fifty of *B*'s shares for $5,000:

Assets		Liabilities	–0–
Cash	$15,000		
		Equity:	
		Capital Surplus	$14,800
		(20,000 less 5,000	
		restricted to reflect	
		treasury shares)	
		Stated Capital	200
Total	$15,000	Total	$15,000

3. No Par Shares

Most states that have par value statutes authorize *no par* shares. Although no par shares may be issued at any price that the board of directors may set in the exercise of its business judgment, they are otherwise subject to par value rules relating to stated capital, the payment of dividends, etc. In other words, no par shares are a variation of nominal par value shares. They are very different from common shares issued under statutes such as the MBCA which have eliminated par value.

a. No par shares are shares authorized in the articles of incorporation as shares *without par value*. No par shares may be issued for any amount of consideration specified by the directors. There is no minimum price. Watered stock liability may arise if shares are issued for cash or property worth less than the price set by the board of directors.

Example: The articles of incorporation of a corporation state that the corporation is authorized to issue "500,000 shares of common stock without par value." A and B decide to contribute $1,000 each. The directors may set the price at which the shares are to be issued, at $.01 per share (in which case 100,000 shares are issued), $1.00 per share (in which case 1,000 shares are issued) or $100 per share (in which case 10 shares are issued).

b. The entire consideration is initially allocated to stated capital but in most states the directors may allocate a specified amount to capital surplus. If no part of the consideration is allocated to capital surplus, the no par alternative is equivalent to the high par alternative. If all or nearly all of the consideration is allocated to capital surplus, the no par alternative is equivalent to the low par alternative. No par shares have no significant advantage over low par shares in most states.

c. Where property (other than cash) is received for no par shares, the directors must usually specify in dollars the consideration received. In some states, the directors may simply specify the property to be received without a dollar value. Thus, no par shares may have an advantage where property of highly uncertain value is contributed because the directors may be able to specify the property that is to be received without setting a dollar value on it.

d. Under the now-repealed federal documentary stamp tax, no par shares were valued at the price at which the shares were actually issued but par value shares were valued at par value. Some states continue to use this model in connection with franchise taxes. In these states there is a strong tax incentive to issue low par rather than no par shares.

Caveat: It is important to distinguish conceptually between no par shares in states that retain the par value structure, and shares issued in states with statutes that have eliminated par value. The issuance of no par shares in par value states affects the stated capital and capital surplus accounts, may create a watered stock liability in certain circumstances, and may affect the capacity of a corporation to make distributions to its stockholders. States that have eliminated par value have also eliminated mandatory capital accounts and have established rules relating to distributions that are independent of any allocation of the consideration received when shares are issued.

F.   PERMISSIBLE CONSIDERATION

Under many state statutes, only certain types of property qualify as valid consideration for shares. A typical statute provides that consideration may be paid, in whole or in part, in cash, in other property, tangible or intangible, or in labor or services actually performed for the corporation. MBCA (1969) § 19. Many statutes add that neither promissory notes nor future services shall constitute payment or part payment for the issuance of shares of a corporation. MBCA (1969) § 19.

Caveat: In a few states, these statutory provisions are based on state constitutional provisions.

Caveat: Most states that retain these restrictions on eligible consideration for shares also retain par value provisions. But these requirements are independent of par value. Some states, including California, have eliminated the par value rules but have retained restrictions on eligible consideration. *See* CCC 409.

G.   WATERED STOCK

Watered stock is a generic term used to describe the issuance of shares at a price below par value. The phrase *watered stock* originated from the practice of getting cattle to drink large amounts of water immediately before being weighed for sale. If stock is issued for no consideration at all, it is sometimes called *bonus stock*. If stock is issued for some consideration but less than par value, such shares are often called *discount shares*. In either case, under common law and the statutes of states that still follow the par value system, one who purchases stock directly from an issuing corporation and pays less than par value is liable to the corporation (or in some cases creditors as well) for the difference between the price paid and the par value.

1.   Theories of Watered Stock Liability

Several different theories have been advanced to explain stockholder liability for watered stock.

a.   The par value of issued shares was early viewed as a public representation that at least that amount of equity capital has been received by the corporation. From this it may be argued that stockholders who knowingly receive watered shares are involved in a potential misrepresentation to creditors and should be liable to them for any short-fall between the par value and the amount actually paid for shares. This is the historical explanation for watered stock liability.

b. Watered stock liability has also been rationalized on the theory that the capital of a corporation is a trust fund for creditors who rely on the capital of the corporation when extending credit to it. Under the *trust fund* theory any creditor might bring suit against the recipient of watered shares for failing to make the required payment to this trust fund. This theory is largely a fiction. The capital of a corporation is not a trust fund in any meaningful sense. The capital of a corporation may be invested in the business and may be lost if the business does not succeed. No one is liable if the capital is lost. The creditors simply go unpaid.

c. In an early case, watered stock liability was based on a *holding out* theory. *Hospes v. Northwestern Mfg. & Car Co.,* 50 N.W. 1117 (Minn.1892). The practical differences between the holding out and the trust fund or classic theories are that under a holding out theory are: (i) only creditors who extend credit subsequent to the issuance of the watered shares may enforce the liability, (ii) creditors who know that the shares were watered when they extended credit may not recover at all., and (iii) the burden is on the plaintiffs to establish that they qualify under (i) and (ii), but they do not have the burden of establishing that they in fact relied on the capital of the corporation in extending credit.

> *Caveat:* The holding out theory is fictional in the sense that reliance on the capital of the corporation by a creditor is presumed. Indeed, defendants can avoid liability only by making an affirmative showing that the plaintiffs knew that the stock was watered or that they did not rely on the capital of the corporation when they extended credit.

> *Caveat:* In modern practice, creditors almost never rely on par values and capital accounts in determining whether to extend credit. Rather, to the extent they investigate the credit standing of a possible borrower at all, commercial creditors rely on credit reporting services or the general reputation of the borrowers. Banks usually require a financial statement from the potential borrowers, but in analyzing that statement the bank normally pays no attention to par value.

d. Another rationale for enforcing minimum pay-in requirements is that it affords some guaranty to the stockholders that other stockholders have contributed a similar amount for their shares. In other words, watered stock liability may protect stockholders from dilution to some extent. Par value works well in this way, however, only when par is set at or near selling price, which may create other problems over time. Nevertheless, watered stock liability probably made some sense to promoters and investors at a time when the use of pre-incorporation subscriptions was common and par value was thought of as a target price.

e. Some par value statutes substitute a statutory liability for the common law theories. These statutes obligate every stockholder to pay at least par value for shares, and if a stockholder fails to do so, the corporation or any creditor may enforce this statutory liability.

f. The issuance of watered stock leads to the creation of fictitious assets or the inflation of asset values on the balance sheet.

Example: A corporation issues 1,000,000 shares of $10 par value common stock for an aggregate consideration of $5,000,000 in cash. Because the capital accounts automatically reflect stated capital equal to the number of shares issued (1,000,000) times the par value ($10.00 per share), the asset accounts must be inflated or *watered* in some way if the balance sheet is to balance.

Example: In the foregoing example, under some statutes the corporation itself might recover $5.00 per share from each recipient as the basic statutory liability each shareholder owes to the corporation for issuance of shares. This liability may be enforced by the corporation, a creditor, or a bankruptcy trustee or similar representative of the corporation, apparently without limitation. *Bing Crosby Minute Maid Corp. v. Eaton,* 297 P.2d 5 (Cal.1956); *Frink v. Carman Distributing Co.,* 48 P.2d 805 (Colo.1935).

2. Other Situations Giving Rise to Watered Stock

a. Depending on the language of the statute, watered stock liability may also arise if shares are issued for any price below the price set by the directors for the issuance of such shares. In other words, under some statutes, shares may be viewed as watered whenever the consideration for which the shares are actually issued is less than the price set by the board of directors. *Milberg v. Baum,* 25 N.Y.S.2d 451 (1941) (low par shares); *G. Loewus & Co. v. Highland Queen Packing Co.,* 6 A.2d 545 (N.J.Ch.1939) (no par shares).

Caveat: Even where a dollar value must be set for the value of property, the directors' good faith valuation is accepted for purposes of watered stock liability under the statutory provisions that make the determination of the directors as to value conclusive in the absence of fraud. *Johnson v. Louisville Trust Co.*, 293 Fed. 857 (6th Cir.1923). That is, the purchasing stockholder may not be held liable as long as she pays at least the agreed consideration. The board of directors on the other hand may be liable to the corporation if the shares are sold for inadequate consideration.

b. Shares issued in exchange for ineligible property or services may also be said to be watered.

Example: In a state with these statutory provisions, A and B agree to form a corporation each to have one half of the stock. A is to contribute $100,000 in cash and B is to work full time for the corporation without remuneration for one year. The consideration for the shares is recited to be $100,000 each, A to pay cash and B to perform services which the board of directors determines to have the value of $100,000 over the next year. B's services are not eligible consideration for the issuance of shares, and if B's shares are issued immediately, they are viewed as having been issued for no consideration at all. A watered stock liability on the part of B has been created by which B may be obligated to pay eligible consideration of $100,000 to the corporation despite the agreement by A and B that B is to contribute only services. The amount of this watered stock liability may depend on the par value of the issued shares in some states. In other states, the watered stock liability may be $100,000, the value of the issued shares as determined by the board of directors.

Example: In the previous example, if B's shares are to be issued only after B has performed services for one year, no watered stock liability is created. Because the services have been actually performed, $100,000 of eligible consideration has been received by the corporation. *Eastern Oklahoma Television Co. v. Ameco, Inc.*, 437 F.2d 138 (10th Cir.1971). But B does not have the rights of a stockholder during the period she is rendering services, although B may have contract rights against A.

Example: In the previous example, if B's shares are to be issued immediately for a promissory note which is to be repaid by the performance of services over the year, a watered stock liability has again been created because a promissory note does not constitute permissible consideration for the issuance of shares. *Cahall v. Lofland,* 114 A. 224 (Del.Ch.1921).

Example: B's shares are to be issued for a one year promissory note for $100,000 secured by a lien on valuable real estate. B plans to repay this note, together with interest, in cash when it comes due. While a promissory note is not eligible consideration for the issuance of shares, some courts have held that a secured promissory note is eligible consideration for shares, because the security granted is itself eligible property. *General Bonding & Cas. Ins. Co. v. Moseley,* 222 S.W. 961 (Tex.1920).

Example: In the previous example, B receives shares in exchange for an unsecured promissory note. Even though the shares are not validly issued because ineligible consideration was received, the note itself is not void and may be sued upon by the corporation.

Example: In the previous example, the board of directors decides to issue B's shares immediately, not for services, but for store fixtures having the value of $100,000. In fact, the store fixtures are worthless. If this transaction is not fraudulent, the values established for the store fixtures must be accepted. If the directors have established the valuation of the fixtures in order to defraud another stockholder or a third party, watered stock liability would arise. *See v. Heppenheimer,* 61 A. 843 (N.J.Ch. 1905); *Pipelife Corp. v. Bedford,* 145 A.2d 206 (Del.Ch.1958). But if B does not know that the valuation is fraudulent, B may rely on the decision of the board of directors to accept the fixtures as conclusive.

Example: B's shares are to be issued, not for services, but for secret contract rights. The board of directors establishes in good faith a value of $100,000 for those services. State statutes refer to intangible property as qualifying for the issuance of shares, and hence, it is likely that such a transaction involves eligible consideration and the value established for such consideration by the board of directors is conclusive. There is, however, some risk that a court may accept the argument that secret contract rights are so ephemeral that they do not qualify as intangible property and that therefore the shares were not issued for eligible consideration and are watered. Moreover, if the secret contract rights derive their value primarily from services to be performed in the future, it is unlikely that the fact that the obligation to perform services has been reduced to a contract will convert the services into property even though the contract itself may have some value. Such property is sometimes called *services flavored property*.

H. USES OF TREASURY STOCK

Corporations often use treasury shares to circumvent the par value rules.

a.   Treasury shares, having once been issued for at least par value and still outstanding for legal capital purposes, may be resold by the corporation without regard to par value.

b.   Treasury shares, having once been issued for eligible consideration, may be resold by the corporation in exchange for future services, promissory notes, or other consideration that is not eligible consideration for new shares.

>   *Example:*   Traditionally, corporations used treasury shares to satisfy obligations to issue shares pursuant to compensation plans. Although there was once some doubt about whether shares issued pursuant to options or as compensation were legally issued because of restrictions on permissible consideration, it is now settled that shares issued pursuant to options and other compensation plans are validly issued, because the shares are issued after the services are performed. But it may be desirable to use treasury shares when issuing shares for services performed (as contrasted with shares issued for cash upon the exercise of an option) because of the need to place a dollar value on the services received.

c.   Stated capital is not reduced by the par value of treasury shares. Rather, such shares are reflected on the balance sheet by a special (negative) entry showing that they are held as treasury shares and restrictions are placed on a surplus account (such as earned surplus) to reflect the purchase price of the treasury shares. Accounting for treasury shares is based on the assumption that the shares are not permanently retired but will be reissued at a later date.

Example: Corporation A wishes to contribute 10 shares as a door prize for a benefit for an employee who has been seriously injured in an automobile accident. It may not use authorized but unissued shares for this purpose under the state statute that permits shares to be issued only for money or property actually received or services actually performed. Corporation A may lawfully contribute treasury shares for this purpose.

Caveat: One court has applied the limitations on the issuance of authorized shares to the reissuance of treasury shares. *Public Inv. Ltd. v. Bandeirante Corp.,* 740 F.2d 1222 (D.C.Cir.1984). This result may be reasonable on the facts of that case, but it is not consistent with generally understood principles relating to treasury shares. *See also Byrne v. Lord*, 1996 WL 361503 (Del.Ch.).

Caveat: Treasury shares are shares of the *issuing* corporation that have been repurchased by the corporation. If the corporation acquires shares of *other* corporations, those shares maybe held in the treasury of the acquiring corporation, but they are investments and are listed as assets on the left-hand side of the balance sheet. Treasury shares are listed as negative equity in the lower right-hand portion of the balance sheet together with the other accounts relating to the stock of the corporation.

I. ISSUANCE OF SHARES BY A GOING CONCERN

A corporation may issue shares at any time during its life—not simply at the time of organization. Shares issued by a going concern affect outstanding stockholders. Shares issued at bargain prices may *dilute* the financial interests of existing stockholders. When shares are issued at fair market value, the voting rights of existing stockholders are diluted if the shares issued are voting shares.

1. Preemptive Rights

A *preemptive right* gives holders of outstanding shares the right to buy a proportionate part of any new issue of securities by the corporation. *Stokes v. Continental Trust Co.,* 78 N.E. 1090 (N.Y.1906). Preemptive rights protect existing stockholders against dilution of their control interest or financial interest in the issuing corporation. If all stockholders exercise their preemptive rights, no dilution occurs and the additional capital needed by the corporation is raised entirely from its present stockholders.

> *Caveat:* Preemptive rights are generally more important as a way of protecting control rights than as a way of protecting financial rights. If shares are issued at a fair price, the consideration received by the corporation should offset the effects of financial dilution.

> *Example:* A corporation is formed and issues 250 shares: 100 shares to A, 100 shares to B, and 50 shares to C. The corporation is a financial success. A and B decide to issue 200 additional shares to themselves at $50 per share. C as the owner of 20 per cent of the outstanding shares has a preemptive right to acquire 20 per cent of the new shares at the same price per share. If C exercises this preemptive right, C will be entitled to purchase 40 shares at $50 per share, and after the new shares are issued, will continue to own 20 per cent of the outstanding shares.

a. In about half of the states, a stockholder has a preemptive right unless a specific opt-out provision appears in the articles of incorporation. MBCA 6.30 and the statutes of about half of the states make preemptive rights an opt-in provision. Corporations in these states have preemptive rights only if the articles of incorporation so provide.

b. MBCA 6.30 contains a model provision relating to preemptive rights that may be elected by a simple clause in the articles of incorporation, stating that the corporation elects to have preemptive rights.

c. In some states preemptive rights do not apply to treasury shares on the theory that the dilution has already occurred. Some statutes extend preemptive rights to treasury shares. And some cases reject the exception for treasury shares in the absence of express statutory language. *Fuller v. Krogh,* 113 N.W.2d 25 (Wis.1962).

> *Caveat:* The issue does not arise under the MBCA which treats previously issued shares as authorized but unissued shares when they are reacquired by the corporation.

d. Preemptive rights generally do not extend to shares issued for consideration other than money. Some courts have construed this exemption narrowly if the corporation can sell shares for cash and use the cash to acquire the property. *Dunlay v. Avenue M Garage & Repair Co.*, 170 N.E. 917 (N.Y.1930).

e. Preemptive rights do not extend to authorized but unissued shares to the extent they represent part of the contemplated initial capitalization of the corporation. For example, MBCA 6.30 exempts sales during the first six months after incorporation.

f. Preemptive rights generally do not extend to shares of different classes unless the other class is convertible into the class held by the stockholder.

> *Example:* Common stockholders do not have a preemptive right to acquire shares of preferred stock unless the preferred is convertible into common.

> *Example:* Preferred stockholders may have a preemptive right to acquire new preferred shares of the same class. They do not, however, have preemptive rights to acquire common shares. Most early case law to the contrary has been overruled by statute. *Thomas Branch & Co. v. Riverside & Dan River Cotton Mills,* Inc., 123 S.E. 542 (Va.1924).

g. Preemptive rights serve little purpose in publicly held corporations because they complicate the raising of capital. Also, the availability of a public market for shares renders the preemptive right less important because any stockholder may add to shareholdings simply by purchasing shares in the open market.

2. Fiduciary Restrictions on the Oppressive Issuance of Shares

Where preemptive rights are unavailable (either because the transaction falls within an exception to the preemptive right or because the right itself has been eliminated by the corporation), the power of the board of directors of a closely held corporation to issue new shares on terms that are unfair to minority stockholders may be limited by a general fiduciary duty. *Schwartz v. Marien*, 373 N.Y.S.2d 122, 335 N.E.2d 334 (N.Y. 1975); *Ross Transport, Inc. v. Crothers*, 45 A.2d 267 (Md.1946).

a. Fiduciary duty may preclude issuance of shares in the absence of a compelling business purpose even where preemptive rights exist but circumstances are such that it is unreasonable to expect some stockholders to exercise their preemptive rights.

Example: X is a 20 per cent stockholder not involved in day-to-day management. With the specific intent of reducing X's interest in the corporation, the board of directors proposes to issue new shares that will require X to invest $100,000 in cash to retain her current percentage interest by exercising her preemptive right. The other stockholders plan to pay for their portion of the new issue by canceling loans they have previously made to the corporation. X declines to purchase the additional shares. As a result of the new issue, X's proportional interest in the corporation is reduced to less than one per cent. Some courts have enjoined transactions of this type on the theory that they are oppressive and serve no business purpose. *Katzowitz v. Sidler*, 301 N.Y.S.2d 470, 249 N.E.2d 359 (N.Y. 1969). Not all courts have agreed though factual differences may partially explain the result. *Hyman v. Velsicol Corp.*, 97 N.E.2d 122 (Ill.App.1951).

b.   Issuance of shares to controlling stockholders at unfair prices may be set aside even though the transaction has a valid business purpose. *Adelman v. Conotti Corp.*, 213 S.E.2d 774 (Va.1975); *Bennett v. Breuil Petroleum Corp.*, 99 A.2d 236 (Del.Ch.1953).

c.   Transactions that affect the balance of power within a corporation may also be set aside if they have no apparent business purpose. *Schwartz v. Marien*, 335 N.E.2d 334 (N.Y. 1975).

d.   If there is a good faith business purpose and no personal benefit to controlling stockholders, shares may be issued on terms that benefit one class at the expense of another. *Bodell v. General Gas & Electric Corp.*, 140 A. 264 (Del. 1927).

3. Stockholder Approval Requirements

In 1999, the MBCA was amended to require that any new issue of shares that increases aggregate voting power of stockholders by 20 percent or more (including increases that may result from conversion) must be approved by the existing stockholders.

a.   This provision closely tracks the rules of the stock exchanges that require a stockholder vote in similar situations. It is arguable, however, that stock exchange rules are designed primarily to give the markets a chance to absorb information about the new issue of shares in order to allow prices to adjust in an orderly fashion. In contrast, the MBCA rule is intended to apply to all corporations whether or not they are publicly traded.

b. The amendment to MBCA § 6.21 was adopted in conjunction with a change in the rules regarding stockholder voting in connection with mergers. Formerly, the MBCA required a vote of the stockholders of the surviving corporation only if the surviving corporation proposed to issue new shares in connection with the merger equal to 20 percent or more of those outstanding before the merger. The MBCA no longer requires a vote by the stockholders of the surviving corporation in connection with the merger, but it does require a vote whenever additional shares are issued that increase voting power by 20 percent or more regardless of the reason for the new issue.

Caveat: State takeover laws may preclude the voting of shares issued by the corporation in excess of 20 percent in the absence of a stockholder vote. *See Simon Property Group, Inc. v. Taubman Centers, Inc.,* 240 F.Supp.2d 642 (E.D. Mich. 2003) (discussing conflicting cases and holding that newly issued shares may be voted under Michigan law).

J. DEBT SECURITIES

Corporations often raise a significant portion of their capital by borrowing rather than by selling shares. Generally, such capital is called *debt capital*. A corporation may borrow debt capital from individuals (including stockholders), a bank, other companies, or any other source. A corporation may also borrow debt capital by issuing *debt securities*. Debt securities may be sold in a public offering (in which case a registration statement must be filed with the SEC) or they may be privately placed with a limited number of large investors (often institutional investors such as insurance companies, pension plans, and mutual funds). With debt securities, the corporation in effect borrows from a group of lenders, although in some cases a single investor may buy an entire issue of debt securities. Debt securities may be of any duration. Debt financing may be short term (for example, bank loans or lines of credit) or long term (for example, bonds that may have maturity dates 20 to 50 years or more in the future). A short term debt security with a maturity of nine months or less from the date of issue is called *commercial paper* and is generally exempt from SEC registration. Corporations also may issue a variety of medium term notes that may be publicly traded. Longer term debt securities are called *bonds* or *debentures* and often have maturities of ten years or more. A stockholder may also be a creditor, particularly in a small closely held corporation. That is, a stockholder may choose to lend some portion of his or her investment (capital contribution) to the corporation rather than invest it in the form of equity. Stockholder loans may have many of the characteristics of equity capital and may be treated as equity capital for some purposes. There is little chance that a bona fide loan from a third party creditor will be treated as equity capital, even though some bonds (such as *junk bonds*) have economic characteristics that make them similar to equity capital.

1. Bonds and Debentures

Technically a *bond* is secured whereas a *debenture* is unsecured. But in practice the word *bond* is often used to refer generically to all long term debt securities issued by a corporation whether secured or not. Bonds are typically secured by a lien on specific property of the issuer (such as land, buildings, equipment, inventory, receivables, *etc.*).

a. Bonds and debentures are written obligations to pay a specific amount at a future date usually with periodic interest payments due in the interim

b. Bonds and debentures are usually negotiable instruments. Historically, debt securities were payable to the *bearer* (that is, the person in possession of the certificate) and the obligation to pay periodic interest was represented by *coupons* that could be clipped from the bond certificate and cashed much as an ordinary check and which were themselves negotiable instruments payable to bearer. Such debt securities are typically called *bearer bonds.* Because of changes in tax law, bonds and debentures today are issued in registered form in the name of a specific holder. Interest payments are not represented by coupons but rather are paid by check directly to the registered holder. Registered debt instruments are transferable only by endorsement rather than by mere delivery.

c. The rights of holders of debt securities are set forth in an *indenture* which typically vests in a *trustee* the rights to enforce the terms of the indenture, including the right to foreclose on security. *United States Trust Co. v. First Nat. City Bank,* 394 N.Y.S.2d 653 (App.Div.1977). An indenture (sometimes called a *trust indenture*) is essentially a contract between the issuer and investors. Because bondholders are not viewed as owners of the corporation, they do not have the right to vote on matters of corporate governance as stockholders do. Bondholders may sometimes have the right to vote on matters relating solely to the bonds, such as whether to permit the issuer to delay an interest payment. It is fairly clear as a matter of case law that the board of directors owes no fiduciary duty to bondholders (although there are a few cases in which courts have held that a limited fiduciary duty is owed to the holders of bonds that may be converted into stock). Bondholders are not entitled to information about the issuer and its business except to the extent specified in the indenture or as may be required by the registration statement (if any) filed with the SEC. In other words, the rights of bondholders are almost entirely contractual. But these contractual rights include an obligation of *good faith* (as under any contract) on the part of the issuer, which means that the issuer agrees implicitly not to subvert the terms of the contract. As a result of these limited rights, bondholders must depend on a trustee to monitor the finances of the issuer. The federal Trust Indenture Act of 1939 (administered by the SEC) sets minimum standards for indentures under which $10 million or more in bonds may be issued.

d. Debt securities are usually issued in units of $1,000 or larger round numbers. If they are publicly traded, their market price is a function of prevailing interest rates and the risk of default by the issuer. Bonds are generally traded by and among dealers for their own account rather than on an exchange. Thus, an investor who wants to buy or sell a bond, typically buys from or sells to a dealer rather than having the transaction handled by a broker who finds an investor to take the other side of the trade. Such a market is called a *dealer market* or an *over the counter* (OTC) market. Because of this market structure, there is less reliable information about bond prices than about stock prices.

e. Bonds are usually rated by a rating agency such as Moody's or Standard & Poors. The highest ratings (A through AAA) are referred to as *investment grade* and institutional investors are sometimes prohibited by law or contract from investing in any lower grade instruments. Preferred stock may also be rated.

f. Debt securities are usually issued at or close to the *face amount* of $1,000 per unit, also called *par*. Market prices of debt instruments fluctuate with market conditions. When interest rates rise, bond prices fall because (other things being equal) the fixed interest payment on a bond becomes less attractive compared to other investments when those other investments offer a higher rate of return. As the price of a bond falls, however, the fixed interest rate relative to par become a higher interest rate relative to market price. Similarly, when interest rates fall, bond prices generally rise. But regardless of movements in market price during the life of a bond, when the bond matures the issuer must repay the face amount.

g.   The fixed relationship between the *face amount* of a debt security and the amount the issuer must pay each year in interest is called the *coupon rate.* When market prices fluctuate an investment in a debt security will yield an effective return that may be greater or less than the coupon rate.

Example: A $1,000 debt security with an 8 per cent coupon rate is trading at par. That means that the market price is $1,000 and the yield on the purchase of such a bond is 8 per cent per year, the same as the coupon rate.

Example: A debt security has a coupon rate of 8 percent per year. Market interest rates rise to 10 percent for a bond of similar risk and maturity. The market price of the outstanding bond will fall so that an investor who purchases the bond will receive approximately 10 percent in return at the lower market price.

h.   Debt securities are usually redeemable by the corporation at a premium over the face amount of the instrument. They may also be made convertible into common stock at the election of the holder. The market price of a convertible bond will depend on the value of the bond as a debt instrument and the value of the securities into which it can be converted. Generally speaking, the bond will trade at the greater of the two and possibly slightly more if it cannot be redeemed immediately.

Example: In *Van Gemert v. Boeing Co.,* 520 F.2d 1373 (2d Cir. 1975), cert. *denied,* 423 U.S. 947, 96 S.Ct. 364, convertible debentures were called for redemption giving the minimum notice to holders required by the trust indenture. The conversion was "forced" in the sense that the conversion securities were worth significantly more than the redemption price. The court held that the corporation owed a duty to convertible debenture holders to give them reasonable notice so that bondholders could elect to convert. In this case a significant number of bondholders had failed to exercise the conversion privilege. *But see Meckel v. Continental Resources Co.,* 758 F.2d 811 (2d Cir.1985) (notice by mail adequate for registered bonds). *See also Broad v. Rockwell International Corp.,* 642 F.2d 929 (5th Cir.1981).

i.   In the 1980s, numerous types of novel debt instruments were developed.

- *zero coupon bonds* or *zeroes* are debentures that do not carry interest payments. They are issued at deep discounts from par and interest is reflected in the discount.

- *income bonds* are debt instruments, but the obligation to pay interest is conditioned on the existence of earnings to cover the interest.

- *participating bonds* are debt instruments, but the obligation to pay interest fluctuates with the earnings of the corporation.

- *PIK (payment in kind)* bonds pay interest in the form of promissory notes or additional bonds for a stated period of time.

- *reset bonds* are bonds that require the issuer to adjust (reset) the interest rate on a specific date in the future if the bonds are selling below par so as to return the bonds' market value to par value.

- *junk bonds* (or high yield bonds) are bonds that are below investment grade when issued.

    Caveat: A *fallen angel* is a bond or debenture that was investment grade when issued but downgraded thereafter because of increased risk in the business of the issuer. In contrast, junk bonds are issued as such. In the 1980s, junk bonds were often issued to raise cash for purposes of funding a takeover. As a result of changes in tax law, interest payable on junk bonds became nondeductible unless the bonds were secured. Today, junk bonds are issued largely as an alternative to common stock.

2. Debt Instruments Compared With Preferred Shares

Bonds and debentures are debt securities. They differ from preferred shares, which are equity securities, in several basic respects:

a.   Interest on bonds (sometimes called *debt service*) is an unconditional obligation of the corporation, whereas dividends on preferred shares are discretionary with the board of directors. But dividend payments may be made mandatory under circumstances specified in the articles of incorporation subject to statutory limitations on distributions to stockholders.

b.   A bond usually has a maturity date at which time the principal becomes due. Preferred shares never become due. But preferred shares may be made subject to mandatory redemption at a specified time or at the option of the holder (in effect on demand) subject again to statutory limitations on distributions to stockholders.

c. A bond may have legal rights of foreclosure in the event of default. Preferred stock does not.

d. Bonds are created pursuant to indentures that usually appoint a trustee to handle the rights of security holders whereas classes of preferred stock are created by provision in the articles of incorporation of the corporation. Debt securities need not be authorized in the articles of incorporation. A corporation has the inherent power to borrow money. But if debt is to be convertible into stock, there must be explicit authorization in the articles of incorporation to issue the conversion securities.

e. Despite these legal differences the economic differences between these two types of securities may be slight.

K. ADVANTAGES OF DEBT CAPITAL

There are both tax and non-tax advantages in using a judicious amount of debt to capitalize a corporation. The ratio between a corporation's equity capital and its long term debt is called the *debt/equity ratio. A corporation with a high debt/equity ratio is called* is said to be *thinly capitalized* or *highly leveraged.*

Example: A corporation is capitalized with $50,000 of long-term bonds and 1,000 shares of common stock issued for $10 each, for an aggregate of $10,000. The debt/equity ratio of the corporation is 5/1.

1. Tax Advantages of Debt

a. Interest on debt is deductible by the corporation whereas dividends on stock are not. Thus, the use of debt permits the corporation to pay out more of its available cash to investors, because interest payments are a deductible business expense and are therefore paid in pretax dollars. In a closely held corporation, stockholder debt is an important way to zero out corporate income, minimize income tax, and increase ultimate return for owners.

    Caveat: The deductibility of interest is irrelevant if the corporation has elected S Corporation status under the IRC. An S Corporation pays no tax on operating income at the corporation level. Rather such income passes through to the stockholders as income taxable to them (whether or not the corporation pays a dividend in that amount).

b. A repayment of debt may be a tax-free return of capital rather than a taxable distribution. The use of debt may therefore permit the tax-free return of a portion of a stockholder's investment, whereas a partial redemption of a taxpayer's common or preferred shares may give rise to ordinary income or capital gain.

c. Because the existence of stockholder debt in the capital structure reduces taxes, stockholders usually want to use the greatest amount of debt possible.

> *Caveat:* A debt/equity ratio of greater than 4 to 1 increases the risk that a court will treat the debt as equity capital and disallow deduction of interest by the corporation for tax purposes. *See John Kelly Co. v. Commissioner,* 326 U.S. 521, 526, 66 S.Ct. 299, 302 (1946). If the debt is excessive, it is usually reclassified as equity in its entirety. *See Taft v. C.I.R.,* 314 F.2d 620 (9th Cir.1963).

2. Non-Tax Advantages of Debt

a. An important advantage of debt financing is that it simplifies planning where some investors contribute more capital than others.

> *Example:* A proposes to contribute $10,000 in cash; B proposes to contribute $6,000 in property of various types. A and B each want to own 50 percent of the shares. In order to equalize contributions, the attorney suggests that common shares be issued to reflect a $6,000 contribution by A and B, and that A separately lend the corporation $4,000.

b. Debt financing may permit the stockholders to obtain parity with general trade creditors if the business fails. But, as in the tax context, if too much of the stockholders' investment is in the form of debt, a court may recharacterize the debt as equity, that is, *subordinate* it to obligations owed to third-party creditors. *See Costello v. Fazio,* 256 F.2d 903 (9th Cir.1958).

c. Corporations often borrow some portion of their capital to create *leverage* and increase return on common stock. For example, if a company can generate a 10 percent return on its total capital, and it can borrow half of its capital at 8 percent, then the excess 2 percent generated on the debt goes to the common stock increasing its return to 12 percent. (The same end can be accomplished by issuing preferred stock at 8 percent.) But because debt and interest thereon must generally be paid no matter how the business fares, debt also increases the risk in the common stock. For example, if the business above were to generate a total return of 6 percent, the debt would still need to be paid at 8 percent, and the return on the common stock would be reduced to 4 percent.

Caveat: Miller and Modigliani demonstrated that the aggregate value of a corporation's securities (the market value of its equity securities plus the market value of its debt securities) is independent of the corporation's debt/equity ratio (ignoring tax effects). In other words, any enhanced value of the common stock because of the advantages of leverage should be precisely matched by a decline in value of the bonds. That is, the return on common stock may be enhanced if the corporation can borrow part of its capital at a low enough interest rate, and the increased return may make the common stock more attractive to investors, hence increasing its market price, albeit at the expense of debtholders. Because interest on debt is deductible from a corporation's income for tax purposes (as a business expense), total return to investors may in fact be increased by the use of debt. In effect, return on debt is taxed only once (to the recipient of the interest) whereas dividends are taxed twice (once when the corporation pays tax on its income and once when the stockholder receives the dividend). Thus, a corporation that pays out some of its return in the form of interest is worth more in the aggregate after-tax than one that does not. Accordingly, leverage may increase the total value of the corporation when the effect of income taxes is taken into account, but not *because* of leverage.

Caveat: Leverage depends on the use of *other people's money*. Leverage cannot be created for a given stockholder as a result of that stockholder lending a portion of her investment to the corporation, because any advantage created for the common stock portion of the investment is offset by a disadvantage for the debt portion of the investment.

Caveat: Although one apparent advantage of debt financing in an inflationary economy is that debt may be paid off in inflated dollars, if the market for debt is efficient, this effect will be offset by an increase in the interest rate payable on the debt.

L.   FEDERAL AND STATE SECURITIES LAWS

The federal Securities Act of 1933 is designed to protect public investors from fraud and misrepresentation in connection with the offer and sale of securities in interstate commerce by requiring the registration of public offerings. State securities laws (blue sky laws) serve a similar purpose for small issues of securities within a state. The goal of federal securities law is full disclosure of all *material* facts about the securities being sold. The federal Securities Act is a disclosure statute. No evaluation of the investment quality of securities is involved. The federal Securities Exchange Act of 1934 focuses on trading and publicly traded companies (as opposed to the offering of securities). It mandates periodic reporting by publicly held companies, establishes various rules relating to trading and stockholder voting, and provides for regulation of the securities business.

Caveat: Many state blue sky statutes also are disclosure statutes. Several, however, involve *merit review*—they authorize the state securities administrator to block the sale of a security in the state if the transaction is not *fair, just and equitable*, even if all information is accurately disclosed.

Caveat: In 1996 Congress enacted the National Securities Markets Improvement Act (NSMIA) which preempts state law with respect to virtually all offerings that are registered with the SEC or made pursuant to SEC rules relating to private offerings. Although state blue sky laws remain on the books, they may be enforced only with regard to certain small offerings and wholly intrastate offerings.

1.   Registration of Securities Offerings

The 1933 Act generally requires registration of securities before they may be publicly offered. Registration involves the filing of detailed information about the offering, its review by the SEC, and public dissemination of that information to potential investors in the form of a prospectus. The federal registration process is expensive and thus impractical for most offerings of less than $20 million. As a result, for small offerings it is essential to find an applicable exemption from registration. Most *initial public offerings (IPOs)* of stocks to be listed on an exchange must be registered on the SEC's long form registration statement, Form S–1. Forms S–2 and S–3 are shorter and simpler than Form S–1 and are available to issuers who are already publicly held. Such issuers must register for purposes of continuous reporting under the Securities Exchange Act of 1934 and reports filed under that act may be incorporated by reference in the short form registration statements under the *integrated disclosure system.*

a. In the absence of an exemption, the sale of unregistered securities gives rise to substantial civil liabilities and may give rise to criminal prosecution as well. Moreover, under § 11 of the 1933 Act, if the registration statement contains a material misrepresentation of fact or fails to disclose a material fact, the company is absolutely liable in damages and all signers of the registration statement, together with all directors of the issuer, the CEO, the CFO, the underwriters, and the various experts (including accountants and attorneys) whose opinions are incorporated in the registration statement are liable in damages unless they demonstrate that they exercised *due diligence* or reasonably relied on another to do so depending on the circumstances. Under § 12, one who sells securities by means of a false prospectus is liable for rescission or damages.

b. Under federal law those who prepare and sign a registration statement represent not only that they believe the registration statement to be correct but also that they have conducted an investigation into the facts (that is, they have exercised *due diligence*) and that the registration statement contains all *material information* (that is, information that would be important to a reasonably investor in deciding whether to invest).

    Caveat: The 1933 Act requires the registration of public *offerings* as opposed to securities. All public offerings by an issuer, underwriter, or dealer are subject to registration. An *underwriter* is someone who distributes securities. A *dealer* is someone who is in the business of buying and selling securities. The term *issuer* has been construed to include both the corporation (or other entity) that issues securities and any one who controls the issuer, a *controlling person.* Thus, a controlling stockholder who seeks to resell a substantial block of stock may be required to register the offering even though the stock to be sold was originally issued in a registered offering, because the controlling person is deemed to be the issuer. An offering by a stockholder is called a *secondary offering* whereas an offering by the issuer is called a *primary offering*. Many registered offerings include shares to be sold by both the issuing company and one or more stockholders. *Escott v. BarChris Const. Corp.*, 283 F. Supp. 643 (S.D.N.Y. 1968); *SEC v. National Student Marketing Corp.*, 457 F.Supp. 682 (D.D.C.1978)

2. Exemptions From Registration Requirement

There are several exemptions from the registration requirement. The two primary exemptions are known as Regulation A and Regulation D. Roughly speaking, Regulation A focuses on small offerings, whereas Regulation D focuses on private offerings. There are several other more specialized exemptions, as well as several open-ended statutory exemptions.

a.   SEC Regulation A exempts offerings of up to $5,000,000 that comply with a simplified registration scheme. Under Regulation A, an issuer may *test the waters* by distributing a written document to prospective issuers to determine whether there is investor interest in the contemplated offering without fear that the document will itself be deemed to constitute an offer.

b.   SEC Regulation D sets forth the primary exemptions from registration for private offerings. It contains three discrete parts, together with accompanying definitions, terms, and conditions. Regulation D is often used in connection with the *private placement* of securities with large institutional investors.

• Rule 504 exempts sales of up to $1,000,000 in any one year if the offer is registered under state law and that law requires delivery of a disclosure document.

• Rule 505 exempts sales of up to $5,000,000 in any one year to a maximum 35 accredited investors. No general solicitation or advertising may be used. Under Rule 505, there is no limit on the number of accredited investors. Specified information about the issue must be given to all unaccredited investors.

• Rule 506 permits sales in unlimited amounts to accredited investors and to not more than 35 unaccredited investors. Each purchaser who is not an accredited investor must have such knowledge and experience in financial and business matters that the purchaser is capable of evaluating the merits and risks of the prospective investment. No general solicitation or general advertising may be used, and specified information must be delivered to each purchaser who is not an accredited investor. Rule 501(a) lists eight categories of accredited investors, including institutional investors, private business development companies, tax exempt organizations, directors, executive officers or general partners of the issuer, large purchasers high net worth individuals and trusts, and entities owned by accredited investors.

Regulation D applies only to sales by issuers. It is not available to investors for purposes of resale. Securities sold under Rule 505 and 506 are *restricted*. They may not be resold by the purchaser except pursuant to an exemption permitting their sale. Regulation D is a *safe harbor* rule, in that it sets forth the conditions that the SEC views as sufficient to qualify for various statutory exemptions (as well as establishing other exemptions). The statutory exemptions remain available, but it is relatively uncommon for issuers to rely on them when a safe harbor rule is available.

c. Section 4(2) of the Securities Act of 1933, exempts transactions by an issuer not involving any public offering. Offerings not complying with Regulation D may nevertheless be exempt under § 4(2) if they meet the tests established by case law for the availability of the exemption. The test is not dependent on the number of offerees. Rather, the basic requirement is that all offerees must have sufficient access and sophistication so that they do not need the protection of the act. *SEC v. Ralston Purina Co.*, 346 U.S. 119, 73 S.Ct. 981 (1953).

   Caveat: Regulation D relates to *purchasers* of securities whereas the § 4(2) exemption requires *offerees* to meet the requirements of access and sophistication.

d. Section 4(6) of the Securities Act, added in 1980, exempts offerings or sales solely to one or more accredited investors if the aggregate amount does not exceed $5 million and there is no advertising or public solicitation. Most offerings exempt under this section are also exempt under Regulation D, but there are a number of technical differences.

e. Section 3(a)(11) of the Securities Act exempts securities which are part of an issue offered and sold only to persons resident within a single state where the issuer is incorporated and doing business in that state.

> *Caveat:*   This so-called intrastate exemption is narrowly construed under case law and SEC Rule 146. A single offer to a nonresident destroys the availability of the exemption.

f.   Rule 701 provides an exemption for specified offers of securities by an employer to employees as compensation or pursuant to employment contracts. Securities issued may not exceed the lesser of 15 percent of the employer's assets or $5,000,000 and must be made subject to limitations on resale.

> *Caveat:*   Rule 701 is applicable to employers that are not registered under the Securities Exchange of 1934. For companies that are registered under the 1934 Act, a simplified registration process on Form S–8 is available to register securities to be issued to employees.

3. Restrictions on Transfer of Unregistered Securities

In order to ensure that buyers of exempt securities are the ultimate investors and do not buy with a view toward further distribution, SEC regulations require restrictions to be imposed on resale of securities sold pursuant to many exemptions. Securities that must be made subject to such restrictions are called *restricted securities*. The restrictions are noted by a *legend* on certificates issued pursuant to the exemption, and *stop transfer* orders are issued to the issuer's transfer agent to prevent unauthorized transfers.

a.   Rule 144 permits limited resales of restricted securities after one year and unlimited sales by unaffiliated investors after two years if the company is registered under the 1934 Act for purposes of continuous reporting. The term *affiliate* includes directors, officers, controlling stockholders, employees, and agents of the issuer or of a controlling or related entity and family members of those persons.

b.   Rule 144A permits unlimited resales of restricted securities to *qualified institutional buyers*, often referred to as *QIBs*.

4. What Constitutes a Security

The question whether a specific scheme or economic arrangement constitutes a security under federal or state law is an issue that is often litigated.

a.   The term *security* includes investment contracts and other instruments that evidence a financial investment. The term *investment contract* has been construed to include any contract, transaction, or scheme by which a person invests money in a common enterprise with the expectation that profits will be derived primarily from the efforts of others. A scheme may involve a security even if the investor is required to exert some individual effort.

Example: An owner of a citrus grove sells land in units consisting of a row of trees. The original owner usually enters into a contract with the investor purchasing the unit by which the owner agrees to provide services such as cultivation, pruning, insect control, and protection from freezing. The owner also usually harvests and markets the crop, dividing the proceeds with the investors purchasing the units. The units constitute securities even though an investor theoretically might cultivate and harvest his own row of trees on his own and use or sell the crop as he sees fit. *S.E.C. v. W.J. Howey Co.*, 328 U.S. 293, 66 S.Ct. 1100 (1946).

Example: Golf club memberships, condominiums, scotch whiskey receipts, chain letters, pyramid schemes, fractional royalty interests, earthworm farms, commodity options, and other schemes have been held to constitute securities in some circumstances. Because such investment schemes are almost never registered as securities, these cases make unlawful the public sale of most such schemes.

b. In *Landreth Timber Co. v. Landreth*, 471 U.S. 681, 105 S.Ct. 2297 (1985), the Supreme Court rejected the *sale of a business doctrine* and held that the sale of all or a majority of the shares of a closely held corporation constituted the sale of a security subject to the federal securities acts. Even though a controlling interest in a business arguably does not meet the *Howey* test, the Court held that common stock was plainly within the class of instruments Congress intended to include within the category of securities. The holding in cases such as *Landreth* is of importance primarily because it makes available the protections of federal antifraud provisions to all sales of closely held shares (assuming that the facilities of interstate commerce are used) even where the purchaser intends to acquire control of a business rather than to make a passive investment.

c. In *Reves v. Ernst & Young*, 494 U.S. 56, 110 S.Ct. 945 (1990), the Court held that a promissory note is presumptively a security, but that the presumption may be rebutted by a showing that the transaction in which the note was issued was not of a type normally used for raising capital, and that the note was not an instrument likely to give rise to trading for speculation or investment by the general public. The court also considered the expectation of the trading public as to whether the note in question was within the coverage of the securities acts, and whether other regulatory schemes provide protection to the investing public similar to that provided by the securities acts.

5. State Blue Sky Laws

Most state blue sky statutes roughly parallel the federal securities acts. Many states have adopted the Uniform Securities Act in whole or part.

a. Some state statutes do not require registration of issues sold within the state but only contain antifraud provisions or provisions requiring the registration of securities professionals. Many state securities statutes apply to the provision of financial services beyond those involving securities.

b. The definition of security under many state statutes is broader than that under federal law.

c. Some states impose substantive standards over and above the full disclosure philosophy of the federal law. These *merit review* states permit distributions to be registered and sold in the state only if the terms are *fair, just, and equitable.*

d. The National Securities Markets Improvements Act of 1996 (NSMIA) preempts many aspects of these blue sky statutes.

M. DIVIDENDS AND DISTRIBUTIONS

Traditionally, the word *dividend* refers to a payment to stockholders out of current or past undistributed earnings that is distributed in proportion to the number of shares owned. In other words, traditionally a dividend is a periodic or special payment out of earnings made by a corporation in some specified amount per share—a *pro rata* payment to stockholders. In some cases, a dividend may also be paid out of capital. In other words, a corporation may make a distribution to stockholders even though the corporation has no earnings. Such a distribution amounts in effect to a return of capital to the stockholders. Typically, dividends and distributions are discretionary with the board of directors. A dividend may be paid in the form of cash or property or even a promise to pay cash or property in the future—a distribution of indebtedness. In other words, a dividend may take the form of a distribution of just about anything of value. In addition, a stockholder may receive cash or property from a corporation in connection with the repurchase or redemption of shares. Such payments are not usually pro rata. But a pro rata repurchase of shares is economically equivalent to a dividend. Thus, the MBCA uses the word *distribution* to refer to both dividends and repurchases. And the rules relating to distributions are more or less unified in MBCA 6.40. In contrast, many state statutes, particularly those in par value jurisdictions, contain two separate provisions that deal with dividends and repurchases respectively. In the MBCA, the word *dividend* is used primarily in connection with *stock dividends,* that is, distributions of additional stock to existing stockholders. Although stock dividends are similar in form to cash and property dividends, stock dividends do not involve the distribution of property by the corporation. In other words, a stock dividend is usually a *paper transaction* in which the primary effect is simply to increase the number of shares outstanding. Thus, stock dividends are typically regulated by a separate provision. *See* MBCA 6.23.

Caveat: The terminology in this area is not precise. The words dividend and distribution are used more or less interchangeably. For example, a liquidating distribution following dissolution of a corporation may be referred to as a liquidating dividend even though the payment constitutes a return of capital. Similarly, a return of capital may be called a dividend or a *capital distribution,* or a *distribution in partial liquidation,* or by other names that may or may not indicate that they are distributions of capital, not distributions of earnings.

Example: A corporation announces that it has ceased paying dividends and probably will not resume dividends for at least five years in order to accumulate funds for expansion and modernization. Although some stockholders may have relied on the corporation's dividend policy in buying their shares, and although the change in the policy may be motivated by the financial needs of the controlling stockholder, dividend policy is almost always protected by the business judgment rule. *See Sinclair Oil Corporation v. Levien,* 280 A.2d 717 (Del. 1971); *Berwald v. Mission Development Co.,* 185 A.2d 480 (Del.1962). *But see Dodge v. Ford Motor Company,* 170 N.W. 668 (Mich. 1919) (requiring payment of dividend where the company retained cash well in excess of its foreseeable needs).

1. Dividend Policies in Publicly Held Corporations

Publicly held corporations generally adopt stable dividend policies that permit regular periodic distributions even though corporate income fluctuates. Changes in dividend payment rates by publicly held corporations are, not made lightly. They tend to reflect only important and usually permanent changes in the profitability of the business. An action to compel the payment of a dividend is rarely successful in a publicly held corporation because the payment of dividends is a matter of business judgment and thus within the discretion of the board of directors. *Sinclair Oil Corp. v. Levien*, 280 A.2d 717 (Del.1971). But it is clear that a court has the power to order that a dividend be paid in an appropriate case.

Example: A publicly held corporation announces a regular dividend of $0.25 per quarter. This rate will most likely be maintained despite fluctuations in earnings. In the event of a temporary decline in earnings, the regular dividend may be omitted for one or two quarters and then resumed consistent with the general philosophy of preserving a stable dividend policy.

Example: In the prior situation, the corporation suffers a loss in one year but continues to pay the regular dividend of $0.25 per quarter. If the corporation has accumulated undistributed earnings from earlier years, the payment is a dividend out of those earlier years' accumulated earnings for tax and accounting purposes.

Example: If excess cash accumulates, the corporation may declare a special or extra dividend of perhaps $1.50 per share. A special dividend carries with it no promise that anything more than the regular dividend will be paid in the future.

Caveat: Miller and Modigliani have shown that (with significant simplifying assumptions) the value of a corporation's common shares is independent of the dividend policy adopted by the corporation. Under these assumptions, the retention of corporate earnings increases the market value of the corporation's common shares by precisely the amount the payment of a dividend would have reduced that value.

2. Dividend Policies in Closely Held Corporations

In a closely held corporation dividend policies are heavily influenced by the tax status of the corporation. The disadvantage of dividends in C corporations is that they lead to double taxation. Corporate income is subject to the corporate income tax and amounts paid in dividends to stockholders are subject to tax a second time when the dividends are included in the individual stockholders' tax returns (albeit at the relatively low rate of 15%).

a. In a C Corporation, the payment of dividends carries a higher tax cost than the payment of the same amount in the form of salaries, rents, interest, or other payments that are deductible by the corporation. If the entire potential income of the corporation can be distributed to stockholders in the form of payments that are deductible by the corporation, the taxable income of the corporation can be *zeroed out* and the corporation will pay no income tax.

Caveat: The IRS may challenge payments in the form of salary, rent, *etc.* if the amounts are unreasonable, that is, in excess of amounts paid by comparable businesses for similar goods and services. *See Hatt v. CIR*, 457 F.2d 499 (7th Cir. 1972). If the challenge is successful, the payments may be recharacterized in whole or part as dividends which may entail the payment of interest and penalties in addition to the tax owed.

Caveat: It was common in the past for a corporation to retain cash so as to increase the value of shares which could then be sold by the stockholder at a gain with the gain taxed at the lower rates applicable to capital gains. In 2003, the same tax rate was made applicable to dividends and to capital gains. There is no longer a tax advantage in holding shares while the corporation retains cash. But it may be advantageous to do so for other reasons: (a) timing, (b) because the capital gains tax applies only to the increase in value of shares over the cost basis of the shares, or (c) because upon death heirs receive shares with a stepped-up basis equal to their fair market value and may thus avoid all taxes on the increase (other than estate taxes that may be paid by the decedent's estate).

Caveat: Under IRC § 1202, capital gains on small business stock obtained directly from the corporation and held for at least five years are taxed at half of the otherwise applicable rate (up to a total of $50 million).

Caveat: Retention and bailout strategies depend on the ability of the stockholder to sell shares. If the shares are repurchased by the corporation, the payment may be recharacterized as a dividend under IRC § 302.

Caveat: The Internal Revenue Code contains a penalty tax applicable to corporations that unreasonably accumulate surplus. IRC § 531 imposes the penalty tax on accumulations that exceed the reasonable needs of the business but a minimum accumulation of $250,000 is permitted in any case.

b.   In a corporation that has elected S Corporation treatment, all corporate income is directly taxed to the stockholders, whether or not distributed, so that payment of dividends has no effect on the aggregate tax bill.

Caveat: Because stockholders must pay income tax on S Corporation earnings allocated to them, whether or not distributed, it is customary in S Corporations to make sufficient distributions to cover income tax liability.

Caveat: S Corporation treatment differs from true partnership tax treatment in several technical respects. For example, an S Corporation pays tax on any gain from the sale of corporate assets, whereas a partnership never pays income tax at the partnership level. Partnership tax treatment is more advantageous than S Corporation treatment.

c.   The distribution of corporate income in the form of salaries, rent, etc. in order to zero out corporate income may give rise to internal dispute because some stockholders may receive larger payments than others and the payments may bear no relationship to relative shareholdings. Excluded stockholders may prefer distributions in the form of dividends despite the additional tax cost.

Example: Virtually all corporate income is used to pay salaries to officers and employees who are either stockholders connected with the management or family members of such stockholders. Some stockholders are excluded entirely from management and receive nothing with respect to their shares. As a result, the favored stockholders benefit from substantially the entire corporate income.

d.   In the context of a closely held corporation, the courts have ordered dividends to be paid in many cases if the plaintiff has been able to show (i) the availability of surplus cash not needed in the corporate business and (ii) affirmative indications of bad faith on the part of management.

Dodge v. Ford Motor Co., 170 N.W. 668 (Mich.1919); *Miller v. Magline,* Inc., 256 N.W.2d 761 (Mich.App.1977); *Keough v. St. Paul Milk Co.,* 285 N.W. 809 (Minn.1939).

Example: Excessive compensation to insiders may be an indication of bad faith. A corporation pays bonuses to four of its employees who constitute the original incorporators but not to one person who later became an employee and a stockholder. The bonuses are computed on the basis of the excess earnings of the corporation and without a review of the employment performance of any of the employees. The bonuses are disguised dividends and are not pro rata. As a result the stockholder who did not receive a dividend may recover his pro rata share. *Murphy v. Country House, Inc.,* 349 N.W.2d 289 (Minn.App.1984).

Example: The corporation may adopt a no dividend policy in an effort to soften up minority stockholders and persuade them to sell their shares at a low price either to the corporation or to other stockholders. This tactic may be particularly effective in an S Corporation in which minority stockholders must pay tax on their share of corporate income even though they receive no cash from the corporation. Such *freeze out* tactics may lead to litigation seeking the payment of a dividend or a mandatory buy-out at a judicially determined price. *White v. Perkins,* 213 Va. 129, 189 S.E.2d 315 (1972). *See also Giannotti v. Hamway,* 239 Va. 14, 387 S.E.2d 725 (1990).

e. Language in articles of incorporation may be construed as requiring the mandatory payment of dividends, particularly on preferred stock. *Crocker v. Waltham Watch Co.,* 53 N.E.2d 230 (Mass.1944); *New England Trust Co. v. Penobscot Chemical Fibre Co.,* 50 A.2d 188 (Me.1946); *Arizona Western Insurance Co. v. L.L. Constantin & Co.,* 247 F.2d 388 (3d Cir.1957). *But see L.L. Constantin & Co. v. R.P. Holding Corp.,* 153 A.2d 378 (N.J.Super.Ch.Div. 1959).

3. Legal Restrictions on Dividends and Distributions

State statutes impose widely varying tests for the legality of dividends and distributions. The tests differ depending on whether the state retains the par value system and the related concepts of *stated capital* and *capital surplus* or rather has eliminated the par value system as under the MBCA. Even among states that retain the par value system in whole or part, the tests may differ significantly in detail.

a. MBCA 6.40 imposes two tests to determine whether a distribution may be lawfully made: (1) an *equity insolvency test* that requires the corporation to be able to pay its debts as they become due in the ordinary course of business after giving effect to the distribution, and (2) a *balance sheet test* that prohibits a distribution if, after giving it effect, the corporation's total assets would be less than the sum of its total liabilities plus (unless the articles of incorporation provide otherwise) the amount that would be needed to satisfy preferential liquidation rights of senior classes of shares.

Caveat: The requirement under MBCA 6.40 that net assets be sufficient to cover liquidation preferences on shares senior to those receiving the distribution is somewhat similar to a requirement that stated capital be preserved with respect to senior shares.

Caveat: The word *insolvent* and its variations may be used in two ways. In corporation law, the word refers to the *equity sense* described above. This is a dynamic concept that may be likened to a *cash flow* test. The word *insolvent* may also be used to mean that liabilities exceed assets on the balance sheet. This is usually called *insolvency in the bankruptcy sense.* Generally speaking, accountants use the word *insolvent* in the bankruptcy sense. In other words, when an accountant says that a company is insolvent, the accountant typically means that the company would fail the balance sheet test.

Caveat: A corporation may easily pass one of these tests but not the other. For example, a distiller of scotch whiskey may have assets in the form of inventory well in excess of liabilities, but because its scotch may not be sold for eight or twelve years or longer it has no way of paying its bills as they come due. Similarly, an airliner manufacturer may have booked profitable contracts for sales and may show a surplus on its balance sheet because of hefty accounts receivable, but may not receive any of the cash for these contracts for months or years. In contrast, a retail business that sells all of its goods on consignment, may have virtually no assets but still be very profitable. It may therefore be able to borrow money to hire more employees and may have liabilities in excess of assets, but still be quite confident of being able to pay all of its bills on time.

b. All states apply some form of equity insolvency test for distributions. The equity insolvency test is the only test under Massachusetts law. Other states combine the insolvency test with some form of balance sheet test. In states that continue to follow the par value system, the balance sheet test requires reference to the various capital accounts that make up stockholder equity. In effect, the capital accounts created under the par value system control the extent to which distributions of capital may be made in these states.

> *Caveat:* The various tests for dividends may be partly a matter of statutory law and partly a matter of case law. For example, there is no express statutory requirement of solvency under Delaware law.

c. A few states continue to follow the 1969 MBCA and permit dividends to be paid only out of *earned surplus,* a term that is defined as the sum of net accumulations of income from all earlier periods reduced by dividends paid in earlier years and similar items. The theory of the earned surplus test is to permit dividends to be paid from earnings but not from contributed capital. These states usually also permit distributions out of *capital surplus* or other surplus accounts (subject to certain limitations) but not from *stated capital.* For example, the corporation may be required to identify distributions other than those from earned surplus so that the stockholders will know that the distribution does not necessarily indicate that the corporation has been profitable. Some statutes refer to such a dividend as a *partial liquidation.*

d. Some state statutes permit dividends or distributions that do not *impair capital.* Generally these statutes permit dividends to be paid as long as assets exceed liabilities plus stated capital. These states may be called *simple surplus jurisdictions* in that a dividend may be paid out of any form of surplus. Delaware and New York are such jurisdictions.

> *Caveat:* Statutes that permit dividends only out of earned surplus but also permit distributions from capital surplus or other surplus accounts come out at about the same place as statutes that broadly permit all dividends or distributions that do not impair capital.

e. Some state statutes may not fit neatly into the above classification. For example, California requires assets to be equal to 125 percent or more of liabilities after giving effect to a dividend.

f. Under the par value system, there are several well recognized wrinkles in the general rules that may affect the dividend-paying capacity of a corporation depending on the language of the specific statute.

- Many statutes permit a so-called *nimble dividend* to be paid out of current earnings (or earnings from the immediately preceding year) even though a deficit exists from prior years. *United States v. Riely,* 169 F.2d 542 (4th Cir.1948); *Goodnow v. American Writing Paper Co.,* 69 A. 1014 (N.J.Err. & App.1908); *Morris v. Standard Gas & Electric Co.,* 63 A.2d 577 (Del.Ch.1949).

- In most jurisdictions, a company that is engaged in exploiting natural resources (*wasting assets*) may pay dividends to the extent of accumulated depletion.

- In most jurisdictions, dividends may be paid out of *reduction surplus* created by the reduction of stated capital by amendment to the articles of incorporation or by the retirement and cancellation of shares.

- A *quasi reorganization* is essentially a bookkeeping entry by which a deficit in earned surplus is eliminated by the transfer of capital surplus to earned surplus. Future earnings are thereafter available for the payment of dividends without requiring that they be first applied against any deficit in earned surplus.

- In some jurisdictions, a dividend may be paid out of *revaluation surplus* created by a *write up* in the value of appreciated assets. *Randall v. Bailey,* 23 N.Y.S.2d 173 (1940); *Dominguez Land Corp. v. Daugherty,* 238 P. 697 (Cal.1925).

- Surplus may also be created by recognizing and placing a value on goodwill or other intangible assets not previously shown in the corporation's books. The use of such surplus for distributions has been permitted in some cases. *See Klang v. Smith's Food & Drug Centers, Inc.,* 702 A.2d 150 (Del. 1997).

Caveat: These various concepts are not recognized in all states. Most of these concepts have no applicability in states that have adopted statutes like the 1984 MBCA that eliminate the par value system and the legal capital accounts. But the MBCA does retain a balance sheet test. Thus, there may be situations even under the MBCA in which a corporation seeks to revalue assets in order to create dividend paying capacity.

Caveat: Dividends are not in fact paid out of equity accounts. A company may have substantial surplus but no cash with which to pay dividends. For example, if a company has used all available free cash flow to reinvest in additional inventory or other assets, it may be rendered insolvent by paying a cash dividend—which is why there is also an insolvency test. Thus, to say that a dividend is paid out of earned surplus (for example), is merely a short hand way of saying that the company has sufficient earned surplus to cover the dividend.

Caveat: The ability to create artificial capital surplus by writing up assets or transmuting stated capital into capital surplus by amending articles of incorporation to reduce the par value of outstanding shares makes it relatively easy for a corporation to adjust its accounts to permit any distribution consistent with the insolvency test.

4. Contractual Restrictions on Dividends and Distributions

Because state statutes provide few practical restrictions on distributions and therefore little or no protection for creditors, creditors often impose contractual restrictions on dividends and distributions in loan agreements.

Example: ABC Company plans to borrow $15,000,000 from Perpetual Life Insurance Company by issuing bonds in a private placement. Perpetual Life declines to make the loan unless ABC Corporation agrees to the following limitations on dividends and distributions: (a) ABC Corporation may pay a regular dividend of 25 cents per share per quarter if its annual income in the preceding year is $5,000,000 or more; (b) ABC Corporation may pay an extra or special dividend not to exceed $1.00 per share if its net earnings exceed $25,000,000 and not to exceed $2.00 per share if its earnings exceed $50,000,000 in the preceding year; (c) no other dividend or distribution or redemption or reacquisition of shares by ABC Corporation may be made without the prior written approval of Perpetual Life; and (d) earnings shall be determined in accordance with generally accepted accounting principles as determined by independent auditors.

N. REDEMPTIONS AND REPURCHASES OF OUTSTANDING SHARES

A corporation may repurchase its own shares by negotiating with a stockholder. A redemption of shares by a corporation is a reacquisition that occurs pursuant to the terms of the shares themselves, with the redemption price established by, or in the manner specified by, the articles of incorporation. Redemptions are usually at the option of the issuer but may also be at the option of the holder. A redemption or repurchase by a corporation has the same economic effect as a dividend or distribution in that it constitutes a transfer of property to stockholders.

Caveat: The IRC uses the term *redemption* to refer to all transactions by which a corporation reacquires its own shares.

1.   Relationship Between Repurchases and Distributions

When a corporation repurchases or redeems some of its own shares, the assets of the corporation are reduced by the purchase price of the shares. But such shares do not constitute an asset in the hands of the corporation. Such shares are akin to authorized but unissued shares (and are so treated under the MBCA). A redemption or repurchase of its own shares by a corporation is thus similar to a dividend in that it constitutes a gratuitous transfer of cash to one or more stockholders in exchange for their shares. Indeed, a pro rata redemption or repurchase has the same economic effect as a dividend.

Example: A, B, and C are the sole stockholders of ABC Corporation. Each own 100 shares. They decide that each will sell 10 shares back to the corporation for $100 per share, or a total of $1,000 each. When the sale is completed, each stockholder continues to own one-third of the outstanding shares (90 shares each) and the corporation is $3,000 poorer. The stockholders each have $1,000 and shares presumably worth $9000.

Caveat: Under IRC § 302, a *pro rata* repurchase is taxed as if the entire amount paid out is a dividend to the extent of a corporations earnings and profits.

a.   The MBCA uses the term *distribution* to refer to all transfers of cash or property in respect of shares. MBCA 1.40(6). The legal restrictions applicable to dividends are also generally applicable to share repurchases or redemptions. MBCA 6.40. Thus, as with dividends, redemptions and repurchases are subject to a balance sheet test and a solvency test.

b.   Under the MBCA (1969), dividends were treated under a separate section (§ 45) from repurchases (§ 6) and redemptions (§ 66). Each section included a balance sheet test and a solvency test albeit with slight variations. Many states continue to follow this pattern.

c. Unlike a distribution, a redemption or repurchase may affect the voting power of the remaining shares.

Example: In the preceding example, C decides to retire, and ABC Corporation agrees to repurchase all of her shares for $10,000 in total. The repurchase increases the voting power of A and B from 33 1/3 percent each to 50 percent each, and the corporation is $10,000 poorer. The increase in voting power of A and B as a result of the purchase of shares from C may be viewed as an indirect dividend to A and B. The same economic result could have been reached if the transaction had been structured as a purchase of shares by A and B from C followed by a cash dividend to A and B. The IRS has asserted this theory, in an effort to improve tax on the constructive dividend, but the theory has been rejected by the courts.

2. Repurchases of Shares by Publicly Held Corporations

Share repurchases may occur in publicly held corporations for several reasons and by several methods.

a. A corporation may redeem redeemable shares if the terms of redemption are attractive. Or the corporation may repurchase the shares of a particular stockholder by agreement.

Example: A corporation has redeemable preferred stock outstanding that pays a dividend of 8 percent. The corporation can borrow funds at 5 percent to buy back the stock. The corporation will likely redeem the preferred stock if permissible under the terms of the stock as set forth in the articles of incorporation. The redemption will increase the value of the common stock by reducing payout to senior security holders (from 8 percent to 5 percent). Preferred stockholders will not be happy about the redemption, because they probably will not be able to reinvest the funds they receive at as high a rate of return as paid by the redeemed stock. It is common, however, when issuing preferred stock for a corporation to provide that the stock may only be redeemed at a premium. In addition, it is common for preferred stock to be convertible into common stock at some specified ratio if the preferred stock is called for redemption. If the stock is called for redemption because interest rates have fallen since the stock was issued, then it is likely that the common stock will have increased in value and that conversion may be attractive (and preferable) alternative to redemption for the preferred stockholder.

Example: A corporation issues shares in connection with a merger. The former controlling stockholder of the acquired corporation becomes a major stockholder of the acquiring corporation and sits on its board of directors. He finds that he disagrees with the policies of the acquiring corporation and begins to criticize publicly the acquiring corporation. In order to eliminate this area of contention, the corporation agrees to buy back his shares at a premium. *See Grobow v. Perot,* 591 A.2d 194 (Del. 1991).

Example: A hostile bidder acquires ten percent of the shares of a target corporation. The target corporation agrees to buy back the bidder's shares at a price 50 percent above the market price (which has already risen sharply in reaction to news of a possible takeover) in exchange for an agreement that the bidder will refrain from buying additional shares and will vote the shares acquired as target management instructs. This strategy is called *greenmail* (presumably because of its analogy to blackmail). The agreement itself is called a *standstill agreement.*

Caveat: Repurchases by agreement are often effected at a *premium,* that is, at a price that is higher than the prevailing market price at the time of the repurchase. Such transactions often trigger lawsuits by the remaining stockholders who claim either that the payment of the premium constitutes waste of corporate assets or that the premium is paid primarily for the personal benefit of the board of directors in seeking to maintain control over the corporation (or both). The board of directors typically responds that the payment is necessary because the acquirer threatens to change existing business policies which the board believes to be optimal or that the acquirer intends in some way to loot the corporation by extracting benefits from it to the detriment of remaining stockholders after obtaining control. *See Cheff v. Mathes,* 199 A.2d 548 (Del.1964).

Caveat: Many states have enacted takeover statutes that require a hostile bidder to disgorge greenmail payments or that preclude a hostile bidder who acquires a specified percentage of shares from voting those shares. In the latter situation, it may be difficult for the target board to argue credibly that a repurchase was justified in order to prevent an undesirable change in business policy. There is case law that holds that the recipient of a greenmail payment may be required to hold the payment in trust (and presumably return it to the corporation) if the recipient knows that the payment constitutes a breach of fiduciary duty by the corporation. *See Heckmann v. Ahmanson,* 168 Cal.App. 3d 119 (1985). In addition, IRC § 162 prohibits the paying corporation from deducting any portion of the payment as a business expense, and IRC § 5881 imposes a 50 percent excise tax on the recipient's income from greenmail (in addition to any tax otherwise due).

b. A corporation may engage in open market repurchases as an alternative to paying dividends if the corporation has no better internal use for the funds or if the board of directors believes that the prevailing market price is attractive. Both of these justifications are usually problematic.

Example: Although a repurchase program is generally viewed as good news by investors because it tends to support stock price, it may also be seen as bad news if the market expects the company to grow through internal expansion. The use of cash by the corporation to purchase shares may indicate that the corporation has been unable to find attractive new investment opportunities.

Example: A company may know that its shares are underpriced in the market because it has favorable inside information that it has not released into the market. A repurchase of shares by the corporation from the market in such circumstances may constitute illegal insider trading on the part of the company. If a repurchase of shares by the issuing corporation is intended to either stabilize or increase the share price, the corporation may also be charged with illegal stock price manipulation. But SEC provides a safe harbor for such open market repurchases by setting forth terms and conditions under which they can be effected. Under Rule 10b–18, an open market repurchase program may be announced publicly or may be implemented without public notice. If the program is announced publicly, and the share price improves significantly, and the corporation decides not to purchase the shares, it may be argued that the announcement was manipulative, but the corporation may argue that repurchases are no longer desirable.

Caveat: Some commentators have argued that an unannounced repurchase program constitutes a violation of fiduciary duty to selling stockholders because the existence of the repurchase program constitutes material information. The implications of the ECMH are also unclear in this area. If the market is in fact efficient, it may be difficult to credit management assertions that the market price is too low. On the other hand, if one assumes that shares react to forces of supply and demand, one would expect repurchase to increase price by reducing supply.

c. A corporation may repurchase shares in order to limit dilution created by the issuance of shares pursuant to stock options or conversion rights.

d. A corporation may announce a public offer to repurchase its own shares. Such an offer is called a *self tender offer.* A self tender offer is often made at a range of prices slightly above the prevailing market price, with the ultimate price dependent on how many shares are offered to the corporation at various prices. Such an offer is called a *Dutch Auction.*

e. A self tender offer may also be undertaken as a defense to a hostile takeover bid. *See Unocal Corporation v. Mesa Petroleum Co.,* 493 A.2d 946 (Del.1985). By purchasing shares from its own stockholders, a target corporation may be able to reduce the number of shares available for a hostile bidder to purchase (sometimes called the *public float)* and at the same time increase the relative voting power of controlling stockholders or those who may have agreed to support management. On the other hand, by purchasing its own shares, the target corporation also increases the relative voting power of a hostile bidder.

Caveat: As with third-party tender offers, self tender offers are subject to regulation under federal securities law. For example, although the Delaware court in *Unocal* upheld a self tender offer made to all the stockholders other than the hostile bidder, the SEC subsequently adopted Exchange Act Rule 14d–10, requiring that such tender offers be open to all stockholders.

Caveat: There is no settled definition of what constitutes a tender offer. Thus, where a corporation in reaction to a hostile third-party tender offer announced that it would buy back shares at the prevailing market price (without placing a time or quantity limit on the offer), the transaction was found not to be a tender offer and therefore not subject to federal regulation. *See SEC v. Carter Hawley Hale Stores, Inc.* 760 F.2d 945 (9th Cir. 1985). *See also Hanson Trust PLC v. SCM Corp.,* 774 F.2d 47 (2nd Cir. 1985).

f.   A self tender offer may be used when a corporation seeks to buy back enough shares to reduce the number of stockholders below some specified number.

Example: By reducing the number of stockholders to 75 or fewer, the corporation may become eligible to elect S Corporation status.

Example: A corporation can *go private* by reducing the number of stockholders to fewer than 300, whereupon the corporation will no longer be required to remain registered with the SEC as a public company and may thus escape reporting requirements and regulations and the expenses that go with them. *See Kaufman v. Lawrence,* 386 F.Supp. 12 (S.D.N.Y. 1974). A going private transaction is often done in two steps: first a self tender offer and second a merger with a *shell corporation* owned by those who plan to continue to be stockholders of the successor private corporation. By acquiring most of the shares in a voluntary tender offer, the corporation avoids the possibility that those shares will dissent from the transaction and seek judicial appraisal.

Caveat: The SEC has adopted rules requiring extensive disclosures in connection with such *going private* transactions.

g.   There are a few situations in which a corporation is permitted (or even required) to reacquire its own shares even though the corporation does not meet the statutory tests for making a distribution. In many states a corporation may repurchase fractional shares for cash. Fractional shares may be created by a *reverse stock split*. For example, one new share may be issued for every 10,000 shares outstanding. All holders of less than 10,000 shares end up owning a fractional share of the corporation, and in most states those fractional shares may be bought back by the corporation. *See* MBCA 6.04. A reverse stock split may be undertaken as a way of going private by creating fractional shares that the corporation must purchase at a specified fair price.

h.   Every state provides a right of dissent and appraisal for stockholders who object to the terms of a merger (and in some cases, other transactions). *See* MBCA 13.02. Under these statutes, a stockholder may be entitled to have his or her shares be purchased at fair value by the corporation. Generally, the requirement that the corporation repurchase a dissenting stockholder's shares is not subject to statutory limitations on distributions.

Caveat: Although the MBCA and many states have largely eliminated appraisal rights for publicly traded corporations, such rights are retained for going private transactions and reverse share splits.

3.   Repurchases of Shares by Closely Held Corporations

Because there is no public market for shares in a closely held corporation, a stockholder who wishes to sell shares has only limited options. Usually the only potential buyers are other stockholders or the corporation itself. In a closely held corporation, repurchase of shares by the corporation may serve several purposes, including retirement of a stockholder from active employment, the cash-out of a stockholder who has agreed to a limited term investment, or the resolution of disagreements about business policy among stockholders. One of the most common disagreements relates to whether the corporation will pay dividends or reinvest available cash to grow the business. If the corporation has elected S Corporation status, the failure to pay dividends may create a financial hardship for stockholders who must nonetheless pay tax on their share of corporate income. In some cases, controlling stockholders may cause the corporation to withhold dividends in order to force minority stockholders to sell their shares to the corporation at a bargain price.

a.   It is important in most settings for stockholders in a closely held corporation to enter into an agreement governing the purchase and sale of shares. Such an agreement is usually called a *buy-sell agreement*. A buy-sell agreement may be incorporated in the articles of incorporation, or in the bylaws, or set forth in a separate contract among the stockholders. (A stockholder agreement may also cover many other matters including election of directors and officers, dividend policy, etc.) Most buy-sell agreements address restrictions on transfer by stockholders, circumstances under which the corporation or the stockholder may compel repurchase of shares by the corporation, and valuation.

> *Caveat:*   A buy-sell agreement is subject to statutory restrictions on distributions.

b. Many states have statutes that permit stockholders in closely held corporations to seek judicial dissolution on the grounds that fellow stockholders have engaged in oppressive conduct. *See* MBCA 4.34. In a case in which dissolution is sought, the corporation or the non-petitioning stockholders may have the right to redeem the shares of the petitioning stockholder.

> *Caveat:*   If the shares are the subject of a buy/sell agreement, the stockholder may be required to sell the shares either to the corporation or the remaining stockholders pursuant to the terms of that agreement.

c. By definition, there is no public market price by which the fairness or reasonableness of repurchase prices for minority shares in a closely held corporation can be judged. Thus, both buy/sell agreements and judicial dissolution may require valuation of the company or its shares—which can be expensive, time-consuming, and subject to widely varying opinions—unless the parties have agreed in advance on a valuation formula or method.

d. If several stockholders plan to remain involved with the corporation and one stockholder desires to sell his shares, the purchase of those shares by any other single stockholder will affect the relative voting power of all the remaining stockholders. Thus, repurchase by the corporation is usually preferable to purchase by a remaining stockholder, because it preserves the balance of power among the remaining stockholders. Repurchase by the corporation also solves the problems that may arise if some stockholders find it difficult or impossible to raise the funds to purchase their pro rata part of the shares.

e. The corporation may acquire life insurance policies on the lives of its stockholders to have funds available to acquire their shares upon their deaths. The premiums may be deductible by the corporation.

f. Repurchases by the corporation may be made on an installment basis over a period of years with the stockholder accepting a promissory note of the corporation for part of the purchase price. The payment of the purchase price by the corporation over time may allow the corporation to pay for the shares out of future cash flow.

4. Statutory Restrictions on Repurchases

In order for a corporation to repurchase its own shares, the corporation must meet essentially the same tests that would be applicable to a dividend or distribution of the amount of the purchase price. In par value states the corporation must have available earned surplus or capital surplus to cover the repurchase, and the corporation must not be rendered insolvent by the transaction. In some states, repurchases may be made on the basis of available capital surplus, whereas ordinary dividends may be paid without stockholder approval only on the basis of earned surplus. MBCA 6.40 applies the same balance sheet and solvency test to all distributions, including both dividends and repurchases.

5. Repurchase by Promissory Note

If the corporation repurchases shares in part by issuing a promissory note to the selling stockholder, the statutory tests may be applied in either of two ways: (i) once, at the time of the note is issued, or (ii) repeatedly, at the time of each payment on the note. It is common in connection with such a repurchase over time for the selling stockholder to negotiate for some sort of security interest in connection with the note.

a. Early case law generally tested the validity of each payment separately. *In re Trimble Co.*, 339 F.2d 838 (3d Cir.1964); *Robinson v. Wangemann*, 75 F.2d 756 (5th Cir.1935).

> *Caveat:* It is unclear that such an obligation is a true debt and can be secured by a valid security interest. The obligation is more akin to preferred stock with a mandatory dividend and redemption provision.

b. MBCA 6.40(e) and some cases take the position that the tests should be applied only once, at the time of the original purchase. *Mountain State Steel Foundries, Inc. v. C.I.R.*, 284 F.2d 737 (4th Cir.1960) (holding that a promissory note covered by earned surplus when it came due was enforceable even if not covered by earned surplus at the time it was issued); *Williams v. Nevelow*, 513 S.W.2d 535 (Tex.1974); *Neimark v. Mel Kramer Sales, Inc.*, 306 N.W.2d 278 (Wis.App.1981). Under the MBCA a promissory note representing the purchase price of shares has the same status as any other ordinary corporate obligation if there is sufficient surplus to cover the note at the time it is issued.

c.   The rationale for the rule adopted by the MBCA is that the corporation might obtain a loan from a third party and use the proceeds to repurchase the shares. Such a loan would typically be on parity with other creditors. The same should arguably be true of a loan made by the selling stockholder. The opposing theory is that the selling stockholder knows that each payment on the notes is essentially a distribution by the corporation and should be evaluated as though it were a distribution.

Caveat: If the corporation ends up in bankruptcy, it is not uncommon for unsecured creditors to challenge a secured third party obligation on the theory that the lender knew or should have known that the proceeds of the loan were to be used to buy back shares and that the corporation would be rendered insolvent as a result. When such a challenge succeeds, the result is usually that the security interest is nullified and the claim of the lender is subordinated to those of other creditors.

d.   California apparently takes an intermediate position and invalidates the note if there is not available earned surplus at the time of payment but allows a lien securing the note to be enforced. *Matter of National Tile & Terrazzo Co., Inc.*, 537 F.2d 329 (9th Cir.1976).

e.   Arguably, these same issues arise with regard to any distribution of indebtedness by a corporation to its stockholders, but no statutes expressly address the issue outside the context of repurchase debt.

f.   Contractual obligations by the corporation to repurchase shares at fixed prices are enforceable despite the potential unfairness to the selling stockholder or to other stockholders.

Example: A corporation's president persuades an investor to purchase shares of the corporation by promising that the corporation will repurchase them at cost at any time. The purchase price of the shares is $45 per share. This promise is enforceable even though the value of the shares thereafter drops to $15 per share. *Grace Securities Corp. v. Roberts*, 164 S.E. 700 (Va.1932).

g. If remaining stockholders have agreed to contribute additional funds to the corporation to enable it to purchase shares consistent with legal capital requirements, the courts have ordered specific performance if the remaining stockholders are able to make the necessary contributions. *Neimark v. Mel Kramer Sales, Inc.*, 306 N.W.2d 278 (Wis.App.1981).

6. Status of Reacquired Shares

Under the MBCA, reacquired shares become authorized but unissued shares. If the articles of incorporation prohibit the reissue of reacquired shares, reacquired shares are cancelled, and the number of authorized shares is reduced. In par value states, reacquired shares become treasury shares and remain on the balance sheet as issued but not outstanding shares. Surplus in an amount equal to the repurchase amount is restricted from use to back up other distributions. When treasury shares are cancelled, the stated capital attributable to those shares is also cancelled together with enough surplus to equal the amount for which the shares were reacquired. Any further restriction on the use of surplus with respect to the cancelled shares is removed.

7. Redeemable Shares in General

State statutes expressly permit corporations to issue preferred shares that are redeemable by the corporation upon terms set forth in the articles of incorporation.

a. In some states common shares may not be made redeemable at all or may be made redeemable only if there exists another class of common shares that is not redeemable. *See Lewis v. H.P. Hood & Sons, Inc.*, 121 N.E.2d 850 (Mass.1954).

b. MBCA § 6.01 permits redeemable common shares without limitation or restriction.

Caveat: Under the MBCA, after incorporation is complete there must be at all times at least one share outstanding with plenary voting rights and one share outstanding with residual financial rights. The same share may fulfill both requirements.

c. If redeemable shares have voting power, the redemption may affect control of the corporation. Such redemptions, however, have been permitted if made in good faith. *Hendricks v. Mill Engineering & Supply Co.*, 413 P.2d 811 (Wash.1966).

d. Some commentators have argued that redeemable voting shares should be prohibited as a matter of public policy because of their potential to be used coercively.

e. Many states prohibit the repurchase of redeemable shares at a price higher than the redemption price.

f. The corporation may purchase redeemable shares from individual stockholders at a negotiated price below the redemption price without necessarily triggering the redemption obligation. *Snyder v. Memco Engineering & Mfg. Co.*, 257 N.Y.S.2d 213 (App.Div. 1965).

8. Redemptions at Option of Stockholder

The MBCA and the statutes of many states permit shares to be made redeemable at the option of the stockholder. In some states the statutes are silent on this question. Presumably, such rights are permitted if not specifically prohibited. Such shares are sometimes called *put-able* shares because they give the stockholder the power to compel the issuer to repurchase the shares at a designated price. Shares that are redeemable by the corporation are *callable* in the sense that the corporation has a call option that permits it to require the holder of the shares to sell them to the corporation at a designated price. These features may also be incorporated into debt securities.

> *Caveat:* Redemptions may involve third parties and forms of consideration other than cash. For example, a corporation may issue *exchangeable bonds* (or debentures) that can be exchanged for shares or debt securities of an unrelated corporation. Typically, the corporation holds the exchangeable shares for investment.

a. Such shares have many of the characteristics of debt. Nevertheless, distributions in respect of such shares must be consistent with the applicable balance sheet and solvency tests. Payments in respect of debt are mandatory in the sense that they must be made as agreed irrespective of operating results with two possible exceptions: (i) agreement by the debtholder to defer payment or (ii) a declaration of bankruptcy by the corporation. Accounting rules require that putable shares be listed on the balance sheet in a special category of quasi-liabilities falling between true liabilities and equity.

b.   Putable shares may be more attractive than debt if the investor is a corporation entitled to the dividend received deduction under federal tax law.

9. Fiduciary Duties in Connection With Repurchases of Shares

Case law in most jurisdictions holds that controlling stockholders in a closely held corporation are subject to a strong fiduciary duty to minority stockholders when repurchasing shares. The leading case is *Donahue v. Rodd Electrotype Co. of New England, Inc.*, 328 N.E.2d 505 (Mass.1975), in which shares owned by the retiring CEO (and father) of the controlling stockholder were redeemed by the corporation. No similar offer was made to the minority stockholders, although the corporation had offered on earlier occasions to buy back shares owned by the minority at significantly lower prices. The court held this conduct violated the fiduciary duty that majority stockholders owe to the minority. Subsequent cases have followed this holding. *See Estate of Meller v. Adolf Meller Co.*, 554 A.2d 648 (R.I.1989); *Sundberg v. Abbott*, 423 N.W.2d 686 (Minn.App.1988); *Balvik v. Sylvester*, 411 N.W.2d 383 (N.D.1987). *But see Toner v. Baltimore Envelope Co.*, 498 A.2d 642 (Md.1985), where the court rejected a *per se* rule that selective repurchase was improper and held that an examination of all relevant facts was necessary. *See also* Nixon v. Blackwell, 626 A.2d 1366, 1376 (Del. 1993).

a.   The holding in *Donahue* is premised on the fact that the corporation is closely held. The primary feature of a closely held corporation is the lack of a public market for shares, a feature that requires stockholders to rely on the good faith of controlling stockholders for access to the financial return of the business. Some commentators have likened the *Donahue* rule to a *reverse preemptive right*.

b.   *Donahue* holds that the controlling stockholder owes a duty of good faith and loyalty directly to other stockholders. This duty permits an aggrieved stockholder to maintain a direct action against a fellow stockholder and does not limit his remedies to a derivative action on behalf of the corporation seeking to compel the return of the distribution to the corporation.

c.   The *Donahue* rule has been modified by subsequent case law in Massachusetts. *See Wilkes v. Springside Nursing Home, Inc.* 353 N.E.2d 657 (Mass.

1976)(founding stockholder is not necessarily entitled to continuing employment where the majority shows a business purpose for dismissal but aggrieved stockholder may show that tactics of majority exceeded business need); *Merola v. Exergen Corp.*, 648 N.E.2d 1301, 1305 (Mass.App. 1995)(an arrangement under which an employee is permitted to purchase shares subject to the condition that the shares may be sold back to the corporation upon termination of employment does not entitle the stockholder to continuing employment).

O. ILLEGAL DIVIDENDS OR DISTRIBUTIONS

Generally, a director is jointly and severally liable to the corporation for any amount distributed in excess of the amount that could legally be distributed if it is established that the director did not comply with the required standard of conduct. MBCA 8.33. Some case law holds stockholders who receive an illegal dividend or distribution must return it to the corporation if they know the distribution was unlawful when they received it. *Reilly v. Segert*, 201 N.E.2d 444 (Ill.1964). In contrast, MBCA 8.33 provides that a director is entitled to contribution from a stockholder who knowingly receives an illegal dividend.

1. Reliance by Directors

Directors who rely in good faith on officers, employees, board committees, or outside experts retained by the corporation (such as lawyers or accountants) in determining whether a distribution may be made, usually do not incur liability for an illegal dividend. MBCA 8.30, 8.33.

> *Caveat:* Under the MBCA and most state statutes, the board of directors may base the decision to pay a dividend on any reasonable accounting method. Thus, even though GAAP requires that assets be shown on the balance sheet at historical cost, the board of directors may choose to restate the balance sheet in terms of current value which may result in an increase in the balance sheet value of assets and may thus create dividend paying capacity.

2. Recovery by Creditors

Liability for illegal dividends or distributions generally run to the corporation rather than to individual creditors. *Schaefer v. DeChant*, 464 N.E.2d 583 (Ohio App.1983). Creditors may be able to force a defaulting corporation into bankruptcy or receivership in order to compel the corporation to recover illegal dividends or distributions for the benefit of creditors.

3. Settlement Payments

Courts have held that amounts distributed to stockholders in a self-tender offer or in a going private merger cannot be recovered from the recipients because such distributions are protected under § 546 of the Bankruptcy Code as settlement payments made through the securities clearing system. *See Kaiser Steel Corp. v. Charles Schwab & Co., Inc.*, 913 F.2d 846, 850 (10th Cir. 1990) (paying agents not personally liable); *Kaiser Steel Corporation v. Pearl Brewing Co.*, 952 F.2d 1230 (10th Cir. 1991) (recipients not liable). *But see Munford, Inc. v. Valuation Research Corp.*, 97 F.3d 456 (11th Cir. 1996) (directors liable). *Cf. C–T of Virginia, Inc. v. Barrett*, 958 F.2d 606 (4th Cir. 1992) (payment in connection with merger is not a distribution).

P. SHARE DIVIDENDS AND SHARE SPLITS

Unlike dividends or distributions that are payable in cash or property, a *share dividend* or *share split* does not dissipate corporate assets. Rather, the total number of shares is increased but corporate assets are neither increased nor decreased.

1. Definitions

The terms *share dividend* and *share split* (or *stock dividend* and *stock split*) connote subtly different transactions, but it is quite common even for sophisticated corporate lawyers to use the terms somewhat interchangeably.

a. In par value states, a share split differs from a share dividend. In a share split, the par value of each old share is divided among the new shares whereas in a share dividend the par value of each share is unchanged and the stated capital of the corporation is increased by the number of shares issued. MBCA 6.23 refers only to *share dividends* and does not address *share splits*.

b. The New York Stock Exchange defines a *stock dividend* as a distribution of less than 25 per cent of the outstanding shares (as calculated prior to the distribution). A *partial stock split* is defined as a distribution of 25 per cent or more but less than 100 per cent of the outstanding shares (as calculated prior to the distribution). And a *stock split* is defined as a distribution of 100 per cent or more of the outstanding shares (as calculated prior to the distribution).

c. A share dividend is usually described as a percentage increase in the number of shares while a share split is usually described in the form of a new-for-old ratio.

Example: A corporation declares a 6 per cent stock dividend. Each stockholder receives six shares for every 100 shares held. Fractional shares may be paid in cash or in the form of *scrip* which may be sold for cash. In par value states, funds must be transferred from earned surplus (or some other surplus account) to stated capital to reflect the increase in the number of outstanding shares. Thus, a corporation may be precluded from effecting a share dividend if it has too little surplus on the balance sheet. The MBCA imposes no balance sheet test on share dividends. The solvency test is irrelevant in this context.

Example: A corporation declares a 2 for 1 stock split. Each stockholder is issued two new shares for each old share held. In par value states, the par value of capital represented by each share is cut in half and as a result, the aggregate stated capital is not increased by the stock split. In many cases, such a stock split is in fact effected by a stock dividend, because a true stock split would require that the old shares be turned in for cancellation. If the transaction is effected by a stock dividend, however, an appropriate amount of surplus must be transferred to stated capital.

2.   Effect of Share Splits or Share Dividends on Market Prices

Market price after a share dividend or share split may be somewhat greater than one might expect simply from the mechanical adjustment for dilution. For example, following a two-for-one split shares often trade at more than half of the price of the old shares. Similarly, following a five percent share dividend, shares may continue to trade at the pre-dividend price even though one would expect the price to fall to about 95 percent of the pre-dividend price. Several explanations have been offered for these anomalies. A share dividend or share split may be viewed as a signal to the market that the corporation is doing well financially, because corporations often maintain a constant per share dividend even though the number of outstanding shares has been increased. Another plausible explanation is that investors prefer shares that trade in the $20 to $30 range because that range permits the purchase of round lots of 100 shares for a reasonable total investment. Shares that trade at lower prices may be viewed as risky because a relatively small decline in the price represents a larger loss on one's investment. Also, shares that trade for less than $5 per share usually may not be used as collateral for a loan. Thus, share dividends and share splits may be used by management as a signal that they believe that the share price is more likely to rise than to fall. Finally, some stockholders may choose to sell dividend shares as a way of rolling their own dividend and nonetheless maintaining an investment in a round lot of shares. This strategy was especially attractive when capital gains rates were lower than dividend rates, but it may still make sense in that it permits stockholders to choose whether to withdraw some cash and pay tax or let it ride, whereas a cash dividend visits a tax on all including those who would prefer to reinvest returns.

3. **Treatment of Share Dividends and Splits as Principal or Income**

    Share dividends and share splits have some characteristics of both income and principal. Litigation has arisen over the proper classification of such distributions in various contexts. The intention of the creator of the interest controls, if clearly expressed.

    a. A recurring question that arises in trusts or testamentary bequests is whether a share dividend should be awarded to the life tenant or to the remainderperson when the instrument is silent on the subject. One view is that share dividends should be classified as income and not principal if earnings are capitalized (on the corporation's books) to reflect the dividend. *In re Fosdick's Trust*, 176 N.Y.S.2d 966, 152 N.E.2d 228 (N.Y. 1958). A second view is that share dividends should be classified as income to the extent they are paid out of income that accrued subsequent to the creation of the life interest. This is referred to as the Pennsylvania rule. A third view is that share dividends should be treated as income up to an amount equal to six per cent of the principal each year. A fourth view is simply that share dividends should be treated as principal. This is referred to as the Massachusetts rule.

    b. A similar issue is whether a testamentary gift of a specified number of shares should be deemed to carry with it shares later received in a share split. Again, the intent of the testator ultimately controls. Was it intended to give a specified number of shares or a specified interest in the corporation? *Compare In re Marks' Estate*, 255 A.2d 512 (Pa.1969) *with In re Howe's Will*, 224 N.Y.S.2d 992 (App.Div.1962).

    c. Under federal tax law, share dividends are generally not regarded as income, but there are important exceptions to this rule. For example, a dividend of common stock paid on preferred stock constitutes taxable income to the extent of the value of the common shares. Moreover, where a stockholder has the option to receive either a cash dividend or a stock dividend, the stock dividend is taxable on the theory that the stockholder could have opted for the cash dividend and used the cash to buy the stock. See generally IRC § 305. A dividend of preferred stock on common is not taxable at the time of receipt but is taxed as if the entire value of the stock is a dividend at the time of sale. *See* IRC § 306.

d. The issue may also arise in community property states where dividends are typically viewed as community income irrespective of who brought the stock to the marital estate, but capital gains typically remain the property of the spouse who originally owned the shares.

e. Under GAAP, a stock dividend of 20 percent or less must be treated as an expense for income statement purposes, whereas a stock dividend of 25 percent or more is treated as a capital transaction. The amount in the middle is a matter of discretion for the accountant.

REVIEW QUESTIONS

5.1. How does a corporation obtain its capital?

5.2. What function does par value serve today?

5.3. Why doesn't the use of no par shares solve all problems of corporate capitalization?

5.4. True or False: Watered stock is a historical concept that has no practical importance today.

5.5. What does the MBCA do about par value?

5.6. In what sense is preferred stock preferred?

5.7. What is the difference between a bond and debenture?

5.8. True or False: In these days of inflation, Ben Franklin's old statement that the best corporation is a debt-free corporation is more true than ever.

5.9. True or False: So long as one offers shares to fewer than 35 persons, there can be no problem under the federal or state securities acts.

5.10. What are preemptive rights?

5.11. True or False: A corporation that eliminates preemptive rights may issue shares at any time in the future at any price the directors decide appropriate.

5.12. Why is a repurchase of outstanding shares by a corporation similar to a dividend?

5.13. True or False: Creditors should always impose restrictions on dividends by contract. The protection given creditors by the legal restrictions on making distributions or paying dividends by state corporation statutes are almost totally illusory.

5.14. True or False: A publicly held corporation decides to pay a dividend in the form of shares of stock rather than in the form of money. As a matter of economics, there is no significant difference in these two types of distributions.

5.15. Commerce, Inc. is incorporated in a state with a par value statute; it has a single class of shares listed on the New York Stock Exchange. It has recently engaged in an extensive mail-order sales campaign in order to stimulate its sagging economic fortunes. Commerce, Inc., although it had a large accumulated deficit in earned surplus from losses from prior years, declared and paid a dividend out of its net profits for last year. Commerce, Inc. was not insolvent at the time of the declaration or payment of the dividend. Commerce, Inc. now finds itself in deep financial trouble. Plagued by creditors and unable to meet presently due liabilities, it files a petition in bankruptcy. Its bankruptcy trustee sues both the directors and the stockholders of Commerce, Inc. who received the dividend. What are the potential liabilities of the directors who authorized the dividends and the stockholders who received them? Would it make any difference if Commerce, Inc. were incorporated in a state that has enacted the MBCA (1984)?

5.16. B owned a mining claim worth $100,000. She formed X corporation in a state with a par value statute and transferred to X the mining claim for shares having a par value of $250,000. The corporation became insolvent and R was appointed its receiver. R sued B for $150,000. May R recover? Explain your answer.

5.17. P entered into an agreement with D Corporation whereby P agreed to sell to D 150 shares of D's stock for $40,000. D Corporation was to pay the purchase price in installments of $1,000 every 3 months. At the time of the purchase D Corporation has sufficient surplus to make the purchase without impairing capital. After the corporation had paid $13,000 on the purchase price it became insolvent. Is P entitled to file a claim for $27,000 as a creditor in a subsequent bankruptcy?

5.18. X corporation has been in business for 10 years, has made substantial profits every year, and yet has never paid a dividend. In addition to its capital of

$2,000,000 it has accumulated $8,000,000 surplus without clear plans to expand its business. Of its $10,000,000 in assets, $2,000,000 is cash. Z, a stockholder, sues to have the court order the board of directors of X to declare a dividend. Should the order issue?

*

VI

Corporate Governance

A. THE STATUTORY SCHEME IN GENERAL

State corporation statutes provide for a standard distribution of the powers of management and control among the three tiers of a corporation: stockholders, directors and officers. But this scheme can be varied considerably in the articles of incorporation, the bylaws, and by stockholder agreement. The statutory scheme described here is an idealized model of corporate governance that does not accurately reflect the exercise of power in either large publicly held corporations (where shares may be owned by thousands of stockholders) or in a closely held corporation (with few stockholders). Moreover, there are many corporations that have some characteristics of both. The idealized statutory scheme may be a reasonable description of the allocation of power and control within such a corporation. The special problems of closely held and publicly held corporations is discussed in separate chapters.

1. Stockholders

The stockholders are generally regarded as the owners of a corporation. Nevertheless, the stockholders have only limited powers of management and control in the corporation, including:

a.   The power to elect directors.

b.   The power to remove (and replace) directors.

Caveat: At common law stockholders could remove directors only for cause, a term that implies dishonesty, misconduct, or incompetence. Hence, at common law directors could be removed and replaced only at an annual meeting. *Auer v. Dressel,* 118 N.E.2d 590 (N.Y.1954). Today, most statutes permit removal without cause. *Scott County Tobacco Warehouses, Inc. v. Harris,* 201 S.E.2d 780 (Va. 1974); *Campbell v. Loew's Inc.,* 134 A.2d 852 (Del.Ch.1957). *See* MBCA 8.08; DGCL 141(k). In most states, if the board of directors is classified (staggered) directors may be removed only for cause unless the articles of incorporation provide to the contrary.

c. The power to make recommendations to the board of directors about business and personnel matters. *Auer v. Dressel,* 118 N.E.2d 590 (N.Y.1954).

Caveat: SEC Rule 14a–8 requires publicly held (registered) corporations to submit certain proposals to stockholders. Otherwise, a stockholder probably cannot compel a proposal to be submitted to the stockholders for consideration. *Carter v. Portland General Electric Co.,* 362 P.2d 766 (Ore.1961).

d. The power to amend or repeal bylaws. MBCA 10.20.

Caveat: *Somers v. AAA Temporary Services, Inc.,* 284 N.E.2d 462 (Ill.App.1972), held that under the Illinois statute then in effect, the stockholders lose power to amend bylaws to the extent authority to do so is vested in the board of directors. In most states, stockholder power to amend bylaws is concurrent with the board of directors although it may be superior in some circumstances.

e. The power to approve fundamental corporate changes as proposed by the board of directors, including amendments to articles of incorporation (MBCA 10.03), mergers, consolidations or share exchanges with other corporations (MBCA 11.03), sales of substantially all the assets of the corporation (MBCA 12.02), and dissolution (MBCA 14.02).

f. The power to inspect corporate books and records for proper purposes. MBCA 16.02.

g. The power to elect (or ratify the appointment of) the corporate auditor (in corporations subject to SEC regulation).

h. The power maintain a derivative action on behalf of the corporation subject to numerous substantive and procedural restrictions.

i. Standing to attend and participate in a meeting of the stockholders (either in person or by proxy).

> *Caveat:*   The stockholders may reserve greater powers in the articles of incorporation or in some cases in the bylaws. Those powers may also be subject to a stockholder agreement. *See* MBCA 7.32. In most jurisdictions, such a reservation of powers to the stockholders is limited to corporations that are not publicly traded. Some state statutes authorize the stockholders rather than the directors to establish the consideration for which shares are to be issued if the power to do so is reserved to the stockholders by the articles of incorporation. *See* MBCA 6.21(a). As a practical matter, this option is almost never exercised, and that function is performed by the board of directors.

2. Directors

The role of directors is specified by statute. The board of directors is entrusted with the power of management of the business and affairs of the corporation. *Continental Securities Co. v. Belmont,* 99 N.E. 138 (N.Y.1912). The board may delegate authority to make many decisions to officers or agents. Individual directors are not agents or representatives of stockholders. Rather, they are *members* of the board of directors. They may act only as a board or as a committee of the board appointed by the board. The corporation acts by action of the board of directors. The role of directors is discussed in more detail in a separate chapter.

a. More traditional statutes provide that powers of the corporation *shall be exercised by* and the business and affairs of a corporation *shall be managed by* the board of directors. This description may reflect the role of the board of directors in some small closely held corporations in which day to day management by the board of directors is feasible. In a closely held corporation, directors are usually substantial stockholders and principal officers. But typically they act informally without clearly designating in which capacity they act.

b. In many states, statutory language has been modified to state that the powers of the corporation may be *exercised by or under authority of* and its business and affairs may be *managed by or under the direction of* the board of directors. *See* MBCA 8.01; DGCL 141(a). This broader language reflects the role of the board of directors in a publicly held corporation where control and management is largely entrusted to professional managers. In a publicly held corporation most directors are not officers of the corporation and neither the officers nor the directors typically owns a controlling interest in the stock of the corporation.

c. The board of directors selects the corporate officers and has the power to remove them. The board also may employ employees or agents, or create new officers and employ persons to fill them. It is customary for boards of directors to delegate the power of employing lower level employees and agents to the corporate officers.

d. Certain corporate decisions, such as determining the amount that should be distributed as dividends to stockholders, must be made by the board directors and may not be delegated to officers or a committee of the board.

e. The directors are not agents of the stockholders and may not be compelled to approve transactions merely because a majority or even all the stockholders approve them. *Continental Securities Co. v. Belmont*, 99 N.E. 138 (N.Y.1912). The sole remedy of the majority stockholders in this situation is to elect different directors.

> *Example:* A, owner of a majority of the shares of a corporation, desires that the corporation buy a piece of land. The directors decline. *A* cannot compel the directors to do so but may elect more compliant directors at the next election of directors and resubmit the proposal then. *Automatic Self–Cleansing Filter Syndicate Co., Ltd. v. Cuninghame*, 2 Ch. 34 (Ct.App. Eng. 1906).

3. Officers

Officers of the corporation have a limited statutory role. They carry out the policies and decisions of the board of directors. They are not themselves formulators of policy. The role of officers is discussed in more detail in a separate chapter.

a. Officers have limited ministerial authority to bind the corporation. For example, the secretary of the corporation typically has the power to certify that the board has adopted a resolution. This power is not broadly construed.

b.   In most corporations, the actual role and discretion of officers is greater than contemplated by the statutory scheme.

B.   STOCKHOLDER MEETINGS & VOTING

The rules with respect to stockholder meetings are rather straight forward. There is a considerable degree of uniformity from state to state in these statutory requirements.

1.   Annual Meetings

Annual meetings are required to be held for the purpose of electing directors and conducting other business. The time and place of the annual meeting may be specified in or fixed in accordance with the bylaws. The failure to hold an annual meeting does not affect the validity or continued existence of the corporation. The failure to hold an annual meeting does not affect the incumbency of sitting directors. MBCA 7.01.

2.   Special Meetings

All meetings other than the annual meeting are special meetings. Special meetings may be called by the board of directors, and under many state statutes by the President, the holders of a specified number of shares (often 10 percent), and other persons named in the bylaws. MBCA 7.02.

3.   Notice

Stockholders who are entitled to vote must be given written notice of annual or special meetings as provided in the statute or in the bylaws. Many statutes require 10 to 50 days notice. MBCA 7.05 requires 10 to 60 days notice.

a.   The purposes of a special meeting must be stated in the notice and the business to be conducted at the meeting is limited to what is specified in the notice. MBCA 7.02(d). No purpose needs to be specified for an annual meeting, and any business may be conducted at such a meeting.

b.   Notice may be waived by a written document executed before, at, or after the meeting in question. MBCA 7.06.

c.   In the absence of statute or SEC regulation, there is no common law requirement that matters not required to be considered by stockholders be noticed or submitted to a vote of stockholders. *Carter v. Portland General Electric Co.*, 362 P.2d 766 (Ore.1961).

C. QUORUM AND VOTING REQUIREMENTS

In order for action to be taken at a stockholders' meeting, there must be a quorum at the meeting and the action must be approved by the required percentage of the votes of stockholders.

1. Quorum Requirements

A quorum is typically a majority of the voting shares although some statutes allow the quorum to be reduced either without limitation or to a specified fraction (e.g. one third) by provision in the articles of incorporation. MBCA 7.25(a) permits the quorum requirement to be reduced without limitation.

> *Example:*   A quorum by statute consists of a majority of the voting shares. A corporation has 100 shares outstanding and 51 shares are represented at the meeting. A quorum is present and therefore a majority of those present—26 shares—may validly approve actions unless a greater percentage is required by the statute, articles of incorporation, or bylaws.

a.   Statutes permit the quorum requirement to be increased up to and including unanimity. Unanimity is a popular control device in closely held corporations because it assures minority participation. A unanimity requirement for a quorum enables any stockholder to prevent undesired action simply by refusing to attend the meeting. It thereby increases the likelihood of deadlock.

b.   Shares represented by proxy are deemed present for purposes of a quorum. *Duffy v. Loft, Inc.,* 151 A. 223 (Del.Ch.1930).

c.   The majority view is that if a quorum is once present, the meeting may continue even though a faction leaves the meeting in an effort to break the quorum. MBCA 7.25(b) codifies the majority view. *See Levisa Oil Corp. v. Quigley,* 234 S.E.2d 257 (Va.1977) (minority view).

2. Shares Entitled to Vote & Class Voting

All shares are entitled to vote one vote per share on any matter to be voted on by the stockholders unless the articles of incorporation specify that a class of shares shall have no voting rights. Generally, shares other than common shares are non-voting. A corporation may also issue non-voting common shares. But if the corporation has issued any shares, there must be outstanding at all times at least one common share with plenary voting rights. MBCA

§ 6.03. (Similarly, there must be outstanding at least one common share with residual financial rights.) Preferred shares are typically non-voting.

> *Caveat:* It must be specified in the articles of incorporation that a class or series of shares carry no voting rights. In the absence of specification, all shares are presumed to be voting shares.

a. Treasury shares and shares owned by a majority-owned subsidiary of the corporation are not eligible to vote under most state statutes. But if a corporation holds shares of its own stock in a fiduciary capacity (for example, in a pension plan), those shares may be voted. (Voting of shares in a pension plan may be subject to regulation under laws governing such plans, primarily ERISA). Shares called for redemption generally cannot vote. MBCA 7.21.

b. A class or series of nonvoting shares may be entitled to vote on specific matters that affect the rights of the class or series in ways specified by statute. Most state statutes refer to such voting as *class voting*. The MBCA uses the phrase *voting by voting groups* to describe the same concept. *See* MBCA 1.40(26). Where class voting on a specific matter is required, that matter is approved only if it receives the necessary affirmative votes from stockholders of that class as well as the necessary affirmative votes of all shares entitled to vote generally on matters coming before the meeting.

c. Under the MBCA only shares may vote. The statutes of some states permit corporations to grant voting power to bond or debenture holders. *See* DGCL 221. Authorization for non-stockholders to vote under these statutes must appear in the articles of incorporation.

3. Vote Required

The traditional rule is that the affirmative vote of a majority of the votes present at a meeting at which a quorum is present is necessary to adopt a measure.

a. The MBCA 7.25(c) changes the approval requirement from a simple majority to the votes cast favoring the action exceed the votes cast opposing the action. This change was designed to eliminate the treatment of abstentions as votes against the question.

> *Example:* A corporation has 100 common shares outstanding. A quorum consists of 51 shares. If 60 shares are represented

and the vote on a proposed action is 28 in favor, 23 opposed, and 9 abstaining, the action is not adopted under the traditional requirement because the affirmative vote by 28 shares is not a majority of the shares present. On the other hand, if the 9 abstaining shares were not present at all, the action would have been approved because 51 shares were present and 28 voted in favor of the proposal.

Example: In the previous example, under MBCA (1984) the proposal would be approved because the number voting in favor (28) exceeds the number opposed (23).

b. Many states and MBCA 7.28 establish a plurality vote requirement for the election of directors in order to take into account the possibility of three or more factions competing for directorships. Many states do not have a special rule for elections of directors.

Caveat: The MBCA phrases quorum and voting requirement in terms of voting groups in order to cover situations in which different classes of shares are entitled to vote separately on an issue. In most meetings, there is only one voting group, consisting of the common shares.

4. Supermajority Requirements

Statutes generally permit the quorum and voting requirements to be increased up to and including unanimity. *See* MBCA 7.27.

a. One case finding such an increase in voting or quorum requirements to be against public policy, *Benintendi v. Kenton Hotel*, 60 N.E.2d 829 (N.Y.1945), was promptly over-ruled by legislative enactment.

b. Supermajority requirements may be imposed in closely held corporations to ensure that a minority stockholder has a veto power over matters coming before the stockholders.

Example: An owner of 20 per cent of the outstanding shares may obtain a veto power by insisting that the articles of incorporation provide that a quorum consists of 90 per cent of the outstanding shares and that actions to be approved must be voted upon affirmatively by all stockholders present at a meeting at which a quorum is present.

Caveat: Supermajority provisions increase the prospect of a deadlock at the stockholders' level because any minority stockholder may be able to block action.

c. Supermajority requirements are also used as defensive weapons to protect publicly held corporations against unwanted takeover attempts. *See Centaur Partners IV v. National Intergroup, Inc.,* 582 A.2d 923 (Del.1990).

Example: A publicly held corporation amends its articles of incorporation to provide that if any person obtains a majority of the outstanding shares of a corporation without the approval of the board of directors, the voting requirement for all actions by the stockholders is increased to 70 percent. This provision deters takeovers because an outsider does not obtain voting control of the corporation unless he either obtains approval of the current board of directors or purchases at least 70 percent of the outstanding shares of the corporation.

d. Statutes often require a greater majority for fundamental corporate actions, including amendments to articles of incorporation, mergers, dissolution, and similar transactions. Until 1999, the MBCA required a majority of all outstanding shares. Some states require a higher percentage of votes (typically 2/3) and may permit nonvoting as well as voting shares to vote on such matters. The MBCA was amended in 1999 to permit mergers and other fundamental changes to be approved by the affirmative vote of a majority of the shares voted.

5. Action Without a Meeting

In lieu of a meeting, the stockholders may act by written consent signed by all the stockholders. MBCA 7.04. As a practical matter, the requirement of unanimity ensures that this procedure will be used only by corporations with relatively few stockholders.

6. Action by Majority Consent

Delaware and a few other states provide that a consent signed by the percentage of shares needed to approve a transaction is effective. DGCL 228. This majority consent procedure may be used in publicly held as well as closely held corporations and permits a purchaser of a majority of the shares of a publicly held corporation immediately to replace the board of directors and take control of the corporation.

Example: A corporation with 120,000 shares outstanding receives a consent signed by holders of 61,000 shares in a state with a majority consent procedure. The consent removes the current board of directors and replaces them with different individuals. The action is validly taken. No account is taken of the quorum requirement in this computation.

Caveat: Because of the effect of the majority consent procedure in takeover struggles, many Delaware corporations have sought to limit the use of the majority consent procedure by defining and limiting in their bylaws the manner in which the majority consent procedure operates. *Datapoint Corp. v. Plaza Securities Co.,* 496 A.2d 1031 (Del.1985); *Empire of Carolina, Inc. v. Deltona Corp.,* 514 A.2d 1091 (Del.1985); *Allen v. Prime Computer, Inc.,* 540 A.2d 417 (Del.1988).

7. Multiple or Fractional Votes Per Share

The traditional rule is one vote per share. A number of state statutes now permit multiple or fractional votes per share. In these states all computations including quorum counts must be based on aggregate votes rather than aggregate shares. MBCA 6.01, 7.21.

Example: Articles of incorporation provide that for purposes of determining a quorum, a stockholder has one vote for each share owned up to fifty shares and one vote for each twenty shares owned in excess of fifty shares, but no stockholder may cast more than one fourth of all the votes at a meeting (except as proxy for other stockholders). The provision, which prevents a single stockholder from constituting a quorum no matter what size his holdings, is valid under the DGCL. *Providence & Worcester Co. v. Baker,* 378 A.2d 121 (Del.1977).

a. Publicly held corporations with strong minority interests held by a single family often create classes of shares with multiple votes per share. Shares with multiple votes are then assigned to family members. Generally, these shares may be sold to third persons only after they are converted to shares with a single vote per share.

Example: A publicly held corporation has a board of directors of seven outside directors who collectively own less than one percent of the common shares and three family members who collectively own 12.6 percent of the common shares. Other family members, family trusts, and an employee benefit plan own over 40 percent of the remaining shares. Fearing takeover, the board recommends an amendment to the articles of incorporation providing that all shares owned at the time of the amendment would be reclassified so that they were entitled to 10 votes per share but any shares thereafter sold revert to a single vote per share until held by a new stockholder for 36 months. Transfers upon death, divorce, or gift do not trigger the reduction in voting power. The amendment is approved by the non-family directors and by 68 percent of the stockholders after full disclosure of its effects, but not by a majority of the non-family related stockholders. The plan is valid because it was approved by disinterested directors and fully informed stockholders. *Williams v. Geier*, 671 A.2d 1368 (Del.1996).

Caveat: The SEC adopted Rule 19c–4 designed to limit such voting rights recapitalizations but the rule was held to exceed the powers of the SEC because it did not relate to disclosure. *Business Roundtable v. SEC*, 905 F.2d 406 (D.C.Cir.1990). Although the rule was invalidated, the stock exchanges had already adopted implementing rules prohibiting the listing of any company that undertook a voting rights recapitalization. Those exchange rules remain in force and effectively prohibit such transactions among publicly traded companies.

8. Manipulation of Meeting Dates

Cases are divided on whether a court should intervene if those in control of a corporation manipulate the meeting date in order to make a proxy fight more difficult.

a. *Schnell v. Chris–Craft Industries, Inc.*, 285 A.2d 437 (Del.1971) holds that such manipulation may constitute a breach of fiduciary duty by those in control of the corporation. *See Stahl v. Apple Bancorp., Inc.*, 579 A.2d 1115 (Del.Ch.1990) (decision to defer meeting date and rescind record date when faced with threatened proxy fight and tender offer not a breach of duty when no proxies had been solicited and the place of meeting not yet established); *see also Alabama By–Products Corp. v. Neal*, 588 A.2d 255, 258 (Del.1991) (*Schnell* "should be reserved for those instances that threaten the fabric of the law or which by an improper manipulation of the law would deprive a person of a clear right.")

b. *In re Unexcelled, Inc.,* 281 N.Y.S.2d 173 (App.Div. 1967) permits such manipulation based on a literal reading of the applicable business corporation act.

D. AMENDMENTS TO THE ARTICLES OF INCORPORATION

Under the law of most states, the articles of incorporation may be freely amended by board resolution followed by stockholders ratification. In a few situations, the board of directors may amend the articles of incorporation without stockholder action. In most states, an amendment to the articles of incorporation must be approved by a majority of the stockholders eligible to vote. But under the MBCA as amended in 1999, a simple majority suffices. MBCA 10.03 (d). A few states continue to follow the traditional rule which requires a two-thirds majority. In most states, the articles of incorporation may be amended so as to include any provision that may be included in the articles of incorporation (AOI), or to eliminate any provision that may be omitted. MBCA 10.01. That is, the AOI may be amended to read in any way that would be legal if the corporation were being formed at the time of the amendment. In other words, the AOI does not create any *vested rights* that cannot be changed by subsequent amendment. As a general rule, only shares with voting rights may vote on an amendment to the AOI. But if the amendment would change the rights of a particular class of shares, that class may vote as a class on the amendment. In some states, an amendment of the AOI that changes certain fundamental stockholder rights, triggers appraisal rights for shares eligible to vote on the amendment. In 1999, the MBCA eliminated appraisal rights in most such situations.

1. Constitutional and Substantive Limitations

MBCA 10.01 states that a shareholder of the corporation does not have a vested property right resulting from any provision in the articles of incorporation, including provisions relating to management, control, capital structure, dividend entitlement, or purpose or duration of the corporation. Many state statutes contain similar provisions.

a. The argument that rights in the articles of incorporation are *vested rights* or *property rights* is basically a constitutional argument. In *Trustees of Dartmouth College v. Woodward,* 17 U.S. (4 Wheat.) 518 (1819), the Supreme Court held that a state could not adopt a statute that had the effect of amending previously issued articles of incorporation. But the Court also recognized that states might avoid this problem by a reservation of power to amend statutes applicable to all corporations created thereafter. Today, all states reserve the power to amend state law even if the amendment has the effect of changing fundamental stockholder rights. *Dentel v. Fidelity Sav. & Loan Ass'n*, 539 P.2d 649 (Ore.1975).

b. Nevertheless, some cases have adopted the view (on non-constitutional grounds) that certain provisions of articles of incorporation may not be altered by stockholder vote. In effect, these cases require unanimous agreement by the stockholders to amend the articles of incorporation in certain ways. *See Cowan v. Salt Lake Hardware Co.*, 221 P.2d 625 (Utah 1950). It is probable that most of these cases have been overruled by statutes similar to MBCA 10.01(b), but the doctrine may continue to have limited vitality in a few states.

c. One issue on which this theory was applied as late as the 1930s is whether arrearages of cumulative dividends on preferred stock may be eliminated by amendment to the articles of incorporation. *Keller v. Wilson & Co.*, 190 A. 115 (Del.1936). An amendment that runs afoul of the vested rights theory may nonetheless be valid if it is accomplished by merger of a corporation into a newly created and wholly owned subsidiary. *See Federal United Corporation v. Havender*, 11 A.2d 331 (Del. 1940); *Hottenstein v. York Ice Machinery Corp.*, 136 F.2d 944 (3d Cir. 1943); *Bove v. Community Hotel Corp. of Newport, R. I.*, 249 A.2d 89 (R.I.1969).

d. The requirement of unanimous consent for amendments to the AOI permits individual stockholders to block amendments unless they receive special consideration or payment. *See, e.g., Matteson v. Ziebarth*, 242 P.2d 1025 (Wash. 1952). Thus, in lieu of the vested rights theory, some courts have developed a broad equitable principle that an amendment may be challenged if it is not reasonable or in good faith or if it does not serve a valid business purpose. *Dentel v. Fidelity Sav. & Loan Ass'n*, 539 P.2d 649 (Or.1975). *See also Singer v. Magnavox Co.*, 380 A.2d 969 (Del. 1977) (freezeout merger on grounds that stockholders were entitled to maintain investment in shares in the absence of business purpose for merger). *But see Weinberger v. UOP, Inc.*, 457 A.2d 701 (Del. 1983) (overruling Singer on this point).

2. Procedural Requirements

State statutes relating to the amendment process vary widely. And most states permit amendments to be made in different ways.

a. In most states, the board of directors must initiate a proposal to amend the articles of incorporation. (In Delaware and a few other states, shareholders may act by majority written consent without preliminary action by the board of directors.) After proposal by the board of directors, the proposed amendments must be submitted to the shareholders for approval. Notice of the proposed amendment and a copy or summary thereof must be given to all shareholders (voting and nonvoting). MBCA 10.03(d).

b. MBCA requires approval by a simple majority of shares present and voting at a meeting of the stockholders. MBCA 10.03 Some states require a two-thirds vote of *outstanding* shares to approve an amendment. Other states require a majority of *outstanding* shares.

> *Caveat:* Prior to 1999, the MBCA provided for the right of dissent and appraisal in connection with certain amendments. Such amendments required approval by a majority of shares entitled to vote.

c. The board of directors, when it approves amendments to be presented to shareholders, may condition the submission on such terms as it desires, e.g., that the amendment be approved by each class of shares, voting as separate voting groups, even though not specifically required by statute.

d. Most states permit minor amendments to be made by the incorporators or initial directors before shares have been issued. MBCA 10.05. Many states also authorize the board of directors, acting alone, to adopt certain minor amendments. *See* MBCA 10.02 (authorizing amendment by the board of directors acting alone to extend the duration of the corporation if incorporated at a time when limited duration was required by law, to delete the names and addresses of the initial directors and the initial registered agent, to change each issued share of the only outstanding class of shares into a greater number of whole shares of the same class, to reduce the number of authorized shares to reflect the reacquisition of shares that may not be reissued, to eliminate classes of shares of which none are outstanding, and to make minor changes to the corporation's name). In addition, when the corporation issues shares with rights specified by the board of directors pursuant to blank check authority under MBCA 6.02, the AOI must be amended by the board of directors in effect to record the rights of the shares issued. Such an amendment is sometimes called a certificate of designation, but it nonetheless becomes part of the articles of incorporation.

e. The statutes of many states authorize amendments to articles of incorporation of corporations in bankruptcy or reorganization to be made by order of court without requiring approval of either shareholders or directors. MBCA 10.08.

f. After an amendment is approved, articles of amendment must be filed with the secretary of state. If an amendment makes a change in outstanding shares or rights of shareholders, or an exchange, reclassification or cancellation of shares or rights is to be made pursuant to the amendment, the articles of amendment must set forth the provisions necessary to effect the transaction. For example, it may be required that holders of reclassified shares surrender old shares before new shares may be issued. Such implementing provisions may appear in the articles of amendment rather than in the amendments themselves. MBCA 10.06.

g. A corporation that has filed several articles of amendments at various times may restate the articles of incorporation so as to create a unified document and eliminate superseded provisions. MBCA 10.07. Restated articles of incorporation that do not make any substantive change may be approved by the board of directors acting alone.

3. **Procedural Protections Against Abusive Amendments**

An amendment to the articles of incorporation may adversely affect the holders of one class of shares to the advantage of holders of another class. For example, an amendment to the articles of incorporation may eliminate the right of a class of preferred stock to cumulative dividends and may even do so retroactively.

a. The primary protection against abuse is the requirement that such an amendment be approved by the separate vote of any class of shares that would be adversely affected by the amendment or that would be affected in a specified way. The MBCA refers to this procedure as *voting by voting group*.

b. Under Delaware law, a class is entitled to vote as a class only if it would be adversely affected by the amendment. This can give rise to nice questions of whether a change constitutes an adverse change. *See Dalton v. American Investment Co.*, 490 A.2d 574 (Del.Ch. 1985).

c. Under MBCA 10.04, a class is entitled to vote as a separate group only if the amendment would: (1) effect an exchange or reclassification of all or part of the shares of the class into shares of another class; (2) effect an exchange or reclassification, or create the right of exchange, of all or part of the shares of another class into shares of the class; (3) change the rights, preferences, or limitations of all or part of the shares of the class; (4) change the shares of all or part of the class into a different number of shares of the same class; (5) create a new class of shares having rights or preferences with respect to distributions or to dissolution that are prior or superior to the shares of the class; (6) increase the rights, preferences, or number of authorized shares of any class that, after giving effect to the amendment, have rights or preferences with respect to distributions or to dissolution that are prior or superior to the shares of the class; (7) limit or deny an existing preemptive right of all or part of the shares of the class; or (8) cancel or otherwise affect rights to distributions that have accumulated but not yet been authorized on all or part of the shares of the class.

d. The underlying objective of class voting is to require voting by voting groups on all amendments that are uniquely burdensome to the voting group. *Levin v. Mississippi River Fuel Corp.*, 386 U.S. 162, 87 S.Ct. 927 (1967). The basic idea of voting by voting groups is that if a majority of a class of shares adversely affected by an amendment is willing to accept that amendment, it should be approved. For example, where an amendment is proposed that would eliminate dividend arrearages on a class of cumulative preferred stock by converting that stock into common stock constituting a majority of the common stock that would be outstanding if the merger is approved, the transaction may be seen as akin to a sale of control to the preferred as a class in exchange for giving the prospect of payment sometime in the future. *See Bove v. Community Hotel Corp. of Newport, R. I.*, 249 A.2d 89 (R.I.1969). Whether the transaction is fair or desirable may be a matter of differing opinion among the affected preferred stockholders. A majority vote in favor would seem to indicate that the tradeoff represents a gain for the affected class and should go forward. In other words, the requirement of a class vote may be a good substitute for a market based resolution.

e. Where a class of shares is specially affected by an amendment, a vote of that class is required even if shares are otherwise nonvoting shares. MBCA 10.04. Similarly, when two corporations merge and the non-surviving corporation has a class of nonvoting preferred stock outstanding, the preferred stock may usually vote as a class on the merger if its rights under the AOI of the surviving corporation would differ from its existing rights.

f.   Many statutes extend the right to vote by class only to classes of shares and not to series within a class. The theory is that the class of blank shares (out of which series are created) is itself a single class of shares. This theory is unrealistic as a practical matter since differences between series may be as great as or greater than differences between classes. MBCA 10.04 extends the right to vote by voting groups to classes or series that are affected in different ways but states that if an amendment affects two or more classes or series in essentially the same way, the classes or series vote as a single voting group on the amendment.

4.   Appraisal Rights

Many states provide for appraisal rights instead of the right to vote as a voting group on an amendment to the articles of incorporation. This right permits certain dissenting shareholders to have the value of their shares ascertained by judicial proceeding and paid to them in cash by the corporation. Prior to 1999, the MBCA provided for the right of dissent and appraisal with respect to "an amendment of the articles of incorporation that materially and adversely affects rights in respect of a dissenter's shares because it: (1) alters or abolishes a preferential right of the shares; (2) creates, alters, or abolishes a right in respect of redemption, including a provision respecting a sinking fund for the redemption or repurchase, of the shares; (3) alters or abolishes a preemptive right of the holder of the shares to acquire shares or other securities; (4) excludes or limits the right of the shares to vote on any matter, or to cumulate votes, other than a limitation by dilution through issuance of shares or other securities with similar voting rights; or (5) reduces the number of shares owned by the shareholder to a fraction of a share if the fractional share so created is to be acquired for cash".

E.   AMENDMENTS TO THE BYLAWS

In most jurisdictions, the bylaws of a corporation may be amended either by the board of directors or by the stockholders. In some jurisdictions, power to amend the bylaws may reside exclusively in the stockholders or the board of directors unless the articles of incorporation provide otherwise. Under the MBCA, the articles of incorporation may reserve the power to amend the bylaws, exclusively to the stockholders but not to the board of directors. MBCA 10.20. Moreover, the stockholders in adopting a bylaw may provide that it may not be amended by the board of directors.

Caveat: In this context, *amendment* refers to all changes to the bylaws, including amendment, repeal, and reinstatement of a bylaw provision.

a. Where the stockholders have the power to amend the bylaws, there is no need for an amendment to be proposed by the board of directors as there is with an amendment to the articles of incorporation. Thus, the stockholders may amend the bylaws by the solicitation of consents. Under the MBCA, however, the stockholders may not act outside a meeting except unanimously. Thus, the power to amend by consent is limited. There is no such limitation under Delaware law.

b. Under the MBCA, a stockholder-adopted bylaw that increases a quorum or voting requirement for the board of directors may be amended only by the stockholders unless the bylaw provides otherwise. (The bylaw may provide that it may be amended only by a specified vote of the stockholders or the board of directors.) A director-adopted bylaw that increases a quorum or voting requirement for the board of directors may be amended by the directors but only if the board of directors meets the same quorum and voting requirements specified in the bylaw. MBCA 10.21.

c. Although statutory law appears to permit amendments to the bylaws for virtually any purpose, the courts have limited the power of the board of directors and even the stockholders where they seek to exercise this power for purposes of entrenchment or unduly limiting the power of the board of directors to manage the corporation. *See Black v. Hollinger International, Inc.,* 872 A.2d 559 (Del.Supr. 2005); *Blasius v. Atlas Corp.,* 564 A.2d 651 (Del. Ch. 1988); *Schnell v. Chris–Craft Industries, Inc.,* 285 A.2d 437 (Del. 1971). *See also Carmody v. Toll Bros., Inc.,* 723 A.2d 1180 (Del. Ch. 1998); *Quickturn Design Systems, Inc. v. Mentor Graphics Corp.,* 721 A.2d 1281 (Del. 1998).

F. VOTING FOR DIRECTORS

Elections of directors may be by *straight voting* or *cumulative voting*. In a few states constitutional or statutory provisions mandate cumulative voting in all elections of directors. In most states a corporation may elect by appropriate provisions in its articles of incorporation whether or not to have cumulative voting. MBCA 7.28. Default rules vary by state. The default rule in most commercially important states is straight voting. In some states, cumulative voting is permitted (even if apparently mandated by the articles of incorporation) only if proxy materials state that the election will be so conducted or a stockholder notifies the corporation of intent to vote cumulatively at least 48 hours before the meeting. In elections for directors, all directors run at large and not for a particular seal. Thus, stockholders may not vote against a candidate except by voting in favor of other candidates.

1. Straight Voting

In straight voting, a stockholder may cast the number of votes equal to the number of shares held for candidates for each position to be filled on the board of directors.

> *Example:* Stockholder A with 30 voting shares in an election to fill three directorships may cast up to 30 votes for each of three candidates.

a. Under straight voting, stockholders holding a majority of the voting shares can always elect the entire board of directors.

b. Straight voting is simple and easy to understand. As a result, it is widely used in publicly held corporations.

2. Cumulative Voting

In cumulative voting, each stockholder determines the aggregate number of votes by multiplying the number of shares held by the number of positions to be filled. Each stockholder may cast that number of votes for one or more candidates. MBCA 7.28(a).

> *Example:* In the foregoing example, stockholder A may cast an aggregate of 90 votes because there are three positions to be filled. Under cumulative voting the stockholder may cast all 90 votes for a single candidate or divide them between two or more candidates.

a. Cumulative voting permits minority stockholders to elect one or more directors in certain circumstances.

> *Example:* In the foregoing example, if stockholder A votes all 90 votes for herself, she will be elected to the board unless three other candidates receive 91 or more votes each. If the other stockholders own a total of 85 shares, they cannot prevent her election. The other stockholders are entitled to cast a total of 255 votes (3 × 85) but that is not enough to give each of three candidates 91 votes each. They may give candidates X and Y 91 votes each, but they then have only 73 remaining votes to give to Z and hence cannot prevent the election of A as the third director.

b. The formula for determining the number of shares required to elect one director under cumulative voting is:

$$N = S / (D + 1) + 1$$

where N equals the required number of shares, S equals the total number of shares outstanding, and D equals the total number of directors standing for election. For example, if there are 1000 shares outstanding and four directors to be elected, the formula shows that the number of shares required to elect one director is (1000 / 5) + 1 or 201. The formula may be modified to determine the number of votes to be cast to assure the election of one director:

$$N = V / (D + 1) + 1$$

where V equals the total number of votes to be cast at the meeting: For example, if there are 1000 shares outstanding, there are 4000 total votes that may be cast in an election for four directors, and the formula shows that the number of votes required to elect a single director is (4000 / 5) + 1 or 801. Whether solving for shares or votes, the required number for the election of one director is a fraction of the total votes to be cast equal to 1 / (D + 1) plus one vote. Thus, if twelve directors are to be elected, the number of shares or votes required to assure the election of one particular person to the board of directors is 1/13 plus one vote.

3. Advantages and Disadvantages of Cumulative Voting

The primary advantage of cumulative voting is that it is more democratic in that it permits minority representation on the board. It also may permit the election of a watchdog director to oversee the majority's management of the corporation. The primary disadvantage is that it may increase partisanship on the board. Moreover, cumulative voting is complex and may be confusing to stockholders.

> *Example:* Bruce and Howard each own 12,500 shares of a family corporation. Bruce is the president and the active manager. The board of directors consists of three directors: Bruce, Howard, and Bruce's wife, Eva. In prior years, the board was elected by straight voting, but cumulative voting is required by the state statute provided that one stockholder announces in advance that he will vote cumulatively. The statute provides that directors are elected by a plurality of the vote. At the election, Howard announces that he plans to vote cumulatively, but Bruce does not change his voting strategy.

Bruce votes as follows:

Bruce	12,500 votes
Sarah	12,500 votes
Eva	12,500 votes

Howard votes as follows:

Howard	18,750 votes
Clara	18,750 votes

Howard and Clara are elected and now control the corporation. There is a three way tie for the third place on the board of directors and no third director is elected. *See Stancil v. Bruce Stancil Refrigeration, Inc.,* 344 S.E.2d 789 (N.C.App.1986).

Caveat: Under MBCA 8.05, directors serve until a successor is elected. Thus, Bruce and Eva may claim that they remain on the board.

a. Although the general rule is that a director may be removed without cause by a majority vote of the stockholders, most states limit the power to remove a director elected by cumulative voting to situations in which the vote to retain the director is insufficient to have elected him if the vote were cast in an election for directors in which cumulative voting was permitted. MBCA 8.08(c).

Example: In the earlier example above, stockholder A has elected one director with 30 shares (90 votes.) The stockholders with 85 shares have elected X and Y. The stockholders with 85 shares call a special meeting of stockholders to remove the minority director. On the removal motion, A casts her 30 shares against removal. Because that vote would have been enough to elect one director at an election of directors, the removal motion fails even though 85 shares were voted to remove the director.

b. The effects of cumulative voting can be minimized in several ways.

- In states where it is not mandatory, the stockholders may amend the articles of incorporation to eliminate cumulative voting. *Maddock v. Vorclone Corp.,* 147 A. 255 (Del.Ch.1929).

- The board of directors may be reduced in size to reduce the impact of cumulative voting.

- The work of the board may be delegated to a committee that does not have a minority-elected member.

- The board may be stage managed so that all important decisions are made through informal discussions that do not include the minority directors. The formal meeting thereafter may be entirely *pro forma* without discussion and conducted with a quick gavel.

  Caveat: A committee may not amend bylaws or approve or propose a resolution that requires stockholder action. MBCA § 8.25.

  Caveat: Such a procedure does not comply with the default requirement that the corporation be managed by or under the direction of the board of directors, and decisions made in such a backroom fashion may not be held to be valid action by the corporation.

4. Staggered Terms for Directors

Under many state statutes, if the board of directors consists of nine or more members, the board may be or *staggered* or *classified* so that members are elected for two or three year terms with one half or one third being elected each year. Under MBCA § 8.06 there is no minimum size board required. Even a board of three may be staggered so that each director serves a three year term. Some state statutes provide that a board of directors consisting of three or more members may be classified if cumulative voting is not permitted.

a. Usually the formal justification for classification is to ensure continuity of service on the board of directors. *Bohannan v. Corporation Com'n,* 313 P.2d 379 (Ariz.1957). The practical justification may be to minimize the effect of cumulative voting. *Stockholders Committee v. Erie Technological Products, Inc.,* 248 F.Supp. 380 (W.D.Pa.1965).

   Example: A publicly held corporation in a state in which cumulative voting is mandatory has 10,000,000 voting shares outstanding and a board of directors consisting of 17 members. If all members of the board are elected each year, a bloc of 555,556 shares is sufficient to elect one director. If the election is staggered so that six members are elected in each of two years and five are elected in the third year, it takes a bloc of 1,428,572 shares to elect a single director in a year in which six directors are to be elected. A dissident group might find that beyond its vote generating capacity.

b.   In the 1980s, staggered boards of directors removable only for cause became a popular defense against unwanted takeover attempts in publicly held corporations. These provisions prevent the purchasers of a majority of the shares through a cash tender offer from immediately replacing a majority of the board of directors.

> *Example:*   In the prior example, if directors cannot be removed without cause, a bidder who purchases more than 5,000,000 voting shares cannot elect a majority of the entire board of directors until at least two annual elections of directors have been held.

> *Caveat:*   One case, *Wolfson v. Avery,* 126 N.E.2d 701 (Ill.1955), invalidated a staggered board on the ground that it violated the right of cumulative voting granted at the time by the state constitution.

> *Caveat:*   One case, *Humphrys v. Winous Co.,* 133 N.E.2d 780 (Ohio 1956), upheld a staggered board that placed only a single director in each class.

G.   RECORD OWNERSHIP AND RECORD DATES

Eligibility to vote shares at a stockholders' meeting is determined by *record ownership* on a specified date called the *record date.*

1.   Record Ownership

Corporations traditionally issue share certificates in the name of each stockholder and the names and addresses of stockholders are recorded in the share register of the corporation. That person is called the record owner.

a.   A person who buys shares becomes a record owner by obtaining possession of the certificate (endorsed by the selling stockholder) and presenting the certificate to the corporation, which cancels the old certificate and issues a new certificate in the name of the purchaser. The purchaser thereby becomes the new record owner. The mechanics of share transfer are generally governed by UCC Article 8. Publicly held corporations usually retain a share transfer agent (often a commercial bank) to process transactions and maintain the share register. Most corporations do not issue a formal certificate for shares unless specifically requested. The common practice is to issue to the stockholder a written statement of the information required to be contained in the certificate. *See* MBCA 6.26.

b. Most stockholders in publicly held corporations leave their shares on deposit with a broker-dealer. And most broker-dealers leave their shares on deposit with a clearing house or share depository (usually the Depository Trust Corporation (DTC)) which officially registers the shares in the name of a nominee corporation (Cede & Company in the case of DTC). In most cases the clearing house or depository is the *record owner* of the shares and the individual stockholder is the *beneficial owner* or *equitable owner* of the shares. Such shares are usually described as being held in *street name*. Ownership of the shares can be transferred simply by a *book entry* in the records of the broker, the clearing house, or the depository. No delivery of certificates is required.

c. Under current practice, securities transactions settle on the third day after execution, a practice known as T + 3 *(trade plus three)*. If a customer places an order to buy or sell, payment or delivery of the certificate or documentation must occur no later than the third day after the trade. And the trade is posted in the customer account on that date. The book entry system permits much more efficient trading and transfer of shares. If an individual owner of shares keeps shares registered in his own name, the sale of the shares requires additional paper-work. The stockholder must endorse the certificates and deliver them to the broker-dealer (within three days). Shares held in book entry form may be bought and sold by a phone call. No physical signature and delivery of certificates is necessary. Moreover, the broker-dealer may lend shares left on deposit to traders who want to effect a short sale. Thus, broker-dealers strongly encourage their customers to keep shares on deposit in book entry form, and may even impose a fee for obtaining a share certificate on behalf of a customer.

Caveat: Technically, nominee ownership was first used by institutional investors to avoid complex rules about the transfer of securities by a fiduciary. The practice of registration in street name was somewhat different in that it involved endorsing share certificates so as to convert them into bearer instruments that could be traded by physical delivery. As trading volume increased, the practice of physical delivery became impractical and led to the so-called *back office crisis* in the 1960s. The result was that the securities industry developed the book entry system, which undoubtedly would have evolved anyway with the advent of computer technology. Nevertheless, shares continue to be registered formally in the name of a nominee corporation and that is usually called a street name.

2. Record Date for Voting

The identity of stockholders entitled to vote at a meeting is determined by the ownership of shares of the corporation on a specific date called the *record date*. The record date may be established by a provision in the bylaws or by designation by the board of directors (which may not set it more than 70 days before the meeting). If no record date is set, the record date is the day before the notice of meeting is delivered to stockholders of record. MBCA § 7.05. A similar record date system governs the payment of dividends.

a. Holders of shares transferred on the books of the corporation after the record date do not receive notice of the meeting and are not entitled to vote shares in their own name. The vote of the record owner is viewed by the corporation as the vote of those shares. *See Salgo v. Matthews*, 497 S.W.2d 620 (Tex.Civ.App.1973) (rules relating to record ownership are designed to simplify stockholder voting process and to minimize disputes).

b. In a few states, the corporation may also establish entitlement to vote by closing the transfer books on a specific date and refusing to recognize all subsequent transfers of shares until after the meeting. This procedure is seldom used today and has been eliminated as an option in the MBCA.

c. The beneficial owner of shares on the meeting date may compel the record owner to vote shares as the beneficial owner directs. This is usually done by the record owner granting a proxy to the beneficial owner to permit the beneficial owner to vote the shares. In addition, a court may compel the record owner to execute a proxy appointment in favor of the beneficial owner.

d. The book entry system complicates communication between corporations and their stockholders because corporations do not know the true identity of most stockholders. Thus, in order to hold a stockholder vote, the corporation ordinarily must send proxy materials in bulk to the various brokerage firms that maintain the records of beneficial owners.

The brokerage firms then forward the materials to the beneficial stock-holders (as required by SEC rule) who then mail in the proxy forms. Obviously, this procedure takes time, and in the case of a meeting to be held after minimal notice, there may not be time to complete the process. Thus, SEC rules allow for the record owner to vote the shares in circumstances in which it is unlikely that the beneficial owners will be able to return proxy forms in time to be counted. There are several proxy solicitation firms that are in the business of assisting corporations in connection with finding and communicating with stockholders particularly in the context of a proxy fight or tender offer.

e. The SEC has adopted regulations that permit issuers of publicly held shares to communicate directly with assenting beneficial owners of shares held in book entry form by brokerage firms on behalf of their customers. The brokerage firms must poll their customers stating that their identities and addresses will be provided to the issuer unless the beneficial owner objects to that disclosure. Beneficial owners who do not object are known as NOBOs (nonobjecting beneficial owners). An issuer may be compelled to create a list of NOBOs at the request of a person also seeking the stockholders' list as a prelude to mounting a takeover attempt. *Sadler v. NCR Corporation*, 928 F.2d 48 (2d Cir.1991). SEC also amended its rules in 2000 to permit delivery of one set of proxy materials to any given household.

f. Given that most shares are held in street name, each record owner usually represents many beneficial owners. As a result, a company may have relatively few record owners. Under SEC rules, a company with fewer than 300 stockholders which is not listed for trading on a stock exchange may de-register as a public company and cease filing public reports as well as complying with numerous SEC rules that are triggered by the requirement to report. Given that reporting is expensive and creates a variety of opportunities for stockholder litigation, several companies have chosen to deregister under these circumstances.

g. The MBCA also has addressed the problems of book ownership to some extent by permitting corporations to adopt rules by which beneficial stockholders may register with the corporation and exercise the rights of record owners. MBCA 7.23 (Shares Held by Nominees). The laws of many states, however, confer rights only on record owners. Thus, only a record owner may bring a derivative action or exercise the right of dissent and appraisal. Under Delaware law, for example, an appraisal proceeding must be commenced in the name of the record owner. On the other hand, not all beneficial owners may want to exercise their appraisal rights. Thus, Delaware law allows the record owner to seek appraisal on behalf of some stockholders but not others, but only for all of the shares held by an individual beneficial stockholder.

h. Prior to 1986, practically all corporate bonds were issued in bearer form and could be sold or negotiated only by physical delivery of the certificate itself. Typically, neither the issuer nor the bond trustee had any record of who actually owned specific bonds. This system created serious problems in communicating with bondholders other than by newspaper notice. But because bondholders cannot vote on matters of corporate governance, this seldom mattered to the issuing corporation except in limited circumstances relating to the modification of bond terms or if the bonds were called for redemption. The 1986 Tax Act prohibited deduction of interest payments on bearer bonds issued thereafter because it was difficult to determine who received the interest and was subject to tax thereon. As a result, virtually all corporate bonds are now issued in registered form, which has also greatly simplified the notice and communication process for bondholders.

3. Voting Lists

Corporations must prepare an accurate voting list of the record owners entitled to vote at a meeting. This list must be available for inspection at the meeting, and under most statutes must also be available for inspection for a period of time before the meeting. MBCA 7.20. The failure to prepare this list does not affect the validity of any action taken at a meeting. Some state statutes impose a penalty on the corporate officer who is obligated to prepare a voting list but fails to do so.

4. Miscellaneous Voting Rules

Statutes of many states set forth rules as to who may vote shares in certain circumstances. MBCA(1984) 7.24 contains more elaborate rules than most statutes addressing acceptance of votes of shares owned by other entities, fiduciaries, pledges, beneficial owners, and co-owners.

5. Inspectors of Election

In a publicly traded corporation, it is standard practice to appoint inspectors of election to determine the number of shares outstanding and the voting power of each, the number of shares represented at the meeting, and the validity of ballots and proxies. Inspectors of election also count the votes and determine the result. Under the MBCA it is required for a public corporation to appoint inspectors of election. MBCA 7.29. A non public corporation may also appoint inspectors of election, but it is not required. Inspectors of election may be officers or employees of the corporation. Disputes as to entitlement to vote are usually resolved by inspectors of election on the basis of statutory voting rules and records of the corporation. *Salgo v. Matthews,* 497 S.W.2d 620 (Tex.Civ.App. 1973).

> *Caveat:* Delaware permits an election inspector to consider supplemental evidence as to intention when inconsistent proxies are filed on behalf of a beneficial owner. *Preston v. Allison,* 650 A.2d 646 (Del.1994). Under MBCA 7.24 and MBCA 7.29, it appears that inspectors of election may consider undisputed evidence as to such matters as beneficial ownership, but it is not clear that they have the power to resolve disputes involving, for example, conflicting proxies. On the other hand, § 7.24 does give inspectors of election the power to determine the result.

H. PROXY VOTING

A *proxy* is the grant of authority by a stockholder to someone else to vote the shares. The relationship is one of principal and agent.

1. Terminology

Depending on the context, the term *proxy* may refer to the piece of paper granting the authority, to the grant of authority itself, or to the person holding the authority. The MBCA (1984) uses the term in the last sense. The MBCA uses the term *proxy appointment* and *proxy appointment form,* respectively, to refer the other senses. *See* MBCA 7.22. Voting by proxy is the norm in publicly held corporations where the large number of stockholders makes personal voting impractical. Voting by proxy may also be used in closely held corporations if a stockholder will not attend a meeting.

> *Caveat:* The use of proxies in registered public corporations is regulated by the SEC as described below.

2. Formal Requirements

A proxy appointment must be in writing. Under many statutes a proxy appointment is valid for eleven months only, thus necessitating a new appointment for each annual meeting. Under MBCA 7.22(c) a proxy appointment is valid for a longer period if specified in the appointment form.

3. Revocability

The general rule is that a proxy appointment is revocable.

a. The act of revocation may consist of any action inconsistent with the continued existence of the grant of authority.

> *Example:* A stockholder executes a proxy appointment form solicited by management on April 1. Four days later he executes a competing appointment form on behalf of an insurgent group. The later appointment revokes the earlier one and the shares may be voted by the insurgent group.

> *Example:* A stockholder executes an appointment form but later decides to attend the meeting in person. If she votes in person, her act constitutes a revocation of the earlier proxy appointment.

b. To be irrevocable a proxy appointment must (i) state that it is irrevocable; and (ii) be *coupled with an interest*. Examples of appointments that are coupled with an interest include:

- A proxy who is a pledgee under a valid pledge of the shares.

- A proxy who is a person who has agreed to purchase the shares under an executory contract of sale.

- A proxy who is a person who has lent money or contributed valuable property to the corporation.

- A proxy who is a person who has contracted to perform services for the corporation as an officer.

- A proxy appointment given in order to effectuate the provisions of a valid pooling agreement (described below).

c. Some courts have upheld irrevocable proxy appointments that do not squarely fall within any of the above categories or meet the above requirements. Some statutes provide that these five situations are the only ones in which an irrevocable proxy appointment may be recognized.

d. A proxy appointment is revocable even if it is stated to be irrevocable and even if consideration for the appointment is paid. *Stein v. Capital Outdoor Advertising, Inc.*, 159 S.E.2d 351 (N.C.1968).

Example: A stockholder executes an appointment form that states it is irrevocable for five years. The appointment is valid for five years under MBCA (1984) but it may be revoked at any time.

e. Vote selling is generally thought to be against public policy and unenforceable. There are relatively few cases addressing naked vote selling, and most hold that purchased votes are void. NYBCL § 609(e) expressly prohibits a stockholder from selling his vote. But in *Schreiber v. Carney,* 447 A.2d 17 (Del.Ch.1982), the court refused to invalidate an arrangement in which a major stockholder contracted, for consideration, to vote in the same manner as a majority of the independent stockholders. There was full disclosure of the arrangement to the independent stockholders.

I. STOCKHOLDER VOTING AGREEMENTS

Agreements among stockholders that they will vote their shares cooperatively or as a unit are generally enforceable. MBCA 7.31. These are called *pooling agreements* or *pooling arrangements* in older cases.

1. Scope of Valid Stockholders Agreements

Stockholder voting agreements are valid so long as they relate to issues, such as the election of directors, on which stockholders may vote. *E. K. Buck Retail Stores v. Harkert,* 62 N.W.2d 288 (Neb.1954); *Weil v. Beresth,* 220 A.2d 456 (Conn.1966); *Ringling Bros.-Barnum & Bailey Combined Shows v. Ringling,* 53 A.2d 441 (Del.1947). If the agreement deals with issues that are within the discretion of directors, the agreement may be invalid.

Example: Two stockholders agree that in the future (i) they will vote for each other as directors, (ii) they will use their best efforts to elect one as president and the other as secretary, and (iii) they will cause the corporation to pay each of them a salary of $10,000 per month. The first agreement is a valid voting agreement. The other two are invalid unless enforceable under special statutes such as where a close corporation election has been made. Whether or not the first agreement is severable depends on the language of the agreement and the extent to which the valid portions standing alone are sufficient to effectuate the underlying purpose of the agreement.

2. Formal Requirements

A few states have adopted statutes regulating voting agreements, limiting the period during which a voting agreement may continue (*e.g.*, to ten years), requiring that copies of the voting agreement be deposited at the principal office of the corporation, and so forth. In most states, a voting agreement is seen as a simple private contract subject to few limitations.

3. Determination of How Shares Should Be Voted

Voting agreements may provide that the shares be voted on a specified proposal or motion. Or such matters may be the subject of subsequent negotiation and decision by the stockholders with some method of determining how the shares are to be voted in the event of a failure to agree. Resolution of disagreements is often by arbitration.

4. Enforcement of Voting Agreements

Enforcement of a voting agreement creates special problems because the shares are registered in the names of the individual stockholders on the books of the corporation.

a. In a leading case the Delaware Supreme Court enforced a voting agreement by disqualifying the shares sought to be voted in violation of the agreement. *Ringling Bros.–Barnum & Bailey Combined Shows v. Ringling*, 53 A.2d 441 (Del.1947). The effect was to permit a minority stockholder to elect half of the board under cumulative voting even though the minority stockholder would ordinarily have been able only to elect two of seven directors.

b. Some state statutes specifically address the enforcement issue by authorizing specific performance of pooling agreements. *See* MBCA 7.31(b).

c. New York makes a proxy granted in connection with a pooling agreement irrevocable. To take advantage of this enforcement device, the agreement should contain specific reference to the irrevocable nature of the proxy appointment, and should designate who may exercise the irrevocable proxy and under what circumstances.

J. VOTING TRUSTS

A voting trust is a device by which the power to vote may be temporarily but irrevocably severed from title to shares. A voting trust is a formal arrangement by which shares are registered in the name of one or more voting trustees on the books of the corporation. In most jurisdictions, a voting trust is the only way one may effectively create an irrevocable proxy without coupling it with an economic interest. A voting trust is a control mechanism that may be abused but generally no more so than other control devices. *Oceanic Exploration Co. v. Grynberg*, 428 A.2d 1 (Del.1981).

1. Common Law

At common law there was suspicion of voting trusts. While this attitude has been partially reversed by state statutes recognizing and validating voting trusts, some of the rules discussed below can be traced to early judicial hostility to this device. *See Tankersley v. Albright*, 514 F.2d 956 (7th Cir.1975) (refusing to grant summary judgment on the validity of a common law voting trust.)

2. Statutory Requirements

State statutes uniformly recognize the validity of voting trusts that meet statutory requirements. *See* MBCA 7.30. The most common such requirements are:

a. The agreement may not extend beyond ten years.

b. The agreement must be in writing.

c. A copy of the agreement must be deposited with the corporation at its registered office and be available for inspection by stockholders and holders of beneficial interests in the trust.

d. Some states have imposed the further requirement that the essential purpose of the trust must be a proper one.

Example: The creator of a voting trust testifies that the purpose is to secure control of the corporation and to preserve her employment with the corporation. This is not a proper purpose for a voting trust, and a trust formed for this purpose is invalid in some states.

Example: The creator of the trust testifies that its purpose is to assure the continued benefit of skilled and experienced management of the corporation. This is a proper purpose of a voting trust and a trust created for this purpose would be valid in the same states.

e. Because of the common law attitude toward voting trusts, discussed above, a voting trust agreement that fails to comply with all statutory requirements is invalid in its entirety in most states. Even though these requirements are simple ones that may be easily satisfied, there are numerous cases in which the requirements have been ignored with the result that the voting trust has been struck down.

f.   An arrangement that has most of the characteristics of a voting trust must fully meet the applicable statutory requirements if it is to be upheld even though it is formally a voting agreement or proxy appointment rather than a voting trust. *Abercrombie v. Davies*, 130 A.2d 338 (Del.1957). A limited partnership formed in order to obtain voting control of a corporation may be a voting trust and is valid only if statutory requirements have been complied with. *Hall v. Staha*, 800 S.W.2d 396 (Ark.1990).

g.   A voting trust may be set aside if later events frustrate its essential purpose. *Selig v. Wexler*, 247 N.E.2d 567 (Mass.1969).

3.   Financial Rights

Voting trust agreements usually provide that all dividends or other corporate distributions pass through to the beneficial owners of the shares so that all attributes of ownership other than the power to vote remain in the beneficial owners. Trustees may issue voting trust certificates to represent the beneficial interests; these certificates may be traded much as shares of stock are traded.

4.   Uses of Voting Trusts

Voting trusts may be used for a wide variety of purposes:

a.   The preservation, retention or securing of control.

b.   Assurance of temporary stability in control of a corporation coming out of bankruptcy or receivership or being created as the result of divestment from another corporation pursuant to the anti-trust laws. *Brown v. McLanahan*, 148 F.2d 703 (4th Cir.1945).

c.   Elimination of a troublesome stockholder from participation in control of a corporation.

d.   Obtaining credit, when required by creditors as a condition of providing needed financing to the corporation.

5. Voting Trusts in Publicly Held Corporations

Voting trusts are generally considered to be inconsistent with corporate democracy in corporations with publicly traded securities. The New York Stock Exchange refuses to list for trading a security that is partially held in a voting trust.

6. Powers of Trustees

The power of trustees to vote on fundamental corporate matters depends on the specific language of the voting trust, *Clarke Memorial College v. Monaghan Land Co.*, 257 A.2d 234 (Del.Ch.1969). Some decisions have imposed equitable limitations on the power of trustees to approve fundamental changes despite clear and broad language in the governing document. *Brown v. McLanahan*, 148 F.2d 703 (4th Cir.1945).

K.   CLASSES OF SHARES

The simplest and most effective device by which the control rights of particular shares may be assured is to create multiple classes of shares. This is a particularly useful device in cases in which it is necessary to allocate voting power in different proportions from financial interests, as when one stockholder contributes cash and one contributes services but both desire equal control rights. Classes of shares may be created without voting rights, with fractional or multiple votes per share, with power to select one or more directors, or with limited financial interests in the corporation. MBCA § 6.01 provides that the articles of incorporation may authorize shares with special voting rights, and MBCA § 8.04 provides that if the articles authorize dividing shares into classes, the articles may also authorize the election of all or a specified number of directors by the holders of one or more classes.

Example: Two stockholders each own 50 percent of the stock of a corporation. After a dispute, they agree to restructure the corporation. Two classes of shares are created, each with the power to elect two directors. Each stockholder holds all the shares of one class of shares. In addition a third class of shares consisting of one share is created and issued to the corporation's attorney. The third class has a par value of $10 per share, is not entitled to receive dividends, may be redeemed at any time by unanimous vote of the other stockholders for its par value, and may receive only its par value upon dissolution of the corporation. This third class has the power to elect one director. A class with such limited financial rights but significant voting rights is a valid class of shares. *Lehrman v. Cohen*, 222 A.2d 800 (Del.1966).

Example: Two people form a corporation, one investing $100,000 and the other investing $50,000. They want to share equally in control but in proportion to their contributions for financial purposes. Thus, an equal number of shares of two classes of common stock, Class A common and Class B common, are authorized. Each class is entitled to elect two directors, but the dividend and liquidation rights of the Class A are twice those of Class B. The corporation then issues all the Class A common to one stockholder for $100,000 and all the Class B common to the other stockholder for $50,000. Alternatively, the corporation might authorize and issue 100 shares of Class A common and 50 shares of Class B common, with each class entitled to elect two directors and otherwise having identical rights. Or, if permitted under applicable law, Class B might be given two votes per share while Class A is given one vote per share.

Caveat: The fact that each class of shares is entitled to elect a specified number of directors does not affect the voting power of the shares for other purposes. Thus, a stockholder who owns a majority of shares may still be able to exercise complete control over all matters requiring a stockholder vote.

Caveat: If the number of directors is increased, presumably any new directors beyond the original four will be elected by the two classes of shares voting together as a single class. Thus, it is important in setting up a scheme of share classes to include appropriate restrictions in connection with amendment of the articles of incorporation or bylaws.

Example: A minority stockholder wishes to be assured of being treasurer of the corporation and to have a veto over all amendments to the articles of incorporation. A special class of common shares is created that provides that (1) the treasurer must be a holder of that class of shares, and (2) the articles may be amended only by an affirmative vote of two-thirds of each class of shares, voting by classes. In other respects the classes have equal rights. All shares of the new class are issued to the minority stockholder.

Example: There are three stockholders A, B, and C who each contribute the same amount of cash. But C also contributes significant intellectual property and wants the same voting power as A and B combined. To effectuate this structure, voting and non-voting common shares (with equal dividend and liquidation rights) are issued in the following amounts:

| | Shares | |
Shareholder	Voting	Non–Voting
A	50	50
B	50	50
C	100	–0–

REVIEW QUESTIONS

6.1. If a corporation's governing documents are silent, what is the minimum number of shares necessary to enact an ordinary resolution at a stockholders meeting?

6.2. May a corporation create shares with more or less than one vote per share?

6.3. What is the difference between record ownership and beneficial ownership?

6.4. Why does a corporation need to set a record date for voting at a meeting or for payment of dividend?

6.5. True or False: Cumulative voting encourages minority representation on the board.

6.6. In a struggle for control, stockholder A gives a proxy appointment to the management faction. A week later A receives a solicitation from the insurgent faction and signs and returns their proxy appointment form. Which appointment form will control?

6.7. True or False: A proxy appointment may be made irrevocable if it is supported by consideration and is stated to be irrevocable.

6.8. What is the difference between a pooling agreement and a voting trust?

6.9. The president of Compliance Corp. calls a special meeting of stockholders expressly for the purposes of considering a merger with Ready, Ltd., and such other matters as might come before the meeting. Notice to this effect is sent to all stockholders of record. At the meeting the holders of a majority of shares are present. Two stockholder directors, N.E. Gative and Ken Servative, voice strong opposition to the merger. A stockholder then proposes that Gative and Servative be removed as directors without cause. This proposal is passed by a majority vote. L. I. Berl and Red Stamp are then elected as successor directors. The stockholders decide that the board should retain counsel and continue negotiation with Ready, Ltd. concerning the proposed merger. Several months later, the plan of merger is finalized, approved by the board of directors, and proposed to the stockholders of Compliance Corp. The plan receives the necessary stockholder vote of both Ready, Ltd. and Compliance Corp. Meanwhile, prior to the filing of the articles of merger, Gative and Servative commence an action to enjoin the merger and for their reinstatement as directors. What result?

6.10. The stockholders of D Corporation request in writing that the president of the corporation call a meeting for the following purposes: (1) to vote upon a resolution endorsing the administration of the former president who had been removed by the directors and demanding that he be reinstated as president; and (2) to vote upon a proposal to hear charges against certain directors and vote upon their removal. The president refuses to call the meeting on the ground that neither of the proposals are proper for a meeting of the stockholders. Will an order in the nature of mandamus lie to require the president to call the meeting?

6.11. True or False: An amendment to articles of incorporation may be freely made so long as it does not eliminate vested rights.

6.12. D corporation has a provision in its articles of incorporation providing for cumulative voting for directors. The corporation law of D's state of incorporation does not require that shareholders be afforded cumulative voting. In addition the state statute gives the corporation the right to amend, alter or repeal any provisions in the articles of incorporation. D has sent a notice to its shareholders of a meeting at which a resolution to amend its articles of incorporation to eliminate the provision for cumulative voting will be considered. P is a minority shareholder who has enough shares to elect one director voting cumulatively but will be unable to do so if the cumulative voting provision is eliminated. P brings an action to restrain D from amending its article of incorporation by eliminating the cumulative voting provisions. Is P entitled to an injunction?

6.13. P is a dissident shareholder who is attempting to replace the management of corporation X. X's bylaws provide that the annual meeting shall be held on January 11 of each year. The board of directors in accordance with statutory provisions that permit the directors to change the date of the annual meeting have advanced the date to December 8 of the prior year. P brings an action against X Corporation for an injunction preventing the advancement of the meeting date. P contends that management has attempted to use the provisions of law and the corporate machinery to perpetuate itself in office and to obstruct the efforts of the dissident stockholder to undertake a proxy contest against management. These contentions are not disputed. Management contends that it has complied strictly with the provisions of state law in changing the date which is all that is required. Is P entitled to an injunction?

VII

Directors & Officers

A. NUMBER AND QUALIFICATIONS OF DIRECTORS

In most states today the board of directors may consist of one or more members. MBCA 8.03(a). Residence and shareholding requirements for directors, while once common, have been largely eliminated. MBCA 8.02. MBCA 8.03 states expressly that only individuals may serve as directors. Delaware law was amended in 2002 to make it clear that only natural persons may be directors. DGCL 141(b). In some European legal systems an entity may serve as a director. Although it is common practice in the United States for a corporation to serve as a general partner in a limited partnership, it does not appear that any states permit non natural persons to serve as directors. Directors need not be full-time employees of the corporation and are not required to devote their efforts exclusively to the corporation. (Of course, a full-time employee may also be a director, but the role of director as such is not a full-time responsibility.)

1. **Board Size**

   Historically, three directors were required and a few states retain this requirement.

   a. The New York Business Corporation Law, § 702, and the statutes of a few other states allow boards of one or two directors only where there are one or two stockholders.

   b. Most states simply state that the board may consist of one or more members without qualification.

   c. The number of directors is usually established in the bylaws; if the bylaws are silent the number may be set by the statute as either the minimum permitted in the state or the number of initial directors set forth in the articles of incorporation.

2. Increase or Decrease

The number of directors may be increased or decreased by amendments to the bylaws, but a decrease does not have the effect of eliminating or shortening the term of any sitting director.

a. Because the board of directors generally has power to amend bylaws, the board of directors in effect has power to determine its own size under most state statutes.

b. The statutes of some states impose limits on the extent to which a board of directors may exercise its power to amend bylaws to increase or decrease its own size without stockholder approval.

B. MEETINGS OF DIRECTORS

Regular meetings of the board occur at the times specified in the bylaws. Special meetings may be called as specified in the bylaws.

1. Notice

No notice of regular meetings is required. MBCA 8.22(a). Special meetings may be called upon two days notice unless a longer or shorter notice is required or permitted by the bylaws. MBCA 8.22(b).

2. Quorum

A quorum of directors consists of a majority of the directors except that a greater or lesser number (but no less than one-third) may be specified by the bylaws. MBCA 8.24(b).

a. Generally, only lawfully elected directors may be counted toward quorum or voting requirements. *Dillon v. Scotten, Dillon Co.*, 335 F.Supp. 566 (D.Del.1971).

b. A board of directors may act on a specific matter only if a quorum is present when the action is taken. MBCA 8.24(c). Many state statutes are silent on this question.

Caveat: This rule for directors' action is the opposite of the rule prescribed for stockholders. MBCA 7.25(b) provides that at a stockholders meeting, once a quorum is present the meeting may proceed to its conclusion and the withdrawal of one or more stockholders does not destroy the quorum. The opposite rule is established for directors in MBCA 8.24(c).

c. The board of directors may sometimes be able to act even though a quorum is not present where vacancies exist and the action to be taken is the filling of those vacancies. Depending on the language of the specific statute, this power may exist only when the number of directors *in office* is less than a quorum; or when the number of directors *acting* is less than a quorum even though the number *in office* is greater than a quorum. *Jacobson v. Moskowitz*, 313 N.Y.S.2d 684, 261 N.E.2d 613 (N.Y. 1970). MBCA 8.10(a)(3) adopts the former position.

> *Example:*   A board consists of eleven members. A quorum is six. Because of deaths and resignations the number in office is five. Under both constructions, the five remaining directors may meet and fill the six vacancies.

> *Example:*   In this example, the number in office is eight. The directors are bitterly divided, five-three, and the three minority directors refuse to attend meetings in order to prevent the existence of a quorum and the approval of actions that they do not favor. Under statutes of the second type described above, the five directors, even though less than a quorum, may fill the vacancies. Under statutes of the first type described above, the five directors could not act because the number of directors in office (eight) is more than a quorum.

d. Some courts have treated a willful refusal to attend a meeting as a breach of fiduciary duty. *Gearing v. Kelly*, 227 N.Y.S.2d 897, 182 N.E.2d 391 (N.Y. 1962). Other courts have recognized that this tactic may be part of a struggle for control and have held that it should not be viewed as improper.

e. In a closely held corporation, an important planning device that creates a veto power on the part of minority stockholders is to increase the quorum requirement for the board of directors to all of the directors, and to require a unanimous vote to approve specific actions. If a minority stockholder has power to elect at least one director, these provisions assure minority participation on all matters, but they also increase the likelihood of deadlock.

3. Voting

Directors traditionally vote on a per capita basis. A majority vote of those present at a meeting where a quorum is present is necessary for the board to act. MBCA 8.24(c). The bylaws may increase the vote necessary for approval of an action up to and including unanimity. DGCL 141(d) permits certificates of incorporation to provide that some directors may have a fractional vote or multiple votes based on shareholdings rather than a per capita one. These voting arrangements may mirror the relative shareholdings of individual stockholders.

4. Objection

A director waives objection to the adequacy of notice of a meeting by attending the meeting, unless he or she attends for the sole purpose of objecting to the transaction of any business and does not participate in the business undertaken at the meeting. Even minimal participation is likely to be construed as a waiver. MBCA 8.23(b).

5. Delegation of Duties

The directors may not delegate their duties to third persons and agreements entered into by the corporation which purport to do so may be unenforceable.

> *Example:* A corporation enters into a management contract with a third person which vests "sole and exclusive power to manage all affairs of the corporation" for a period of 25 years. Such an agreement is against public policy and unenforceable. *Sherman & Ellis v. Indiana Mutual Cas. Co.*, 41 F.2d 588 (7th Cir.1930); *Kennerson v. Burbank Amusement Co.*, 260 P.2d 823 (Cal.App.1953).

> *Example:* A corporation enters into a management contract but the agreement reserves to the board of directors the power to fire the third person for cause. It is doubtful that such a limited power would save such an agreement from invalidity.

> *Example:* A corporation enters into a management contract but the agreement reserves to the board the power to review the performance of the manager annually and to replace him if the board considers it appropriate (although such an action would trigger a substantial severance payment). The size of

the severance payment is a matter of business judgment, and the ultimate power to replace the manager makes the agreement valid because the delegation of authority is not total. *See Grimes v. Donald,* 673 A.2d 1207 (Del.1996).

Caveat: The board of directors may delegate most of its duties to committees of the board.

6. Voting Agreements and Directions

a. The directors may not enter into agreements among themselves relating to how they will vote and generally may not vote by proxy.

Example: A and B are directors. They agree that B will support proposals presented by A and that A will support proposals presented by B. Such an agreement is against public policy and unenforceable, but, A and B may vote together on a voluntary basis.

b. A majority stockholder may seek to guide the fortunes of a corporation after death by testamentary directions to their trustees. Such directions are generally unenforceable on the ground they restrict the discretion of directors.

Example: Z, a 68 per cent stockholder has power to elect the entire board of directors of A Corporation. Z's will bequeaths his shares in A Corporation to a testamentary trust and directs his trustees (i) to elect themselves as directors, (ii) to name Z's widow chairman of the board of A Corporation at a salary of $10,000 per month, and (iii) to elect Z's son as president, at a salary of $8,000 per month. Instructions (ii) and (iii) violate public policy and are unenforceable. *Matter of Hirshon,* 233 N.Y.S.2d 1018 (App.Div. 1962), *modified* 192 N.E.2d 174 (N.Y. 1963).

Caveat: If trustees name themselves as directors, testamentary instructions may create unavoidable conflicts between the duty of the trustee to follow the directions of the testator and the duty of a director to make decisions based on the best interests of the corporation. Trustee-directors faced with such a conflict may petition a court for instructions, but this is an expensive, cumbersome and time-consuming process.

C. COMPENSATION

Traditionally, directors served without compensation on the assumption that their financial interest in the corporation was sufficient inducement. In publicly held corporations today, outside directors receive significant compensation as an inducement to devote substantial attention to corporate affairs and in recognition of the danger of liability. *See* MBCA 8.11. Typically, director compensation consists of an annual payment and a per meeting fee (plus expenses). It may also include grants of stock or the right to participate in a retirement plan. In the 1990s, there was a trend toward compensating outside directors with options. That trend appears to have abated as a result of criticism that it tended to induce directors to approve business strategies that were too risky.

D. REMOVAL AND RESIGNATION

1. Removal

Directors may be removed by stockholders, with or without cause, under the statutes of most states. MBCA 8.08. The articles of incorporation, however, may limit the power of removal to removal for cause. Removal by judicial action is also authorized under the statutes of some states.

a. The power to remove directors without cause tends to assure fealty by the board to the majority stockholder.

b. Many publicly held corporations have eliminated the power of stockholders to remove directors without cause as a defensive measure against hostile takeovers. This provision is usually coupled with the staggering of the term of directors.

> *Caveat:* A corporation may amend its articles of incorporation to restore the power of the stockholders to remove directors without cause. *Roven v. Cotter,* 547 A.2d 603 (Del.Ch.1988).

c. Under the statutes of some states, a court may also remove a director for cause specified in the statute. MBCA 8.09, for example, permits court removal for fraudulent or dishonest conduct, or gross abuse of authority or discretion. Removal for cause by judicial action is appropriate in at least two types of situations. In a publicly held corporation, a judicial proceeding to remove a director for cause, when the director refuses to resign, may be simpler and less expensive than holding a stockholders' meeting to remove the director, an action that must be preceded by a proxy solicitation. In a closely held corporation, judicial removal may be used where the director charged with misconduct declines to resign and possesses the voting power as a stockholder to prevent his own removal.

2. Resignation

The resignation of directors in most states is not expressly covered by statute. MBCA 8.07 permits resignation either immediately or at a future date. A resignation at a future date permits the departing director to participate in the selection of a successor.

E. FILLING VACANCIES

Vacancies created by resignation, death or removal of a director, may be filled either by the board of directors or the stockholders. MBCA 8.10(a). Under older statutes, vacancies created by increasing the size of the board could only be filled by the stockholders, but most modern state statutes permit all vacancies to be filled by the board of directors without regard to the way the vacancies is created.

F. TERM OF OFFICE

Directors serve for the term for which they are elected and a director continues to serve, despite the expiration of the term, until a successor is elected and qualifies or until there is a decrease in the number of directors. MBCA 8.05(e).

G. HOLDOVER DIRECTORS

If directors are not elected at an annual meeting for any reason, or the required annual meeting is never held, the directors then in office hold over until their successors are selected. This principle applies (1) where meetings are held erratically, if at all, and (2) in deadlock situations where the stockholders are evenly divided and unable to elect successors. *Gearing v. Kelly*, 227 N.Y.S.2d 897, 182 N.E.2d 391 (N.Y. 1962).

Example: A and B are the sole stockholders in a corporation, each owning fifty per cent of the shares. There are four directors, elected by straight voting, two in effect having been named by A and two by B. One of A's directors dies, and the vacancy is validly filled by the board of directors by a 2 to 1 vote with a person acceptable to B but not to A. The person so elected remains in office indefinitely because in the next election for directors the election will be deadlocked when B casts votes for three or four directors.

Example: In the foregoing example, directors are elected by cumulative voting. By casting all his votes for two candidates, A is able to restore the prior two-two division of the board and the hold-over director provision will have no application.

H. MEETING REQUIREMENT

The common law rule is that the power invested in directors to control and manage the affairs of a corporation is not joint and several, but joint only, and that directors may take action only as a body at a properly constituted meeting. The theory is that stockholders are entitled to a decision reached only after group discussion and deliberation. Views may be changed as a result of discussion, and the sharpening of minds as a result of joint deliberation improves the decisional process. Moreover, unlike stockholders who may vote based on self-interest, a director is required to exercise business judgment on behalf of the corporation. As a result, the board of directors is effectively required to reach a decision, whereas a stockholder may simply decline to vote.

1. Implications

This rule has several important implications. Perhaps most important is that directors may not vote by proxy. Moreover, formalities as to notice, quorum, and similar matters must be fully observed.

> *Example:* The independent, seriatim approval of an act by each director individually, is not effective directoral action. *Baldwin v. Canfield*, 1 N.W. 261, modified, 1 N.W. 276 (Minn.1879).

a. The rule has the undesirable consequence of permitting a corporation to use its own internal procedural defects as a sword to undo undesired transactions even though a person dealing with a corporation usually has no way of verifying that formalities were in fact completely and fully followed. *Mosell Realty Corp. v. Schofield*, 33 S.E.2d 774 (Va.1945).

b. Several exceptions have been created, including estoppel, ratification, and acquiescence. *See Meyers v. El Tejon Oil & Refining Co.*, 174 P.2d 1 (Cal.1946).

> *Example:* The directors of a corporation informally agree that a particular transaction is desirable. Even though such informal directoral action is ineffective to authorize the transaction under the common law rule, it constitutes acquiescence in and ratification of the very same transaction, thereby binding the corporation. *Sherman v. Fitch*, 98 Mass. 59 (1867);

Phillips Petroleum Co. v. Rock Creek Mining Co., 449 F.2d 664 (9th Cir.1971); *Mickshaw v. Coca Cola Bottling Co.,* 70 A.2d 467 (Pa.Super.1950).

c.   The common law rule will likely be applied today in situations where it appears that no benefit was received from the transaction by the corporation. *Hurley v. Ornsteen,* 42 N.E.2d 273 (Mass.1942); *Mosell Realty Corp. v. Schofield,* 33 S.E.2d 774 (Va.1945).

2.   Variations

a.   Most state statutes permit the board of directors or a committee of the board to participate in a meeting by conference call or similar means enabling all persons participating in the meeting to hear each other at the same time. *See* MBCA 8.20(b). Such participation constitutes presence in person at a meeting so as to satisfy the quorum requirement.

b.   Most state statutes now permit directors to act by unanimous written consent without a formal meeting. MBCA 8.21. A written consent has the same effect as a unanimous vote.

> *Caveat:*   An informal action, not evidenced by a written consent, has been held to be invalid on the ground that the statute has preempted the field. *Village of Brown Deer v. Milwaukee,* 114 N.W.2d 493 (Wis.1962). This holding is also consistent with the traditional common law rule.

> *Caveat:*   The unanimous consent procedure is not available if one director is unwilling to sign the consent. Even though that director is in the minority, a formal meeting of the board of directors should thereafter be held to approve the transaction.

I.   DIRECTOR LIABILITY

Under some circumstances a director can be held personally liable for decisions that cause a loss to the corporation or that are otherwise illegal. In general, all members of the board are presumed to have assented to the action of the board (even if voting against the resolution in question) and are jointly and severally liable in such cases.

1.   Written Dissent

Statutes provide that a director is presumed to have assented to an action unless he or she votes against the action or abstains and his or her dissent appears in the written minutes or a written dissent is thereafter timely filed. MBCA 8.24(d).

a. Abstention or silence without registering a formal dissent is taken is the equivalent of voting in favor of the action.

b. A written dissent must be filed with the presiding officer of the meeting or with the corporation immediately after the meeting.

> *Caveat:* These requirements may have a psychological effect upon the other directors who realize that at least one director considers the conduct sufficiently questionable so as to seek legal protection. These requirements may also afford notice to stockholders or others examining the records that the transaction should be examined carefully because at least one director questioned the propriety of the transaction.

2. Resignation

The director fearing liability may resign as director, though if the resignation occurs after the objectionable transaction is approved, liability may be avoided only if the director files appropriate dissent.

3. Limitation of Liability

The statutes of many states permit corporations to limit the liability of directors by specific provision in articles of incorporation. MBCA 2.02(b)(4); DGCL 102(b)(7).

> *Caveat:* Although individual directors of large publicly held companies have seldom been held liable in connection with claims of mismanagement not involving self-dealing (or failure to manage), it appears that as a result of the numerous corporate scandals of the early 2000s, individual directors may find themselves exposed to personal liability for simple breaches of the duty of care even in cases in which they did not personally benefit. For example, in January 2005, ten former WorldCom Inc. outside directors agreed to pay a total of $18 million to settle securities fraud class action claims arising from the concern's massive accounting irregularities. In addition, a 2005 Delaware case suggests that individual directors may be held liable depending on their expertise and the nature of decision made by the board. Traditionally, the courts have viewed the board of directors as a unit—consistent with the fact that the board may only act as a unit and that individual directors have no inherent authority—and have

declined in most cases to consider the actions of individual directors in the absence of a director's filing a formal dissent or objection.

J. RELIANCE ON ADVICE OF OTHERS

Depending on the language of the specific statute, a director may be able to avoid liability in some situations by showing good faith reliance on the advice of others. MBCA 8.30(c).

Generally, a reliance defense is not available to a director who has actual knowledge about, or expertise with respect to, the issue in question. MBCA 8.30(c). Statutes permit reliance on one or more of the following:

- The written opinion of legal counsel for the corporation.

- Financial reports prepared by the corporation or by its auditors or accountants.

- Statements by officers or employees of the corporation with respect to matters within their authority.

- Reports by committees of the board other than committees on which the director serves.

K. COMMITTEES

It may be convenient to appoint one or more committees to perform certain of the functions of the board of directors. MBCA 8.25. The committee may specialize on one area of concern to the board (for example, a compensation committee or an audit committee) or may function as a substitute for the full board between meetings (an executive committee).

Caveat: Committees are particularly important when assessing the balance of power between management and the board of directors in a publicly held corporation. CEOs in the past have tended to dominate boards of directors. The extent to which the board of directors has developed independence from the CEO varies widely from corporation to corporation. As the independence of the board of directors increases, the power and importance of committees has also increased.

1. Committee Authority

MBCA 8.25 authorizes only committees composed exclusively of members of the board of directors which are authorized to exercise functions of the board of directors.

a. The board of directors may create advisory committees consisting of directors and possibly others. These committees may render advice or make recommendations to the board of directors but do not have power to exercise the directorial function.

b. A committee formed under MBCA 8.25 may be created only by board action.

> *Caveat:* A committee may by unanimous vote appoint a replacement in the event of the absence or disqualification of a committee member.

c. A committee formed under MBCA 8.25 may have a single member. Some statutes require that a committee have at least two members.

d. The creation of a committee and the delegation to it of authority does not of itself constitute compliance with the directors' statutory duty of care.

e. MBCA 8.25(e) lists four functions that must be exercised by the full board of directors and may not be delegated to a committee:

- declaration of distributions except pursuant to a formula

- proposal of matters requiring a stockholder ratification vote

- filling vacancies on the board or committees

- adoption, amendment, or repeal of bylaws

All other matters may be decided by committees acting on behalf of the board of directors.

> *Example:* A derivative action is filed by a stockholder seeking to set aside a transaction between the corporation and a trust created by the chief executive officer for the benefit of her children. A demand is made on the board of directors, and the board responds by creating a committee of disinterested directors to determine whether maintenance of that suit is in the best interests of the corporation. The committee decides that it is not in the best interests of the corporation to pursue this litigation and that a motion to dismiss the litigation with prejudice should be filed. This decision has the same force as though it were made by the board of directors itself.

> *Caveat:* Some courts have found that a committee of one may be too easily influenced to be considered independent.

2. Executive Committee

An executive committee generally provides oversight over general corporate matters during periods when the board of directors is not sitting.

a. An executive committees usually consists only of directors who are executive officers of the corporation.

b. Under older statutes, an executive committee may be created only if specific provision therefor appears in the articles of incorporation or bylaws. Under MBCA 8.25, any committee, including an executive committee, may be created by a corporation unless the articles of incorporation or bylaws specifically provide otherwise.

c. Some statutes that specifically refer to executive committees impose limitations on the powers of such committees.

d. Delegation of authority to an executive committee generally does not relieve the board of directors, or any member, of any responsibility imposed upon it or them.

3. Audit Committee

An audit committee is now required by SEC rules for publicly held companies. The audit committee perform functions such as the following:

a. Recommends the accounting firm to be employed by the corporation as its independent auditor.

b. Consults with the accounting firm so chosen to be the independent auditors with regard to the plan of audit.

c. Reviews, in consultation with the independent auditors, the report of audit and the accompanying management letter of response, if any.

d. Consults with the independent auditors (out of the presence of management) with regard to the adequacy of the internal accounting controls and similar matters.

e. Reports to the full board of directors the results of the audit and make recommendations for changes to improve the adequacy of the control processes.

> *Caveat:* The Public Company Accounting Reform and Investor Protection Act of 2002 (the Sarbanes–Oxley Act) requires that

stock exchanges adopt listing standards requiring listed companies to have an audit committee composed entirely of independent directors. At least one of the members must qualify as a financial expert. Moreover, the audit committee is responsible for the appointment, compensation, and oversight of the company's auditor who must report directly to the audit committee. The Act also gives the audit committee the power to retain counsel and other experts at the expense of the company. In addition, the audit committee must adopt procedures for the receipt of anonymous submissions by employees. The audit committee is also designated as a backup authority to which an attorney must report any evidence of illegality if after reporting to the chief legal officer or the CEO they have failed to take appropriate action. These rules effectively supplant state corporation law by granting authority to the audit committee that is not reviewable by the board of directors or the stockholders (though in practice committees such as special litigation committees are often given non-reviewable authority even in the absence of a legal requirement).

4. Nominating Committee

Most publicly held corporations have a nominating committee that performs some or all of the following functions:

a. Establish qualifications for directors.

b. Establish procedures for identifying possible nominees who meet these criteria.

c. Review the performance of current directors and recommend, where appropriate, that sitting directors be removed or not reappointed.

d. Recommend the appropriate size and composition of the board of directors.

> *Caveat:* Under SEC rules proposed in 2003, the stockholders may have the power to nominate a limited number of candidates for election to the board of directors in the event of certain accounting irregularities.

5. Compensation Committee

Most publicly held corporations have a compensation committee whose role is to set compensation and retirement benefits for high level executive officers. Most compensation committees consist entirely of non-management directors. The compensation committee may perform some or all of the following functions:

a. Review and approve (or recommend to the full board) the annual salary, bonus and other benefits, direct and indirect, of the CEO and other designated members of senior management.

b. Review and submit to the full board of directors recommendations concerning new executive compensation plans.

c. Establish and periodically review the corporation's policies with regard to management perquisites.

d. Review compensation policies relating to members of the board of directors.

e. Review the operation of retirement plans for employees.

f. Review conflict of interest transactions between the corporation and a director.

6. Special Litigation Committee

When derivative litigation is filed by a stockholder on behalf of the corporation, a litigation committee composed of disinterested directors may be created to review the litigation and determine whether its pursuit is in the best interest of the corporation. The courts generally respect the decision of an independent litigation committee and will dismiss derivative litigation based on the decision of such a committee. As discussed further below, if the derivative action is based on a claim of negligence, the courts will usually apply the business judgment rule to the decision of the litigation committee. If the derivative action is based on a duty of loyalty claim, however, the court may review the substance of the committee decision to seek dismissal. In both cases, the court will review whether the committee has conducted an adequate investigation into the matter. *Aronson v. Lewis*, 473 A.2d 805 (Del. 1984).

L. STATUTORY DESIGNATIONS OF CORPORATE OFFICERS

State corporation statutes contain only skeletal provisions dealing with corporate officers. The officers of a corporation, and the functions they are to perform, are usually defined in the bylaws or in resolutions adopted by the board of directors rather than by statute.

1. Traditional Statutes

Traditional statutes such as the MBCA (1969) provide that each corporation shall have a president, a treasurer, a secretary, and (usually) one or more vice-presidents.

a. Under these statutes a person may fill two or more offices simultaneously except the offices of president and secretary. This exception was based on the belief that execution of documents required signatures of two officers, one executing the document and the other attesting to the execution.

b. These statutes also grant unlimited authority to the board of directors to create such additional offices as the board deems appropriate.

2. Flexible Statutes

Neither the MBCA nor the DGCL specifies officer titles. Both grant the corporation freedom to determine which officers it chooses to have. MBCA 8.40(a); DGCL 142. Problems of implied or apparent authority based on titles are avoided under these statutes.

a. Both statutes recognize that there must be an officer performing the functions usually associated with the office of the corporate secretary. *See* MBCA 1.40(20), 8.40(c); DGCL 142(a).

b. Both statutes permit any individual to hold two or more offices at the same time without limitation or restriction. MBCA 8.40(d); DGCL 142(a).

M. NON–STATUTORY OFFICERS

Boards of directors or bylaw provisions may create new or different offices under both types of statutes. These various offices are sometimes created by specific provisions in the bylaws. But more typically these titles are created by a simple resolution of the board of directors.

1. Publicly Held Corporations

Publicly held corporations use functional designations such as: Chairman of the Board of Directors, Chief Executive Officer (CEO), Chief Financial Officer (CFO), Chief Legal Officer (CLO), and Chief Operations Officer (COO).

a. If the corporation is formed in a state that requires that every corporation have a "president," the person holding that office may be a senior officer subordinate to other officers such as the CEO.

2. Assistant Officers

Most corporations find it convenient to designate numerous assistant officers, particularly assistant secretaries or treasurers. In a corporation with several officers in different locations a vice president and assistant officers may be named for each office to permit decision-making and the execution of documents at the local level.

N. AUTHORITY OF OFFICERS IN GENERAL

Corporate officers, including the president, have relatively little inherent power by virtue of their offices. The principal repository of power to conduct the business and affairs of the corporation is in the board of directors not the officers.

1. Sources of Authority

Corporate officers may draw authority from the following sources:

a. Statutes (to a limited extent).

b. Articles of incorporation (though provisions dealing with officers in this document are uncommon).

c. Bylaws (which usually outline the functions of officers in some detail).

d. Resolutions of the board granting authority to officers.

e. Specific resolutions of the board authorizing corporate officers to enter into specific transactions reviewed and approved by the board.

f. Course of conduct.

g. Many cases recognize that some authority may be implied from the office held by the person acting. This is referred to as inherent authority.

h. Many cases find that authority exists in specific circumstances by the application of amorphous doctrines such as ratification, estoppel, or implied consent inferred from inaction by the board of directors.

   Caveat: It may be unclear whether authority implied on the basis of informal conduct or acquiescence is implied actual authority or apparent authority.

   Caveat: The statutes of many states specify that the secretary has the authority to perform certain ministerial acts such as to certify that the board of directors has validly adopted a resolution.

MBCA 8.41 provides that an officer has such authority as is set forth in the bylaws or, to the extent consistent with the bylaws, the duties prescribed by the board of directors or by direction of an officer authorized by the board of directors to prescribe the duties of other officers.

2. Inherent Authority From Description of Office

The bylaws of the corporation usually describe in general terms the roles of traditional corporate officers. The brief descriptions that follow, taken from typical bylaw provisions, define the authority of corporate officers.

a. The president is the principal executive officer of the corporation, and, subject to the control of the board, in general supervises and controls the business and affairs of the corporation.

b. The vice president performs the duties of the president in his absence or in the event of his death, inability or refusal to act. Vice presidents act in the order designated at the time of their election, or in the absence of designation, in the order of their election.

c. The secretary keeps the minutes of meetings of the stockholders and the board of directors, sees that all notices are duly given as required by the bylaws, is custodian of the corporate records and of the corporate seal, sees that the seal of the corporation is properly affixed on authorized documents, attests to the execution by the president or vice president of certificates for shares of the corporation, important contracts, and other documents, and has charge of the stock register and transfer books of the corporation if there is no transfer agent.

d. The treasurer has charge and custody of and is responsible for all funds and securities of the corporation, and receives, gives receipts for, and deposits, all moneys due and payable to the corporation. The treasurer may be required to give a bond to ensure the faithful performance of his duties. The treasurer, however, does not have inherent or apparent authority to execute a loan guarantee. *General Overseas Films, Ltd. v. Robin Intern., Inc.*, 542 F.Supp. 684 (S.D.N.Y.1982).

3. Inherent Authority of the President

It is a popular belief that the president of a corporation has wide discretion to enter into not only ordinary business transactions, but extraordinary transactions as well.

a. Most courts have held that this view is erroneous. The traditional position is that the president has only limited authority. *Black v. Harrison*

Home Co., 99 P. 494 (Cal.1909); In *re Westec Corp.*, 434 F.2d 195 (5th Cir.1970). The power to approve significant transactions is in the board of directors, not the president. *Schwartz v. United Merchants & Manufacturers*, 72 F.2d 256 (2d Cir.1934).

b. This construction of the president's authority may lead to injustice because persons relying on appearances may discover that their reliance was ill-advised. Persons aware of the limited authority of a president are forced to demand an exhibit of the president's authority before dealing with him.

c. There is a trend to broaden the implied authority of the president. Some courts have concluded that a president presumptively has any powers which the board of directors could give him. Others have held that the president has authority to enter into transactions arising in the usual and regular course of business, and have construed that phrase broadly.

> *Example:*   The corporate president hires a salesman on a commission basis that is customary in the industry. Because the hiring of agents and employees is within the regular course of business, most courts today would find the president has inherent authority to bind the corporation to transactions entered into by the salesman. *See Lind v. Schenley Indus., Inc.*, 278 F.2d 79, 89 (3d Cir. 1960).

> *Example:*   The president of the corporation negotiates a settlement of a lawsuit in which the corporation is a defendant. The settlement involves the payment of a material amount. That action exceeds the inherent authority of the president. *Covington Housing Development Corp. v. City of Covington*, 381 F.Supp. 427 (E.D.Ky.1974), *aff'd*, 513 F.2d 630 (6th Cir.1975). The board of directors should approve the settlement. A similar rule applies to the decision to file a major lawsuit that may have important business impact.

> *Example:*   The president of a corporation promises a 30 year old person a pension of $1,500 per year commencing in thirty years if he will leave his present employment and become an employee of the corporation. Such a promise is within the inherent authority of the president. *Lee v. Jenkins Bros.*, 268 F.2d 357 (2d Cir.1959).

Example: The president of a closely held family corporation executes a guarantee of a debt of a wholly owned subsidiary of the corporation. The president of such a corporation has the authority of a "general agent" and therefore has apparent authority to execute the guarantee. *Foote & Davies, Inc. v. Arnold Craven, Inc.,* 324 S.E.2d 889 (N.C.App.1985).

Caveat: Even though many cases reflect the broadening of the inherent authority of the president of a corporation, the scope of the president's inherent power is often uncertain in application and reliance on inherent authority therefore may be risky.

4. Determination of an Officer's Authority

A person dealing with a corporate officer who purports to represent the corporation should verify the officer's authority.

a. Reliance on oral representations is hazardous because an agent's representation about his or her authority without more is not binding on the principal.

b. Reliance on the office held by an individual is also hazardous because of the common law view described above that such offices carry with them only very limited authority to bind the corporation.

Example: The president of an oil drilling corporation orders 45 miles of plastic pipe. Without more, it cannot be determined whether or not such a transaction is within the president's actual or apparent authority.

Example: In the preceding example, the corporation is a multi-billion dollar publicly held corporation. The president is also the CEO and the corporation follows the practice of having business matters conducted by the management with the board of directors serving only an oversight role. The president has actual authority to enter into a transaction of this nature.

Example: In the preceding example, the corporation receives and uses the pipe. The corporation is liable to pay for the plastic pipe under principles of quasi-contract or unjust enrichment.

c. The formal way to ensure that the corporation is bound is to require the person purporting to act for the corporation to deliver, prior to the closing of the transaction, a certified copy of a resolution of the board of directors authorizing the transaction (although such formalities may be uneconomic in a small transaction). The certificate should be executed by the secretary of the corporation. There is no reason to go behind the certificate. The corporation is estopped to deny the secretary's certificate, because keeping and certifying corporate records is within the actual authority of the secretary. *In re Drive–In Development Corp.*, 371 F.2d 215 (7th Cir.1966). Nevertheless, lawyers often conduct *due diligence* reviews of contemplated transactions which may include verification of the authority of the officer entering into the transaction. This review may include examination of the corporation's minute book to ensure that an appropriate resolution has been entered in the official corporate records.

> *Caveat:* The binding nature of the certificate rests on an estoppel. Therefore a detailed inquiry into the circumstances behind the certificate may be counterproductive because it may develop information that may destroy the basis of estoppel. If one knows or should know that the representations in a certificate are untrue, one cannot rely on estoppel. *Keystone Leasing Corp. v. Peoples Protective Life Insurance Co.*, 514 F.Supp. 841 (E.D.N.Y. 1981).

O. APPARENT AND IMPLIED AUTHORITY OF OFFICERS

Where the authority of a person purporting to act for a corporation has not been specifically granted by action of the board of directors, the following doctrines may be available to a third person seeking to bind the corporation.

1. Ratification

The board of directors of a corporation may learn that an officer has entered into a transaction without being specifically authorized to do so. If the board of directors does not promptly repudiate the transaction, the corporation may be bound on a theory of *ratification*. Or the knowledge of the officer-agent may be imputed to the corporation. *See Scientific Holding Co., Ltd. v. Plessey Incorporated*, 520 F.2d 15 (2d Cir. 1974). Acquiescence by the board of directors may also indicate that an an actual grant of authority was informally made. *Hessler, Inc. v. Farrell*, 226 A.2d 708 (Del.1967). It is sometimes said that ratification is merely an after-the-fact grant of authority. An officer may also be deemed to have implied authority to take action necessary to complete actions that are in fact authorized by the board. Such authority is actual authority and sometimes described as *implied actual authority* (or *lesser included authority*).

2. Estoppel or Unjust Enrichment

When the corporation retains the benefit of a transaction or a third party relies to its detriment, concepts of *unjust enrichment* or *estoppel* may be applied. Estoppel differs from ratification primarily because of reliance by third persons.

> *Example:* One or more directors know that a third person is relying on the authority of the president in approving a questionable transaction. Failure to speak up promptly constitutes ratification. *Yucca Mining & Petroleum Co. v. Howard C. Phillips Oil Co.,* 365 P.2d 925 (N.M.1961).

> *Caveat:* Courts are reluctant to find ratification of an unauthorized act by an officer where the act is fraudulent, unfair to minority stockholders, or against public policy.

3. Implied Authority

An officer may be deemed to have implied authority to take action necessary to complete actions that are in fact authorized by the board. Such authority is *actual* authority and thus is sometimes called *implied actual authority.*

4. Apparent Authority

Apparent authority exists where there is conduct on the part of the principal that leads a reasonable person to suppose that the agent has the authority he purports to exercise.

a. A classic example of apparent authority involves a third person who knows that an officer has exercised authority in the past with the consent of the board of directors.

b. Apparent authority involves conduct on the part of the *principal* (the corporation) which creates the appearance of authority. A mere representation by a corporate officer that he possesses the requisite authority is not sufficient.

c. Apparent authority differs from implied actual authority. For apparent authority, the third person must show that she was aware of the prior acts or holding out and that she relied on appearances, while implied actual authority may be found even in the absence of knowledge on the part of the third person.

> *Caveat:* The same conduct may often tend to prove either implied actual authority or apparent authority.

Example: A corporate president has purchased pipe from a supplier four times in the past; each time the corporation has routinely paid for the pipe. The fifth time, involving a transaction of the same general order of magnitude, the corporation declines to accept or pay for the pipe. In a suit for damages, a court may rest a decision against the corporation on either apparent authority or implied actual authority and may rely on the prior transactions to justify either conclusion.

Caveat: A corporate officer or agent may be liable to the corporation if he exceeds his actual authority and binds the corporation in a transaction with a third person.

P. DUTIES OF OFFICERS

Corporate officers and agents owe a fiduciary duty to the corporation of honesty, good faith, and diligence. The scope of an officer's or agent's obligation to the corporation is determined in part by the nature of his employment with the corporation. MBCA 8.42 imposes a duty of care on officers analogous to the duty of care imposed on directors. Other duties of officers are not codified. State statutes permitting corporations to limit monetary liability for due care violations may cover officers as well as directors.

Q. OFFICERS' LIABILITY ON CORPORATE OBLIGATIONS

An officer or agent who acts within the scope of authority in a consensual transaction is not personally liable on the transaction solely by virtue of so acting. See MBCA § 8.42. The common law of agency is the same.

1. Express Guarantee

The officer or agent may expressly guarantee the performance by the corporation, intending to be personally bound on the obligation.

a.   To be enforceable, a guarantee must be supported by consideration.

b.   Whether or not a guarantee must also be in writing may depend on the statute of frauds as applied to promises to answer for the indebtedness of another.

2. Confusion of Roles

An officer or employee may not intend to be personally bound, but may become bound by creating the impression that she is negotiating as an individual rather for the corporation or if the agreement is executed in such a way as to indicate personal liability.

a. If a person negotiates a transaction without disclosing that she is acting on behalf of a corporation, she is liable to the third person on general agency principles relating to undisclosed principals.

b. If the existence of the corporation is disclosed, the corporation and the officer may both be bound because of carelessness in the manner of execution. *See Harris v. Milam*, 389 P.2d 638 (Okl.1964). *Benjamin Plumbing, Inc. v. Barnes*, 470 N.W.2d 888 (Wis.1991).

> *Caveat:* In cases involving ambiguous forms of execution, courts appear to be more willing to allow officers or agents to testify about the real intention of the parties in executing general contracts than in executing promissory notes. This principle, however, is not applicable when the existence of the corporation does not appear at all in the form of execution.

3. Statutory Liability

Liability may be imposed by statute. For example, some state statutes impose personal liability for corporate obligations if officers fail to pay franchise taxes or to publish a notice upon incorporation.

> *Example:* The Internal Revenue Code provides for a personal penalty of one hundred per cent of the tax if a corporation fails to pay over income taxes withheld from employees. This penalty tax may be imposed on any person required to collect, truthfully account for, and pay over the tax. IRC 6672.

4. Personal Participation in Tortious Conduct

An officer or agent is personally liable if he or she personally participates in tortious conduct.

5. Authority

An officer or agent may be personally liable on contracts or other obligations entered into in the name of the corporation if the officer or agent exceeds his actual authority to bind the corporation. The corporation is also bound if the action is within apparent authority, but the corporation may have an action over against the officer or agent for exceeding his actual authority.

R. CORPORATE NOTICE OR KNOWLEDGE

A corporation can *know* or *have notice of* something only if one or more persons who represent the corporation know or have notice. The issue is whether knowledge or notice should be imputed to the corporate entity.

1. General Rule

Knowledge acquired by a corporate officer or employee while acting in furtherance of the corporate business or in the course of employment is imputed to the corporation.

> *Example:* If the president knows of a transaction, the corporation ratifies it if the corporation accepts the benefits of the transaction, even though one or more directors or other officers may not know the details of the transaction.

> *Example:* Service of process on an authorized agent of the corporation supports a default judgment against the corporation even though the agent fails to forward the papers to the corporation's attorney.

2. Agent Acting Adversely to Principal

Difficult problems arise when it is sought to impute knowledge of an agent to the corporation if the agent is acting adversely to the corporation. Generally, information or knowledge may be imputed from an agent who has ultimate responsibility for the transaction to his corporation even if the agent is acting adversely to the corporation.

3. Corporate Criminal Responsibility

An agent's wrongful intent may be imputed to a corporation so that a corporation may be subject to criminal prosecution, including prosecution for traditional crimes such as murder or rape. For the corporation to be prosecuted, such acts must be connected with or in furtherance of the corporation's business.

S. TENURE OF OFFICERS AND AGENTS

Corporate officers and agents serve at the will of the board of directors. Corporate officers are elected by the board of directors and may be removed by the board of directors with or without cause. MBCA 8.43(b). Agents appointed by officers or other agents may be discharged by the persons with authority to employ them.

1. **Employment Contracts in General**

    An officer or agent may be given an employment contract, and removal of that officer or agent may give rise to a cause of action for breach of contract.

    a. The mere election or appointment of an officer or agent, even for a definite term, does not of itself give rise to a contract of employment. MBCA 8.44(a).

    b. Bylaws sometimes provide that specified officers shall be elected by the board of directors for a term of one year. A provision of this nature does not prevent a corporation from granting an officer an employment contract extending beyond the term of office.

    c. Despite a contract, the officer may be relieved at any time (as is the general rule for agents). *But see Staklinski v. Pyramid Elec. Co.,* 188 N.Y.S.2d 541, 160 N.E.2d 78 (N.Y. 1959). The corporation may be liable for breach of contract for the premature termination of the employment period if the officer is discharged without cause. MBCA 8.44(b).

    d. Long-term employment contracts for officers may be upheld on the same theory applied to other long-term contracts, such as long term leases that bind subsequent boards of directors. *Staklinski v. Pyramid Elec. Co.,* 188 N.Y.S.2d 541, 160 N.E.2d 78 (N.Y. 1959); *In re Paramount Publix Corp.,* 90 F.2d 441 (2d Cir.1937).

    e. Even if a bylaw provision is deemed to be a restraint on the power of the board of directors to grant an officer a long term employment contract, a long term employment contract may be deemed to be an implied amendment of the bylaws. *Realty Acceptance Corp. v. Montgomery,* 51 F.2d 636 (3d Cir.1930). This assumes that the board of directors has power to amend the bylaws.

        Caveat: At least one court has invalidated a long term employment contract as being inconsistent with a bylaw provision that limits the terms of officers. It is not clear whether the board of directors had the power to amend the bylaws. *Pioneer Specialties, Inc. v. Nelson,* 339 S.W.2d 199 (Tex.1960).

2. **Lifetime Employment Contracts**

    The claim that an officer or agent has been given a lifetime employment contract by a corporation has been treated with hostility by courts. Such contracts are usually oral and arise within the context of a family-run business.

a. Although such a contract is not invalidated by the statute of frauds, courts have found such open-ended commitment to be inherently implausible.

b. Many cases that have refused to enforce lifetime arrangements have done so on the ground that the officer making the arrangement had no actual or apparent authority to enter into the arrangement. *See Lee v. Jenkins Bros.*, 268 F.2d 357 (2d Cir.1959).

3. Discharge for Cause

An officer or employee with an employment contract may always be discharged for cause.

a. Cause may consist of dishonesty, negligence, refusal to obey orders, refusal to follow rules, or a variety of other acts such as engaging in an unprovoked fight.

b. In effect, such conduct constitutes a breach of an implied (or express) covenant in the employment contract.

c. If an officer does not have an employment contract, it is irrelevant whether or not cause for discharge exists.

4. Executive Compensation

High level officers are often compensated based on earnings or sales or on an increase in the market price of the corporation's shares rather than by a flat salary. No legal problem is raised by such contracts so long as the total amount of compensation is not so excessive as to constitute waste.

a. A common question arising with respect to bonus arrangements based on earnings or profits is one of computation. Profits may be computed in various ways and may lead to different results.

b. Corporate officers and employees may also be paid with stock or options to purchase stock. Some executive compensation plans measure compensation on the basis of stock price but do not involve the actual purchase of shares. These devices are often called *phantom stock options* or *stock appreciation rights* (SARs).

c. Such equity compensation arrangements are designed to give officers employees a long term investment interest in the corporation that is similar to the interest of stockholders and that will thus induce the officers to maximize stockholder value. They are more common in publicly held corporations (where a market for shares exists) than in closely held corporations.

d. Long term employees of closely held corporations may be granted or permitted to buy a small number of shares of the corporation as an incentive. Typically, these shares are subject to an agreement between the corporation and the officers by which the officer agrees to sell them back to the corporation and the corporation agrees to repurchase them when the employment arrangement ends, often at a preset price or a price determined by a formula.

e. Employment contracts for highly paid officers usually provide for deferred compensation, fringe benefits, reimbursement of business expenses, and other benefits. Such benefits may also be provided to lower paid employees on a more limited basis.

f. In a closely held corporation, an employment agreement may be an integral part of the basic understanding between stockholders. Terms relating to employment are often included in stockholder agreements so that they will be binding on all other stockholders as well as on the corporation. In the absence of such an agreement or an employment agreement, the majority may be able to exclude the minority from financial and managerial participation in the business, although such tactics may constitute a breach of fiduciary duty or grounds for dissolution in many states.

REVIEW QUESTIONS

7.1. True or False: Directors who are unavoidably absent should vote by proxy.

7.2. True or False: Directors may only act collegially in meetings.

7.3. The reason that most persons believe that the president of a corporation has considerable authority is that the president is the most important person within the corporation and owns the most shares. Does this view accurately reflect the power of a president in a corporation?

7.4. True or False: An officer of a corporation cannot be given an employment contract for a period that exceeds the term for which the person was elected.

7.5. M is the president of P Corporation. P Corporation entered into a contract with D Corporation (which owned 1/2 the stock of P Corporation) to distribute D Corporation's products. D Corporation failed to deliver the product. M suggested to the board of directors of P Corporation that suit be instituted against D Corporation. A resolution to that effect was defeated by a tie vote of P Corporation's board of directors, directors affiliated with D corporation voting against the motion. M then instituted suit against D Corporation on behalf of P Corporation. Did M have power to institute the action under these circumstances?

7.6. A, the president of D Corporation, without the consent of D Corporation's board of directors entered into a contract with P Corporation for the purchase of 45 miles of 6 5/8? gas pipe. D Corporation refused to accept the pipe and P Corporation sued for breach of contract. At the trial the judge charged the jury that the corporation is bound by the act of the president in signing a contract. Is the jury charge correct?

*

VIII

Fiduciary Duties of Directors, Officers & Stockholders

A. DUTIES IN GENERAL

Directors and officers owe fiduciary duties to the corporation and to the stockholders and in some cases to other constituencies such as creditors. Controlling stockholders may also owe a fiduciary duty to the corporation and other stockholders not to use their power inappropriately. These duties are generally a matter of state law, but federal securities law may also impose duties that are similar to state law duties.

1. Directors

Directors have the broad responsibility of overseeing the management of the corporation. They occupy a unique position within the corporate structure, and owe both a duty of care and a duty of loyalty to the corporation.

a. The duties of directors are sometimes analogized to those of a trustee of a trust. *Guth v. Loft, Inc.*, 5 A.2d 503 (Del.1939); *Litwin v. Allen*, 25 N.Y.S.2d 667 (1940). Directors of corporations are not strictly trustees, because they are not automatically liable for consequences of actions which exceed their powers. Further, the area of their discretion and judgment is considerably greater than that possessed by traditional trustees. Directors may enter into transactions with the corporation under some circumstances.

b. In most instances, directors owe duties to the corporation as a whole rather than to individual stockholders or to individual classes of stockholders. Moreover, directors act as a group, although in some cases a court may conclude that one or more individual directors have breached a duty to the corporation.

> *Caveat:*   It is not entirely clear whether the directors and officers owe a duty to the corporation or to the stockholders. The stockholders are generally seen as the owners of the corporation. Accordingly, many legal scholars argue that the duty to the corporation is a duty to the stockholders. In the UK, on the other hand, it is quite clear that directors and officers owe a duty to the corporation. This subtle distinction may make a difference in some cases.

2. Officers and Agents

The duties owed by corporate officers and agents to the corporation depend to some extent on the position occupied by the officer or agent and the type of liabilities that are being imposed. A full-time, high-level managing officer may owe substantially the same duties to the corporation as a director. Agents or employees in subordinate or limited positions owe a correspondingly lesser degree of duty, though even the lowest agent owes the principal certain minimum duties of care, skill, propriety in conduct, and loyalty in matters connected with his agency.

3. Stockholders

Stockholders as such have no power to manage the business and affairs of the corporation and do not perform services for the corporation in that capacity. But they do select the directors and have power to approve or ratify certain transactions. Their fiduciary relationship to the corporation therefore differs from the relationship of a director or officer.

a. Many cases state that a stockholder owes no fiduciary duty to the corporation. Such statements are too broad, because stockholders, particularly controlling stockholders, clearly owe a duty to the corporation or fellow stockholders in some circumstances.

b. A number of states hold that controlling stockholders in a closely held corporation owe a duty to other stockholders that is akin to that owed by partners to each other. *See Matter of TJ Ronan Paint Corp.*, 469 N.Y.S.2d 931, 936 (App.Div. 1984); *Fender v. Prescott*, 476 N.Y.S.2d 128 (App.Div. 1984).

    c.   Controlling stockholders may also owe duties to minority stockholders when they transfer control of the corporation to a third party. *See Perlman; Jones.*

    d.   Transactions between a controlling stockholder and the corporation must be fair to the corporation and the controlling stockholder has the burden of proving entire fairness unless the transaction has been ratified by the stockholders after full disclosure of all material facts. *Kahn v. Lynch Communication Systems,* 638 A.2d 1110 (Del.1994); *Lewis v. S.L. & E., Inc.,* 629 F.2d 764 (2d Cir.1980); *Sinclair Oil Corp. v. Levien; Weinberger v. UOP, Inc.*

    e.   Even though a stockholder is under no general obligation to vote in the best interest of the corporation and may vote with a view to personal interests or indeed on the basis of whim or caprice, a stockholder may not sell his or her vote. *Ringling Brothers v. Ringling; Schreiber v. Carney.*

        Caveat: The prohibition on vote selling is very narrow. It is clear that a stockholder may properly vote for a transaction that carries economic benefit for the stockholder. *Schreiber v. Carney.*

    f.   Stockholders are not subject to the same conflict-of-interest rules as directors, but the courts have generally declined to count the votes of stockholders who vote their shares in favor of ratification of their own self-dealing transactions. *Fliegler v. Lawrence. See Weinberger v. UOP, Inc.* This rule has been codified in MBCA 8.63.

B. DUTY OF CARE

Directors and officers owe a duty to the corporation to exercise reasonable care in performing their duties with respect to the corporation's affairs.

1. General Tests

MBCA 8.30 states that the standard test for directors' duty of care is that the duties must be discharged (1) in good faith, (2) with the care an ordinarily prudent person in a like position would exercise under similar circumstances, and (3) in a manner he reasonably believes to be in the best interests of the corporation.

    a.   This standard of care is justified on various grounds. A stricter test might unduly discourage individuals from serving as directors. And the courts are reluctant to second-guess corporate managers with the benefit of hindsight.

b. A number of older cases state that bank directors owe a higher degree of care than directors of ordinary business corporations. *See Bates v. Dresser*, 251 U.S. 524, 40 S.Ct. 247 (1920). On the other hand, this rule may simply be a reflection of the nature of the banking business, that is, that the business of a bank is among other things to provide a safe depository.

c. The test of skill and prudence is based on an average person of reasonable intelligence and competence. *See Selheimer v. Manganese Corp. of America*, 224 A.2d 634 (Pa.1966).

2. Business Judgment Rule

The business judgment rule is a common law principles that provides that honest business decisions made in good faith and on the basis of reasonable investigation are not actionable, even though the decision is mistaken, unfortunate, or even disastrous. *Shlensky v. Wrigley*, 237 N.E.2d 776 (Ill.App.1968) (decision not to play night games at Wrigley Field); *Kamin v. American Express Co.*, 383 N.Y.S.2d 807 (1976), aff'd, 387 N.Y.S.2d 993 (decision to pay dividend in property on which tax loss was available).

a. Section 4.01(c) of the ALI Principles of Corporate Governance (PCG) codifies the business judgment rule: "A director or officer who makes a business judgment in good faith fulfills [the duty of care] if (1) he is not interested in the subject of his business judgment; (2) he is informed with respect to the subject of his business judgment to the extent he reasonably believes to be appropriate under the circumstances; and (3) he rationally believes that his business judgment is in the best interests of the corporation."

b. The relationship between the duty of care and the business judgment rule is unclear. The business judgment rule may be seen as a presumption or burden shifting device. That is, in the absence of the business judgment rule it is not clear that the plaintiff would bear the burden of proof given that the defendant director controls the evidence. Under the business judgment rule, the burden of pleading specific facts falls on the plaintiff. Otherwise, the court will dismiss the case without discovery.

c. As a practical matter, the most common way to overcome the business judgment rule has been to show that the decision in question was tainted by a conflict of interest and thus may not have been made in good faith.

d. There are a few cases in which plaintiffs have prevailed by showing that the decision in question was a no win proposition or could only lead to a financial loss. Litwin v. Allen; Selheimer v. Manganese Corporation of America; Joy v. North.

e. An *ultra vires* act is probably not protected by the business judgment rule.

f. The business judgment rule is not applicable unless a decision has been made. A failure to manage is not protected by the business judgment rule.

> *Caveat:*   However, a decision not to take action is itself a decision that may be protected by the business judgment rule.

g. Issues relating to dividend policies and distributions are often said to be especially appropriate for the application of the business judgment rule. *Kamin v. American Express Co.*, 383 N.Y.S.2d 807 (1976).

3. Failure to Manage

A director may be liable for failure to manage. Liability is not precluded by the business judgment rule because no judgment or decision is involved.

> *Caveat:*   Causation may be difficult to prove in failure to manage cases. *Barnes v. Andrews,* 298 Fed. 614 (S.D.N.Y.1924), holds that a figurehead director who attended few meetings breached his fiduciary duty of care to the corporation but he could be held liable only if the plaintiff could show a causal relationship between the director's inattention and the losses suffered by the corporation. *See also Allied Freightways, Inc. v. Cholfin,* 91 N.E.2d 765 (Mass.1950) (housewife-director is not liable for losses suffered by a corporation as a result of her husband's defalcations because her negligence was not the proximate cause of the loss, it being doubtful that she could have prevented the loss in any event). *But see Francis v. United Jersey Bank,* 432 A.2d 814 (N.J.1981) (elderly and alcoholic widow of corporation founder serves as a director and receives financial statements that indicate sons are misappropriating funds but takes no steps to stop these transactions; she is liable for the misappropriations because simple question or objection would likely have prevented loss). [*See also Smith v. Atlantic Properties, Inc.,* 422 N.E.2d 798 (Mass.App.1981).]

Caveat: The Delaware Supreme Court has stated that causation is irrelevant to a determination whether the business judgment rule applies, specifically distinguishing *Barnes v. Andrews. Cede & Co. v. Technicolor, Inc.,* 634 A.2d 345 (Del. 1993). Although, this holding is subject to varying interpretations, the court subsequently explained that causation is irrelevant in determining whether the business judgment rule precludes consideration of the merits of a business decision, suggesting that causation may nonetheless be relevant in determining whether a director is liable. *Cinerama, Inc. v. Technicolor, Inc.,* 663 A.2d 1156 (Del.1995).

4. Knowing Authorization of Wrongful Act

Liability has sometimes been imposed where a director knowingly authorizes or participates in a wrongful act, for example, where a director authorizes the improper use of corporate funds, knowing that the use is not in furtherance of corporate affairs.

a.   Attempts to hold non-participating directors or officers personally liable for antitrust fines imposed on the corporation, or for bribes, improper payments or illegal campaign contributions made by the corporation, have generally been unsuccessful. *Graham v. Allis–Chalmers Mfg. Co.,* 188 A.2d 125 (Del.1963).

b.   In *Miller v. American Telephone & Telegraph Co.,* 507 F.2d 759 (3d Cir.1974), the court upheld a stockholder's complaint against AT & T that that corporation had failed to try to collect a debt of $1,500,000 owed to the company by the Democratic National Committee for communications service provided during the 1968 Democratic Convention. The decision was based in part on a statute prohibiting campaign contributions by corporations to political parties.

c.   In some cases, the courts appear to have been reluctant to hold a director liable for a wrongful or illegal action on the part of the corporation, because the action may nonetheless have generated a benefit for the corporation. *See Auerbach v. Bennett* (bribes to foreign officials). This does not mean, however, that the corporation itself cannot be held liable for the wrongful or illegal act. In this situation, the status of the director is similar to that of an agent who negotiates a contract on behalf of a principal who later breaches the contract. In such a case, the agent cannot be held liable as long as the principal was disclosed and the contract was made in good faith.

Caveat: A director may be held liable for a tortious or unlawful act of the corporation if the director personally participated in the act. But liability in such a case rests on the fact that the director as an individual participated in the illegal act and not on the director's status as a director who authorized or assented to the act.

5. Reliance on Experts and Committees

MBCA 8.30(b) permits directors to rely on information, opinions, reports, or statements, including financial statements and other financial data prepared or presented by responsible corporate officers, employees, legal counsel, public accountants, or committees of the board of directors. Liability cannot be imposed on directors if the conditions of MBCA 8.30 are met.

a. Reliance is justified only if the director reasonably believes that the officers or directors are reliable and competent on the matters presented, and in the case of legal counsel, public accountants, and other professionals, the director reasonably believes that the matters are within the person's professional or expert competence.

b. A director may also rely on the reports of committees of the board of directors (of which the director is not a member) if the director reasonably believes the committee merits competence.

c. If the director makes a judgment that the source of information on which she proposes to rely is reliable and competent, then the decision to rely is itself protected by the business judgment rule.

6. *Smith v. Van Gorkom* and its Consequences

Prior to 1985, relatively few cases imposed liability upon directors for failure to comply with their duty of care. But in *Smith v. Van Gorkom*, 488 A.2d 858 (Del.1985), the Delaware Supreme Court imposed liability upon the directors of TransUnion Corporation for accepting an outside offer to purchase the corporation without investigating whether a higher price might be obtained and without making an investigation into the value of the company. The directors relied on the opinion of Van Gorkom, the CEO, that the price being offered was a reasonable one and approved a sale of the corporation within a three day period with virtually no discussion of possible alternatives and no assistance from outside experts. The corporation was sold at $55 per share. While the sale was pending it received an inquiry that indicated that a sale at $60 per share might be possible. Since there were more than 12,000,000 shares outstanding, the potential liability of the directors arising from this $5 differential was more than $60,000,000.

a. The Delaware Supreme Court held that the test for applying the business judgment rule was gross negligence. Further, the business judgment rule did not protect the directors of TransUnion because they had been grossly negligent in not adequately informing themselves of the transaction they approved.

b. The court decided that all directors, outside as well as inside directors, were responsible for the potential loss to stockholders but did not consider the measure of damages.

c. The decision in *Smith v. Van Gorkom* came at the height of a takeover boom involving immense transactions and was widely criticized by practicing lawyers on several grounds.

- The possibility of director liability with respect to such transactions was a deterrent to any outside person agreeing to serve as a director.

- Directors' and officers' liability insurance premiums soared, though whether caused by the decision or independent factors was disputed.

- Many feared that the decision would lead to overly cautious decision-making by directors, to emphasis on creating a paper trail that would appear to demonstrate informed decision-making, and to increased reliance on experts, including legal counsel.

- Many commentators were appalled that liability could be imposed on directors for simply following the recommendation of the CEO for whom they had great respect with respect to a transaction that did not involve self dealing by directors.

7. Director Liability Statutes

In 1986, in direct response to *Smith v. Van Gorkom*, the Delaware General Assembly enacted DGCL 102(b)(7), which authorizes in a certificate of incorporation:

"A provision eliminating or limiting the personal liability of a director to the corporation or its stockholders for monetary damages for breach of fiduciary duty as a director, provided that such provision shall not eliminate or limit the liability of a director (i) for any breach of the director's duty of loyalty to the corporation or its stockholders, (ii) for acts or omissions not in good faith or which involve intentional misconduct or a knowing violation of law, (iii) under [the section of the DGCL making directors liable for unlawful distributions] or (iv) for any transaction from which the director derived an improper personal benefit. No such provision shall eliminate or limit the liability of a director for any act or omission occurring prior to the date when such provision becomes effective."

The requirement that this or a similar provision appear in a certificate of incorporation means a stockholders' vote is necessary in connection with existing corporations if the liability of directors is to be eliminated or limited.

a. Virtually all states have enacted similar statutes since 1986. A few states, including Indiana, have adopted self executing statutes that automatically limit the liability of directors without requiring an amendment to the articles of incorporation.

b. Thousands of corporations incorporated in Delaware, including most publicly held corporations, have taken advantage of DGCL 102(b)(7) and eliminated directoral liability to the maximum extent permitted by that section.

c. This section makes it clear that the directors of a corporation adopting an appropriate provision are not personally liable for damages even in the case of gross negligence. *Boeing Co. v. Shrontz*, 1992 WL 81228 (Del.Ch.1992).

d. DGCL 102(b)(7) applies only to actions for monetary damages. An action for equitable relief to enjoin a transaction is not precluded. As a result litigation in due care cases continue to arise despite the enactment of DGCL 102(b)(7). Similar statutes in a few other states apply to actions for equitable relief as well as to actions for monetary damages.

e. MBCA 2.02(b)(4) permits a provision in the articles of incorporation providing for the limitation or elimination of liability of directors for gross negligence. The exceptions are narrower than DGCL 102(b)(7): liability may not be eliminated or limited for (A) the amount of a financial benefit received by a director to which he is not entitled; (B) an intentional infliction of harm on the corporation or the stockholders; (C) a violation of section 8.33 (relating to illegal distributions); or (D) an intentional violation of criminal law.

f. MBCA 8.31(a) provides in essence that a director may not be held liable to the corporation unless it is established that the director's conduct (1) is not immune and has not been ratified, and (2) is either a violation of the duty of care, or a violation of the duty of loyalty, or the result of sustained inattention, or involves the receipt of a financial benefit to which the director was not entitled or which resulted from unfair dealing with the corporation. MBCA 8.31(b) provides that it must also be established that the corporation suffered harm (presumably financial harm) and that the harm was proximately caused by the conduct challenged.

C. DUTY OF LOYALTY

Whereas the duty of care focuses on the responsibility of directors and officers to manage a corporation competently, the duty of loyalty (sometimes called the duty of fairness) focuses on the responsibility of directors and officers to avoid or at least scrutinize conflicts of interest. Conflicts of interest may take many forms.

• In a self-dealing case, a director or officer enters into a transaction with the corporation. For example, a director may sell a piece of property to the corporation. The obvious danger is that the director may use his position to cause the corporation to overpay.

• In a corporate opportunity case, a director or officer may come across a valuable business opportunity in his capacity as a director or officer and may seek to exploit the opportunity for his own benefit rather than offering it to the corporation. The harm to the corporation is a loss of profits.

• In a competition case, a director or officer engages in a new business venture that seeks to exploit the same market as the old corporation. The harm to the corporation is in the form of reduced profits.

1. In General

If a transaction is tainted by a conflict of interest that triggers duty of loyalty analysis, the burden shifts to the defendant to prove that the transaction is fair to the corporation. Some courts use the phrase *entire fairness* or *inherent fairness* or *intrinsic fairness*.

Caveat: Although fiduciary duty subsumes both a duty of care and a duty of loyalty, some courts use the phrase fiduciary duty to refer to the duty of loyalty alone. Careful attention to the context will usually reveal the court's meaning.

Caveat: In some cases, the courts seem to look to the good faith requirement of the duty of care to determine whether the business judgment rule applies. In other words, a transaction tainted by a conflict of interest may be motivated by the prospect of personal financial return rather than the best interests of the company. The requirement of good faith may extend to a broader range of factors as well.

Caveat: A decision may fail to be protected by the business judgment rule without necessarily triggering duty of loyalty analysis. If so, the defendant may be required to prove that the transaction was merely reasonable or rational.

a. The key question in many cases is whether or not the transaction in question should be analyzed as a duty of care case or a duty of loyalty case. Often the answer to this question is outcome determinative, because the business judgment rule does not apply if a director or officer has a personal financial interest in the transaction.

Caveat: The precise definition of a disabling interest may vary depending on the language of the statute and nature of the transaction.

b. The burden of proof may be shifted back to the plaintiff if the decision is ratified by unconflicted directors (or a committee thereof) or by the stockholders in a fully informed vote (without counting the votes that may be cast by a conflicted stockholder).

c. Generally speaking, the remedy in a duty of care case is damages, whereas the remedy in a duty of loyalty case is rescission or the equivalent. The pattern is the same as under the common law of agency. An agent must account to the principal. In cases in which it is impossible to rescind the transaction, the courts may apply a constructive trust on the proceeds from the offending transaction or award the monetary equivalent of rescission–sometimes called *rescissory damages.* In some cases, a transaction may give rise to both types of liability. If rescission is ordered, the corporation will ordinarily also be required to surrender whatever it received in connection with the transaction. *See Meinhard v. Salmon.*

d. Proof of fairness of a complex transaction may be difficult and expensive, involving a protracted trial. Moreover, the potential liability may be significant in that a fiduciary may be required to disgorge all profits from a transaction occurring years before judgment is finally rendered. Hence, there is a strong incentive to obtain review and approval of transactions by directors or stockholders rather than requiring the interested director to establish the fairness of the transaction.

2. Self–Dealing

A self-dealing transaction is one between a director and corporation. The test for self-dealing transactions developed by the courts in absence of statute combines procedural and substantive requirements. Some courts describe the test as requiring both "fair dealing" and "fair price".

a. The early common law took the position that because of the risk inherent in self-dealing transactions, all such transactions were void or voidable at the election of the corporation. *Stewart v. Lehigh Valley R. Co.*, 38 N.J.L. 505 (1875). This approach has been abandoned as overbroad, because many self-dealing transactions are entirely fair and reasonable. Indeed, directors may give their corporations terms that are more favorable than the corporation might obtain elsewhere. *Robotham v. Prudential Ins. Co. of America*, 53 A. 842 (N.J.Ch.Div.1903). Moreover, the strict approach may have the effect of precluding a director or officer from a mutually beneficial deal simply because of status and effectively creating a presumption in favor of outsiders who presumably are less well informed.

Example: A director may make a loan to the corporation when the corporation cannot borrow elsewhere or can borrow only on terms that are less favorable. The director may be willing to make the loan because the director has a better understanding of the prospects of the business. Moreover, the opportunity to lend money to the corporation may be more lucrative than other investments available to the director at the time. Such transactions should obviously be encouraged.

b. Generally speaking, there are three ways that a tainted transaction may be upheld or ratified. First, if the transaction is approved by the board of directors after full disclosure of material terms and without the participation of the interested director (except possibly for purposes of establishing a quorum), the transaction is deemed to be ratified. Second, if the transaction is approved by the stockholders after full disclosure of material terms, the transaction is deemed to be ratified and enforceable. Third, in the absence of ratification, the transaction may be upheld if a court determines that the terms of the transaction are fair. Some authorities have required ratification or approval even for fair transactions.

Caveat: If a transaction involves waste of corporate assets it may not be ratified except possibly by a unanimous vote of the stockholders. The term *waste* connotes the disposition of corporate assets for a clearly inadequate return, including gift or theft.

Caveat: It is not always clear whether the effect of ratification is to trigger applicability of the business judgment rule or simply to shift the burden of disproving *fairness* to the plaintiff. But it is not clear that the distinction matters in many cases.

Caveat: The Delaware Supreme Court has held that ratification of a tainted transaction does not trigger DGCL 102(b)(7) and that accordingly an action challenging the transaction cannot be summarily dismissed as immunized from attack. *Emerald Partners.* The court reasoned that ratification merely shifted the burden of proof with respect to the issue of fairness, and that the issue of whether a director had received an improper benefit was not one that could be immunized under DGCL 102(b)(7).

Caveat: Where approval by disinterested directors is sought, the interested director, if present, should not be counted toward the quorum requirement, and she should not vote on or participate in the discussion of the merits of the transaction. She also should not informally lobby disinterested directors in an effort to persuade them to support the transaction. Any of these actions on the part of the interested director may make the transaction voidable by the corporation and require the interested director to establish the intrinsic fairness of the transaction.

3. Ratification by Stockholders

Ratification by stockholders of a transaction between a director and the corporation may validate a self-dealing transaction. At common law, interested directors may vote their shares as stockholders in favor of the transaction. *North-West Trans. Co. v. Beatty,* 12 App.Cas. 589 (Eng. 1887); *Gamble v. Queens County Water Co.,* 25 N.E. 201 (N.Y.1890); *Allaun v.*

Consolidated Oil Co., 147 A. 257 (Del.Ch.1929). The modern view is to disqualify the vote of the interested stockholder and permit ratification by a majority of the remaining stockholders. This may lead to ratification by a *majority of the minority* (MOM).

4. Statutory Treatment of Self–Dealing Transactions

Statutes in many states address the issue of self-dealing transactions. Most such statutes are similar to old MBCA 8.31 though individual state statutes vary widely in details:

Director Conflict of Interest

(a) A conflict of interest transaction is a transaction with the corporation in which a director of the corporation has a direct or indirect interest. A conflict of interest transaction is not voidable by the corporations solely because of the director's interest in the transaction if any one of the following is true: (1) the material facts of the transaction and the director's interest were disclosed or known to the board of directors or a committee of the board of directors and the board of directors or committee authorized, approved, or ratified the transaction; (2) the material facts of the transaction and the director's interest were disclosed or known to the stockholders entitled to vote and they authorized, approved, or ratified the transaction; or (3) the transaction was fair to the corporation.

(b) For purposes of this section, a director of the corporation has an indirect interest in a transaction if (1) another entity in which he has a material financial interest or in which he is a general partner is a party to the transaction, or (2) another entity of which he is a director, officer, or trustee is a party to the transaction and the transaction is or should be considered by the board of directors of the corporation.

(c) For purposes of subsection (a)(1), a conflict of interest transaction is authorized, approved, or ratified if it receives the affirmative vote of a majority of the directors on the board of directors (or on the committee) who have no direct or indirect interest in the transaction, but a transaction may not be authorized, approved, or ratified under this section by a single director. If a majority of the directors who have no direct or indirect interest in the transaction vote to authorize, approve, or ratify the transaction, a quorum is present for the purpose of taking action under this section. The presence of, or a vote cast by, a director with a direct or indirect interest in the transaction does not affect the validity of any action taken under subsection (01) if the transaction is otherwise authorized, approved, or ratified as provided in that subsection.

(d) For purposes of subsection (a)(2), a conflict of interest transaction is authorized, approved, or ratified if it receives the vote of a majority of the shares entitled to be counted under this subsection. Shares owned by or voted under the control of a director who has a direct or indirect interest in the transaction, and shares owned by or voted under the control of an entity described in subsection (b)(1), may not be counted in a vote of stockholders to determine whether to authorize, approve, or ratify a conflict of interest transaction under subsection (a)(2). The vote of those shares, however, shall be counted in determining whether the transaction is approved under other sections of this Act. A majority of the shares, whether or not present, that are entitled to be counted in a vote on the transaction under this subsection constitutes a quorum for the purpose of taking action under this section.

a. Section 8.31 was withdrawn in 1988 and replaced by sections 8.60 to 8.63, discussed below.

b. These statutes simply exonerate or remove a cloud from self-dealing transactions based on the early common law rule of automatic voidability. It merely removes an interested director cloud when its terms are met and protects against invalidation of an agreement solely because such a director or officer is involved. *Fliegler v. Lawrence*, 361 A.2d 218, 222 (Del.1976); *Cookies Food Products, Inc. v. Lakes Warehouse Distributing, Inc.*, 430 N.W.2d 447 (Iowa, 1988).

c. These statutes involve the business judgment rule. The conditions for approval set forth in MBCA 8.31 are similar to the requirements of the business judgment rule. In *Marciano v. Nakash*, 535 A.2d 400 (Del.1987), the Delaware Supreme Court stated that under DGCL 144 approval by fully-informed disinterested directors or disinterested stockholders permits invocation of the business judgment rule and limits judicial review to issues of gift or waste with the burden of proof upon the party attacking the transaction.

d. Compliance with these statutes generally requires full disclosure of both the existence of conflicting interests and the details of the transaction.

e. Old MBCA 8.31 excluded interested stockholders from voting to approve conflict-of-interest transactions but many state statutes do not expressly do so. In *Fliegler v. Lawrence*, 361 A.2d 218 (Del.1976), interested stockholders voted to ratify a transaction as literally permitted by DGCL 144. The court applied an intrinsic fairness test and set aside the transaction, stating that nothing in the statute "sanctions unfairness * * * or removes the transaction from judicial scrutiny." At 222.

f. Under the California statute (which differs significantly from MBCA 8.31 in that fairness is the sole test for invalidity), unfair or unreasonable transactions may not be validated. *Remillard Brick Co. v. Remillard–Dandini Co.*, 241 P.2d 66 (Cal.App.1952); *Kennerson v. Burbank Amusement Co.*, 260 P.2d 823 (Cal.App.1953).

5. MBCA Subchapter F

In 1988, the Committee on Corporate Laws withdrew MBCA 8.31, discussed above, and substituted a new and more comprehensive statute dealing with conflict of interest transactions. This new treatment appears in sections 8.61 through 8.63, and is often referred to as Subchapter F. Chapter F is a complex and elaborate statute that cannot be easily summarized. The following comments and examples describe only the broad outlines of this statute.

a. Subchapter F is structured similarly to MBCA 8.31: a conflict of interest transaction is not voidable by the corporation if (a) it has been approved by disinterested directors or stockholders, or (b) the interested director establishes the fairness of the transaction. Unlike § 8.31, however, Subchapter F is designed to create a series of bright line principles that increase predictability and enhance practical administration.

b. Subchapter F deals only with transactions between a director and the corporation.

Example: The corporation decides to establish a divisional headquarters in a director's home town. This is not a transaction between the director and the corporation and is not governed by subchapter F.

c. MBCA 8.60 defines a conflicting interest in terms that are exclusive. MBCA 8.60(1)(i) defines a direct conflicting interest to be when the director knows at the time of commitment that he or a related person is a party to the transaction or has a beneficial interest in or so closely linked to the transaction and of such financial significance to the director or a related person that the interest would reasonably be expected to exert an influence on the director's judgment if he were called upon to vote on the transaction.

MBCA 8.60(1)(ii) adds limited classes of indirect interests to the definition of conflicting interest: transactions that would in the normal course of events be brought to the board of directors for decision and involve (i) an entity of which the director is a director, general partner, agent, or employee or (ii) an entity that controls, is controlled by, or is under common control with one of those entities or (iii) a person who is a general partner, principal, or employer of the director.

MBCA 8.60(2) defines a related person to include spouses, children, grandchildren, siblings, parents, and any trust of which the director is a trustee.

Example: If D (a director of X Co.) is a major creditor of Y Co., and the issue is some transaction between X Co. and Y Co., D's creditor interest in Y Co. does not fall within the definition of conflicting interest unless it is so large that it would reasonably be expected to affect his judgment if he were called to vote on the transaction.

d. A director's conflicting interest transaction is a transaction effected or proposed to be effected by the corporation in which a director of the corporation has a conflicting interest. MBCA 8.60(2). This definition is also exclusive. MBCA 8.61(a) provides that a court may not enjoin, set aside or award damages or impose another sanction with respect to a transaction that is not a director's conflicting interest transaction on the ground that the director has a personal interest in the transaction.

Example: D, a director, votes to approve a transaction between the corporation and D's cousin. Since a cousin is not a related person, the transaction is not a director's conflicting interest transaction and may not be invalidated on the ground of conflict of interest.

Example: D, a director, votes to approve a transaction between the corporation and the president of a golf club D desperately wishes to join. The transaction is not a director's conflicting interest transaction and may not be invalidated on the ground of conflict of interest.

Caveat: Subchapter F deals only with claims based on conflict of interest. The transactions described above may be attacked on the ground they were not approved at a lawful meeting, or that they constitute fraud or waste.

e.   MBCA 8.61(b)(1) provides that approval of a transaction by disinterested directors, following full disclosure by the interested director, is protected by the business judgment rule and MBCA 8.30.

> *Caveat:*   The Official Comment to this section is unusual in that it stresses the substantive requirements of the business judgment rule, stating that if the transaction is approved merely as an accommodation to the director with the conflicting interest, that approval would not be given preclusive effect under the business judgment rule. Similarly, if the terms of a director's conflicting interest transaction are manifestly unfavorable to the corporation, that fact would be relevant to the question whether the approval of the transaction was in good faith.

> *Example:*   The board of directors of a manufacturing corporation approves a cash loan to a director, the terms of which—the duration, security, and interest rate—are at prevailing commercial rates. The loan, however, is not made in the course of the corporation's ordinary business and its effect is to require a commitment of limited working capital that would otherwise have been used in furtherance of the corporation's business activities. The loan is not protected by subchapter F since the board of directors did not comply with the requirement of § 8.30(a) that the action be, in the board's reasonable judgment, in the best interests of the corporation.

6.   Loans to Directors or Officers

Most state statutes contain a provision restricting or prohibiting loans to directors or officers. MBCA 8.32 contained a liberalized prohibition similar to these state statutes, but that section was withdrawn in 1988 when subchapter F was approved. That subchapter now governs loans to directors or officers.

> *Example:*   A corporation desires to provide low cost housing loans for officers, employees and directors who are compelled to relocate as a result of a decision to change the location of the home office. Under the statutes of some states, such loans are unlawful if made to directors or officers even though the

program benefits the corporation and the loans proposed to be made to officers and directors are consistent with loans granted to lower level employees. Compensation arrangements with the officers and directors, however, may be adjusted to give substantially the same benefits as the prohibited loans. Such loans are valid under subchapter F if the requirements of that subchapter are met.

7. Waiver by Provision in the Articles of Incorporation

Provisions may be placed in the articles of incorporation of a corporation to validate transactions between directors and the corporation that otherwise might be voidable under the above principles. These clauses are not construed literally, and do not validate fraudulent or manifestly unfair acts. *Spiegel v. Beacon Participations*, 8 N.E.2d 895 (Mass.1937). Such clauses may be effective to permit an interested director to be counted in determining whether a quorum is present and exonerate transactions between corporation and director from adverse inferences which might be drawn against them. *Everett v. Phillips*, 43 N.E.2d 18 (N.Y.1942).

> *Caveat:* There is no express statutory authorization for provisions exonerating directors from the duty of loyalty. Compare the provisions relating to the duty of care authorized by DGCL 102(b)(7).

D. CORPORATE OPPORTUNITIES

As a fiduciary, a director owes a duty to further the interest of the corporation and to give it the benefit of her uncorrupted business judgment. She may not take a secret profit in connection with corporate transactions, compete unfairly with the corporation, or take personally profitable business opportunities which belong to the corporation. If the opportunity is not a corporate opportunity the director may take advantage of it personally for his or her own private gain and need not share it with the corporation or with other participants in the corporation.

1. What is a Corporate Opportunity?

Several competing tests exist as to when an opportunity should be considered a corporate opportunity.

a. An early test was that the opportunity must involve property wherein the corporation has interest already existing or in which it has an expectancy growing out of an existing right. *See Burg v. Horn*, 380 F.2d

897 (2d Cir.1967); *Litwin v. Allen,* 25 N.Y.S.2d 667 (N.Y. 1940). This narrow test of corporate opportunity and has been rejected by most courts. *See Kerrigan v. Unity Sav. Ass'n,* 317 N.E.2d 39 (Ill. 1974).

b. Some courts have adopted a test that the opportunity must arise out of the corporation's business as it is then conducted. The *line of business* test compares the opportunity to the businesses in which the corporation is engaged. The more similar the opportunity, the more likely it is to be seen as a corporate opportunity. This test tends to be expansive and has been categorized as too broad. *Burg v. Horn,* 380 F.2d 897 (2d Cir.1967).

c. Some courts simply apply a test of fairness. *Durfee v. Durfee & Canning, Inc.,* 80 N.E.2d 522 (Mass.1948). This test has been rejected by most courts as providing little or no practical guidance. *Northeast Harbor Golf Club, Inc. v. Harris,* 661 A.2d 1146 (Me.1995)

d. A leading Minnesota case combines a line of business test with consideration of whether it is fair for the director under the circumstances to appropriate the opportunity. *Miller v. Miller,* 222 N.W.2d 71 (Minn.1974).

e. Delaware law holds that an opportunity is a corporate opportunity if (1) the corporation is financially able to exploit the opportunity, (2) the opportunity is within the corporation's line of business, (3) the corporation has an interest or expectancy in the opportunity and (4) by taking the opportunity for his own, the corporate fiduciary will thereby be placed in a position inconsistent with his duties to the corporation. *Broz v. Cellular Information Systems, Inc.,* 673 A.2d 148 (Del.1996), *citing Guth v. Loft, Inc.,* 5 A.2d 503 (Del.1939).

f. PCG 5.05 defines a corporate opportunity *for a director or officer* as an opportunity offered with the expectation that it would be offered to the corporation or discovered with the use of corporate information or property, and is an opportunity that is reasonably closely related to the business in which the corporation is engaged or expects to engage. *See Northeast Harbor Golf Club v. Harris,* 661 A.2d 1146 (Me.1995) (reviewing competing tests and adopting PCG test). *See also Klinicki v. Lundgren,* 695 P.2d 906 (Ore.1985) (adopting earlier and stricter version of test).

Example: A corporation is planning to build a new plant at a specified location. An officer buys up a portion of the land on which the plant is to be built and resells it at a profit to the corporation without disclosing his identity. The opportunity is a corporate opportunity under all the above tests and the officer must account to the corporation for his entire profit.

Example: A corporation is in the boat building business and does not buy or sell used boats. The corporate president learns that a used boat is for sale at a favorable price. She buys the boat personally and resells it profitably. The used boat is not a corporate opportunity under any of the above tests and she need not account to the corporation for her profit.

g. Several factors are considered in evaluating the status of an opportunity.

- Whether there were prior negotiations with the corporation about the opportunity.

- Whether the opportunity was offered to the corporation or to the director as an agent of the corporation. *See Rapistan Corp. v. Michaels,* 511 N.W.2d 918 (Mich.App.1994) (Delaware law).

- Whether the director disclosed the opportunity to the corporation or took advantage of it secretly.

- Whether the director learned of the opportunity by reason of his or her position with the corporation.

- Whether the director used corporate facilities or property in taking advantage of the opportunity.

- Whether as a result of taking advantage of the opportunity the director is competing with the corporation, thwarting corporate policy, or acting unfairly with respect to the corporation. *Zidell v. Zidell, Inc.,* 560 P.2d 1091 (Ore.1977).

- Whether the director acquired at a discount claims against the corporation when the corporation could have done so. *See Weissman v. A. Weissman, Inc.,* 97 A.2d 870 (Pa.1953); *Manufacturers Trust Co. v. Becker,* 338 U.S. 304, 70 S.Ct. 127 (1949).

- Whether the need of the corporation for the opportunity was substantial.

- Whether the director was involved in several ventures and the opportunity in question was not uniquely attributable to one such venture. *See Johnston v. Greene,* 121 A.2d 919 (Del.1956).

Example: X is a director and controlling stockholder of Y Co., a publicly owned company, which in turn owns as its principal asset Z Co., a profitable business. X is approached as a director of Y Co. by B Co which is interested in purchasing Z Co. X does not present this proposal to Y Co., but instead negotiates with B Co. to purchase his interest in Y Co. In connection with this negotiation X receives option payments from B Co. and Y Co. incurs some expenses in providing information to B Co. X has the ability to block Y Co.'s purchase of Z Co. since stockholder approval by Y Co. would be necessary. The corporate opportunity doctrine does not require X to give up his blocking power as a stockholder, but he is an interested director and breaches his duty of loyalty to Y Co. by failing to communicate B Co.'s interest in purchasing Z Co. directly to Y Co. As a result X is liable to Y Co. for the payments he received from B Co. and for the expenses incurred by Y Co. *Thorpe v. CERBCO, Inc.,* 676 A.2d 436 (Del. 1996).

Example: The president of a corporation operating a retail department store learns that a competitive store is for sale two blocks away. He secretly buys the competing store, and uses his knowledge of inventory control and relations with suppliers to make the new store more competitive. The new store is a corporate opportunity and the president must account for his profit.

Example: In this example, the corporation has previously decided not to expand into new locations in the community in question. The competing store is not a corporate opportunity but the president may be liable for conversion of trade secrets or unfair competition if he improves the competitive nature of the store on the basis of proprietary information obtained from the corporation. *Lincoln Stores v. Grant,* 34 N.E.2d 704 (Mass.1941).

Caveat: There is always a danger that a corporation (or other principal) may wait to assert claims relating to an arguable corporate opportunity until after it is apparent whether the opportunity will prove profitable. In such cases, the corporation (or other principal) may seek to use the corporate opportunity doctrine as a sword rather than a shield. As a general rule, a corporation should act promptly to object to the diversion of an opportunity (or any act in competition with the corporation). Although some commentators have suggested that the benefits of free enterprise dictate that corporate opportunities should be narrowly construed, a better approach might be to deny relief if it appears that the director or officer (or other agent) assumed a substantial business risk in connection with pursuing the opportunity. *Cf. Lincoln Stores v. Grant*, 34 N.E.2d 704 (Mass.1941).

2. Rejection of Corporate Opportunity

Even if an opportunity is a corporate opportunity, directors may take advantage of it if the corporation elects not to do so. *Zidell v. Zidell, Inc.*, 560 P.2d 1091 (Ore.1977).

a. The corporation may voluntarily relinquish a corporate opportunity, though such a relinquishment is a self-dealing transaction and is scrutinized by the courts on the basis of principles described earlier. *Johnston v. Greene*, 121 A.2d 919 (Del.1956).

b. A persuasive reason for the relinquishment helps to make it clear that the corporation voluntarily decided not to pursue the opportunity.

Example: The corporation operating the retail department store referred to above receives a proposal from the competing store that it purchase the competing store's business; the board of directors of the department store reviews the proposal and decides that under the circumstances it would be unwise to expand the corporation's business. The opportunity is no longer a corporate opportunity and individual directors may thereafter take advantage of the opportunity and purchase the competing store.

c. As is the case with self-dealing transactions generally, effective approval by the board of directors requires compliance with the standards of the business judgment rule as applied to self dealing transactions. Requirements include full disclosure of all the surrounding facts by the interested directors and their non-participation in the decision-making process.

3. Inability or Incapacity of Corporation

Directors may take advantage of a corporate opportunity if the corporation is unable or incapable of taking advantage of the opportunity.

> *Example:*   A third person refuses to deal with the corporation but is willing to deal with one or more directors individually. The opportunity is not a corporate opportunity.

a.   Most courts permit directors to take advantage of a corporate opportunity if the corporation is financially unable to capitalize on the opportunity. *A. C. Petters Co. v. St. Cloud Enterprises, Inc.*, 222 N.W.2d 83 (Minn.1974). The financial inability defense is troublesome because it may tempt directors to refrain from exercising best efforts on behalf of the corporation if they thereafter may take advantage personally of a profitable opportunity. *Irving Trust Co. v. Deutsch*, 73 F.2d 121 (2d Cir.1934). Thus, when courts permit a director to utilize a corporate opportunity on this basis, they require a convincing showing that the corporation in fact lacks the independent assets to take advantage of its opportunity.

> *Caveat:*   Directors do not have the obligation to lend funds to the corporation in order to permit it to take advantage of a corporate opportunity.

> *Caveat:*   If the opportunity is sufficiently attractive, the corporation should normally be able to borrow funds to develop the opportunity on the security of the opportunity.

b.   The PCG does not recognize a defense of financial inability. *See Klinicki v. Lundgren*, 695 P.2d 906 (Ore.1985). Under the PCG, before a director or officer may take advantage of an opportunity, the corporation must voluntarily renounce its interest in the opportunity or unreasonably fail to act on the proposal.

c.   An absolute prohibition on directors taking advantage of a corporate opportunity may mean that directors would have to forgo an opportunity entirely if they are unable to persuade the corporation to forgo the transaction and are unwilling to lend the necessary funds to the corporation.

E.   COMPETITION WITH THE CORPORATION

Directors may engage in a similar line of business in competition with the corporation's business where it is done in good faith and without injury to the corporation. A director is not a full-time employee and may utilize his or her time as the director sees fit.

a.   Cases have found a competing director or officer to be guilty of a breach of fiduciary duty on several possible theories: conflict of interest, corporate opportunity, misappropriation of trade secrets or customer lists, or wrongful interference with contractual relationships. *Duane Jones Co. v. Burke,* 117 N.E.2d 237 (N.Y.1954).

b.   Tort concepts of unfair competition in this area are close to fiduciary duties.

c.   Judicial notions of fairness or fair play are dominant, and cases require a close appraisal of the fiduciary's conduct in light of ethical business practice. *Aero Drapery of Kentucky, Inc. v. Engdahl,* 507 S.W.2d 166 (Ky.1974).

F.   EXECUTIVE COMPENSATION

Decisions regarding executive compensation by their very nature raise duty of loyalty issues. The board of directors must approve the compensation paid to the CEO, who is invariably a director and usually is also chairman of the board of directors. Most publicly held corporations have created compensation committees composed of independent directors to review all compensation issues for highly compensated executives. Because the conflicts of interest involved are structural and cannot be avoided, and because most publicly traded corporations have established standing compensation committees composed solely of outside directors, decisions regarding executive compensation are not usually treated as duty of loyalty problems.

1.   Test for Excessive Compensation

Courts are reluctant to inquire into issues of executive compensation in publicly held corporations. In such corporations, the test for excessive compensation is whether the payments are so large as to constitute spoliation or waste. *Rogers v. Hill,* 289 U.S. 582, 53 S.Ct. 731 (1933).

Example: A bylaw duly approved by the stockholders provides that a stated percentage of the profits are to be set aside each year and paid as a bonus to specified executive officers. Twenty-five years later, the business of the corporation has increased many-fold; the profits payable to the executive officers under the bylaw are roughly ten times higher than the compensation payable by comparable corporations to comparable officers. The payments constitute waste and may be reduced by the court to a reasonable amount. *Rogers v. Hill,* 289 U.S. 582, 53 S.Ct. 731 (1933).

Example: A corporation creates a non-discriminatory pension plan for its employees, including its chief executive officer. Because of his nearness to retirement and large pension that he commands, over $10,000,000 of the initial payment of $14,000,000 is attributable to the inclusion of the CEO in the plan, an amount far in excess of his reasonable compensation. The plan constitutes waste. *Fogelson v. American Woolen Co.,* 170 F.2d 660 (2d Cir.1948).

Example: A chief executive of a corporation receives a salary of $4,000,000 per year. This salary is at the high end of the range of salaries for chief executive officers for corporations of an equivalent size in the same industry. The salary is not so out of line as to constitute waste.

Caveat: During the 1990s there has been increased criticism of the salaries paid to senior executives, particularly CEOs. Levels of executive compensation are of direct concern to institutional investors who are substantial stockholders in publicly held corporations. Internal control, rather than judicial intervention, seems more appropriate to deal with this issue if indeed it needs to be dealt with.

Caveat: Courts are reluctant to review compensation levels of executives of publicly held corporations. A reasonableness test for measuring excessiveness of compensation has been rejected as being unworkable and involving courts in business decisions with respect to which courts have little or no competence. *See Heller v. Boylan,* 29 N.Y.S.2d 653 (1941).

2. Compensation Issues in Publicly Held Corporations

A controversial aspect of modern corporation law is the level of the compensation paid to senior executives of publicly held corporations. In the 1990s average salaries of senior executives were in the high six or low seven figures usually supplemented by stock options and incentive compensation arrangements. Incomes of senior executives were increasing more rapidly than average income levels throughout society and the spread between average wage levels and the salaries of senior executives was increasing.

a. In 1992, the SEC mandated more elaborate and complete descriptions of executive compensation in disclosure documents, including a specific discussion of compensation levels.

b. The SEC required corporations to place stockholder proposals with respect to compensation levels in proxy statements under Rule 14a–8.

c. The SEC required footnote disclosure of the value of stock options granted to senior executives.

d. In 1993, Congress enacted IRC 162(m) capping the deductibility of executive compensation at $1,000,000 million per year. Performance based compensation such as bonuses and stock options is excluded from the cap. This provision has not reduced the level of executive compensation and may actually have encouraged increases in compensation levels.

3. **Compensation Based on Stock Performance**

    Courts have upheld compensation arrangements based on the price or value of shares. Economists generally favor these arrangements because they tend to align management interests with the maximization of stockholder wealth.

    a. Stock option plans, stock purchase plans, and stock bonus plans may have special tax benefits. Such plans are upheld if approved by disinterested directors or by stockholders, and the benefits being conferred bear a reasonable relationship to the services being performed. *Beard v. Elster, 160 A.2d 731 (Del. 1960); Eliasberg v. Standard Oil Co.,* 92 A.2d 862 (N.J.Super.Ch.Div. 1952). *See also Cohen v. Ayers,* 596 F.2d 733 (7th Cir.1979) (cancellation of out-of-money options and substitution of valuable options valid if effectively ratified by disinterested directors or stockholders).

    b. A *phantom stock plan* provides compensation that is computed over a period of time as though the officer had owned a specified number of shares. Such an arrangement is a legitimate form of compensation. *Lieberman v. Koppers Co., Inc.,* 149 A.2d 756 (Del.Ch.1959); *Berkwitz v. Humphrey,* 163 F.Supp. 78 (N.D.Ohio 1958).

    c. *Stock appreciation rights* (SARs) are bonus payments computed on the basis of growth of value of the corporation's shares. In recent years bonus payments based on the attainment of a predetermined goal (e.g. a ten per cent increase in gross sales of the division) have become popular. These are sometimes called *performance unit payments* (PUPs).

4. Benefit to Corporation

Services must be given or promised in exchange for compensation. A post-death payment to the estate of a deceased employee or surviving spouse not made pursuant to a preexisting plan has been invalidated on this ground. *Adams v. Smith,* 153 So.2d 221 (Ala.1963); *Alexander v. Lindsay,* 152 So.2d 261 (La.App.1963).

> *Caveat:* The court usually can find some way to avoid this technical objection to the enforceability of a compensation arrangement if it wishes to do so. Regular pension or profit sharing plans, for example, are not subject to this objection because they are part of an overall plan of compensation entered into while services are being performed.

> *Example:* A retiring employee agrees to be available for consultation after his retirement at the corporation's request in exchange for specified payments for life. The employee is never requested to consult. The payments are nevertheless supported by consideration. *Osborne v. Locke Steel Chain Co.,* 218 A.2d 526 (Conn.1966).

G. CONTROLLING STOCKHOLDERS

Minority stockholders in a corporation may be injured by a variety of transactions authorized by the controlling stockholder or by the board of directors elected by such stockholders. The test usually applied to such transactions is fairness or intrinsic fairness. However, to an increasing extent, courts are willing to accept the decision of disinterested directors as to the reasonableness of such transactions under the business judgment rule.

1. Transactions With a Partially Owned Subsidiary

A clear example of a potentially injurious transaction is a transaction between a corporation and its partially owned subsidiary. The minority stockholders of the subsidiary are injured by any transaction that in effect transfers assets from the subsidiary to the parent on less than a fair and equivalent exchange.

a. The parent corporation usually has the power to nominate and elect all the directors of the subsidiary and thereby to name all members of the subsidiary's management.

b. If the transaction involves a proportionate distribution of assets by the subsidiary to all of its stockholders, the minority has no basis for complaint on the ground of domination of the management by the parent corporation.

c. The proper standard for evaluating transactions between parent and subsidiary is that it must be entirely fair or intrinsically fair to the subsidiary.

Example: Plaintiffs are minority stockholders of a corporation which is 97 per cent owned by the parent corporation. They attack decisions (1) to pay large dividends by the subsidiary to ease the cash needs of the parent (the plaintiffs received their proportionate share of these distributions) and (2) to cause the subsidiary not to pursue claims for breach of contract against the parent or other subsidiaries of the parent. The question of the excessive dividends should be evaluated by the business judgment rule since all stockholders are being treated proportionately. However, the refusal to enforce the contract claim should be judged on the basis of an intrinsic fairness test since it involves self dealing, the parent receiving something from the subsidiary to the exclusion and detriment of the minority stockholders. *Sinclair Oil Corp. v. Levien,* 280 A.2d 717 (Del.1971).

Caveat: Problems of this type arise only when there are minority stockholders of the subsidiary. They do not arise when the subsidiary is 100 per cent owned by the parent corporation.

d. A common problem is the allocation of tax benefits resulting from the filing of a consolidated, return. As a result of the consolidation of the financial operations of the subsidiary with the parent, it is possible that valuable tax benefits owned by the partially owned subsidiary will be realized by the parent corporation. *Case v. New York Central R. Co.,* 256 N.Y.S.2d 607, 204 N.E.2d 643 (N.Y. 1965). In order to avoid conflicts of interest in this situation, parent corporations usually enter into tax sharing agreements with their partially owned subsidiaries, requiring each subsidiary to pay the portion of the total tax shown on the consolidated return resulting from the subsidiary's operations and requiring the parent corporation to compensate the subsidiary for any tax benefits utilized by the parent to reduce or eliminate its tax obligation as reflected in the consolidated return.

e. Similar allocation problems may arise whenever parent and partially owned subsidiary share office space or utilize common services. They also arise whenever the parent corporation provide services to subsidiaries. To avoid claims of conflict of interest, parent and subsidiary usually enter into formal agreements providing how these costs should be shared and reimbursements made.

Caveat: Formal agreements dealing with cost sharing and reimbursements may also be entered into between parent and wholly owned subsidiaries. The purposes of these formal agreements are to preserve the corporate separateness and to permit the parent to evaluate the profitability of individual subsidiaries by allocating costs on a rational basis.

f. Because of conflict of interest problems, a parent corporation with a partially owned subsidiary may place outside unaffiliated directors on the board of directors of the subsidiary. When a transaction between subsidiary and parent is proposed, the subsidiary may be represented solely by the outside directors. In this way, the transaction may be subject to the business judgment rule rather than the rule of intrinsic or entire fairness.

g. A parent corporation with a partially owned subsidiary may lawfully eliminate the minority stockholders in the subsidiary through a cash-out merger, thereby making the subsidiary wholly owned rather than partially owned.

2. Miscellaneous Transactions

The fairness test is applicable to a variety of transactions that defy precise categorization and are best illustrated by example. These situations also generally involve duties of controlling stockholders or of directors named by controlling stockholders.

Example: Preemptive rights are excluded in X Co; directors elected by a controlling stockholder cause X Co. to issue to the controlling stockholder new or treasury shares that increases her ownership from 62 per cent to 90 per cent of all outstanding shares. The shares are issued at a bargain price. The transaction is unfair to minority stockholders since it dilutes their economic interest and should be invalidated.

Example: In the previous example, the price for the additional shares is fair but the purpose is to give the controlling stockholder enough shares to approve unusual corporate transactions. The transaction is unfair since it has no valid business purpose and dilutes the voting power of the minority stockholders and should be invalidated.

Example: Directors of a corporation know that inventory owned by the corporation has appreciated greatly in value over the value reflected on the books of the corporation. To obtain the greatest portion of this appreciation for itself, the directors elected by the majority stockholder cause the corporation to call for redemption at $80 per share a class of convertible preferred shares. If the called shares were converted into common they would have a value of $160 per share because of the appreciation in value of the inventory. The corporation does not disclose the inventory appreciation to the preferred stockholders, and, as a result, most of the holders of the preferred shares elect to have their holdings redeemed at $80.00 per share. This transaction violates a duty of fairness owed to the minority stockholders: in effect, the directors must fully and fairly disclose the financial consequences of the alternatives available to the preferred stockholders and not mislead them. *Zahn v. Transamerica Corp.*, 162 F.2d 36 (3d Cir.1947); *Speed v. Transamerica Corp.*, 235 F.2d 369 (3d Cir.1956).

Caveat: In the previous example, the directors' decision whether or not to call the preferred is itself not subject to a fairness test. Since the preferred stockholders do not have the power to elect directors, they should realize that when they acquire shares that are subject to redemption, the decision to redeem may be based solely on what maximizes the wealth of the common stockholders. The directors must treat the preferred holders fairly only in the sense of not misleading them as to which option they should elect.

Example: In the previous example, before the preferred is called the directors elected by the common stockholders declare extra dividends on the common shares reflecting most of the inventory appreciation, after making the required provision for the senior securities. The holders of senior securities cannot complain of the extra dividends paid to the common stockholders.

Example: The directors in a closely held corporation agree to repurchase shares owned by the father of the majority stockholder at a price of $600.00 per share. Previously, the corporation offered to repurchase shares of other minority stockholders at $300.00 per share. The transaction is voidable unless the other minority stockholders are also given an opportunity to sell shares to the corporation at the favorable price. Cf. *Donahue v. Rodd Electrotype Co.*, 328 N.E.2d 505 (Mass.1975).

Example: A majority of the directors of a corporation have been named by the bank supplying most of the credit needed by the corporation to operate and the other directors have acquiesced in the prior credit transactions. The credit instruments require the majority stockholders to grant the bank an irrevocable proxy appointment that continues so long as credit is outstanding. The bank has named its own officers to be a majority of the directors of the corporation. The bank decides it needs a pledge of all the corporate assets as security for a further loan that has been applied for. This pledge does not require stockholder approval under state law. The stockholders should be advised of the demand and that the board of directors may not simply authorize the pledge; a failure to give the notice to stockholders makes the transaction voidable. *Wright v. Heizer Corp.*, 560 F.2d 236 (7th Cir.1977).

H. STATE STATUTORY LIABILITIES

State business corporation acts may impose personal liability on directors for transactions that violate specific statutory provisions. This liability is usually in addition to other liabilities and not dependent on bad faith.

1. Acts for Which Liability Is Imposed

While provisions vary from state to state, liability for the following actions are typical:

a. Paying dividends or making distributions in violation of the act or in violation of restrictions in the articles of incorporation. *See* MBCA 8.33. Liability is usually limited to the excess of the amount actually distributed over the amount which could have been distributed without violating the act or restriction.

b. Authorizing the purchase of its own shares by a corporation in violation of statute. The liability is usually limited to the consideration paid for the shares which is in excess of the maximum amount that could have been paid without violating the statute.

c. Distributing assets to stockholders during the dissolution and winding up of the corporation without paying and discharging, or making adequate provision for the payment and discharge of, all known debts, obligations, and liabilities of the corporation.

d. Permitting the corporation to commence business before it has received the minimum required consideration for its shares.

e. Permitting the corporation to make a loan to an officer or director, or to make a loan secured by shares of the corporation when such transactions are prohibited. The liability is limited to the amount of the loan until it is repaid.

> *Caveat:* Many of these liability provisions appear in older statutes that contain restrictive requirements that have been eliminated from more modern statutes. Most modern state statutes, like the MBCA (1984), do not contain minimum capital requirements for new corporations, and do not prohibit loans to officers and directors, loans secured by shares of the corporation, or have otherwise relaxed older prohibitions.

2. Directors Who Are Liable

Business corporation acts usually provide that joint and several liability is imposed on all directors present at a meeting at which an action in violation of the statute is taken, unless a director's negative vote is duly entered in writing in the corporate records or the secretary is notified in writing by registered mail of the negative vote.

REVIEW QUESTIONS

8.1. What is meant by a duty of care?

8.2. What is meant by the business judgment rule? By the business judgment doctrine?

8.3. A director offers to sell his corporation a piece of land owned by a family trust at a questionable price. What standards are applicable to determine the validity of such a transaction?

8.4. If the board of directors in the previous question conclude that the transaction is in the best interests of the corporation, may the transaction be protected against later attack by a dissatisfied stockholder?

8.5. What rule is applicable to determine the validity of a transaction between two corporations with common directors?

8.6. May the stockholders ratify a self dealing transaction that does not meet the standard of fairness?

8.7. Today many executives in publicly held corporations receive executive compensation of more than a million dollars per year. Is this self dealing? What is the standard for determining the validity of such very large compensation?

8.8. How may executive compensation be tied directly to the performance of the stock in the stock market?

8.9. What is meant by the doctrine of corporate opportunity?

8.10. What is the test for determining when an opportunity is a corporate opportunity?

8.11. True or False: May a director take advantage of a corporate opportunity if the corporation is unable or unwilling to do so?

8.12. A corporation enters into a transaction with its subsidiary of which it owns 98 per cent of stock. Which standard should be applied to such a transaction, the business judgment rule or the fairness standard of self dealing transactions?

8.13. Corporation A owns 93 per cent of the outstanding shares of Corporation B. The remaining 7 per cent of the shares are held by 50 individuals. Corporation A desires to raise capital for itself by pledging certain liquid assets of Corporation B. May it do so?

8.14. A corporation has. two classes of authorized shares: 1,000 preferred shares and 3,000 common shares. Outstanding are: (1) 1,000 noncumulative $100 par value preferred shares with full voting rights with a liquidation preference of $200 per share; the preferred shares are also redeemable at $105 per share and each share is convertible into two common shares; and (2) 1,000 common shares without par value with full voting rights. The corporation has net assets of $210,000, of which $105,000 is earned surplus. It is about to dissolve. What should the board of directors do in fairness to both classes?

8.15. A is a large corporation with over 30,000 employees at 100 plants scattered around the country or overseas. The corporation and certain employees have entered pleas of guilty to indictments charging violations of the federal antitrust laws. The directors of the corporation were not charged with any violation of the anti-trust laws in the proceeding against the corporation. P brings an action on the corporation's behalf to hold the directors liable for the losses sustained by the corporation by reason of the violations of its employees. There is no evidence presented to the effect that the directors knew or had any knowledge that would have put them on notice that violations were occurring. Are the directors liable to the corporation?

8.16. X corporation, a mining company, entered into a contract with M corporation, a smelting company, which provided that M should smelt all of X's ore for a period of 10 years at a specific price per ton of ore. The price agreed to be paid by X to M was 10 per cent higher than the regular and customary price for smelting. A, B and C were directors of X corporation and also of M corporation. When this contract came up for approval before the boards of directors of the two corporations, the directors A, B and C, refrained from voting, but the contract was approved by the board of directors of X corporation because the directors other than A, B and C, were advised that A, B and C wanted such contract approved. The metal market was dropping when this contract was made and continued to drop thereafter. Usually the price of smelting drops with the market. X corporation elected a new board of directors which made an investigation and found that the contract with M was causing the company to lose money. The new board voted to cancel the contract with M and brought suit for a declaratory judgment to determine that the cancellation was legal. M's defense is that the contract is valid because the directors who were common to both corporations, A, B and C, abstained from voting on the contract. Is the defense valid at common law? Under a conflict of interest statute?

8.17. X corporation, in which D is the majority stockholder but not on the board of directors, is engaged in mining copper. X corporation is in very precarious financial shape, being barely able to meet its day-to-day obligations as they come due. D completely controls the board of directors of X corporation and regularly consults with members of the board and visits X's mining operation. D learns that a vein of ore that X is mining runs directly into B's property which adjoins X's property. An opportunity to buy B's property arises and without mentioning the opportunity to X corporation, D buys B's mines for $100,000 cash. T, a minority stockholder in X, sues D on behalf of the corporation to compel him to turn over to X at cost the mining property he purchased from B. D's defense is that B would sell his property only for cash and that at the time D bought the mines from B the X corporation was unable to raise more than $10,000 in cash. Is the defense valid?

IX

Stockholder Derivative Litigation

A. DERIVATIVE ACTIONS GENERALLY

A *derivative action* is a lawsuit brought by one or more stockholders to remedy or prevent a wrong *to the corporation*, rather than a wrong to the stockholders individually. In contrast, a *direct* action involves the enforcement by a stockholder of a claim based on injury to the stockholder as an individual as an owner of shares. This is a fundamental distinction, but it is fuzzy at the edges because some types of claims may be characterized either as direct or derivative actions, depending on the way the claim is described.

1. The ultimate rationale for the derivative action as a procedural device is that in a case in which the corporation has a claim against a director, officer, or controlling stockholder, the claim may not be pursued directly because it would in effect require these parties to sue themselves. In other words, there is an inherent conflict of interest in such situations. The plaintiff stockholder thus serves as an outside agent (similar to an independent prosecutor) to protect the rights of the corporation. In addition, a derivative action brought in the corporation's name avoids a multiplicity of actions by stockholders. Thus, some courts have questioned whether the derivative action makes much sense in the context of a closely held corporation.

2. In a derivative action, a stockholder sues in a representative capacity on a cause of action that belongs to the corporation. Accordingly, the stockholder must be an adequate representative of all the stockholders. The real party in

interest is the corporation. But for most procedural purposes the corporation is treated as a defendant in derivative litigation. *Koster v. Lumbermens Mut. Cas. Co.*, 330 U.S. 518, 67 S.Ct. 828 (1947). The rules relating to derivative actions are sometimes found in corporation law and sometimes included in procedural rules of court. *See* MBCA 7.40-7.47; FRCP 23.1. (Many states have adopted the FRCP and retain its numbering.) In some cases these two authorities may conflict. The rules relating to class actions are found primarily in procedural rules, but many rules relating specifically to federal securities fraud actions are incorporated into federal securities law by PSLRA and SLUSA.

3. In a derivative action, the claim belongs to the corporation and recovery if any should usually go to the corporation rather than to the stockholders individually, although in extraordinary cases individual recovery may be ordered. The rationale for the general rule is that where an injury is done to the corporation each stockholder is made whole if the corporation recovers damages from the wrongdoer. If the stockholder suffered damage in the form of a decrease in share price, share price should increase when the corporation recovers. In addition, damages recovered by the corporation derivatively are available for the payment of claims by the corporation's creditors while a direct recovery by stockholders may adversely affect creditors.

4. A derivative action may be settled or dismissed only with the approval of the court because of the danger that in a privately negotiated settlement, the corporation may in effect bribe the plaintiff, or the plaintiff's attorney, to drop the action. *See* MBCA 7.45; FRCP 23.1.

5. Commentators disagree about the ultimate value of the derivative action as a device for protecting stockholder interests. Some observers see the derivative action as an important check on management discretion. Others argue that most derivative litigation is without substantive merit and is instituted primarily for the settlement value and for the benefit of the plaintiff attorneys whose fee must be paid by the corporation if the action is successful. Critics often refer to derivative actions as *strike actions.*

a. Plaintiff attorneys may look for and find possible litigation situations and then seek to find a plaintiff in whose name action may be brought. Plaintiff attorneys usually advance the expenses of litigation costs and accordingly have a substantial financial interest in the litigation that usually exceeds that of any single stockholder. The litigation is directed and controlled by the plaintiffs' attorneys who are motivated at least in part by their financial interest in the litigation.

Caveat: The same arguments may also be made about direct class actions.

b.   Most derivative actions are dismissed or settled. Few cases are litigated to final judgment. The corporation usually receives some benefit, either in the form of monetary recovery or changes in management practices. Nevertheless, most studies have found little or no financial benefit from successful derivative litigation in terms of share price movement.

c.   Where the action is settled without payment but rather in the form of agreed changes in management practices, the plaintiff attorney is nevertheless entitled to recover a fee from the corporation for the benefit conferred on the corporation. This is an exception to the usual American rule regarding attorney fees. The rationale is that because all of the stockholders benefit from the recovery by the corporation, all should pay proportionally, which they do in effect by charging attorney fees against corporate assets which should result in a pro rata charge against the value of each stockholder's shares. The same rationale applies in connection with a (direct) class action where attorney fees are paid out of the class recovery.

B.   DISTINGUISHING DERIVATIVE ACTIONS AND DIRECT ACTIONS

One of the key questions in many cases is whether the action is derivative or direct, because if the action is derivative, the corporation is the real party in interest and the board of directors may be able to assume control of the action. In *Tooley v. Donaldson, Lufkin, & Jenrette, Inc.*, 845 A.2d 1031 (Del.Supr.2004), the Delaware Supreme Court held that the issue of whether an action is direct or derivative must turn *solely* on (1) who suffered the alleged harm (the corporation or the suing stockholders, individually), and (2) who would receive the benefit of any recovery or other remedy (the corporation or the stockholders, individually). Tooley involved a claim by a stockholder that a delay in completing a merger deprived the stockholders of the interest on the consideration paid during the delay. The court held that because the stockholders had no right to receive the consideration until the merger was accomplished, they had no right to the interest thereon. The claim, if any belonged to the corporation and the stockholders lost the right to pursue it by virtue of having been cashed out in the merger.

1.   Anything that harms the corporation also harms its stockholders by reducing the value of their shares. But a stockholder cannot transmute a derivative claim into a direct one merely by alleging that he suffered a reduction in value of his shares as a result of injury to the corporation. *Armstrong v. Frostie Co.*, 453 F.2d 914 (4th Cir.1971).

2. Usually a direct action is pursued as a class action on behalf of all stockholders. Stockholders who are members of the class in those cases may claim they were injured by an act which did not itself injure the corporation. *Green v. Wolf Corporation*, 406 F.2d 291 (2d Cir. 1968). Nevertheless, a derivative action usually has some aspects of a class action because a stockholder, when suing to right a wrong done to the corporation, is also usually suing to protect the interest of all stockholders who are not plaintiffs. In other words, in both types of actions, the plaintiff is acting as a representative, and therefore must qualify as an adequate representative of the stockholders.

3. In actions under the proxy rules, Federal courts have tended to ignore the distinction between direct and derivative actions. *See J.I. Case Co. v. Borak*, 377 U.S. 426, 84 S.Ct. 1555 (1964). On the other hand, it is clear that courts treat securities fraud class actions under Rule 10b–5 as direct rather than derivative actions.

Example: An action charging officers and directors with misapplication of corporate assets or breaches of duty is usually derivative in character. An action to examine corporate books and records or to compel the registration of securities is a direct action. An action claiming a conspiracy to injure the business of a corporation is a derivative claim. But if it is alleged that the conspiracy was designed to compel a stockholder to sell her shares at less than actual value, a direct claim is stated. *Green v. Victor Talking Machine Co.*, 24 F.2d 378 (2d Cir.1928).

Example: An action to compel the payment of a dividend may be either direct or derivative. Compare *Knapp v. Bankers Securities Corp.*, 230 F.2d 717 (3d Cir.1956) with *Gordon v. Elliman*, 119 N.E.2d 331 (N.Y. 1954) (later overruled by statute). An action to recover improperly paid dividends from third parties or to require a controlling stockholder to account for a premium received on the sale of shares is derivative because the benefit inures to the corporation.

Example: An action challenging the price negotiated by the board of directors in a merger is a direct action. *Smith v. Van Gorkom*, 488 A.2d 858 (Del.1985). But an action challenging a delay in completing a merger that led to a delayed payment of merger consideration to stockholders is a derivative action. *Tooley v. Donaldson, Lufkin, & Jenrette, Inc.*, 845 A.2d 1031 (Del.Supr.2004).

An action alleging that a plan of merger or reorganization was designed to dilute a stockholder's voting power states a direct claim. *Eisenberg v. Flying Tiger Line, Inc.*, 451 F.2d 267 (2d Cir. 1971).

Example: An action claiming the corporation issued shares without honoring preemptive rights is a direct claim, but it may also be viewed as derivative if it is alleged that the corporation issued shares for inadequate consideration. *Shaw v. Empire Sav. & Loan Assn.*, 9 Cal.Rptr. 204 (Cal.App.1960).

C. PREQUISITES FOR MAINTAINING DERIVATIVE ACTION

The procedural rules governing derivative actions are extensive and complicated. The purpose of these rules is to assure that the plaintiff is a faithful representative of the stockholders and to prevent the pursuit of purchased claims or claims brought solely for their settlement value.

Caveat: These procedural requirements are designed for corporations with many stockholders and make little sense for closely held corporations with few stockholders. Statutes in some states and the PCG direct courts to treat derivative actions in closely held corporations as direct actions where all the parties are before the court and the dispute is essentially among two or more groups of stockholders. *Schumacher v. Schumacher*, 469 N.W.2d 793 (N.D. 1991).

1. Demand on the Corporation or Board of Directors

Generally in a derivative action, the plaintiff must allege and prove a good faith effort to obtain redress from the corporation. A demand on the board of directors is the traditional device that satisfies this requirement.

a. The traditional rule still followed in many states and in federal courts is that a demand must be made unless it would be futile because members of the board of directors are interested in the transaction in question and a demand would in effect require the directors to sue themselves. MBCA 7.42 and the statutes of several states require that demand be made in every case.

Caveat: MBCA 7.42 requires that demand be made *on the corporation.* The demand should be addressed to the board of directors if the issue is one to be dealt with by the board. If the issue may be dealt with by an officer of the corporation, the demand may be addressed to the chief executive officer or the secretary of the corporation.

b. Statutes generally require that the plaintiff allege in his complaint either that a demand has been made on the board of directors or that such a demand would be futile. Historically, this was only a pleading requirement: The worst that could happen is that the court might conclude that a demand should have been made and that the proceeding should be suspended until a demand was actually made. As a result, the demand requirement usually did not significantly affect the progress of the litigation. More recent cases require more than *pro forma* allegations. An action that recites only conclusory reasons for not making a demand will likely be dismissed. *Grossman v. Johnson,* 674 F.2d 115 (1st Cir. 1982); *Gonzalez Turul v. Rogatol Distributors, Inc.,* 951 F.2d 1 (1st Cir. 1991).

c. Delaware is the most important single state with respect to derivative litigation because of the number of corporations organized there. In Delaware, the distinction between cases in which demand is required and cases in which demand is excused often determines the outcome of the case. If demand is required, the board of directors or a committee thereof (usually called a *special litigation committee*) may decide whether to pursue the action and its decision will usually be protected by the business judgment rule. Many Delaware cases consider the circumstances when demand is required and when it is excused. *See Aronson v. Lewis,* 473 A.2d 805 (Del.1984); *Rales v. Blasband,* 634 A.2d 927 (Del.1993). Litigation over the demand issue in Delaware is time-consuming. It requires a virtual trial on the merits before discovery is undertaken. *See Starrels v. First Nat. Bank of Chicago,* 870 F.2d 1168 (7th Cir.1989) (concurrence by Easterbrook stating that the Delaware demand rule creates more litigation than it avoids.) *See also Kaplan v. Wyatt,* 484 A.2d 501 (Del.Ch.1984), *aff'd on other grounds* 499 A.2d 1184 (Del.1985).

d. MBCA 7.42 and the statutes of several states require that demand be made in all cases.

Caveat: Section 7.42 requires that the demand be made on the corporation. The demand should be addressed to the board of directors if the issue is one to be dealt with by the board; if the issue may be dealt with by an officer of the corporation, the demand may be addressed to the chief executive officer or the secretary of the corporation.

e. FRCP 23.1 requires that a plaintiff allege with particularity the efforts, if any, made by the plaintiff to obtain the action he or she desires from the directors or comparable authority and the reasons for his or her failure to obtain the action or for not making the effort. In *Kamen v. Kemper Financial Services, Inc.*, 500 U.S. 90, 111 S.Ct. 1711 (1991), the Court held that the demand futility exception, as defined in the law of the state of incorporation, applies to derivative actions brought under federal statutes. State law also controls in actions brought on the basis of diversity of citizenship. *RCM Securities Fund Inc. v. Stanton*, 928 F.2d 1318 (2d Cir.1991); *Hausman v. Buckley*, 299 F.2d 696 (2d Cir.1962).

f. Although some older statutes require demand upon stockholders, the MBCA and most states have dropped this requirement. The FRCP and the statutes of several states provide that if a demand on stockholders is not made, the plaintiff must show some adequate reason for not making the effort. Expense or difficulty may be justifiable reasons. In most states with stockholder-demand requirements, cases have held that demand may be omitted in appropriate circumstances. *Levitt v. Johnson*, 334 F.2d 815 (1st Cir. 1964). Courts generally have proceeded on a case-by-case basis, not requiring a demand when there are thousands of stockholders, and considering other factors such as the motives of the plaintiff, the number of stockholders joining in the action, and the proximity to the next stockholders' meeting.

g. Massachusetts appears to have adopted the most stringent rule, requiring a demand in every case where a majority of stockholders are not wrongdoers. *S. Solomont & Sons Trust v. New England Theatres Operating Corp.*, 93 N.E.2d 241 (Mass.1950); *Pomerantz v. Clark*, 101 F.Supp. 341 (D.Mass. 1951).

h. If a demand is made on stockholders, and the stockholders reject the demand, the action may nevertheless be brought by the minority stockholders in many cases. *Rogers v. American Can Co.*, 305 F.2d 297 (3d Cir.1962). For example, demand may be excused if the wrongdoers own a majority of the shares and hence favorable stockholder action is unlikely. In addition, if the challenged transaction cannot be ratified by the stockholders, demand on the stockholders is useless. *Mayer v. Adams*, 141 A.2d 458 (Del.1958). *But see Claman v. Robertson*, 128 N.E.2d 429 (Ohio 1955).

2. Contemporaneous Ownership

MBCA 7.41 provides that one may not commence a derivative action unless one was a stockholder of the corporation at the time the cause of action arose or one became a stockholder through transfer by operation of law from a person who was a stockholder at that time. This statute is typical of requirements in many states. This is usually referred to as the contemporaneous ownership rule.

a. The contemporaneous ownership rule is often justified as necessary to prevent buying into a lawsuit. If buying into a lawsuit is the concern, the contemporaneous ownership requirement might be safely liberalized to allow action by plaintiffs who discover the facts giving rise to the lawsuit only after becoming a stockholder. *Pollitz v. Gould,* 94 N.E. 1088 (N.Y.1911). California has adopted this approach. Cal.Corp.Code 800(b)(1). Most state statutes, however, have not accepted this liberalizing principle. *See Goldie v. Yaker,* 432 P.2d 841 (N.M. 1967); *Jepsen v. Peterson,* 10 N.W.2d 749 (S.D.1943). On the other hand, where an action seems reasonable, the time of the transaction has been construed flexibly to permit the action to be maintained. *Maclary v. Pleasant Hills, Inc.,* 109 A.2d 830 (Del.Ch. 1954).

b. Another rationale for the contemporaneous ownership rule is that a stockholder is presumed to have bought shares at a fair price. Thus, in cases in which the cause of action is known to the market at the time of purchase, the market price should already reflect the harm and the stockholder pays a fair discounted price. This rationale, however, assumes that the market is efficient.

Caveat: The derivative action may nonetheless be maintained by another contemporaneous stockholder for the benefit of all stockholders (including those who may have bought into the lawsuit). In egregious cases, a court may therefore order the recovery to be allocated among the affected stockholders on some equitable basis.

Caveat: The rule does not apply in connection with actions by holders of debt instruments.

c. A principle related to the contemporaneous ownership rule prohibits a stockholder (who purchases all or substantially all the shares of a corporation at a fair price) from causing the corporation to bring action against the selling stockholders on grounds of prior corporate mismanagement. *Bangor Punta Operations, Inc. v. Bangor & Aroostook R. Co.,* 417 U.S. 703, 94 S.Ct. 2578 (1974); *In re REA Express, Inc.,* 412 F.Supp. 1239 (E.D.Pa. 1976); *Courtland Manor, Inc. v. Leeds,* 347 A.2d 144 (Del.Ch.1975); *Capital Wine & Spirit Corp. v. Pokrass,* 98 N.Y.S.2d 291 (App.Div.1950). This is an equitable principle that bars action *by the corporation* after the sale rather than simply barring a stockholder from serving as a plaintiff. In *Rifkin v. Steele Platt,* 824 P.2d 32 (Colo.App.1991) the court held that subsequent stockholders could sue on a pre-existing claim only if the purchase price did not reflect the prior wrongdoings.

d.   A stockholder plaintiff who sells or disposes of his shares during the pendency of derivative litigation thereafter loses the right to maintain or continue the action. *Tenney v. Rosenthal,* 189 N.Y.S.2d 158, 160 N.E.2d 463 (N.Y.1959).

e.   A stockholder plaintiff who is cashed out by merger may not thereafter continue a derivative action. *Lewis v. Anderson,* 477 A.2d 1040 (Del.1984); *Kramer v. Western Pacific Industries, Inc.,* 546 A.2d 348 (Del.1988). On the other hand, a stockholder plaintiff who receives stock in the surviving corporation following the merger may be able to continue the action on the theory that the action belongs to the surviving corporation by virtue of the merger. *See Schreiber v. Carney.* If the original corporation survives as a subsidiary, the stockholder may be able to maintain the action as a *double derivative* action.

3.   Security for Expenses

Many state statutes require that the plaintiff stockholder post security for expenses as a condition of maintaining a derivative action. These statutes authorize the corporation and individual defendants to recover their expenses (including attorney fees) from such security in some circumstances. These statutes were designed to deter derivative actions in that plaintiffs may be unable or unwilling to post security. The constitutionality of security-for-expenses statutes was upheld in *Cohen v. Beneficial Indus. Loan Corp.,* 337 U.S. 541, 69 S.Ct.1221 (1949). These statutes have not been particularly effective, and some states have repealed them.

a.   Under statutes requiring security for expenses, the amount of the security is fixed by the court in light of reasonable expenses that the corporation may incur, including the expenses of other defendants for which the corporation may become liable by indemnification or otherwise. The security is usually in the form of a bond, but it may also be in the form of cash or securities.

b. Stockholder plaintiffs who are required to post security-for-expenses are defined in different ways in state statutes. In the older statutes (where the purpose to discourage derivative litigation is most manifest), the size of the plaintiff's holding is determinative. A typical provision is that plaintiffs must post security-for-expenses unless their holdings are more than five percent of the outstanding shares or exceed a specified market value, e.g. $25,000. MBCA (1969) 49. This provision was eliminated in part on the ground that basing the requirement on the size or value of the plaintiff's holdings rather than on the apparent good faith of the claim unreasonably discriminates against small stockholders. Some state statutes require security for expenses only upon a finding that the action appears to lack merit.

Caveat: A corporation may not issue additional shares to reduce the plaintiff's holdings to less than five percent and then seek security-for-expenses.

c. Security-for-expenses statutes usually provide that the corporation may have recourse to such security in such amount as the court thereafter determines. Under such statutes, courts usually allow reimbursement only if the plaintiff is unsuccessful and the action was brought without reasonable cause. Where reimbursement is allowed, an unsuccessful stockholder plaintiff posting security-for-expenses ends up paying the expenses of both sides of the litigation. If no security is posted and the case is dismissed, the plaintiff is not liable for the defendant's expenses in securing the dismissal. *Tyler v. Gas Consumers Assn.,* 231 N.Y.S.2d 15 (N.Y. 1962).

d. MBCA 7.46(2) provides that the court, upon termination of a derivative action, may require the plaintiff to pay any defendants' reasonable expenses (including counsel fees) incurred in defending the proceeding if it finds that the proceeding was commenced or maintained without reasonable cause or for an improper purpose.

e. Security-for-expenses statutes are not applicable to actions in federal court based on violations of the federal securities acts, though a state claim made in connection with a federal claim under the doctrine of pendent jurisdiction may be subject to the security-for-expenses requirement.

Caveat: Under FRCP 11, a court may impose sanctions against a party or attorney who files a frivolous case or pleading. These sanctions may include reimbursement of fees and expenses of the opposing side. In addition, FRCP 23.1 requires that the complaint in a derivative action be verified (sworn). Thus, filing a false complaint may constitute perjury.

f. Security-for-expenses statutes are not applicable to class actions. *Eisenberg v. Flying Tiger Line, Inc.*, 451 F.2d 267 (2d Cir. 1971); *Knapp v. Bankers Securities Corp.*, 230 F.2d 717 (3d Cir.1956).

D. DEFENDING A DERIVATIVE ACTION

The defendant in a derivative action has all of the defenses that would be available in a direct action based on the same claim. For example, the corporation may establish that the claim is barred by the statute of limitations. Because the corporation is the nominal plaintiff in a derivative action, these defenses may need to be asserted by the defendant. But the corporation may also argue that the individual plaintiff is an inadequate representative of the stockholders based on laches, participation in the fraud, or conflicts of interest. The most common and effective defensive tactic is for the board of directors to seek dismissal of the lawsuit on the grounds that the action ultimately belongs to the corporation and thus may be *voluntarily* dismissed by the corporation because it is contrary to the best interests of the corporation to pursue it. This is a relatively recent development, and although it remains controversial, it now appears to be well established.

1. Dismissal by the Corporation

A derivative action is a lawsuit for the benefit of the corporation. The right to pursue the action is an asset like any other under the authority of the board of directors. As a general rule the corporation acting through the board of directors may choose whether or not to pursue the action on behalf of the corporation.

a. Where a derivative action seeks recovery by the corporation from third persons unrelated to the corporation, it is clear that a decision by the directors not to pursue such litigation is protected by the business judgment rule.

b. If the cause of action is one that is based on a decision by the board of directors itself or on the actions of one more individual directors, an adverse decision by the board may be seen as conflicted and therefore subject to scrutiny under the duty of loyalty. Under well-established rules, however, the board of directors may nonetheless act even when conflicted. Conflicted directors may be required to recuse themselves, or the matter may be referred to a committee of directors who are free of conflict, or the stockholders may ratify the matter, or a court may determine that the action of the board was fair. The most common practice is for the board of directors to appoint a special litigation committee.

c. Early decisions on the dismissal issue involved actions in which stockholders sought to recover improper foreign payments or domestic political contributions from the directors or officers who authorized them (or who failed to prevent them). The courts initially ruled with little reservation that the decision to seek dismissal of derivative litigation was no different than other questions to be resolved by disinterested directors as a matter of business judgment. *Gall v. Exxon Corp.*, 418 F.Supp. 508 (S.D.N.Y. 1976); *Auerbach v. Bennett*, 419 N.Y.S.2d 920, 393 N.E.2d 994 (N.Y. 1979); *Burks v. Lasker*, 441 U.S. 471, 99 S.Ct. 1831 (1979). It is doubtful that the plaintiffs in some of these cases would have prevailed if a trial on the merits had been held.

d. The primary argument against the uncritical application of the business judgment rule is based on *structural bias*—that directors may be reluctant to sue each other. This argument has been consistently rejected by the courts. *See Auerbach v. Bennett*, 393 N.E. 994, 1001–1002, 419 N.Y.S.2d 920 (N.Y.1979); *Beam ex rel. Martha Stewart Living Omnimedia, Inc. v. Stewart*, 833 A.2d 961 (Del.Ch. 2003); *Beam v. Stewart*, 845 A.2d 1040 (Del.Supr. 2004) (personal friendship or family relationship alone is insufficient to show interestedness). *Cf. United States v. Chestman*, 947 F.2d 551, 566 (2d Cir. 1991) (en banc) (family relationship insufficient to establish a fiduciary duty not to use inside information). Rather, one must show a financial interest. MBCA 7.44(c) specifically rejects structural bias as grounds for interestedness.

e. Either the board of directors itself (excluding directors who are defendants in the proceedings) or a special litigation committee composed of independent directors who are not involved in the matters complained of should investigate the matters complained of in the stockholders complaint.

- Where a special litigation committee is formed, the full powers of the board of directors are delegated to the SLC without any express reservation by the board to review the recommendation of the committee. In other words, the SLC is authorized to act on its own recommendations.

- The board of directors or the committee may hire independent counsel to investigate the complaint and make a recommendation as to the position the board of directors or the litigation committee should take.

- If the board of directors or litigation committee concludes that it is not in the best interests of the corporation to pursue the derivative action, the corporation may file a motion to dismiss the stockholders' action on the ground that the decision whether or not to pursue litigation is itself an important business decision that is subject to the business judgment rule.

    Caveat: If the business judgment rule applies, the decision to discontinue the litigation is binding on the plaintiff stockholders who therefore never obtain a decision on the merits of their lawsuit. They may, however, independently litigate questions such as whether the board or committee were truly independent and whether the board or committee reasonably informed itself in good faith of the facts before reaching its decision.

    Caveat: Many statutes require that a committee of the board consist of at least two directors. And even if a committee of one is permitted the court may find that such a committee is incapable of independent judgment. *See Lewis v. Fuqua*, 502 A.2d 962 (Del.Ch. 1985). Thus, probably the usual practice today is to have a committee of two or more directors, in part in order to avoid the result reached in cases where a decision by a single director was held not to be protected by the business judgment rule.

f. Delaware courts have developed a complex set of rules with respect to the dismissal of derivative litigation. The test for the application of the business judgment rule in Delaware depends on whether the case is a *demand excused* or a *demand required* case.

- *Zapata Corp. v. Maldonado*, 430 A.2d 779 (Del.1981), holds that where a demand on directors is excused, the action is properly filed without a demand, but the corporation may thereafter appoint a committee to consider the merits of the plaintiff's claim. If the committee recommends that the litigation be dismissed (as litigation committees almost invariably do) the court should review the independence of the committee and may thereafter exercise its own independent business judgment to determine whether litigation should be dismissed over the objection of the plaintiff on the basis of the recommendation of the litigation committee.

- *Aronson v. Lewis*, 475 A.2d 805 (Del.1984) holds that the *Zapata* rule is applicable only where demand is excused. Where demand is required, the decision whether or not to pursue the litigation is vested in the board of directors, and the business judgment rule applies. If action is filed without making a demand, it should be dismissed for failing to make a demand. If a demand was made, the decision by the litigation committee should be evaluated under the business judgment rule.

- Under *Aronson,* demand is excused only if (1) there is a reasonable doubt that the board of directors has the independence and disinterestedness necessary for application of the business judgment rule, or (2) if the facts (alleged with particularity) when taken as true, support a reasonable doubt that the challenged transaction was the product of a valid exercise of business judgment. To avoid the business judgment rule the plaintiff must overcome one of the two requirements set forth in *Aronson.* If both requirements have been met, a demand is required and the decision of the board or committee is thereafter entitled to the protections of the business judgment rule. *See also Levine v. Smith,* 591 A.2d 194, 205–208 (Del.1991): "The premise of a stockholder claim of futility of demand is that a majority of the board of directors either has a financial interest in the challenged transaction or lacks independence or otherwise failed to exercise due care. . . . When lack of independence is charged, a plaintiff must show that the Board is either dominated by an officer or director who is the proponent of the challenged transaction or that the board is so under his influence that its discretion is sterilize[d]. Assuming a plaintiff cannot prove that directors are interested or otherwise incapable of exercising independent business judgment, a plaintiff in a demand futility case must plead particularized facts creating a reasonable doubt as to the soundness of the challenged transaction sufficient to rebut the presumption that the business judgment rule attaches to the transaction."

Caveat: The decision as to whether demand is futile is made on the basis of the particularized facts set forth in the pleadings without the benefit of discovery. Conclusory allegations are insufficient.

Caveat: If plaintiff makes a demand, the demand may constitute a concession that the case is a demand required case. *Stotland v. GAF Corp.,* 469 A.2d 421 (Del. 1983); *Spiegel v. Buntrock,* 571 A.2d 767 (Del.1990). If the board of directors appoints a special litigation committee with the ultimate power of decision without moving to dismiss for failure to make a demand, that may constitute a concession by the board of directors that demand is futile. *Abbey v. Computer & Communications Technology Corp.,* 457 A.2d 368 (Del.Ch. 1983).

g. Most Delaware cases since *Aronson* have concluded that demand is required and therefore that the business judgment rule is applicable to the decision of the independent litigation committee or the board of directors to discontinue the litigation even though the cause of action is based on a business decision that appears to be questionable. In *Aronson,* demand was required even though the challenged decision by the board was to grant to the controlling stockholder a lucrative employment and consulting contract that did not require the performance of any specific services. The controlling stockholder did not himself sit on the board, but had hand-picked each of the directors. *See also Grobow v. Perot,* 539 A.2d 180 (Del.1988)(decision to repurchase shares of dissenting stockholder and director Ross Perot at a premium was described by Perot as obscene.) But *See RCM Securities Fund, Inc. v. Stanton,* 928 F.2d 1318 (2d Cir. 1991)(decision to borrow heavily against corporate assets in order to buy back shares of stock to be contributed to employee share ownership plan (ESOP) that would then control corporation and insulate it from a threatened takeover).

Caveat: In *Alford v. Shaw,* 358 S.E.2d 323, 327 (N.C. 1987), the court first uncritically accepted the *Gall* approach but then decided that it was error to rely blindly on the report of a corporation-appointed committee which assembled materials on behalf of the corporation. The court stated that although the recommendation of the special litigation committee is not binding on the court in making this determination the court may choose to rely on such recommendation. To rely blindly on the report of a corporation-appointed committee which assembled such materials on behalf of the corporation is to abdicate the judicial duty to consider the interests of stockholders imposed by the statute. The decisions in *Auerbach* and *Aronson* therefore should not be blindly followed and courts should apply their independent business judgment when reviewing such decisions.

Caveat: Several states have enacted statutes authorizing a court to appoint an independent committee to review derivative litigation and recommend dismissal of a derivative action.

h.   The Delaware approach has led to extensive pretrial skirmishing because the decision as to whether demand is excused is likely to be outcome-determinative. Some judges have questioned the desirability of the Delaware approach. *See Starrels v. First Nat. Bank of Chicago*, 870 F.2d 1168 (7th Cir. 1989) (concurrence by Easterbrook); *Kaplan v. Wyatt*, 484 A.2d 501 (Del.Ch. 1984), aff'd, 499 A.2d 1184 (Del.1985).

i.   Delaware law applies in federal cases that involve Delaware corporations. *Kamen v. Kemper Financial Services, Inc.*, 500 U.S. 90, 111 S.Ct. 1711 (1991); *RCM Securities Fund, Inc. v. Stanton*, 928 F.2d 1318 (2d Cir. 1991). *See also Joy v. North*, 692 F.2d 880 (2d Cir. 1982) (construing Connecticut law and applying the *Zapata* test rather than the *Auerbach* test; the court also rejected the decision to seek dismissal as unlikely to be a valid exercise of business judgment).

j.   MBCA 7.42 requires a written demand on the corporation in all cases. A derivative action may nonetheless be commenced despite a refused demand. Also the board of directors or a committee of two or more independent directors thereof may seek to have the action dismissed if after a reasonable investigation they conclude in good faith that the action is not in the best interests of the corporation. If a majority of the board is independent at the time the determination to seek dismissal is made, the plaintiff bears the burden of proof with regard to the determination to seek dismissal. If a majority of the board is not disinterested at the time the determination is made, the committee bears the burden of proof as to the determination to seek dismissal. The business judgment rule does not appear to apply even when the board is majority independent. Thus, the MBCA appears to favor derivative actions more than Delaware law. *See also Beneville v. York*, 769 A.2d 80,

85–86 (Del.Ch. 2000), holding that demand may be excused where a board is evenly divided between interested and disinterested directors.

k. PCG also requires demand be made in virtually all cases unless irreparable injury to the corporation would result from delay. Under the PCG 7.04, if the board rejects a demand, it must deliver a written reply to the plaintiff stating the reasons for the rejection and identifying the directors who reviewed the demand. PCG 7.09 provides that the board may appoint a committee of two or more disinterested directors to review the action. Although the comments suggest that disinterested directors should appoint the committee, the PCG does not specifically so require. PCG 7.10 provides that the standard of review upon a motion to dismiss generally should be the same as that which applies to the challenged transaction.

l. The business judgment rule does not appear to apply even when the board is majority independent. Thus, the MBCA appears to favor derivative actions slightly more than Delaware law. *See also Beneville v. York*, 769 A.2d 89, 85–86 (Del.Ch. 2000)(holding that demand is excused where a board is evenly divided between interested and disinterested directors).

m. The PCG also requires demand in virtually all cases unless irreparable injury to the corporation would result from delay. Under PCG 7.04, if the board rejects a demand, it must deliver a written reply to the plaintiff stating the reasons for the rejection and identifying the directors who reviewed the demand. PCG 7.09 provides that the board may appoint a committee of two or more disinterested directors to review the action. Although the comments suggest that the committee should be appointed by disinterested directors, the Principles do not specifically so require. PCG 7.10 provides that the standard of review upon motion to dismiss should generally be the same as that which applies to the transaction challenged.

n. Both the MBCA and the PCG contain provisions permitting the Court to stay discovery proceedings on motion by the corporation if the corporation undertakes to review the merits of the action with a view toward seeking dismissal. As a practical matter, the stay of discovery often precludes the representative plaintiff from obtaining information that would permit pleading with particularity. Similar provisions apply in connection with securities fraud class actions.

o. *Miller v. Register & Tribune Syndicate, Inc.*, 336 N.W.2d 709 (Iowa 1983) holds that if a majority of directors are named as defendants, the board of directors may not establish a litigation committee with the power of the board to terminate derivative litigation. Rather, the board must apply to a court for the appointment of a trustee or receiver if it wishes to discontinue the litigation. *See also* MBCA 7.44(f) (authorizing the court to appoint an independent panel to determine whether to seek dismissal). PCG 7.12 (same).

Caveat: MBCA 7.42 requires that the demand be made on the *corporation.* The demand should be addressed to the board of directors if the issue is one to be dealt with by the board. If the issue may be dealt with by an officer of the corporation, the demand may be addressed to the chief executive officer or the secretary of the corporation.

Caveat: FRCP 23.1 requires that a plaintiff must allege with particularity the efforts, if any, made by the plaintiff to obtain the action he or she desires from the directors or comparable authority and the reasons for his or her failure to obtain the action, or for not making the effort. In *Kamen v. Kemper Financial Services, Inc.*, 500 U.S. 90 (1991), the Court held that the demand futility exception, as defined in the law of the state of incorporation, applies to derivative actions brought under federal statutes. State law also controls actions brought on the basis of diversity of citizenship. *RCM Securities Fund Inc. v. Stanton*, 928 F.2d 1318 (2d Cir. 1991); *Hausman v. Buckley*, 299 F.2d 696 (2d Cir. 1962).

E. SETTLEMENT

A derivative action may be settled only with judicial approval. In the absence of such a requirement, the corporation might attempt to settle with a representative plaintiff alone, in effect paying a bribe to the plaintiff to drop his action.

a. Notice of the proposed dismissal or compromise must be given to stockholders or members in such manner as the court directs. *Saylor v. Bastedo*, 594 F.Supp. 371 (S.D.N.Y.1984); *Lewis v. Newman*, 59 F.R.D. 525 (S.D.N.Y.1973); *Perrine v. Pennroad Corp.*, 47 A.2d 479 (Del.1946); *Shlensky v. Dorsey*, 574 F.2d 131 (3d Cir.1978).

b. Where a secret settlement has led to a payment to a derivative plaintiff, other stockholders may bring derivative actions in the name of the corporation against the settling stockholder to recover the payment. *Clarke v. Greenberg,* 71 N.E.2d 443 (N.Y. 1947).

c. The corporation itself may settle a claim without court approval and without the consent of the plaintiffs' attorneys, but a sweetheart settlement may become the basis of a later derivative action. *Wolf v. Barkes,* 348 F.2d 994 (2d Cir.1965).

F. RECOVERY

Recovery in a derivative action is usually payable to the corporation rather than to individual stockholders. The theory is that payment to the corporation increases the value of the corporation and its shares for the benefit of all stockholders. In some cases, courts have ordered a pro rata recovery to be paid to the stockholders if payment to the corporation would effectively result in payment to the wrongdoers. *See* PCG 7.18.

Example: In *Perlman v. Feldman,* 219 F.2d 173 (2d Cir.1955), a control premium paid to a former controlling stockholder was held to be recoverable and payable to the non-selling stockholders on a pro rata basis on the theory that it was improper for those who had paid a control premium to the defendants (and who subsequently controlled the corporation) to share in the recovery. The selling stockholder (who had owned 37 percent of the shares) was permitted to keep his own share of the premium and ordered to pay the remaining 63 percent of the premium to the stockholders (other than the new controlling stockholders).

a. Most courts are reluctant to order stockholder recovery. Indeed, some have suggested that pro rata recovery is inconsistent with the idea of a derivative action and can never be awarded.

b. A pro rata recovery often gives rise to practical and conceptual problems. *Keenan v. Eshleman,* 2 A.2d 904 (Del.1938); *Norte & Co.v Huffines,* 416 F.2d 1189 (2d Cir. 1969); *Schachter v. Kulik,* 547 N.Y.S.2d 816, 547 N.E.2d 71 (N.Y. 1989)[recovery should go to the corporation even where there were only two stockholders]. *See also Tooley v. Donaldson, Lufkin, & Jenrette,* 845 A.2d 1031 (Del.Supr. 2004) (determination of whether claims are direct or derivative depends on who suffered harm and who will recover). *Cf. Bangor Punta Operations, Inc. v. Bangor & Aroostook R. Co.,* 417 U.S. 703, 94 S.Ct. 2578 (1974)(rejecting pro rata recovery on behalf of holdover minority stockholders and dismissing action brought by injured corporation on theory that control had changed hands at a fair price following mismanagement by former controlling stockholder and that new stockholders could not therefore have maintained derivative action because of the contemporaneous ownership rule).

> *Example:* In *Perlman*, if the buyers of control (who paid a control premium) resell for another control premium, can they argue that the noncontrol stockholders, having already been compensated for the absence of control by sharing in Feldmann's premium, cannot complain of the second sale?

The controlling shares in Perlman were sold for a premium constituted 37 per cent of the outstanding shares. The remaining 63 per cent of the shares were widely held. If a hostile bidder acquires the 63 per cent by tender offer at a premium it may become the control block. Does it have any responsibility to return the premium it previously received?

A direct recovery for a derivative injury has a mandatory dividend feature. Arguably, the courts should thus determine that a distribution would be permissible under the circumstances.

In appropriate cases plaintiffs may obtain non-monetary relief. *White v. Perkins,* 189 S.E.2d 315 (Va. 1972) (dissolution); *Robinson v. Thompson,* 466 S.W.2d 626 (Tex.Civ.App.1971) (receiver).

G. RES JUDICATA

The *res judicata* effect of the termination of a derivative action depends on the manner or basis for the termination. A final judgment on the merits is *res judicata* and binding on all other stockholders.

1. Settlement

A court-approved settlement ordinarily has the same effect as a final judgment on the merits. *Berger v. Dyson,* 111 F.Supp. 533 (D.R.I.1953). But stockholders may not be bound if they were not notified of the proposed settlement or if the settlement was based on nondisclosure of relevant evidence or collusion between plaintiff and defendant. *Manufacturers Mut. Fire Ins. Co. of Rhode Island v. Hopson,* 25 N.Y.S.2d 502 (N.Y. 1940); *Shlensky v. Dorsey,* 574 F2d 131 (3d Cir. 1978); *Alleghany Corp. v. Kirby,* 333 F.2d 327 (2d Cir.1964).

2. Dismissal

The *res judicata* effect of a dismissal of a derivative action depends on the reason for the dismissal. A voluntary dismissal, or a dismissal because the plaintiff stockholder does not qualify as a proper plaintiff is usually without prejudice and does not bind the class. For example, dismissal for failure to post security for expenses or to answer interrogatories does not bind the class. *Papilsky v. Berndt*, 466 F.2d 251 (2d Cir. 1972).

a. In some situations, the court may order that notice be given to all other stockholders before a derivative action is dismissed voluntarily. Such action may then be continued by intervening stockholders. If none appear, the action may be dismissed with prejudice.

b. A dismissal on the merits, as where the complaint does not state a claim on which relief can be granted or where the decision of a litigation committee not to pursue the litigation is protected by the business judgment rule, binds all members of the class.

H. LITIGATION EXPENSES

If the plaintiff is successful, the court usually awards expenses, including attorney fees, to be paid by the corporation. Expenses are typically paid out of the award or settlement obtained by the corporation as a result of the action. Expenses may also be paid by the corporation where the corporation receives no money as a result of the litigation if the action was of some benefit to the corporation. *Bosch v. Meeker Co–Op Light & Power Assn.*, 101 N.W.2d 423 (Minn.1960); *Fletcher v. A.J. Industries, Inc.*, 72 Cal.Rptr. 146 (1968). MBCA 7.46(1) adopts a substantial benefit standard.

Caveat: Payment of the representative plaintiff's expenses by the corporation does not compel the losing party to pay the other's expenses because the corporation is technically the winning party.

1. Amount

The amount of the attorney fees to be awarded to a successful plaintiff counsel depends on a variety of factors: the nature and character of the litigation, the skill required, the amount of work actually performed, the size of the recovery, the nature of the harm prevented, and other factors.

a. The fee must be reasonable. Its size is determined or approved by the court and is a question of fact on which evidence may be taken.

b. Where derivative litigation is settled, attorney fees may be negotiated as part of the settlement. Such fees are subject to judicial review and approval. As a practical matter, it may be difficult for a judge to review the reasonableness of an agreed fee if all settling parties support the negotiated fee.

2. Defendant Expenses

In limited circumstances defendants may be entitled to have their fees and expenses paid by the plaintiffs or by the corporation.

a. If the plaintiff has posted security for expenses, the defendants may have recourse to that security if authorized by the court. Or if a court determines that the plaintiff has filed action or pleadings not in good faith, expenses may be recoverable from the plaintiff or plaintiff's attorney if authorized by the court.

b. Individual defendants may be entitled to be indemnified *by the corporation* for their expenses. Defendants may also be protected by a directors and officers (D & O) insurance policy obtained by the corporation. Such policies usually cover litigation expenses.

3. Miscellaneous Procedural Issues

The corporation is the nominal plaintiff in a derivative action. And often the board of directors is the defendant. In such a case, the corporation and the board of directors are technically adverse parties. But the reality is that the corporation and the board are usually allied at least in the early stages of litigation. This gives rise to several peculiar problems.

a. The corporation is technically the plaintiff in a derivative action and its interest is therefore technically adverse to the interest of the other defendants. *Cannon v. U.S. Acoustics Corp.*, 398 F.Supp. 209 (N.D.Ill.1975); *Marco v. Dulles*, 169 F.Supp. 622 (S.D.N.Y. 1959). Nevertheless, a single attorney may represent both the corporation and the directors or officers who are defendants in the early stages of a derivative action until it becomes clear that the interests of the two are in fact adverse. Multiple representation may be permitted only if it is clear that there are no possible conflicts. *Seifert v. Dumatic Industries, Inc.*, 197 A.2d 454 (Pa.1964).

b. The attorney-client privilege between corporation and counsel usually may not be invoked by management defendants. *Garner v. Wolfinbarger*, 430 F.2d 1093 (5th Cir. 1970).

c. An attorney involved in an investigation of wrongdoing for a client corporation may be disqualified to serve later as a derivative plaintiff based on that wrongdoing. *Richardson v. Hamilton Intern. Corp.*, 469 F.2d 1382 (3d Cir.1972); *Cannon v. U.S. Acoustics Corp.*, 398 F.Supp. 209 (N.D.Ill. 1975).

d.   Although a derivative action is technically an action at equity, in *Ross v. Bernhard*, 396 U.S. 531, 90 S.Ct. 733 (1970), the Supreme Court held that a right to jury trial may exist in a derivative action in federal court where the ultimate issue is one at law rather than at equity.

e.   If the independent existence of the corporate plaintiff disappears by merger or similar transaction during the pendency of the action, the action must be dismissed unless the surviving entity is added as a party defendant. *Niesz v. Gorsuch*, 295 F.2d 909 (9th Cir. 1961). A representative plaintiff who has been cashed-out ceases to be a stockholder and may no longer maintain a derivative action.

f.   A stockholder in a parent corporation may maintain a derivative action on behalf of a wholly-owned subsidiary corporation. Such an action is often called a *double derivative action.*

g.   The corporation is a necessary party; without it the action cannot proceed. *Dean v. Kellogg,* 292 N.W. 704 (Mich. 1940).

h.   A derivative action has class as well as derivative aspects; multiple derivative actions may be filed by several different stockholders. Courts may consolidate proceedings, or permit one proceeding to continue and stay the others. *Res judicata* applies to preclude retrial of issues previous decided.

i.   The representative plaintiff in a derivative action may be seen as a fiduciary which may give rise to a duty not to enter into other transactions with the corporation that entail special benefits not enjoyed by all stockholders.

I.   INDEMNIFICATION GENERALLY

In the context of corporation law, indemnification refers to payment or reimbursement by the corporation of a director, officer, or agent for expenses incurred in defending against a civil claim or criminal prosecution that arises in connection with service to the corporation, including claims by the corporation itself in the context of a derivative action. If indemnification is permitted or required, it normally covers legal fees and other expenses. It may also cover a monetary award or settlement, amounts needed to satisfy a judgment entered against defendant officers or directors, or even a criminal fine. A corporation may also advance expenses to a defendant prior to a determination of liability. Liability insurance for directors and officers (D&O insurance) is also available.

There are fundamental policy questions posed by indemnification. On he one hand, the practice encourages responsible persons to accept a position as a director. Given litigation costs today, few responsible persons would be willing to serve as directors in the absence of indemnification. Moreover, it encourages innocent directors to resist unjust charges, and it discourages groundless stockholder litigation. There can be little objection to indemnification of expenses if a director is absolved of liability or misconduct. *In re E. C. Warner Co.*, 45 N.W.2d 388 (Minn.1950). On the other hand, indemnification in connection with some wrongful acts such as self-dealing would effectively nullify fiduciary duty and would presumably therefore violate public policy. The problem is to sort out the situations where indemnification is proper and should be encouraged and situations where it is against public policy and should be prohibited.

J. SCOPE OF INDEMNIFICATION UNDER STATE STATUTES

State statutes attempt to work out a compromise of these various competing considerations. Statutes on indemnification vary from skeletal authorization to elaborate procedural and substantive requirements.

Caveat: Some state indemnification statutes are expressly made not exclusive, so that corporations may create more generous policies than described below. In states with non-exclusive statutes, the outer limits of indemnification are set by considerations of public policy and not the statute.

1. Mandatory Indemnification

A defendant is entitled to indemnification *as a matter of statutory right* if he is wholly successful, on the merits or otherwise. MBCA 8.52.

Example: A defendant prevails because of the statute of limitations or because of pleading defects. He is entitled to indemnification as a matter of right.

Example: In a criminal securities case, a defendant pleads *nolo contendere* on one count in a plea bargain that results in the dismissal of other counts. *Merritt-Chapman & Scott Corp. v. Wolfson,* 321 A.2d 138 (Del.Super.1974) holds that the defendant is entitled to indemnification for expenses with respect to the dismissed counts. It is doubtful if this was the intention of the statutory draftsmen, and the Model Business Corporation Act (1984) reverses this result by requiring the defendant to be wholly successful on the merits or otherwise. MBCA 8.52.

Example: An individual has all claims against him dismissed as part of a settlement under which the corporation paid a substantial amount. The individual is entitled to mandatory indemnification for his expenses because no liability was imposed on him. *Waltuch v. Conticommodity Services, Inc.,* 88 F.3d 87 (2d Cir.1996).

a. The language on the merits *or otherwise* may result in some directors being entitled to indemnification even though they were successful because of a procedural defense that does not go to the merits of the claim against the director. In some of these instances, further investigation might show that the director had engaged in conduct that would have prevented indemnification if the procedural defense had not been available.

b. If a director is entitled to mandatory indemnification but the corporation refuses to make the required payment, the director may petition a court for an order compelling the payment of indemnification. MBCA 8.54(l). If such an order is entered, the director is entitled also to recover expenses incurred in obtaining the order.

c. Corporations may opt out of indemnification statutes by restricting or eliminating indemnification in the articles of incorporation or bylaws. A corporation may do this in order to conserve limited resources or to limit the rights of former directors or officers to demand indemnification.

2. Permissive Indemnification

Indemnification is permitted *as a matter of discretion but not as a matter of right* in a variety of situations. Directors cannot compel corporations to grant indemnification for conduct falling within the category of permissive indemnification. *Tomash v. Midwest Technical Development Corp.,* 160 N.W.2d 273 (Minn.1968). Permissive indemnification is authorized in the following situations:

a. Liabilities that may be indemnified against include the obligation to pay a judgment, settlement, penalty, fine, tax, or reasonable expenses. For actions in the official capacity of a person, indemnification is permitted only if the person acted in good faith and can establish that she reasonably believed that her conduct was in the corporation's best interest. MBCA 8.51(a)(2)(i). For all other actions, indemnification is permitted only if the person acted in good faith and can establish that she reasonably believed that her conduct was *at least not opposed to* the corporation's best interest. MBCA 8.51(a)(2)(ii).

b. In the case of a director, official capacity means only the office of director in a corporation. In other cases, official capacity means the office in the corporation or the employment or agency relationship undertaken by that individual for or on behalf of the corporation. All relationships other than the foregoing do not involve actions in official capacity.

> *Example:* A director serves at the request of the corporation as an officer of a trade association. That service is not in the official capacity of the director.

c. In the case of a criminal proceeding, the person must also have had no reasonable cause to believe her conduct was unlawful. MBCA 8.51(a)(3).

d. Even though an individual meets these standards, indemnification is not permitted in two situations: (1) in a action or proceeding by or in the name of the corporation in which the person is adjudged liable to the corporation; and (2) in a proceeding charging the receipt of an improper personal benefit in which the person is adjudged liable for receiving that personal benefit.

> *Caveat:* MBCA 8.51(c) provides that the termination of a proceeding by judgment, order, settlement, plea of nolo contendere, or similar terminating event is not of itself determinative that the director failed to meet the required standards of conduct.

> *Caveat:* A few states permit indemnification where the person is adjudged liable to the corporation, despite the obvious circularity that is involved.

e. Many corporations, by bylaw provision, grant a contractual right of indemnification in all cases in which indemnification is permissive. Some state statutes make this the default rule unless the articles of incorporation provide the contrary.

3. Court–Approved Indemnification

MBCA 8.54(2) recognizes that a person ineligible for indemnification under the technical requirements of the statute may in some circumstances be fairly entitled to indemnification and provides that a person otherwise not eligible for indemnification may petition a court (which may be either the court in which the proceeding occurred or another court) for a determination that the person is fairly and reasonably entitled to indemnification. Court-approved indemnification is limited to the indemnification of reasonable expenses.

> *Example:* A director is named as a defendant in an action charging violation of the insider trading rules because of sales by the defendant of more than 100,000 shares of stock in a two-month period. After a trial, the court concludes that with respect to the sales of 99,800 shares, the director did not violate the insider trading rules because he did not have material inside information when the sales were made; with respect to the sale of 200 shares, however, the court concludes that a violation of rule 10b–5 occurred. The latter holding renders the defendant director ineligible for indemnification under the statute. But a court might conclude that the director is fairly and equitably entitled to indemnification of his expenses because the violation of Rule 10b–5 was minor in comparison to the essential vindication of the defendant on the bulk of the litigation.

4. Advance for Expenses

MBCA 8.53 authorizes a corporation to pay or reimburse the expenses of a proceeding *as* they are incurred without waiting for a final determination that the person is eligible for indemnification. This provision recognizes that as a practical matter, adequate legal representation and adequate preparation of a defense often requires substantial payments of expenses before a final determination. If advances are not permitted less affluent officers and directors might be unable to finance their own defense. On the other hand, advances for expenses may lead to payments to defendants who are ultimately determined to be ineligible for indemnification.

a. In the absence of specific statutory authorization to make such advances, a court may not order them. *Gross v. Texas Plastics, Inc.,* 344 F.Supp. 564 (D.N.J.1972), *aff'd* 523 F.2d 1050 (3d Cir. 1975).

b. A director seeking an advance must furnish the corporation a written affirmation of the director's good faith belief that he meets the standard of conduct that permits indemnification, MBCA 8.53(a)(1), and a written undertaking to repay the advance if it is ultimately determined that the director did not meet the applicable standard of conduct. MBCA 8.53(a)(2).

Caveat: The written undertaking must be unlimited and general, but need not be secured and may be accepted without regard to the financial ability of the defendant to make repayment. MBCA 8.53(b).

c. Before making an advance, a determination must be made that indemnification is not precluded. MBCA 8.53(a)(3).

e. A corporation may make advances for expenses mandatory. A few courts have refused to order advances under a mandatory provision where it appeared probable that the defendants had engaged in misconduct. *Fidelity Fed. Sav. & Loan Ass'n v. Felicetti,* 830 F.Supp. 262 (E.D.Pa.1993), but most courts have accepted at face value a mandatory provision. *Ridder v. CityFed Fin. Corp.,* 47 F.3d 85 (3d Cir.1995).

Caveat: A mandatory advances provision may result in the corporation being required to finance both sides of a lawsuit brought by the corporation against directors or officers.

5. Officers, Employees & Agents

Officers, employees, and agents of a corporation may have rights of indemnification based on contract, corporation policy, or general principles of agency that are broader than the right of directors. MBCA 8.56.

Example: An officer and an employee of a corporation are indicted personally for antitrust violations. They plead *nolo contendere* at the request of the corporation. The corporation may properly indemnify them for the fines imposed. *Koster v. Warren,* 297 F.2d 418 (9th Cir.1961). The court stated in this case that an agreement in advance to indemnify all employees convicted of antitrust violations might be against public policy.

a. A corporation has the same discretionary right to indemnify an officer, employee or agent of the corporation as it has to indemnify directors. MBCA 8.56(2).

b. An *officer* of the corporation (but not employees or agents generally) has the same right to mandatory indemnification as a director and also may apply for court-ordered indemnification to the same extent as a director. MBCA 8.56(1).

c.   In some states, a director who is also an officer, agent, or employee of the corporation has only the indemnification rights of a director. The purpose of this limitation is to ensure that all directors are treated alike with respect to indemnification.

6.   Modification of Statutory Indemnification Policies

Delaware and several other states provide that the indemnification statute is not exclusive. That means that a corporation may include broader indemnification provisions in its articles of incorporation or bylaws.

a.   In states with non-exclusive statutes, the only limitation on indemnification rights granted by contract or bylaw provision is public policy.

> *Caveat:*   *Waltuch v. Conticommodity Services, Inc.*, 88 F.3d 87 (2d Cir.1996) reads the non-exclusive provision of the Delaware statute as being qualified by a good faith requirement in connection with permissive indemnification.

b.   MBCA 8.58(a) makes the statute exclusive, but provides that a contractual or voluntary provision relating to indemnification that goes beyond the statute is valid only to the extent the provision is consistent with the statute. The Official Comment states that this position is believed to be a more accurate description of the limited validity of nonstatutory indemnification provisions. As a practical matter there may be little difference between the Model Act and non-exclusive statutes, because public policy probably does not permit indemnification significantly broader than that permitted by the Model Act.

> *Example:*   A bylaw provision provides that indemnification decisions shall be made by an outside committee consisting of law professors with no interest in the proceeding. That provision is valid under both types of statutes.

> *Example:*   A corporation agrees to grant indemnification on a mandatory basis whenever it may do so on a voluntary basis. The provision is valid under both types of statutes.

7.   Indemnification of Witnesses

MBCA 8.50-8.58 applies only when a director is named or threatened to be named as a defendant in a proceeding. MBCA 8.50(6).

a.   MBCA 8.58(b) states that it does not limit the power of a corporation to pay or reimburse the expenses of a director in connection with an appearance as a witness.

b.   Most statutes are silent on whether indemnification of expenses of directors who are not parties to litigation is permitted.

8. Notification of Indemnification
MBCA 16.21(a) requires the corporation to notify stockholders of all indemnifications or advances of expenses to defendants in connection with actions brought by or in the name of the corporation.

a.   The notification must be in writing and must be given with or before notice of the next annual meeting.

b.   The statutes of many states do not require notice to be given stockholders in these situations.

9. Indemnification in Federal Proceedings
Indemnification of liabilities incurred under federal statutes may raise additional questions of public policy.

a.   The SEC has long taken the position that it is against public policy for a corporation to indemnify officers or directors against liabilities imposed by the Securities Act of 1933. Rule 460 provides that acceleration of the effective date of a registration statement may be denied unless a waiver of right to indemnification is filed.

b.   Some cases indicate that indemnification is also less broadly available for liabilities imposed by federal securities law than under common law or state statutory provisions. *See Globus v. Law Research Serv. Inc.,* 418 F.2d 1276 (2d Cir.1969). *S.E.C. v. Continental Growth Fund, Inc.,* 1964 Fed.Sec.L.Rep. ¶ 91,437 (S.D.N.Y.Oct. 7, 1964). *See also Gould v. American–Hawaiian Steamship Co.,* 387 F.Supp. 163 (D.Del.1974), vacated on other grounds 535 F.2d 761 (3d Cir.1976).

K. D & O LIABILITY INSURANCE

Directors and officers (D & O) liability insurance provides useful but limited protection against costs and liabilities for negligence or misconduct not involving dishonesty or knowing bad faith, and for false or misleading statements in disclosure documents. Most candidates would decline to serve as a director of a publicly held corporation unless protected by a D & O policy.

1. Structure of D & O Policies
D & O policies are complementary to indemnification. Most publicly held corporations provide both indemnification and insurance for its directors.

a. D & O insurance is *claims made* insurance. It insures only for claims that are presented to the insurer during the period of insurance (and a short period thereafter if the insurance is not renewed) even though the actions giving rise to the claim may have occurred months or years earlier. When the period of insurance ends, if no claim has been made the insurer has no responsibility for events occurring during the period. *McCullough v. Fidelity & Deposit Co.*, 2 F.3d 110 (5th Cir.1993).

b. D & O insurance consists of two different parts. (1) The Corporate Reimbursement portion of the policy insures the corporation against payments it is obligated or permitted to make to officers or directors under its indemnification obligations. This portion of the policy does not insure the corporation against direct claims made by stockholders or others. (2) The Directors and Officers portion of the policy insures directors and officers against obligations that are not indemnifiable by the corporation as long as they are not excluded by the policy.

> *Example:* The corporation issues a press release that contains false statements and violates rule 10b–5. It is sued by stockholders who sold shares before the press release was corrected. Claims made in those actions against the corporation are not covered by the insurance policy.

> *Example:* An officer is also named as a defendant in the stockholder actions described in the previous example. The officer retains a lawyer and incurs other expenses in connection with her defense. The corporation indemnifies the officer. If the corporation is permitted to indemnify the defendant, the insurance policy covers these payments. *Raychem Corp. v. Federal Ins. Co.*, 853 F.Supp. 1170 (N.D.Cal.1994).

> *Example:* A director is named as a defendant in a derivative action action. The action is settled by the director agreeing to pay a small sum to the corporation. The corporation is not permitted to indemnify the director for this payment in most states. The amount paid in settlement is covered by the D & O insurance policy.

2. Policy Exclusions

Policy exclusions in D & O policies fall into three broad categories.

a. Conduct exclusions deal with conduct that is sufficiently self-serving or egregious that it is not insurable.

> *Example:* Claims based on conduct for personal advantage or illegal remuneration are not insurable.

b. Other insurance exclusions cover conduct for which insurance is available under other policies.

> *Example:* Bodily injury or property damage are excluded from D & O insurance coverage.

c. Laser exclusions are exclusions unique to the specific firm or industry.

d. Reckless, willful, or criminal conduct may not be insurable as a matter of law. *Raychem Corp. v. Federal Ins. Co.,* 853 F.Supp. 1170 (N.D.Cal.1994).

3. State Statutes

Many state statutes specifically authorize corporations to purchase D & O insurance. *See* MBCA 8.57. Where no statutory authorization exists, the power to purchase such insurance is usually thought to be implicit in the general corporate power to provide executive compensation. Corporate bylaws often specifically authorize the purchase of such insurance.

REVIEW QUESTIONS

9.1. What is the difference between direct and derivative litigation?

9.2. Is there a clear distinction between direct and derivative litigation?

9.3. What is a class suit?

9.4. Is a derivative suit a class suit?

9.5. In a derivative suit, is the corporation named as a plaintiff or a defendant?

9.6. A stockholder brings a derivative suit complaining that the board of directors approved the payment of a bonus of $20,000,000 to the chief executive officer of the corporation, who is also chairman of the board of directors and owner of 45 per cent of the voting stock of the corporation. The complaint alleges that payment of a bonus of this magnitude was unrelated to the value of the services provided by the chief executive officer and constituted waste. The complaint further alleges that no demand was made because it would be futile since all the directors are personal friends of the chief executive officer and will not do anything that the chief executive officer opposes. The corporation moves that the complaint should be dismissed for failing to make a demand on directors. Should that motion be granted?

9.7. In the preceding question, before filing the suit, the stockholder makes a demand on the board of directors that the bonus paid to the chief executive officer be rescinded on the ground that it is unrelated to the value of the services provided by the chief executive officer and constitutes waste. The board of directors appoints a litigation committee of two directors, neither of whom were on the board of directors at the time the bonus was approved, to consider the demand made by the stockholder. The two members of the litigation committee also have no direct connection with the corporation other than serving as outside directors. The litigation committee reviews the circumstances under which the bonus was paid and concludes in a written report that it is not in the best interests of the corporation to seek to rescind the bonus. The stockholder then files suit. The corporation moves that the suit be dismissed on the ground the decision of the litigation committee is final and conclusive. The plaintiff opposes this motion on the ground that he is entitled to a judicial decision on the merits of his claim. Should the corporation's motion be granted?

9.8. To what extent are federal courts involved in derivative litigation?

9.9. What is the contemporaneous ownership requirement and what is its justification in federal and state courts?

9.10. What are the procedural prerequisites for maintaining a derivative suit?

9.11. Why are derivative suits often treated with mistrust or skepticism?

9.12. What are the policy considerations underlying a state legislative decision whether or not to eliminate the security-for-expenses statute?

9.13. What are the consequences of a decision that a derivative plaintiff must comply with the security-for-expenses statute?

9.14. Is the state security-for-expenses statute applicable in the federal courts?

9.15. Is the security-for-expenses statute applicable to direct and class litigation?

9.16. Is a final decision in a derivative suit *res judicata* and binding on all stockholders?

9.17. Are any limitations placed on the power of a plaintiff to accept a settlement offer in a derivative suit?

9.18. What is a strike suit and how are such suits handled under modern practice?

9.19. May a plaintiff who is successful in a derivative suit recover attorneys fees and other expenses even if the corporation does not receive any money from the suit?

9.20. Is there any situation in which a derivative suit recovery is paid directly to the stockholders?

9.21. Ps are stockholders in X corporation which is incorporated in State A. They have brought a derivative action on behalf of X in the courts of State B against X's majority stockholder, a director of X, and another corporation also owned by X's majority stockholder. Ps claim that the majority stockholder has looted X by a series of transactions with the other corporation and that X is entitled to an accounting. Ps have obtained service of process on all defendants except X. The defendants have moved to dismiss Ps' petition on the ground that the court lacked jurisdiction of X, an essential party. Ps claim that if the suit may not be maintained in personam it may be brought as an action in rem in that the cause of action is property of X within the state. Are the defendants who were served entitled to dismissal?

9.22. P brought an action against the directors of D corporation on D's behalf for breach of fiduciary duties. The court found the directors liable in an amount of $4,355,595, in that they had appropriated an opportunity of D to purchase shares in another corporation. The defendant directors contend the award of damages should be limited to those who were stockholders at the time of the share transaction. Are the defendants correct in their contention?

9.23. What does indemnification mean?

9.24. Should not all indemnification be considered to be against public policy?

9.25. Is it against public policy to indemnify a defendant who has been found guilty of criminal or improper conduct?

9.26. What is D & O insurance?

9.27. Should not D & O insurance be prohibited as being against fundamental public policy?

X

Disclosure & Corporate Records

Under federal securities law, a publicly held company is required to file periodic reports with the Securities & Exchange Commission (SEC or Commission). Most of the information contained in these reports is also required to be distributed to stockholders. A corporation subject to these rules is often called a *reporting company*. State law also requires corporations to maintain certain books and records and to make them available to stockholders under specified conditions. State law relating to books and records applies to all corporations, whether or not publicly traded. But state law also imposes disclosure obligations in connection with particular transactions.

A. CORPORATIONS SUBJECT TO FEDERAL PERIODIC REPORTING REQUIREMENTS

Periodic reporting requirements under federal securities law are applicable to corporations (1) that must register under Section 12 of the Securities Exchange Act of 1934, or (2) that have made a public offering of securities registered under the Securities Act of 1933. The latter requirement is found in § 15(d) of the 1934 Act. The distinction between the two reporting requirements is important. A company that is registered under § 12 is also subject to a variety of other SEC rules including the rules governing proxy solicitations. Section 15(d) does not trigger these requirements. Thus, for example, a company that has registered only an offering of debt securities is not required to comply with the proxy rules.

Caveat: A company need not be a corporation to be subject to federal securities law. Rather, the applicability of federal securities law depends on whether a company offers *securities* to the public or has *equity securities* outstanding. Still, the vast majority of reporting companies are corporations.

Caveat: The terms *register* and *registration* are used in two distinct ways under federal securities law. Under the Securities Act of 1933 (1933 Act or Securities Act) a company must file a *registration statement* with the SEC in connection with any public offering of securities. Such an offering is said to be *registered*. It is the offering—not the company—that is registered. Under the Securities Exchange Act of 1934 (1934 Act or Exchange Act), a company must *register* with the SEC if it has 500 or more stockholders and $10 million or more in assets. The former form of registration applies to *offerings* (not the securities themselves) whereas the latter form of registration applies to *companies.*

Caveat: Although these two forms of registration are conceptually distinct, they are also related under the SEC's *integrated disclosure system.* If a company is registered under the 1934 Act, it may be able to use an abbreviated form of registration (SEC Forms S–2 and S–3) for purposes of making subsequent offerings of securities to the public by incorporating by reference information on file with the SEC in a registration statement covering a subsequent offering. Moreover, a registered company may also be eligible to use additional *methods* of offering securities to the public, such as a *shelf registration* (under SEC Rule 415) by which securities may be sold incrementally over a period of time in an *at the market offering* rather than being sold all at once in a *fixed price offering* as is the usual method in an *initial public offering* (IPO). In addition, filings must be current to take advantage of many exemptions under federal securities law such as Rule 144 and Regulation D.

Caveat: The penalties for nondisclosure under the 1933 Act are quite severe as compared to those under the 1934 Act. Thus, one downside of the integrated disclosure system is that incorporation by reference of a document filed under the 1934 Act may effectively increase the penalties for a failure of disclosure under the 1934 Act if the information is incorporated by reference in a 1933 Act registration statement. For this reason, among others, the SEC follows the practice of deeming some required documents (such as the annual report to stockholders) not to be officially *filed* documents.

1. Section 12 Registration

Section 12 of the 1934 Act requires registration by corporations (1) that have securities that are registered on a national securities exchange, or (2) that have a class of equity securities held of record by 500 or more persons and assets of $10 million or more. In order to register under § 12 a company must file SEC Form 10.

> *Caveat:* Although § 12(g) sets the asset requirement at $1,000,000, that figure has been increased by SEC rule from time to time over the years and now is at $10 million. *See* SEC Rule 12g–1. In practice, the 500 stockholder trigger is much more important than the asset trigger in that the vast majority of corporations with 500 stockholders have assets well in excess of $10 million. (The asset requirement relates to gross assets and not to net worth.) On the other hand, a company whose stock trades at a very low price—a *penny stock*—may have many stockholders and relatively little in the way of assets. Prior to 1998, many such stocks were traded on the OTC Bulletin Board (a service owned and operated by the NASD but not part of NASDAQ). Since 1998, corporations whose stock is traded on the OTC Bulletin Board have been required to register with the SEC under § 12 of the 1934 Act in order to be so traded even though such companies are not legally required to register under the terms of § 12.

> *Caveat:* Registration under § 12(g) is based on the number of stockholders of record rather than beneficial stockholders. Given that most investors leave their shares on deposit with their brokers and thus hold their shares in the name of brokers—in *street name*—a large company may have relatively few stockholders of record. The SEC has the power to adopt rules designed to prevent intentional circumvention of registration requirements in this way, as well as through the issuance of similar securities in separate classes.

2. Section 15(d) Reporting

If a company issues securities pursuant to a registration statement filed under the 1933 Act, it must file and distribute periodic reports under § 15(d) of the 1934 Act. Whereas § 12(g) is triggered by the equity securities only, the reporting requirement under § 15(d) is triggered by any offering of securities, including debt securities.

> *Caveat:* Most corporations that make an initial public offering of securities under the 1933 Act have more than 500 stockhold-

ers and $10,000,000 in assets as a result of the public offering and therefore must also register under section 12 of the 1934 Act. It is possible, however, for a corporation to make a public offering of securities and not thereafter meet these requirements. For example, a company may make an offering of debt securities. Similarly it is possible for a corporation to become subject to section 12 of the 1934 Act without ever making a public offering under the 1933 Act.

3. Implications of § 12 Registration

Registration under § 12 of the 1934 Act triggers the applicability of several other requirements under the 1934 Act, including:

- the proxy solicitation rules under § 14.

- the tender offer rules under §§ 13 and 14.

- reporting and trading rules under § 16.

- beneficial ownership rules under § 13.

In other words, these rules apply only to companies that are registered under § 12 of the 1934 Act. They do not apply to companies that are required to file reports under § 15(d).

Example: Corporation X has 400 stockholders of record holding common stock, and another 400 stockholders of record holding preferred stock, but no shares are registered on a national securities exchange. The preferred shares were sold pursuant to a 1933 Act registration. Corporation X is not required to register under section 12 even though it has an aggregate of 800 stockholders because no class of shares is held by 500 persons. It is, however, subject to the periodic reporting requirements because it has sold shares under a 1933 Act registration.

Example: Corporation Y has 520 stockholders of record of common shares and $7,000,000 of assets. The shares are traded infrequently by a single broker-dealer in Topeka, Kansas. Corporation Y is required to register under section 12 of the 1934 Act even though shares are not traded on any exchange. It is therefore subject to both the periodic reporting and registration requirements.

Example: Corporation Z has $100,000,000 in assets and 440 common stockholders. Corporation Z has never made a public offering of shares. Corporation Z is not required to register under section 12 and is not subject to periodic reporting requirements.

Example: Corporation Z's stockholders increase in number because of gifts of shares to children and grandchildren until there are 525 common stockholders. Corporation Z must register under section 12 and therefore becomes subject to periodic reporting requirements.

Example: The common shares of Dow Corning Corporation are owned 50 percent by Dow Chemical Corporation and 50 percent by Corning Glass Corporation. In order to raise needed capital, Dow Corning Corporation sells $50 million in debentures through a public offering registered under the 1933 Act. Dow Corning is subject to the periodic reporting requirements of the 1934 Act but is not required to register under section 12.

4. Termination of Section 12 Registration

Once a corporation is required to register under section 12, it remains subject to that section even though the number of stockholders drops below 500. Registration under section 12 may be terminated if the corporation has no class of shares held of record by more than 300 persons. A corporation may also terminate registration if it has fewer than 500 stockholders and if its assets are valued at less than $10,000,000 on the last day of its fiscal year for the last three years. SEC Rule 12g–4. In order to terminate registration, a company must file SEC Form 15. Reporting requirements are immediately suspended, but the termination becomes effective 90 days later after SEC review.

Caveat: A corporation with less than $10 million in assets is exempt from registration under § 12(g). SEC Rule 12g–1.

Caveat: A corporation that remains listed on a national securities exchange may not terminate its registration, although as a practical matter it is likely to be delisted from the exchange if it is eligible for termination. NASDAQ is not an exchange. (It is an electronic over the counter market.) Thus, corporations listed there are technically eligible to terminate registration if they meet SEC standards. But NASDAQ rules require listed companies to maintain registration.

5. Termination of Section 15(d) Reporting

The reporting requirement under § 15(d) is automatically suspended if a company has fewer than 300 stockholders of any class as of the beginning of any fiscal year after the year of an offering. There is no asset standard. A company must file SEC Form 15 within 30 days in order to notify the SEC of the suspension.

B. PERIODIC REPORTING REQUIREMENTS

Companies subject to § 12 or § 15(d) are required to file periodic reports with the SEC. These reports, are designed to update continually the information that is publicly available about the company. These reports are publicly available. They are on file in SEC reading rooms and are available electronically under the SEC's Electronic Data Gathering and Retrieval (EDGAR) system. These reports are subject to detailed formal requirements set forth in § 13 of the 1934 Act and rules thereunder. The SEC does not routinely review 1934 Act reports, but may do so if the report is incorporated by reference in a 1933 Act registration statement or in connection with selective enforcement program.

Caveat: The rules relating to the form and manner of textual disclosures under both the 1933 Act and the 1934 Act are contained in SEC Regulation S–K. The rules relating to financial disclosures are contained in SEC Regulation S–X, although to a large extent financial disclosures are also governed by generally accepted accounting principles (GAAP) as determined by the accounting profession under authority delegated by the SEC. These unified regulations operate as a disclosure cookbook of sorts and form the basis of the SEC's integrated disclosure system. Generally speaking, under SEC parlance, the word *regulation* is used to refer to a collection of *rules*. Regulations S–K and S–X are, however, composed of a series of *items* relating to particular matters subject to disclosure requirements and are widely distributed by electronic means (called EDGAR) to investors, brokerage firms, and the like. Information in these reports also form the basis of reports and stories in financial and other newspapers and magazines.

1. Form 10–K

Form 10–K is an annual report that provides the same information about the issuer that appears in a 1933 Act registration statement except for information that would relate to an offering of securities (such as stockholder rights, use of proceeds, underwriting arrangements, method of offering, pricing, and so forth). It must include full audited financial statements. Information required in Form 10–K, including:

- description of business and properties.

- management's discussion and analysis of financial condition and results of operations.

- full audited financial information together with independent auditor opinion.

- description of material legal proceedings.

- quantitative and qualitative disclosures about market risk.

- information regarding directors and officers and their compensation.

In addition, the Sarbanes Oxley Act requires that Form 10–K include:

- information relating to the company's code of ethics (if any).

- information relating to financial experts on the company's audit committee and whether they are independent.

- a table of contractual obligations.

- information relating to internal controls over financial reporting.

Many companies also include a discussion of risk factors in the 10–K (and 10–Q). By doing so, the company can take advantage of statutory defenses for forward looking statements (whether in the filed form or elsewhere) that turn out to be incorrect. Form 10–K must be signed by the CEO, CFO, principal accounting officer, and a majority of the members of the board of directors. Moreover, under the Sarbanes Oxley Act, the CEO and CFO both must certify (1) that they have reviewed the report and that the report is fair and accurate to their knowledge, and (2) that the company has designed and implemented internal controls over financial reporting and disclosure. In addition the CEO and CFO must certify that the report complies with the requirements of the 1934 Act.

> *Caveat:* Form 10–K includes much of the same information as the *annual report to stockholders* and the *proxy statement*, both of

which must be distributed to stockholders if the company is registered under § 12. SEC rules allow for these other documents to be incorporated by reference in Form 10–K. In such cases, it is typical for the reporting company to file Form 10–K simply by reporting on matters outside the scope of these other documents and attaching a copy of the materials distributed to stockholders. In some cases, documents incorporated by reference may not be filed or distributed until some later time. This is particularly true in the case of the proxy statement which typically is not distributed until well after the 10–K must be filed. Form 10–K itself is not required to be distributed to stockholders. Some companies follow the practice of incorporating the full Form 10–K in the annual report to stockholders even though SEC rules permit a much more limited annual report. Some companies also combine materials required in the proxy statement simply in order to save on distribution costs. Although Form 10–K is required only to be filed with the SEC and is not required to be distributed, it is widely used by financial analysts and readily available via EDGAR.

2. Form 10–Q

Form 10–Q is a quarterly report containing unaudited interim financial data. It must also disclose material nonrecurring events that occurred during the quarter, such as commencement of significant litigation. Under the Sarbanes Oxley Act, Form 10–Q reports must be certified by the CEO and CFO in the same fashion as Form 10–K reports.

3. Form 8–K

Form 8–K is a report that must be filed only when a reportable event occurs. A reportable event generally involves matters of major significance such as significant financial developments, changes in control, material acquisitions or dispositions of assets, changes in and resignations of directors. Generally, a Form 8–K must be filed within two days of a reportable event. Specifically, a company must file a Form 8–K if any of the following events occur:

- change in control.

- acquisition or disposition of significant assets other than in the normal course of business.

- bankruptcy or receivership.

- resignation or dismissal of auditor or engagement of new auditor.

- resignation of director or principal officer and reasons therefore

- election of new director or appointment of principal officer.

- change in fiscal year.

- material events regarding employee benefit plans including temporary suspension of trading under employee stock ownership plan.

- earnings release under Regulation G.

- amendment to or waiver under code of ethics.

- establishment or termination of material agreement or business relationship.

- change in securities rating.

- amendments to articles of incorporation or bylaws.

A company may voluntarily file a Form 8–K relating to any other material event.

> *Caveat:* The title page of these reports typically states that the report is filed pursuant to Section 13 or 15(d) of the 1934 Act without specifying which section applies.

4. Management's Discussion and Analysis (MD & A)

One of the most important items of information provided in periodic reports and proxy statements is the Management Discussion and Analysis of Financial Condition and Results of Operations (MD & A). SEC rules require that the MD & A focus specifically on material events and uncertainties known to management that would cause reported information not to be necessarily indicative of future results or conditions.

a. The MD & A must include a discussion of liquidity, capital resources and results of operations, including any unusual or infrequent events or transactions, as well as any other information necessary to understanding a company's financial condition and changes therein. *See* SEC Regulation S–K, Item 303.

b. The SEC tends to focus on the MD & A in reviewing periodic reports and has identified several common deficiencies including:

- failure to discuss revenue recognition policies, one-time charges, and assumptions used.

- failure to discuss or quantify reasons for material changes year to year in financial report line items.

- failure to discuss known material trends and uncertainties that diverge from historical patterns.

- failure to discuss business segment information.

See Matter of Caterpillar, Inc., SEC Rel. No. 34–30532 (1992) (SEC enforcement proceeding resulting from failure to disclose and discuss significance of profits from Brazilian subsidiary on overall financial results).

c.   As a result of the Sarbanes Oxley Act, the MD & A must now also include a discussion of material off balance sheet financings, critical accounting estimates, and adoption of new accounting policies.

C.   OTHER DISCLOSURE RULES

The reporting requirements discussed above are mandatory for companies subject to § 12 or § 15(d). There are, however, other disclosure requirements that may be triggered in situations in which the company speaks publicly.

1.   Regulation FD

Regulation FD, adopted in 1999, requires that when a company discloses material nonpublic information to certain stockholders or investment professionals—whether intentionally or inadvertently—it must also disclose the information to all stockholders unless the original disclosure is subject to a confidentiality agreement. The rule is designed to prevent selective disclosure. (FD stands for *fair disclosure.*) The disclosure may be made by via Form 8–K.

2.   Regulation G

Regulation G requires that a company that issues an earnings report using non GAAP methods furnish the information to the SEC on Form 8–K. It is common for companies to issue so-called *pro forma* earnings reports that show what earnings from ordinary operations would have been but for the inclusion of extraordinary items.

> *Caveat:*   Reports under Regulation FD and G are *furnished* rather than *filed.*

3. Press Releases

Public companies often issue press releases to the public in addition to filing required reports. Although press releases may not be required as a technical matter, they may be required, practically speaking, if the company or its directors, officers, agents, or controlling stockholders engage in trading of company shares. In the absence of disclosure, a transaction in shares may give rise to liability for insider trading. A company may also be required to issue a press release to correct an earlier statement that has become incorrect or to deal with rumors that may have originated from a source within the company. In addition, the company may be required by exchange or NASDAQ rules to make disclosures to stockholders or the public beyond those required by SEC rules. When a company communicates with its stockholders or the public via press release or otherwise, it may be liable under SEC Rule 10b–5 for any misstatement or omission of a material fact in the press release or communication.

> *Caveat:* Under § 18 of the 1934 Act an investor who buys or sells in reliance on a report filed with the SEC (such as a 10–K) has a private cause of action for damages. Section 18 applies only to documents *filed* with the SEC (not documents merely *furnished* to the SEC). Thus, § 18 typically applies only to companies that are subject to 1934 Act reporting requirements. On the other hand, Rule 10b–5 applies to all transactions in securities in interstate commerce, and may thus apply even to a non-reporting company.

D. BOOKS & RECORDS UNDER STATE LAW

State law requires corporations to maintain a record of stockholders' ownership. In addition many states require corporations to keep certain minimum records, such as minutes of meetings, and books and records of account. Unlike most state statutes the MBCA contains detailed rules with respect to the maintenance of minimum records.

1. Mandatory and Discretionary Records

a. MBCA 16.01(a) requires every corporation to *keep* certain basic records, such as minutes of meetings and records of actions taken by directors and stockholders. MBCA 16.01(b) and (c) require every corporation to *maintain* appropriate accounting records and a record of stockholders. MBCA 16.01(e) also requires that specified records be kept at its principal office where they may be inspected by stockholders. MBCA 16.02(a).

b. Most records maintained by corporations, such as financial records, tax returns, and samples of advertising are not covered by corporation statutes, but their retention may be required by other statutes. Depending on their character and the purpose of the stockholder, discretionary records may be subject to inspection by a stockholder.

2. Record of Stockholders

MBCA 16.01(c) requires that a corporation maintain a record of its stockholders, in a form that permits preparation of a list of the names and addresses of all stockholders, in alphabetical order by class of shares, showing the number and classes of shares held by each.

a. Many states require a voting list to be compiled immediately before each meeting. The voting list must be available to stockholders for inspection for a limited period of time during or immediately before a meeting.

b. The record of stockholders consists of the names of record owners only. It does not attempt to list beneficial owners. Where shares are held in the names of nominees, only the name of the nominee appears.

3. Disclosure to Stockholders

a. MBCA 16.20 requires every corporation to furnish stockholders with annual financial statements, containing at a minimum an income statement, a balance sheet, and a statement of changes in stockholders' equity.

> *Caveat:* Unlike financial statements included in SEC filings, these financial statements need not be prepared by an accountant or be consistent with GAAP. If not prepared in accordance with GAAP, however, financial statements must contain a description of the basis on which they were prepared and describe whether they were prepared in a manner consistent with the statements for the preceding year. If GAAP statements are prepared for any purpose they must be provided to stockholders.

b. MBCA 16.21 requires disclosure to stockholders of (1) transactions involving issuance of shares for promissory notes or promises of future services and (2) indemnification transactions in proceedings in which the corporation is a party.

c.   MBCA 16.22 requires every corporation to file an annual report with the Secretary of State. The annual report must disclose the nature of the corporation's business, the identity of its directors and officers, and the number and classes of outstanding shares. MBCA 16.01(e)(7) also requires corporations to maintain a copy of its most recent annual report at its principal office where it must be made available for inspection by stockholders.

> *Caveat:*   The MBCA and most state statutes specify the Secretary of State as the officer with which corporation reports must be filed. Some states specify other officers. For simplicity, it is assumed here that the Secretary of State is the designated officer.

d.   Most states do not contain these disclosure requirements, though many states require disclosure of various types of information, usually by way of a required annual report of the corporation. There is great diversity of requirements in this regard. Some states require disclosure of franchise tax reports or other documents that provide basic financial information.

E. INSPECTION OF BOOKS & RECORDS

1. Inspection by the Public
Corporations that are not registered under the federal securities acts generally need not make public disclosures except to the extent required by corporation and state tax statutes.

> *Caveat:*   Federal proxy rules and tender offer rules give alternative access to the record of stockholders. Rule 14a–7 requires a corporation registered under § 12 either to supply a copy of the record of stockholders or to mail solicitations to stockholders on behalf of a stockholder upon payment of the postage by that stockholder.

a.   Documents typically available at the Secretary of State's office include articles of incorporation, designation of registered office and agent, articles of amendment, and articles of merger. MBCA (1984) also requires every corporation to file an annual report with the Secretary of State containing current information about the corporation's business, directors, and capitalization.

> *Caveat:*   Bylaws are not generally required to be filed in any public office.

b. Information may also be publicly available from franchise tax returns and other filings, but in most states relatively little information is available. Information may also be obtained from state securities commissions.

2. Inspection by the Government

The government of the state of incorporation has broad visitorial powers under many state incorporation statutes, but as a practical matter, those powers are seldom exercised. Specific state or federal offices may also have visitorial powers under substantive statutes.

3. Inspection by Directors

A director has a broad right of inspection of books and records. A director is a manager of the corporation and owes certain duties to it and to all the stockholders. A director has a duty to be acquainted with the business and affairs of the corporation. Some decisions state that the directors' right of inspection is absolute and unqualified. *See Pilat v. Broach Systems, Inc.*, 260 A.2d 13 (N.J.Super.Law Div. 1969); *Brenner v. Hart System, Inc.*, 493 N.Y.S.2d 881 (App.Div. 1985); *Davis v. Keilsohn Offset Co.*, 79 N.Y.S.2d 540 (App.Div.1948). Other courts have sometimes denied inspection rights to directors where it was clear that the director was acting with improper motives.

4. Inspection by Stockholders

The right of a stockholder to inspect corporate books and records is narrower than the right of a director. A stockholder has a financial interest in the corporation and the law recognizes a right to inspect books and records to protect this interest. But a stockholder is not charged with management responsibility, is not subject to a broad fiduciary duty, and may have conflicting or inconsistent financial interests. As a result, a stockholder's right to inspect is limited to inspection for a *proper purpose*.

a. A stockholder may have either a common law or a statutory right of inspection, or both. A stockholder may also have rights of discovery if in litigation with the corporation. In many states, stockholders also have a special statutory right to inspect a list of stockholders before or during a stockholder meeting. MBCA (1984) 7.20. The right of stockholders to inspect books and records may not be eliminated in the articles of incorporation. *Cochran v. Penn–Beaver Oil Co.*, 143 A. 257 (Del.1926).

b. A common law inspection right is available to any stockholder of record who establishes a proper purpose for examining the books and records of the corporation. The burden of proof of a proper purpose is on the stockholder. *Fleisher Dev. Corp. v. Home Owners Warranty Corp.*, 856 F.2d 1529 (D.C.Cir.1988).

c. In an effort to make the right of inspection available without litigation, the statutes of many states supplement the common law right of inspection with a statutory right of inspection.

- The statutory right of inspection is typically available to persons (a) who have been stockholders of record for at least six months prior to the demand or (b) who own a specified number of shares.

- The statutory right of inspection often also requires a proper purpose for the inspection which must be stated in a written demand. But the corporation has the burden of showing the plaintiff does not have a proper purpose.

- Some statutes specifically provide that a record of stockholders need not be produced if the applicant has sold or offered for sale a stockholders list within the preceding five years.

- Under many statutes a corporate officer or agent who refuses to grant a statutory right of inspection maybe liable for a penalty equal to a specified per cent of the value of the shares owned by the stockholder or some other fixed amount.

   Caveat: The relationship between the common law right of inspection and these statutory rights of inspection is not clear in many states.

d. MBCA 16.01–16.04 adopts a somewhat different approach toward inspection rights than traditional statutes. Stockholders have an unrestricted and unqualified right to inspect documents that the corporation must preserve at its principal office. MBCA 16.02(a). This right of inspection is absolute and not subject to a proper purpose limitation. The documents are listed in MBCA 16.01(e) and include:

- Articles or restated articles of incorporation.

- Bylaws.

- Resolutions creating classes or series of shares.

- Minutes of stockholders' meetings and records of action taken by consent of the stockholders for the past three years.

- Written communications to stockholders within the past three years, including financial statements required to be provided to stockholders.

- A list of the names and business addresses of directors and officers.

- The corporation's most recent annual report.

MBCA 16.02(b) authorizes a stockholder to inspect and copy additional records only upon a showing of proper purpose and good faith, and upon providing a statement setting forth with reasonable particularity his purpose and the records he desires to inspect. The records must be directly connected with that purpose. The records subject to this additional inspection right include:

- Excerpts from minutes of the board of directors, records of actions of committees of the board of directors, and minutes of stockholders meetings more than three years old.

- Accounting records of the corporation.

- The record of stockholders.

Caveat: The classes of records available for inspection under MBCA 16.02 are narrower than the scope of inspection permitted by many courts under earlier statutes. Some courts, for example, have permitted inspection of correspondence or internal records that do not fall within any of the categories set forth there.

e.   The rights of inspection set forth in MBCA 16.02 are inspection rights that may not be restricted or eliminated by provisions in the articles of incorporation or bylaws.

f.   The inspection right includes the right to make copies. MBCA 16.03. The corporation may impose a reasonable charge for making copies but may not limit the inspection right to taking notes or making longhand copies. MBCA § 16.03(b), (c). The stockholder is entitled to be accompanied by an attorney or accountant. MBCA 16.03(a).

g.   A stockholder who is denied the right of inspection may seek a summary judicial order compelling inspection. MBCA 16.04. Further, the court must order the corporation to pay the stockholder's costs in compelling inspection unless the corporation proves that it refused inspection in good faith because it had a reasonable basis for doubt about the right of the stockholder to inspect the records demanded.

h. A court may impose restrictions on the use of information by a stockholder. It may, for example, prohibit the stockholder from disclosing it to a competitor. Courts have inherent power to restrict the use of information obtained by stockholders independent of specific statutory authority to do so. *See, CM & M Group, Inc. v. Carroll*, 453 A.2d 788 (Del.1982); *Helmsman Management Services, Inc. v. A & S Consultants, Inc.*, 525 A.2d 160 (Del.Ch.1987).

i. A purpose is proper if it is directed toward obtaining information bearing upon or seeking to protect the stockholder's interest and that of other stockholders of the corporation. A stockholder may have a proper purpose even though it is unfriendly to management.

> *Example:* A stockholder demands a list of stockholders in order to communicate with other stockholders about matters of corporate concern, to solicit proxies, to determine the value of one's shares or the reasons for a decline in profits, to discuss a derivative suit, to discuss proposals of management or to form a protective committee. These are all proper purposes. *General Time Corp. v. Talley Industries, Inc.*, 240 A.2d 755 (Del.1968); *Compaq Computer Corp. v. Horton*, 631 A.2d 1 (Del.1993); *Conservative Caucus v. Chevron Corp.*, 525 A.2d 569 (Del.Ch.1987).

> *Example:* The mere fact that the stockholder making the request is a competitor of the corporation does not necessarily make his or her purpose improper though such a demand may raise suspicions. But a desire to obtain trade secrets for a competitor is not a proper purpose.

> *Example:* It is not a proper purpose to seek the list in order to communicate one's own personal social or political views to stockholders. *State ex rel. Pillsbury v. Honeywell, Inc.*, 191 N.W.2d 406 (Minn.1971). Similarly, it is not a proper purpose to seek inspection in order to obtain the list of stockholder names and addresses for sale to a mail solicitation firm.

Example: Idle curiosity is probably not a proper purpose, but a stockholder can almost always assert a purpose that would be considered proper. A court may examine the true motives of the stockholder and disregard stated purposes for which there is no credible basis. *Thomas & Betts Corp. v. Leviton Mfg. Co.,* 681 A.2d 1026 (Del.1996).

j. A person who is a beneficial owner of shares but not the record owner has a common law right of inspection. Whether or not a beneficial owner has a statutory right depends on the precise wording of the statute. Under some state statutes, pledgees or judgment creditors have a statutory right to inspect. Under the MBCA 16.02(f), a beneficial owner of shares has a statutory right of inspection. Holders of voting trust certificates also have a statutory right to inspect under the MBCA and many state statutes.

F. FEDERAL REGULATION OF PROXY SOLICITATIONS

Under § 14(a) of the 1934 Act, it is unlawful to solicit proxies with respect to corporations registered under § 12 in contravention of rules and regulations that the SEC may prescribe as necessary or appropriate in the public interest or for the protection of investors. Pursuant to this broad grant of authority to regulate proxies, the SEC has issued comprehensive and detailed regulations. Historically, the proxy solicitation rules were particularly important because they forced public companies to communicate directly with stockholders. Although federal securities law focuses on disclosure and not substantive rights of stockholders, the proxy solicitation rules work because state law requires an annual meeting of stockholders to elect directors. Thus, the theory behind federal regulation of proxy solicitations is that stockholders should be informed as to the matters on which they may vote. Moreover, and perhaps more important today, the proxy rules tend to focus on the financial interests of the soliciting group. They require detailed disclosures on such matters as conflicting interest transactions and executive compensation. Thus, the proxy statement is a major source of stockholder information about corporate affairs. Federal law also requires that if a solicitation is made on behalf of management, the company must also distribute an annual report to stockholders. In contrast to Form 10–K which is filed with the SEC and available for review, the proxy statement and annual report are sent directly to stockholders (although for the majority of stockholders who hold their shares in street name they are sent through a broker-dealer). The proxy solicitation rules are collected in Regulation 14A which comprises Rules 14a–1 through 14b–2.

Caveat: The proxy solicitation rules apply only to companies registered under § 12 of the 1934 Act (whether such registration is mandatory or voluntary). The rules do not apply to companies reporting solely under § 15(d) of the 1934 Act. Thus, a company with fewer than 500 stockholders that has made a public offering of debt securities is not subject to the proxy solicitation rules even though the company is required to file periodic reports.

Caveat: The proxy rules apply (with certain narrow exceptions) to anyone who solicits proxies. Although the vast majority of proxy solicitations are made by incumbent management in connection with a regular annual meeting of stockholders, occasionally an insurgent group may seek to take control of the corporation by soliciting proxies for a competing slate of directors or in a narrower effort to compel a particular transaction—a *proxy fight* or *proxy contest*. In such a case, both groups must distribute proxy materials.

Caveat: Although the stockholder voting process is sometimes likened to the democratic process, incumbent management may use corporate funds to solicit proxies seeking reelection of a friendly slate of directors and recommending votes in favor of various resolutions proposed by management or against resolutions proposed by others (subject to a very lenient state law limitation that require only that the solicitation relate to business policies rather than a merely personal desire to remain in power). Nothing in federal or state law prohibits incumbent management from recommending that stockholders vote in a particular way. And management almost always makes a recommendation as to how stockholders should vote. (Indeed, in some cases a management recommendation is effectively required.) Although SEC rules create a limited right for stockholders to propose resolutions that must be included in the proxy materials distributed by management, an individual or group that seeks election to the board or opposes a management position, must ordinarily conduct (and pay for) an independent proxy solicitation. In short, stockholders have no inherent right to access to the corporate ballot or the proxy machinery.

1. Proxy Statements

a. SEC rules provide that with certain exceptions solicitation of a proxy must be accompanied or preceded by the delivery of a proxy statement setting forth detailed information about the solicitation and the group soliciting proxies. Schedule 14A of the SEC rules sets forth the matters that must be addressed in the proxy statement:

- date, time, and place of meeting, and deadline for submitting stockholder proposals.

- identity and detailed background information relating to nominee and incumbent directors.

- voting information including matters subject to a vote (if any), the manner of voting, the required vote for each matter, shares entitled to vote, method for counting votes, and the record date.

- the identity of the party for whom proxies are being solicited (for example, incumbent management), revocability of proxies, and the cost of the solicitation

- detailed information about compensation of the CEO and the four next most highly compensated officers, about stock performance compared to the market and peer companies, about equity compensation plans generally and whether such plans have been approved by a stockholder vote.

- related party transactions (a related party is defined as a director, officer, five-percent stockholder, or family member)

As a result of the Sarbanes Oxley Act and beginning in 2004, NYSE and NASDAQ companies must have boards comprising a majority of independent (non-management) directors and must disclose in their proxy statements the basis on which that determination is made. Moreover, independent directors must meet in regular executive sessions, and the proxy statement must disclose who presides at those sessions. Proxy statements must also include a description of and report by the company's audit committee and compensation committee.

> *Caveat:*   A company that is controlled by a single controlling stockholder or group need not comply with the independence rules.

b.   The proxy statement usually also incorporates the state-law-required notice of the meeting to stockholders. Most states require notice at least 10 days (but no more than 60 days) in advance of the meeting. Thus, state law effectively dictates when the proxy statement will be distributed.

c.   The proxy rules apply to all solicitations seeking stockholder approval. Thus, they apply to the solicitation of stockholder consents as permitted under Delaware law even though such consents are not proxies.

d.   The rules apply in connection with all solicitations not just those in connection with a regular annual meeting. Thus, the rules apply whenever a vote of the stockholders is to be taken, including in connection with mergers and other fundamental changes, amendments to the articles of incorporation or bylaws, ratification of board actions, and removal of directors. The proxy rules are thus particularly important in connection with mergers and acquisitions in that they provide stockholders with material information about the merits of the deal. (In a merger in which the stockholders of both corporations must vote, it is common for the two corporations to issue a joint proxy statement in order to avoid inconsistencies.) Proxy materials may thus also be important as a matter of state law in connection with an appraisal proceeding or an action challenging the validity of a corporate level transaction. Moreover, as discussed further below, there is a private cause of action under federal law for violations of the proxy rules, which may also give rise to parallel federal litigation.

2.   Annual Report to Stockholders

The proxy regulations require the distribution of an annual report to stockholders (ARS).

a.   Rule 14a–3 provides that if a solicitation is made on behalf of management relating to an annual meeting of stockholders at which directors are to be elected, the proxy statement must be accompanied or preceded by an annual report of the corporation.

b.   Rule 14c–3 extends this requirement to registered companies that do not solicit proxies.

c.   SEC rules specify the minimum content of the ARS:

- financial statements for the two most recent years

- stock and dividend information

- operation and industry segment information

- director and officer information

d. NYSE rules require that annual reports also include information relating to corporate governance, the charters of important committees of the board of directors, and a certification by the CEO that the company meets NYSE listing standards. NYSE rules require that the annual report be distributed no later than 120 days after the close of the fiscal year or 15 in advance of the annual meeting. Thus, the annual report may be distributed separately from the proxy statement.

e. Because the ARS serves a public and stockholder relations function in addition to a disclosure function (as distinct from the Form 10–K), companies may and usually do include additional information in the annual report.

f. The ARS must be furnished to the SEC but is not technically a filed document unless it is incorporated by reference in Form 10–K. If the company is listed for trading, the ARS must also be filed with the NYSE or NASDAQ.

g. Most state statutes do not require the distribution of annual information to stockholders.

3. Form of Proxy

SEC regulations prescribe the form of proxy appointments by specifying the information that must appear on the proxy card to be returned by the stockholder (as well as details about the form of its presentation) and prohibit certain tactics such as undated or post-dated appointments or broad grants of discretionary power to proxy holders. Stockholders must be given the option to vote for candidates for directors (or to withhold a vote for some or all of the candidates).The persons appointed as proxy (the proxy holder) must vote as directed by the appointing stockholders for the election of directors and on other issues presented for decision to the stockholders. In short, the proxy holder is simply an agent for the appointing stockholder. Thus, the proxy holder is typically required to vote some shares FOR and some shares AGAINST any given proposition. (The individual who is to serve as proxy holder is typically designated by the soliciting group. The proxy holder may be a lower level officer of the company or an attorney or accountant retained by the company or group.)

Caveat: The proxy holder may vote in his or her discretion (or as directed by the soliciting group) on any matter that arises from the floor of the meeting.

4. Presolicitation Review

Prior to 1992, the SEC required a presolicitation review of all for proxy documents. Drafts of proxy statements and other soliciting materials (such as letters, press releases, and the like), were required to be filed with the SEC at least ten days prior to the date it was proposed to mail definitive copies to securities holders. In 1992, the SEC sharply reduced the scope of presolicitation review to out-of-the-ordinary matters. While the SEC does not pass upon the accuracy or adequacy of the disclosures, it does indicate that revisions should be made if it concludes that some materials are incomplete or inaccurate.

5. What Is a Solicitation?

The SEC has consistently argued, and most courts have agreed, that the definitions of *solicitation* and *proxy* should be broadly construed to ensure the widest protection provided by the proxy regulations. Thus, any communication that is reasonably calculated to result in the granting, withholding, or revocation of a proxy, consent, authorization, or other action by a stockholder is covered by Regulation 14A.

> *Example:* An authorization to obtain a list of stockholders signed by 42 stockholders is a solicitation subject to the proxy regulations. *Studebaker Corp. v. Gittlin*, 360 F.2d 692 (2d Cir.1966).

> *Example:* Advertisements urging the approval or disapproval of certain transactions may constitute solicitations, though some courts have disagreed. *Brown v. Chicago R. I. & P. R. Co.*, 328 F.2d 122 (7th Cir.1964); *Long Island Lighting Co. v. Barbash*, 779 F.2d 793 (2d Cir.1985).

6. Exempt Proxy Solicitations

a. SEC proxy rues exempt certain narrow classes of solicitations. The principal exceptions are:

- Solicitations other than on behalf of registrant to fewer than 10 persons.

- Solicitations by a record owner to a beneficial owner to obtain instructions on how to vote.

- Solicitation by a beneficial owner to obtain proxy materials from the record owner.

- Newspaper advertisements that merely describe how holders may obtain copies of the proxy documents.

- Proxy advice furnished by a person who renders financial advice in the ordinary course of business and receives no special remuneration for the proxy advice.

b. In 1992 the SEC amended rules 14a–1 and 14a–2 to exempt most communications by persons who do not seek the power to act as proxy. The amendments permit communications that state how a stockholder intends to vote and communications directed to persons to whom the stockholder owes a fiduciary duty or is in response to an inquiry from another stockholder. These amendments are designed to permit discussion of corporate governance issues among institutional investors such as mutual funds and pension plans. Prior to these amendments institutional investors—who own more than 60 percent of all shares—were effectively precluded from communicating with each other about how to vote, because such communications would have been deemed to be proxy solicitations subject to all of the formalities of Regulation 14A. (Failure to comply with the proxy rules may result in votes being voided.) Thus, SEC rules originally designed to promote stockholder democracy arguably impeded the process and conferred an additional advantage on management beyond the considerable edge afforded by incumbency and the ability to use corporate funds to solicit proxies.

7. Corporations That Need Not Solicit Proxies

Most publicly held corporations need to solicit proxies if there is to be a quorum at a stockholders' meeting. In some corporations, one or a few stockholders may own or control an outright majority of shares and accordingly may not need to solicit proxies from other stockholders. Section 14(c) of the 1934 Act requires corporations that do not solicit proxy appointments to supply stockholders with information substantially equivalent to the information that would have been required if a proxy solicitation to its stockholders had been made.

> *Caveat:* This provision goes somewhat beyond the narrow principle of mandating disclosure where stockholder action is sought.

8. Problems Created by Book Entry and Nominee Holdings

The widespread practice of holding shares in street names creates problems for the proxy solicitation process because beneficial owners of shares are not the record owners.

a. Under § 14(b) of the 1934 Act and SEC rules, a broker-dealer, bank, or other entity that exercises fiduciary powers (street name holder) must forward proxy materials to beneficial owners and afford them a reasonable opportunity to vote either by executing proxy forms in blank (and delivering them to the beneficial owners so that the shares may be voted) or by soliciting directions as to how to vote the shares and voting them as the beneficial owners direct.

b. A street name holder transmits proxy information to beneficial owners if the solicitor reimburses forwarding expenses. The solicitor must provide sufficient copies of the proxy materials so that a copy can be transmitted to each beneficial owner.

c. SEC regulations require street name holders to determine whether a beneficial owner objects to disclosure of their names to the issuer in order to permit direct communication.

- Beneficial owners who do not object are known as non-objecting beneficial owner (NOBOs.)

- Many brokerage firms recommend that customers do not elect to become NOBOs in part because of concern that the customers may be solicited by other brokerage firms if their names appear on a NOBO list.

- Some investors prefer to maintain their anonymity in order to avoid unwanted communications or pressure or recrimination in connection with voting decisions.

- A corporation may be required to prepare a NOBO list and make it available to a stockholder for inspection. *Sadler v. NCR Corp.*, 928 F.2d 48 (2d Cir.1991).

d. Studies by the SEC reveal that beneficial owners generally receive proxy solicitation material on a timely basis and that there are not widespread abuses of the proxy solicitation process as a result of street name ownership. Thus, although there have been various proposals to create a direct registration system for beneficial owners, none have progressed far.

Because of the difficulties created by holdings in street name as well as the complexity of the SEC proxy rules, many companies find it useful to retain one of the several proxy solicitation firms to help organize and conduct the process, particularly if a proxy fight is likely.

9. Stockholder Proposals

Rule 14a–8 establishes procedures by which a stockholder may submit one proposal each year for inclusion in a company's proxy statement.

a. If the proposal is an appropriate one for stockholder action, the company is required to include the proposal even if opposed to it.

b. The stockholder submitting the proposal must have owned for a period of at least one year either (i) one per cent of the outstanding shares or (ii) shares with a market value of at least $2,000. The shares may be owned beneficially or of record.

c. A stockholder submitting a proposal may also submit a supporting statement which the company is required to publish if the proposal and the supporting statement do not exceed 500 words in the aggregate. Management may explain the basis of its opposition to a proposal without limitation on the number of words.

d. Proposals that fail in one year may be resubmitted within the following five years only if they meet specific standards based on votes received in the past.

e. Because stockholders may seek action on proposals of dubious relevance or propriety, or simply for personal publicity, the SEC has imposed specific requirements and limitations on stockholders' proposals. A proposal may be omitted if:

- It is not a proper subject for action by stockholders.

- It would require the company to violate any law, if implemented.

- It is contrary to proxy regulations.

- It relates to the redress of a personal claim or grievance or is designed to result in a benefit to the proponent not shared with other security holders.

- It deals with operations which account for less than 5 per cent of the company's total assets net earnings, and gross sales and is not otherwise significantly related to the registrant's business.

- It deals with a matter that is beyond the company's power to effectuate.

- It deals with a matter relating to the conduct of ordinary business operations.

- It relates to election of a director or officer.

- It is moot the company has substantially implemented the proposal.

- It is either counter to a proposal by management or substantially the same as a proposal by another stockholder which will be included in the proxy materials.

- It relates to specific amounts of cash or stock dividends.

f. The SEC has issued numerous rulings applying these exclusions. As a result, phrases such as *proper subject* or *ordinary business operations* have been given considerable practical content, and the tests are not as vague and open-ended as the language might indicate. In *SEC v. Transamerica Corp.*, 163 F.2d 511 (3d Cir.1947) the court rejected the argument that these terms should be construed restrictively or legalistically.

> *Example:* Important business-related proposals are proper subjects for stockholder action under state law if they are phrased as recommendations to the board of directors rather than specific directions to the corporation. As a result, most proposals that are approved by the stockholders are not binding on the corporation unless the board approves. These proposals are usually referred to as *precatory resolutions*.

> *Example:* A proposal to institute cumulative voting must be included in a proxy statement.

> *Example:* A proposal that an electric utility not build a nuclear power plant may not be omitted on the ground that it involves only ordinary business operations.

> *Caveat:* Some proposals are phrased in terms of amendments to bylaws. If such a proposal is approved by the stockholders it would appear to become immediately effective without di-

rector action. There is no situation in which a stockholder proposal phrased as an amendment to the bylaws has been approved. In one case the SEC ruled that such a proposal might be excluded because it related to the *ordinary business operations* of the registrant.

Example: A proposal that the bylaws of an oil company be amended to disqualify citizens of OPEC from service on the board of directors may be omitted from the proxy statement because one such citizen was already a director and running for reelection so that the proposal related to an election to office. *Rauchman v. Mobil Corporation,* 739 F.2d 205 (6th Cir.1984).

g. In 1989, the SEC ruled that a proposal recommending that a company dismantle its affirmative action program must be included in the company's proxy statement. In 1991, the SEC held that a company could omit a proposal that required the registrant to report on its equal employment opportunity programs, including data on work force composition and affirmative action timetables and programs on the ground it dealt with the ordinary business operations of the registrant. The SEC staff subsequently agreed that employment matters concerning the work force could be omitted even though they involved social as well as economic issues. *In re Cracker Barrel Old Country Store, Inc.,* 1992 WL 289095 (1992). A court subsequently refused to accept this conclusion on the ground that *Cracker Barrel* was inconsistent with a published policy statement of the SEC. *Amalgamated Clothing & Textile Workers v. Wal–Mart Stores, Inc.,* 821 F.Supp. 877 (S.D.N.Y.1993). In a subsequent case involving the same corporation, an injunction requiring the inclusion of a proposal that Cracker Barrel not discriminate on the basis of sexual orientation was overturned on the ground that this interpretation by the staff was a legislative rule that could not be implemented without notice and comment. *New York City Employees' Retirement System v. SEC,* 45 F.3d 7 (2d Cir.1995).

h. *Roosevelt v. E.I. DuPont de Nemours & Co.,* 958 F.2d 416 (D.C.Cir.1992) holds that stockholders have a private cause of action to enforce Rule 14a–8. But *Roosevelt* also held that a proposal relating to the defendant's plan to phase out chlorofluorocarbons was excludable as involving ordinary business operations.

i. Institutional investors have submitted numerous proposals. In many instances, these proposals have been voluntarily implemented without a vote by stockholders. In other instances these proposals have been adopted outright or have received significant stockholder support. Proposals made by institutional investors include:

- confidential voting (approved outright by stockholders of two companies in 1990 and voluntarily implemented by management at several others)

- independent tabulation of votes,

- requiring stockholder approval for poison pills and other defensive tactics relating to takeovers,

- requiring stockholder approval of management compensation arrangements following a takeover (so-called golden parachutes),

- requiring issuers to opt out of undesirable provisions of state law, and

- requiring the redemption of poison pills when faced with a desirable tender offer.

Proposals by institutional investors under rule 14a–8 have declined since 1992 in favor of direct contact with directors.

j.   Some academic commentary during the 1980s and early 1990s has been critical of the stockholder proposal rule. Here SEC rules extend somewhat beyond the narrow principle of mandating disclosure where stockholder action is sought. Some SEC Commissioners have expressed concern that the numerous social policy proposals being included in proxy statements provide little or no benefit to stockholders generally.

10. Extension of SEC Authority Over Stockholder Voting

The SEC has attempted to use its power to regulate proxy solicitation as a foundation for protecting stockholder democracy generally.

a.   In 1990, an SEC rule purporting to require stock exchanges to adopt listing standards prohibiting alterations in stockholder voting rights was struck down as an unwarranted intrusion on state corporation law and beyond the Commission's authority to foster disclosure.

b.   In 2003, the SEC proposed new rules that would require disclosures about the process of nominating candidates for election as director and about stockholder communications with the board of directors. In addition the SEC staff recommended that stockholders be permitted access to the company's proxy machinery to nominate candidates for director after certain triggering events, including failure of the company to act on stockholder proposals that receive a majority of votes or the election of an unopposed director by fewer than 65 percent of the votes cast. These proposals have been quite controversial, and have prompted counter proposals that state law be amended instead to require election of directors by majority vote. The proposals may have contributed to campaigns by institutional investors to withhold votes from specific directors, including Michael Eisner of Disney and Warren Buffett of Coca Cola.

G. FALSE AND MISLEADING STATEMENTS IN PROXY COMMUNICATIONS

Rule 14a–9 makes it unlawful to solicit proxies by means of communication that contains any statement that is false or misleading with respect to any material fact, or which omits to state any material fact.

1. Private Cause of Action

This broad prohibition creates an implied private cause of action by stockholders. *J. I. Case Co. v. Borak*, 377 U.S. 426, 84 S.Ct. 1555 (1964). *Borak* held that Rule 14a–9 created a private cause of action because, private enforcement of the proxy rules provides a necessary supplement to Commission action. This is sometimes called the *private attorney general* doctrine.

a. Since the mid 1970s the courts have been reluctant imply further private causes of action (particularly for damages) under the federal securities laws. It is, however, clear that there is also a private cause of action under Rule 10b–5 relating to misstatements and omissions of material facts in connection with the purchase or sale of securities (such as insider trading and the like) as discussed further in the chapter on transactions in shares. Generally speaking, the law relating to what constitutes a material fact under Rule 14a–9 also applies to actions under Rule 10b–5 (and vice versa). State courts also rely heavily on federal case law relating to materiality in opinions dealing with the validity of stockholder ratification votes and the like. On the other hand, although it is clear that some level of *scienter* (knowingness) is required to state a cause of action under Rule 10b–5, it appears that negligence will suffice under Rule 14a–9. *Wilson v. Great Am. Indus.*, 855 F.2d 987 (2d Cir. 1988); *Herskowitz v. Nutri/System*, 857 F.2d 179 (3d Cir. 1988).

b. Actions arising under the 1934 Act are subject to exclusive federal jurisdiction. *See* § 27. But the settlement of state class actions dealing with related claims may include within the settlement claims based on federal law such as Rule 14a–9. *Matsushita Electric Industrial Co. v. Epstein*, 516 U.S. 367, 116 S.Ct. 873 (1996).

c. A private action under Rule 14a–9 may take the form of either a derivative action or a direct action (usually a class action), depending on the precise nature of the claim. In either case, federal law also applies to the procedural aspects of the case. Thus, a state law requirement that a bond be posted in connection with a derivative action does not apply.

d. The SEC may maintain a civil enforcement action under any of the proxy rules. Willful violations may be prosecuted criminally by a United States Attorney.

2. Materiality

Most of the leading cases regarding private actions under Rule 14a–9 have dealt with stockholder votes in connection with mergers and have focused on whether an alleged failure of disclosure involved a material fact.

a. In *Mills v. Electric Auto–Lite Co.*, 396 U.S. 375, 90 S.Ct. 616 (1970), the Court held that it is not necessary to show that the omission of a material fact actually influenced votes. Rather, it is enough to establish that the vote itself was an *essential link* in the transaction being questioned. This is sometimes called *transaction causation* and is distinct from *loss causation*. *Mills* also suggested that a fact is material if it might be of interest to a stockholder.

b. In *TSC Industries, Inc. v. Northway, Inc.*, 426 U.S. 438, 96 S.Ct. 2126 (1976), the Court held that a fact is material if there is a substantial likelihood that a reasonable stockholder *would* consider it important in deciding how to vote and rejected the *might* test. TSC also held that in order to be material a fact must change the *total mix* of information available to stockholders. Thus, proxy materials need not provide characterizations and interpretations but rather should set forth just the facts. The Court also held that it was error to grant summary judgment on the issue in favor of the plaintiff, although a warning to lower courts to limit Rule 14a–9 to substantial misstatements was added. Prior to this decision some courts had tended to find relatively minor misstatements or omissions to be material and therefore violations of Rule 14a–9. The test adopted in *TSC* is generally accepted as the definition of materiality in securities litigation as well as under state law cases relating to stockholder voting.

Example: In a proposed merger, the proxy statement does not disclose that the largest single stockholder needs funds immediately in order to meet estate tax liabilities. Whether such an omission meets the test of materiality set forth in *TSC* is an issue that should be submitted to a jury and not resolved on a motion for summary judgment. *Mendell v. Greenberg*, 927 F.2d 667 (2d Cir.1990).

c.   In *Virginia Bankshares, Inc. v. Sandberg*, 501 U.S. 1083, 96 S.Ct. 2749 (1991), the Court held (1) that a statement couched in terms of opinion or belief may be materially misleading in violation of Rule 14a–9, but (2) that a false statement in a proxy solicitation may not meet the essential link (transaction causation) test if it is addressed solely to stockholders whose combined votes are not sufficient to prevent the action being taken.

Example: A statement that the plan of merger has been approved by the board of directors because it provides an opportunity for the bank's public stockholders to achieve a high value for their shares is materially misleading if in fact the directors did not hold the belief that a high value was being offered.

Caveat: Under state corporation law, the vote of minority stockholders may have the (material) effect of insulating the transaction from review as a violation of the duty of loyalty or at a minimum of shifting the burden of proof away from the defendant directors and back to the plaintiffs. The Court in *Virginia Bankshares* rejected this argument because the plaintiff could still maintain an action in state court but expressly left open the possibility that a fact could be material if it led stockholders to forgo appraisal rights.

Example: In a cash-out merger, the corporation solicits proxies from all stockholders even though the controlling stockholder owns 85 per cent of the outstanding shares and only a majority vote is needed to approve the merger. The minority stockholders' vote cannot affect the outcome of the vote, and therefore a misstatement cannot be material and made the basis of a private suit brought by minority stockholders under Rule 14a–9.

Caveat: Minority stockholders may be able to claim compensable injury under Rule 14a–9 if the false statement caused them to lose appraisal remedies under state law even if their vote was not necessary to approve the proposal. *Wilson v. Great American Industries, Inc.*, 979 F.2d 924 (2d Cir.1992).

3. Remedies in Rule 14a–9 Cases

As a practical matter the test in *TSC* seems to turn on whether the fact in question would have affected the price of the transaction, even though in *Mills* the Court reversed a decision that no cause of action had been stated because the price was fair. Ironically, after remand, the court in *Mills* found that even though a cause of action had been stated and the plaintiff established liability, the stockholders had not suffered financial harm and no damages were awarded because § 28 of the 1934 Act limits awards to actual damages (which has generally been interpreted as requiring an out-of-pocket measure). Some federal courts have suggested that injunctive relief should be the norm in order to avoid this result.

a.   A court may grant injunctive relief in a Rule 14a–9 case, but it rarely happens, because the plaintiff must show irreparable harm, and because the plaintiff may be required to post a large bond in order to obtain a TRO or temporary injunction. Moreover, most Rule 14a–9 cases involve stockholder votes in connection with mergers and similar transactions in which the ultimate issue is the price paid for the acquired company. The usual remedy in such cases is money damages.

Caveat: It is unclear in many Rule 14a–9 cases whether the action should be characterized as direct or derivative. The federal courts have tended to minimize the significance of the differences between the two in part because there is no requirement under federal law for a bond to be posted in connection with a derivative action as there is in many states. Nevertheless, a bond may be required in connection with an action for an injunction.

b.   Many state courts (in particular the Delaware courts) award *rescissory damages* (benefit of the bargain (BOBs)) in such cases, making state law more attractive than federal law even though it may be more difficult to establish liability in a state law action than in a federal action under the proxy rules in which mere negligence will suffice. (If a cause of action based on Rule 10b–5 is also asserted, that claim must allege that the defendant acted with *scienter*, that is, at least recklessly.) In addition, a state court in an appraisal action may sometimes include a premium for control. Moreover, some state courts (including those of Delaware and California) have held that failure to disclose a material fact may be actionable even in the absence of any action in reliance thereon by a stockholder. On the other hand, the federal courts have awarded BOBs in a few cases in which the deal promised a specific amount higher than the consideration actually paid.

c. In some cases, the courts may order that improperly obtained votes be sterilized and not counted. This remedy may be favored where it is workable because of judicial reluctance to mandate that a stockholder vote in a particular way (possibly because of concern that such an order would run afoul of the general rule that proxies are revocable). Sterilization may also be favored because of reluctance to attach a dollar value to stockholder votes (which might be likened to illegal vote selling).

d. In theory, a court may order that a merger be reversed (or *unwound*), but this remedy is seldom if ever used, because once a merger is effected, it quickly becomes impossible to determine which assets and liabilities would go with which predecessor business. In other words, it is extremely difficult to unscramble eggs.

e. If a derivative action or class action is successful (or partially successful), attorney fees may be awarded to the plaintiff attorneys against the defendant even though the action does not result in the award of damages. Although *Mills* suggested that attorney fees might be awarded based on the private attorney general theory, that rationale has since been rejected by the Supreme Court. In an action in which damages are awarded or a monetary settlement results, attorney fees are typically paid out of the damages or settlement.

H. PROXY CONTESTS

In a proxy context, an insurgent group competes with management in an effort to obtain proxy appointments. In the classic proxy fight the goal of insurgents is to elect a majority of the board of directors and thereby obtain control, but in some cases contests are waged solely to obtain representations on the board.

1. Strategy and Tactics

a. It is important for an insurgent group to obtain a stockholder's and NOBO list so that substantial stockholders may be identified and contacted personally. A court proceeding under state law may be necessary to obtain these lists. An insurgent group also has limited rights under SEC rule 14a–7, which requires management to provide minimal assistance either by providing a list of stockholder names and addresses or by mailing a communication directly to stockholders at the expense of the insurgent group. Large stockholders may be courted individually. In addition mutual funds and many other institutional investors are required regularly to disclose their portfolio holdings showing their beneficial ownership in all corporations.

b. An insurgent group usually purchases a substantial block of shares in the open market before announcing its intentions. Under the 1934 Act an insurgent group must file schedule 13D with the SEC within ten days if it acquires over five percent of any class of the target corporation's equity securities. The Schedule 13D must also be furnished to the target company and to the relevant stock exchange and must be amended within ten days of any purchase of additional shares (or sale of shares).

Caveat: An insurgent group may be required to file and furnish a Schedule 13D simply as a result of forming a group representing a five percent or more of shares in the aggregate.

c. Within a broad range, management may finance its solicitation from the assets of the corporation, because management controls the proxy machinery and is free to use it to seek reelection, while the insurgent group must finance its campaign from outside sources. In addition, many stockholders routinely vote as recommended by management (or do not at all). Although SEC rules are often said to be intended to protect stockholder democracy, stockholder apathy is arguably rational on the part of a well diversified investor.

Caveat: With increasing concentration of shares in the hands of institutional investors, successful proxy contests may become more common.

d. Although incumbent management may use its control over the proxy machinery with relative freedom in an attempt to defeat a challenger, such tactics are permissible only if supported by a reasonable business purpose.

Example: A board of directors has authority to set the annual meeting date within certain limits set forth in the bylaws. The board elects to move the meeting date forward as much as possible solely in order to make the successful solicitation of proxies by the insurgents more difficult. Such an action is invalid because it has no business purpose. *Schnell v. Chris–Craft Indus.*, 285 A.2d 437 (Del.1971).

Example: Shortly before a scheduled meeting of stockholders at which a proxy fight is to be resolved, the board of directors learns that the election is too close to call. The board of directors announces that the election will be deferred for several months and a new record date is established. Because the delay does not benefit stockholders generally and requires the dissident faction to make a new solicitation the change in meeting date may be enjoined. *Aprahamian v. HBO & Co.*, 531 A.2d 1204 (Del.1987).

e.   There are several firms that specialize in proxy solicitations, which are available to assist both management and insurgents in connection with a proxy contest.

2.   Regulation of Proxy Contests

Proxy contests in corporations registered under section 12 of the Securities Exchange Act of 1934 are subject to regulation by the SEC under its proxy regulations.

a.   SEC regulations require all participants in a proxy contest (including non-management groups) to file a proxy statement with the SEC and the relevant securities exchange at least ten days before it is disseminated.

b.   A proxy statement in connection with a proxy fight must contain all of the information required in an ordinary proxy statement (as specified in SEC Schedule 14A) although an insurgent group need not include information about incumbent management that would appear in an ordinary proxy statement. In addition, a proxy statement in connection with a proxy contest must include disclosures relating to the identity and background of the participants, their interests in securities of the corporation and when they were acquired, financing arrangements, participation in other proxy contests, and understandings with respect to future employment with the corporation. Other materials such as advertisements, press releases, and direct mailings must be filed with the SEC as they are disseminated.

c. SEC regulations reject the view that proxy contests should be viewed as political contests with each side free to hurl charges with comparative unrestraint on the assumption that the opposing side may refute misleading charges. Rather, each participant's statements are subject to objective standards of accuracy and truthfulness. *SEC v. May*, 229 F.2d 123 (2d Cir.1956).

d. State law is applicable to proxy contests in unregistered corporations but there are few reported state cases dealing with proxy fights. See, however, *Salgo v. Matthews*, 497 S.W.2d 620 (Tex.Civ.App.1973).

3. Who Pays the Cost of a Proxy Contest?

The corporation usually pays the costs of the defense of a proxy contest. Where a change in control occurs, the corporation may also pay the costs of the successful campaign to oust incumbent management.

a. It is clear that the corporation should pay for the cost of printing and mailing the notice of meeting, the proxy statement required by federal law, and the proxy appointment forms themselves. These are legitimate corporate expenses necessary to ensure the existence of a quorum of stockholders.

b. Most courts have allowed management also to charge to the corporation the reasonable expenses of educating stockholders if the controversy involves a *policy* question rather than a mere *personal* struggle for control. *Rosenfeld v. Fairchild Engine and Airplane Corp.*, 128 N.E.2d 291 (N.Y.1955); *Levin v. Metro–Goldwyn–Mayer*, Inc., 264 F.Supp. 797 (S.D.N.Y.1967). Virtually every issue may be dressed up as a policy rather than personal issue. The combined effect is probably to permit the deduction of all reasonable management expenses.

c. A successful challenger may seek to have the corporation reimburse expenses. As with management expenses, the reimbursement of successful insurgents are permitted if the dispute can be characterized as one over business policy and involving policy rather than personalities. *Rosenfeld v. Fairchild Engine and Airplane Corp.*, 128 N.E.2d 291 (N.Y.1955). As a result the corporation may end up paying for the expenses of both sides if the challenger is successful.

d. Although one might argue that the system is biased against insurgents, it would be difficult to structure an unbiased system. Although proxy fights arguably constitute an important check on managerial behavior, a system that required insurgents to be reimbursed would arguably encourage too many proxy fights, while a system that prohibited management from using corporate resources to defend itself might discourage competent managers from agreeing to serve and would operate as an effective presumption that an insurgents is as worthy as incumbent management.

REVIEW QUESTIONS

10.1. True or False: Since the solicitation of proxy appointments in publicly held corporations is an internal function of corporate management, this subject is largely governed by state law.

10.2. When is a corporation subject to federal proxy regulation?

10.3. When is a corporation subject to SEC periodic disclosure requirements?

10.4. What is the constitutional basis for federal regulation of proxies?

10.5. How does federal proxy regulation attempt to assure the transmission of complete and adequate information about corporate affairs to stockholders?

10.6. If a corporation includes false or misleading statements in its proxy solicitation statement, may the individual stockholders object and bring suit if the statement is used to obtain stockholder approval of a transaction?

10.7. In a suit by a stockholder, does the false or misleading statement have to be material and, if so, how is materiality defined?

10.8. May a stockholder plaintiff obtain attorneys' fees in a suit described in question 10.6 if his suit is successful?

10.9. May the prohibitions on false or misleading statements be avoided by phrasing them in terms of opinion or estimate rather than fact?

10.10. A minority stockholder in a publicly held corporation subject to SEC regulation requests that the corporation include in its proxy statement a proposal that the corporation not develop nuclear energy facilities. May the corporation reject out of hand such a request?

10.11. Even though a corporation is required to include a stockholder proposal in its proxy statement, history demonstrates that most such proposals that are presented by individuals are rejected by large pluralities. Why is any attention paid at all to such proposals?

10.12. Have any stockholder proposals ever been adopted?

10.13. Expansion, Ltd. is a growing corporation that speculates in the recent boom in rural real estate. Its success has been erratic. The acquisition of Hideaway Ranch, Inc., a popular tourist resort, became its next objective. To this end, Expansion bought 39 percent of Hideaway's shares from a few large stockholders and then proposed a merger to the Hideaway management, which was inclined to support the merger, particularly because of Expansion's promise to retain them in managerial capacities in Expansion, the surviving corporation. Hideaway has a total of 78 stockholders, all children, grandchildren, nephews or nieces of the founder. Hideaway solicited proxies for the proposed merger and received the necessary stockholder vote. However, the proxy material failed to disclose Expansion's erratic past or its speculative plans; nor did it mention the commitment made to Hideaway management. Under the merger Hideaway stockholders received two shares of Expansion for each of their Hideaway shares. No independent appraisal was made. An examination of Expansion's history reveals that its shares rarely reached a value as high as referred to in the prospectus. Expansion's securities are registered under section 12 of the federal Securities Exchange Act of 1934 but Hideaway's are not.

What rights and remedies might be available to Jack Case, a stockholder of Hideaway who dissented and is now seeking appraisal?

10.14. Assume that Hideaway is a publicly held corporation registered under section 12 and Expansion does not attempt to complete the merger until after it has acquired more than 50 per cent of Hideaway stock, thereby assuring that the merger will be approved. If the proxy statement fails to make the disclosures referred to in question 13, will Case be able to bring a suit under the federal proxy regulations?

10.15. What is the test for determining the propriety of a stockholder's demand to inspect corporate records?

10.16. If the test is a proper purpose, why are further restrictions on the right of inspection necessary?

10.17. What is the test for a director's right to inspect?

10.18. To what extent must a corporation provide routine information to all stockholders, such as financial reports and the like?

10.19. The stockholders of X corporation adopt a bylaw which requires that all stockholders, as a condition precedent to a right to inspect the books of the corporation, give at least three months notice before the proposed inspection. The bylaw further provides that inspection should be granted only if the purpose of the inspection is approved by the board of directors. The state corporation statute provides for a traditional statutory right of inspection but is silent on whether the right may be limited in any way by the corporation. P, a stockholder of X, demands the right to inspect the books of X within two weeks of the date of the demand and states that his purpose for inspection is to determine whether there has been mismanagement, a purpose that is clearly proper under applicable state law. The demand is refused by the directors under the above bylaw because it is untimely. P seeks a writ of mandamus to compel the officers and directors to permit his inspection of the books. Should the writ issue?

10.20. In a successful proxy fight in which the insurgents triumph, who pays the expenses and costs?

10.21. The argument has been made that all proxy fight contestants should have their expenses reimbursed by the corporation. What is the basis of this argument and what is its weakness?

10.22. How are proxy contests regulated?

XI

Closely Held Corporations

A. CHARACTERISTICS OF CLOSELY HELD CORPORATIONS

The statutory scheme does not accurately reflect the manner of operation of closely held corporations owned by a very small number of stockholders. The stockholders in closely held corporations are usually simultaneously officers and directors. Business decisions may be made by consensus and without regard to whether the person is acting as officer, director, or stockholder. Requirements of meetings, appointments, elections, and so forth are all likely to be considered meaningless formalities. Indeed, many such corporations go for years without ever having a formal stockholders' or directors' meeting. Accordingly, a number of states have adopted statutes relaxing the statutory requirements applicable to closely held corporations.

1. Stockholder Domination of Management

In a closely held corporation, the controlling stockholders usually operate the business in an informal manner, more as though it were a partnership rather than a corporation. Indeed, closely held corporations are sometimes called *incorporated partnerships* to reflect the close similarity in management that exists between partnerships and closely held corporations. The majority stockholders name the board of directors, and through them, the officers and employees. Usually they name themselves as directors and officers, including the most important and highest paying positions. A major aspect of planning is to develop devices that assure minority stockholders of meaningful participation in management despite the power of majority stockholders to name a majority or all of the directors, officers and employees.

a. Stockholders' meetings may be held infrequently if at all. Unanimous consents may be prepared to record who is serving on the board of directors from time to time.

b. Formal directors meetings may also be held infrequently. Meetings may consist of informal discussions or simple decision-making by the majority stockholder (who may also be the sole director of the corporation) or by the controlling stockholders. The controlling stockholders may or may not consult with other officers, directors, or stockholders.

c. The attorney for a closely held corporation should assure that minimal records are kept as to the identity of stockholders, directors, and officers, the manner of their election or appointment, and the periods they serve. The attorney should also assure that documents executed on behalf of the corporation clearly reflect corporate execution by the persons who hold the positions described in the form of execution.

2. No Market for Shares

Because a closely held corporation has only a relatively small number of stockholders, there is no public trading in, or public market for, its shares. Majority or controlling shares are salable to the same extent the underlying business is salable, because they represent control of that business. Minority or non-controlling shares, however, have only very limited marketability even if the business is highly profitable. The power of minority stockholders to participate in the business and its profits may be at the sufferance of the majority or controlling stockholder.

a. Potential purchasers of minority blocks of shares usually must be found among the corporation and its present stockholders, or rarely, among outsiders willing to take a gamble.

b. The market for minority blocks of shares is at worst non-existent and at best a buyer's market. Because there are few alternative purchasers there is little or no incentive for buyers to offer reasonable prices for shares. Minority shares have some value because they constitute a nuisance, may serve as the basis for litigation, and have residual rights in the event the corporation is dissolved or sold.

c. If the minority shares offered for sale represent the balance of control between factions, they are readily salable to one faction or another.

d. Transferability of shares is usually restricted by contractual restrictions limiting free transferability. A stockholder desiring to sell his shares may have to comply with the restrictions before offering shares to outsiders.

3. Dividend Policy

In a closely held corporation, dividend policy is heavily influenced by the tax status of the corporation and is often manipulated to favor controlling stockholders.

a. Large salary payments may be designed to limit the double tax problem of doing business as a C corporation. But the IRS may disallow excessive payments of salaries, bonuses, or fringe benefits as business expenses (deductions) of the corporation treating the excess as income to the corporation and as a dividend to the recipient stockholder. The test is whether the compensation is for services and is reasonable. *Charles McCandless Tile Service v. United States*, 422 F.2d 1336 (Ct.Cl.1970), *Herbert G. Hatt*, 28 T.C.M. 1194 (1969). Minority stockholders may use such a tax determination in an effort to obtain a court order requiring the payment of a dividend or the return of the excess funds to the corporation. *See, Wilderman v. Wilderman*, 315 A.2d 610 (Del.Ch.1974); *Fendelman v. Fenco Handbag Mfg. Co.*, 482 S.W.2d 461 (Mo.1972).

b. Controlling stockholders may divert the bulk of corporate income to themselves by adopting a no dividend policy, refusing to employ the minority stockholders in the business, and paying the bulk of the earnings to themselves in the form of salaries, bonuses, benefit plan contributions, and fringe benefits (free use of automobiles, country club memberships and the like). These policies may be adopted in an effort to soften up minority stockholders and persuade them to sell their shares at a low price either to the corporation or to other stockholders. Such a strategy—often called a freeze out or squeeze out—may lead to litigation seeking the payment of a dividend or other relief against the controlling stockholders on grounds of oppressive conduct.

4. Stockholder Oppression

In the absence of a binding stockholder agreement, the foregoing factors may result in oppression of minority stockholders who are locked into the corporation but excluded from management and deprived of investment return. Minority stockholders in a closely held corporation ordinarily have no power to force dissolution of the corporation because corporation statutes typically require the consent of at least a majority of the outstanding shares.

In this respect a closely held corporation differs significantly from a partnership, in which each partner possesses inherent power to dissolve the partnership.

a. Advance planning—usually in the form of a buy/sell agreement—may avoid many of these problems. Important functions of stockholder agreements are they assure minority stockholders that (i) they will be able to dispose of their shares when they die, retire, or wish to leave the corporation, (ii) they will have a voice in management, (iii) they will be entitled to a financial return from their investment, and (iv) they will have the benefits of estate planning.

b. Nonetheless, there are many cases in which advance planning may not occur. Over the long haul, the possibility that hostility will develop within a closely held corporation as a result of falling out, withdrawal, or death among the stockholders is fairly high. These situations include family businesses which have devolved down through one or two generations, particularly when deaths of controlling stockholders occur unexpectedly and without adequate planning, and situations where the participants enter the venture fully trusting each other and believe it is unnecessary to provide legal protection.

B. ALLOCATION OF CONTROL IN A CLOSELY HELD CORPORATION

In the absence of special statutory treatment of closely held corporations, such corporations must establish control devices through the use of traditional and accepted control techniques.

1. Traditional Control Techniques

There are many planning devices that may be used to allocate control in a closely held corporation, including multiple classes of shares, supermajority quorum and voting requirements (at both the stockholder level and the board level), stockholder voting agreements, voting trusts, proxy appointments, employment agreements between stockholders and the corporation,and share transfer restrictions. These devices are discussed in this and subsequent chapters.

2. Supermajority Quorum & Voting Requirements

Minority participation may be assured by increased voting and quorum requirements in order to give minority interests effectively a veto power. This veto power may be applicable at the stockholder level, at the board level, or at both levels.

a.   It is usually important to increase both the quorum requirement and the minimum vote requirement to make sure that it is impossible for the corporation to act without the assent of the minority stockholders.

b.   Unanimity may be required for both, although some courts seem to be reluctant to enforce such an extreme requirement. In many circumstances a lesser percentage is sufficient to give the desired veto power.

Example: A 25 per cent stockholder may feel secure if an 80 per cent quorum and voting requirement is imposed. However, it is essential that decisions permitting the issuance of additional voting shares themselves be subject to this supermajority requirement if the 25 per cent stockholder is to be protected.

Caveat: Creation of a veto power through these devices greatly increases the possibility of deadlock within the corporation.

Example: A 25% stockholder has a veto power over certain transactions because of an 80% voting requirement. The stockholder exercises this power arbitrarily to prevent the payment of dividends thereby causing the corporation to incur a penalty tax for unreasonable accumulation of surplus. The minority stockholder has breached his duty to the other stockholders. *Smith v. Atlantic Properties, Inc.,* 422 N.E.2d 798 (Mass.App.1981).

3.   Legal Problems Created by Informal Management

In most small closely held corporations, corporate matters are likely to be resolved by unanimous consent with a minimum of formality and regard for statutory niceties. Meetings may be held infrequently, if at all, corporate records may be kept on an erratic basis, and decisions may be made without any recognition that the corporation theoretically consists of different layers with different rights and responsibilities. Failure to follow corporate formalities may create several legal issues. Ignoring corporate formalities may be grounds for piercing the corporate veil, with the result that the participants may be held personally liable on corporate obligations. Decisions that are made informally and without following statutory norms may not be binding. The participants' control arrangements may be unenforceable.

C.   ATTEMPTS TO VARY THE STATUTORY SCHEME

Attempts to reallocate the corporate powers in ways significantly different from the statutory scheme historically were viewed with suspicion and many were held to be against public policy and unenforceable.

1. Strict Common Law Approach

The strict common law approach was that agreements among stockholders to make decisions that are the responsibility of the board of directors were against public policy as expressed in the corporation statute and were unenforceable. *McQuade v. Stoneham,* 189 N.E. 234 (N.Y.1934). The traditional view was that all corporations should be governed by essentially the same rules set forth in the corporation statutes, and that no special rules could or should be developed for the closely held corporation. *See Kruger v. Gerth,* 263 N.Y.S.2d 1, 210 N.E.2d 355 (N.Y. 1965). The rationale for the strict common law approach is that corporation law is designed to protect minority stockholders who are not parties to the contract by assuring that they receive the protection of the unfettered best judgment of the board of directors.

> *Example:* In a corporation with 30 stockholders, two stockholders, A and B, together own a majority of the voting shares. A and B enter into a written agreement that provides: (a) They will vote for themselves as two of the three directors, (b) they will establish and maintain A as president and B as vice president, (c) the salary of the president will be $50,000 per year and the salary of the vice president will be $40,000 per year. A and B have a falling out and B is summarily discharged. B has no claim against A for breach of contract, because the agreements referred to in (b) and (c) invade the power of the board of directors and are unenforceable. The stockholder level voting agreement does not interfere with the discretion of directors and is not subject to attack on the same ground. Enforceability depends on whether it is severable from the unenforceable portions of the agreement.

> *Example:* A stockholder's agreement providing that each stockholder has an option to purchase shares offered by other stockholders also contains provisions relating to the naming of officers and the fixing of their compensation. These provisions were in fact never implemented. The court may ignore the provisions dealing with the officers (which violate the statutory scheme) and enforce the remainder of the agreement. *Triggs v. Triggs,* 413 N.Y.S.2d 325, 385 N.E.2d 1254 (N.Y. 1978).

> *Example:* C agrees to invest in a corporation only if the other two stockholders, A and B, agree that the corporation will not

borrow in excess of $10,000 without the prior consent of C. A and B agree in writing to this proposal and C purchases the shares. Because borrowing money is within the discretionary power of the board of directors to manage the business, the agreement by the stockholders is against public policy and unenforceable. The board of directors may ignore the agreement and borrow money in excess of $10,000 without obtaining the prior consent of C. *See Burnett v. Word, Inc.,* 412 S.W.2d 792 (Tex.Civ.App.1967).

Caveat: Some courts distinguish between agreements to which all the stockholders are a party and those between some but not all of the stockholders. The former are more likely to be enforced. Moreover, an existing agreement among all of the stockholders may be enforced against a new stockholder if the new stockholder knows of it when he becomes a stockholder. In many states, the articles of incorporation must contain a provision that authorizes a stockholder agreement in order for the agreement to be valid. It is also possible that the actions of A and B in the example above may constitute fraud independent of corporation law.

2. Relaxation of Strict Common Law Approach

The strict common law rule sometimes leads to significant injustice because apparently reasonable and sensible contracts are invalidated even though they do not affect non-parties. As a result, shortly after *McQuade* the New York court modified the strict common law approach by holding that contracts among all stockholders that involves only minor infringement on the statutory scheme are enforceable. *Clark v. Dodge,* 199 N.E. 641 (N.Y.1936). Some courts and statutes have relaxed even further the test for invalidating such agreements, and uphold substantially any stockholders agreement, so long as all stockholders agree to it. *Galler v. Galler,* 203 N.E.2d 577 (Ill.1964). *See also* MBCA 7.32 (authorizing broad ranging stockholder agreements even to the extent of management by the stockholders rather than a board of directors but only if authorized in the articles of incorporation and only for non-publicly traded corporations).

Example: All stockholders agree that the corporation should pay dividends of $50,000 per year if there are funds available after the board of directors has set aside whatever funds it believes necessary for future contingencies and growth. In most states such an agreement today would be valid.

Example:　All stockholders agree that all internal decisions within the corporation shall be made as though the stockholders were partners and that the corporation shall not have a board of directors. Absent specific statutory authorization, such an agreement is probably not enforceable.

Example:　All stockholders agree that directors must agree to and accept all transactions that a majority of the stockholders approve. Such an agreement is probably not binding on the board of directors.

D. STATUTES RELATING TO MANAGEMENT OF CLOSELY HELD CORPORATIONS

Many states have adopted statutes relating to management problems within the closely held corporation. These statutes may be traced to judicial dissatisfaction with the application of traditional corporation law principles to closely held corporations. They fall into three general categories: statutes of general applicability dealing with variations in management structure, special statutes applicable only to corporations making a formal election, and hybrid statutes such as MBCA 7.32. These statutes permit numerous kinds of control arrangements for closely held corporations.

1. General Statutes Permitting the Elimination of the Board of Directors

The statutes of many states permit any corporation to modify the traditional role of its board of directors by appropriate provision in its articles of incorporation. The provision may permit a corporation to dispense entirely with the board of directors and have the business and affairs managed directly by its stockholders or place restrictions on the discretion of directors. As a practical matter, this option is almost solely utilized by closely held corporations.

a.　DGCL 141(a) provides that the business and affairs of every corporation shall be managed by or under the direction of a board of directors except as may be otherwise provided in this chapter or in its certificate of incorporation. If any such provision is made in the certificate of incorporation, the powers and duties conferred or imposed upon the board of directors by this chapter shall be exercised or performed to such extent and by such person or persons as shall be provided in the certificate of incorporation.

Example:　Lehrman and Cohen each own 50 per cent of the stock of X Corporation. They have numerous disagreements and finally agree that Danzansky, X Corporation's general counsel, whom they both trust, shall be given the power to vote as a director to break any deadlocks on the board of directors. An appropriate provision in the articles of incorporation granting Danzansky a tie breaking vote on the board of directors is valid. *Lehrman v. Cohen*, 222 A.2d 800 (Del.1966).

b.   MBCA 8.01(c) contained a provision similar to DGCL 141(a), but that provision was repealed in 1991 and a more general provision, MBCA 7.32, discussed below, was substituted.

2.   Statutes Applicable Only to Electing Close Corporations

a.   The statutes of several states contain special provisions applicable only to corporations that make a formal election. These statutes permit an electing close corporation, among other things, to dispense entirely with the board of directors, to restrict the discretion of directors, and to permit the business and affairs of the corporation to be conducted as though it were a partnership. *See* DGCL 341–355.

b.   The definition of an eligible corporation usually involves a limitation on the number of stockholders and a requirement that share transfer restrictions be imposed. Many such statues are limited to corporations with fewer than 35 stockholders or some other specified number. Some statutes, however, do not limit the corporations that may elect to become close corporations. A qualified corporation becomes a statutory close corporation by including in its articles of incorporation a statement to the effect that the corporation is a statutory close corporation.

c.   A statutory close corporation may adopt a variety of internal control arrangements, including restrictions on the discretion of directors and even dispensing with the board of directors entirely. If this option is elected, the liabilities otherwise imposed on directors are imposed on the stockholders as if they were directors. Where the board of directors has been eliminated the stockholders may be called *managing stockholders* and have the rights and duties of directors. *Graczykowski v. Ramppen*, 477 N.Y.S.2d 454 (App.Div. 1984). These statutes also permit an electing close corporation to eliminate bylaws, to broaden the power to create share transfer restrictions, to create mandatory buyouts upon the death of a stockholder, to require dissolution at the election of a minority interest, and so forth. These statutes contain special provisions to resolve dissension or deadlock such as the appointment of receivers, custodians or provisional directors.

d. Even though many states have adopted special close corporation statutes and this development has been widely praised, the actual experience in California, Delaware, Florida, Texas and other states indicates that this election is not widely used. It is probable that most attorneys are able to work out basic control relationships under the general corporation statutes and therefore do not feel it is necessary to use or experiment with these largely untried statutes. The complexity of some of these statutes may also have discouraged their widespread use.

e. Some lawyers may be concerned that the use of the close corporation election may have adverse tax consequences or may result in the possible loss of limited liability. Many of these statutes expressly attempt to negate this result.

f. Despite the broad remedial purposes underlying modern close corporation statutes, some courts have given them narrow and literalistic readings not consistent with the underlying purposes. *See, Blount v. Taft,* 246 S.E.2d 763 (N.C.1978). Other courts have been more generous. *See, Zion v. Kurtz,* 428 N.Y.S.2d 199, 405 N.E.2d 681 (N.Y. 1980). In *Nixon v. Blackwell,* 626 A.2d 1366 (Del. 1993) the court held that special rules for close corporations in Delaware are applicable only to corporations making the election as required by the Delaware Close Corporation Statute. In an earlier case, *Zion v. Kurtz,* 428 N.Y.S.2d 199, 405 N.E.2d 681 (N.Y. 1980), the court upheld an agreement under Delaware law even though the corporation's certificate of incorporation did not contain the required language. The court ordered the certificate of incorporation reformed to include the mandatory language. It is doubtful that the Delaware courts would accept the *Zion* approach.

Caveat: The term *close corporation* is often regarded as a term of art referring only to a corporation that makes a formal statutory election as distinguished from a *closely held corporation* which is simply a corporation with no public market for its shares.

3. Hybrid Statutes

In 1991, the MBCA was amended by withdrawing a provision similar to DGCL 141 and adding the more general MBCA 7.32 entitled *Stockholder Agreements* and providing that an agreement that complies with that section is effective among stockholders and the corporation even though it is inconsistent with one or more specified provisions of the act.

a. MBCA 7.32 rejects the older line of cases relating to statutory norms and adds an element of predictability theretofore absent from the MBCA (1984). It recognizes that many of the corporate norms contained in corporation statutes were designed with an eye towards public companies where management and share ownership are quite distinct.

b. MBCA 7.32 validates virtually all stockholders' agreements relating to corporate governance and business arrangements, including agreements relating to: governance of the entity; allocation of the return from the business; and other aspects of relationships among stockholders, directors, and the corporation.

c. MBCA 7.32 creates a broad but not universal mandate to customize the management of closely held corporations. Agreements that affect third parties and agreements that violate fundamental principles of public policy may not be validated.

   Example: A provision in a stockholders' agreement that the directors have no duty of care or loyalty is not within the scope of that section.

d. The agreement under MBCA 7.32 must be unanimously approved by the stockholders; it may appear in the articles of incorporation, the bylaws, or a stockholders' agreement.

e. The existence of an agreement under MBCA 7.32 must appear on the share certificates or information statements reflecting shares. A purchaser of shares without notice of the existence of the agreement has the sole remedy of recission within 90 days after learning of the existence of the agreement.

f. An agreement under MBCA 7.32 is valid for 10 years unless otherwise provided in the agreement. It automatically terminates if the shares of the corporation become publicly traded on a national securities exchange or public market for securities.

E. OPPRESSION AND DEADLOCK

It is common for disagreements to arise among stockholders in closely held corporations about business policies and practices. One of the more common problems arises when one group prefers reinvestment of available cash and growth of the company while another group prefers a generous payout policy. It is also common for personality conflicts to arise. In many cases, differences of opinion about business may evolve into personality conflicts so that it becomes difficult to determine the nature of the difficulty. If two stockholders or factions of stockholders have equal control or veto power, such conflicts may lead to deadlock. If one stockholder or faction has effective working control and the power to exclude other stockholders from meaningful participation in management or the economic benefits of the business, the faction with control may sometimes use its power inappropriately to infringe the legitimate interests of the minority. Advance planning may prevent such difficulties or reduce their severity. One common solution is to have a binding buy/sell agreement that is triggered by certain defined events, such as the failure to elect directors for a stated period.

1. Oppression

a. The word *oppression* does not necessarily mean imminent disaster; it has been construed to mean lack of fair dealing or fair play, and in any event is a question for the trier of fact to resolve. *Mardikos v. Arger,* 457 N.Y.S.2d 371 (1982); *White v. Perkins,* 189 S.E.2d 315 (Va.1972); *Gidwitz v. Lanzit Corrugated Box Co.,* 170 N.E.2d 131 (Ill.1960).

b. A recent development in closely held corporation law discussed below is that the term oppression is being defined by some courts in a broader fashion as meaning any action that is inconsistent with the expectations of the minority stockholders with respect to their roles in the corporation or that constitutes burdensome, harsh, or wrongful conduct.

Example: Davis owns 55 percent of a corporation's shares; Sheerin owns the remaining 45 percent. For many years Davis operates the corporation and Sheerin is inactive. When Sheerin requests to examine the corporation's records. Davis refuses and falsely claims that Sheerin donated his shares back to the corporation many years earlier. This argument constitutes oppression of Sheerin. *Davis v. Sheerin,* 754 S.W.2d 375 (Tex.1988).

c. Where a corporation has been in existence for a generation or more, oppression should not be defined in terms of original expectations but in terms of whether conduct is inherently oppressive. *Gimpel v. Bolstein,* 477 N.Y.S.2d 1014 (Sup. 1984).

2. Deadlock

a. Deadlock typically involves two stockholders (or two factions) in a control structure that does not permit either faction to have effective working control. It is also possible for a corporation with more than two factions to become deadlocked if each individual stockholder and/or director has a veto power but that is not common.

b. A corporation is potentially subject to deadlock if two stockholders (or two stockholder factions) both own exactly fifty per cent of the outstanding shares, if there are an even number of directors and two factions each have the power to select the same number, or if a minority stockholder has retained a veto power.

c. A deadlock may occur either at the stockholders' level or at the directors' level. If the stockholders are deadlocked, the corporation may continue to operate under the guidance of the board of directors in office when the deadlock arose. The general rule is that directors serve until their successors are qualified; if the deadlock prevents a subsequent election, those in office remain in office indefinitely. A deadlock at the directoral level may prevent the corporation from functioning at all, though more commonly the president or general manager may continue to operate the business, often to the complete exclusion of the other faction.

Example: Two stockholders each own 50 per cent of the outstanding shares. Shares are not entitled to vote cumulatively. There are four directors, A, her spouse, Mr. A, B, and her spouse, Mr. B. Mr. B resigns as a result of marital discord with B. Control of the corporation has been turned over permanently to A and Mr. A. In subsequent elections, an attempt by B to elect two directors (and return to parity on the board) can itself be deadlocked by A.

Example: In the foregoing example, A and Mr. A, acting as directors, fill the vacancy by electing their son, XX. Even though A and Mr. A may not constitute a quorum of directors, under the statutes of many states they may fill a vacancy. B is now outvoted on the board, three to one. There may be no way for B to return to parity because XX remains in office until his successor is elected and all such elections continue to be deadlocked. *See Gearing v. Kelly,* 227 N.Y.S.2d 897, 182 N.E.2d 391 (N.Y. 1962).

Example: In the foregoing example, if cumulative voting is permitted, B may restore her former position by dividing her votes between herself and Mr. B. However, if an odd number of directors were to be elected, cumulative voting leads to a deadlock in any attempt to fill a vacancy in the last position on the board of directors.

3. Advance Planning to Avoid Oppression and Deadlock

Although it is always possible for the stockholders to agree to a fair business divorce after a dispute arises, it is preferable for the possibility of dissension, oppression, and deadlock to be addressed by the stockholders in advance while in amity. It is ordinarily preferable to preserve a going corporation rather than to dissolve it. The business and assets of a corporation, including intangible good will, are ordinarily worth more as a unit than fragmented. Thus, the most sensible solution usually is a buyout agreement by which one faction buys out the other at a fair price in the event a serious disagreement arises. Such an agreement is usually called a buy/sell agreement. Such an arrangement must resolve several basic questions.

a.   What events triggers the power to buy or sell? Some kind of objective standard as to what constitutes dissension or deadlock sufficient to trigger the buyout obligation is desirable, such as the failure to agree on a slate of directors for some specified period. But one must be careful not to create opportunities on the pretext of a minor dispute for stockholders who simply want to cash out.

b.   Who is to buy out whom if both desire to continue the business? Often the senior stockholder retains the right to buy out the junior stockholder. But if the age discrepancy is large, it may be more sensible to reverse the order and have the junior buy out the senior. An agreement may provide that one stockholder sets a price at which she is willing to buy out the other stockholder or to sell her own shares, and the other stockholder has the election to buy or sell.

c.   What pricing formula should be used? The formula chosen should not rely on an agreement to agree about the price. Presumably, the formula should yield as fair a price as possible rather than one that arguably creates a bargain for one faction or the other. On the other hand, some discount from full value may be appropriate to discourage opportunism.

d. May the person who is bought out form a competing business, and if so, where and on what terms? A non-competition agreement is usually enforceable if it is reasonable under the circumstances.

F. SHARE TRANSFER RESTRICTIONS

In a corporation, a transfer of shares conveys both financial and voting rights. Shares in a corporation are freely transferable unless there is an express restriction on the transferability of shares. In contrast, partnership interests may not be transferred without the consent of all the other partners, although a partner may always assign any financial benefits he may receive from the partnership. Although free transferability of shares is usually considered an advantage of the corporate form, there are many situations in which it is desirable to limit the transferability of shares, particularly in a closely held corporation.

1. Reasons for Imposing Share Transfer Restrictions

a. Share transfer restrictions enable stockholders to decide who may participate in the venture. This is important in a closely held corporation in which there is substantial stockholder participation in management and where the shares carry the ability to elect one or more directors.

b. Share transfer restrictions may protect against changes in the proportionate interests of stockholders, which may occur if one stockholder is able to purchase shares owned by other stockholders.

c. Share transfer restrictions may simplify the estate tax problems of a deceased stockholder. If the corporation or other stockholders are obligated to purchase the shares owned by the deceased stockholder, the estate is assured that a large illiquid asset will be reduced to cash and that funds will be available to pay taxes.

   Example: Cash required to pay estate and other taxes upon the death of a stockholder may be provided for by a life insurance policy purchased by the corporation. In most cases, the purchase price specified in a buy-sell agreement will be accepted by the Internal Revenue Service as conclusive for valuation purposes in connection with calculation of estate and other death taxes, unless there is reason to suspect that the price was set collusively.

d. Share transfer restrictions may be imposed to maintain S Corporation status, for example, to ensure that the 75 stockholder maximum is not exceeded or that shares are not transferred to an ineligible stockholder.

e. Share transfer restrictions may be imposed where there are substantive limitations on who may be a stockholder or where governmental authorities wish to review, and possibly limit, who is participating in the ownership of the business.

> *Example:* A professional corporation that is engaged in the practice of law may impose share transfer restrictions prohibiting the transfer of shares to a person who is not an attorney.

> *Example:* The New York Stock Exchange for many years reserved the right to determine who may participate in the ownership of brokerage firms. This restriction was enforced by share transfer restrictions that prohibited transfers of share of brokerage firms to persons without the prior consent of the Exchange. *See Ling & Co. v. Trinity Savings & Loan Ass'n*, 482 S.W.3d 841 (Tex. 1972).

f. Share transfer restrictions may be used to prevent violations of federal securities law where the corporation has issued shares pursuant to an exemption from registration requirements. In many cases, the exemption would be lost if the shares were transferred to ineligible persons, and the offering would be rendered illegal because it is unregistered. (i) In addition to placing a legend on certificates of restricted securities, the issuing corporation may require the purchase to execute a representation or agreement stating that the securities have been acquired for investment and not for redistribution and will not be transferred without the written permission of the issuer. Moreover, the issuing corporation typically instructs its transfer agent to refuse to accept restricted securities for transfer. (ii) Rule 144 under the Securities Act of 1933 is the principal rule establishing when restricted securities may be sold on the public market. Under Rule 144, limited quantities of restricted securities may be sold after they have been held for at least one year. In addition, Rule 144A permits the sale of restricted securities to qualified institutional buyers without significant restrictions. Finally, under SEC Regulation S, securities originally sold to non-US investors may be resold in the United States after specified waiting periods.

> *Caveat:* A corporation may have outstanding securities of a given class that are publicly traded and freely transferable.

g. A temporary share transfer restriction (*lock-up*) may be imposed in connection with shares sold in an initial public offering (IPO) in order to ensure an orderly market for shares following the offering. For example, if shares are offered both to employees and outside investors, the employees' shares may be frozen for trading purposes for some specified period of time, typically 180 days.

2. Permissible Restraints

Under the common law, the validity of a share transfer restriction depends on whether it unreasonably restrains transferability. Several states have adopted legislation broadening the types of restrictions that may be enforced.

a. DGCL 202(c) expressly validates restrictions that require consent by the corporation or the holders of a specified class of securities, that require the approval of the proposed transferee by the corporation, or that prohibit a transfer to designated persons or classes of persons if not manifestly unreasonable.

b. DGCL 202(d) provides that a restriction imposed to insure the continued availability of S Corporation status or any other tax advantage to the corporation is conclusively presumed to be for a reasonable purpose.

c. MBCA 6.27 follows the broad outline of the Delaware statute. It authorizes share transfer restrictions to maintain the legal status of the corporation, to preserve exemptions under securities laws, or for any other reasonable purpose.

d. Both the DGCL and the MBCA expressly authorize share transfer restrictions requiring the sale of shares to the corporation or other stockholders without limitation.

3. Forms of Transfer Restrictions

The power to transfer or dispose of corporate shares may be restricted by provisions in the articles of incorporation, the bylaws, or a stockholder agreement. MBCA 6.27(a). There are several different forms of transfer restrictions:

a. A *right of first refusal* gives the corporation or other stockholders an opportunity to meet the best price the stockholder has been able to obtain from a third party.

   Caveat: A right of first refusal may have a chilling effect on the ability to sell shares because a buyer knows that the corporation or other stockholders have the power to buy shares on whatever terms are negotiated.

> *Caveat:* A third party offeror may be required to demonstrate that the offer is made in good faith and not in collusion with the seller whose real goal may be to induce the corporation or other stockholders to purchase shares.

b. The corporation or other stockholders may retain an *option* to purchase shares owned by another stockholder at a designated or computable price upon the occurrence of a triggering event. *See Allen v. Biltmore Tissue Corp.,* 161 N.Y.S.2d 418, 141 N.E.2d 812 (N.Y. 1957) (option at original purchase price enforceable upon death of stockholder despite fact that price was far below the market value of the shares).

c. A *consent restriction* requires approval of a proposed transfer by the board of directors, the stockholders, or in some cases a third party.

> *Caveat:* Share transfer restrictions not coupled with an obligation on the part of the corporation or other stockholders to purchase are often disfavored by the courts. They may be found to be unenforceable in the absence of a reasonable justification.

> *Example:* A restriction that prohibits transfer without the consent of the directors or other stockholders is probably not valid unless there is some express or implied limit on the discretion to grant or deny consent. *Rafe v. Hindin,* 288 N.Y.S.2d 662 (App.Div. 1968) (unrestricted right to consent invalid).

d. An outright prohibition on transfer is probably invalid unless a compelling need can be shown.

e. A *buy-sell agreement* is an agreement by which a stockholder is obligated to sell, and the corporation or other stockholders are obligated to buy, shares at a designated or computable price upon the occurrence of specified triggering events. A buy-sell agreement differs from an option in that the buyer is required to buy the shares of the selling stockholder.

> *Caveat:* The terms of a buy-sell agreements must be carefully crafted to avoid the possibility of opportunism. If the terms of an agreement are favorable, a stockholder may be tempted to trigger the agreement in order to compel the corporation to buy simply as a means of cashing out his interest.

f. Many close corporation statutes also impose standard share transfer restrictions.

4. Terms

The option or obligation to purchase shares usually runs either to the corporation or to some or all of the stockholders. MBCA § 6.27(d) also expressly permits the option or obligation to run to other persons.

a.   There are several advantages of an option or obligation running first to the corporation. The corporation may be able to raise the necessary cash more easily than the stockholders individually. The proportionate interests of the remaining stockholders are unaffected by a corporate acquisition of shares. If life insurance is to be used to provide funds to purchase shares on the death of a stockholder, it is usually simplest to have the corporation pay the premium and own the policies on the lives of each stockholder rather than having each stockholder attempt to insure the life of every other stockholder. Finally, purchase by the corporation may be more attractive from a tax standpoint.

b.   The primary disadvantage of an option or obligation running to the corporation is that is that if the corporation lacks the necessary legal capital to lawfully repurchase the shares, the restriction may be unenforceable. In this situation, it is usually possible to arrange for the corporation to repurchase the shares over time. *See* MBCA § 6.40. The agreement may also permit or require the stockholders or some of them to agree to buy the shares.

   Caveat: In an option arrangement running to the corporation alone, the corporation may decline to purchase the shares, and anticipated control arrangements may be adversely affected. Interested stockholders may also participate in the decision whether or not the corporation should purchase and may vote their own self-interest. *Boss v. Boss,* 200 A.2d 231 (R.I.1964).

c.   The primary disadvantage of having a share option run to other stockholders is that one or more of the stockholders may be unable or unwilling to purchase their allotment of shares. If so, the proportionate interests of the remaining stockholders will be affected if some purchase and some do not. The agreement may provide that shares not purchased should be offered proportionately to the remaining stockholders. In the absence of such a requirement, it is likely that unpurchased shares are thereafter considered free of all repurchase obligations. The agreement may also provide that the offer may be withdrawn if some decline to accept. *Helmly v. Schultz,* 131 S.E.2d 924 (Ga.1963).

> *Caveat:* If the number of stockholders is large, it becomes complicated for an option or obligation to run to stockholders. It is usually preferable for the restrictions to run to the corporation.

> *Caveat:* A stockholder may not always desire that his shares be offered proportionately to the other stockholders. For example, a controlling stockholder with a son and daughter who are minority stockholders may wish to provide that all shares be first offered to his son and then to his daughter (or vice versa) rather than be offered proportionately.

5. Formalities and Notice

A restriction on transfer is enforceable against a transferee only if the transferee has actual knowledge of the restriction or notice in the form of a conspicuous statement (usually called a *legend*) on the share certificate or document. UCC 8–204; MBCA 6.27(b). Copies of restrictions appearing in contracts but not in the articles of incorporation or bylaws may be required to be filed with the corporation and be available for inspection under the statutes of some states.

> Example: A restriction imposed by amendment to the articles of incorporation or bylaws does not apply to holders of outstanding shares or their transferees unless the holder assents to the restriction. *B & H Warehouse, Inc. v. Atlas Van Lines, Inc.*, 490 F.2d 818 (5th Cir.1974). There is some contrary authority but MBCA 6.27(a) codifies this result.

6. Duration of Restraints

There is no absolute limit on the duration of share transfer restrictions. It is probable that a restriction remains enforceable without regard to the rule against perpetuities or similar limitations. Share transfer restrictions may terminate in several ways.

a. By express agreement of the stockholders involved.

> *Example:* All stockholders decide to sell their shares to an outside purchaser despite a restriction against sales to third persons unless the shares are first offered to the corporation. The restriction is abandoned by agreement.

b. By abandonment or disuse.

> *Example:* Shares are sold or transferred by two or three stockholders in isolated transactions without compliance with the restric-

tions and without objection by the various parties. The restrictions probably have been abandoned and later sales or transfers may be made free of the restrictions.

7. Strict Construction

Share transfer restrictions are restraints on alienation. Many courts have stated that they therefore should be strictly construed.

Example: An option or buy/sell agreement that applies to sales or donations of shares to third persons is not violated by a transfer or gift to children or grandchildren.

Example: A restriction against sales to the public does not prohibit a sale to another stockholder.

Example: A prohibition against sale to an officer-stockholder does not prohibit a sale to a corporation owned by an officer-stockholder.

Example: A restriction without specific language of survivability may expire on the death of a stockholder. *Vogel v. Melish*, 196 N.E.2d 402 (Ill.App. 1964).

Caveat: Strict construction may defeat legitimate expectations. As a result a trend toward more liberal interpretation has developed in some states. *Bruns v. Rennebohm Drug Stores, Inc.*, 442 N.W.2d 591 (Wis.App.1989). When creating share transfer restrictions, an attorney must assume the worst and draft the clause on the assumption that a court will adopt the traditional strict construction approach.

8. Price

The price provisions of buy-sell agreements raise difficult and important problems. Closely held shares have no easily determined market price. Thus, the usual goal is to establish a fair price defined as the price that would be agreed between a willing buyer and seller. The following methods are widely used to establish a purchase price:

- a stated price.

- book value.

- capitalization of earnings.

- best offer by an outsider.

- appraisal or arbitration.

- a percentage of profits.

- prior transactions in shares.

- sales of similar businesses.

a. A price fixed in the agreement or by periodic negotiation is enforceable in the absence of fraud, overreaching, or breach of fiduciary duty. *Yeng Sue Chow v. Levi Strauss & Co.*, 122 Cal.Rptr. 816 (App. 1975); In *re Mather's Estate*, 189 A.2d 586 (Pa.1963).

> *Example:* Two stockholders agree that the shares of the one who dies first shall be bought by the other at $1.00 per share. That agreement is enforceable even though at the time of death the shares are worth over $1000 per share.

> *Example:* A contract provides for the periodic adjustment of a fixed purchase price. A willful refusal by a younger stockholder to renegotiate the price under such an agreement might be considered fraudulent. A convenient forgetfulness on the part of such a stockholder might also be grounds for setting aside the obsolete price. *See Helms v. Duckworth*, 101 U.S. App. D.C. 390, 249 F.2d 482 (1957); *Collins v. Universal Parts Co.*, 260 So.2d 702 (La.App.1972). Essentially contra is *Concord Auto Auction, Inc. v. Rustin*, 627 F.Supp. 1526 (D.Mass.1986) (estate obligated to tender shares for purchase even though annual meeting that was required to review the price was never held and contract price was substantially less than actual value.)

> *Example:* The two stockholders agree that if they have a dispute over policy, A will set a price on his shares, and B will have the option either to purchase A's shares at that price or sell her shares to A at that price. The agreement is enforceable.

b. Book value is a popular method of valuation. This value is typically computed by a simple division of stockholder equity as shown on the balance sheet by the number of outstanding shares. Book value tends to increase as the profitability of the business increases, assuming that earnings are retained in the business. But book value tends to decrease if the corporation pays liberal dividends. Thus, otherwise identical corporations may have radically different book values that may not accurately reflect the value of a business in terms of its ability to generate returns for its stockholders.

Caveat: Book value is based on accounting conventions and may not be a realistic estimate of the value of a business as a going concern. In extreme situations a court may require book value to be adjusted so as to be a more realistic estimate of value in the absence of specific directions as to how the calculation should be made. *Aron v. Gillman,* 128 N.E.2d 284 (N.Y.1955); *Jones v. Harris,* 388 P.2d 539 (Wash.1964).

Example: Accounting convention requires assets to be valued at historical cost rather than current market value. A corporation which owns real estate acquired decades earlier at a low price may have a book value that considerably understates the true liquidation value of the assets.

Example: Accounting conventions often permit a business to record certain assets that may never be realized on liquidation. For example it may be appropriate to eliminate such assets as costs of initial formation or good will from the purchase of another business from the balance sheet before computing book value.

Example: If a corporation uses accelerated depreciation for tax purposes, it may be desirable to specify that straight line depreciation should be used to compute book value for valuation purposes.

c.   The most widely accepted method of valuation in the finance industry is going concern value (GCV). GCV is the value of a business based on the returns it is likely to generate for investors into the future. Projected returns are discounted to present value to give a lump sum value expressed in current terms. GCV can be based on several different measures of return. Traditionally, it was based on income or earnings as calculated under generally accepted accounting principles (GAAP). It may also be based on projected dividend payments. The method preferred by most appraisers today, however is discounted cash flow (DCF).

d. Cash flow is essentially the measure of how much cash a business could theoretically distribute to its owners without disrupting the business. Cash flow is calculated by adjusting GAAP earnings for various accounting conventions (such as depreciation) that cause earnings to vary from actual cash inflows and outflows. In most businesses, cash flow will differ from year to year. Thus, it is common to calculate individual present values for expected cash flows for the first five years and to calculate a lump sum residual value for cash flows after five years on the assumption that annual cash flow will level off at some average. On the other hand, if the business is relatively stable and can be expected to generate roughly the same return each year under normal circumstances, it may be acceptable to estimate its value based on a single calculation that assumes a consistent level of cash flows going forward. In such a case, the value of the business may be calculated by dividing the annual predicted cash flow by a rate of return (the capitalization rate) that would be required by a reasonable investor given the riskiness of the business:

return / required rate of return = value.

The required rate of return is usually calculated by adding a premium to the prevailing riskless rate of return (usually the yield on a long term government bond).

Example: If a corporation has average cash flow of $50,000 a year, and it is reasonable to capitalize those earnings at 10 percent, the capitalized value of the corporation is:

$50,000 / .10 = $500,000.

If the capitalization rate is 8 percent, the value of the business would be:

$50,000 / .08 = $625,000.

If the capitalization rate is 15 percent, the value of the business would be:

$50,000 / .15 = $333,333.

Caveat: Cash flow is based on the theoretical *ability* of the business to distribute cash taking into consideration its needs. It does not matter whether the business does in fact distribute the cash or instead retains it and reinvests in the business. But if reinvestment causes returns to increase in the future (as it should), one must be careful not to double count reinvested cash as available for distribution *and* to use projected increases in returns that result from that reinvestment.

e. The reciprocal of the capitalization rate is often called the multiplier. For example, the reciprocal of 8 percent (.08) is 1/.08 or 12.5. In other words, one can figure the value of a company with an 8 percent capitalization rate by multiplying the periodic return by 12.5. In concept, the multiplier is the same thing as the price/earnings ratio in a publicly traded company. Accordingly, appraisers often estimate the capitalization rate by comparison to the price/earnings ratio(P/E) of comparable publicly held businesses.

> *Caveat:* Publicly held companies tend to be larger and less risky than closely held companies. Thus, it is likely that a lower multiplier should be applied to a closely held company. In a publicly held company, on the other hand, an appraisal proceeding may arise because a minority stockholder believes that the market price of the shares is too low and does not reflect the true value of the company (notwithstanding the ECMH). In such a case, it makes little sense to rely on the P/E ratio which itself is based on market price and thus may reflect an inherent discount.

f. Appraisers often consider various possible methods of valuation, including (i) book value, (ii) capitalized value, (iii) estimated liquidation value if the assets were to be sold and (iv) sales prices of shares in isolated transactions in the past, and may take an average of these values. This is sometimes called the Delaware Block Method. This method is not favored today and has in fact been abandoned by the Delaware courts.

g. After the value of the overall business is obtained, a tentative per share value is usually obtained by a simple division by the number of outstanding shares.

> *Caveat:* The foregoing discussion assumes an all common stock capital structure. If there are senior securities such as bonds or preferred stock, it is usually appropriate to value the business as if the company has no such senior securities outstanding and then to calculate the value of these securities (at a somewhat lower capitalization rate reflecting the fact

that these securities are safer than common stock because their returns are paid first) and then to subtract that calculated value from the total value of the business in order to estimate the lump sum value of the common stock. If comparable companies are used to determine the capitalization rate, however, it is important to apply a similar adjustment to those companies. This is often called an *unleveraged* capitalization rate.

h.   An appraiser may apply one or more discounts from the tentative per share value in order to reflect lack of marketability (if there is no ready market for the shares) or minority status (if the shares have no control value), and a variety of other factors that may affect the value of the shares. Where controlling stockholders dictate the terms of a transaction, courts are usually reluctant to accept discounts on the theory that all stockholders own shares that have the same value per share. On the other hand, a discount of some sort may be appropriate in a buy-sell agreement in which the exiting stockholder determines the timing of a transaction and receives a benefit that is not available to other stockholders. It may also be appropriate to apply a discount in connection with valuation for estate tax or in other situations in which non stockholders are involved.

G. INVOLUNTARY DISSOLUTION

In the absence of a buy/sell agreement, the traditional remedy for problems of oppression and deadlock is involuntary dissolution by judicial decree at the request of a stockholder. In order to obtain dissolution a petitioning stockholder must establish that statutory grounds for dissolution have been met. In addition, the court may withhold this remedy on equitable grounds.

1. Statutory Grounds

Generally, dissolution may not be available to a stockholder unless the stockholder can establish that the situation comes within the precise language of the statute.

a.   There is no general common law right of involuntary dissolution and statutes authorizing this remedy are strictly construed. *Johnston v. Livingston Nursing Home, Inc.,* 211 So.2d 151 (Ala.1968); *Kruger v. Gerth,* 263 N.Y.S.2d 1, 210 N.E.2d 355 (N.Y. 1965); *Nelkin v. H. J. R. Realty Corp.,* 307 N.Y.S.2d 454, 255 N.E.2d 713 (N.Y. 1969).

b. Statutory grounds for involuntary dissolution vary to some extent from state to state. MBCA 14.30 provides that dissolution may be ordered by a court if (1) the acts of the directors or those in control of the corporation are illegal, oppressive, or fraudulent; (2) the directors are deadlocked in the management of the corporate affairs, the stockholders are unable to break the deadlock and irreparable injury to the corporation is threatened or being suffered, or the business and affairs of the corporation can no longer be conducted to the advantage of the stockholders generally, because of the deadlock; (3) the stockholders are deadlocked and have failed to elect successors to directors whose terms have expired during a period that includes at least two consecutive annual meeting dates; or (4) The corporate assets are being misapplied or wasted.

> *Example:*   Wisconsin authorizes dissolution if the corporation is deadlocked so that its business can no longer be conducted with advantage to its stockholders. Refusal to dissolve a deadlocked corporation that is unable to elect directors may itself be an abuse of discretion under this statute. *Strong v. Fromm Laboratories, Inc.*, 77 N.W.2d 389 (Wis.1956).

> *Example:*   The California statute authorizes dissolution if reasonably necessary for the protection of the rights or interests of any substantial number of the stockholders, or of the complaining stockholders. Dissolution may be ordered under this statute even in the absence of deadlock, mismanagement, or unfairness. *Stumpf v. C. E. Stumpf & Sons, Inc.*, 120 Cal.Rptr. 671 (Cal.App.1975).

c. Even if statutory grounds for involuntary dissolution are established, the statute usually provides or is interpreted to provide that the court has discretion to grant dissolution upon finding that grounds exist. Discretion is necessary because dissolution may benefit one faction of stockholders at the expense of another. *Wollman v. Littman*, 316 N.Y.S.2d 526 (App.Div. 1970); *In re Radom & Neidorff, Inc.*, 119 N.E.2d 563 (N.Y. 1954).

> *Example:*   Radom and Neidorff are equal stockholders in a profitable business that has operated successfully by them for many years. Neidorff dies and his shares are inherited by his wife, Radom's sister. Brother and sister do not get along. Mrs. Neidorff does not participate in the management of the business but is an officer and must countersign all checks. She refuses to permit the corporation to pay Radom's salary.

Radom petitions the court for involuntary dissolution. Even though the court recognizes that grounds for dissolution exist, dissolution is denied because it will give Radom an unfair advantage in the future. Radom's personal abilities largely explain the corporation's current success, and it is unlikely that a purchaser could continue to operate the business at the same level of success. But the value of the business is also in part explained by Neidorff's contribution to the business before his death. If the corporation were dissolved and the assets sold, Radom could buy in the operating assets at a favorable price and thereafter continue to operate the business without sharing the fruits with Mrs. Neidorff. He thereby would capture the contribution made by Neidorff before his death without compensating her for this contribution. It is unlikely that Mrs. Neidorff will obtain the true value of her shares in this scenario. After dissolution is denied, Radom is compelled to negotiate with his sister to purchase her shares. (If Radom simply abandons the corporation and starts a new business in competition with it, he may be subject to suit for unfair competition or usurpation of corporate opportunity.) *In re Radom & Neidorff, Inc.*, 119 N.E.2d 563 (N.Y.1954) (denying judicial dissolution even though statutory grounds existed).

d. Other remedies short of involuntary dissolution may sometimes be available and courts have declined to order dissolution until such other remedies have been tried. *Jackson v. Nicolai–Neppach Co.*, 348 P.2d 9 (Or. 1995); *Masinter v. WEBCO Co.*, 262 S.E.2d 433 (W.Va.1980).

H. JUDICIALLY ORDERED BUYOUTS

There is a significant trend toward recognition that courts may order a buyout of shares rather than involuntary dissolution in order to resolve problems of oppression or deadlock. Buyout orders are specifically authorized by statute in some states, and may be viewed as part of the inherent judicial power in states where they do not have express statutory sanction.

1. Judicial Recognition of the Buyout Remedy

In several cases, courts have ordered a buyout remedy in involuntary dissolution suits even when not expressly authorized by statute. *See Balvik v. Sylvester*, 411 N.W.2d 383 (N.D.1987); *Davis v. Sheerin*, 754 S.W.2d 375 (Tex.App.1988).

2. Statutory Provisions

In 1991, MBCA 14.34 was added expressly authorizing the buyout of shares owned by a stockholder who has filed a petition for involuntary dissolution. When a petition for involuntary dissolution is filed, the corporation or one or more stockholders may elect to purchase the shares of the petitioning stockholder. If one or more stockholders make this election, the remaining stockholders are entitled to purchase on a pro rata basis.

a. MBCA 14.34 is applicable to all corporations whose shares are not publicly traded whether or not the corporation has opted into the statute. There is no provision for opt out.

b. Once the election is made, the stockholder originally petitioning for dissolution may not withdraw the petition.

c. The price at which the shares are to be sold is the fair value of the shares. The parties are given an opportunity to reach a voluntary agreement as to the price, but if they fail to reach agreement on the price, the court determines the fair value of the shares. In determining fair value of shares under MBCA 14.34, neither minority status nor lack of marketability should be considered. *Charland v. Country View Golf Club, Inc.*, 588 A.2d 609 (R.I.1991).

d. If the court establishes the fair value of the shares, it may also establish terms for the purchase, including payment in installments and appropriate security.

e. If a judicially ordered purchase does not occur within ten days of the order, the corporation is deemed to be voluntarily dissolved.

f. MBCA 14.34 is one sided. Only the shares of the petitioning stockholder are subject to purchase.

   Caveat: At least one case suggests that courts should have flexibility in determining which stockholder should be the purchaser and which the seller. *Muellenberg v. Bikon Corp.*, 669 A.2d 1382 (N.J.1996) (court has discretion to require majority stockholder to sell shares to minority stockholder).

g. In some states, the remedy of mandatory buyout is available only to corporations that have elected close corporation status.

h.   Some courts have ordered remedies short of a mandatory buy-out. *Gimpel v. Bolstein*, 477 N.Y.S.2d 1014 (Sup. 1984) (corporation may elect to resume payment of substantial dividends in lieu of a buyout).

I.   OTHER SOLUTIONS FOR OPPRESSION OR DEADLOCK

1.   Minority Dissolution Provisions

Close corporation statutes of a few states authorize corporations to elect dissolution provisions that permit a minority stockholder to compel the dissolution of a corporation.

a.   In the absence of specific statutory authorization, a minority dissolution right may be created through the use of a voting trust or other device that permits the minority stockholder to compel the majority stockholder to vote in favor of dissolution under specified circumstances.

b.   A minority dissolution provision may permit a minority stockholder to use, or threaten to use, this power at an inconvenient time in order to opportunistically seek some additional benefit from the corporation.

2.   Receivership

In some states, the courts may appoint a receiver for a deadlocked corporation. Some statutes contemplate the appointment of a receiver as an interim measure before dissolution is decreed.

a.   If a corporation is placed in receivership, control passes from the hands of the stockholders to a court-appointed receiver; even if the business and assets are preserved during the receivership, it is unlikely that the causes of deadlock or dissension will be corrected and the business ever returned to its owners. In such situations, dissolution is usually the ultimate step in the receivership.

b.   Receivership may encourage the warring stockholders to reach an agreement by which one agrees to buy out the other's interest; in such situations, the receivership may be terminated when sale is consummated. *Shaw v. Robison*, 537 P.2d 487 (Utah 1975).

3.   Custodians

Some state statutes authorize courts to appoint custodians for corporations that are deadlocked or otherwise threatened with irreparable injury. *See* DGCL 226. A custodian differs from a receiver in that the goal is to continue the business of the corporation and not to liquidate it or distribute its assets.

If a custodian is appointed and the cause of the deadlock or irreparable injury is not eliminated, a custodianship may be converted into a receivership.

a.   This provision is designed to provide a simpler, more flexible and less drastic solution for corporations than either the appointment of a receiver or dissolution. *In re Jamison Steel Corp.*, 322 P.2d 246 (Cal.App.1958); *Giuricich v. Emtrol Corp.*, 449 A.2d 232 (Del.1982).

b.   The mere threat of the appointment of a custodian may encourage quarreling stockholders to make some kind of a mutual accommodation. But it is doubtful that the appointment of a custodian can cure deep-seated and fundamental differences of views among stockholders. Again, a buyout or involuntary dissolution may be the ultimate remedies.

> *Example:*   Two stockholders each own 50 of the stock of a corporation. One stockholder is in control of the board of directors and the deadlock prevents the other stockholder from attaining parity. A custodian may be appointed under DGCL 226 despite the absence of irreparable injury. *Giuricich v. Emtrol Corp.*, 449 A.2d 232 (Del.1982).

4.   Provisional Directors

A provisional director is an impartial person appointed by a court to serve on the board of directors of a corporation if the board itself is so divided that it cannot make decisions with the consequence that the business and affairs of the corporation can no longer be conducted to the advantage of the stockholders generally. *See* DGCL 353.

a.   Provisional directors are authorized in some states only in the case of corporations that have elected close corporation status.

b.   A petition for the appointment of a provisional director may be made by one-half of the directors or by a specified fraction of the voting stockholders.

c.   A provisional director may be removed by majority vote of the voting stockholders.

> *Example:*   In an appropriate case it may be appropriate to appoint a relative of one of the stockholders as provisional director in order to ensure business decisions are made on an informed basis.

> *Caveat:*   While stockholders may not wish to have outsiders take over the business of the corporation through a receivership or custodian, or participate in management as a provisional director, these remedies generally may not be disclaimed in advance by a corporation.

5. Additional Remedies

Close corporation statutes may expressly authorize a variety of additional remedies, including the performance, prohibition, alteration, or setting aside of any action of the corporation or of its stockholders, directors, or officers of or any other party to the proceeding; the cancellation or alteration of any provision in the corporation's articles of incorporation or bylaws; the removal of any individual as a director or officer; the appointment of any individual as a director or officer; an accounting with respect to any matter in dispute; the payment of dividends; the award of damages to any party.

J. FIDUCIARY DUTIES AMONG STOCKHOLDERS

The traditional view is that stockholders have no fiduciary duty to each other and that transactions that are unfair to minority stockholders cannot generally be attacked as a breach of a duty of loyalty or good faith by a majority stockholder. More recent decisions recognize that such duties exist and that many cases involving oppression or deadlock may be resolved by application of principles of fiduciary duty.

1. Strict Equal Treatment

The idea that there is a fiduciary duty running between stockholders was first adopted in *Donahue v. Rodd Electrotype Co.*, 328 N.E.2d 505 (Mass.1975). The court analogized the closely held corporation to a partnership and held that fiduciary duty required that where the controlling stockholder family caused the corporation to repurchase shares at an attractive price from a family member who had served as CEO, the same opportunity to sell shares back to the corporation should be afforded to minority stockholders.

     a.   Many cases support the result reached in *Donahue* on share buy-backs at different prices. *See Estate of Meller v. Adolf Meller Co.*, 554 A.2d 648 (R.I.1989); *Sundberg v. Abbott*, 423 N.W.2d 686 (Minn.App.1988); *Balvik v. Sylvester*, 411 N.W.2d 383 (N.D.1987).

     b.   The *Donahue* doctrine has also been widely applied by courts in other situations as creating a basic fiduciary duty among stockholders and viewing freeze-out tactics as constituting a breach of that duty. *See 68th*

Street Apts., Inc. v. Lauricella, 362 A.2d 78 (N.J.Super.Law Div.1976), *Knaebel v. Heiner*, 663 P.2d 551 (Alaska 1983), *Russell v. First York Savings Co.*, 352 N.W.2d 871 (Neb.1984), overruled on other grounds, *Van Pelt v. Greathouse*, 364 N.W.2d 14 (Neb.1985); *Muellenberg v. Bikon, Corp.*, 669 A.2d 1382 (N.J.1996); *Pedro v. Pedro*, 489 N.W.2d 798 (Minn.App.1992) (controlling stockholders breached fiduciary duty when they fired minority stockholder who had a legitimate expectation of lifetime employment and majority stockholders had engaged in misconduct).

Example: Minority stockholders in a closely held corporation establish (1) that they requested but were denied employment with the corporation, (2) the corporation never paid dividends, (3) compensation to the majority stockholders and their families in the form of salary, bonuses, and pension benefits was excessive, and (4) majority stockholders offered to buy out minority's shares at an unreasonably low price. *Sugarman v. Sugarman*, 797 F.2d 3 (1st Cir.1986).

Caveat: The idea that a controlling stockholder (or any stockholder) may owe a fiduciary duty to other stockholders is not entirely unique to the closely held corporation setting. There are numerous cases involving publicly traded corporations that turn on the duty of controlling stockholders. The difference is that in a closely held corporation the duty may be asserted by one stockholder directly against another, thus circumventing any need to maintain a derivative action. It is also arguable that the duty of a controlling stockholder may extend to matters that would ordinarily be considered under the duty of care not simply the duty of loyalty.

2. Business Purpose Test

The rule of strict equal treatment has been somewhat modified by subsequent Massachusetts cases addressing other situations. For example, where a dispute arose over a business decision leading to extreme hostility among stockholders, three of four equal stockholders declined to reelect the fourth stockholder to the board of directors and terminated him as salaried employee. The court held (1) that majority stockholders must show business purpose for actions and (2) that minority stockholder could show that less drastic alternative resolution was possible. *Wilkes v. Springside Nursing Home, Inc.*, 353 N.E.2d 657 (Mass.1976). Following *Wilkes*, the Massachusetts courts have continued to struggle to establish the line between appropriate majority action and breaches of the *Donahue* fiduciary duty.

a. In *Hallahan v. Haltom Corp.*, 385 N.E.2d 1033 (Mass.App.1979), the court ordered shares acquired by an equal co-owner of shares in an effort to change the balance of power to be returned to the seller at cost.

b. In *Smith v. Atlantic Properties, Inc.*, 422 N.E.2d 798 (Mass.App.1981), a minority stockholder had veto power over most decisions because of a unanimity requirement. The stockholder exercised the power arbitrarily to prevent the payment of all dividends, thereby causing the corporation to incur a penalty tax for unreasonable accumulation of surplus. The court held the minority stockholder liable because he breached his duty to the other stockholders.

c. In *Leader v. Hycor, Inc.*, 479 N.E.2d 173 (Mass.1985) the court upheld a reverse stock split at the ratio of one new share for each 4,000 old shares, with fractional shares to be purchased for cash at a specified amount per share.

d. In *Goode v. Ryan*, 489 N.E.2d 1001 (Mass.1986), the court held that the *Donahue* duty did not permit the estate of a minority stockholder to compel the corporation to repurchase its shares in order to simplify the settlement of the estate. In this case, there was no prior contractual obligation to repurchase the shares.

e. In *Evangelista v. Holland*, 537 N.E.2d 589 (Mass.App.1989), the court held that a preexisting contract for the corporation to repurchase minority shares on the death of a stockholder at a set price should be enforced despite the argument that *Donahue* required the corporation to negotiate a price closer to the current value of the shares owned by the deceased stockholder. The court stated that there was a mutuality of risk and no violation of the *Donahue* duty.

f. In *Crowley v. Communications for Hospitals, Inc.*, 573 N.E.2d 996 (Mass.App.1991), controlling stockholders paid themselves excessive compensation while excluding the minority stockholders. The court ordered the excessive compensation restored to the corporation and ordered a mandatory dividend to all stockholders if the creditors were adequately protected. It did not order a direct payment be made to the minority stockholders.

g. In *Merola v. Exergen Corp.*, 668 N.E.2d 351 (Mass. 1996), an employee who purchased stock in corporation was fired and later sold his stock back to the majority stockholder (at a profit) on terms apparently continuously available to all minority stockholders. The court held that stock ownership does not create entitlement to continued employment.

3. Other Approaches

In *Nixon v. Blackwell*, 626 A.2d 1366 (Del.1993), the Delaware Supreme Court rejected the *Donahue* approach, saying it would do violence to normal practice of corporation law to create a broad fiduciary duty among stockholders and noting that the corporation had not elected statutory close corporation status. The case involved the claim of a non-employee minority stockholder that the sellback option under an employee stockownership plan should be available to all stockholders. Delaware nonetheless appears to recognize a somewhat enhanced fiduciary duty to the corporation in the context of a closely held corporation.

> *Example:* H and W are equal stockholders and the two directors in a corporation. H is the president and manager and W the secretary and bookkeeper, each receiving a salary. H and W divorce. H thereafter excludes W from participation in the business and increases his own salary. These actions constitute self dealing and under Delaware law H must establish that the increased salary was intrinsically fair. *Wilderman v. Wilderman*, 315 A.2d 610 (Del.Ch.1974).

a. In *Toner v. Baltimore Envelope Co.*, 498 A.2d 642 (Md.1985), the court rejected a *per se* rule of strict equal treatment in connection with a stock buyback intended to resolve a dispute between two stockholder factions and focusing on business purpose and feasibility, noting that the corporation had not elected statutory close corporation status.

b. New York recognizes a fiduciary duty within closely held corporations. *See Alpert v. 28 Williams St. Corp.*, 473 N.E.2d 19 (N.Y. 1984). But the New York courts have held that a stockholder who is an at-will employee may be fired without cause. *Ingle v. Glamore Motor Sales, Inc.*, 535 N.E.2d 1311 (N.Y. 1989). The power to fire an at-will employee who is also a stockholder may be exercised in order to avoid the application of a new valuation formula for the purchase of the employee's shares. *Gallagher v. Lambert*, 549 N.E.2d 136 (N.Y. 1989).

c. Cases from other jurisdictions recognize that a fiduciary duty may exist but generally have not followed the implications of the strict *Donahue* duty. *Zidell v. Zidell, Inc.*, 560 P.2d 1091 (Or.1977), and *Masinter v. WEBCO Co.*, 262 S.E.2d 433 (W.Va.1980).

K. ALTERNATIVE DISPUTE RESOLUTION (ADR)

Mandatory *arbitration* is sometimes used as a device to avoid a deadlock short of dissolution. The advantages of arbitration are speed, cheapness, informality (as contrasted with a court proceeding), and the prospect of a decision by a person with knowledge and experience in business affairs. Where the reason for deadlock is a question not involving basic personal or policy matters, arbitration may satisfactorily resolve a dispute and permit the corporation to continue. In addition, many courts today routinely require parties to business disputes to undertake *mediation*. The difference is that the decision of an arbitrator is binding whereas a mediator seeks only to facilitate a settlement between the parties.

   a.   Arbitration is a matter of contract. The parties must agree to it. Thus, the parties must agree on the nature of disputes that an arbitrator may decide and the remedies that the arbitrator may order. Arbitration statutes contain virtually no restrictions on the types of disputes that may be resolved pursuant to arbitration.

   b.   The agreement to arbitrate may be entered into at any time. Thus, it may be part of a stockholder agreement or the parties may agree to arbitration after a dispute has arisen. The courts will ordinarily enforce the decision of an arbitrator as long as the arbitrator has acted within the scope of the agreement to arbitrate.

   c.   Traditionally, courts were reluctant to enforce agreements to arbitrate as an improper delegation of duty by the board of directors. Most courts today will enforce an agreement to arbitrate as long as all affected stockholders are party to the agreement. *Vogel v. Lewis*, 268 N.Y.S.2d 237 (App.Div.1966), aff'd, 224 N.E.2d 738 (N.Y.1967) (disagreement whether a corporation should exercise option to purchase is arbitrable); *Moskowitz v. Surrey Sleep Products, Inc.*, 292 N.Y.S.2d 748 (App.Div. 1968). On the other hand, a court might consider the corporation itself a necessary party to the dispute in some cases.

   d.   Many disputes leading to deadlock in a closely held corporation involve personality conflicts or broad differences in policy. An arbitrator may have no criteria for resolving such disputes, and even if she does resolve a specific dispute, it is unlikely that the decision will cure the basic disagreement which led to the original deadlock. Nevertheless, the courts routinely order arbitration in closely held corporation disputes when provided for by contract without consideration of the probable success of the arbitration. Ultimately, if deep personal or policy conflicts continue, dissolution appears to be the only suitable remedy because arbitration cannot cure the root cause of the disagreement.

> *Example:* A minority stockholder in a corporation deadlocked because of a unanimity requirement seeks arbitration of a claim that the majority stockholder should be removed as director. A decision by the arbitrator to remove the majority stockholder in effect turns control of the corporation over to the minority stockholder, and because there is a unanimity requirement for the election of directors, the turnover of control is permanent. Even if the majority stockholder has committed acts that constitute cause for removal, it is doubtful whether an arbitrator should favor permanently one faction over another in a pure struggle for control. *Application of Burkin,* 154 N.Y.S.2d 898, 136 N.E.2d 862 (N.Y. 1956). In this situation, a derivative suit for damages against the majority stockholder might be a more appropriate remedy than removal.

REVIEW QUESTIONS

11.1. True or False: In a closely held corporation the stockholders today have essentially the same fiduciary duties to each other as partners in a partnership.

11.2. True or False: So long as an even division of shares between two stockholders is avoided, there is no possibility of a deadlock in a corporation.

11.3. Why isn't dissolution an adequate solution to deadlock and oppression problems in the closely held corporation because it appears to be an adequate solution for the same problems in the case of a partnership?

11.4. Are there better solutions to the deadlock problem than dissolution?

11.5. True or False: Every state should adopt a close corporation statute, because the experience in the states that have enacted them indicate that they are almost widely and universally used.

11.6. What is the statutory scheme or statutory norm in the law of corporations?

11.7. True or False: In a corporation with two stockholders, it is silly to talk about the statutory scheme. The stockholders should simply run the corporation in the same way that they run a partnership.

11.8. X corporation has a provision in its articles of incorporation that states, no act of the board of directors of this corporation concerning the management of its business affairs shall be of any effect unless consented to or ratified by a unanimous vote of all its stockholders. A, B and C were the sole stockholders and the sole directors of X corporation. They had earlier elected A president, B vice president and C secretary-treasurer of the corporation. They now meet as a board of directors and vote to relieve C of his duties as secretary-treasurer and make B secretary-treasurer in addition to his being vice president. C votes against his removal as secretary-treasurer and contends that he cannot be removed under the above charter provision without unanimous vote of the stockholders, and he does not consent to his own removal. C brings suit against A and B to compel them to admit him to the office of secretary—treasurer and to compel them to deliver to him the books of such office. What result?

11.9. True or False: Small corporations that are eligible for special treatment under close corporation statutes usually elect such treatment.

11.10. Why are share transfer restrictions commonly used in closely held corporations?

11.11. Are share transfer restrictions ever used in publicly held corporations? If so, why?

XII

Publicly Held Corporations

A. CONTROL IN THE PUBLICLY HELD CORPORATION

Corporate governance in a large publicly held corporation bears little relationship to the system contemplated by state corporation statutes or to the procedures followed by most closely held corporations. Who controls large publicly held corporations and for whose benefit are among the most controversial issues in corporation law.

1. Limited Role of Individual Stockholders

The number of voting shares in the large publicly held corporation is so large that the votes of any single investor are almost always irrelevant on any issue. With respect to the election of directors, the small stockholder is usually presented with a ballot and a list of candidates for the board of directors equal in number to the positions to be filled. The stockholder may vote for these candidates or withhold a vote for some or all of them. But because the overwhelming majority of the stockholders almost always vote in favor of the proposed directors, it seldom makes a difference whether or not an individual stockholder exercises the right to vote.

Caveat: Proxy appointments from small stockholders are significant in the aggregate in that they may be necessary to establish a quorum and obtain sufficient votes.

Caveat: Many individuals today do not own shares of individual companies. Rather, they own shares of mutual funds or through other investment vehicles that create portfolios of shares from numerous individual companies. Thus, many shares are voted by mutual fund managers and other investment advisers for institutional investors without the knowledge or consent of individual investors in those funds. In 2004, the SEC adopted rules that require disclosure of voting policies by mutual funds, albeit after the fact. (Most mutual funds and other investment companies are themselves corporations, and investors who own shares in them may vote *those* shares as in any other corporation to elect directors of the fund and on other matters.)

2. The Board of Directors and the Chief Executive Officer (CEO)

In large publicly held corporations, professional managers run the business even though as a matter of statutory law the board of directors retains ultimate and complete authority to manage the business. In practice, the board of directors does not participate directly in management but serves a more limited role as a monitor of management. Rather, the chief executive officer (CEO) has the ultimate working responsibility for management of the enterprise. And in *very* large enterprises, even the CEO may have limited involvement with day-to-day operations. Instead, he or she may be primarily involved with financial matters, long term planning, the selection of operating personnel, and the like. Still, significant decisions are likely to be made by the CEO or in consultation with the CEO.

a.   The board of directors in publicly held corporations is particularly important in the following areas:

- They provide general review and oversight of management.

- They select the CEO, set his compensation, and may replace him if overall performance is unsatisfactory.

- They assure that the corporation has in place working and effective auditing and accounting systems.

- They provide advice and counsel to management.

- They provide intellectual discipline for management (which must appear before the board and present views and defend proposals).

- They set dividend rates, approve significant financial transactions, approve stock option plans for managers and employees, and so forth.

- They act in crisis situations, where the CEO unexpectedly dies or is incapacitated, or where significant misconduct, fraud, or theft of corporate assets is discovered.

    Caveat: Under most state corporation statutes there are certain specified decisions that may be made only by the entire board of directors and thus may not be delegated to an officer or committee of the board. *See* MBCA 8.25. These include issuing shares, authorizing distributions, approving a merger or any transaction that must be ratified by the stockholders, filling vacancies on the board or its committees, amending the articles of incorporation, or adopting, amending, or repealing bylaws.

b. Although they do not establish objectives, strategies and policies of the corporation, many boards of directors are involved in strategic planning through participation on board committees dealing with specific problem areas. These committees may work closely with the CEO and management and may become directly involved in defining and establishing long term goals for the corporation.

c. Although it is clear that most boards of directors do not actually manage the company, neither do they act as adversaries or even a devil's advocate. Rather, most decisions are made by consensus. Indeed, caselaw effectively mandates that the board of directors reach a consensus. *See Smith v. Atlantic Properties, Inc.* Corporation law presumes that board decisions are unanimous unless a director formally registers dissent. *See* MBCA 8.24. Moreover, corporation law generally prohibits action by the board without a meeting unless the decision is unanimous. *See* MBCA 8.21. It also effectively prohibits a director from voting by proxy. *See* MBCA 8.20.

3. Composition of the Board of Directors

Historically, the board of directors was viewed largely as a rubber stamp for management. Directors were viewed as having limited responsibilities.

Today, stock exchange rules mandated by the SEC require that the board of directors of listed companies be composed of a majority of independent members. Thus, most boards of directors consist partly of management representatives—*inside directors*—and partly of *outside directors* who are not officers or employees of the corporation

a. The Chief Executive Officer (CEO) is often also the chairman of the board of directors, though in an increasing number of corporations these positions are held by different people. If the CEO is also chairman of the board of directors he or she may control the agenda. However, it has also been recognized that it is often preferable for these two offices to be held by different persons. Where that is the case the chairman of the board rather than the CEO may largely develop the agenda.

b. Inside directors are high level executive officers employed by the corporation. Because they are subordinate to the CEO, they are generally assumed to largely reflect and support the CEO's policies.

c. Outside directors are often CEOs (or retired CEOs) of other corporations, though they may also include major investors, well known public figures, politicians, educators (such as university presidents and business school deans), and others. Experience with the management of complex bureaucratic structures and lack of prior economic involvement with the specific corporation are usually desirable characteristics for outside directors. Nevertheless an outside director is not likely to have detailed knowledge of company affairs. Thus, briefing books are distributed to directors in advance of a meeting so that they may become informed in connection with issues on the agenda. Most boards meet monthly as a board. Committees may meet more often. Special meetings may be held by conference call. As the role of outside directors has increased in importance, it has become recognized that they should raise significant issues for discussion at board or committee meetings. Many important questions are first raised informally with the CEO or at meetings of committees of boards prior to a discussion of them at a meeting of the board of directors. Recommendations with respect to these matters are usually discussed by management in advance of the meeting.

d. Under NYSE rules a director is not considered to be independent if:

   •   The director is or has been within the last three years an employee of the listed company, or an immediate family member is or has been within the last three years an executive officer of the listed company.

- The director or an immediate family member has received more than $100,000 in compensation from the listed company during any twelve-month period within the last three years other than director and committee fees and pension or other forms of deferred compensation for prior service.

- The director or an immediate family member is a current partner of a firm that is the company's internal or external auditor; the director is a current employee of such a firm; the director has an immediate family member who is a current employee of such a firm and who participates in the firm's audit, assurance or tax compliance (but not tax planning) practice; or the director or an immediate family member was within the last three years a partner or employee of such a firm and personally worked on the listed company's audit within that time.

- The director or an immediate family member is or has been within the last three years employed as an executive officer of another company where any of the listed company's present executive officers at the same time serves or served on that company's compensation committee.

- The director is a current employee or an immediate family member is a current executive officer of a company that has made payments to or received payments from the listed company for property or services in an amount that exceeds the greater of $1 million or 2% of such other company's consolidated gross revenues in any of the last three fiscal years.

e. Under NYSE rules non-management directors must meet at regularly scheduled executive sessions without management representatives being present.

f. A variety of factors has contributed to the emphasis on the role of independent directors. Officers and inside directors were blamed for corporate misconduct in the 1970s (particularly following Watergate) and even more significant criminal misconduct in 2000 and 2001, leading to federal legislation tightening internal financial controls at publicly traded corporations and requiring oversight by independent directors. In addition, the courts have tended to respect decisions by disinterested directors in connection with stockholder derivative actions and takeover defenses.

Caveat: For purposes of fiduciary duty analysis, a director may be described as *interested* with respect to a specific issue or transaction irrespective of whether that director is or is not considered to be independent under stock exchange rules. An interested director is one with a financial interest in the issue or transaction that is of sufficient importance to him that it might reasonably be expected to influence his judgment.

4. Committees of the Board of Directors

In a publicly traded company, the board of directors must appoint several standing committees.

a. Under the Sarbanes Oxley Act stock exchange rules must provide that all listed companies have an audit committee that is directly responsible for the appointment, compensation, and oversight of the work of any registered public accounting firm employed by that issuer for the purpose of preparing or issuing an audit report or related work, and each such registered public accounting firm shall report directly to the audit committee. The audit committee must also establish procedures for the receipt, retention, and treatment of complaints received by the issuer regarding accounting, internal accounting controls, or auditing matters, the confidential, anonymous submission by employees of the issuer of concerns regarding questionable accounting or auditing matters. The audit committee must also have the authority to engage independent counsel and other advisers, as it determines necessary to carry out its duties.

b. Under NYSE rules, each listed company must have a *Nominating Committee or Corporate Governance Committee* and a *Compensation Committee*. Both of these committees must be composed entirely of independent directors. Comparable rules apply to NASDAQ companies.

Caveat: The NYSE rules that a majority of board members must be independent and that the board must appoint an independent nominating/corporate governance committee and compensation committee does not apply to a company in which more than 50 percent of the voting power is held by an individual or control group. A company that elects this exemption must disclose that fact to its stockholders in its proxy statement or annual report.

5. Statutory Duties of Officers Under Federal Law

Under the Sarbanes Oxley Act, the CEO and the chief financial officer (CFO) of each *SEC registered company* must certify in each annual or quarterly report filed with the SEC (1) that they have reviewed the report; (2) that based on the officer's knowledge, the report does not contain any untrue statement of a material fact or omit to state a material fact necessary in order to make the statements made, in light of the circumstances under which such statements were made, not misleading; (3) that based on such officer's knowledge, the financial statements, and other financial information included in the report, fairly present in all material respects the financial condition and results of operations of the issuer as of, and for, the periods presented in the report; (4) that the signing officers (A) are responsible for establishing and maintaining internal controls, (B) have designed such internal controls to ensure that material information relating to the issuer and its consolidated subsidiaries is made known to such officers by others within those entities, particularly during the period in which the periodic reports are being prepared, (C) have evaluated the effectiveness of the issuer's internal controls as of a date within 90 days prior to the report, and (D) have presented in the report their conclusions about the effectiveness of their internal controls based on their evaluation as of that date; (5) that the signing officers have disclosed to the issuer's auditors and the audit committee of the board of directors (or persons fulfilling the equivalent function) (A) all significant deficiencies in the design or operation of internal controls which could adversely affect the issuer's ability to record, process, summarize, and report financial data and have identified for the issuer's auditors any material weaknesses in internal controls, and (B) any fraud, whether or not material, that involves management or other employees who have a significant role in the issuer's internal controls; and (6) that the signing officers have indicated in the report whether or not there were significant changes in internal controls or in other factors that could significantly affect internal controls subsequent to the date of their evaluation, including any corrective actions with regard to significant deficiencies and material weaknesses.

> *Caveat:* The above rules have been controversial for several reasons. In particular, the rules relating to audit committee independence have been seen as infringing on the ultimate authority of the board of directors under state corporation law. In

addition, the rules relating to director independence have led to the reclassification of some directors who thought they were independent because of jobs held by family members. And the requirement that the CEO and CFO certify the financial statements of the company have led to fears of criminal prosecution for negligent errors. Other provisions in the Sarbanes Oxley Act require that the CEO and CFO refund to the company any incentive compensation they receive if the company is required as a result of misconduct to restate its financial results for the previous twelve month period.

6. CEO Succession

The ultimate power and duty to name the CEO rests with the board of directors. Traditionally, management of most publicly-held corporations has tended to be self-perpetuating. In most cases, the incumbent CEO, in consultation with the board of directors, recommends a successor and that recommendation is accepted by the board of directors. Major stockholders including institutional investors may have an important voice in the selection. With the requirement of an independent nominating/corporate governance committee, it is likely that boards of directors will exercise significant and increasing independence in reviewing recommendations by incumbent management and the outgoing CEO.

a. In many corporations, managers rise gradually through the ranks until one ultimately becomes CEO. But there are many examples of outsiders being named CEO.

b. The board of directors may also remove the CEO. Such actions, which may be based on dissatisfaction with profitability of the business, failure to eliminate corruption or misconduct, or unpopular actions by the CEO, have become more common since the 1980s. Studies indicate that CEO tenure has become shorter and shorter in recent years.

7. Nominees for the Board of Directors

Historically, candidates for the board of directors were identified by the CEO. This practice permitted the CEO to assure that the board of directors remained friendly. Today, most publicly held corporations must have an independent nominating committee to select new director candidates. As a result, the formal role of the CEO in selecting members of the board of directors has been significantly reduced, but the CEO may still have considerable voice in who is nominated to be a director on the management's slate.

a. Except in the case of a proxy fight, stockholders have no real choice in voting for alternative candidates. There is no requirement that management include competing candidates in its proxy materials even though the expense of the proxy solicitation is borne by the company. (A competing candidate (or slate of candidates) is free to solicit votes at his or her own expense and in compliance with SEC rules.) Thus, a stockholder may withhold her vote, vote for management's slate, or waste her vote on a write-in candidate. Accordingly, the role of stockholders when voting for directors is effectively to ratify the persons nominated by the corporation to serve as its directors.

b. Although institutional investors could in theory dictate the outcome of many board elections, most institutional investors support management nominees. In some cases, institutional investors have announced that they will not vote for one or more incumbent directors. Such an announcement is taken very seriously by current management, because it is likely that other institutional investors will also withhold their votes or demand changes in governance of the corporation.

c. In 2003, the SEC proposed to permit outside candidates to be nominated for election to the board of directors in the management proxy materials under specified circumstances including financial misconduct or the withholding of a 35 percent or more of stockholder votes from an individual candidate. As an alternative, it was proposed that Delaware corporation law be amended to require election by a majority of votes cast for director. The SEC proposal was withdrawn and is not likely to be raised again in the near future.

B. STOCKHOLDERS IN PUBLICLY TRADED CORPORATIONS

A great deal of attention has been given to the place of stockholders in corporate governance, the role they should play, and the implications of the growth of institutional investors in the modern American economy. Scholars have several different views as to the appropriate role of stockholders.

1. Berle & Means View

In 1933, Adolph Berle and Gardiner Means, published *The Modern Corporation and Private Property,* a revolutionary book at the time, which pictured stockholders as scattered, isolated, and disorganized individuals who typically vote blindly in favor of management or as management recommends. Because management has total control of the enterprise in this view, the business is often operated as much for the benefit of the managers as it is for the benefit of the stockholders–a model that is often called *managerialism*. This *separation of ownership from control* could be traced to several factors according to Berle and Means:

a. Management has control of the proxy machinery and the views of management are therefore routinely set forth before the stockholders as the institutional voice of the corporation. Challengers must locate and communicate with stockholders largely at their own expense and without the benefit of access to corporate information. Hence, it is expensive to challenge incumbent management, and the chances of success are slim.

b. The CEO not only controls who is nominated to serve as director but also dominates the meetings of the board by reason of being its chairman, by controlling its agenda, and by limiting the circulation of information to the directors.

c. There is a natural process of self-selection by stockholders. Most stockholders think first of their own financial interest. If they are dissatisfied with management, they sell their shares. Thus, dissatisfied stockholders tend to disappear by a process of self-elimination, and the remaining stockholders tend to be pro-management. This is often called the Wall Street Rule or the Wall Street Option.

d. On the other hand, it is always possible for stockholders to bring a derivative action challenging specific transactions or for an insurgent group to undertake a proxy fight seeking to oust management. These devices are usually seen as a last resort, because they are expensive and unlikely to succeed except in the most extreme cases.

e. Finally, several other forces may serve to discipline management. Perhaps most important, management is concerned with its own reputation in the company, the business world, and the community. There is almost always a better job to which even a CEO may aspire. In addition, poor management may cause large investors or even creditors to demand changes. Internal dissension or competition among senior officers may lead to a shake up of management.

> *Caveat:* Such reputational considerations do not seem to have generated much restraint in connection with executive compensation. On the other hand, high levels of pay may be the result primarily of a broad shift to using options and stock as compensation.

2. The Market for Corporate Control

In the late 1970s, some scholars began to argue that the Berle and Means thesis ignored market forces that serve to discipline management. To be sure, it is only natural for a manager to work less hard to maximize the wealth of stockholders than it would be for him to maximize his own wealth. Moreover, a manager may be inclined to engage in a variety of tactics—ranging from exacting excessive salary and benefits to withholding dividends in order to grow the company through questionable acquisitions *(empire building)* to self-dealing or appropriation of corporate opportunities—designed to divert profits of the corporation to himself. Such shirking and opportunistic behaviors are often called *agency costs* because they reduce returns to stockholders. But if agency costs are too high, and stockholder return is too low, stock price will suffer and the company may become the target of a takeover attempt. In other words, if stock price falls because management is inefficient or self-serving, someone will emerge to make an offer to buy the company on the theory that the stock would be worth more if the company were better managed. In such a situation, the bidder may be able to offer a premium over the market price to target stockholders and gain control of a company that will be worth more than the price paid once better management is installed.

a. Stockholders can reduce agency costs by monitoring the performance of managers and by devising incentive systems that encourage managers to maximize the wealth of stockholders rather than their own personal wealth. Incentive devices such as bonuses, stock option and stock purchase plans, and long term incentive compensation, and even golden parachutes may link manager self-interest to owner wealth maximization and may limit agency costs by aligning the interests of the manager with the interests of owners. Outside directors can also serve as monitors particularly if they are required to own stock or are paid in stock rather than in cash, practices which became increasingly common in the 1990s. In addition, mandatory disclosure requirements under federal securities law facilitate monitoring, although some legal scholars have argued that publicly traded companies already have adequate incentive to communicate with investors and the market in order to keep stock price as high as possible.

b. In the 1980s, cash tender offers for large publicly-held corporations became relatively common, because new sources of cash (such as junk bonds) became available and because shares have become relatively concentrated in the hands of institutional investors. In a significant number of cases, such takeover attempts proved successful and were followed by the replacement of the board of directors and management by presumably more competent managers.

> *Caveat:* The market for corporate control assumes that the stock market is relatively efficient in that market prices accurately reflect the value of potential target companies. If the market is often incorrect in setting stock prices, then takeovers may not have the effect of maximizing stockholder wealth.

c. Needless to say, the market for corporate control threatens managers who do not maximize stockholder wealth with the possibility of hostile takeovers that may lead to their ouster from positions of control. This led to the development of a variety of takeover defenses and the adoption of state takeover legislation. Many legal scholars argued that such defenses were largely inappropriate because they were in fact designed to entrench incumbent management. Some argued that management should not be permitted to engage in any defensive tactics at all, because the fact that a bidder offers a premium constitutes an increase in stockholder wealth and since the stockholders own the company, the goal of management should be to increase stockholder wealth. These same scholars also argued that state takeover statutes and indeed federal tender offer law, were unwise. The courts tended to take a middle view and to strike down defensive tactics that did not serve a business purpose and appeared to be motivated primarily by a desire for entrenchment. Generally, the courts did not mandate that management must seek to maximize stockholder wealth except in cases in which it was clear that the company would be sold to a new control group.

d. Cash tender offers became much less common after 1990 in part because market prices increased significantly (possibly because the market for corporate control had increased management solicitude for the interests of stockholders) and in part because takeover defenses became more sophisticated. In addition, companies appeared to be quite willing to divest operations if divestiture would likely lead to an increase in aggregate stockholder wealth. Thus, although many target managers had opposed takeover attempts on the grounds that bidders sought to break up the target company (and undo the corporate empire), would-be target managers began to undertake break-ups voluntarily, possibly because of a general shift to compensation primarily in the form of stock options (which effectively aligned management interest with stockholder interest) and away from compensation based on earnings or other measures based on size. An increase in takeover activity beginning in the mid–1990s largely involved combinations of independent businesses. These transactions in some cases also may have led to the elimination of less effective managers and their replacement by more competent managers.

e. The collapse of the dotcom market as well as Enron, WorldCom, and other companies beginning in the year 2000, led to significant new regulation focused primarily on improving financial reporting. It also led many scholars and commentators to question the use of stock options as compensation and to question market efficiency generally.

3. Stockholder Wealth Maximization as the Goal

The traditional view is that the objective of a corporation is to maximize the wealth of its stockholders. This view is expressed in early cases. *See Dodge v. Ford Motor Co.,* 170 N.W. 668, 684 (Mich.1919). It is also implicit in the Berle & Means thesis. And it is the basic premise on which the analysis of corporate governance by law and economics scholars is founded.

a. Nevertheless, as a result of takeover activity in the 1980s, most states adopted *other constituency statutes* that permit (and in a few cases require) management to consider interests other than those of the stockholders in making decisions on behalf of the corporation. These other constituencies may include employees, customers, suppliers, creditors, and the communities in which the corporation has facilities. They are often called *stakeholders* to distinguish them from stockholders. These statutes were enacted by state legislatures without extensive consideration in response to fears that corporations incorporated in their states might become the target of unwanted takeover bids. Management of threatened companies believed that constituency statutes might permit them to reject takeover bids at even above-market prices by relying expressly on the interests of stakeholders. There have been few reported instances of the actual application of these statutes. Delaware has not enacted such a statute.

b. These statutes have been widely criticized from various different perspectives. They have also had their defenders.

• Law and economics scholars have criticized these statutes on the grounds that stakeholders can protect themselves by contract and that aggregate wealth is maximized if managers are required to maximize the return to stockholders as residual claimants.

- The ABA's Committee on Corporate Laws and the Business Roundtable have criticized these statutes because they increase uncertainty and raise the specter of possible lawsuits brought by other stakeholders who are adversely affected by director or management decisions. In other words, by effectively giving management the choice of which constituency to serve in any given situation, management is in fact relieved of all effective responsibility.

- These statutes have been defended as being consistent with long term stockholder interests and as stating a traditional view of corporate citizenship and social responsibility.

- Stockholder wealth maximization is easy to state as a goal but difficult to apply in light of stockholder diversification and the development of options and derivative securities that can affect share values.

c. Some legal scholars have suggested that an alternative model of the corporation as an organization focused on problems of *team production* may be more accurate than the traditional stockholder-owner model. The premise of the team production model is that in most corporations (1) it is necessary to commit goods and services to production and to forgo the right to withdraw those assets for a substantial period and (2) it is difficult to determine how much of the profits are attributable to individual contributions. Thus, the various contributors of inputs agree to distribute profits to the stockholders and the board of directors serves as a largely disinterested mediator to determine the returns to be paid to the various contributors of inputs. Although the team production model has been offered as an explanation for why stockholders should not be the ultimate claimants to residual corporate returns, it does not address the fact that other constituencies all bargain for fixed returns. On the other hand, it suggests that management itself should be seen as an important claimant, particularly where compensation is paid primarily in the form of gains from stock options.

C. INSTITUTIONAL INVESTORS

Institutional investors—including mutual funds and other investment companies, pension and retirement funds, insurance companies, bank trust departments, foundations, university endowments, and others—have grown tremendously in importance since the 1950s. Today, individual investors own only about one-third of all corporate equities. Moreover, in many listed companies, a relatively small number of institutional investors own a majority of all outstanding voting shares.

a. Traditionally, institutional investors have not been active in the control and management of publicly held corporations despite their potential voting power. Rather, they have tended to view themselves as passive investors and have not attempted to influence management decisions. On the other hand, institutional investors have generally been quite eager to sell at a gain in the event of a takeover, because such sales increase the returns to the fund and enhance the competitive position of the fund compared to other funds. Moreover, in a struggle for control, shares held by institutional investors may be the critical swing votes and may effectively determine who will control the corporation. In addition, institutional investors have objected to management decisions to implement takeover defenses. As a result, some corporations have declined to adopt defenses such as the poison pill or have submitted proposed defenses to a stockholder vote.

  Caveat: It is usually possible for a corporation to adopt a poison pill on short notice in the event of an announced takeover attempt. Thus, the market may assume that all corporations are in fact protected by a poison pill.

b. The traditionally passive attitude of most funds may also be changing because of several other factors.

  • Changes to the SEC proxy regulations now permit institutional and other investors to communicate freely with each other with respect to corporate governance matters. Before 1992, communication among institutional investors was impeded by the worry that such efforts might be viewed as a proxy solicitation requiring filing with and approval by the SEC. In 1992, the SEC amended its proxy regulations to it make clear that institutional investors could freely communicate with each other without violating SEC regulations, so long as proxy appointments were not solicited.

  • Some institutional shareholdings have become so large that it may no longer be possible to sell without an adverse effect on the market price.

  • Legal scholars have suggested that institutional investors should consider increased activism on corporate governance matters.

  • With the increasing number of independent directors, institutional investors may be able to raise issues with individual directors without approaching management directly.

c. Pension funds appear to be more willing to participate in corporate governance. Public employee retirement systems such as the California system (CALPers) in particular have been leaders in seeking to increase the voice of institutional stockholders in decisions relating to corporate governance.

d. Institutional investors have used a variety of tactics to express their views.

- Many institutional investors (particularly charitable organizations) have submitted stockholder proposals for inclusion in proxy statements under SEC Rule 14a–8. Some of these proposals have been approved and others have received substantial percentages of the vote, thereby calling management's attention to the dissatisfaction of large stockholders. In some cases, a corporation may negotiate with these organizations before the proposal is disseminated in order to work out a mutually acceptable compromise that avoids the need for negative publicity.

- In several cases, institutional investors have announced their intention to withhold votes for some or all incumbent directors. These campaigns to withhold votes prompted the SEC to propose a rule (discussed above) that would have given large stockholders the power to nominate candidates for the board of directors in certain circumstances. The rule was ultimately withdrawn and does not appear likely to be adopted in the near future.

- Federal securities law provides that in the case of a private securities fraud class action, the largest stockholder should be presumed to be the best representative of the class and thus should be deemed to be the lead plaintiff authorized to direct the action including selecting counsel for the class. This provision was seldom invoked during the period before 2004, but it appears that institutional investors have shown some interest recently in assuming a leadership role in such actions. On the other hand, several legal actions were filed against mutual funds in 2004 alleging that they had neglected to submit claims in some cases even though they may have been entitled to participate in the recovery.

e. In 2003, it was discovered that several mutual fund groups had permitted favored investors to engage in a variety of abusive trading strategies that had the effect of skimming returns away from ordinary investors. As a result, the SEC adopted a series of reforms designed to ensure the independence of mutual fund boards of directors from the investment advisers who manage the funds day to day. In addition, the SEC has independently adopted rules requiring enhanced disclosure of how mutual funds vote their shares.

f. Many institutional investors rely on third parties such as Institutional Stockholder Services (ISS) to advise them about the corporate governance practices of the companies in which they invest and about how to vote their shares. This has raised the question whether these advisers may be in a position to dictate corporate governance policies and if so how they determine what position to take on the issues. In addition, such agencies issue "scores" for publicly traded companies in connection with their governance practices and advise companies about how to improve their scores. Some commentators have suggested that this dual role constitutes a serious conflict of interest and may give such agencies undue leverage.

REVIEW QUESTIONS

12.1. What is the Wall Street Option in publicly held corporations?

12.2. In a publicly held corporation, who selects the directors?

12.3. True or False: The major role of directors in the publicly held corporation is to establish general business policies for the corporation.

12.4. True or False: A major function of directors is to decide who is to run the business, that is to select the chief executive officer.

12.7. What role do institutional investors play in modern financial practice?

12.8. Do institutional investors usually support management or insurgents?

*

XIII

Securities Fraud & Insider Trading

This chapter deals generally with securities fraud. Although there are many forms of securities fraud, most cases involve either (1) trading by officers, directors, and other persons who have access to material non-public information about the corporation (referred to as insider trading), or (2) injuries to investors caused by reason of false or misleading information disseminated by the corporation.

Caveat: The term *insider* broadly includes directors, high level officers, and major stockholders, as well as the corporation itself. It also may include agents of the corporation such as lawyers, accountants and investment bankers who are privy to non-public information. Some federal statutes set forth precise definitions. For example, § 16 of the 1934 Act creates a corporate cause of action for short swing trading (buying and selling shares within short time intervals in order to capitalize on price movements), and applies it to directors, officers, and persons who own ten percent or more of the corporation's common shares. Other federal statutes apply a five percent test, while some provisions, such as Rule 10b–5, assume that anyone entrusted with non-public information is an insider.

A. STATE LAW REGULATING TRANSACTIONS IN SHARES

State law relating to trading in shares has been largely overshadowed by federal law. But the protection afforded by federal law to private plaintiffs has been scaled back significantly by a series of Supreme Court decisions dating from the 1970s and by several statutes enacted by Congress. As a result, state law has become more important in this regard in recent years.

1. Insider Trading

A director, officer or manager of a corporation may have material non-public information about corporate affairs that will likely affect the price of shares when it is disclosed. As a result, an insider may be tempted to purchase or sell shares (depending on the nature of the information) without publicly disclosing the information. Such trading is called insider trading.

a. State law generally permitted such trading in the absence of fraud on the assumption that the corporation itself was not harmed by insider trading. Moreover, in an anonymous public market, it was often difficult to determine precisely who took the other side of the trade in question. And, even if a particular outsider could be matched with the insider executing a trade, presumably the outsider had decided to enter into the transaction because he believed it was a desirable one in any event. He had simply made a poor decision. Hence, it seemed doubtful that he should be viewed as having been injured at all. In other words, if the insider does nothing to induce the outsider to trade, it is difficult to see how that transaction can constitute common law fraud by the insider. The leading case for this position is *Goodwin v. Agassiz*, 186 N.E. 659 (Mass. 1933).

b. If an affirmative misrepresentation was made by an insider, however, normal fraud principles dictate that the defrauded person should be able to rescind the transaction or sue for damages.

c. Where certain facts are of critical importance and are within the sole knowledge of the insider because of his official capacity, some courts found an affirmative duty on the part of the insider to disclose these special facts before entering into a transaction with an uninformed investor. This duty is called the "special facts rule." *Strong v. Repide*, 213 U.S. 419, 29 S.Ct. 521 (1909); *Taylor v. Wright*, 159 P.2d 980 (Cal.App.1945).

d. Kansas adopted a stricter rule of fiduciary duty designed to protect all outsiders in *Hotchkiss v. Fischer*, 16 P.2d 531 (Kan. 1932). However, the difference between cases involving the strict duty rule of *Hotchkiss* and those applying the special facts rule appeared to be one of degree.

e. This strict duty rule arose in cases involving closely held corporations and is apparently still the majority rule in such cases. *See Van Schaack Holdings, Ltd. v. Van Schaak*, 867 P.2d 892 (Colo. 1994).

f.   Another principle is set forth in *Diamond v. Oreamuno*, 248 N.E.2d 910 (N.Y. 1969), where the court permitted the corporation to recover losses avoided by insiders who became aware of negative information and sold their shares before the negative information was disclosed. The court reasoned that inside information was corporate property and insiders should not be permitted to profit from the use of that property even though the corporation was not itself injured thereby.

> *Caveat:*   This view has not been widely accepted. It has been expressly rejected by at least two courts. *Schien v. Chasen*, 313 So.2d 739 (Fla. 1975); *Freeman v. Decio*, 584 F.2d 186 (7th Cir. 1978) (Indiana law). Two federal district courts, however, have concluded that New Jersey probably would recognize the *Diamond* principle. *In re ORFA Securities Litigation*, 654 F.Supp. 1449 (D.N.J. 1987); *National Westminster Bancorp NJ v. Leone*, 702 F.Supp. 1132 (D.N.J. 1988).

2.   Other Settings

a.   State law may apply in cases where an insider competes with his corporation by buying or selling corporate shares when the corporation would have been financially benefited if it had entered into the same transactions directly. These cases are essentially corporate opportunity cases. Examples include: *Brophy v. Cities Service Co.*, 70 A.2d 5 (Del.Ch.1949) (purchase of shares when corporation was planning to make a repurchase); *Weissman v. Weissman*, 97 A.2d 870 (Pa. 1953) (purchase of creditor claims at a discount); *Manufacturers Trust Co. v. Becker*, 338 U.S. 304, 70 S.Ct. 127 (1949) (same, addressing treatment in bankruptcy); *People v. Floretino*, 456 N.Y.S.2d 638 (Crim.Ct. 1982) (criminal proceeding against bidder attorney who bought target shares ahead of client); *Perlman v. Feldmann*, 219 F.2d 173 (2d Cir. 1955) (sale of controlling shares at a premium to major customers when corporation was subject to price controls and could not raise prices).

b.   Under federal law only stockholders who actually buy or sell shares have standing to assert a claim for securities fraud against the offending corporation. But some state courts have held that stockholders who are misled and fail to buy or sell may sue as well. *Malone v. Brincat*, 722 A.2d 5 (Del. 1998); *Small v. Fritz Cos.*, 30 Cal.4th 167 (2003).

B. FEDERAL LAW AND RULE 10b–5

Rule 10b–5, promulgated by the SEC under § 10(b) of the Securities Exchange Act of 1934, is the source of most of the current principles relating to transactions in shares by insiders. The Rule states:

> It shall be unlawful for any person, directly or indirectly, by the use of any means or instrumentality of interstate commerce, or of the mails or of any facility of any national securities exchange, (a) To employ any device, scheme, or artifice to defraud, (b) To make any untrue statement of a material fact or to omit to state a material fact necessary in order to make the statements made, in light of the circumstances under which they were made, not misleading, or (c) To engage in any act, practice, or course of business which operates or would operate as a fraud or deceit upon any person, in connection with the purchase or sale of any security.

Rule 10b–5 is the broadest antifraud provision in the federal securities laws and is sometimes called a *catch-all* antifraud rule. It is common for the SEC, the DOJ, and private plaintiffs to add a claim based on Rule 10b–5 even though another provision of federal securities law is more on point.

1. Development of Rule 10b–5

Rule 10b–5 was originally promulgated because the express antifraud provisions of the federal securities laws applied only to sales of securities. But it is also quite possible for an insider to defraud an existing stockholder by purchasing the outsider's shares at a bargain price or by disseminating untrue bad news about the corporation before seeking to purchase the shares. Thus, the SEC promulgated Rule 10b–5 under its broad authority to adopt rules designed to prevent and remedy fraud, and to the extent possible, make a level playing field for transactions in shares. Prior to the mid–1970s courts generally interpreted Rule 10b–5 liberally in part because state law principles were seen as not providing adequate protection for stockholder interests. As a result, plaintiffs increasingly chose to file law suits in Federal courts under Rule 10b–5 rather than in state courts under state law. Beginning in 1975, however, the United States Supreme Court began to issue opinions that limited the scope of Rule 10b–5 and other provisions of federal securities law that had been interpreted as providing a general private cause of action for injured stockholders. When reading cases relating to Rule 10b–5 and related principles, it is important to consider the period in which the decision was issued. Nevertheless, Rule 10b–5 still is the single most important source of federal law in connection with trading in securities.

2. General Principles

Rule 10b–5 has the same force as a federal statute. Its violation may be made the basis of a criminal prosecution, an enforcement action brought by the SEC, or a private civil action by an injured stockholder. Although the Supreme Court has been reluctant since the mid–1970s to recognize implied private rights of action under the federal securities laws, it is clear that the private cause of action under Rule 10b–5 continues to exist. *See Herman & MacLean v. Huddleston,* 459 U.S. 375, 103 S.Ct. 683 (1983). The Court also recognizes a private cause of action under Rule 14a–9. *See J.I. Case v. Borak,* 377 U.S. 426, 432, 84 S.Ct. 1555 (1964).

a. Section 27 of the 1934 Act provides that all actions arising under that Act are subject to exclusive federal jurisdiction. Thus, state courts do not have jurisdiction to adjudicate Rule 10b–5 claims. While the doctrine of pendent jurisdiction permits the joinder of both state and federal claims arising from the same transaction in a Rule 10b–5 case, a Rule 10b–5 claim cannot be joined with a state cause of action in a state court.

> *Caveat:* In *Matsushita Electric Industrial Co., Ltd. v. Epstein,* 516 U.S. 367, 116 S.Ct. 873 (1996) the Supreme Court held that a state court settlement of all claims set forth in a class action might terminate pending federal claims based on the same facts. The Securities Litigation Uniform Standards Act of 1998 (SLUSA) provides, however, that state law *class* actions based on facts that might give rise to a claim under federal securities law are preempted by federal law. *Matsushita* may still have some force in non-class action cases.

b. There is worldwide service of process in Rule 10b–5 cases. There are also liberal venue provisions. State security for expenses statutes and other state procedural rules are not applicable in suits brought under federal law. Procedure in federal court is generally simpler than in state court and discovery rights are broader.

> *Caveat:* The Private Securities Litigation Reform Act of 1995 curtailed many of the advantages that had been available in federal court in connection with securities fraud cases.

c. Rule 10b–5 is applicable to fraud in connection with the purchase or sale of any security, including those issued by closely held corporations. *Landreth Timber Co. v. Landreth,* 471 U.S. 681, 105 S.Ct. 2297 (1985) (fraudulent sale of stock in connection with sale of a small business).

Caveat: The 1934 Act contains a slightly different definition of security from the 1933 Act. For example, short term notes (commercial paper) are not deemed to be securities under the 1934 Act are deemed to be securities under the 1933 Act.

d.   *Blue Chip Stamps v. Manor Drug Stores,* 421 U.S. 723, 95 S.Ct. 1917 (1975) holds that only purchasers or sellers of securities may sue under Rule 10b–5. This doctrine is based on the early decision of *Birnbaum v. Newport Steel Corp.,* 193 F.2d 461 (2d Cir. 1952) and is sometimes referred to as the *Birnbaum* rule.

e.   The plaintiff in a Rule 10b–5 action must allege and prove *scienter,* a term that is defined as a mental state embracing some level of intent to deceive, manipulate or defraud. Negligence is not sufficient. *Ernst & Ernst v. Hochfelder,* 425 U.S. 185, 96 S.Ct. 1375 (1976). *See also Aaron v. S.E.C.,* 446 U.S. 680, 100 S.Ct. 1945 (1980) (SEC enforcement action).

Caveat: Under Rule 10b–5, *scienter* is required even if the offense is based on the breach of an affirmative duty of the defendant. For example, *Hochfelder* involved a negligent audit by the defendant accountants. Under Rule 14a–9 (which addresses fraud in connection with proxy solicitations), *scienter* is not required to establish a violation. Courts generally have concluded that negligence will suffice given that the disclosures required in connection with a proxy solicitation are mandatory. In addition to Rule 10b–5, section 18 of the 1934 Act creates an express cause of action for any misstatement of material fact that appears in a document filed with the SEC. However, section 18 does not apply to discretionary statements such as those that may be included in a press release. In addition, section 18 also requires that a plaintiff establish reliance on the alleged misstatement.

Caveat: Many cases have involved allegations of aiding and abetting against accountants, lawyers, investment bankers, and other independent agents. In 1992, the Supreme Court ruled that there was no cause of action for aiding and abetting under the 1934 Act. *Central Bank of Denver N.A. v. First Interstate Bank of Denver N.A.,* 511 U.S. 164, 114 S.Ct. 1439 (1994). In 1995, Congress created a statutory cause of action for aiding and abetting as part of the Private Securities Litigation Reform Act, but limited its scope to actions brought by the SEC.

However, private plaintiffs are still free to argue that independent agents have liability because they participated directly in the fraud.

f. *Santa Fe Industries v. Green,* 430 U.S. 462, 97 S.Ct. 1292 (1977), involved a short form merger at an allegedly unfair price. The case sets forth the basic principle that Rule 10b–5 applies only to situations involving deception. Unfair transactions that are adequately disclosed cannot be attacked under Rule 10b–5.

g. The statute of limitations for Rule 10b–5 cases was set as one year after discovery or three years after the transaction in question in *Lampf, Pleva, Lipkind, Prupis & Pettigrow v. Gilbertson,* 501 U.S. 350, 111 S.Ct. 2773 (1991). Before this decision, lower federal courts had generally held that the applicable statute of limitations should be borrowed from state law. The Supreme Court ordered that the *Lampf* holding be applied retroactively. Congress then enacted a statute that sought to make this holding prospective only, but in *Plaut v. Spendthrift Farm, Inc.,* 514 U.S. 211, 115 S.Ct. 1447 (1995), the Court held that this statute was unconstitutional to the extent it sought to revive cases that had been finally dismissed pursuant to the *Lampf* holding. In 2002, section 804 of the Sarbanes–Oxley Act extended the statute of limitations for private securities fraud claims to the earlier of two years after discovery of the facts constituting the violation or five years after the violation. This new statute of limitations applies to proceedings commenced after July 30, 2002.

h. Claims may be brought under Rule 10b–5 even though under the same factual situation a claim could also be brought under the more specific provisions of the Securities Act of 1933 or the Securities Exchange Act of 1934. *Herman & MacLean v. Huddleston,* 459 U.S. 375, 103 S.Ct. 683 (1983).

i. Rule 10b–5 proscribes not only affirmative misrepresentations and half-truths, but also a failure to disclose material facts that are necessary in order to make the statements made, in light of the circumstances under which they were made, not misleading. Rule 10b–5 does not itself impose a duty to disclose. Rather it affords a federal remedy in connection with misrepresentations and omissions that are otherwise in violation of a duty to speak the truth.

• Courts agree that there is a clear duty to refrain from making affirmative misrepresentations. Thus, if a corporation chooses to issue a press release, it must tell the whole truth. For example, the financial analyst who touts a stock without disclosing that he has a financial interest in selling that stock violates Rule 10b–5. *Zweig v. Hearst Corp.,* 594 F.2d 1261 (9th Cir. 1979).

- A duty to disclose may arise as a result of a requirement to file a public document.

- A duty to disclose (or refrain from trading) may arise if a corporation or its agent possesses material non-public information about the corporation's business. The theory is that the corporation and its agents have a general fiduciary duty to use such information only for the benefit of all stockholders.

- Disclosure is required if undisclosed information renders previous public statements by the corporation misleading or if rumors can be traced to a source within the issuer. *In re Time Warner, Inc. Securities Litigation,* 9 F.3d 259 (2d Cir. 1993).

    Caveat: No fiduciary duty is owed to creditors. Thus, bondholders have no standing to sue under Rule 10b–5 for an omission to state a material fact, although they presumably do have standing in connection with an affirmative misrepresentation.

j. Rule 10b–5 applies only if there is failure to disclose a *material* fact. The test of what is material is whether a reasonable person would regard the information as important in deciding how to act. *TSC Industries v. Northway, Inc.,* 426 U.S. 438, 96 S.Ct. 2126 (1976). Disclosure of pending merger negotiations has been a particularly troublesome issue. Several courts held that disclosure was required only when an agreement in principle had been reached and that prior to that time a general denial was not misleading. *Greenfield v. Heublein, Inc.,* 742 F.2d 751 (3d Cir. 1984). The Supreme Court rejected this bright line test. *Basic Inc. v. Levinson,* 485 U.S. 224, 108 S.Ct. 978 (1988). Although the court agreed that it may sometimes serve the interests of stockholders for the company to deny that it is in negotiation in order to complete the deal on favorable terms, the Court nonetheless held that the general rule as stated in TSC applies. The practical effect may be to cause issuers to adopt a no comment policy with respect to all inquiries about negotiations.

k. In a case of failure to disclose a material fact, proof of reliance on the omission may be inferred and need not be separately established.

Affiliated Ute Citizens v. United States, 406 U.S. 128, 92 S.Ct. 1456 (1972). In the case of a misrepresentation relating to a publicly traded security, a purchaser or seller may be able to recover without establishing reliance on the misrepresentation under the principle of *Basic v. Levinson.* The theory is that investors rely on the efficiency of the securities markets in establishing an appropriate price for the shares. This principle is generally referred to as the fraud on the market theory. In *Basic,* the Court adopted this theory to the extent of creating a rebuttable presumption of reliance, thereby placing the burden of showing a lack of reliance upon the defendants.

l. The SEC has adopted safe harbor rules designed to permit corporations and insiders to engage in trading without fear of running afoul of Rule 10b–5. For example, it might be argued that a corporation's repurchase of its own shares is a per se violation because it indicates that the corporation likely has information indicating that the price should be higher. Thus, the SEC adopted Rule 10b–18 providing guidelines for such transactions.

3. Securities Fraud Class Actions

A corporation may violate Rule 10b–5 if it makes a false statement in a filing, a press release, or a conference call. Although *Blue Chip Stamps* requires that a *plaintiff* be a purchaser or seller of shares, there is no similar requirement for *defendants.* A person may violate Rule 10b–5 even though he neither purchases nor sells a security. For example, a publicly traded corporation that issues a press release knows that the market will react. By definition, such a press release is *in connection with* the purchase of sale of securities. It has long been clear that stockholders who buy or sell in actual reliance on a false press release may recover damages from the corporation. *See Mitchell v. Texas Gulf Sulphur Co.,* 446 F.2d 90 891 (10th Cir. 1971). A class action on behalf of all who bought or sold during the fraud period under FRCP 23 is also possible. Indeed, the official commentary to FRCP 23 notes that the rule may be particularly useful for such cases. The problem is that questions of individual reliance may make a class action impractical. This issue was avoided by *Affiliated Ute Citizens v. United States,* 406 U.S. 128, 92 S.Ct. 1456 (1972). As for cases based on affirmative misrepresentations, class actions became practical with the 1988 decision by the United States Supreme Court in *Basic v. Levinson,* 485 U.S. 224, 108 S.Ct. 978 (1988) (upholding the fraud on the market theory presuming reliance on the integrity of market prices). *See also Blackie v. Barrack,* 524 F.2d 891 (9th Cir. 1975).

a. Federal securities law requires corporations registered under § 12 of the 1934 Act periodically to file (and disseminate publicly) information about their business and finances. Prior to 1979, the SEC strongly discouraged the inclusion in such reports of *forward-looking information*, such as projections of future performance even though such information can be quite important to investors. In 1979, the SEC reversed its policy and adopted safe harbor rules for forward-looking information under both the 1933 Act (Rule 175) and the 1934 Act (Rule 3b–6). Under these safe harbor rules, a forward looking statement in a filed document is false and misleading only if it is made or reaffirmed without a reasonable basis or disclosed other than in good faith.

b. Nevertheless, many companies—particularly growth companies—became the target of class actions if they made optimistic projections that failed to materialize. Defendants complained that plaintiff law firms often filed suit in order to extort settlements. Defendants also claimed that these law firms kept a stable of plaintiffs in whose name suit might be filed whenever a significant change in the price of a stock indicated that there may have been false information at work in the market. The courts also generally permitted the plaintiff who was first to file to be the lead counsel, prompting races to the courthouse in many cases. The filing of a suit was followed immediately by a demand for extensive discovery that many defendants saw as a fishing expedition to find a more solid basis for the action.

c. Federal courts faced with proliferating securities fraud class actions attempted to discourage them in several ways. They tightened the requirement for pleading by insisting that fraud be pleaded with particularity (as required by FRCP 9) and that allegations give rise to a strong inference that the statements were made with scienter (fraudulent intent). They adopted the so-called *bespeaks caution doctrine* that precludes reliance on forward-looking statements if the document contains specific warnings that the investment is risky and that projections might not be fulfilled. *See In re Donald J. Trump Casino Securities Litigation–Taj Mahal Litigation*, 7 F.3d 357 (3d Cir. 1993).

d. In 1995 Congress enacted the Private Securities Litigation Reform Act of 1995 (PSLRA) to deal with the perceived evil of class action law suits brought against publicly held corporations for false or misleading statements or projections. This legislation was vetoed by President

Clinton but the veto was overridden. PSLRA tightened the requirements for class action securities litigation and created several novel or experimental litigation devices.

- Plaintiffs must file a sworn statement that they reviewed and authorized the filing and did not purchase securities at the direction of counsel or to qualify to act as plaintiff. A lead plaintiff may not serve as such more than three times in the previous five years. The lead plaintiff's compensation is also limited to a proportionate share of any recovery.

- Courts are directed to select the lead plaintiff and lead counsel based on a presumption that the plaintiff with the largest financial stake should be lead plaintiff.

- A statutory safe harbor for projections is created. A defendant is not liable for misrepresentations or omissions if a statement is (1) identified as a forward looking statement and (2) is accompanied by meaningful cautionary statements identifying factors that might cause results to differ materially from those protected in the statement. Alternatively, a defendant is protected by the statutory safe harbor unless the plaintiff can show that the person made the statement with actual knowledge that it was false or misleading.

- Courts must stay all discovery pending the disposition of a motion to dismiss. It is unlawful for any defendant to destroy relevant evidence during the stay.

- To avoid the naming of "deep pockets" as defendants (even though their involvement may be slight), PSLRA provides for proportionate liability for parties who are found not to have committed knowing violations.

- Notice of proposed settlements must be given to all members of the class involved.

- PSLRA creates a presumption that sanctions should be imposed on plaintiff counsel for violations of FRCP 11. A similar presumption is not imposed on defendants' counsel.

- PSLRA mandates a strict standard that the facts must be pleaded with particularity and establish a strong inference that the misstatements were made with *scienter*.

- Independent public auditors must report illegal conduct that they discover to the appropriate level of management, the board of directors, or the SEC. While auditors have no personal liability to third persons for failing to comply, the SEC may impose civil penalties for failing to comply with these requirements.

- PSLRA contains a formula for limiting damages to the loss attributable to the fraud by determining the post-fraud price on the basis of average prices for 90 days following the corrective disclosure.

- PSLRA also provides that the SEC (but not private plaintiffs) may sue aiders and abettors, thus partially overruling *Central Bank.*

  Caveat: The legislative history states that safe harbor protection is available even though (a) all important factors have not been listed or (b) the factor that actually caused the failure to achieve the predicted results was not listed. The inter-relationship between the two branches of the safe harbor test raises the possibility that this safe harbor creates a license to lie. The statutory safe harbor is not available for several listed types of securities.

e. Although fewer securities fraud class actions were filed immediately after enactment of PSLRA, the number of actions has since increased. However, PSLRA seems to have had little lasting effect in terms of discouraging such actions.

f. In response to PSLRA, some securities fraud class actions were filed in state court in an effort to avoid the limitations of PSLRA. As a result, Congress enacted the Securities Fraud Litigation Uniform Standards Act of 1998 (SLUSA) which preempts all state law securities fraud class actions based on failure of disclosure. SLUSA applies to state law actions based on the same facts and involving 50 or more plaintiffs whether or not the action (or actions) are formally styled as a class action (or are consolidated into a single action). SLUSA permits the defendant in a covered state law action to remove the action to federal court in order to have it dismissed. SLUSA contains an exception for state law actions— the so-called Delaware carve out—involving questions of internal affairs such as duty of care and duty of loyalty issues. Although such actions are almost always styled as derivative actions in which the corporation itself is the single nominal plaintiff, a derivative action may involve significant disclosure issues particularly if a stockholder vote is involved.

Caveat: Several important states have ruled that the fraud on the market theory does not apply for state law purposes. *Mirkin v. Wasserman*, 5 Cal. 4th 1082 (1993). In addition, the Delaware Supreme Court shortly after passage of SLUSA upheld a stockholder's derivative suit grounded solely on failure to disclose material facts to existing stockholders. *Malone v. Brincat*, 722 A.2d 5 (Del. 1998).

4. Mismanagement

Rule 10b–5 is potentially applicable when a corporation issues or acquires its own shares or the shares of another company because the phrase *purchase or sale* is broad enough to cover all such transactions. Also, if shares are issued or acquired by a corporation as a result of deception or a failure of someone (such as a director or officer or agent) to disclose material facts to the corporation, the corporation may have a claim under Rule 10b–5, and this claim may be asserted derivatively by a minority stockholder. *Drachman v. Harvey*, 453 F.2d 722 (2d Cir. 1971).

Example: Stock options granted to officers who knew of a major favorable development may be canceled if the recipients do not advise the members of the option committee of the development. *SEC v. Texas Gulf Sulphur Co.*, 401 F.2d 833 (2d Cir.1968).

a. A Rule 10b–5 violation also occurs if the corporation is fraudulently induced to issue shares for inadequate compensation even though such conduct also constitutes a violation of state-created fiduciary duties.

b. The potential use of Rule 10b–5 in connection with corporate level transactions is largely limited to mergers and other fundamental transactions because it is in such transactions that the corporation in effect purchases or sells shares (whether its own or those of another corporation). Although it appeared that the use of Rule 10b–5 in such settings was precluded by the Supreme Court's holding in *Santa Fe Industries, Inc. v. Green*, 430 U.S. 462, 97 S.Ct. 1292 (1977) (short form merger in which plaintiff had no material use for the withheld information), a few such cases have since arisen. *See Goldberg v. Meridor*, 567 F.2d 209 (2d Cir. 1977). The dearth of such cases is attributable to several factors. First, such cases usually involve a proxy solicitation, triggering Rule 14a–9. They may also raise questions about whether the plaintiff has a material use for the undisclosed information. *See Virginia Bankshares, Inc. v.*

Sandberg, 501 U.S. 1083, 111 S.Ct. 2749 (1991). Second, state law has become much more responsive to such cases. *See Weinberger v. UOP,* Inc., 457 A.2d 701 (Del. 1983). In addition, if the case involves the issuance of securities by the defendant corporation, the 1933 Act may apply.

> *Caveat:* The Supreme Court has suggested in recent cases that it may take a relatively liberal view of when a fraud may be said to be *in connection with* a purchase or sale of stock. *United States v. O'Hagan,* 521 U.S. 642, 117 S.Ct. 2199 (1997); *Wharf (Holdings) Ltd.* v. *United Int'l Holdings, Inc.,* 532 U.S. 588, 121 S.Ct. 1776 (2001); *SEC v. Zandford,* 535 U.S. 813, 122 S.Ct. 1899 (2002).

5. Other Applications

Rule 10b–5 has many applications outside the context of corporation law. For example, it provides a remedy for individual investors in connection with the mismanagement of an investment account. It may also apply to fraud in connection with the sale of a business where the sale is accomplished by a transfer of stock.

C. INSIDER TRADING

A director, officer, agent, or major stockholder of a corporation may have material non-public knowledge about corporate affairs that is likely to affect the price of the shares when it is disclosed. As a result, such an insider may be tempted to buy or sell shares, depending on the nature of the information, without first disclosing the information. Such trading is called *insider trading*. Rule 10b–5 is applicable to such trading by individuals, and constitutes a broad prohibition against trading on the basis of inside information by anyone who receives the information from the issuer in connection with a relationship to the issuer that gives rise to a duty not to use the information for personal gain. Accountants, lawyers, investment bankers, and other constructive insiders all may become subject to Rule 10b–5.

1. Early Cases—Disclose or Abstain

The basic principle that trading on inside information violates Rule 10b–5 was first established in *Cady, Roberts & Co.,* 40 S.E.C. 907 (1961), and *SEC v. Texas Gulf Sulphur Co.,* 401 F.2d 833 (2d Cir. 1968).

    a.   Cady Roberts was an SEC enforcement proceeding arising from a broker's sales of stock on the basis of non-public information that a corporation planned to cut its dividend. The information was obtained from a partner who sat on the board of directors of the issuing corporation. *Cady, Roberts* seems to take the absolute position that trading while in possession of non-public information regardless of the source of the information or the trader's relationship to the source is a violation.

b.   *Texas Gulf Sulphur* was an appeal from an SEC enforcement proceeding arising from purchases by directors, officers, and employees of TGS on non-public information that TGS had discovered an unusually rich deposit of ore in Ontario. In addition, the corporation itself issued a false press release essentially denying the rumors about the ore strike. *TGS* holds that officers, directors, and employees of an issuer who know of a material favorable development as a result of their position with the corporation violate rule 10b–5 if they purchase shares or options before the information is released. *TGS* also holds that insiders must wait until the information has been reasonably disseminated to the investing public through wire services and the like before they may trade and suggests that *tippees* (persons who obtain material information before it is publicly released) have an obligation not to trade on that information.

> *Caveat:*   In these early cases, the SEC appeared to have taken the position that all trading on the basis of material non-public information constituted insider trading. This gave rise to the belief that an insider must *disclose or abstain* from trading, even though in many instances the individual was in no position to disclose. Later cases have made it clear that there are many situations in which a person may trade on material non-public information if the information was not improperly obtained. Nevertheless, the phrase *disclose or abstain* continues to be widely used. Several aspects of these holdings have been affected by later caselaw.

c.   In *Shapiro v. Merrill Lynch, Pierce, Fenner & Smith, Inc.*, 495 F.2d 228 (2d Cir. 1974), a brokerage firm obtained information about a corporation in connection with a contemplated debt financing before the information was publicly available. The brokerage firm violated Rule 10b–5, because it traded before the information was released. To avoid violations of Rule 10b–5 in this situation, brokerage firms try to maintain separation (a *Chinese Wall*) between their investment banking (underwriting) operations and their brokerage (sales) operations. The failure to maintain such separation was also central to many of the abuses that arose in connection with IPOs in the late 1990s.

2. Later Cases—The Misappropriation Theory

In the late 1970s, the Justice Department (largely under the direction of Rudolph Giuliani who was at the time the United States Attorney for the Southern District of New York) began a vigorous campaign to prosecute insider trading cases as crimes. These cases raised difficult issues with the definition of what constitutes insider trading and with the scope of federal securities law generally.

a. *Chiarella v. United States*, 445 U.S. 222, 100 S.Ct. 1108 (1980), was the first insider trading case to reach the Supreme Court. It involved the criminal conviction of a low level employee of a legal printing firm who regularly handled disclosure documents in connection with planned tender offers and who bought stock in the target companies before announcement of the offers. The Supreme Court reversed the conviction because the defendant owed no duty to the target or its stockholders (other than a general duty to refrain from affirmative misrepresentations). The court reasoned that the bidder was free to purchase shares before announcement of the offer and that therefore the printer and its employees violated no duty to the sellers of the shares, because the printer had been retained by the bidder. Chief Justice Burger dissented, arguing that the employee had a duty to his employer not to use information entrusted to the printer for business use only and thus should be held liable for having misappropriated the information for personal gain.

b. Following *Chiarella*, the SEC adopted Rule 14e–3 making it unlawful for any person who obtains advance information about a tender offer to use that information in connection with a securities transaction. This rule (together with the misappropriation theory advocated by Chief Justice Burger) was ultimately upheld in *United States v. O'Hagan*, 521 U.S. 642, 117 S.Ct. 2199 (1997), as a reasonable antifraud rule even though it might capture some instances of insider trading not involving a breach of fiduciary duty.

c. In *Dirks v. S.E.C.*, 463 U.S. 646, 103 S.Ct. 3255 (1983), the Supreme Court held that a tippee violates Rule 10b–5 only if the tipper breaches a fiduciary duty in disclosing the information to the tippee and the tippee is aware of the breach. Such a breach may be established for this purpose by showing that the insider-tipper disclosed the information for the purpose of obtaining an improper benefit. The tipper is also liable for unlawful insider trading by the tippee. In Dirks, the tipper was an employee of an insurance company that had fraudulently overstated its assets, and the employee was apparently motivated only by a desire to expose the fraud and not by the prospect of any monetary gain.

> *Example:* While attending a track meet, the coach of the University of Oklahoma football team overhears a corporate officer describing a corporate matter that involves material non-public information. The football coach subsequently trades profitably on the basis of this information. The football coach does not violate Rule 10b–5 even though it later turns out that the officer had intended to confer a benefit on the coach by letting the information appear to have been disclosed inadvertently. *SEC v. Switzer*, 590 F.Supp. 756 (W.D.Okl.1984).

> *Caveat:* Under Rule 14e–3, an eavesdropper may be liable for trading on inside information with respect to a tender offer.

> *Caveat:* Federal securities law requires many entities and individuals (such as broker-dealers and investment advisers) to register with the SEC, which in turn subjects the registrant to a variety of rules aimed at the securities industry. Thus, in some cases the applicability of federal securities law depends on whether one's registered or required to register. *Dirks v. S.E.C.* was such a case: Dirks himself was a registered investment adviser and the SEC brought its case as a disciplinary action. But it does not appear that Dirk's status as a registered investment adviser was relevant to the holding of the Supreme Court.

d. *Carpenter v. United States*, 484 U.S. 19, 108 S.Ct. 316 (1987) involved a criminal prosecution of Foster Winans, a Wall Street Journal writer who told friends that certain corporations would be favorably commented on in his *Heard on the Street* column. His friends traded on the information, and Winans shared in the profits. Winans was convicted on two theories: (1) insider trading under the misappropriation theory, and (2) mail and wire fraud. The Supreme Court split four to four on the insider trading theory, but agreed unanimously on the mail and wire fraud theory.

e. *United States v. Chestman*, 947 F.2d 551 (2d Cir. 1991), holds that disclosure of inside information by one family member to another, who in turn discloses the information to a broker, does not violate Rule 10b–5 because a mere family relationship does not give rise to a fiduciary duty.

f. In *United States v. O'Hagan*, 521 U.S. 642, 117 S.Ct. 2199 (1997), the Supreme Court upheld the misappropriation theory (as well as Rule 14e–3) in a case involving a lawyer who gave information about a planned tender offer to a client for another company. But consistent with *Dirks*, the court based its holding on a duty not to use business information for personal profit.

3. Insider Trading Legislation and Rules

a. In 1984, Congress enacted the Insider Trading Sanctions Act (ITSA) which provides that the SEC may recover the profit made (or loss avoided) from insider trading plus an additional fine equal to three times that amount. In 1988, Congress enacted the Insider Trading and Securities Fraud Enforcement Act (ITSFEA) extending ITSA in a variety of ways. By the enactment of ITSA and ITSFEA, Congress has expressly endorsed the basic policy of enforcing sanctions against insider trading under Rule 10b–5.

b. ITSA and ITSFEA address a fundamental problem with respect to the remedies for insider trading. If the insider is liable only for the amount of the gain made or loss avoided, there is little reason not to trade on inside information. If one is caught one simply gives back the gain. Thus, simple disgorgement of ill-gotten gains is not a significant deterrent. On the other hand, if an insider is liable for the losses of all who traded at or about the same time, the damages imposed would often far exceed the actual harm. ITSFEA imposes for individuals a minimum fine of $100,000 and five years imprisonment and a maximum fine of up to $1,000,000 and 10 years imprisonment. For defendants other than natural persons fines may range up to $2,500,000. ITSFEA also adds a bounty provision that awards informants in amounts not to exceed 10 percent of the penalties recovered as a result of the informant's efforts.

c. Under § 20A of the 1934 Act (added by ITSFEA) a person violating the insider trading prohibitions is liable to contemporaneous traders of the security even though there may be no privity between the insider and the person trading. Liability under § 20A is limited to the total profit gained or loss avoided by the person violating the insider trading prohibitions, and is further reduced by any disgorgement of profits ordered by a court at the instance of the SEC.

d. Under ITSFEA the employer of an individual who engages in insider trading may also be liable as a controlling person. In order to recover from a controlling person, the SEC must establish either that the controlling person knew or recklessly disregarded the fact that such controlled person was likely to violate the Act or (for firms in the securities industry) knowingly or recklessly failed to establish, maintain or enforce policies or procedures designed to prevent insider trading.

e. The SEC has taken the position that trading while in mere possession of inside information may constitute insider trading, but the courts have ruled that a violation requires actual use of the information. *SEC v. Adler*, 137 F.3d 1325 (11th Cir. 1998). Thus, an insider who plans in advance to sell shares periodically pursuant to a plan may proceed with the plan despite coming into possession of new (adverse) information. In 2000, the SEC adopted a safe harbor rule (Rule 10b–5–1) providing guidelines for such plans.

4. Criminal Prosecution and Civil Enforcement Actions

The Federal Government generally views insider trading as a serious offense that should be prosecuted vigorously, both civilly and criminally. This is true despite extensive academic commentary that suggests that insider trading in many instances harms no one and may be beneficial in some cases. The SEC has pursued individuals making relatively small profits on the basis of inside information.

a. Although the SEC has the authority to enforce the securities laws by means of civil action for an injunction or fine (an *enforcement action*), the Department of Justice (DOJ) has jurisdiction over criminal prosecution. It is quite common, especially in high profile cases, for both agencies to act. Moreover, many offenses may give rise to a private right of action and may also violate state law. Thus, a defendant may be subject to multiple sanctions for any given violation.

b. A violation of federal securities law must be *willful* in order to be prosecuted criminally. But given that a violation of Rule 10b–5 involves *scienter*, virtually every violation of Rule 10b–5 is also a crime.

c. The primary goal of many SEC enforcement actions is to impose an injunction on the defendant prohibiting future violations of the securities laws. Although an injunction that merely requires compliance with the law may seem to be a rather mild sanction, it has the effect of criminalizing any future violation and affording a summary remedy in the form of civil contempt.

D. SECTION 16 OF THE SECURITIES EXCHANGE ACT

Section 16 of the 1934 Act addresses trading by directors, officers, and ten percent stockholders of SEC registered companies. Section 16(a) requires reporting of all transactions in issuer shares by such persons and prohibits their engaging in any short sale of such shares. Section 16(b) provides that the gain (or loss avoided) from a purchase and sale (or sale and purchase) of such shares within a six month period may be recovered by the issuer.

1. General Principles

a. Section 16(a) requires all persons subject to Section 16 to file reports with the SEC. The first report must be filed within ten days of the date one becomes subject to the requirement and must describe the person's initial ownership of the issuer's shares. Subsequent reports must be filed within two days of any purchase or sale thereafter. The SEC publishes this information so that it is possible to identify violations from the public record. Registered companies are required to disclose failures to comply with § 16(a). In 1991 and 1996, the SEC adopted rules identifying which officers are subject to § 16(a). Officers covered by § 16 include officers referred to in the corporation's 10K and officers designated by the corporation as having significant policy making roles. Effectively these regulations determine the scope of § 16(b) as well as § 16(a) because persons exempt from the reporting requirements of § 16(a) are also exempt from § 16(b).

b. Section 16(b) is applicable only to directors, officers, and ten percent stockholders of companies registered under § 12 of the Securities Exchange Act. In contrast, Rule 10b–5 covers all persons and all companies. Section 16(b) is a bright line rule that creates automatic liability. It is unnecessary to show actual use of inside information. A sale for entirely justifiable reasons (such as to cover unexpected medical expenses) triggers § 16(b) if there has been any offsetting purchase within the previous six months or there is a subsequent purchase within the following six months. In contrast, Rule 10b–5 requires proof of *scienter*. A recovery under § 16(b) is payable only to the corporation. In contrast, Rule 10b–5 authorizes private damage recovery in many situations by buyers or sellers.

c. Attribution rules apply to § 16(b) so that transactions in the name of spouses, relatives, or nominees may be attributed to an officer, director, or ten percent stockholder. In *Blau v. Lehman,* 368 U.S. 403, 82 S.Ct. 451

(1962), a partner in Lehman Brothers was a director of the issuer. Unknown to him, Lehman Brothers engaged in purchases and sales of the issuer's stock (but never became a ten per cent holder). The Court held that the partnership might be considered a director only if the partnership deputized the partner to represent the partnership on the issuer's board of directors. *See also Feder v. Martin Marietta Corp.*, 406 F.2d 260 (2d Cir. 1969).

d. Section 16(b) is applicable to offsetting paired purchases and sales (or sales and purchases) of an equity security of the issuer within any six-month period. But a sale made six months plus one day after the purchase does not trigger section 16(b). Section 16(b) differs from Rule 10b–5 in that Rule 10b–5 may be violated by a single transaction or a single sale without any off-setting requirements.

> *Example:* A purchase on January 2 will be matched with an offsetting sale made at any time from six months before to six months after January 2. All profits from such a pairing are recoverable by the corporation. A sale made on the following May 1 will be matched with a January purchase even though the shares sold on May 1 had been owned for five years by the seller.

e. The words *purchase* and *sale* are construed broadly. A transaction is considered to be a purchase or a sale for purposes of § 16(b) if it is of a kind that can lend itself to the abuse of short swing trading. Under some circumstances a sale may occur as a result of a gift, redemption, conversion or exchange pursuant to a merger. In 1991, the SEC adopted regulations addressing derivative securities under § 16(b). The acquisition of a warrant to acquire a security may be treated as a purchase of the underlying security. The purchase of a derivative security, such as a call or put, may also be the purchase or sale of the underlying security. Section 16(a) does not prohibit a *covered* short sale—also called a *short sale against the box*—as a way of *hedging* against the decline in price of issuer stock. The SEC has authority to exempt classes of transactions from § 16(b). It has exercised this authority in a number of circumstances. The most important is rule 16b–3, relating to stock option plans, stock purchase plans, and compensation plans of various types that are based on stock prices.

f. A purchase and sale matched under § 16(b) must generally be of the same class of stock. But if preferred is convertible into common and is trading at or close to the conversion price, matching may be permitted because the two securities then are essentially trading as economic equivalents.

> *Caveat:* In *Gund v. First Florida Banks*, 726 F.2d 682 (11th Cir. 1984), the court matched sales of convertible debentures with purchases of common stock even though the two were not trading as market equivalents. The court computed profits by comparing the actual purchase price of the common stock with the highest price the common attained within six months before or after the debentures were sold.

g. Purchases and sales are matched so as to squeeze out all possible profit by matching the highest sale price with the lowest purchase price, the next highest sale price with the next lowest purchase price, and so forth.

> *Example:* A director buys 100 shares for $60 per share ($6,000) on January 10 and sells them for $50 per share ($5,000) on January 19. On April 5, the same director buys 100 shares for $10 ($1,000). All purchases and sales have taken place within a six-month period. Although most people would conclude that the director has lost $1000, under § 16(b) the highest sale price of $5,000 is matched with the lowest purchase price of $1,000 to produce a profit of $4,000. *Gratz v. Claughton*, 187 F.2d 46 (2d Cir. 1951).

h. Even though profits are recoverable by the corporation, corporations may be reluctant to enforce § 16(b) against its own directors, officers, and substantial stockholders. However, § 16(b) expressly recognizes that enforcement by a derivative action brought by a single stockholder is permissible. Like Rule 10b–5, the jurisdiction of § 16(b) is exclusively federal.

2. Application of Section 16(b) in Takeover Situations

During the 1970s, the United States Supreme Court struggled with the application of § 16(b) to takeover situations where an unsuccessful bidder acquires more than ten percent of the target's shares and then sells that interest (or has it merged out) within six months thereafter.

a. *Reliance Elec. Co. v. Emerson Elec. Co.*, 404 U.S. 418, 92 S.Ct. 596 (1972), holds that a 13.2 per cent stockholder could dispose of its holdings by first selling just over 3.2 per cent of the target's shares subject to § 16(b) and then disposing of the remainder free of § 16(b) requirements because it was no longer a ten percent stockholder.

b. *Kern County Land Co. v. Occidental Petroleum Corp.*, 411 U.S. 582, 93 S.Ct. 1736 (1973) holds that a forced sale pursuant to a merger is not covered by § 16(b).

c. *Foremost–McKesson, Inc. v. Provident Securities Co.*, 423 U.S. 232, 96 S.Ct. 508 (1976), holds that the purchase by which a bidder exceeds the ten percent threshold is not a § 16(b) purchase. The rationale is that a ten percent stockholder is covered by § 16(b) because a ten percent stockholder is presumed to have access to inside information. Thus, a purchase by which one *becomes* a ten percent stockholder is presumed to be made without the benefit of inside information.

3. Section 16(b) in Perspective

People do not knowingly violate § 16(b). The penalties are simply too great and the chance of discovery almost certain. Most violations appear to be a result of mistake or ignorance rather than actual misuse of inside information.

a. Most inadvertent violations probably are a result of a failure to keep track of precisely when the six month period ends. Other causes of inadvertent violations include a failure to appreciate how broadly the words "purchase and sale" are construed in the case of unusual transactions, uncertainty as to whether a specific person is covered by § 16(b), and the failure to recognize that attribution rules may apply. For example, it is not clear whether a director who resigns from a board and then immediately sells his shares should be viewed as within § 16(b).

b. Despite its shortcomings, § 16(b) has effectively eliminated the evil of in-and-out trading that existed prior to 1934. In the 1990s, proposals have been made to repeal this section because its application is erratic and insider trading is now more broadly delineated and policed under Rule 10b–5.

c. Reports under § 16(a) are often published in the financial press and have been used by some to attempt to devise trading strategies on the theory that reported insider trades contain implicit information about company prospects. Generally, these strategies have not led to gains.

REVIEW QUESTIONS

13.1. What is meant by insider trading?

13.2. Are the rules relating to insider trading based on state or federal law?

13.3. Should not every transaction by an insider that is based on personal use of non-public information be subject to attack on the theory that it involves misuse of corporate assets?

13.4. True or False: Rule 10b–5 is applicable only to publicly held corporations that are subject to registration under section 12 of the Securities Exchange Act of 1934?

13.5. True or False: A Colorado corporation has three stockholders, all of whom reside in Denver. Its business is located in Denver and all of its sales are made to Denver residents. The majority stockholder defrauds minority stockholders by inducing them to sell shares on the basis of false representations. This transaction involves only Colorado law and not rule 10b–5.

13.6. What kinds of transactions are subject to rule 10b–5?

13.7. What limiting factors have been applied to rule 10b–5?

13.8. How does section 16(b) of the Securities Exchange Act differ from rule 10b–5?

13.9. How are profits to be determined in a section 16(b) case?

13.10. Dynamic, Inc. is a successful computer component manufacturer whose excellent engineering staff is developing a seemingly matchless production technique. Partially because of its engineering expertise, Dynamic, Inc.'s shares, which are registered under section 12 of the Securities Exchange Act of 1934 and actively traded over-the-counter, sell at about $180 per share. Ian Sider, director and vice president of Dynamic, Inc., learns at a board of directors' meeting that the cream of the engineering staff of Dynamic, Inc. is threatening to leave and establish their own computer operation. Rather than wait to see if the threat materializes, Sider calls his broker and directs the sale of his 10,000 shares of Dynamic, Inc. The shares are sold for $170 per share. One week later the disgruntled engineering faction publicly announces its intention to leave. The shares of Dynamic, Inc. drop to $100 per share. Ben Taken, a new stockholder of Dynamic, Inc., who purchased one day prior to the public announcement for $175 per share, consults you as to possible recourse against Sider. What is your advice?

13.11. Maggie M. is a paralegal with the law firm of Jones and Smith, a firm with a substantial corporate practice. She is asked to work on certain documents from which she infers that Apex Corporation is to announce the successful settlement of a major lawsuit. Maggie M. tells her boyfriend about what she has learned and together they purchase calls on Apex Corporation stock. Has Maggie M. violated Federal law? Has her boyfriend?

13.12. In the situation described in question 13.11, would it make any difference if the information Maggie M. obtained related to a takeover bid by a client of Jones and Smith and Maggie M. bought stock in the target corporation?

13.13. Peter Jones is a vice president of Apex Corporation. His college roommate, John Smith, is a stock broker and old personal friend. Peter Jones tells Smith of the successful settlement of the law suit; Jones then purchases calls on Apex Corporation Stock. Has either Peter Jones or John Smith violated Federal law?

13.14. Who were the principal proponents of the PSLRA?

13.15. What were the principal criticisms of securities class action litigation that gave rise to the PSLRA?

13.16. What are the pleading requirements for claims of fraud under the PSLRA and the Federal Rules of Civil Procedure?

13.17. What is a lead plaintiff and what role does he play in class action litigation?

13.18. What sanctions are imposed under the PSLRA for filing a class action without reasonable cause?

13.19. What responsibilities are placed upon independent public accountants by the PSLRA?

*

XIV

Sales of Control & Tender Offers

This chapter addresses the variety of ways by which control of a corporation may be transferred from one party to another, including sales of control and tender offers. Such a transaction may be friendly or hostile. Friendly transfers of control may also be affected by a merger or sale of assets. Such *fundamental transactions* or *organic changes* are addressed in another chapter. If the transaction is hostile, it will almost certainly be accomplished by one of the methods discussed here. But it is quite common following a hostile takeover for a corporation to engage in some sort of merger or sale of assets to complete the transaction. A hostile takeover may also be affected by means of a proxy fight. An insurgent group may undertake a proxy fight without acquiring a significant number of shares, though it is uncommon. Nevertheless, because proxy fights are ultimately about stockholder voting, they are addressed in that chapter and not here.

A. SALES OF CONTROL

The general rule in the United States is that a controlling shareholder may sell a controlling block of shares to a purchaser thereby transferring working control of the corporation to the purchaser. A sale of controlling shares is almost always at a premium over the market price (or the price a minority stockholder would be able to command). Although a controlling stockholder owes a fiduciary duty to the minority not to use control to exact an improper benefit from the corporation, there is no general requirement that a controlling stockholder seek a buyer who is willing to buy all the shares from all the stockholders or that the controlling stockholder share the control premium with the minority or the corporation.

Caveat: The UK and most other countries follow the rule that a transfer of control triggers an obligation on the part of the buyer to offer to buy any and all shares, although it is typical for a controlling shareholder to receive a different form of consideration than that offered to the minority. (For example, the controlling stockholder may get cash, while the minority is offered shares in the purchasing company.) A transfer of control is typically defined as any transaction by which 20 percent or more of shares change hands.

Caveat: Many states have adopted statutes that are triggered by a change in control and that limit the rights of the purchaser in various ways. Although these statutes were intended to apply to hostile takeovers, they also apply to sale of control transactions. A control share acquisition statute suspends the voting rights of control shares when transferred unless the minority votes to re-enfranchise the shares. A business combination statute applies following a transfer of control without the approval of the board of directors and prohibits any disposition of assets for a specified period (such as three years).

Caveat: SEC rules require disclosure of change of control transactions for registered companies in various ways. A change of control triggers the obligation of the company to file a Form 8K. And both the buyer and the seller must file a Schedule 13D if either owns more than five percent of the outstanding shares of any class.

1. Control Premiums

Shares owned by a controlling shareholder command a premium over other shares because they represent the power to control the business. A controlling stockholder typically has the power to elect the entire board of directors, which in turn carries the power to establish business policies, including those with regard to the payment (or not) of dividends, reinvestment of available cash and overall business strategy. A controlling stockholder may also effectively designate the officers of the corporation as well as their compensation.

    a.   This premium is usually referred to as the *control premium* and may be expressed as a per share differential or as an additional lump sum payment for the controlling shares. Shares which carry with them control of the corporation are often called *control shares.*

        Example: A purchaser offered minority shareholders $220 per share and controlling shareholders $460 per share for all the shares of a corporation. The controlling shareholders did not advise minority shareholders of this difference in price. There is nothing fraudulent or improper about this transaction. *Tryon v. Smith*, 229 P.2d 251 (Ore.1951).

b. A controlling stockholder may not use control to extract improper benefits to the exclusion of minority stockholders. *See Sinclair Oil Corp. v. Levien.* But control is valuable for several other reasons:

- the controlling stockholder avoids the risk inherent in management by others.

- the controlling stockholder may change business policies in such a way as to increase the value of the business.

- the seller of control will insist on some premium if only because it is presumable that the buyer perceives a gain from the transaction whatever the source.

c. It is also possible for a controlling stockholder to use control in such a way as to extract benefits to the exclusion and detriment of minority stockholders. Such tactics are usually referred to as *looting* the corporation.

Example: A controlling shareholder owns 51 percent of a corporation and causes the board of directors to appoint him CEO at a grossly excessive salary. For every dollar gained in excess salary as CEO, the controlling stockholder loses 51 cents in stock value, but the other 49 cents represents a reduction in value to the minority.

Example: A controlling stockholder owns 60 percent of ABC, Inc. and 100 percent of XYZ, Inc. ABC supplies steel to corporation XYZ which builds ships. The controlling stockholder causes ABC to sell steel to XYZ at cost. For every dollar of profit lost by ABC, the controlling stockholder effectively loses 60 cents in ABC value but gains a full dollar in XYZ value.

Caveat: A corporation is managed by its board of directors. Thus, a controlling stockholder must exert control through the board of directors which must approve any transaction proposed by the controlling stockholder. Many looting cases have involved transactions undertaken by a controlling stockholder without board approval. Where the board of directors approves transactions that constitute looting, the board will have breached its duty of care and will be liable to the corporation for the damage caused.

Caveat: Looting is a concern ordinarily only if the controlling stockholder owns less than 100 percent of the shares. *But see Pereira v. Cogan,* 294 B.R. 449 (S.D.N.Y. 2003).

d. In the case of a publicly traded company, the market price of company stock will presumably reflect the danger of looting. If the market perceives that the buyer of control is likely to engage in some form of looting, presumably the stock price will fall. If the stock price rises, presumably the market thinks that the buyer of control is likely to make the company more profitable.

2. Looting

The US rule is generally based on the idea that looting can be addressed when it happens. Eliminating private sales of control would make acquisitions more difficult and expensive than necessary. If looting is suspected, the looter is primarily liable, but the seller of control may be liable on various theories ranging from breach of fiduciary duty, to aiding and abetting, or to conspiracy. Generally a controlling shareholder may sell controlling shares for whatever price he or she can obtain.

a. The virtually unanimous position of courts is that there is nothing inherently wrong in receiving a premium for control shares. *Zetlin v. Hanson Holdings,* Inc., 397 N.E.2d 387 (N.Y. 1979); *Tryon v. Smith,* 229 P.2d 251 (Or.1951); *McDaniel v. Painter,* 418 F.2d 545 (10th Cir.1969). But some courts have imposed duties on the selling shareholder with respect to investigating the honesty of the purchaser.

b. A controlling shareholder who sells his shares to a buyer who thereafter loots the corporation may be liable for any loss suffered by the corporation. Some cases take the position that the controlling shareholder has a duty to make a reasonable investigation of potential purchasers. *Gerdes v. Reynolds,* 28 N.Y.S.2d 622 (N.Y. 1941); *DeBaun v. First Western Bank and Trust Co.,* 120 Cal.Rptr. 354 (Cal.App.1975). Other cases take the position that the controlling shareholder has a duty to investigate potential purchasers only if there is reason to believe that the purchaser may loot the corporation. *Clagett v. Hutchison,* 583 F.2d 1259

(4th Cir.1978); *Swinney v. Keebler Co.*, 480 F.2d 573 (4th Cir.1973). PCG 5.16(b) states that investigation is required when it is apparent from the circumstances that the purchaser is likely to violate a duty of fair dealing. Danger signs include, (1) an obviously excessive price for the shares willingly paid, (2) an unusual interest in the liquid and readily salable assets owned by the corporation, (3) insistence by the buyers on an immediate transfer of control, (4) insistence by the buyers that the liquid assets be made available immediately, and (5) little interest by the purchasers in the current operation of the corporation's business. *Swinney v. Keebler Co.*, 480 F.2d 573 (4th Cir.1973) holds that on the facts of that case no duty to investigate arose even though with hindsight several of these factors existed. Investment companies that have liquid and readily salable assets are a likely target for looting but many looting cases involve regular business corporations.

c. If the duty of reasonable investigation is not met, liability may be imposed on the seller based on negligence. Recovery is based on the damage suffered—the amount looted by the purchasers—rather than by the purchase price paid or the amount of the control premium. *DeBaun v. First Western Bank & Trust Co.*, 120 Cal.Rptr. 354 (Cal.App.1975); *Harris v. Carter*, 582 A.2d 222 (Del.Ch.1990).

3. Other Theories

In addition to arguments based on possible looting, courts have considered other theories that might be used to hold a controlling shareholder liable to return a premium received for a sale of control. Again, most cases hold that a controlling shareholder may retain any control premium paid, but a few cases have compelled the controlling shareholder to share the control premium with minority shareholders.

a. Some cases contain broad statements to the effect that a director owes a fiduciary duty to the corporation and to the minority shareholders, but that does not explain when the premium may be recovered and when it may not. *See Perlman v. Feldmann*, 219 F.2d 173 (2d Cir.1955).

b. Some cases have permitted the recovery of a control premium on a theory of usurpation of corporate opportunity. For example, if the purchaser first offers to buy the assets of the corporation at an attractive price and the controlling shareholder suggests that the transaction be recast in the form of a purchase of the controlling shares, the opportunity to sell the assets may be a corporate opportunity belonging to all the shareholders, rather than to the majority shareholder. *Perlman v. Feldmann* may be explained on this basis. *See also Birnbaum v. Newport Steel Corp.,* 193 F.2d 461 (2d Cir. 1952) (same case under federal securities law). In addition, the subject company in *Perlman v. Feldmann* was precluded from raising the price of steel because of wartime price controls. Thus, the sale of control to steel users at a premium was a way for the controlling stockholder to gain the benefit of customers' willingness to pay higher prices without sharing what would have been higher profits with minority shareholders.

Caveat: The PCG rejects this argument on the ground that the majority shareholder is free to decline the offer in its entirety and therefore the minority shareholders have no power to require that the transaction be completed as proposed.

c. Some cases have viewed the payment of a control premium as a sale of corporate office rather than a sale of shares. A shareholder owning or controlling less than a majority of the shares may have effective working control of the corporation if other shareholders are numerous and disorganized. If the shareholder's interest is very small, the sale of that interest at a premium is more likely to be viewed as a sale of office rather than a sale of shares. Because a sale of office is against public policy, the excess payment may be recovered by the corporation for the benefit of the minority shareholders.

Caveat: This argument may prove too much because all sales of control shares at a premium may be analyzed in this fashion.

Example: The selling shareholder (Roy Cohn) enters into an agreement to sell three per cent of the outstanding shares of Lionel Corporation with the sale to be completed two years hence. The contract provides for the seriatim resignation of directors to permit the immediate transfer of control. The price greatly exceeds the market value of the shares being sold. An improper sale of office may be inferred from these circumstances. *Matter of Caplan v. Lionel Corp.,* 20 A.D.2d 301, 246 N.Y.S.2d 913, aff'd, 14 N.Y.2d 679 (1964).

Example: A selling shareholder holds 28.3 per cent of the shares of a publicly held corporation. The contract provides for a control premium and the seriatim resignation of directors to permit the immediate transfer of control. This agreement is not of itself against public policy. *Essex Universal Corp. v. Yates*, 305 F.2d 572 (2d Cir.1962).

d. Some cases have imposed liability for a control premium on a theory of nondisclosure or misrepresentation.

    Example: A controlling shareholder contracts to sell his shares for $1,500 per share. The purchaser offers to buy minority shares at the same time for $300 per share. The controlling shareholder permits the $300 offer to be made without disclosing that he is receiving five times as much per share. One court has held that this nondisclosure makes the transaction improper and the minority shareholders may share in the control premium. *Brown v. Halbert*, 76 Cal.Rptr. 781 (Cal.App.1969).

    Example: A controlling shareholder contracts to sell more shares than she owns, planning to purchase the additional shares from other shareholders. If she purchases the additional shares without disclosing the contract, she may be liable under Rule 10b–5 or state law on the theory that as a controlling shareholder she owed a duty of disclosure to minority shareholders.

e. Some cases have imposed liability for the control premium on the basis of the extreme unfairness of the transaction.

    Example: The majority shareholders of a savings and loan association create a holding company and exchange their shares for holding company shares. Minority shareholders in the association, however, are not permitted to exchange their shares for holding company shares. The holding company then makes a public offering of its own shares and an active market is created for its shares. The minority shareholders of the association are excluded from this market because they continue to own association shares rather than holding company shares. This conduct violates the majority's fiduciary responsibility to treat the minority fairly. *Jones v. H. F. Ahmanson & Co.*, 81 Cal.Rptr. 592, 460 P.2d 464 (Cal. 1969). This case may also be seen as one in which the opportunity to create a public market for shares was a corporate opportunity, or one in which the appropriation of that opportunity by the majority positively harms the minority by making their shares less liquid than before. This case may also be seen as one in which the opportunity to create a public market for shares is a corporate opportunity, or one in which the appropriation of that opportunity by the majority positively harms the minority by making their shares less liquid than before.

f. Where a control premium is recoverable, courts have permitted either the corporation or the minority shareholders to recover, depending on the theory adopted. If the theory of recovery is looting, corporate opportunity, corporate action, or the sale of corporate office, logically only the corporation should recover and a suit by a shareholder should be considered only derivative in nature. If the theory is misrepresentation or violation of rule 10b–5, the minority shareholders should be able to recover directly in their own right.

Caveat: Recovery by the corporation indirectly enriches the purchaser of control who paid the premium. Because of this, *Perlman v. Feldmann* allowed minority shareholders to recover directly even though the theory adopted in that case apparently was corporate opportunity which would dictate solely a recovery by the corporation.

Caveat: Delaware case law strictly forbids direct shareholder recovery in a derivative action. *See Keenan v. Eshelman,* 2 A.2d 904, 913–14 (Del. Ch. 1938). *See also Bangor Punta Operations, Inc. v. Bangor & Aroostook Railroad Co.,* 417 U.S. 703, 94 S.Ct. 2576 (1974).

g. Delaware courts have tended recently to scrutinize sale of control transactions closely. *Hollinger International, Inc. v. Black,* 844 A.2d 1022 (Del. Ch. 2004) (sale of control enjoined where controlling shareholder had agreed in writing to assist company in divestiture of assets); *Omnicare, Inc. v. NCS Healthcare, Inc.,* 818 A.2d 914 (Del. 2003) (merger in which controlling shareholders agreed unconditionally to vote in favor of was a breach of fiduciary duty where merger at higher price was proposed). *See also McMullin v. Beran,* 765 A.2d 910 (Del. 2000) (board of directors violated their fiduciary duty in recommending sale of company since 80 percent shareholder could dictate terms and he failed to disclose material information to minority shareholders).

B. TENDER OFFERS

In a *tender offer* the prospective *acquirer* (often called the *bidder* or *offeror*) of a *target* corporation makes a public offer to purchase shares directly from shareholders, bypassing the board of directors. The company to be acquired is usually called the *target* company. A tender offer is technically an offer for target stockholders to tender their shares for purchase by the bidder upon the terms of the offer. The shares tendered are not usually purchased immediately by the bidder. Indeed, federal law effectively prohibits the immediate purchase of tendered shares. The price is set at a premium over current market price so as to attract tenders. In many tender offers during the latter part of the 1980s, the premium was set at 50 per cent or more over the current market price of the shares. In other periods smaller premiums were offered, but the historical average is about 50 percent.

a. Such an offer is usually made in exchange for cash and is called a *cash tender offer*. An *exchange offer* differs from a cash tender offer in that the bidder offers a package of its own securities—often a combination of cash, debt, and equity securities—for the securities of the target corporation. Such an offer is subject to registration and disclosure requirements of the Securities Act of 1933 because it involves a public offer of new securities. As a result the target and target stockholders are given advance notice of the offer. A cash tender offer does not require registration, because cash is not a security. Prior to 1968 it was possible to mount a tender offer without advance notice and to give target stockholders minimal time to respond. In 1968, Congress passed the Williams Act, amending the 1934 Act, to regulate tender offers. A number of substantive rules have been established by the Williams Act and SEC regulation with respect to tender offers. For example, tender offers must remain open for specified periods, and shares previously tendered may be withdrawn during specified periods; if the price is increased during an outstanding tender offer, the higher price must be paid for all shares previously tendered. A person making a tender offer must purchase only through that offer and may not make private purchases while the offer is outstanding. In addition, oversubscribed cash tender offers must be accepted pro rata and not on a first-come-first-bought basis.

b. The type of consideration offered in a tender offer (and in mergers generally) tends to depend on whether the stock market is high or low. When stocks are trading at high prices, target stockholders are more willing to accept stock as consideration. When the market is low, cash is usually the only form of payment accepted.

c. A bidder may seek just enough shares to ensure voting control. However, in many instances the bidder offers to acquire all the outstanding shares. Such an offer is called an *any or all* tender offer and is usually conditioned on some minimum number of shares being tendered (typically enough to assure control of the target). If the ultimate goal is to obtain all of the shares of the target corporation, a second transaction to acquire the balance of the outstanding shares shortly follows a successful acquisition of sufficient shares for control.

d. No tender offer ever obtains all of the outstanding shares of a target. If the bidder desires to acquire all of the outstanding shares they may be acquired in a cash-out merger that compels minority shareholders to accept the proffered terms (or follow the statutory dissent and appraisal procedure). Such a second step merger is also called a *mop up* merger or *freeze out* merger.

e. Many tender offers in the 1980s were financed by the bidder's borrowing of large sums of cash from banks or by issuing *junk bonds*. A junk bond is a bond of less than investment grade. Bonds issued to finance a takeover were low rated because there was no assured source of repayment if the takeover did not succeed. And if the takeover did succeed, the bonds would typically be assumed by the target company and subordinated to outstanding bonds. Before the 1980s such bonds were thought to be unmarketable because of their low rating, but the investment bank Drexel Burnham Lambert developed a market for such bonds through cooperation with successful takeover firms such as Kohlberg Kravis & Roberts (KKR).

f. In some cases, a bidder will offer a premium for enough shares to establish control over the company and announce in advance that remaining shares will be bought at a lower price in a back-end merger—possibly even at the market price for target shares before the offer. Such an offer is usually called a front-end loaded two tiered tender offer. Such offers are generally seen as coercive in that they may induce target stockholders to tender their shares for less than their true *reservation price* (price at which they would willingly sell). A partial offer in which the bidder makes no announcement about the fate of minority shares after the transfer of control is arguably even more coercive. Several states have enacted fair price statutes requiring that any mop-up merger be done at the same price is that paid in the front end. But these statutes do not generally *require* a back-end merger.

g. Target managers often argue that coercive tactics used by bidders justify defensive tactics designed to thwart a hostile bid and preserve incumbent control. Target shareholders often object to such tactics because they almost always prefer the opportunity to sell their shares at a premium.

Caveat: Since the late 1980s, most hostile bids have taken the form of any-or-all offers for cash. There is little basis for arguing that such a bid is coercive and thus there is little cause for defensive tactics. Arguably, coercive tactics evolved away because bidders found that non-coercive bids were more likely to succeed.

h.   A tender offer may also be used in a friendly negotiated deal as a way of permitting target stockholders to sell voluntarily and avoiding issues of fiduciary duty as well as appraisal rights for those stockholders who accept the offer. In some cases, a deal may start out friendly and turn hostile or vice versa.

Example: A target corporation is approached by a bidder with a proposal for a voluntary merger. The board of directors of the target corporation declines to consider the deal. A merger is therefore impractical since approval of the board of directors is required before a proposed statutory merger may be submitted to shareholders. The bidder announces it will make a cash tender offer for the shares of the target at an attractive price. The board of directors, fearing that the offer may succeed, reopens negotiations and a mutually satisfactory merger transaction is worked out and subsequently approved by the shareholders. Such a series of events is often called a *bear hug.*

i.   Tender offers provide an important source of discipline for corporate managers in that those who fail to maximize stockholder value may find that their company becomes the target of a hostile offer. In such a case, a bidder may seek to take over the target by offering target stockholders a premium over the market price, and after gaining control, impose new management policies to increase target value, thus recouping the purchase price and then some. In many cases, a successful bidder will sell off parts of the target business, particularly if the tender offer has been financed by borrowing. (Indeed, buyers for pieces of the business may have been lined up even before the offer is announced.) Such a transaction is sometimes called a *bust up takeover.*

j.   A tender offer may also be used by an issuer that seeks to buy back a large number of its own shares—often called a *self tender offer.*

k.   When a cash tender offer is made, the open market price for the shares increases dramatically. Target shareholders thus have the choice of selling their shares in the open market (usually at a discount from the tender offer price) or tendering their shares. (When a competing bid seems likely, the market price for target shares may exceed the price offered in the tender offer.) Most shares sold on the open market are ultimately tendered because of the activity of arbitrageurs.

l. Arbitrageurs are speculators who purchase shares in the open market at prices below the tender offer price in order to tender them and profit by the difference between the two prices. Arbitrageurs are the natural allies of bidders since they profit only if the transaction is consummated. As a result of activities of arbitrageurs, a corporation that is in *play* (the subject bid) is likely to be purchased by someone and not to remain independent.

C. ECONOMIC ANALYSIS OF TAKEOVERS

Generally speaking, target stockholders favor takeover bids because they afford an opportunity to sell shares at a substantial premium. On the average, bidders offer about 50 percent more than the pre-bid market price. Thus, target stockholders generally oppose efforts by target management to resist takeovers, although sometimes resistance may lead to the emergence of a competing bidder who is willing to pay even more. Although resistance may lead to a higher price in a given deal, it may reduce the number of deals proposed overall and thus may reduce overall stockholder wealth.

It is not entirely clear why bidders are willing to pay premiums to acquire target companies. Several theories have been suggested.

1. Inefficient Management

Many commentators views takeover bids as part of the market for corporate control and an important mechanism for improving the quality of management by weeding out inefficient managers and assuring that assets are devoted to their highest and most profitable use. Some have even suggested that management should never attempt to defeat a hostile offer, but should simply stand aside and let the shareholders determine what is in their best interest. Moreover, some suggested that efforts to regulate takeovers, including the Williams Act, ultimately had the effect of making takeovers more difficult to do and thus reducing stockholder wealth. These arguments are ultimately based on the assumption that the stock market is efficient and accordingly that market price accurately reflects the value of the target company as currently managed. Thus, a bidder would be willing to offer a premium over market only if the bidder has a better idea about how to manage the company or if the currently management is inefficient (which is really the same thing).

Caveat: Although target stockholders clearly gain from takeovers, the stock of bidder companies often falls when a bid is announced, possibly because of the tendency of bidders to overpay for targets, particularly if a bidding war or auction arises. Still, studies indicate that stockholders in the aggregate—including both bidders and targets—gain from takeovers, with bidders enjoying roughly a market rate of return and target stockholders receiving the excess. On the other hand, because many takeovers have the effect of increasing the debt load of the target company, the value of any outstanding target debt often falls as the result of a takeover. Thus, bondholders in the aggregate tend to lose from takeovers.

Caveat: It is possible that takeover premiums arise naturally because target stockholders have differing opinions as to the value of target shares and thus set differing reservation prices. In other words, as a simple function of supply and demand, it may be necessary for a bidder to offer a bigger premium to attract a larger percentage of shares.

Caveat: Some studies show that the securities market is *informationally efficient*—in that it reacts quickly to new information—but is not *fundamentally efficient* in that the market may not accurately measure the worth of a business.

Caveat: Some takeovers occur apparently even though the target is efficiently managed. It is not uncommon for the bidder to retain incumbent management.

2. Synergy

Some commentators have suggested that takeovers may provide synergistic benefits by combining complementary businesses that are worth more as a single unit, for example, because of economies of scale.

Caveat: Many takeovers in the 1980s resulted in the breakup of conglomerate companies that had been assembled in the 1960s and 1970s. In these cases, it appears that the parts are worth more than the whole. Thus, the idea of synergy may be an excuse for empire building by managers seeking to build a bigger company for a variety of reasons ranging from increasing market power, to enhanced compensation, to avoiding takeover through sheer size. But if a supposedly synergistic merger does not make economic sense, presumably the stock price will fall and the company will find itself the target of a takeover.

3.　Other Motivations

It is possible that the gains to shareholders are largely due to tax savings caused by the substitution of debt for equity capital. Many takeovers were financed by issuing so-called junk bonds and using the proceeds to purchase target stock, with the target company assuming the obligation to pay off the bonds after takeover. This tactic had the effect of increasing the leverage of the target company and increasing the rate of return to remaining stockholders following the takeover. It also had the effect of requiring the target company to distribute available cash in the form of interest payments to bondholders, albeit at the cost of increasing the chances of bankruptcy. Nevertheless, one common justification for takeovers in the 1980s was that target companies had failed to pay dividends and had used available cash to invest in uneconomic expansion. Thus, in addition to their tax effect, junk bonds may also be seen as a remedy for a form of mismanagement.

Caveat:　Debt financing increases the risk of bankruptcy while also increasing leverage and thus potential return. Although bankruptcy is undesirable, it is arguably not a disaster in connection with a highly leveraged company where the holders of junk bonds are diversified investors who may receive stock in a reorganized company, given that junk bonds and stock carry comparable risks. Moreover, in many cases, such reorganizations can be negotiated by the various security holders and presented to the court for approval with a minimum of disruption to the operations of the company. Such prepackaged bankruptcies are common in connection with default on junk bonds. Thus, the takeover movement may be attributed in part to evolving practices in bankruptcy. In addition, it may be that diversified investors such as mutual funds found that they could increase overall returns if individual investee companies each pursued maximum returns by increasing leverage, because successful companies would more than make up for a few bankruptcies.

Caveat:　The use of junk bonds for such purposes was largely curtailed by changes in the tax law limiting interest deductions for unsecured takeover debt and the ruling on margin loans by the Federal Reserve Board that debt financing of takeovers was subject to limitation under rules governing margin loans. In addition, most junk bonds were distributed through the firm of Drexel Burnham Lambert under the supervision of Michael Milken, both of whom were convicted of securities fraud in connection with these transactions.

D. THE WILLIAMS ACT

The Williams Act was passed by Congress in 1968 in response to perceived abuses in the conduct of tender offers. The Williams Act consists of a series of amendments to the 1934 Act, codified in §§ 13(d), 13(e), 14(d), and 14(e). The Williams Act applies to tender offers *for equity securities* of companies registered under Section 12 of the 1934 Act. The general goal of the Williams Act is not to favor or disfavor takeovers but to assure full disclosure of proposed transactions and provide a fair set of rules for the struggle for control of the corporation. Nevertheless, it is clear that the Williams Act was also intended to reduce the perceived advantages enjoyed by bidders in connection with unregulated offers. Some legal scholars have argued that the Williams Act thus reduces the number of offers made and therefore ultimately reduces aggregate stockholder wealth.

Caveat: Although the Williams Act addresses the wholesale purchase of securities and is designed in large part to prevent fraud in connection with such transactions, it was enacted as part of the proxy regulation system because a tender offer is similar in many respects to a proxy fight.

a. Any person who makes a cash tender offer for a registered corporation must disclose the source of funds used in the offer, the background of persons involved in the offer, the purpose for which the offer is made, plans for the target if successful, and any contracts or understandings it has with, or with respect to, the target corporation. § 14(d). This information must be filed on Form 14D and distributed to target shareholders when the offer begins. In other words, the Williams Act differs from a 1933 Act registration statement in that it does not require advance notice of an offer.

b. Disclosure of similar information is required by any person or group who acquires more than 5 per cent of the outstanding shares of any class of stock of a registered company, whether or not a tender offer is in progress or is contemplated. § 13(d). This information must be filed on Form 13D and furnished to the issuer within ten days. A new Form 13D must be filed and furnished within ten day of any further purchase or sale. This rule provides potential target companies with advance information about potential offers.

Caveat: Form 13D may be required when a stockholder group representing five percent or more of a class of stock is formed or altered even though no one in the group has bought or sold shares. This requirement overlaps in many cases with required filings under § 16(a) of the 1934 Act.

c. Similar information must be disclosed by issuers making an offer for their own shares, or issuers in which a change of control is proposed. § 13(e).

d. Aside from requiring disclosure, the Williams Act and the rules adopted by the SEC thereunder contain a series of substantive rules about the terms of an offer:

- the offer must remain open for 20 business days.

- tendered shares must be purchased no later than 60 business days after the beginning of the offer.

- the offer must be made to all holders of the class of securities for which the offer is made.

- if the offer is for fewer than the number of shares tendered, the bidder must purchase an equal proportion of shares from each tendering stockholder.

- a tendering stockholder has the right to withdraw tendered shares at any time during the course of the offer.

- if the offer price is increased or decreased during the offer the highest price paid to a tendering shareholder must be paid to all tendering shareholders.

- during an offer, the bidder may not purchase any shares outside the offer.

- a stockholder must own all shares tendered.

   Caveat: SEC rules relating to tender offers conflict in several cases with the statutes under which they have been adopted, but to date no rule has been struck down for that reason.

e. Section 14(e) imposes a broad prohibition against the use of false, misleading or incomplete statements in connection with a tender offer. Section 14(e) adopts the standards of materiality, *scienter,* and disclosure of Rule 10b–5. The Supreme Court has held that § 14(e), like Rule 10b–5, relates only to nondisclosure or deception and does not reach unfair practices generally. *Schreiber v. Burlington Northern, Inc.,* 472 U.S. 1, 105 S.Ct. 2458 (1985).

f.   In *Piper v. Chris–Craft Industries, Inc.,* 430 U.S. 1, 97 S.Ct. 926 (1977), the Court held that a defeated tender offeror does not have standing to sue for damages, but injunctive relief may be available. An issuer has standing to enjoin violations of section 14(e) when acting on behalf of shareholders. *Polaroid Corp. v. Disney,* 862 F.2d 987 (3d Cir.1988).

g.   Tendering shareholders have standing to seek injunctive relief and, probably, damages. *Lowenschuss v. Kane,* 520 F.2d 255 (2d Cir.1975). The Supreme Court in *Chris-Craft* specifically left open the question whether a nontendering shareholder might have standing to sue a bidder. Some cases have held that such a shareholder does have standing. *See Plaine v. McCabe,* 797 F.2d 713 (9th Cir.1986).

h.   The Williams Act does not contain a definition of what constitutes a tender offer. A variety of techniques have been devised to acquire control of a target corporation without triggering the Williams Act. The principal legal issue involved in such transactions is whether the transaction should be viewed as a tender offer subject to the requirements of the Williams Act.

> *Example:*   A simultaneous offer to purchase shares of the target corporation made to some 40 institutional and other investors by telephone in a single evening is a tender offer that must be registered under the Williams Act. *Wellman v. Dickinson,* 682 F.2d 355 (2d Cir.1982).

> *Example:*   A purchase of a single 30 per cent block of shares followed by an offer to purchase shares owned by all directors of the company plus purchases on the open market over a securities exchange is not a tender offer. *Nachman Corp. v. Halfred, Inc.,* Fed.Sec.L.Rep. (CCH) 94,455 (N.D.Ill. 1973), *Hanson Trust PLC v. SCM Corp.,* 774 F.2d 47 (2d Cir.1985).

> *Example:*   A plan that involves the purchase of shares through routine transactions on a securities exchange is not a tender offer even though designed to acquire control of the corporation. *Kennecott Copper Corp. v. Curtiss–Wright Corp.,* 584 F.2d 1195 (2d Cir.1978).

> *Example:*   An offer to purchase shares from a small number of institutional investors and arbitrageurs immediately after a cash tender offer

has been withdrawn is not a tender offer. This transaction is called a "street sweep." *Hanson Trust PLC v. SCM Corp.*, 774 F.2d 47 (2d Cir.1985).

Example: An unlimited time offer to repurchase shares at the market price during a hostile tender offer by a third party is not itself a tender offer even though the market price reflects a built-in premium and even though the offer may be withdrawn at any time. *SEC v. Carter Hawley Hale Stores, Inc.*, 760 F.2d 945 (9th Cir. 1985).

E. STATE TAKEOVER STATUTES

Most states have enacted statutes dealing with takeovers. Unlike the Williams Act, these statutes were openly designed to protect corporations against bidders.

a. State statutes enacted before 1982 generally imposed hearing requirements and fairness standards on tender offers made with respect to corporations with significant contacts with the state. The Illinois statute of this type was held unconstitutional in *Edgar v. MITE Corporation*, 457 U.S. 624, 102 S.Ct. 2629 (1982) on the ground that it was an unreasonable burden on interstate commerce.

b. New attempts by states to impose restrictions on tender offers began promptly after the decision in *MITE*. These statutes are often called second generation takeover statutes and they apply only to corporations incorporated in the state in question. They all build on the established power of states to regulate the internal affairs of domestic corporations.

c. The most important of these statutes is DGCL § 203. This statute provides that if a person acquires 15 per cent or more of a corporation's voting stock, that person may not enter into mergers or other specified transactions with the corporation unless (a) the person acquires 85 per cent or more of the corporation's stock, or (b) the transaction is approved by the board of directors and at least two-thirds of the shares other than the shares held by the person acquiring the stock. Section 203 is important because many publicly held corporations are incorporated in Delaware. More than twenty-five other states, including New York, have adopted similar business combination statutes. The Wisconsin statute modeled on the Delaware statute was upheld in *Amanda Acquisition Corp. v. Universal Foods Corp.*, 877 F.2d 496 (7th Cir. 1989).

d. Ohio and Indiana pioneered the *control share acquisition statute*. The Indiana statute was upheld by the Supreme Court in *CTS Corporation v. Dynamics*

Corp. of America, 481 U.S. 69, 107 S.Ct. 1637 (1987). In this type of statute, shareholder approval must be obtained for purchases by an individual or group that crosses the 20 percent, the 33⅓ percent, and the 50 percent thresholds. If a shareholder fails to obtain approval, the acquired shares lose the right to vote and may be reacquired by the corporation on terms set forth in the statute. The net effect of a control share acquisition statute may be to reward holdout stockholders by necessitating a back-end premium. In other words, these statutes may lead to the transfer of a front-end premium to the back-end. Arguably, this is a good result because holdout stockholders presumably attach a higher value to their shares than do stockholders who sell quickly.

e.   Pennsylvania provides that if a shareholder acquires more than 20 per cent of the voting shares of a corporation, other shareholders have the right to compel that shareholder to acquire their shares at fair value. This statute is similar to the rule in the UK and many other countries.

f.   More than 30 states have adopted statutes authorizing boards of directors to consider constituencies other than shareholders when making decisions. These are generally viewed as being motivated by a desire to make takeovers more difficult.

F.   DEFENSIVE TACTICS

Numerous defensive tactics have been devised in order to defeat or deter takeover bids. These tactics increased in sophistication during the 1980s. By 1990, more than 90 per cent of all publicly held corporations had adopted various standing defenses against unwanted takeover attempts. The most successful defense is the poison pill discussed below.

1.   Creating Legal Obstacles

A target corporation may seek to create legal obstacles to takeover. A target might buy a business that increases the chances that the threatened takeover will give rise to anti-trust problems. *See Panter v. Marshall Field & Co.,* 646 F.2d 271 (7th Cir.1981); *Marathon Oil Co. v. Mobil Corp.,* 669 F.2d 378 (6th Cir. 1981). A target might acquire and hold a business that requires governmental approval for its transfer, e.g. a parent corporation owning an insurance subsidiary. A target might institute suit to enjoin the offer for violations of the Williams Act, the antitrust laws, or on other grounds. *See Corenco Corp. v. Schiavone & Sons, Inc.,* 488 F.2d 207 (2d Cir.1973).

2.   Porcupine Provisions

Amendments may be made in the articles of incorporation or bylaws that make it difficult for a bidder who acquires a majority of the voting shares to obtain control of the board of directors. These are sometimes referred to as *porcupine provisions*. Common devices included limiting removal of directors for cause in the articles of incorporation, staggering the election of directors, or requiring a supermajority vote to amend bylaws, or to take other specified actions.

3. Supervoting Stock

The articles of incorporation may be amended to provide for supervoting stock (stock with multiple votes per share) and placing that stock in the hands of members of the founding families or other persons friendly to the incumbent management. Supervoting stock is generally made non-transferable but convertible into ordinary voting stock that is transferable. A person holding supervoting stock is thus unable to convey the supervoting privilege but may sell the shares after they are converted into ordinary voting stock. Supervoting stock permits a target corporation to make itself completely takeover-proof.

a.   Supervoting stock may be created at the time the stock is issued or at some later time by offering to exchange the shares of non-controlling stockholders for lesser voting shares with the same financial rights as ordinary shares. Typically, the company offers additional lesser voting shares to as an inducement to take the exchange. Thus, a stockholder who accepts the exchange offer typically receives enhanced financial rights in exchange for giving up a vote that probably has little value to him or her.

      Caveat: Although such an exchange offer appears to be voluntary, a stockholder who declines the offer forgoes the value of the additional shares in order to maintain voting rights that likely have little value to him. Thus, such an offer may be seen as inherently coercive.

      Caveat: The SEC attempted to prevent the use of supervoting stock by enacting Rule 19c–4 prohibiting the various securities exchanges and NASDAQ from continuing to list the stock of any company that changed the voting rights of outstanding shares. In *Business Roundtable v. SEC*, 905 F.2d 406 (D.C.Cir.1990), the court invalidated this rule on the ground that it exceeded the power of the SEC, but the exchanges and NASDAQ have continued to comply with the rule voluntarily. Ironically, prior to the adoption of Rule 19c–4, the NYSE refused to list any company that did not follow the one-share-one-vote model. With the adoption of the rule, it became common for companies to issue lesser voting shares when going public because such a voting structure was no longer prohibited by NYSE rules. Only subsequent changes in voting rights are prohibited. (It is unclear whether the rule prohibits a listed company from later issuing supervoting stock to a controlling stockholder, though it would likely be difficult for any such transaction to pass muster as a matter of fiduciary duty.)

b. A variation of supervoting stock is tenure voting. For example, as of a specified date a reclassification is effected by which each share of stock becomes entitled to 10 votes. If any shares are transferred, the voting power of the shares is reduced to one vote per share. If the shares are held for a stated period, (say) 36 or 48 months, they again obtain the power to cast 10 votes. A tenure voting plan of this type was upheld In *Williams v. Geier*, 671 A.2d 1368 (Del. 1996).

4. White Knight

A corporation facing an undesired takeover attempt may seek to find a more congenial suitor, a *white knight*. In order to assure the white knight's success, the target may seek to negotiate exclusively with the white knight and in addition may grant the white knight a "lockup".

5. Lockup

Lockups involve entering into transactions with a friendly party on favorable terms to make takeover by others difficult or unattractive. A lockup may involve the sale of shares at a bargain price or the grant of options to purchase shares.

a. A corporation faced with an unwanted tender offer may create an employee stock ownership plan (ESOP) with a trustee friendly to incumbent management, and distribute a significant number of shares to that trustee. *See NCR Corp. v. American Tel. & Tel. Co.*, 761 F.Supp. 475 (S.D.Ohio 1991); *Shamrock Holdings, Inc. v. Polaroid Corp.*, 559 A.2d 278, 290 (Del.Ch.1989). However, some legal restraints apply to this device.

Example: A publicly-held corporation, incorporated in Panama, is threatened with a takeover attempt. It issues two large blocks of its shares, one to a wholly-owned subsidiary, and the other to an Employee Stock Option Plan (ESOP), the trustees of which are directors of the corporation. Neither transaction is protected by the business judgment rule because the primary purpose is entrenchment. In addition, shares owned by a subsidiary of the issuing corporation cannot be voted. *See* MBCA 7.21(b). The voting of both blocks of shares should be enjoined. *Norlin Corp. v. Rooney, Pace* Inc., 744 F.2d 255 (2d Cir.1984).

Caveat: The court applied NY law despite the fact that the Panamanian subsidiary may have been able to vote the shares under the law of Panama. This exception to the internal affairs rule is sometimes called the "pseudo-foreign corporation doctrine." As for the ESOP, federal law (ERISA) imposes strict fiduciary duties on the trustee of an employee benefit plan which arguably would require the trustee to act so as to maximize the value for plan beneficiaries even if it means acting contrary to the interests of the target company.

b. A corporation may find a "white knight" and grant it options to purchase shares at current market prices. *See Smith v. Van Gorkom*, 488 A.2d 858 (Del.1985). The options give the white knight a *leg up* on any competing bidder and also protects the white knight if a competing bidder appears and acquires the target at a higher price, because the white knight may tender the acquired shares for purchase under the competing bid.

c. A corporation facing an unwanted tender offer may sell or grant options to purchase a desirable asset or line of business (*crown jewels*) to a favored bidder at a bargain price. *See Hanson Trust PLC v. ML SCM Acquisition, Inc.*, 781 F.2d 264 (2d Cir.1986); Mobil Corp. v. Marathon Oil Co., 669 F.2d 366 (6th Cir. 1981). This type of lockup is designed to discourage the competing bidder by making the target less attractive, and may be enjoined if it the transaction is unreasonable.

6. Greenmail

A target corporation facing an unwanted tender offer may seek in effect to bribe a bidder by repurchasing bidder shares at a premium. This is called greenmail. *See Heckmann v. Ahmanson*, 214 Cal.Rptr. 177 (1985); *Cheff v. Mathes*, 199 A.2d 548 (Del.1964).

a. In 1987, the Internal Revenue Code was amended to impose a 50 percent nondeductible excise tax on greenmail payments (in addition to the normal income tax payable on sales of shares). IRC 5881.

b.   Some states (notably Pennsylvania) have statutes that prohibit greenmail or require that any premium be returned to the company.

7.   Manipulation of Target Share Price

A corporation facing an unwanted tender offer may seek to defeat it by driving up the price of its shares to make the takeover price unattractive.

a.   The target may buy back its own shares in the open market for ostensibly proper reasons. Such transactions tend to drive up the price and make a purchased takeover more difficult. *Bennett v. Propp*, 187 A.2d 405 (Del.1962); *Herald Co. v. Seawell*, 472 F.2d 1081 (10th Cir.1972).

   Caveat: Although it might be argued that these tactics constitute illegal stock price manipulation under § 9 of the 1934 Act, SEC rules effectively permit repurchases even if they are designed to increase the stock price. If the repurchase is made by tender offer, extensive disclosure is required by Rule 13e–1. Open market repurchases may be made pursuant to Rule 10b–18 so long as they do not account for more than 25 percent of average daily trading volume and are not made at the open or close of the market.

b.   A target may make an offer to repurchase its own shares but limit the offer by excluding shares acquired by the bidder. In *Unocal Corp. v. Mesa Petroleum Co.*, 493 A.2d 946 (Del.1985), the Delaware Supreme Court upheld this type of transaction on the basis of an expanded business judgment rule, discussed below. Shortly thereafter, the SEC adopted Rule 14d–10, the *all holders* rule that requires equal treatment of all shareholders of the same class.

c.   The target may declare an extraordinary dividend or announce an increase in its regular dividends. In some cases, the target may borrow large amounts of money to pay a dividend, thereby effecting a *leveraged recapitalization*. Or the target may distribute debt obligations directly to its own stockholders. Although these tactics will usually have the effect of lowering the stock price, they also drain the company of cash and borrowing power and may make it less attractive as a target. In addition, the target may include a provision in its debt instruments that requires payoff in the event of a takeover. Such debt is usually called *poison pill debt*.

8.   Poison Pills

A poison pill is a new issue of stock that increases in rights if any person makes a cash tender offer or acquires more than a specified percentage of the company's shares.

a.   A poison pill is technically a new series of preferred shares distributed to common shareholders in the form of a dividend. The new series is usually created by the board of directors without shareholder action under blank check authority in the articles of incorporation.

b.   The increased rights of the holders of the poison pill preferred may consist of *flip in* or *flip over* rights, or both. Flip-in rights permit the holder to purchase additional shares or debt securities of the target at a bargain price, to sell shares back to the target at high prices, or to exchange the poison pill preferred for valuable packages of debt and securities issued by the target. Flip-over rights permit the holder to purchase shares of the bidder at a bargain price if there is a subsequent merger or other defined transaction between the target and the bidder. Most poison pills contain both flip-in and flip-over provisions, both of which alone would result in unacceptable dilution of the bidder's interest if triggered.

c.   Before a triggering event occurs, the board of directors may redeem the poison pill preferred at a nominal cost. After a triggering event occurs, the preferred is generally not redeemable. Thus, a poison pill compels the bidder initially to negotiate with the board of directors to neutralize the pill through redemption of the poison pill rights.

d.   The principal case approving the issuance of poison pill preferred is *Moran v. Household International, Inc.*, 500 A.2d 1346 (Del.1985).

e.   Two courts have applied New Jersey law to conclude that the board of directors may not adopt "poison pill" preferred stock that materially changes the voting rights of shareholders without approval of the shareholders. *Asarco, Incorporated v. Court*, 611 F.Supp. 468 (D.N.J.1985); *Minstar Acq. Corp. v. AMF, Inc.*, 621 F.Supp. 1252 (S.D.N.Y.1985). The second case also invalidates a "scorched earth" plan under which the target corporation granted excessive amounts of compensation to high-level employees. As a result of these two decisions, most corporations have not attempted to create poison pills in which voting rights change upon the occurrence of a triggering event.

G. JUDICIAL REVIEW OF DEFENSIVE TACTICS

A large number of cases have considered the validity of defensive tactics in different contexts. No general theory has developed. The lawfulness of defensive tactics is largely governed by state law. Attempts to attack these tactics under Rule 10b–5 was foreclosed by the United States Supreme Court decisions in *Santa Fe Industries, Inc. v. Green*, 430 U.S. 462, 97 S.Ct. 1292 (1977) (limiting Rule 10b–5 to cases of deception rather than unfairness or breach of fiduciary duty), and *Schreiber v. Burlington Northern, Inc.*, 472 U.S. 1, 105 S.Ct. 2458 (1985) (extending the same limitation to suits under § 14(e) of the Williams Act). On the other hand, some of the actions described below have been successfully attacked by regulations promulgated under the Williams Act.

1. Early Tests

The early test of the propriety of defensive tactics was one of underlying purpose. If the action of the board of directors was motivated by a business purpose (such as preserving existing business policies or strategies), the action was protected by the business judgment rule. On the other hand if the board or management acted primarily because of a personal desire to perpetuate or *entrench* itself in office, the defensive tactic may be invalidated. *Cheff v. Mathes*, 199 A.2d 548 (Del.1964). This early test may be criticized on the ground that it is possible to dress up virtually any transaction with a proper business purpose even through the real motive is entrenchment. Nevertheless, entrenchment remains an important basis for invalidation defenses.

2. Business Judgment Rule

In the early 1980s, most courts took the position that defensive tactics were simply a matter of the exercise of the business judgment of the directors and such decisions were immune from judicial review under the business judgment rule. *See Panter v. Marshall Field & Co.*, 646 F.2d 271 (7th Cir.1981); *Gearhart Industries, Inc. v. Smith International, Inc.*, 741 F.2d 707 (5th Cir.1984). *See also Hilton Hotels Corp. v. ITT Corp.*, 962 F. Supp. 1309 (D. Nev. 1997).

3. Intermediate Scrutiny

Beginning in the mid 1980s, the Delaware Supreme Court developed a balancing test that appears to fall somewhere between the business judgment rule applied in connection with the duty of care and the fairness test applied in connection with the duty of loyalty.

a. In *Unocal Corp. v. Mesa Petroleum Co.*, 493 A.2d 946 (Del.1985), the court upheld a self tender offer of debt for stock that excluded the bidder from participation, stating that "If a defensive measure is to come within the ambit of the business judgment rule, it must be reasonable in relation to the threat posed. This entails an analysis by the directors of the nature of the takeover bid and its effect on the corporate enterprise."

b. In *Moran v. Household International, Inc.*, 500 A.2d 1346 (Del.1985), the court upheld the adoption of a poison pill as a defensive tactic in advance of a specific takeover attempt, reasoning that the poison pill did not prevent all takeover attempts, and that the management's invocation of the poison pill in response to a specific takeover attempt could be considered when the occasion arose.

c. In *Revlon, Inc. v. MacAndrews & Forbes Holdings, Inc.*, 506 A.2d 173 (Del.1985), the court held that a lock-up agreement that favored one contestant in a takeover attempt over another was invalid and should be enjoined because the board of directors had resolved to sell the corporation and that upon making that decision, the board had an obligation to get the best possible price for shareholders, and could not arbitrarily favor one contestant over another. In other words, *Revlon* holds that once it is clear that the company will either be sold or broken up, the board of directors must conduct an auction to insure that shareholders receive the best possible price. *See also Ivanhoe Partners v. Newmont Mining Corp.*, 535 A.2d 1334 (Del. 1987) (same rule if board initially resists takeover); *Mills Acquisition Co. v. MacMillan, Inc.*, 559 A.2d 1261 (Del. 1989) (addressing conduct of auction); *Cottle v. Storer Communication, Inc.*, 849 F.2d 570 (11th Cir. 1988) (addressing the end of the auction); *Barkan v. Amsted Industries, Inc.*, 567 A.2d 1279 (Del. 1988) (addressing the use of a market test).

d. In *Paramount Communications, Inc. v. Time, Inc.*, 571 A.2d 1140 (Del.1989), the court held that in a true merger in which two companies seek to combine rather than a takeover in which control of the target company is transferred, the auction requirement is not triggered and the offer of a competing bidders need not be considered. This decision has given rise to the *just say no* defense by which a company may refuse to consider an offer on the grounds that the company is not for sale even if the offer clearly increases stockholder wealth.

Caveat: In *Paramount Communications, Inc. v. QVC Network, Inc.*, 637 A.2d 34 (Del. 1994), the court rejected the *just say no* defense where the proposed merger would have resulted in the transfer of control of a publicly traded company (without a dominant stockholder) to another publicly traded company effectively controlled by a single individual, thus eliminating the opportunity of target stockholders to sell at a premium in future transactions. *See also City Capital Assoc. v. Interco Inc.,* 551 A.2d 787 (Del.Ch.1988); *Grand Metropolitan Public Ltd. Co. v. Pillsbury Co.,* 558 A.2d 1049 (Del.Ch.1988) (both rejecting the "just say no" defense and requiring redemption of a poison pill).

e.   In *Unitrin, Inc. v. American General Corp.,* 651 A.2d 1361 (Del.1995) the court refined the rule of *Unocal* holding that to be proportional to the perceived threat a defensive tactic may not be *coercive* or *preclusive.* In other words, the tactic may not be designed to force target stockholders to reject the bid or to prevent the bid from going forward. Presumably, this means that the target board may take steps to level the playing field or even to favor itself, but may not dictate a result in its own favor. The *Unitrin* court also made it clear that this intermediate level of scrutiny is in addition to scrutiny under the business judgment rule. If management shows that its response is proportional, the plaintiff may nonetheless seek to show that management tactics were not based on a valid exercise of business judgment, but, for example, that they were motivated primarily by a personal desire to remain in office (entrenchment). In other words, the action may not be dismissed solely on the ground that the target board has met an intermediate standard of care.

f.   *Quickturn Design Systems, Inc. v. Shapiro,* 721 A.2d 1281 (Del. 1998), held that a provision limiting the ability of the board of directors to redeem poison pill rights for a period of six months was an unreasonable limitation on the power of the board of directors. *But see Int'l Bd. of Teamsters Gen. Fund v. Fleming Cos., Inc.,* 975 P.2d 907 (Okla. 1999) (stockholders may adopt a bylaw requiring board to obtain stockholder approval before issuing poison pill).

    Caveat: It is unclear whether the rule of *Unocal* and *Unitrin* means that poison pill rights must be made redeemable after they have been triggered.

g.   In *Omnicare, Inc. v. NCS Healthcare, Inc.,* 818 A.2d 914 (Del. 2003), the court held that an unconditional agreement by controlling shareholders to vote in favor of a proposed merger was preclusive and coercive where a merger at a higher price was subsequently proposed by a competing bidder.

H. LEVERAGED BUYOUTS

A leveraged buyout (LBO) is an acquisition of a target usually by a group including existing management and additional private investors, using borrowed funds which are to be later repaid out of the earnings and assets of the target. If incumbent management forms a part of the group that makes the cash tender offer, the transaction may be called a management buyout (MBO). Such deals are often also called *going private transactions*. The spectacular collapse of some leveraged buyout transactions contributed to the cessation of takeovers at the end of the 1980s.

a.   In a leveraged buyout, the bidder creates a new corporation (NEWCO) to acquire the shares of the target (OLDCO). NEWCO receives minimal equity capital from the bidder group and borrows the balance of the purchase price for the publicly held shares of OLDCO. Typically, NEWCO makes a tender offer for any and all of the shares of OLDCO held by stockholders other than the bidder group so that the target becomes a subsidiary of NEWCO.

b.   Following the acquisition of the shares of the target (and a subsequent mop-up merger) the target and NEWCO are merged so that the target's assets become available to service the takeover debt of NEWCO. Alternatively, the separate existence of the target as a subsidiary of NEWCO may be retained, but the target may formally guarantee the payment of the debt of NEWCO (an *upstream guarantee*). The acquisition debt may be paid down by the proceeds of sales of assets by the recapitalized target or out of its cash flow.

c.   In effect a leveraged buyout results in recapitalization of the target by the massive substitution of debt for equity capital. An important factor in the economics of LBO transactions is that the LBO sharply reduces or eliminates income tax liability of the acquired business through the substitution of deductible interest payments for taxable dividend payments.

d.   After a leveraged buyout, the surviving company typically has too few stockholders to be required to report under section 12 of the Securities Exchange Act of 1934. Thus, the company may reduce costs (and increase profits) by eliminating various regulatory requirements that follow from registration.

> *Caveat:*   Many companies acquired through leveraged buyouts in the 1980s later made public offerings of equity securities and again became publicly held corporations.

e.   An LBO differs from a sale of control or a takeover in that the existing controlling stockholders usually remain in control and effectively buy out the interests of the minority, albeit using the assets of the corporation. A sale of control usually involves the payment of a premium to the controlling stockholder and leaves the minority in place, whereas a hostile takeover may involve the payment of a premium to public stockholders leaving management in a minority position.

f.   An LBO may also be seen as a preemptive defensive tactic designed to prevent a takeover or may be proposed following the announcement of a hostile takeover as an alternative to the takeover. In some cases, the proposal of an LBO will prompt a third party offer if the proposed LBO price appears to be attractive.

g.   An LBO is similar to a transaction by which a parent company eliminates the minority stockholders in a subsidiary by means of a freeze out merger.

h.   Several private investment firms specialize in arranging LBOs. The most prominent of these firms is Kohlberg Kravis Roberts (KKR) which arranged the $25 billion buyout of RJR Nabisco in 1989. *See Metropolitan Life Ins. Co. v. RJR Nabisco, Inc.*, 906 F.2d 884 (2d Cir. 1990).

i.   LBOs have been criticized as involving an inherent duty of loyalty problem because the controlling stockholders are privy to more and better information about the value of the company. The SEC has adopted Rule 13e–3 specifically addressing tender offers in connection with going-private transactions.

j.   Delaware law appears to favor LBOs and other going-private transactions. *See In re Siliconix Inc. Shareholders Litigation*, 2001 WL 716787 (in the absence of coercion, a self tender offer by a majority stockholder will not be reviewed for entire fairness but only for full disclosure). Moreover, the Delaware courts have held that where the acquiring company owns 90 percent or more of the target and thus may use a short form merger in the back-end mop-up, the business judgment rule applies. *Glassman v. Unocal Exploration Corp.*, 777 A.2d 242, 248 (Del. 2001) (appraisal is the sole remedy available to a minority stockholder in a short form merger). *But see Smith v. Van Gorkom* (proposed third party buyout by merger violates the business judgment rule).

Caveat: If the proposal of an LBO prompts a competing third party bid, the Revlon rule presumably applies. Thus, premiums paid to stockholders in LBOs tend to be comparable to those paid in third party deals.

k.   A similar transaction is often used to effect the divestiture of a division of a corporation to a subgroup of management. Such a transaction is often called a *split off*. In some cases, a company may choose to *spin off* a division, by forming a NEWCO to hold the assets and then distributing shares of NEWCO to existing stockholders as a dividend. In other cases, a company may split off a division and sell or spin off a small amount of stock in NEWCO in order to create a public market for the shares as a prelude to a public offering of NEWCO. Such a transaction is often called an equity carve-out. As with LBOs, such divestitures may be seen as a defensive tactic designed to preempt a hostile bid financed with borrowed money to be paid back through the break-up and piecemeal sale of the target company.

Caveat: In the 1980s, such transactions were often seen by management as the lesser of evils. In many cases, a break-up was impossible to avoid if a hostile bidder had offered an attractive premium to shareholders. One might think that with the advent of more or less bulletproof takeover defenses, LBOs and divestitures would have largely faded away. To the contrary, such transactions have become more common as management compensation has shifted from mostly cash to mostly equity (often in the form of stock options). As a result, in the 1990s management has tended to gain when stockholders gain and has little incentive to pursue or maintain size for its own sake.

Caveat: Some courts have held that the use of borrowed funds to purchase (or repurchase) target stocks constitutes a fraudulent transfer with respect to creditors because the transaction may render the corporation insolvent and unable to pay its obligations as they become due. *See Wieboldt Stores, Inc. v. Schottenstein*, 94 B.R. 488 (N.D.Ill.1988); *Crowthers McCall Pattern, Inc. v. Lewis*, 129 B.R. 992 (S.D.N.Y.1991). Other courts have avoided the fraudulent transfer argument by holding that payments to shareholders are *settlement payments* for securities transactions that are statutorily excluded from the fraudulent transfer statute. *See Kaiser Steel Corp v. Charles Schwab & Co., Inc.*, 913 F.2d 846 (10th Cir. 1990); *Kaiser Steel Corp. v. Pearl Brewing Co.*, 952 F.2d 1230 (10th Cir. 1991); *Zahn v. Yucaipa Capital Fund*, 218 B.R. 656, 675 (D.R.I. 1998). *But see Munford v. Valuation Research Corp.*, 98 F.3d 604 (11th Cir. 1996).

I. TAKEOVERS AND MERGERS AFTER 1990

Takeover activity (as well as merger activity generally) largely ceased around 1990, because of state takeover laws, more powerful defenses, and lack of funding. Merger activity resumed in the mid 1990s albeit in a very different form. Because of high stock market prices, most mergers and takeovers involved stock rather than cash as consideration. In addition, a general relaxation of the antitrust laws together with globalization encouraged horizontal consolidations in larger S companies. Finally, as a result of the takeovers of the 1980s, managers began to focus on maximizing share value as the best defense against takeover. Indeed, by the year 2000, CEOs of the largest companies received 90 percent of their compensation in some form of equity, primarily stock options. Accordingly, management had to undertake value maximizing transactions such as divestitures of underperforming divisions even if it meant shrinking the size of the company, whereas during the 1980s such transactions could only be forced by an accomplished hostile takeover.

REVIEW QUESTIONS

14.1. True or False: A person who owns a controlling interest in the shares of a corporation may sell those shares for any price that she can get.

14.2. Why not adopt a rule that control is a corporate asset and that the profit from its sale must be divided among all shareholders?

14.3. X corporation was a manufacturer of steel. Because of wartime conditions steel was in short supply and a gray market existed with respect to it although there were government controls on prices. D, the controlling shareholder of X, sold his stock to Y corporation at a premium over the price which non-control shares could command. Y was an end-user of steel and used its control of X to allocate steel to itself at the government prices. P, a minority shareholder of X, brings a derivative action on behalf of the corporation against D for breach of D's fiduciary duty. Is D liable to the corporation?

14.4. What is a tender offer and how are they regulated?

14.5. How does a takeover by tender offer differ from a takeover by merger?

14.6. What is the "Williams Act"?

14.7. Why have states adopted statutes dealing with tender offers despite the existence of the Williams Act?

14.8. What role is played in takeover attempts by risk arbitrageurs?

14.9. What is a leveraged buyout?

14.10. What are "porcupine provisions"?

14.11. What is a "poison pill"?

14.12. True or False: The decisions by the Supreme Court of Delaware on permissible defensive tactics in takeovers are hopelessly confused; the court in effect wanders from one side to another.

14.13. What is the "just say no" defense?

XV

Mergers & Acquisitions

Corporation statutes typically provide for certain kinds of corporate combinations, including (1) the *merger* of one corporation into another corporation, (2) the *consolidation* of two corporations into a single new corporation, (3) merger of a subsidiary of a corporation into the parent corporation, and (4) in some states, a compulsory share exchange. Although the word *merger* may connote that stockholders in the non-surviving corporation receive shares in the surviving corporation, most merger transactions today do not involve the simple amalgamation of two businesses as the term appears to contemplate. A nonstatutory transaction such as a share purchase (possibly through a tender offer) or an asset purchase may achieve the same economic result as a statutory transaction but with different legal consequences. For example, if an acquiring corporation purchases the assets of a target corporation in exchange for shares of the acquiring corporation, and the target corporation then dissolves and distributes the shares to its stockholders, the transaction is economically equivalent to a merger. But under Delaware law, for example, the stockholders of the acquiring corporation do not have a vote or appraisal rights and the stockholders of the target corporation do not have appraisal rights. In a few cases (though not in Delaware), the courts have recharacterized such a transaction as a merger under the *de facto merger doctrine* in order afford stockholders rights they would have in a statutory merger.

Caveat: The word *merger* is often used loosely to refer to any combination of companies. Here the word merger is used in its technical sense to refer to the statutory combination of two companies in which one survives.

The word *target* is used generally to refer the company being acquired. In some mergers, the target may survive in the merger.

Caveat: Although the word *merger* may connote a transaction in which target stockholders become stockholders in the surviving company, most merger statutes today permit target stockholders to be paid any form of consideration, including cash, debt, property, and stock in other corporations, for their shares. Most merger statutes also permit the payment of differing forms (and even amounts) of consideration to different stockholders.

Caveat: Special rules address combinations involving a domestic corporation and a foreign corporation (a corporation formed in a different state or country.) *See* MBCA 11.02. In addition, many states now have provisions addressing the merger of a corporation with a partnership or LLC or other unincorporated form of organization, or with a nonprofit corporation. *See* MBCA 11.02. In such a transaction, each entity typically must follow the rules under which it is organized. Unless otherwise noted, the discussion here assumes a transaction between two corporations incorporated in the same jurisdiction.

A. STATUTORY MERGERS & SHARE EXCHANGES

1. Mergers, Consolidations, and Share Exchanges

a. A *merger* of corporation A into corporation B means that the two corporations are combined and corporation B survives while corporation A disappears. On the effective date of a merger, the assets and liabilities of the non-surviving corporation become assets and liabilities of the surviving corporation automatically by operation of law and are not deemed to be transfers of assets or liabilities. *See* MBCA 11.07. This may be of importance when a corporation has assets that may not be transferred without the prior consent of a governmental agency or third person.

b. A *consolidation* of corporation A and corporation B means that the two corporations are combined but both corporation A and corporation B disappear and a new corporation C is created. The MBCA has eliminated the concept of consolidation. It is seldom used because it is almost always advantageous for one of the entities involved in a transaction to be the surviving corporation, and because a new entity can always be created and the other entities merged into it.

c. In a *share exchange* all stockholders of a class of shares are obligated to exchange their shares for the consideration specified in a plan of share exchange when that plan is approved by a majority of the shares of that class following essentially the same procedure that is applicable to the approval of a merger. The exchange is mandatory. A share exchange is similar in effect to a reverse triangular merger (described below) in that the target corporation survives and becomes a subsidiary of the acquiring corporation.

> *Caveat:* Many states have amended their statutes relating to mergers to permit combinations of differing types of entities, such as a merger between a corporation and partnership. The ABA and NCCUSL have undertaken to develop a model statute dealing with domestication, conversion, merger, and share exchanges between unincorporated entities and between such entities and corporations. The Model Entity Transactions Act (META) does not address transactions between corporations. Many statutes impose arbitrary limits on the forms of organizations that may merge and the types of organizations that must survive the merger. META is designed to eliminate these discrepancies. META was adopted by NCCUSL in August 2004.

2. Basic Procedures

A statutory merger must be approved by the board of directors and by a specific percentage of the stockholders of one or both corporations.

a. A plan of merger must be approved by the board of directors and recommended to the stockholders. MBCA 11.04. The board of directors may condition the plan on such terms as it deems desirable. For example, the plan may require that the merger be approved by one or more classes of shares voting as separate voting groups or that no more than a specified number of stockholders elect the right of dissent and appraisal (described below). Following approval, articles of merger must be filed with the state.

b. The vote of stockholders required for approval of a merger varies from state to state. Under the MBCA, most mergers require a vote of the stockholders of the non surviving corporation only. The stockholders of the surviving corporation need not vote on the merger if (1) the articles of incorporation of the surviving corporation will not be changed in a way that requires a stockholder vote, (2) each stockholder of the surviving corporation will hold the same number of shares rights, and (3) the issuance in the merger of shares does not require a vote under MBCA 6.21(f), (which requires a stockholder vote if the aggregate voting power of the corporation will increase by 20 percent or more as a result of the issuance of new shares). MBCA 11.04. Voting by voting group is required if a class or series would be entitled to vote as a separate group on a provision in the plan that, if contained in a proposed amendment to articles of incorporation, would require action by separate voting groups under MBCA 10.04.

> *Example:* A corporation that is a party to a statutory merger has outstanding a class of nonvoting preferred shares that has unpaid cumulative dividends. The plan of merger provides that each preferred share is to receive one share of common stock in full payment of the unpaid dividends. The preferred shares are entitled to vote as a separate voting group on the merger. *See* MBCA 10.04(a). Further, holders of preferred shares who vote against the plan of merger have a right of dissent and appraisal pursuant to MBCA 13.02. In this example, it makes no difference whether the corporation with the class of preferred shares is to be the surviving corporation in the merger or is to disappear in the merger. In either event the right of the preferred stockholders to cumulative dividends may be eliminated pursuant to the merger subject to the procedural protections described above.

c. Most states follow similar rules except that the 20 percent trigger relates to shares to be issued in the merger by the surviving corporation, while under the MBCA it relates to any 20 percent increase in voting power, whether or not the shares are issued in the context of a merger. In other words, the MBCA provision relates to *all* new issues of a substantial number of voting shares, including rights to purchase such shares. Thus, in most states, a stockholder vote by the surviving corporation may be avoided even if the number of shares is increased by more than 20 per cent by casting the transaction as a triangular merger rather than as a direct merger. (Triangular mergers are discussed below.) As a practical matter, however, because stock exchange rules require stockholder approval of any new issue of shares in excess of about 20 percent of the outstanding number, a stockholder vote will ultimately be required, though technically not in connection with the merger.

d. Under the MBCA, the required vote is a simple majority of shares present and voting at meeting at which there is a quorum of at least a majority of shares eligible to vote. Many states require a majority vote of all outstanding voting shares (as did the MBCA prior to 1999). Older statutes sometimes require the affirmative vote of two-thirds of outstanding shares, which may include both voting and nonvoting shares.

e. Stockholders have a right of dissent and appraisal if the plan of merger must be approved by the stockholders and the stockholders in question have the right to vote on the merger. MBCA 13.02. The rules about voting and the right of dissent and appraisal are technical and vary significantly from state to state. The requirements may sometimes be avoided by casting the transaction in a non-statutory form.

f. If the directors of the two corporations are not acting at arms length (as where one corporation owns enough shares of the other to name a majority or all of the board of directors of the other), the merger is a form of self-dealing and is judicially reviewed for fairness. *See Weinberger v. UOP, Inc.*, 457 A.2d 701 (Del.1983); *Singer v. Magnavox Co.*, 380 A.2d 969 (Del.1977); *Sterling v. Mayflower Hotel Corp.*, 93 A.2d 107 (Del.1952). Approval of the merger by disinterested directors or by a vote of disinterested stockholders may avoid the full scale fairness review.

3. Short Form Mergers, Cash Mergers, and Triangular Mergers

Although it is normal to think of a merger as a deal by which two corporations become one and the two groups of stockholders become stockholders in the surviving corporation, most modern transactions are otherwise. The merger statutes of most states provide expressly that the shares of a party to a merger may be converted into shares, obligations or other securities of the surviving or any other corporation or into cash or other property. *See* MBCA 11.02.

a. Most states permit a parent corporation that owns 90 percent or more of the outstanding shares of a subsidiary corporation to merge the subsidiary into the parent without a stockholder vote of either corporation. This procedure is usually called a *short form merger*. MBCA 11.05 Although they do not have a vote, the stockholders of the subsidiary have the statutory right to dissent and receive the appraised value of their shares. MBCA 13.02(a). The short form merger procedure creates no appraisal rights on the part of stockholders of the parent corporation since those stockholders are not entitled to vote on the transaction.

b. A cash merger is a merger in which some stockholders who are parties to the merger are required to accept cash or property (other than shares) for their shares. A cash merger permits the statutory merger procedure to be used to squeeze out one or more stockholders. It is in effect a compulsory buy-out of the shares of certain stockholders. A cash merger may be used as the second part of a two-step acquisition of all the outstanding shares of a target corporation. Such a merger is usually called a *back end* or *mop up merger.*

> *Example:* A majority of the outstanding shares of the target are obtained by open market purchases or tender offers. Some stockholders of the target decline to sell or tender their shares for purchase. The target is then merged into the bidder or a subsidiary of the bidder by a cash merger in which the remaining stockholders of the target are compelled to accept cash. The bidding corporation thereby becomes the owner of all the outstanding shares of the target. Typically, the cash received in the merger is the same as the amount originally paid in the tender offer. In some cases, a bidder may offer a high price for a majority of the stock and announce in advance that if the offer is successful, it will acquire the balance of the shares in a back end merger at a lower price or for debt securities rather than cash. Such *front end loaded two tier tender offers* were common in the mid 1980s but are now rare.

c. Cash mergers are a relatively recent phenomenon. Before the 1960s, many states limited the consideration payable in connection with a merger to shares of the surviving company. Nevertheless, it was possible to effect something like a cash merger by paying target stockholders in redeemable preferred stock. *See Matteson v. Ziebarth*, 242 P.2d 1025 (Wash.1952).

d. In a *triangular merger,* the acquiring corporation forms a wholly-owned subsidiary with nominal assets—sometimes called a *shell corporation* or *acquisition vehicle*—which then merges with the corporation to be acquired. In most cases, the stockholders of the acquired corporation receive shares or other securities of the acquiring corporation or cash. The acquired corporation becomes a wholly-owned subsidiary of the acquiring corporation. One distinct advantage of a triangular merger is that the acquiring corporation does not assume the liabilities of the acquired corporation.

e. In effect, a cash merger involves the payment of cash to minority stockholders while the controlling stockholder receives stock because the controlling stockholder remains in control of the combined entity. Formally, the controlling stockholder corporation might also receive cash for its shares in the subsidiary, but that would only be taking the cash out of one pocket and putting it in another. Thus, many state statutes provide that the plan of merger may specify differing forms of consideration for different stockholders.

f. These devices may be used in combination to avoid a vote by the stockholders of the acquiring corporation. For example, an acquiring corporation may form a shell corporation to merge with the target and then merge the shell into the parent by means of a short form merger. Given that the parent is the sole stockholder of the subsidiary corporation, it is the board of directors of the parent corporation that technically votes the shares of the subsidiary. Similarly, it is the parent corporation that would have appraisal rights if any. While, individual stockholders of the parent corporation might vote against the deal or even use it as an opportunity to cash out by exercising item appraisal rights, presumably the board of directors that negotiated the deal will have no objections.

4. Reverse Triangular Mergers & Share Exchanges

In some transactions, it is important that the acquired corporation survive. Such a result may be achieved through a *reverse triangular merger.*

a. Survival of the target corporation may be important where that corporation is organized under a special statute that makes incorporation difficult (e.g., banks, or insurance companies) or where the corporation has government licenses or other contracts that do not permit assignment.

b. In a reverse triangular merger, the acquiring or holding company creates a new subsidiary and contributes assets to that subsidiary to be used to acquire the shares of the target corporation. The contribution of assets, which may be cash or parent stock or anything of value, is often called a *drop down*. It does not require special approval, because both the creation of the subsidiary and the drop down of assets transactions are in the normal course of business. The subsidiary is then merged into the target corporation and the assets of the subsidiary corporation are exchanged for the shares of the target corporation. The result is that the target corporation becomes a wholly owned subsidiary of the parent and stockholders of the target receive stock, cash or other consideration for their shares.

> *Caveat:*   It is not necessary under most merger statutes to contribute property to the subsidiary corporation, because most statutes permit the target stockholders to be paid in any form of property, including stock of another corporation.

c.   A compulsory *share exchange* accomplishes the same end as a reverse triangular merger. MBCA 11.03 This procedure permits the mandatory acquisition of all shares of a target corporation upon the affirmative vote of a majority of the shares to be acquired. The consideration for the shares being acquired may consist of cash, property, or shares in another corporation. As with a merger, a compulsory share exchange requires approval of the board of directors and submission of the proposed share exchange to the stockholders of the target corporation. If a majority of the shares being exchanged approve the transaction, it is binding on all holders. Stockholders who object to the share exchange have the statutory right of dissent and appraisal. MBCA 13.02(a).

> *Caveat:*   In a share exchange, the acquiring corporation may acquire one class of shares of the target but not others. For example, the acquiring corporation may acquire the common stock of the target (and thus control of the target) but leave preferred stock in place. The same result is possible with a merger as long as the rights of the preferred vís a vís the surviving corporation are identical to its rights vís a vís the non-surviving corporation even though the surviving corporation may be more or less creditworthy than the non-surviving corporation.

5. Fairness Standards

In a merger between a parent and subsidiary, the parent as the controlling stockholder has the power to force terms on the subsidiary and may thus be tempted to take advantage of its controlling position and impose terms unduly favorable to the parent. In theory, minority stockholders are protected by their right of dissent and appraisal. But the appraisal remedy may provide inadequate protection.

a.   Caselaw holds that such transactions constitute self dealing so that a test of *entire fairness* is applicable and that compliance with statutory formalities alone is not sufficient. *Weinberger v. UOP, Inc.*, 457 A.2d 701 (Del.1983). However, the courts have struggled with the precise test to be applied to such transactions.

b. *Singer v. Magnavox Co.*, 380 A.2d 969 (Del.1977), combines a business purpose test with the test of entire fairness. In essence, the court recognized a residual right of a stockholder to continue to be a stockholder rather than an absolute right of the parent to cash out all minority members at any time. Several non-Delaware cases accept this standard. *Gabhart v. Gabhart*, 370 N.E.2d 345 (Ind.1977); *Coggins v. New England Patriots Football Club*, 492 N.E.2d 1112 (Mass.1986); *Alpert v. 28 Williams St. Corp.*, 483 N.Y.S.2d 667, 473 N.E.2d 19 (N.Y. 1984). In *Tanzer v. International Gen. Indus., Inc.*, 379 A.2d 1121 (Del.1977), the court held that the business purpose requirement may be satisfied by considering only the interests of the majority stockholder. As so construed, the business purpose test has little force in preventing abusive transactions. Nevertheless, the court extended the business purpose test to short form mergers. *Roland Intern. Corp. v. Najjar*, 407 A.2d 1032 (Del.1979).

c. In *Weinberger v. UOP, Inc.*, 457 A.2d 701 (Del.1983), the court rejected the business purpose test and substituted an increased emphasis on the entire fairness of the transaction. *Weinberger* states that entire fairness has two elements: fair dealing and fair price. Fair dealing includes full disclosure of all information relating to fairness. *Weinberger* also holds that the statutory right of dissent and appraisal is normally the sole remedy for minority stockholders complaining about the price in freeze-out mergers. The court, however, significantly liberalized that remedy.

> *Example:* In a cash-out merger, the minority stockholders institute an appraisal proceeding complaining that the price is unfair. While in discovery, the plaintiffs discover evidence of wrongdoing in connection with the merger, including fraud, illegality and unfair dealing. The plaintiffs may then bring an independent suit to set aside the merger on these grounds; the appraisal proceeding is the exclusive remedy only for complaints that the price is unfair. *Cede & Co. v. Technicolor, Inc.*, 542 A.2d 1182 (Del.1988).

d. The burden of proving entire fairness is on the corporation proposing the cash transaction. *Kahn v. Lynch Communication Systems*, 638 A.2d 1110 (Del.1994). *Weinberger* suggests, however, that strong evidence of fairness of a transaction may be derived from (a) approval by independent directors of the acquired corporation and (b) approval of the transaction by a *majority of the minority* of shares being cashed out. If these steps are taken, the burden of proof shifts from the parent corporation to the complaining stockholders.

e.   Federal law provides virtually no protection against unfair cash-out merger transactions unless the merger is accomplished by means of deception. *See Santa Fe Indus., Inc. v. Green,* 430 U.S. 462, 975 S.Ct. 1292 (1977); *Cole v. Schenley Indus., Inc.,* 563 F.2d 35 (2d Cir.1977). *But see Virginia Bankshares, Inc. v. Sandberg,* 501 U.S. 1083, 111 S.Ct. 2749 (1991) (considering possibility that deception in connection with majority of minority vote could give rise to federal cause of action if vote insulates transaction from challenge and there is no remedy under state law). *See also Goldberg v. Meridor,* 567 F.2d 209 (2d Cir.1977); *Healey v. Catalyst Recovery of Pennsylvania, Inc.,* 616 F.2d 641 (3d Cir.1980).

Caveat: Under Delaware law a majority stockholder owes a duty of *full-disclosure* but no duty of *fairness* to minority stockholders in connection with a tender offer for the minority shares. *See In re Siliconix Inc. Stockholders Litigation,* 2001 WL 716787 (Del.Ch.). *But see In re Pure Resources, Inc., Stockholders Litigation,* 808 A.2d 421 (Del. Ch. 2002) (imposing certain conditions to assure that tender offer is not coercive).

B.   SALE OF ASSETS

In most states, a sale, lease, exchange, or other disposition of *all or substantially all* of the assets of a corporation (other than in the usual and regular course of business) must be approved by the stockholders. The MBCA followed this pattern until 1999. MBCA 12.02 now provides that stockholder approval is required only if the disposition would leave the corporation without a significant continuing business activity. More specifically, MBCA 12.02 provides that if a corporation retains a business activity that represents at least 25 percent of total assets *and* 25 percent of *either* income from continuing operations before taxes *or* revenues from continuing operations, the corporation will be deemed conclusively to have retained a significant continuing business activity. These tests are applied on the basis of financial information as of the end of the most recently completed fiscal year and on a consolidated basis including the corporation and its subsidiaries.

1. Sales in Ordinary Course of Business

A sale of all, or substantially all, the property and assets of a corporation in the ordinary course of business (which is not common), does not require stockholder approval. MBCA 12.01(a)(1).

> *Example:* A corporation is in the business of buying and selling improved real estate. It invests substantially all of its assets in an apartment house that it holds for speculation for eight months and then resells. The resale does not require stockholder approval.

a. Many state statutes provide that a pledge, mortgage, or deed of trust covering all the assets of the corporation to secure a debt is in the ordinary course of business. MBCA 12.01(a)(2).

b. MBCA 12.01(a)(3) provides that stockholder approval is not required where a corporation drops down substantially all of its assets to a wholly owned subsidiary. *See Campbell v. Vose*, 515 F.2d 256 (10th Cir.1975) (invalidating such a transaction in the absence of stockholder approval). The MBCA Official Comment states that this provision should not be used as a device to avoid a vote of stockholders.

2. All or Substantially All

The scope of the phrase *all or substantially all* is a matter of dispute.

a. All or substantially all of the assets of a corporation are sold even if the corporation retains some small amount of property as a pretext. *Stiles v. Aluminum Products Co.*, 86 N.E.2d 887 (Ill.App.1949). For example, a sale of all the corporate assets other than cash or cash equivalents is the sale of all or substantially all of the corporation's property. A sale of several distinct manufacturing lines while retaining one or more lines is normally not a sale of all or substantially all even though the lines being sold are substantial and include a significant fraction of the corporation's former business, unless the lines are retained only as a temporary operation or as a pretext to avoid the statutory requirements. A sale of a plant but retention of operating assets (machinery and equipment), accounts receivable, good will, and the like, which permits the operation of the same business at another location is also not the sale of all or substantially all of the corporation's property.

b. Until 1999, the MBCA Official Comment stated that the phrase *all or substantially all* should be read to mean what it literally says and noted that the phrase "substantially all" was added merely to make it clear that the statutory requirements could not be avoided by retention of some minimal or nominal residue of the original assets.

c. Judicial decisions adopt a much broader view of the phrase *all or substantially all*. These cases view the test as whether the change of business activity implicit in the sale is sufficiently important that it should be submitted to the stockholders for approval. *See Gimbel v. Signal Companies, Inc.*, 316 A.2d 599 (Del.Ch.1974), *aff'd per curiam*, 316 A.2d 619 (Del.1974). *But see Murphy v. Washington American League Base Ball Club, Inc.*, 293 F.2d 522 (D.C.Cir.1961).

Example: A corporation plans to sell a Canadian subsidiary that constitutes 51 per cent of the corporation's total assets and 44.9 per cent of the corporation's total revenues. *Katz v. Bregman*, 431 A.2d 1274 (Del.Ch.1981), holds that this is a sale of all or substantially all of a corporation's assets and requires stockholder approval. *See also Sharon Steel Corp. v. Chase Manhattan Bank, N.A.*, 691 F.2d 1039 (2d Cir. 1982) (piecemeal sale of operations followed by proposed merger of stripped down corporation with another corporation that would assume long term debts constituted breach of bond indenture relating to successor obligors).

3. Procedural Requirements

As with a merger or share exchange, a sale of assets must be approved by the board of directors and recommended to the stockholders for approval. The transaction must be approved by a majority of the shares voting at a meeting at which a majority quorum of shares entitled to vote is present. Voting by voting groups is not required, because the proceeds of the sale are payable to the corporation and not to the stockholders directly. Under the MBCA and the laws of most states, stockholders who are entitled to vote and who oppose the transaction have a right of dissent and appraisal. MBCA 12.02. Some states, including Delaware, do not grant the right of dissent and appraisal in connection with sales of asset transactions.

C. NONSTATUTORY COMBINATIONS

A statutory merger or share exchange is only one of several ways of effecting a corporate acquisition or combining or amalgamating two or more corporations into a single operation.

1. Types of Transactions

There are basically two types of nonstatutory combinations: a stock purchase and an asset purchase.

a. A stock purchase transaction is one in which one corporation purchases all or most of the outstanding shares of the other corporation in one or more voluntary transactions (such as a negotiated purchase, an open market purchases, or a tender offer). As a result, the target corporation becomes a subsidiary of the acquiring corporation. Thereafter, the parent may liquidate or merge the acquired corporation into itself using one of the devices discussed above.

b. An asset purchase or asset acquisition is a transaction in which one corporation purchases substantially all the assets of another corporation. The purchase may include all or virtually all of the assets of the acquired corporation, or it may include only the assets used in one line of business. The liabilities assumed by the asset purchaser are a matter of negotiation. Often, all liabilities remain with the seller, though it is common for the purchaser to assume liabilities to trade creditors. In any event, claims not assumed remain the responsibility of the seller. The ability to avoid assuming certain types of liabilities is one of the most important advantages of an asset acquisition.

> *Example:* Claims that an asset purchaser does not wish to assume include product liability claims arising from products sold before the sale, tax liabilities for earlier years, environmental responsibilities, and claims based on undisclosed contractual obligations or pending lawsuits.

c. After the transaction is completed, the selling corporation retains its separate existence as an independent corporation but its assets consist only of the proceeds of the sale, usually cash or stock, and whatever assets were not purchased. Such a corporation may continue in existence operating thereafter essentially as an investment company. The selling corporation may liquidate after making provision for liabilities not assumed by the purchaser and distribute the remaining proceeds of the sale to its stockholders. But it is common for the purchasing corporation to require that the selling corporation remain in existence for a number of years to avoid the possibility that the transaction will be recharacterized as a merger.

d. There is no right of dissent and appraisal for stockholders of the purchasing corporation even though stockholder approval would be required if the transaction were cast as a statutory merger.

Example: Corporation A plans to acquire Corporation B, a closely held corporation. Stockholders of Corporation B are to receive one share of Corporation A stock for each share of Corporation B stock they own. Corporation A has sufficient authorized shares to complete the transaction without amending its articles of incorporation. All stockholders of Corporation B approve the transaction. The board of directors of Corporation A simply authorizes the issuance of its shares in exchange for shares of B corporation. The transaction is not a statutory merger and none of the procedures for statutory mergers need to be followed by Corporation A.

2. Selection of Form of Transaction

Non-statutory transactions may have the same economic effect as a statutory merger or share exchange. For example, a sale of assets in exchange for stock of the buyer corporation followed by dissolution of the seller and distribution of the buyer stock to seller stockholders amounts to the same thing as a merger of the two corporations.

a. The choice of form for a particular transaction involves a variety of business and tax considerations. The parties to a specific transaction may have different views on this question, one preferring an asset purchase, the other a stock purchase or statutory merger, often depending on the tax consequences. Generally the controlling stockholder may structure the transaction according to its own interests. *Grace v. Grace Nat. Bank of New York*, 465 F.2d 1068 (2d Cir.1972).

b. It is perfectly legal to structure a transaction in one form rather than another in order to simplify the procedures to be followed or to avoid granting dissenting stockholders the right of dissent and appraisal. *Hariton v. Arco Electronics, Inc.*, 188 A.2d 123 (Del.1963). On the other hand, because the transactions may be economically equivalent, some courts have held that a sale of assets may be treated as a merger in some circumstances under the *de facto merger doctrine. See Farris v. Glen Alden Corp.*, 143 A.2d 25 (Pa. 1958) (purchase of assets for stock by small Pennsylvania corporation from larger Delaware corporation recast as merger where structure of deal avoided appraisal rights for Pennsylvania corporation stockholders as well as real estate transfer taxes and stockholders of Delaware corporation constituted large majority of stockholders following transaction). *See also Applestein v. United Bd. & Carton Corp.,* 159 A.2d 146 (N.J.Super.Ch.Div.1960). The Pennsylvania statutes were later amended to reverse the result in *Farris. See Terry v. Penn Central Corp.,* 668 F.2d 188 (3d Cir.1981) (challenging series of triangular mergers designed to avoid vote of preferred stockholders). *See also Orzeck v. Englehart,* 195 A.2d 375 (Del.1963).

c. The *de facto merger doctrine* has been applied more recently in connection with cases involving products liability claims and environmental harms in order to hold the purchasing corporation liable as it would be if the transaction had taken the form of a statutory merger. Some courts reach the same result under a variety of theories: (1) there is an express or implied agreement to assume the liabilities; (2) the transaction amounts to a consolidation or merger; (3) the successor entity is a mere continuation or reincarnation of the predecessor entity; or (4) the transaction was fraudulent, not made in good faith, or made without sufficient consideration; or (5) continuity of enterprise. *See North Shore Gas Co. v. Salomon, Inc.,* 152 F.3d 642, 651 (7th Cir. 1998); *Nissen Corp. v. Miller,* 323 Md. 613, 594 A.2d 564, 565–66 (Md. 1991). In addition, under some circumstances it may be possible to argue that the two corporations have entered into a partnership with each other. *See Good v. Lackawanna Leather Co.,* 233 A.2d 201 (N.J.Super.Ch.Div.1967).

> *Example:* A closely held manufacturing corporation sells its assets to a large publicly held corporation, discharges its known liabilities, distributes the remaining proceeds to its stockholders, and dissolves. The acquiring corporation does not assume liabilities of the manufacturing corporation (other than specific liabilities spelled out in the agreement itself). The acquiring corporation continues the business of the acquired corporation using the same plant, same work force, and the same name. Four years later an action is filed for personal injuries caused by a defective product sold by the old manufacturing company. Despite express disclaimer of the assumption of liabilities, the court holds the purchasing corporation liable on the products liability claim on the basis of the *de facto merger doctrine. Knapp v. North American Rockwell Corp.,* 506 F.2d 361 (3d Cir.1974).

d. Under most state statutes, suit against a dissolved corporation must be brought within three years of public notice of dissolution, MBCA 14.07, and the stockholders may be held liable to the extent that assets of the dissolved corporation have been distributed to them.

3. Divisive Transactions

A few states have adopted statutes permitting corporations to divide into two or more corporations. The ABA and NCCUSL have undertaken jointly to draft model legislation in this area.

a. Such transactions constitute about half of all corporate deals but have not traditionally been addressed by statute. Rather, in most cases such a division is accomplished by a transfer of assets to a newly formed subsidiary corporation (or an existing subsidiary) followed by a distribution of the subsidiary's shares.

b. If the distribution of the subsidiary's shares is made to all stockholders of the parent (a spinoff), the distribution will likely be treated as a distribution of property (such as a cash dividend). Such a distribution of stock is not a stock dividend because the stock distributed is stock of another corporation (the subsidiary). It is property of the distributing corporation. If the distribution of subsidiary stock is made to some stockholders but not others and the distributee stockholders give up their stock in the distributing corporation (a split off), then the transaction will likely be treated as a repurchase of stock. In many states, the same basic rules apply to both types of transactions, but there may be subtle variations even in those states. In other states, the rules may vary considerably between the two. In some cases, if the operations to be shed are quite significant in comparison to those remaining with the distributing corporation, the transaction may arguably qualify as a sale of assets, triggering the rules relating to such transactions.

c. One important issue in such deals is the division of liabilities between successor entities. In most cases, the offshoot corporation will assume minimal current liabilities, while the distributing corporation will retain most long term liabilities. (The corporation cannot shed its own liabilities even if another corporation assumes them, but a new corporation is not obligated to creditors except to the extent that it assumes such obligations.) Thus, the creditors will have a strong interest in the deal. In extreme cases, the deal may be unwound by means of piercing the corporate veil or theories of successor liability.

D. GOING PRIVATE & LEVERAGED BUYOUTS

The term *going private* refers to a transaction by which a publicly held corporation cashes out its public stockholders and becomes privately held. The transaction permits deregistration of the corporation under the Securities Exchange Act of 1934, thereby eliminating expensive reporting and disclosure requirements. Most corporations considering a traditional going private transaction went public by selling shares publicly at a time when market conditions were favorable. Typically only a minority interest was sold to the public. The going private transaction is likely to occur some years later when stock prices are depressed.

Example: A corporation sells shares in a public offering in 1968 at $5 per share. In 1975, the controlling stockholders propose a going private transaction at a time when the market price is under $2 per share and the price offered the public stockholders is $2 per share. This transaction was enjoined as unfair to minority stockholders. *Berkowitz v. Power/Mate Corp.*, 342 A.2d 566 (N.J.Super.Ch.Div.1975).

1. Form of Going Private Transactions

A going-private transaction may take the form of a cash merger of the publicly held corporation into a corporation wholly owned by the control group, by a cash tender offer followed by a mop-up merger, by a reverse stock split, or by an amendment to articles of incorporation changing the rights of stockholders. If the transaction is accomplished by reverse stock split, the ratio between outstanding shares and post-transaction shares is set at a level that makes the holdings of the largest public stockholder into a fractional share. The corporation purchases all fractional shares at a specified price, as is permitted by most corporation statutes. *See* MBCA 6.04.

Caveat: It is not entirely clear whether the rules relating to distributions apply to the repurchase of fractional shares, though the law of some states appears to exempt such repurchases from the balance sheet and solvency tests.

2. Leveraged Buyouts

A leveraged buyout (LBO) is essentially a going-private transaction involving outside investors. In an LBO, a private corporation acquires all of the outstanding shares of a publicly held corporation. The acquiring corporation may be financed by investors who specialize in such transactions often using borrowed money and often by issuing junk bonds. After the LBO is completed, the corporation is no longer publicly owned. Typically, the corporation assumes the obligation to repay the loans required to accomplish the transaction. Pieces of the acquired company are often sold to help pay down this debt. Thus, such a transaction is often called a bust up takeover, though that term may be used in the context of both friendly and hostile deals.

a. An LBO differs from a going private transaction primarily in that outside investors rather than incumbent managers acquire the predominant equity ownership of the company. Incumbent management may participate in an LBO, usually with a minority stake. Such a transaction may be called a management buy-out (MBO). Still, the economic interest of management in the corporation is usually increased significantly as a result of the transaction.

b. As much as possible of the purchase price is borrowed. The interest payable on LBO debt is tax deductible by the acquired company, subject to limitations imposed by FRB rules. Income taxes may thus be reduced to zero by the LBO and cash flow formerly used to pay taxes may be used to pay interest.

c. Often the hope of the investors in the LBO is that the company will be able to pay down the debt with cash flow and possibly again become a publicly owned company.

3. Regulation

Going private transactions are similar in form to a parent-subsidiary merger and thus are subject to entire fairness review under *Weinberger*. Some states also grant stockholders who are cashed out by a reverse stock split the right of dissent and appraisal. *See* MBCA 13.02(a). In addition, in 1979 the SEC adopted Rules 13e–3 and 13e–4 to assure full disclosure in connection with going private transactions, including a statement as to the belief of the issuer whether the transaction is fair or unfair to the public stockholders and a discussion in reasonable detail of the material factors upon which the belief is based.

E. RIGHT OF DISSENT & APPRAISAL

State statutes give stockholders the right to dissent from certain types of transactions and to obtain the appraised value of their shares in cash through a judicial proceeding. *See* MBCA 13.01-13.31.

1. Scope of the Appraisal Right

The appraisal right is a creature of statute and is available only when the statute specifically so provides. State statutes vary considerably in terms of the transactions that give rise to appraisal rights.

a. MBCA 13.02 extends appraisal rights to (1) a merger in which the stockholder has the right to vote, (2) a short form merger of a subsidiary into its parent as to stockholders of the subsidiary only, (3) a share exchange if the stockholder has the right to vote as a stockholder of the target only, and (4) a sale of assets if the stockholder has the right to vote on the sale, (5) a reverse stock split as to stockholders who will have their shares repurchased, (6) domestication, if the stockholder does not receive shares in the foreign corporation resulting from the domestication that have terms as favorable to the stockholder in all material respects, and represent at least the same percentage interest of the total voting rights of the outstanding shares of the corporation, as the shares held by the stockholder before the domestication; (7) consummation of a conversion of the corporation to nonprofit status; (8) consummation of a conversion of the corporation to an unincorporated entity, or (9) transactions as to which the articles of incorporation, bylaws, or a resolution of the board of directors specifies that dissenters' rights must be provided.

b. Prior to the 1999 amendments, the MBCA also provided for appraisal rights in the case of an amendment to the articles of incorporation that materially and adversely affects stockholder rights in specified ways–roughly similar to the situations in which a stockholder vote is triggered for non-voting shares though somewhat narrower.

Caveat: Not all state statutes provide dissenters' rights in all categories. For example, Delaware law does not provide for appraisal rights in connection with a sale of assets. Some states also provide dissenters' rights in additional classes of cases. For example, Pennsylvania provides for appraisal rights if there is a change of control.

c. The law of many states includes an exception for publicly traded companies on the theory that if there is a liquid market for the shares of the subject company, market price is a reliable measure of value. In other words, stockholders of a publicly traded company do not have appraisal rights even though the transaction is one that would ordinarily trigger such rights. As of 1999, the MBCA also includes such an exception. (The

MBCA also included a similar exception prior to 1984.) Specifically, the MBCA exempts companies that are listed on the NYSE, AMEX, or NASDAQ, or have 2000 or more stockholders and a public float of $20 million or more. MBCA 13.02(b). Delaware law also includes a market exception but only for mergers in which the consideration to be paid is stock of a publicly traded company. (Delaware law also grants appraisal rights to the stockholders of the *surviving* corporation unless it is listed or widely held *and* no stockholder vote is required.) DGCL 262.

d.   Under the MBCA there is an exception to the exception for (1) transactions in which the stockholders will be paid in anything other than cash or shares of a publicly traded company, and (2) transactions in which an insider or insider affiliate acquires the subject company. MBCA 13.02(b). For these purposes, an insider is defined as anyone who (before the transaction) owns 20 percent or more of the subject company stock (excluding shares acquired in an any-or-all offer within the preceding 12 months at an equal or lesser price), or anyone who had the power to elect or appoint one-fourth or more of the company's directors, or anyone who will receive a financial benefit not generally available to other stockholders (other than employment by or a seat on the board of directors of the surviving company). In other words, appraisal is available notwithstanding the market exception in the context of an interested transaction.

2.   Exclusiveness of Appraisal Right

The statutes of some states provide that appraisal is the exclusive remedy for dissenting stockholders. MBCA 13.02(d) provides that appraisal is the exclusive remedy unless the action is unlawful or was procured as a result of fraud or material misrepresentation. In some states, caselaw holds that appraisal is the exclusive remedy. *See Weinberger v. UOP, Inc.*, 457 A.2d 701 (Del.1983); *Glassman v. Unocal Exploration Corp.*, 777 A.2d 242, 248 (Del. 2001) (short form merger). Other states hold that the right of dissent and appraisal is exclusive when the stockholders' only complaint is the inadequacy of the price. *Stringer v. Car Data Systems*, 841 P.2d 1183 (Ore.1992). Several states appear to permit stockholder actions challenging the fairness of terms on a variety of grounds including lack of business purpose even though the statute states that the appraisal remedy is exclusive. *See Alpert v. 28 Williams St. Corp.*, 483 N.Y.S.2d 667, 473 N.E.2d 19 (N.Y. 1984); *Matteson v. Ziebarth*, 242 P.2d 1025 (Wash.1952). It is not entirely clear what it means for the appraisal statute to be the exclusive remedy given that the notion of fraud is broadly construed in the context of corporation law as essentially equivalent to a breach of fiduciary duty.

3. Procedure

State statutes provide elaborate procedures for establishing the right to an appraisal and fixing the price.

a. The corporation has a duty to provide correct information as to the procedures to be followed. *Gibbons v. Schenley Indus., Inc.*, 339 A.2d 460 (Del.Ch.1975). The statutory right may be lost if the statutory procedures are not precisely followed. *Gibson v. Strong, Inc.*, 708 S.W.2d 603 (Ark.1986). If the right is lost, the dissenting stockholder must go along with the transaction.

b. The notice of meeting to stockholders at which the transaction is considered must state that dissenters' rights may arise from the transaction. MBCA 13.20. A written notice of intent to demand payment must be filed by each dissenting stockholder before the vote of stockholders is taken on the proposed action. MBCA 13.21. Following approval of the transaction, the corporation must send a notice to each dissenter. MBCA 13.22. Each dissenting stockholder must then file a demand for payment. MBCA 13.23. A stockholder must dissent with respect to all shares, but record owners who hold shares for more than one beneficial owner may dissent owner by owner. MBCA 13.03. The MBCA permits either the record owner or the beneficial owner to commence an appraisal proceeding. MBCA 13.03. Under Delaware law, only a record owner may do so.

c. In most states, no money is paid by the corporation until the judicial proceeding is concluded. Under the MBCA, the corporation must estimate the fair value of the shares and pay to each dissenter that amount immediately. MBCA 13.24. If the dissenting stockholder is dissatisfied with this payment, he must submit an estimate of the fair value of his shares. MBCA 13.26. If the stockholder and the corporation cannot agree as to an additional amount to be paid, the stockholder or the corporation may obtain a judicial appraisal of the value of the shares. MBCA 13.30. To avoid possible speculation on the outcome of an appraisal proceeding, the MBCA provides that a corporation may refuse to make immediate payment to a stockholder who acquires shares after announcement of the transaction. MBCA 13.27. Such a stockholder is entitled to payment only upon the completion of the appraisal proceeding.

d. The fair value of shares is to be fixed as of a time immediately before the transaction and without consideration of the effect of the transaction on the value of the shares. MBCA 13.01. Some statutes specify that value should be determined as of the day before the announcement of the deal, while other statutes specify the day before the stockholder. The MBCA permits consideration of appreciation or depreciation in anticipation of the transaction if equitable. MBCA 13.01. Caselaw addresses a variety of factors to be considered in this regard. *See Weinberger v. UOP, Inc.,* 457 A.2d 701 (Del.1983) (court may consider premiums in comparable transactions); *Rapid-American Corp. v. Harris,* 603 A.2d 796 (Del.1992) (court should consider control premium that could be commanded by parent in connection with sale of subsidiary).

e. The traditional manner of establishing fair value is the Delaware Block Method. In this method of valuation, the court calculates a weighted average of asset value, market value, and earnings value. Weights are assigned according to the reliability of each factor. *See Gibbons v. Schenley Indus., Inc.,* 339 A.2d 460 (Del.Ch.1975). In a case in which the market value for the stock is based on only a few transactions, market value is given a relatively low weight. *Piemonte v. New Boston Garden Corp.,* 387 N.E.2d 1145 (Mass.1979) (ten percent); *Brown v. Hedahl's-Q B & R, Inc.,* 185 N.W.2d 249 (N.D.1971); *Application of Delaware Racing Ass'n,* 213 A.2d 203 (Del.1965). Earnings value is usually based on the capitalized value for average earnings over the most recent five years. *Francis I. duPont & Co. v. Universal City Studios, Inc.,* 312 A.2d 344 (Del.Ch.1973). There is no assurance under these tests that the court-determined price will be equal to or more than the merger price. *See Gibbons v. Schenley Indus., Inc.,* (merger price was $53.33 per share and appraised value was $33.86 per share).

f. In *Weinberger v. UOP, Inc.,* 457 A.2d 701 (Del.1983), the Delaware Supreme Court abandoned the Delaware block method and adopted a more flexible approach that permits use of valuation techniques acceptable in the financial community. The trial court has broad discretion in the process. The most common method followed by courts today is valuation by means of discounted cash flow (DCM) using the capital asset pricing model (CAPM) to determine the capitalization rate based on the risk inherent in the stock as measured by its beta coefficient (the volatility of the stock compared to the market as a whole).

g. The MBCA provides that the costs of an appraisal proceeding including the fees of a court appointed appraiser are to be borne by the corporation. Attorney fees may be assessed against the corporation if it did not substantially comply with the requirements of the statute or against the dissenting stockholders if they acted arbitrarily, vexatiously, or not in good faith. The court may also order attorney fees paid out of the award to the dissenters. MBCA 13.31. The court also has broad discretion with respect to awards of prejudgment interest.

4. Evaluation of the Appraisal Remedy

The appraisal remedy has a superficial appeal, but from the stockholder's point of view it is not an attractive remedy. Accordingly, stockholders and their lawyers typically look for some way to maintain an action against the corporation based on breach of fiduciary duty or some similar broad claim.

a. Appraisal involves potentially long delays while the price is established. In most states there is no requirement that the corporation make immediate payment of the amount it estimates to be the fair value of the shares. All payments are deferred until completion of the appraisal proceeding. Accordingly, the stockholder may lose the returns that would have been available if the merger price had been taken and the funds reinvested. Although the courts have broad discretion in the award of prejudgment interest, they seldom award it at a rate that would compensate the investor for interim investment returns. The MBCA has sought to alleviate some of these problems, but it has not been widely followed in this regard.

b. Litigation over the value of shares is complicated, expensive and risky. The corporation is an active participant in the judicial proceeding and seeks to establish the lowest possible valuation. The corporation has extensive knowledge about its own affairs and virtually unlimited resources to litigate the issue. There is always a risk that a court will find the appraised value to be less than the price offered in the merger. Practically speaking, a lawyer is likely to prefer to pursue a class action on behalf of all stockholders because if the action is successful, attorney fees will likely be a percentage of a much larger pot and are assured to be paid out of that pot. Thus, it is much more likely that a stockholder will be able to retain effective control of a class action than an appraisal proceeding.

c. Because appraisal rights may constitute a serious cash drain on the corporation, it is common in a merger agreement to provide an escape clause for the parties to a merger if an excessive number of dissents are filed. Arguably, the elaborate procedures to be followed in a appraisal proceeding were developed to permit the corporation to withdraw from a transaction once it learns that a large number of dissents will be filed. But the complex procedural requirements may also create injustice if a relatively minor failure to follow the prescribed procedures results in a loss of the right to dissent.

d. On the other hand, a stockholder has a right to appraisal that cannot be dismissed for failure to state a cause of action or as a result of summary judgment. Moreover, the existence of the appraisal remedy may cause acquiring corporations to offer a fairer price in the first place.

F. VOLUNTARY DISSOLUTION

Generally, a corporation may dissolve if the board of directors so proposes and a majority of stockholders (or some other specified percentage) approves. *See* MBCA 14.02. In this regard, dissolution is similar to other organic changes such as a merger or sale of assets. There are special rules that permit dissolution before commencement of business by the incorporators or initial directors by filing a simple notice of dissolution. MBCA 14.01. Dissolution is permitted in many states at any time with the unanimous consent of the stockholders if suitable provision is made for creditors. This provision is widely used by closely held corporations. The MBCA does not contain a provision to this effect. Even though stockholders may act by unanimous consent under the MBCA, action by the board of directors is still required for dissolution.

Caveat: This section does not address involuntary dissolution. That subject is addressed in the chapter on closely held corporations.

1. Procedure

Some states require the filing of a notice of intent to dissolve, followed by a period in which the business and affairs of the corporation are wound up, followed by the filing of final articles of dissolution. MBCA (1969) followed this multiple step procedure. MBCA 14.03 permits articles of dissolution to be filed at any time during the dissolution process.

a. The corporation must give written notice of the dissolution to known creditors and claimants. MBCA 14.06. The notice must state a deadline for filing claims no fewer than 120 days from the effective date of the notice. If the corporation rejects a claim, the claimant has 90 days from the date of the rejection notice to begin a judicial proceeding to enforce the claim. If a claimant who receives notice fails to make a claim or fails to commence an enforcement proceeding within these specified periods, the claim is barred.

b. As for possible unknown claimants, the corporation may publish a notice of dissolution in a newspaper of general circulation in the county of its principal office or, if it has no office in the state, the county of its registered agent. The notice must specify a procedure for filing claims and state that claims not filed within three years are barred. MBCA 14.07.

> *Caveat:* It is implicit in this provision, that the corporation must follow this procedure in every state in which it is qualified to do business.

> *Example:* An Illinois corporation qualifies to transact business in New Jersey. It later dissolves under Illinois law but takes no steps to withdraw from New Jersey even though that state provides a procedure for withdrawal of dissolved corporations. The corporation remains liable to suit in New Jersey until it follows the required New Jersey procedure. *Dr. Hess & Clark, Inc. v. Metalsalts Corp.,* 119 F.Supp. 427 (D.N.J.1954).

c. State statutes usually provide that the existence of a corporation continues after dissolution for a stated period so that the corporation may be sued on pre-dissolution claims. MBCA 14.07 states simply that the corporation's existence continues indefinitely after dissolution, but bars claims that are not timely filed.

d. A claim that is not barred may be enforced (1) against the dissolved corporation to the extent of its undistributed assets or (2) against a stockholder of the dissolved corporation to the extent of the stockholder's pro rata share of the claim or the corporate assets distributed to the stockholder in liquidation, whichever is less. However, a stockholder's total liability for all claims under this section may not exceed the total amount of assets distributed to the stockholder. MBCA 14.07.

e. MBCA 14.08 provides a procedure by which a corporation may commence a judicial proceeding to determine the necessary security for claims that have not been filed or that may arise after the effective date of dissolution. If the corporation provides such security, unknown claimants may not thereafter enforce their claims against the stockholders.

f. There is no statutory right of appraisal in connection with a voluntary dissolution.

2. Equitable Limitations

Equitable limitations on the power to dissolve have sometimes been imposed in situations where a voluntary dissolution is unfair to minority stockholders or is used to freeze out such stockholders.

a. If the business is losing money dissolution may be reasonable, because the majority should not be required to wait until the corporation is insolvent and their investment is lost. On the other hand, dissolution may lead to the sale of assets at inadequate prices.

b. Cases have arisen where dissolution is part of a broader scheme to eliminate some stockholders from sharing in the future profits of a profitable business. For example, the business may be sold as a going concern to a new corporation which is owned by only some of the original owners. *Lebold v. Inland Steel Co.*, 125 F.2d 369 (7th Cir.1941).

c. In some early cases, dissolution and reincorporation was used to eject a minority from a successful venture. Today, such a transaction is normally cast as a cash-out merger. The tests developed in the cash-out merger cases may have potential applicability to dissolutions that are designed to eliminate unwanted minority stockholders.

REVIEW QUESTIONS

15.1. What is the difference between a merger and a consolidation? Why does MBCA (1984) not recognize consolidations?

15.2. How does a cash merger differ from an ordinary merger?

15.3. What is a short form merger?

15.4. What is the relationship between statutory and non-statutory methods of combining two corporations?

15.5. What is a de facto merger?

15.6. What are appraisal rights?

15.7. May a corporation sell substantially all its assets without the approval of stockholders?

15.8. What are going private transactions and what legal requirements are applicable to them?

15.9. What is a leveraged buyout?

15.10. True or False. If a person has a right of dissent and appraisal he is fully protected and has no reason to complain about the treatment of his interest in the corporation.

15.11. Corporation A owns 93 per cent of the outstanding shares of Corporation B. The remaining 7 per cent of the shares are held by 50 individuals. Corporation A determines to eliminate the minority stockholders of Corporation B before entering into a transaction with Corporation B. It therefore creates a new wholly owned corporation, Corporation C, and merges Corporation B into Corporation C. The merger agreement provides that the minority stockholders of Corporation B are to receive $60 per share in cash, a fair price, and that the transaction is to be approved only if a majority of the minority stockholders approve it. If the required approval is obtained, is the transaction valid? What remedy, if any, do minority stockholders have who are dissatisfied with the $60 price?

15.12. P is the owner of 40 shares of the stock of D corporation which operates the Gray Sox Baseball Team in Fun City, under a league franchise. D's directors have approved the removal of the franchise to another location. P brings an action to enjoin the club's move. He contends that D's directors have agreed to dispose of substantially all D's assets outside the ordinary course of business and that such a transaction is valid only if it complies with the state corporation act that requires owners of 2/3rds of the common stock to consent to the transfer. Is P entitled to an injunction?

15.13. P is a preferred stockholder in D corporation, a State Y corporation. There are accumulated unpaid dividends on P's stock of $1,800 per share. D has adopted a plan of merger by which it plans to merge with its wholly-owned subsidiary DD. Under the plan of merger P's preferred stock would be converted into one share of new preferred and 5 shares of new common. Under the laws of State Y a stockholder who objects to a merger is entitled to dissent and appraisal, but this remedy is specifically not made exclusive. P brings an action to enjoin the merger on the ground that the merger is unfair to preferred stockholders who will lose all their accumulated unpaid dividends. May P obtain an injunction?

*

APPENDIX A

Answers to Review Questions

CHAPTER 1

1.1. *False.* While the corporate entity theory is useful and the assumption set forth in the question usually leads to the correct answer to questions, it is only a partial explanation of the concept of a corporation.

1.2. *False.* While a corporation almost always involves contractual elements, and the economic model of a corporation is basically contractual, there are also mandatory, noncontractual aspects of corporation law. The economists' nexus of contracts approach is a useful analytic device but not a complete explanation of the corporation.

1.3. *False.* Rights and duties within corporations are largely defined by statute and by the governing corporate documents. Answers must be sought in these sources, at least initially.

1.4. *Largely False.* The law treats a wholly owned corporation as a separate entity for many purposes. For example, a wholly owned corporation is a separate taxable entity; it may enter into contracts with its stockholders, it may become insolvent even though its stockholder is still solvent, and so forth.

1.5. *False.* The state grant of corporate authority is itself subject to constitutional restrictions. Further, Supreme Court decisions have granted a corporation many (though not all) of the federal constitutional rights possessed by an individual.

1.6. *Largely true.* The articles of incorporation are generally viewed as the contract which defines the rights of the various classes of stockholders in the corporation. Most case law dealing with rights of preferred stockholders involve construction of specific provisions in articles of incorporation. Statutes, however, give some minimum rights to preferred stockholders independent of their contract and these rights may not be eliminated by provision in the articles of incorporation.

1.7. *False.* The law of the state of incorporation controls many internal relationships within the corporation, but both federal law and the laws of other states regulate corporate conduct generally. Federal law has also superseded state law in many areas of internal corporate governance in publicly held corporations.

1.8. The number of stockholders is the most obvious difference. However, from an economic standpoint the most important difference is that a market exists for shares of a publicly held corporation but no market exists for closely held shares, which may be unsalable except to other persons interested in the corporation. Publicly held corporations must make public disclosures of information about their activities; a closely held corporation does not. The most important analytic difference, however, is the absence of a market for closely held shares.

1.9. States that do not maintain up-to-date corporation statutes discover that more and more corporations that are transacting business in the state are incorporating in Delaware or other states. This leads to a loss of revenue to the state and its citizens, and may result in courts applying the law of the state of incorporation rather than the local law in matters relating to the internal affairs of the corporation.

1.10. Professor Cary's thesis had wide credence until it was subjected to careful empirical and theoretical economic analysis. It appears that the reasons for the success of Delaware in the incorporation race cannot be traced solely to the laxity of its statute or the biases of its judiciary. Indeed, in most respects, Delaware is viewed as a leader in modern corporation law, not a follower.

1.11. There is no simple answer to selection of the best business form. Tax considerations today favor the LLC or LP over the corporation for closely held businesses, but the corporation is the business form of choice, for most successful businesses since it is better understood and more familiar to many people.

CHAPTER 2

2.1. *False.* Most local businesses should incorporate locally rather than in a distant state. While Delaware has advantages, particularly for large, publicly held corporations that do business in every state, a new small business just starting out should usually incorporate in the state in which its principal business is to be conducted.

2.2. *False.* Under most state statutes incorporation today is simple and inexpensive. Over the years most states have made the process even simpler and less expensive.

2.3. *True.* The role of incorporator today has no substantive significance. Corporations may serve as incorporators in many states.

2.4. *False.* Articles of incorporation may contain any provisions relating to the corporation's affairs or governance that the draftsman elects to include, but the articles of incorporation may not contradict mandatory provisions of the applicable corporation statute.

2.5. The most common reason is that articles of incorporation are more difficult to amend than bylaws. A second reason is the belief that important restrictions or limitations should be made a matter of public record.

2.6. *False.* In the absence of fraud or unfair competition a corporation may use an assumed name as freely as an individual. Compliance with assumed name statutes may be required.

2.7. A *reserved name* is a name that has been set aside for a limited period for use by a corporation to be formed. A *registered name* is the name of a foreign corporation that has been publicly recorded in order to prevent a new corporation in the state from using the name.

2.8. *Probably never.* Even in a limited venture, perpetual duration creates no problem and may avoid later difficulties.

2.9. *False.* In most states a corporation may be formed for the purpose of engaging in any lawful business. Such a corporation is not restricted by the articles of incorporation in the businesses in which it may engage. The MBCA does not require any statement of purpose (unless a purpose narrower than "any lawful business" is desired). As a general proposition, narrower purpose clauses should be avoided.

2.10. *False.* While a broad clause minimizes the risk of ultra vires, participants in a corporation may sometimes wish to have their corporation restricted in its activities. However, the practical enforceability of narrow purposes clauses is questionable. Regulatory statutes may sometimes require narrower or qualified purposes clauses.

2.11. The purpose of these requirements is to make sure that the corporation has a place where it may be found for service of process, tax notices, and the like.

2.12. *Generally no.* The only exception is if the statutory list of powers in a particular state does not clearly cover some action that the corporation may wish to engage in.

2.13. The phrase *ultra vires* means beyond the purposes or powers of a corporation.

2.14. The common law of *ultra vires* was erratic and often led to injustice. The modern view is that a corporation should have essentially the same powers as an individual to engage in profit-making conduct, and a person unaware of a restriction on a corporation should not be bound by the restriction.

2.15. Most important are statutes limiting the scope of the doctrine, its widespread use of broad purposes clauses in articles of incorporation, and the broadening of the statutory list of powers of the corporation.

2.16. Adoption of bylaws, sale of stock and election of officers are the most important. Other necessary steps include preparation of minutes, opening of a bank account, obtaining a taxpayer's identification number, and so forth.

2.17. The most likely consequence is that participants will be held personally liable for corporate obligations on a "piercing of the corporate veil" theory. However, many cases have not imposed liability in this situation.

2.18. The principal question is whether the two lawyers should form a professional corporation. A professional corporation to practice law (which may be formed under the laws of all jurisdictions) offers the advantage of limited liability. However, election to be a limited liability partnership provides at least some degree of limited liability without incorporating. There is no tax advantage in incorporating and, depending on the nature of the income provided by the practice, incorporation may actually increase total tax costs. The extra formalities and expenses in forming and operating as a corporation would probably be of little significance since the two lawyers themselves can attend to legal matters. A minor advantage of incorporation would be the provision of tax-free benefits such as group medical insurance, group life insurance and similar employee benefits with pre-tax dollars. All in all, however, incorporation today usually offers no significant advantage over the simple LLP election for a two-person business.

2.19. Some provisions are valid only if they appear in the articles of corporation. In addition, generally, it is desirable to place unusual provisions in the articles of incorporation where they have maximum legal effect (since articles of incorporation are approved by stockholders while bylaws may usually be amended by the board of directors acting alone).

2.20. *False.* Provisions appearing in the articles of incorporation alone are of course effective as a legal matter. However, officers and directors are more likely to be familiar with and consult the bylaws than the articles of incorporation. As a result, provisions relating to corporate governance should usually appear in both the bylaws and the articles of incorporation.

CHAPTER 3

3.1. *False.* An incorporator performs the symbolic role of signing articles of incorporation. A promoter is the organizer of a business.

3.2. *Uncertain.* Many promoters have been held personally liable in litigated cases but theories exist that may excuse them.

3.3. *Uncertain.* While more courts would probably find a novation in these circumstances, some courts have refused to do so, holding both the corporation and the promoter jointly liable on the obligations.

3.4. De facto cases involve transactions entered into in the name of a corporation before it has been formed, and where one or both parties believe the corporation has been formed. Promoters' cases may involve situations where one or both parties know, and the contract recites, that no corporation has been formed. Generally a corporation *de jure* exists only if there is actual filing of valid articles of incorporation.

3.5. *Uncertain.* While earlier versions of the Model Act clearly attempted to eliminate the de facto doctrine, many courts continued to apply common law concepts despite the statute. As a result, the MBCA does not directly address the de facto corporation doctrine; it simply provides that persons who act as or on behalf of a putative corporation knowing that articles of incorporation have not been filed are personally liable on obligations so created.

3.6. The corporation by estoppel analysis accepts the argument that persons who deal with a corporation as such are thereafter estopped from claiming that the individuals are personally liable. The problem with this reasoning is that it reverses the traditional concept of estoppel; the person being estopped is not the one making the representation but the one relying on it. It also results in the possibility that one might obtain the benefits of limited liability without taking any steps to incorporate simply by consistently doing business in the corporate name.

3.7. *False.* A corporation assumes only the promoters' contracts that it elects to assume.

3.8. *Yes.* Promoters have fiduciary duties to each other similar to the duties of partners in a partnership.

3.9. *Uncertain.* If the corporation represents subsequent investors who were unaware of the transactions, the answer is true. If the investors knew of the transaction they cannot compel the corporation to sue since they presumably adjusted the purchase price to take into account the known transaction.

3.10. *Usually False.* While some courts have treated subscriptions as contracts between subscribers, the most common view is that they are mere offers since no corporation is in existence and therefore a bilateral contract cannot exist between the subscriber and the corporation.

3.11. *Yes, D is personally liable.* Whether or not a promoter will be personally liable when acting for a proposed corporation depends on the construction of the contract. The promoter may (1) take on behalf of the proposed corporation an offer from the other party, which being accepted by the corporation after incorporation becomes a contract; (2) enter into a contract initially binding the promoter with the clear understanding that if the corporation is formed it will be substituted and the promoter will be relieved of further responsibility (a novation); or (3) bind himself so that both he and the corporation are thereafter liable but seek indemnity from the corporation. Where, as here, the contract calls for some performance before the corporation is organized it is a strong indication that the promoter intended to be personally liable on the contract. Nothing in the contract authorized D to substitute the corporation as the sole responsible party; therefore D, as well as the corporation, are personally liable on the contract. See *O'Rorke v. Geary*, 207 Pa. 240, 56 A. 541 (1903).

3.12. *Yes, XYZ is liable.* Although a corporation is not liable on a contract made by its promoter for its benefit unless it takes some affirmative act to adopt the contract, it is not necessary that the adoption be express. It may be inferred from the acts of the corporation after incorporation. Here the court should imply that XYZ adopted the contract by reason of the failure of stockholders and directors to object, and the continuation of employment after incorporation. See *McArthur v. Times Printing Co.*, 48 Minn. 319, 51 N.W 216 (1892).

CHAPTER 4

4.1. PCV cases all deal with correctly and fully formed corporations. The issue is, should the shield of limited liability be ignored under the circumstances despite the complete formation of the corporation? The other doctrines referred to in the question deal with formational defects.

4.2. *False.* Motive, by itself, is not a ground for PCV.

4.3. *False.* In contract cases, inadequate capital, by itself, should not be sufficient reason to PCV. There must be some additional abuse of the corporate form or misrepresentation of the capital actually invested in the corporation.

4.4. *Probably false.* Most courts will impose tort liability on stockholders on a PCV theory if the original capital was inadequate in light of expected business needs.

4.5. *Probably true.* Failure to follow corporate formalities and intermingling of corporate assets are classic reasons for PCV. Usually, personal liability is imposed on the stockholder even though no direct harm resulted from the stockholder's conduct.

4.6. *False.* So long as "hats" are properly labeled, a subsidiary and parent may share the same officers and directors without becoming liable for each other's debts.

4.7. *True.* Relatively small amounts of intermingling of parent and subsidiary affairs may give rise to PCV. A few courts have rejected this result and have required a showing that the plaintiff was injured by the transactions in question.

4.8. *False.* The use of corporations to defeat or further governmental policy in this way depends on an analysis of the goals of the governmental policy. Some cases have permitted persons to qualify for social security benefits in this fashion.

4.9. *No.* A holding or parent company has a separate corporate existence and is treated separately from its subsidiary in the absence of circumstances justifying disregard of the corporate entity. The participation of A corporation in the affairs of S did not amount to a domination of the day-to-day business decisions of S even though A corporation had the opportunity to exercise control. Consequently, jurisdiction over A corporation cannot be established by reason of its stock ownership of S. See *Quarles v. Fuqua Indus., Inc.*, 504 F.2d 1358 (10th Cir. 1974).

4.10. *Yes.* This case is a good illustration of an unsuccessful attempt to use corporate process to avoid personal responsibility. The corporation never had any equity capital despite the dangerous nature of the business. There was confusion and intermingling of personal and corporate finances. Formalities were not followed. The case involves a tort not a contract. Principally because of the lack of capital in a tort case, the court should hold the stockholder personally liable. See *Dixie Coal Mining & Mfg. Co. v. Williams*, 221 Ala. 331, 128 So. 799 (1930).

CHAPTER 5

5.1. There are four major sources: the sale of shares, loans from stockholders, loans from third persons, and internally generated funds from operations.

5.2. Very little. Par value today provides a floor on the price of shares. Whether or not this is an advantage is questionable. Par value also establishes the amounts to be allocated to the capital accounts, called stated capital and capital surplus (in the MBCA (1969) nomenclature), when authorized shares are issued. With the virtually universal use of nominal par value shares, it is fair to say that par value serves little purpose today. On the other hand, par value, and the complex rules with respect to capital accounts that it generates, may be affirmatively misleading since it appears to protect creditors against distributions to stockholders when in fact it provides little or no protection to creditors.

5.3. Traditional no par shares do not solve all problems because they are tied to the concept of par value. The artificial problems created by par value therefore also appear in a corporation that uses no par shares.

5.4. *False.* While watered stock liability may easily be avoided by proper planning, the issuance of shares with high par values today may give rise to classic watered stock liability in many states.

5.5. The MBCA abolishes par value (except as a voluntary planning device as a matter of contract or when necessary to minimize tax liability in states that continue to compute taxes on the basis of par values).

5.6. Preferred stock has preference over common stock in connection with either the payment of dividends or distributions on liquidation, or both. Preferred stock usually is nonparticipating and entitled to a fixed distribution and no more.

5.7. A bond is a secured long term debt instrument while a debenture is an unsecured long term debt instrument. The word "bond" is often used as a generic term to describe both bonds and debentures.

5.8. *False.* Many corporations benefit from the leverage created by having a portion of its permanent capital be in the form of debt rather than equity. Also, in periods of inflation, debt financing may become more attractive since money borrowed will be repaid in the future with inflated dollars. Of course, as inflation continues, interest rates tend to rise to offset this phenomenon. Most corporations today desire to maintain a significant amount of debt in their capital structures.

5.9.   *False.* The Federal Securities Act exemption for private offerings is not controlled by the number of offers. An offer to a relatively small number of offerees who need the protection of the Act may require registration under the Securities Act of 1933. In contrast, most state security statutes (blue sky laws) contain numerical exemptions for offers to a small number of persons but these exemptions will usually be lost if the plan of distribution involves a public offer or a public advertisement.

5.10.   Preemptive rights are the rights of existing stockholders to purchase their proportionate share of new issues of securities by the corporation.

5.11.   *False.* Even in the absence of preemptive rights, there is a fiduciary duty applicable to directors that prohibit the issuance of shares at prices that unreasonably dilute the interests of outstanding stockholders. The same fiduciary duty may prevent the issuance of shares at reasonable prices if issued for improper purposes, such as to influence control of the corporation.

5.12.   When a corporation repurchases its own shares, it distributes assets equal to the purchase price to the stockholder from whom the shares are being purchased. However, shares of a corporation are not an asset of the corporation in any real sense. One cannot own shares of oneself. Shares of a corporation that were formerly outstanding but have been reacquired by the corporation are no more an asset of a corporation than are authorized but unissued shares. This can be seen graphically by the accounting treatment for treasury shares: the purchase price of the shares reduces the corporation's assets while an offsetting reduction is made in the equity portion of the right hand side of the balance sheet.

5.13.   *True.* It is generally recognized that modern corporation statutes are so liberal that capital may be freely distributed by a corporation to its stockholders. If a creditor wishes to assure that capital is not distributed to stockholders and that a cushion is available to make sure that its loan will be repaid, it must impose meaningful restrictions by agreement.

5.14.   *False.* A share distribution is purely a paper transaction that does not reduce the real assets available to the corporation or increase the proportionate interest of any stockholder. In contrast, a cash dividend reduces the funds available to the corporation. If a stockholder receives a share dividend and sells the new shares (in order to obtain the cash) that stockholder's proportionate interest in the corporation is thereby reduced by a small fraction.

5.15. The legality of the dividend last year out of current profits of that year, at a time when there was an accumulated deficit in earned surplus, depends on whether or not the state of incorporation has a "nimble dividend" statute. A nimble dividend is one paid out of current earnings before those earnings are applied against the deficit in earned surplus from other years. If the state does have such a statute, the dividend was lawful because Commerce was not insolvent at the time of the dividend. If the state of incorporation does not have a nimble dividend statute, the dividend was unlawful (unless current earnings are large enough both to wipe out the earlier deficit in earned surplus and to cover the dividend). If the dividend is unlawful, the directors are jointly and severally liable to the corporation for the benefit of its creditors or stockholders. Directors who fail to dissent from the action are also liable. The directors are entitled to contribution from other directors who concurred in the action. Moreover, stockholders who received the dividend with knowledge that it was unlawful are also liable for their pro rata share of the dividend. In some states, Commerce, Inc. might be able to treat the distribution as a distribution of capital rather than as a dividend. If Commerce, Inc. were incorporated in a state that has adopted the MBCA, the distribution would be lawful if the dividend was made at a time when Commerce was solvent in both an equity and a balance sheet sense. The MBCA completely eliminates the concept of earned surplus and, as a result, of nimble dividends as well.

5.16. *Yes.* The stock was par value stock and the property which was transferred to the corporation as consideration for the stock was worth only $100,000. It therefore cannot constitute full payment for shares issued with a par value of $250,000. Thus, the stockholder remains liable on the suit of a creditor or creditors' representative. Two theories on which to base B's continued liability are (1) if there is no statute expressly making B liable to pay at least the par value for the newly issued shares, then B impliedly agreed to pay the par value of the shares being issued to her; or (2) if there is a statute imposing such liability on B, then the provisions of the statute make B liable. This debt is a corporate asset which can be enforced by a creditor of the corporation. If the valuation of $250,000 is made non-fraudulently by the board of directors (which seems implausible on the stated facts), B can argue that valuation is conclusive and cannot be attacked by R.

5.17. *Yes.* The stockholders may not use corporate assets to repurchase their shares and thus recover their investment if to do so would leave the corporation without sufficient funds to pay its creditors. If, however, the corporation has sufficient assets to pay its creditors in full and also pay the purchase price of the stock it may enter into an agreement to purchase the shares. Instead of paying cash, the corporation may be able to issue notes for all or part of the purchase price, in which case the stockholder becomes a creditor of the corporation rather than a stockholder. In any subsequent insolvency proceeding the former stockholder should be able to share proportionally with other creditors. Here, the purchase of shares was effected at a time when the corporation was solvent and subsequent insolvency does not affect the validity of the transaction. Several early cases agree with this rationale but several others do not; it is possible that a court might subordinate the claim of P in the above situation. MBCA 6.40 accepts the rationale set forth above and permits P to share in the assets on a parity with other creditors.

5.18. *Yes.* Whether or not to declare a dividend is usually within the sound discretion and business judgment of the board of directors. The courts will usually interfere with the exercise of such discretion, unless there is a clear case of abuse of discretion, bad faith or dishonesty. There is an implied obligation on the part of the board of directors and managers of the corporation to exercise good faith and reasonable business judgment in distributing dividends to the stockholders. Of course, sound discretion dictates that there should be kept in reserve enough money to carry on the corporate business, make replacements of worn-out machinery, pay taxes and insurance, and provide for unforeseen losses and expenses. But here there was a surplus built up over a period of 10 years which is four times the capital, a continued annual profit, a continuing prosperity, and not a single dividend during the entire 10 year period. With $2,000,000 cash on hand and the corporation in the condition disclosed by these facts, there seems to be a clear abuse of discretion on the part of the board in not declaring a dividend. *Dodge v. Ford Motor Co.*, 170 N.W. 668 (Mich.1919); *Gottfried v. Gottfried*, 73 N.Y.S.2d 692 (1947).

CHAPTER 6

6.1. Under most statutes, a quorum consists of a majority of the outstanding shares; a majority of the shares present at a meeting at which a quorum is present is necessary to adopt a resolution. As a result, in the absence of a specific provision by the corporation, one half of one half, or one quarter plus one, of the outstanding shares, may adopt an ordinary resolution at a stockholder's meeting.

6.2. *Yes.* The common law view was one vote per share but most state statutes today authorize a corporation to create a class of shares with multiple or fractional votes per share. Virtually all states also permit nonvoting common shares. However, the statutes of the specific state must be consulted before such a question can be answered definitively.

6.3. Record ownership refers to the status of the ownership of shares as shown on the books and records of the corporation. Beneficial ownership refers to the person who actually owns the shares. That person may or may not be the record owner. The corporation generally treats the record owner as the sole owner of shares without consideration of who the beneficial owner may be. A beneficial owner should have shares transferred to his or her name as record owner if unhappy with the current record owner.

6.4. The corporation must set record dates for these actions in order to establish clearly, as between transferor and transferee of shares, who is entitled to vote or who is entitled to receive a dividend.

6.5. *True.* The effect of cumulative voting is to permit a large minority bloc of shares to obtain representation on the board. The size of the minimum bloc necessary to obtain representation may be determined mathematically by a relatively simple formula.

6.6. Since proxies are revocable, the latest one revokes earlier ones. In this situation, A's shares will be voted for the insurgents.

6.7. *False.* A proxy appointment is irrevocable only if it is coupled with an interest in the underlying shares or in the corporation.

6.8. A pooling agreement is a simple contract between stockholders to vote shares in a certain way while a voting trust involves a formal transfer of the shares to trustees so that the trustees have the legal power to vote.

6.9. At issue are the validity of the removal of directors and of the merger. The notice of the special meeting referred to consideration of a proposed merger but did not refer to the removal of specific directors. Therefore, the removal of the directors should not have been considered because specific reference to proposed removals of directors must appear in the notice of meeting. MBCA 8.08(d) provides that only matters related to those specified in the notice of meeting ordinarily may be entertained at a special meeting. Under MBCA 8.08, a director may be removed with or without cause by a vote of the holders of a majority of the shares then entitled to vote at an election of directors at a meeting called expressly for that purpose. When Gative and Servative were elected, their tenure as directors was subject to the statutory power of removal. However, because the meeting was not expressly called for removing directors, the purported removal is invalid and the two directors should be reinstated. The effect of this invalid action on the status of the merger is not so easily resolved. The substituted directors, Berl and Stamp, exercised their functions under at least a color of office and arguably can be considered to be de facto directors whose actions as directors are not subject to collateral attack. The action of the board during their tenure may thus be binding on the corporation. Also, an agreement of merger has been entered into with a presumably innocent party who has no notice of the infirmity of the action taken by the directors. It is therefore likely that the merger could not be set aside. The corporation may also argue that there was no causal relationship between the merger and the defective removal of directors if the votes of Berl and Stamp were not necessary for approval of the merger. This argument increases the likelihood that the merger could not be set aside.

6.10. *Yes.* As to proposal 1, even though the stockholders do not have the power to effect a change in the officers of a corporation such power being reserved to the board of directors, they may express their opinion to the board of directors. As to proposal 2, stockholders have the inherent power to remove directors for cause. *See Auer v. Dressel*, 118 N.E.2d 590 (N.Y.1954). Hence both proposals are proper for consideration by the stockholders.

6.11. *False.* Amendments are permitted without limitation since in most states there is no vested rights doctrine in corporation law. Stockholders are protected from adverse amendments by class voting (referred to as voting by voting groups in the MBCA), and by the right of dissent and appraisal.

6.12. *No.* Since the state statute does not provide for mandatory cumulative voting, the stockholders may properly abandon the system without unanimous consent. Although the right to vote cumulatively is a valuable one, the corporation law that allows amendment of the articles of incorporation is a part of P's contract with the corporation and he or she may not complain if the action is taken in the proper form with the requisite majority. *Maddock v. Vorclone Corp.*, 147 A. 255 (Del.Ch. 1929).

6.13. *Yes.* There are equitable limitations to provisions governing the operation of a corporation. Here the management of X attempted to perpetuate itself in office and to obstruct the legitimate efforts of stockholders to obtain new management. Inequitable action does not become permissible simply because it is legally possible. *Schnell v. Chris–Craft Indus., Inc.*, 285 A.2d 437 (Del. 1971).

CHAPTER 7

7.1. *False.* Unlike stockholders, directors may not vote by proxy. This rule is based broadly on the common law view that directors may act only at a meeting of directors.

7.2. *False.* There are many statements in early cases to this effect. However, many cases now recognize informal ratification or estoppel as binding the board of directors without a formal meeting. Statutes today also authorize directors to act by unanimous written consent without a meeting.

7.3. *No.* This lay view of the president does not reflect the traditional legal relationship, though the trend appears to be in the direction of recognizing broader inherent authority. In a corporation, the directors rather than the president, have the principal power of decision-making. However, many corporate presidents in fact exercise a great deal of power by virtue of their office, as a member of the board of directors, or as a stockholder.

7.4. *False.* The period of the officer's employment contract and the term of the office are independent of each other. If a board of directors grants an officer a contract for a period longer than the term of his office and a subsequent board refuses to elect the officer to that office, the corporation has breached the employment contract.

7.5. *No.* Although in general there may be a presumption that the president of a corporation has authority to institute litigation and engage counsel, absent a provision in the bylaws to the contrary, any actual or implied authority which M had to do so was terminated when a majority of the board of directors failed to sanction it. The fact that the directors were deadlocked or that the directors who voted against the suit were interested in the transaction does not affect the result. If a stockholder wishes to file a derivative suit against D corporation, he may do so, and the issue of the validity of the contract will be adjudicated in that proceeding.

7.6.   *No.* The president of a corporation is an agent for the corporation. In any given situation whether the president acted within the scope of that agency is a question of fact for the jury. The president's authority may be derived from: (a) certain powers implied by virtue of the office which allow the president to perform the acts necessary for the convenient management of the day-to-day business of the corporation, (b) express grants of power found in statutes, the corporate charter and bylaws and resolutions of the board of directors, and (c) powers which arise by reason of a course of conduct of both the president and the corporation showing that the president had acted on similar matters in the past, and that the corporation had acquiesced in, approved and ratified such former actions. The charge to the jury that was held to be appropriate was: "If you find from the evidence that the president . . . was not acting within the usual scope of his office and that he had not in the past acted alone in the signing of contracts and that the defendant company had never recognized any acts of the president alone or had not held him out as qualified to transact singly and alone all business dealings for the company, then your verdict must be for the defendant, for I say to you it is only upon these principles, upon the proven facts of the case that the act of the president could bind the corporation. If, however, you find . . . that the president was acting within the usual scope of his employment or that he had on prior occasions entered into contracts and bound the corporation which recognized and approved such acts and held him out as authorized to deal with the company's affairs, then your verdict may be for the plaintiff." *See Joseph Greenspon's Sons Iron and Steel Co. v. Pecos Valley Gas Co.,* 156 A. 350 (Del. 1931). To avoid questions of this nature it is customary to require the President to supply a certified copy of an express resolution of the board of directors authorizing the execution of the transaction.

CHAPTER 8

8.1.   The duty of care requires directors to exercise a minimum degree of skill and attention toward corporate affairs. While monetary damages for breach of this duty have been sharply limited by statute and judicial decision, this duty is nevertheless one of the fundamental duties owed by directors to corporations. Breaches of this duty may give rise to monetary liability in cases involving knowing authorization of wrongful acts by directors or to a lesser extent in cases of a failure to pay attention to corporate affairs. Directors who are elderly or infirm must meet a minimum standard of care applicable to everyone. An attorney, or a director with specialized knowledge, must use care in light of that specialized knowledge.

8.2. The business judgment rule is a common law doctrine related to the duty of care that immunizes directors from liability for decisions that turn out badly if they act without conflict of interest, exercise good faith judgment in making the decision, and reasonably inform themselves of the facts relating to that decision. The business judgment rule has been applied in recent years to novel issues such as to authorize the dismissal of derivative suits by disinterested directors or to validate self-dealing transactions. The business judgment rule or doctrine makes the business decision itself (as contrasted with the liability of the directors) immune from judicial review.

8.3. Such a transaction is known as self-dealing. The common law test for the validity of a self-dealing transaction is whether the transaction is fair and whether the director's interest has been fully disclosed. The burden of establishing fairness may be placed on the director, who should not participate in the corporate decision whether or not to enter into the transaction. Most states have enacted statutes relating to self-dealing transactions that uphold the transaction if it is approved by disinterested directors or stockholders in accordance with the business judgment rule or, if there has been no approval, if it is intrinsically fair to the corporation.

8.4. *Yes*, by arranging for the transaction to be reviewed and approved by the disinterested directors after full disclosure of the fact of the conflict of interest and of the facts surrounding the transaction. Such an action is preclusive under modern statutes in the absence of fraud or waste, and the common law rules would doubtless lead to the same result.

8.5. Such a transaction is an indirect self-dealing transaction and is also judged by the standards for self-dealing transactions. Many transactions of this nature are innocent in the sense that the common director did not participate in the approval of the transaction by either corporation, and indeed may have been unaware that such transactions were occurring.

8.6. The general view is that stockholders may not ratify a transaction which is fraudulent, oppressive, or overreaching. However, it is possible that a nonfraudulent transaction that may not be upheld under the fairness test may be validated if it is approved by the disinterested vote of the stockholders. At the very least, such a vote shifts the burden of proof to those seeking to avoid the transaction, and, under conflict of interest statutes, may be given preclusive effect.

8.7. The test for executive compensation is that such compensation is valid unless it is so large as to constitute spoliation or waste. Such compensation is not generally viewed by the same standards as self-dealing transactions. As a practical matter, most corporations arrange to have compensation arrangements approved by outside, nonmanagement directors through a compensation committee; information about executive compensation levels is widely available and provides a yardstick. If a problem exists with respect to the level of executive compensation it is unlikely that judicial intervention is the appropriate response.

8.8. Such arrangements may take the form of stock options or stock appreciation rights, stock bonuses, phantom stock plans, or stock purchase plans.

8.9. Corporate opportunity is a fiduciary duty that directors and officers owe to the corporation to offer the corporation profitable business opportunities to which the corporation has a reasonable claim.

8.10. No single test has been generally accepted. The traditional view is that an opportunity is a corporate opportunity only if it is something in which the corporation has an interest or expectancy. Modern formulations of the corporate opportunity doctrine emphasize the fairness or unfairness of allowing an officer or director to take advantage of the opportunity and whether the opportunity arises out of the corporation's line of business. Other factors may be relevant, such as whether the opportunity was addressed to the corporation when it was received by the director or officer.

8.11. *Yes.* If the corporation decides not to take advantage of the opportunity after full consideration, a director may do so. The burden, however, is on the director to establish the underlying premise that the corporation has elected not to pursue the opportunity.

8.12. Either standard may be applied depending on the nature of the transaction. If the transaction involves a contract or other arrangement between the parent and the subsidiary, the fairness test is applied. If the parent's action does not discriminate against the minority stockholders of the subsidiary, the business judgment rule is generally applicable. For example, a dividend paid by the subsidiary to all stockholders will be judged by the business judgment rule not the fairness standard. If the subsidiary's board of directors has outside unaffiliated directors, it is likely that a judgment by them alone will meet the standard of the business judgment rule and will be given preclusive effect binding the subsidiary.

8.13. *No.* The transaction is a self dealing transaction since Corporation A is receiving something not received by all stockholders of Corporation B. Since the transaction is not intrinsically fair to the minority stockholders of Corporation B, it is voidable by them.

8.14. The directors may: (1) propose dissolution, subject to stockholder approval; or (2) first redeem the preferred shares, without the necessity of stockholder approval, in which case the preferred stockholders prior to the redemption date may convert each of their preferred shares into common shares. The corporation may then dissolve. Since there are 1,000 outstanding shares of each class and all shares have equal voting rights, the directors are elected by the combined votes of the two classes. The facts do not indicate the respective shareholdings of the several directors. However, the directors are under a fiduciary duty, not only to do what is in the best interests of the corporation, but also to be fair to the stockholders of both classes. Normally this would permit the full redemption of the preferred shares before the dissolution of the corporation. There are two alternatives. If the corporation were dissolved without redemption of the preferred, the preferred stockholders would receive their liquidation preferences of $200 per share or a total of $200,000 ($200 × 1,000 shares), leaving $10 for each common share ($10,000 × 1,000 shares). Voluntary dissolution generally would require approval by the holders of at least a majority of all the outstanding shares, depending on the applicable corporate statutory requirements. If the preferred shares were redeemed (which would require only board of directors action), the preferred stockholders would receive the redemption price of $105 per share or a total of $105,000; there would then be available $105 for each common share ($105,000 × 1,000 shares). However, each preferred share is convertible into two common shares, which conversion privilege ordinarily would terminate on the redemption date set forth in the notice sent to the preferred stockholders of the intended dissolution. However, the economics should cause the preferred stockholders to convert (if they are given accurate information), since, upon conversion, each would have two new common shares for each converted preferred share. If all shareholders convert, the former preferred stockholders would hold 2,000 or two-thirds of the then 3,000 outstanding common shares, and each former preferred stockholder would receive $70 for each new common share or $140 for each old preferred share or a total of $140,000 (2/3rds of $210,000). Each old common stockholder would also receive $70 for each of his shares or a total of $70,000 ($70 × 1,000 shares). The latter course appears to be most appropriate under all the circumstances. This problem is patterned after *Zahn v. Transamerica Corp.*, 235 F.2d 369 (3d Cir. 1956).

8.15.   *No.* Directors of a corporation are not generally liable for losses suffered by the corporation by reason of its employees' violations of law. In managing the corporate affairs a director is required to use the care which ordinary careful and prudent men would use in similar circumstances. Whether or not they have failed to exercise proper care depends upon the circumstances. Here the size of the enterprise and its wide geographical distribution made it necessary that directors confine their oversight to broad policy matters, and they should have no responsibility for employee misconduct unless something occurs to put them on notice that misconduct is occurring. Until that time they are entitled to rely on the honesty and integrity of their employees. Hence no liability is imposed. *Graham v. Allis–Chalmers Mfg. Co.*, 188 A.2d 125 (Del.Ch. 1963).

8.16.   Under common law principles, the contract should be cancelled. This contract was made between two corporations having an interlocking directorship, the directors, A, B and C, being common to the boards of both companies. In such a case the two corporations may contract with each other and the contracts made are valid and enforceable if the contract is fair to both. If it is not fair to one corporation that one may avoid it. It is immaterial whether the common directors vote or refrain from voting on the approval of the contract. The fact that this contract provided that X corporation should pay M 10 per cent more for smelting ore than was the usual and customary price for such service, and the additional fact that the contract was to continue for 10 years without providing for any change in the price when the price of metals dropped made the contract unfair to X corporation and therefore gave it a right to cancel the contract. *Globe Woolen Co. v. Utica Gas & Elec. Co.*, 121 N.E. 378 (N.Y. 1918). A transaction between corporations with common directors may involve an indirect conflict of interest. Since the transaction was brought before the board of directors, it is valid if the action of the board of directors of X corporation (excluding

A, B, and C) meets the standards of the business judgment rule. The facts state that the directors approved the transaction because they thought that A, B, and C wanted the transaction approved. This is not a decision made in good faith and in the reasonable belief that it is in the best interest of the corporation; therefore the decision is not entitled to the protection of the business judgment rule. The test again becomes one exclusively of fairness, and the analysis in part (a) presumably would control on this issue.

8.17. Possibly if D can persuasively establish that X in fact lacked the ability to finance the purchase. The opportunity was probably a corporate opportunity since D learned of it through the corporation and the opportunity is in X's line of business. D, as the controlling stockholder in X corporation in complete control of the board of directors of X corporation, owes a fiduciary duty to X corporation. Hence, when D learned of the value of B's properties and that it could be purchased at an advantageous price to the direct benefit of X corporation, D had a duty to give X corporation the first opportunity to buy that property for its own purposes. D violated his fiduciary duty in not letting X know of that opportunity. However, if it is assumed that such duty had been performed by D, it would have been futile because X was wholly incapable financially to take advantage of the opportunity. D's duty to X does not require him to lend money to X so that X can buy the property of B. And D does not have to let the opportunity pass simply because X could not realize upon it. He may buy it for himself for his own personal benefit. See *Zeckendorf v. Steinfeld*, 100 P. 784 (Ariz. 1909). However, not all cases agree with this analysis; the ALI Corporate Governance Project also would not accept a defense of financial inability under these circumstances but would require the opportunity to be presented to X corporation since it is possible that the corporation might have been able to finance the purchase of B's property. In this case, the majority stockholder had a fiduciary duty by virtue of his complete control of the board of directors. In typical cases of corporate opportunity, where officers or directors are involved, the fiduciary duty is similar to that imposed on D in this case.

CHAPTER 9

9.1. Direct litigation is a claim brought by a stockholder for injury as a stockholder; a derivative claim is a claim brought by a stockholder on behalf of the corporation for injury to the corporation that indirectly injures all stockholders.

9.2. *No.* Some claims may be phrased either as direct and derivative, and there is some judicial disagreement over whether certain types of claims, e.g., suits to compel a declaration of a dividend, should be classified as direct or derivative. To some extent this is a matter of pleading.

9.3. A class suit is brought by a member of the class on behalf of the class as a whole. A typical class suit is a direct suit.

9.4. A derivative suit is a class suit to the extent the plaintiff stockholder serves as a representative of the class of stockholders injured by the conduct in question.

9.5. As a defendant, though in fact it is an involuntary plaintiff.

9.6. *Yes.* Under both the Model Business Corporation Act and the Corporate Governance Project demand is required in substantially all cases. Under Delaware law, demand is futile only if the board of directors is interested in the transaction, or if the plaintiff establishes a reasonable doubt, based on particularized allegations, that the decision complained of was not protected by the business judgment rule. The allegations that the directors are friends of the CEO and will not do anything he opposes are not particularized and should not create a reasonable doubt that the directors are not independent or the decision was not made in accordance with the business judgment rule.

9.7. *Yes.* Under both Delaware law and the Model Business Corporation Act, the motion should be granted unless the plaintiff can establish that the decision of the Committee was not a good faith exercise of business judgment or that the Committee was not disinterested. The allegations made by the plaintiff do not go to the valid exercise of business judgment by the committee or to its independence and therefore do not provide grounds for denial of the motion.

9.8. The jurisdiction of the federal courts is not affected by the derivative-direct distinction. A suit brought under the Federal securities acts may be direct or derivative and in either event may or must be brought in Federal court. A direct or derivative claim based on state law may be brought in Federal court if there is diversity of citizenship or on the theory of pendent jurisdiction.

9.9. The contemporaneous ownership requirement requires the plaintiff to be a stockholder at the time the cause of action arose. In the federal courts it is imposed to avoid the collusive creation of diversity jurisdiction. In state courts it is justified in part because of dislike of derivative litigation and in part to avoid the purchase and sale of lawsuits. It is believed that relatively few suits are barred from litigation on the ground there is no plaintiff who qualifies under the contemporaneous ownership requirement.

9.10. In addition to the contemporaneous ownership requirement (see Question 9.9), the plaintiff must make a demand on the corporation and its directors, and (in some states) on its stockholders, or show why such a demand should be dispensed with or is futile. In addition, a plaintiff may have to comply with state security-for-expenses statute that require the posting of a bond. The MBCA requires a demand on directors in all cases but does not require a demand on stockholders or the posting of security-for-expenses.

9.11. It is widely believed by members of the corporate bar that a great deal of derivative litigation is instituted without reasonable cause for the benefit of plaintiffs' attorneys rather than for the corporation or its stockholders.

9.12. The purpose of security-for-expenses statutes is to prevent strike suits by plaintiffs with nominal interests in the litigation which itself may be without substantive merit. The security-for-expenses statute makes it more difficult for small plaintiffs to maintain derivative suits without regard to whether the underlying suit has merit. These statutes are illogical in the sense that they tend to bar meritorious as well as groundless suits, and may impose substantive requirements based more on the size of the plaintiff's holdings than the merits of the law suit. The MBCA eliminates these requirements but substitutes other devices in an effort to close off meritless litigation, particularly authorizing the court to impose litigation costs on the plaintiff if the suit is ultimately found to be without merit.

9.13. In most states, the effect is two-fold: (1) the plaintiff is compelled to post a bond to secure the defendants' expenses, and (2) if the defendants are successful, the plaintiff may be required to pay their expenses. The proceeds of the bond may be used for this purpose.

9.14. This statute is substantive under the Erie doctrine; it is applicable in derivative litigation based on diversity of citizenship and pendent jurisdiction. It is not applicable to claims arising under the Federal securities acts.

9.15. In most states, no.

9.16. It depends on the basis of the decision. If it is on the merits it is *res judicata* and binding on all stockholders. A dismissal on the basis of a litigation committee's decision that is entitled to business judgment rule protection is on the merits. If it is based on a defect in the plaintiffs standing to maintain the suit, such as failing to comply with the security-for-expenses statute, it is not *res judicata* and other stockholders may refile the same suit.

9.17. In most states, a proposed settlement must be judicially approved before the suit may be dismissed. This is designed to prevent secret settlements.

9.18. A "strike suit" is a slang term for suits brought solely for their settlement value. The major device now used to prevent such suits is the judicial review of proposed settlements. Also, suits that are believed to be strike suits may be the subject of litigation committee review.

9.19. *Usually, yes.* The test for plaintiffs' expenses is whether the suit yields a substantial benefit to the corporation, not whether it recovers cash, or tangible property.

9.20. There are a few such cases where members of current management were found to be wrongdoers and therefore should not have control over the use of the proceeds. A distribution directly to stockholders has some of the attributes of a compelled dividend and as a result has not been widely required.

9.21. *Yes.* In a stockholders' derivative suit any recovery runs in favor of the corporation because it is in the right of, or on behalf of the corporation, that stockholders sue. If defendants are held liable recovery must be to the corporation and not to the stockholders. The decree also must protect the defendants against any further suit by the corporation. This cannot be done unless the corporation is a party to the action. Hence X is an indispensable party to the action and if it cannot be served with process the action must be dismissed. Since X has not been served with process, it is not within the jurisdiction of the court and the action must be dismissed. *Dean v. Kellogg,* 292 N.W. 704 (Mich. 1940).

9.22. *No.* In a stockholders' derivative action brought for the benefit of the corporation for damages caused by a breach of fiduciary duties to the corporation, the corporation is entitled to recover the entire amount of the damages suffered by it. The identity of the stockholders at the time is not a matter of proof in the action. It is the corporation as an entity which has been harmed and to whom the damages are to be paid. *Norte & Co. v.*

Huffines, 416 F.2d 1189 (2d Cir. 1969). A few courts have permitted the stockholders to recover individually in a derivative suit on the theory that the persons now in control of the corporation should not be permitted to control the proceeds of the recovery since they participated in the wrongful conduct. Certainly, however, the defendants should not be able to restrict their recovery on this theory.

9.23. Indemnification permits the corporation to reimburse expenses incurred by officers or directors arising from litigation over their actions as officers or directors. In some instances it also permits reimbursements for payment of judgments, fines, or amounts paid in settlement of such litigation.

9.24. Indemnification is not against public policy if the defendant is absolved of liability or acted in good faith and did not engage knowingly in wrongful conduct. The underlying reason for permitting indemnification is the concern that persons might refuse to serve as directors if they had to bear the cost of defending against groundless litigation out of their own pockets.

9.25. *Certainly in most cases.* Most indemnification statutes, however, permit indemnification with court approval and in some cases where the defendant settles or successfully prevails on a procedural defense. Indemnification in criminal cases is also permitted where the defendant in good faith believed the conduct was lawful.

9.26. D & O Insurance refers to directors and officers liability insurance. It is commercially available insurance for some of the liabilities discussed above.

9.27. *No.* D & O insurance only covers insurable risks. Most if not all cases of wrongful conduct are not insurable and are expressly excluded from coverage by policy exclusions.

CHAPTER 10

10.1. *False.* For a variety of reasons, including history, the law of proxy regulation in publicly held corporations arises under section 14 of the Securities Exchange Act of 1934, and, most importantly, under the SEC regulations issued thereunder.

10.2. Corporations (1) with a class of security that is traded on a national securities exchange, or (2) with $5,000,000 of assets and a class of shares owned by more than 500 stockholders of record, are subject to federal proxy regulation. These are the requirements for registration under section 12 of the 1934 Act and SEC regulations.

10.3. Corporations that are required to register under section 12 of the 1934 Act or that have made a registered public offering of shares under the 1933 Act are subject to the SEC periodic disclosure requirements.

10.4. The constitutional bases of federal proxy regulation are the power to regulate interstate commerce and the mails. Proxy regulation has been in effect since 1934 and its constitutional validity is beyond question.

10.5. The SEC proxy regulations require both proxy statements and annual reports to be distributed to stockholders by all registered companies even though they do not actually solicit proxies. In the absence of federal requirements, most states do not require the transmission of any information to stockholders.

10.6. *Yes.* Rule 14a–9 forbids false and misleading statements in proxy statements. The early case of *J. I. Case v. Borak* held that a private cause of action is created for violations of this rule. Even though private causes of action have been largely restricted by the United States Supreme Court in recent years, it appears unlikely that *J. I. Case v. Borak* will be overruled. However, *Virginia Bankshares v. Sandberg* limits plaintiffs who are eligible to pursue such claims.

10.7. The requirement of materiality was emphasized by the United States Supreme Court in *TSC Industries v. Northway*, which defined materiality as a fact that *would* influence an investor in making a decision.

10.8. *Yes.* Under *Mills v. Electric Auto–Lite Co.*

10.9. *No.* Virginia Bankshares, Inc. v. Sandberg holds that a statement phrased as opinion is false and misleading if in fact the directors do not hold that opinion.

10.10. *No.* The SEC proxy regulations require certain stockholder proposals to be included in proxy solicitations even though the corporation is opposed to them. A no-nuclear-energy proposal is one that must be included in the proxy statement.

10.11. This regulation is a method of calling management's attention to stockholder concerns. Many corporate officers have stated that they pay considerable attention to stockholder proposals that are presented by institutional investors or by individuals, if they receive a vote of five or ten per cent of the outstanding shares. Management usually has the power as a practical matter to cause all such proposals to be defeated. Recent academic commentary has cast doubt on this justification.

10.12. *Yes.* Some have been approved in recent years as a result of the use of this device by institutional investors to compel changes in corporate governance. Such proposals usually receive significant support. Of course, this is most likely in corporations in which institutional investors have large holdings. Also, if it seems likely to be approved, a proposal may be implemented voluntarily by the corporation.

10.13. The SEC proxy rules do not apply to the solicitation of Hideaway's stockholders since it has no securities registered under section 12 of the 1934 Act. Therefore Case has no remedy. But if the proxy statements are materially misleading, causes of action exist not only under state law but also under rule 10b–5. The questions therefore presented are the lawfulness and fairness of the merger under state law and SEC rule 10b–5. Claims against Expansion or the surviving corporation and against the former controlling stockholders and former management of Hideaway may all be pursued under these alternative principles. Also, a question is raised about Case's standing to attack the transaction since he is a dissenting stockholder of the merged corporation pursuing his appraisal remedy. The proxy statements seem to be clearly misleading in their failure to disclose the financial history of Expansion. This omission would appear to satisfy the conventional deception standard of fraud required by rule 10b–5 and the requirement of *scienter* in *Hochfelder*. There would also appear to be a substantial prospect of attack under state law. Recent decisions of state courts, particularly in Delaware, have adopted the rule of entire fairness for merger transactions. The nondisclosure by Hideaway's management of the commitments it received might well be sufficient to invalidate a merger whose terms are unfair under state law.

10.14. *No.* Under *Virginia Bankshares, Inc. v. Sandberg*, no claim may be asserted by Case and other minority stockholders of Hideaway under Rule 14a–9 since the minority stockholders of Hideaway are unable to defeat the merger and therefore causal necessity is lacking. It is likely that the same argument will prevent a recovery under rule 10b–5; however, the Court in *Virginia*

Bankshares clearly preserved possible remedies under state law to attack this transaction.

10.15. The basic test is that the stockholder's purpose must be a proper one.

10.16. It is relatively easy for a stockholder to allege a proper purpose. Additional restrictions are appropriate to prevent fishing expeditions and to prevent misuse of valuable corporate information. The problem is that a stockholder with an insignificant financial interest in the corporation may have a strong incentive to use corporate information to further private ends.

10.17. A director has a broader right to inspect than a stockholder since directors have management responsibilities. The right of a director is often stated to be absolute; in fact some courts have limited it if the possibility of misuse of the information is high. The Corporate Governance Project adopts a limited right of inspection for directors.

10.18. The traditional view is that virtually no information has to be disclosed. A number of state statutes, however, require some such disclosure, and the trend toward mandatory disclosure appears to be increasing. The MBCA requires financial and other disclosure. If a corporation is subject to the registration requirements of section 12, or has previously made a registered public offering of the Securities Exchange Act of 1934, it is subject to the significantly greater disclosure requirements imposed by federal regulation.

10.19. *Yes.* The bylaw is invalid. First, a requirement that three months notice must be given before an inspection of books is permitted is unreasonable. If the books would disclose mismanagement at the time of the notice, the three months thereafter might permit the management to "cook the books" to reflect a proper state of affairs or condition. Also, the two weeks notice given by P is reasonable. Second, to permit the directors of the corporation to determine on a subjective basis whether or not a purpose of inspection by a stockholder is proper, would nullify the right of inspection in the very cases where inspection is most necessary, that is, when the books would disclose mismanagement on the part of the directors. Narrow restrictions on the right to inspect the books may be valid if they are limited to time, place and proper purpose, and cannot in substance deny or significantly delay the right or make it exercisable only at the whim of the directors. *State ex rel. Healy v. Superior Oil Corp.,* 13 A.2d 453 (Del.1940).

10.20. In a successful proxy fight in which the insurgents take control of the corporation it is likely that the corporation will end up paying both the management's unsuccessful defense costs plus the insurgent's costs. The outgoing management's costs will be paid before the management leaves office and the insurgents' costs will be paid after they take office. This result may be justified on the general view that the corporation may be asked legitimately to pay proxy contest expenses in policy disputes.

10.21. The argument basically is that proxy fights are a device for eliminating inefficient management and that making proxy fights easier will tend to keep management on its toes. The difficulty is that an unlimited right to reimbursement from the corporation would encourage proxy struggles in which there was little chance of success. Such fights could carry a high cost to the corporation.

10.22. Proxy contests are largely controlled by SEC regulations. These regulations impose a truth in campaigning requirement. There is virtually no state law of proxy contests.

CHAPTER 11

11.1. *Partially true.* While not true as a matter of common law, as a result of decisions in the last ten or fifteen years, substantial fiduciary duties have been imposed on stockholders of closely held corporations. While these duties are usually imposed on majority stockholders who are also directors of the corporation, several decisions recognize that stockholders in a corporation have somewhat the same relationship to each other that partners have in a partnership. The leading decision in this regard is the Massachusetts case of *Donahue v. Rodd Electrotype Co.*, discussed in the text. The leading case contra is the Delaware case, *Nixon v. Blackwell*, also discussed in the text.

11.2. *False.* A deadlock situation may be created by high quorum or high voting requirements as well as by an even division of voting power.

11.3. While involuntary dissolution is the traditional remedy for the deadlocked corporation, that solution may destroy a valuable going business. Alternatively, if there is a single stockholder whose skills are essential to the success of the business, that stockholder may use dissolution in order to obtain the bulk of the going concern value of the corporation. It is true that dissolution at the option of any partner is the standard remedy in partnership law, but it is not always a satisfactory solution for the reasons set forth in this answer.

11.4.   It is by no means certain that dissolution is the best solution for partnership problems. Buyouts may be preferable in many situations. But be that as it may, simpler and less damaging solutions to the problems of deadlock and oppression in the closely held corporation have been devised. By advance planning a buy-sell arrangement or arbitration may avoid a deadlock. Many state close corporation statutes also provide for provisional directors, custodians, or temporary receiverships designed to attempt to solve deadlock problems. Some state statutes also provide for a buyout at a judicially established price rather than involuntary dissolution, with the option of dissolution if that price is unacceptable. Even in states without such provisions, courts increasingly are willing to provide an equitable buyout remedy rather than involuntary dissolution, which is usually viewed as a harsh remedy.

11.5.   *False.* The evidence to date indicates that these statutes have not been widely used. In 1991, the drafters of the Model Business Corporation Act added two general provisions—one relating to stockholders' agreements (MBCA 7.32) and the other relating to a mandatory buyout arrangement available if a stockholder sues for involuntary dissolution (MBCA 14.34). It is likely that these generalized provisions will ultimately be the accepted solutions for the problem the closely held corporation.

11.6.   These phrases refer to the statutory requirements that there be a board of directors and officers, that they be selected in a certain way, that they be invested with specific authority, and so forth. The statutory scheme is most realistic in corporations of a middle size and complexity.

11.7.   *False.* While the requirements of directors and officers often make little sense when applied to a closely held corporation, it is important to recognize that in the absence of statutory authorization, two stockholders who run a business as a partnership may well end up personally liable for the corporation's obligations. Also, control agreements that violate the statutory scheme may be unenforceable.

11.8.   Answers to questions such as this depend strongly on the statutes of the state in question. The traditional view, and one that is likely to prevail if there is no express statutory provisions dealing with close corporations or modifications of traditional roles of directors, is that C should lose on the theory that a corporation must have a board of directors and that neither the incorporators nor the stockholders of a corporation may render such board impotent, sterile, helpless, or devoid of power. The quoted provision in the articles of incorporation arguably does just that. It provides that the board of directors shall have no power to bind the corporation without the unanimous consent of the stockholders. This arguably renders the board wholly impotent and without any power to act if a unanimous vote of the stockholders cannot be obtained. Therefore, the provision providing that the board of directors of X corporation has no power to act without the unanimous consent of the stockholders, should be viewed as wholly void, and the board of directors of X corporation may be able to act as though it did not exist. Under statutes such as MBCA 7.32, courts may enforce such a provision today. Even in the case of a traditional statute, a court might accept the argument that the requirement was accepted unanimously, does not hurt anyone, and is not a substantial impingement on statutory norms. *Clark v. Dodge, Galler v. Galler.* As a result of these factors, the chances of enforcing this agreement are significantly higher than they were twenty or more years ago.

11.9. *False.* All data indicates that the close corporation election is rarely utilized today.

11.10. In a closely held corporation share transfer restrictions may: (1) assure each stockholder that she will have a voice in who else participates in the corporation, (2) provide a way for stockholders desiring to withdraw to liquidate their interests in the corporation in a systematic fashion, and (3) establish the value of shares for estate tax purposes. While these advantages may not be assured in every case, they are the typical reasons for share transfer restrictions in closely held corporations.

11.11. *Yes.* Share transfer restrictions are commonly used in publicly held corporations to preserve the availability of securities act exemptions that are dependent on the shares not being reoffered or resold publicly.

CHAPTER 12

12.1. The Wall Street Option is a slang phrase to describe the option of a dissatisfied stockholder to sell his or her shares on the open market. This option is available in the publicly held corporation but of course is not generally available in closely held corporations. The extent to which this option is available to large holders of shares, such as institutional investors, depends on the volume of the market in those securities.

12.2. A question such as this should be answered carefully since it can be answered at different levels. Formally, the stockholders select the directors. However, in most publicly held corporations, the stockholders in fact ratify decisions made earlier as to who should be on the management slate of directors. In a real sense, the persons who put together the management slate determine who the directors of a publicly held corporation are to be. And this usually means either the incumbent management or a committee of the board of directors.

12.3. *False.* All recent studies indicate that the professional management, not the board of directors, establishes the broad business policies of the corporation. The role of directors is more one of oversight than of direction.

12.4. *Generally true.* The board of directors has the ultimate responsibility in this regard. Historically, the normal pattern was that the selection of a successor was largely the prerogative of the outgoing CEO. Since the 1990s, however, the role of the board of directors in selecting the CEO has increased significantly, and an answer of "generally true" is probably most accurate today, whereas it might not have been ten years ago. Answers to broad questions like this should be qualified not only by the time frame under discussion but also by the possibility that a substantial block of shares owned by a single person may affect the locus of power within the corporation.

12.5. "Book entry" refers to the predominant form of registration of publicly held securities today. Shares owned by investors or speculators are reflected only by monthly statements from the brokerage firm; the brokerage firm in turn has an account with Depository Trust Company or other central clearing corporation but all shares are owned of record by a nominee for the central clearing corporation. Transactions in shares are cleared by a simple netting process, first by the brokerage firm, and then by the central clearing corporation, with accounts of members being adjusted on a daily basis. More than 80 per cent of publicly held shares owned by individuals are today owned in book entry form.

12.6. Street name refers to a method of handling publicly traded shares. For many years, shares were registered in the name of brokerage firms with offices on Wall Street in New York City and certificates were endorsed in blank and transferred merely by delivery. Such "street name certificates" were the normal method by which the routine transfer of shares sold on the securities exchanges were effected before the book entry system developed. Most street name certificates were transferred directly between brokerage firms. "Street name" is now often used to refer to the modern system of book entry registration.

12.7. Institutional investors include investment companies, mutual funds, pension funds, insurance companies, bank trust accounts, charitable foundations, university endowments and the like.

12.8. Institutional investors have traditionally supported management on the theory that they simply are acting as investors. In a few instances institutional investors have supported insurgent bids. There has also been increasing institutional investor opposition to shark repellant provisions adopted by management.

CHAPTER 13

13.1. Insider trading refers to transactions by a corporate director, officer or employee in the shares of the corporation on the basis of information that is currently not publicly available. Insider trading may also refer to trading by other persons on the basis of nonpublic information obtained directly or indirectly from a director, officer, or employee. Insider trading is entirely a phenomenon of publicly held corporations.

13.2. *Both.* The early principles were based on state law notions of fraud or deception, and later expanded to a special facts doctrine that required disclosure of special facts. Today, insider trading is based primarily on Rule 10b–5 promulgated under the Securities Exchange Act of 1934.

13.3. *Uncertain.* Such an argument was accepted by the New York Court of Appeals in *Diamond v. Oreamuno* as a matter of state law. This view, however, has not been accepted. In *Chiarella* and *Dirks*, brought under Rule 10b–5, the United States Supreme Court held that the disclosure of the information constituted a breach of duty and was unlawful.

13.4. *False.* Rule 10b–5 applies to transactions in any security involving the use of any facility of interstate commerce. It is applicable to closely held corporations as well as publicly held corporations. The insider trading aspect of Rule 10b–5 is only applicable to publicly held corporations, but Rule 10b–5 is itself an important antifraud statute.

13.5. *False.* If a single telephone call or other use of the facilities of interstate commerce or the mails is involved in connection with this fraudulent sale, the defrauded stockholder may sue in Federal Court under Rule 10b–5.

13.6. Rule 10b–5 is a broad antifraud statute triggered by any purchase or sale of a corporate security through the facilities of interstate commerce. Rule 10b–5 has been applied to insider trading, to fraudulent transactions between stockholders in a closely held corporation, to false press releases issued by corporations which influence the price of a security, to issuance of shares by a corporation at an inadequate price, to a sale of all the stock of a closely held corporation, and to other transactions as well.

13.7. The U.S. Supreme Court has imposed significant limitations on Rule 10b–5. First, *Manor v. Blue Chip Stamps* holds that the plaintiff in a Rule 10b–5 case must be in fact a purchaser or seller of shares. Second, *Hochfelder* holds that a plaintiff must establish scienter (or possibly recklessness) in order to prove a 10b–5 claim. Third, *Santa Fe Industries v. Green* holds that Rule 10b–5 only applies to misrepresentation, fraud or deceit, and not to transactions that are fully disclosed but unfair. Fourth, Rule 10b–5 does not authorize claims based on aiding and abetting. *Gustafson v. Alloyd Co., Inc.* The mere fact that a transaction is unfair does not create a Rule 10b–5 liability so long as that unfairness is fully disclosed. These cases do not significantly affect the core case applications of Rule 10b–5 to insider trading, fraud in connection with sales of shares, and so forth.

13.8. Both of these principles deal with insider trading. However the application of the two is quite different, though to some extent overlapping. Section 16(b) deals only with offsetting transactions within a six-month period by an officer, director, or 10 per cent stockholder of a corporation that is registered under section 12 of the Securities and Exchange Act of 1934. Rule 10b–5 has none of these limitations. A second major difference is that liability under section 16(b) is automatic and not dependent on the actual profiting from the use of inside information in the transaction. Rule 10b–5 requires the proof of scienter and the establishment of the wrongful use of information.

13.9. The theory under which profits are computed on in-and-out transactions under § 16(b) is to squeeze out all possible profit. To this end the highest sales price is matched against the lowest purchase price within each six-month period; the next highest purchase price is matched with the next lowest; all such transactions are sequentially matched until no profit remains. All losses in this computation are ignored.

13.10. The issues are the liability under state and federal law of Sider, an officer and director with insider information, for selling his shares and Taken's standing to assert such liability. *(a) State law.* While the shares in question were registered under the Securities Exchange Act of 1934, the sale by Sider was over-the-counter and impersonal, and without any misrepresentation. Although there was a failure to disclose inside information, Taken was not a stockholder at the time of the nondisclosure. Because the transaction was anonymous and Taken was not a stockholder and thus was owed no fiduciary duty by Sider, the traditional common-law special facts and minority rules requiring disclosure by insiders of inside information in a person-to-person transaction to stockholders probably are not applicable. *Diamond v. Oreamuno* may have renewed the importance of state insider-trading law. In *Diamond*, the inside information was deemed to be a corporate asset. Any profit gained by corporate personnel through use of this asset was held to belong to the corporation. Therefore, under a *Diamond* approach, Sider would be liable to Dynamic, Inc. for the difference between what the shares were actually sold for and what they would have sold for had the information been public. This claim could be asserted directly by the corporation or derivatively by a stockholder or anyone else with standing to sue. Taken might not be able to maintain a derivative action because of the contemporaneous share ownership requirement of FRCP 23.1 since he was not a stockholder at the time of the transaction unless it can be shown that the wrong was a continuing one. This would be difficult since Taken bought his shares several days after Sider sold his shares. *(b) Federal law.* The more likely basis of recovery is under Rule 10b–5, creating a federal remedy for inside trading. Under Rule 10b–5, the use of the mails or a facility of interstate commerce (such as the intrastate use of the telephone system) are the sole jurisdictional requirements; the shares do not have to be listed on an exchange or publicly traded (though the shares of Dynamic, Inc. were). Since Sider is an officer of Dynamic, Inc., his transactions constituted a violation of Rule 10b–5 under the leading cases of *Texas Gulf Sulphur, Chiarella and Dirks.* An implied private right of action exists under Rule 10b–5. This right is also embodied in the recent statutes, ITSA and ITSFEA. Since Taken is a contemporaneous trader, he may bring suit against Sider, who has clearly failed to disclose material information, which, had it been made public, would certainly have dissuaded Taken to buy at the then market price. Moreover, Sider knowingly entered into the insider trading transaction, satisfying the scienter requirement of *Hochfelder*. While there is no privity between Sider and Taken, the statutory remedy does not require privity. Sider should thus be liable to the extent of his profit or loss avoided. Presumably other new stockholders are in the same situation as Taken. However, Sider's maximum liability may not exceed the loss avoided by his insider trading violation, and this may be further reduced by any penalty paid to the SEC under these statutes.

13.11. *Yes.* Maggie M. is guilty of insider trading in violation of Rule 10b–5. The law firm of Jones and Smith is a temporary insider, so that the information obtained by Maggie M. is inside information. She may have breached a duty to the client in using the information to profit personally; even if not, she breached a duty to her employer, Jones and Smith, and this breach of a duty may be used to find a violation of Rule 10b–5. The boyfriend is liable as a tippee if, as appears to be the case, Maggie M.'s disclosure constituted the breach of a fiduciary duty.

13.12. The only difference that the use of inside information about a takeover bid makes is that such use violates an explicit SEC rule, Rule 14e–3, without regard to how the insider or tippee obtained the information.

13.13. Under the *Dirks* case, trading by the tippee in a case such as this is unlawful only if Jones made an improper use of inside information when he divulged it to Smith. This in turn depends on whether Jones obtained a personal benefit from divulging the transaction; an intention to allow Smith to make a profit on the information seems to be the only motive for disclosing the information, and hence it is probable that both Jones and Smith violated Rule 10b–5 in this transaction. Traders in derivative securities, such as puts and calls, are covered under ITSFEA to the same extent as holders of shares themselves.

13.14. The principal proponents of PSLRA were publicly held high tech firms largely involved with computerization and the internet. However, it was also supported by many other publicly traded corporations, auditing firms, and trade associations.

13.15. The principal complaints were that many class actions were in fact strike suits or fishing expeditions designed to extract settlements from corporate defendants that primarily enriched plaintiffs' attorneys. The specific complaints included: Suits were filed solely on the basis of market declines in securities prices; there were unseemly rushes to be the first to file class actions; and the discovery process was being used a club to compel settlements of groundless litigation.

13.16. The basic pleading standard requires allegations of fraud to be pleaded with particularity and that each allegation must be supported by a specification of which statements are alleged to be misleading, and a description of the particular facts on which a belief that the statement is misleading is based.

13.17. The lead plaintiff is appointed by the court on the basis of who is most capable of adequately representing the interests of the class members. The lead plaintiff may be the class member with the greatest financial interest in the outcome. The lead plaintiff may select and retain counsel to represent the class, subject to court approval. This provision is designed to replace the first to file presumption that the attorney that is first to file should be lead counsel.

13.18. Attorney for the plaintiffs may be sanctioned under FRCP 11 for filing a complaint without reasonable cause. An appropriate sanction is presumed to be an award to the opposing party of the reasonable attorneys' fees and other expenses of the defendants in the action. While an attorney for defendants also may be sanctioned under FRCP 11 there is no presumption that a monetary sanction should be imposed.

13.19. Public accountants must adopt auditing procedures designed to provide reasonable assurance of detecting illegal acts that would have a material effect on the financial statements of the firm being audited. If an auditor discovers illegal acts in connection with an audit, it must report that fact to responsible officers or the board of directors of the firm, and if no remedial action is taken, to the Securities & Exchange Commission.

CHAPTER 14

14.1. *True within limits.* A stockholder may generally sell her shares for whatever price she can negotiate and if they carry a control premium she may keep it. However, the law recognizes that a controlling stockholder has certain duties by reason of her unique position with respect to the corporation. This duty is owed to minority stockholders, preferred stockholders, and creditors who are essentially defenseless. The duty is to take steps to avoid selling the shares to a person who may thereafter loot the corporation to the detriment of minority stockholders, preferred stockholders, and creditors. There is disagreement as to when the controlling stockholder must investigate a possible purchaser. In addition there may be situations where a sale of control breaches other fiduciary duties of a majority stockholder.

14.2. The law has not adopted this view even though it has been contended for in several cases. This may be a legislative rather than a judicial issue. In addition, there is a fear that an all or nothing approach may prevent desirable transactions from occurring as argued by economists of the University of Chicago Law School. The cost of such a rule may therefore exceed its benefits.

14.3. *Yes.* This case can be analyzed in a number of ways to reach the result that D breached his fiduciary obligation to the corporation. A controlling stockholder may usually sell a control block of shares for any price he or she can get; however, in disposing of control shares the stockholder owes a fiduciary duty to the corporation and to the minority stockholders not to injure them in so doing. It can be argued that: (a) D's sale of shares was an usurpation of the corporation's business opportunity to use the demand for steel to its advantage in attracting financing and new customers to its business, (b) the sale of the shares at a premium was really an usurpation by D of the grey market premium for steel which was an asset of the corporation, or (c) D's premium on the sale of his shares was actually the sale of control which is a corporate asset that belongs to all stockholders collectively. The best approach is probably (a) or (b) above. The stockholder has breached a duty to the corporation and is liable to account to it for the control premium received by him for the sale of shares. *Perlman v. Feldmann*, 219 F.2d 173 (2d Cir. 1955). However, commentators question the correctness of the result reached in *Perlman v. Feldmann*.

14.4. A tender offer (or cash tender offer, as it is often called) is a public offer by an aggressor to purchase shares of the target corporation. Usually the aggressor will seek working control of the corporation or all the publicly held shares of the corporation. In recent years most struggles for control have been in the form of cash tender offers or a negotiated acquisition. They are partially regulated by the Williams Act, though important aspects of them are also regulated by state law, particularly the validity of defensive tactics.

14.5. A merger is a consensual transaction which requires the approval of the board of directors of the target corporation. A cash tender offer is made directly to the stockholders of the target corporation, bypassing any need to obtain approval of the board of directors of the target corporation.

14.6. The Williams Act is a federal statute enacted in 1970 to regulate cash tender offers. Technically, the Williams Act is part of the Securities Exchange Act of 1934. The Williams Act is essentially neutral legislation, establishing ground rules and disclosure requirements for cash tender offers but not designed to make such attempts easier or more difficult.

14.7. State statutes relating to tender offers were enacted to make successful tender offers more difficult. Unlike the Williams Act, they are largely designed to protect local, incumbent management. The Supreme Court decision in *CTS Corporation v. Dynamics Corp. of* America largely validated state takeover statutes so long as they relate only to corporations formed under the laws of that state.

14.8. Arbitrageurs are speculators or investors who take offsetting positions in a single security selling at price differentials. In connection with cash tender offers, an arbitrageur may purchase the shares of the target corporation on the open market at any price up to the cash tender offer price and submit their shares for tender to take advantage of the price differential. They may also sell short or on a when-issued basis the aggressor's securities. In most takeovers, a very large percentage of the shares traded in the securities market after the announcement of a takeover attempt are purchased or sold by arbitrageurs. As a result of arbitrage transactions, virtually all target shares sold on the open market after the offer is announced are tendered into the offer (or into a competing offer at a higher price).

14.9. A leveraged buyout is a transaction in which the assets and earning power of the target corporation become the source of payment for the shares of the target corporation. A leveraged buyout involves borrowing very large sums of money to be repaid out of the earnings and assets of the target corporation.

14.10. Porcupine provisions is a slang term for defensive provisions in articles of incorporation adopted by potential target corporations to make takeovers more difficult. A typical porcupine provision requires a greater than majority vote for approval of mergers or other transactions that are opposed by the target's board of directors.

14.11. A poison pill is a new class or series of shares that provides valuable rights to stockholders upon the occurrence of a triggering event, such as when an aggressor purchases a specified percentage of shares. A number of varieties of poison pills have been developed but they all have in common the fact that they dilute significantly the interests of an aggressor if the poison pill is not redeemed.

14.12. *Generally false.* In a series of important decisions the Supreme Court of Delaware has created a set of rules as to when the business judgment rule may be relied upon by incumbent management in fighting an unwanted takeover. While there is a clear logic to these cases, the opinions are fact-specific and some doubt exists as to the precise scope of some decisions.

14.13. The "just say no" defense states that a corporation's board of directors may determine that the corporation is not for sale and refuse to redeem poison pills or otherwise negotiate or assist the aggressor, no matter how attractive the proposed transaction is to the target's stockholders. The Delaware courts have flirted with accepting a "just say no" defense but have never formally done so.

CHAPTER 15

15.1. In a merger one of the two combining corporations survive; in a consolidation both combining corporations disappear into a third, new corporation. The Model Business Corporation Act eliminates the concept of consolidations because they are generally not used in practice. It is usually advantageous for tax or other reasons for one of the present entities to be the survivor; if not, it is customary to create a new entity and merge the other entities into it.

15.2. In an ordinary merger, the stockholders of the disappearing corporation receive shares in the continuing entity. In a cash merger, some stockholders receive cash or other property rather than shares of the surviving corporation.

15.3. A "short form" merger is a merger of a subsidiary into a parent corporation subject to special statutory procedural rules applicable to this type of amalgamation. See MBCA 11.04.

15.4. These transactions are often functional equivalents that may have different legal and tax implications. Procedures and protections available in one type of transaction may not be available in other types of transactions even though they have the same economic effect.

15.5. A de facto merger is a nonstatutory amalgamation of two corporations that a court concludes is (a) the functional equivalent of a statutory merger and (b) participants should be accorded the rights they would have had in a statutory merger.

15.6. Appraisal rights (or dissenters' rights, as they are called in the MBCA) or the "right of dissent and appraisal" allow a dissenting stockholder to obtain the value of his or her shares in a judicial proceeding rather than go along with the merger or other transaction that gave rise to the appraisal right.

15.7. In most states, stockholder approval is required if the sale is not in the ordinary course of business.

15.8. A "going private" transaction involves the elimination of the public stockholders of a corporation through a cash merger or similar transaction. Such a transaction is susceptible of unfairness; the only special legal requirements are imposed by the SEC which requires a statement by management as to their opinion of the fairness of the transaction.

15.9. A "leveraged buyout" is a transaction by which an outside group acquires all the shares or assets of a public corporation. Incumbent management may participate in the outside group and thereafter continue to manage the business. Most of the purchase price is in the form of debt which is assumed by the corporation that is acquired at the end of the transaction.

15.10. *False.* In most states the right of dissent and appraisal is hedged with procedural traps and subjects a dissenting stockholder to the risk that a court may significantly undervalue interests in the corporation. Because of the cost of a judicial proceeding, the long delays, and the formidable litigation power of corporations intent on keeping the appraised value as low as possible, dissenters' rights are often viewed as an unattractive remedy.

15.11. This is a freeze-out merger, and must meet the intrinsic fairness tests of *Weinberger*, fair dealing and fair price. In some states, a business purpose requirement may also be imposed. Assuming there was full disclosure, the requirements of *Weinberger* appear to be met. Approval by a majority of the minority is also evidence of the fairness of the transaction. Thus, assuming that there was full disclosure the transaction is valid. Dissatisfied stockholders nevertheless have the right of statutory dissent and appraisal. If the transaction is in a state with a business purpose requirement, that test would also have to be met if the transaction is to be upheld.

15.12. *No.* The transfer of the franchise to another city is not a sale of all or substantially all the corporation's assets. The franchise remains an asset of the corporation with all of its rights and privileges intact. The corporation will continue to operate with substantially the same assets. *Murphy v. Washington American League Base Ball Club, Inc.,* 293 F.2d 522 (D.C.Cir. 1961).

15.13. *No.* A merger of a corporation with its wholly-owned subsidiary may eliminate preferred stockholders' rights to accumulated dividends if the terms of the merger agreement are fair and equitable in the circumstances. State law allows but does not require a stockholder objecting to the terms of a merger to use the remedy of dissent and appraisal. Dissenting stockholders are thus not put to an election by the statute of State Y. While a merger is always subject to nullification for fraud, here P has alleged only that the allocation between the old preferred and common stockholders is so unfair that it amounts to fraud. P has alleged no misrepresentation, concealment or deception. When fraud of this nature is charged, the unfairness must be of such character and must be so clearly demonstrated as to impel the conclusion that it emanates from acts of bad faith or a reckless indifference to the rights of others interested, rather than from an honest error of judgment. *Porges v. Vadsco Sales Corp.,* 32 A.2d 148 (Del.Ch. 1943); *Barrett v. Denver Tramway Corp.,* 53 F.Supp. 198 (D.Del. 1943); *Bove v. Community Hotel Corp.,* 249 A.2d 89 (R.I. 1969).

APPENDIX B

Glossary

A

accredited investor is a defined term in Regulation D promulgated under the Securities Act of 1933. Accredited investors are basically sophisticated investors who do not need the protection of the Securities Act in making investment decisions; sales to accredited investors are not counted in applying exemptions in Regulation D that depend on the number of investors to whom sales are made.

accumulated earnings tax is a special penalty tax imposed on corporations that fail to pay dividends or distribute earnings and accumulate funds in excess of foreseeable needs in order to avoid the taxation of dividends.

adoption is a contract principle by which a person agrees to assume a contract previously made for his or her benefit. An adoption speaks only from the time of the agreement, in contrast to a "ratification" which relates back to the time the original contract was made. In corporation law, the concept is applied when a newly formed corporation accepts a preincorporation contract made for its benefit by a promoter.

advances for expenses are payments by the corporation for expenses incurred by officers or directors as a result of defending against claims brought against them. Advances may be made as the expenses are incurred.

affiliate is a corporation that is related to another corporation by shareholdings or other means of control. It includes not only a parent and a direct or indirect subsidiary but also corporations that are under common control.

aggressor corporation is a corporation that attempts to obtain control of a publicly held corporation, often by a cash offer to shareholders, but also possibly by way of merger or other transaction that requires agreement or assent of the target's board of directors.

all holders' rule is a rule adopted by the SEC that prohibits a public offer by the issuer of shares that is made to some but less than all the holders of a class of shares.

alternative constituencies or **non-stockholder constituencies** are groups other than shareholders that have an interest in the well being of corporations: employees, customers, communities, states, etc. Statutes in more than one half of the states permit directors to consider the interests of alternative constituencies when making major policy decisions with respect to the corporation.

amotion is the common law procedure by which a director may be removed for cause by the shareholders.

antidilution provisions appear in convertible securities to guarantee that the conversion privilege is not affected by share reclassifications, share splits, share dividends, or similar transactions that may increase the number of outstanding shares without increasing the corporate capital.

appraisal. See dissent and appraisal.

arbitrageurs are market investors who take offsetting positions in the same or similar securities in order to profit from small price variations. An arbitrageur, for example, may buy shares on the Pacific Coast Exchange and simultaneously sell the same shares on the New York Stock Exchange if any price discrepancy occurs between the quotations in the two markets. By taking advantage of momentary disparities in prices between markets, arbitrageurs perform the economic function of making markets more efficient.

arbs is a slang term for arbitrageurs.

articles of incorporation is the name customarily given to the document that is filed in order to form a corporation. Under various state statutes, this document may be called the "certificate of incorporation," "charter," "articles of association," or other similar name.

authorized shares are the shares described in the articles of incorporation which a corporation may issue.

B

beneficial holders of securities are persons who have the equitable or legal title to shares but who have not registered the shares in their names on the records of the corporation. See also: record owner.

blank shares. See: series of preferred shares.

blue sky laws are state statutes that regulate the sale of securities to the public within the state.

bond discount. See: discount.

bonds are long term debt instruments secured by a lien on some or all the corporate property. Historically, a bond was payable to bearer and interest coupons representing annual or semiannual payments of interest were attached (to be "clipped" periodically and submitted for payment). Today, most bonds are issued in registered or book entry form. Bondholders are creditors and not owners of the enterprise. The word bond is sometimes used more broadly to refer also to unsecured debt instruments, i. e., debentures. Income bonds are hybrid instruments that take the form of a bond, but the interest obligation is limited or tied to the corporate earnings for the year. "Participating" bonds take the form of a typical debt instrument but the interest obligation is not fixed so that holders are entitled to receive additional amounts from excess earnings or from excess distributions, depending on the terms of the participating bond.

bonus shares are par value shares issued without consideration, usually in connection with the issuance of preferred or senior securities, or debt instruments. Bonus shares are considered a species of watered shares and may impose a liability on the recipient equal to the amount of par value.

book entry describes the method of reflecting ownership of publicly traded securities in which customers of brokerage firms receive confirmations of transactions and monthly statements but not share certificates. Brokerage firms also may reflect their customers' ownership of securities by book entry in the records of a central clearing corporation, principally Depository Trust Company (DTC). DTC reflects transactions between brokerage firms primarily by book entry in its records rather than by the physical movement of securities.

book value is the value of shares determined by using the numbers appearing on the books of the corporation. Using the corporation's latest balance sheet, the liabilities are subtracted from assets, an appropriate amount is deducted to reflect the interest of senior securities (preferred shares), and what remains is divided by the number of outstanding shares to obtain the book value per share. Book value is widely used as an estimate of value, particularly of closely held shares, but has certain fundamental limitations: it is based on accounting conventions, may not reflect unrealized appreciation or depreciation of assets, and does not take into account future prospects of the business.

bust up merger is a slang term for a leveraged buyout in which the acquiring corporation plans to sell off lines of business owned by the acquired corporation in order to reduce or eliminate the loans which were used to purchase the shares of the acquired corporation.

buyout is the purchase of a controlling percentage of a company's shares. A buyout often involves all of the company's outstanding shares. A buyout can be accomplished through negotiation, or through a tender offer or merger.

bylaws are the formal rules of internal governance adopted by a corporation. Bylaws define the rights and obligations of various officers, persons, or groups within the corporate structure and provide rules for routine matters such as calling meetings and the like. State corporation statutes generally contemplate that every corporation will adopt bylaws.

C

call for redemption. See: redemption.

capital stock is another phrase for common shares, often used when the corporation has only one class of shares outstanding.

capital surplus (in the Model Business Corporation Act nomenclature) is an equity or capital account which reflects the capital contributed for shares not allocated to stated capital: the excess of issuance price over the par value of issued shares plus the consideration paid for no par shares allocated specifically to capital surplus. Capital surplus may be distributed to shareholders under certain circumstances or used for the purchase or redemption of shares more readily than stated capital.

capitalization is an imprecise term that generally refers to the amounts received by a corporation for the issuance of its shares. However, it may also be used to refer to the proceeds of loans to a corporation made by its shareholders (which may be in lieu of capital contributions) or to capital raised by the issuance of long term bonds or debentures to third persons. Depending on the context, it may also refer to accumulated earnings not withdrawn from the corporation.

cash flow refers to an analysis of the movement of cash through a business and should be contrasted with the earnings of the business. For example, a mandatory debt repayment is taken into account in a cash flow analysis but such a repayment does not reduce earnings. See: negative cash flow.

cash merger or **cash out merger is** a statutory merger transaction in which certain shareholders in a corporation are required to accept cash for their shares while other shareholders receive shares in the continuing enterprise. Modern statutes generally authorize cash mergers, though courts test such mergers on the basis of fairness and, in some states, business purpose.

cash tender offer is a public offer to purchase a specified fraction (usually a majority) of the target corporation's shares from persons who tender their shares. Cash tender offers are regulated by the Williams Act.

C corporation is a corporation that has not elected (or is disqualified from electing) S corporation tax status. The taxable income of a C corporation is subject to tax at the corporate level while dividends continue to be taxed at the shareholder level. Compare S corporation; double taxation.

Cede and Company is the nominee used by Depository Trust Company.

CEO stands for chief executive officer of a publicly held corporation. CEO is a preferred and useful general designation because official titles vary from corporation to corporation.

CERCLA is the Comprehensive Environmental Response, Compensation, and Liability Act, also known as Superfund. CERCLA provides for liability of owners and operators of waste disposal sites in which hazardous substances have been deposited.

certificate of incorporation in most states is the document issued by the Secretary of State to evidence the acceptance of articles of incorporation and the commencement of the corporate existence. In some states the certificate of incorporation is the name given to the document filed with the Secretary of State, i. e., the articles of incorporation. The Model Business Corporation Act (1984) has eliminated certificates of incorporation, requiring only a fee receipt.

charter may mean (i) the document filed with the Secretary of State, i. e., the articles of incorporation, or (ii) the grant by the State of the privilege of conducting business with limited liability. Charter may also be used in a colloquial sense to refer to the basic constitutive documents of the corporation.

claims made insurance covers only claims presented during the period an insurance policy is in effect without regard to when the facts giving rise to the claim occurred.

class A common shares. See participating preferred shares.

class voting. See: voting group.

class of shares. A class of shares has specific voting and/or financial rights established in the articles of incorporation. Traditional classes of shares include common shares and preferred shares.

close corporation or **closely held corporation** is a corporation with relatively few shareholders and no regular market for its shares. Close corporations also usually have made no public offering of shares and the shares themselves are usually subject to restrictions on transfer. Close and closely held are synonymous.

closed end. See investment companies.

common shareholders are holders of common shares, the ultimate owners of the residual interest of a corporation.

common shares represent the residual ownership interests in the corporation. Holders of common shares vote to select directors to manage the enterprise, are entitled to dividends out of the earnings of the enterprise declared by the directors, and are entitled to a per share distribution of whatever assets remain upon dissolution after satisfying or making provisions for creditors and holders of senior securities.

consolidation is an amalgamation of two corporations pursuant to statutory provision in which both of the corporations disappear and a new corporation is formed. The Model Business Corporation Act (1984) eliminates the consolidation as a distinct type of corporate amalgamation.

control of a corporation by a person normally means that the person has power to vote a majority of the outstanding shares. However, control may be reflected in a significantly smaller block if the remaining shares are scattered in small, disorganized holdings.

control person in securities law is a person who is deemed to be in a control relationship with the issuer. Sales of securities by control persons are subject to many of the requirements applicable to the sale of securities directly by the issuer. In addition, controlling persons have a duty under federal law to prevent insider trading by persons under their control.

control premium refers to the pricing phenomenon by which shares that carry the power to control a corporation are more valuable per share than identical shares that do not carry a power of control. The control premium is often computed not on a per share basis but on the aggregate increase in value of the "control block" over the going market value of shares that are not part of the "control block."

control share acquisition is the name for state antitakeover statutes that require a shareholder who acquires shares that causes his ownership to break through specified percentages (e.g. 20 per cent, 33 per cent, 50 per cent) to obtain shareholder approval of the acquisition or the acquired shares lose their voting right. The constitutionality of these statutes was upheld in *CTS Corporation v. Dynamics Corporation of America*.

conversion securities are the securities into which convertible securities may be converted.

convertible securities are securities, usually preferred shares or debentures, that may be exchanged for a designated number of shares of another class (usually common shares), called the conversion securities. The ratio between the convertible and conversion securities is fixed at the time the convertible securities are issued, and is usually protected against dilution.

co-promoters. See: promoters.

corporate opportunity is a fiduciary concept that limits the power of officers and directors to take personal advantage of opportunities that are available to the corporation.

corporation by estoppel is a doctrine that prevents a third person from holding an "officer," "director," or "shareholder" of a nonexistent corporation personally liable on an obligation entered into in the name of the nonexistent corporation on the theory that the third person relied on the existence of the corporation and is now "estopped" to deny that the corporation existed.

cumulative dividends on preferred shares carry over from one year to the next if a preference dividend is omitted. An omitted cumulative dividend must be made up in a later year before any dividend may be paid on the common shares in that later year. However, cumulative dividends are not debts of the corporation but merely a right to priority in future discretionary distributions.

cumulative to the extent earned dividends on preferred shares are cumulative dividends that are limited in any one year to the available earnings of the corporation in that year.

cumulative voting is a method of voting that permits a shareholder to cast all of her available votes in an election in favor of a single candidate or to allocate them among various candidates.

D

D & O insurance refers to directors' and officers' liability insurance. Such insurance, which is widely available commercially, insures against claims based on negligence, failure to disclose, and to a limited extent, other defalcations. Such insurance provides coverage against expenses and to a limited extent fines, judgments, and amounts paid in settlement. D & O insurance also insures the corporation against its obligation to indeminfy officers and directors.

deadlock in a closely held corporation arises when a control structure permits one or more factions of shareholders to block corporate action if they disagree with some aspect of corporate policy. A deadlock often arises with respect to the election of directors, e.g., by an equal division of shares between two factions, but may also arise at the level of the board of directors itself.

debentures are long term unsecured debt instruments. Historically, a debenture was payable to bearer and interest coupons representing annual or semiannual payments of interest were attached. Most debentures today are issued in registered or book entry form. See: bonds.

deep rock doctrine is a principle in bankruptcy law by which unfair or inequitable claims presented by a controlling shareholder of a bankrupt corporation are subordinated to claims of general or trade creditors; this doctrine is now codified in the Bankruptcy Code. The doctrine receives its name from the corporate name of the subsidiary involved in the leading case articulating the doctrine.

de facto corporation at common law is a partially formed corporation that provides a shield against personal liability of shareholders for corporate obligations; such a corporation may be attacked only by the state of incorporation.

de facto merger is a transaction that has the economic effect of a statutory merger but is cast in the form of an acquisition of assets or an acquisition of voting stock and is treated by a court as if it were a statutory merger.

de jure corporation at common law is a corporation that is sufficiently formed to be recognized as a corporation for all purposes. A de jure corporation may exist even though some minor statutory requirements have not been complied with.

delectus personae is a Latin phrase used in partnership law to describe the power each partner possesses to accept or reject proposed new members of the firm.

derivative suit is a suit brought by a shareholder in the name of and on behalf of a corporation to correct a wrong done to the corporation.

dilution of outstanding shares results from the issuance of additional shares. The dilution may be of voting power, if shares are not issued proportionately to the holdings of existing shareholders, or it may be financial, if the price at which the new shares are issued is less than the market or book value of the outstanding shares when the new shares are issued.

directory requirements are minor statutory requirements. At common law, a de jure corporation may be created despite the failure to comply with directory requirements relating to its formation. Important statutory requirements are called mandatory requirements.

discount shares are par value shares issued for cash less than par value. Discount shares are a species of watered shares and may impose a personal liability on the recipient equal to the difference between the par value and the cash for which such shares were issued.

dissension in a closely held corporation refers to personal quarrels or disputes among shareholders that may make business relations unpleasant and interfere with the successful operation of the business. Dissension, however, may occur without constituting oppression or creating a deadlock or otherwise adversely affecting the corporation's business.

dissent and appraisal is a limited statutory right granted to minority shareholders who object to specified fundamental transactions, e.g. mergers. In an appraisal proceeding a court determines the value of the shares being appraised and the corporation pays the appraised value to the dissenting shareholder in cash. This right also may be referred to as the "appraisal right" or "dissenters' rights." The Model Business Corporation Act (1984) uses the term "dissenters' rights to obtain payment for their shares" to describe this right. The right of dissent and appraisal exists only to the extent provided by statute.

dissenters' rights. See: dissent and appraisal.

distribution is a payment to shareholders by a corporation. If out of current or past earnings (called "earned surplus" in the MBCA (1984)) it is often called a dividend. The word "distribution" in the MBCA indicates virtually all transfers of assets to shareholder. It is sometimes accompanied by a word describing the source or purpose of the payment, e.g., Distribution of Capital Surplus, or Liquidating Distribution.

dividend is a distribution to shareholders from or out of current or past earnings (called "earned surplus" in the MBCA (1984)). The word dividend is also sometimes used more broadly to refer to any payment to shareholders though a more appropriate term for all payments out of capital is "distribution."

double taxation refers to the structure of taxation under the Internal Revenue Code of 1954 which subjects income earned by a C corporation to an income tax at the corporate level while a second tax at the shareholder level is enforced if the previously taxed income is distributed to shareholders in the form of dividends.

down stream merger is the merger of a parent corporation into its subsidiary.

E

efficient capital market hypothesis posits that securities markets are efficient so that current securities prices accurately reflect all publicly available information about the security.

equity or **equity interest** are financial terms that refer in general to the extent of ownership interest in a venture. In this context, equity refers not to a legal concept but to the financial or accounting definition that an owner's equity in a business is equal to the business's assets minus its liabilities.

equity financing is raising money by the sale of common shares or preferred shares.

equity security is a security that represents an interest in the equity of a business. Equity securities are usually considered to be common and preferred shares.

ESOP is an acronym for employee stock ownership plan. ESOPs acquire shares of the employer for the benefit of employees usually through contributions by the employer to the plan and contributions by the employee to the plan.

ex dividend refers to the date on which a purchaser of publicly traded shares is not entitled to receive a dividend that has been declared and the seller of such shares is entitled to retain the dividend. The ex dividend date is a matter of agreement or of convention to be established by the securities exchange. On the first day shares are traded without the right to receive a dividend, the price will decline by approximately the amount of the dividend; such shares are referred to as "trading ex dividend."

ex rights refers to the first date on which a purchaser of publicly traded shares is not entitled to receive rights that have been declared on the shares.

F

face value is the nominal value of a bond, note, mortgage, or other security, as stated on the certificate or instrument, payable upon maturity of the instrument. The face value is also the amount on which interest or coupon payments are calculated. Thus, a 10 percent bond with a face value of $1000 pays bondholders $100 per year. Face value is also often referred to as the par value or nominal value of the instrument.

forced conversion refers to a conversion of a convertible security that follows a call for redemption at a time when the value of the conversion security is greater than the amount that will be received if the holder permits the security to be redeemed. Usually, a holder of a convertible redeemable security has a period of time after the call for redemption to determine whether or not to exercise the conversion privilege.

fraud on the market is a principle by which a plaintiff may presumptively establish reliance on a false statement in connection with the purchase or sale of securities by relying on the accuracy of the stated price of the security. This principle is based on the efficient capital market hypothesis. The presumption may be negated by the defendant proving the plaintiff in fact relied on considerations other than the current market price of securities when deciding to enter into the transaction.

freeze out refers to a process, usually in a closely held corporation, by which minority shareholders are prevented from receiving any direct or indirect financial return from the corporation in order to persuade them to liquidate their investment in the corporation on terms established by the controlling shareholders. See: squeeze out.

freeze out merger. See: cash merger.

G

going private refers to a transaction in which all public shareholders of a publicly held corporation are compelled to accept cash for their shares so that the business becomes wholly owned by officers, directors, or inside shareholders.

going public refers to the first public offering of securities by an issuer pursuant to its registration under the securities acts. The offering itself is called an "initial public offering" or ("IPO").

greenmail is a slang term that refers to a purchase by the target at a premium over market priced shares that have been acquired by a potential aggressor. The aggressor in exchange agrees not to pursue its takeover bid.

H

holding company is a corporation that owns a majority of the shares of one or more other corporations. Usually a holding company is not engaged in any business other than the ownership of shares. See: investment companies.

hybrid securities are securities that have some of the attributes of both debt and equity securities.

I

income bonds. See bonds.

incorporators are the person or persons who execute the articles of incorporation to form a corporation. In modern statutes only a single incorporator is required, and the role of the incorporator is largely limited to the act of executing the articles of incorporation. Restrictions on who may serve as incorporators have largely been eliminated.

indemnification refers to the practice by a corporation to pay the expenses of officers or directors who are named as defendants in litigation relating to the corporation. In some instances corporations may indemnify officers and directors for fines, judgments, or amounts paid in settlement as well as expenses. Broad indemnification rights may raise issues of public policy; but may also be justified on the ground, it is usually difficult or impossible to persuade persons to serve as directors in the absence of indemnification protection.

indenture is the contract that defines the rights of holders of bonds or debentures as against the corporation. Typically, the contract is between the corporation and an indenture trustee whose responsibility is to protect the bondholders. The indenture usually constitutes a mortgage on specified corporate property to secure payment of the bonds or debentures.

independent directors are directors of a publicly held corporation who are not officers of the corporation and have no direct or indirect business relationship with the corporation.

initial public offering (IPO) is the first public offering of securities by a corporation or other business entity that is registered under the Securities Act of 1933.

in pari delicto is a common law principle known as the "unclean hands" doctrine. The principle limits a person intending to engage in wrongful conduct from suing another wrongdoer when things do not work out as expected.

inside directors are directors of a publicly held corporation who hold executive positions within the corporation.

insider is a term of uncertain scope that refers to persons having some relationship to an issuer, and whose securities trading on the basis of nonpublic information may be a violation of law.

insider trading refers to transactions in shares of publicly held corporations by persons who have inside or advance information on which the trading is based. Usually the trader is an insider with an employment or other relationship of trust and confidence with the corporation. See: tip.

insolvency may refer either to "equity insolvency" or "insolvency in the bankruptcy sense." Equity insolvency means that the business is unable to pay its debts as they mature while insolvency in the bankruptcy sense means that the aggregate liabilities of the business exceeds its assets. Since a business may be unable to meet its debts as they mature and yet have assets that exceed in value its liabilities, or vice versa, it is important to specify in which sense the term "insolvency" is being used.

institutional investors are substantial investors, such as mutual funds, pension funds, insurance companies, endowments, foundation, and others who largely invest other people's money. Since World War II, institutional investors have accounted for an increasing portion of all public securities ownership.

integration in securities regulation is the principle that requires all offerings of securities over a period of time to be created as a single offering for purposes of determining the availability of an exemption from registration.

interlocking directors are persons who serve simultaneously on the boards of directors of two or more corporations that have dealings with each other. Federal antitrust law prohibits interlocking directors of competing businesses; such directors may also involve violations of fiduciary duties.

intra vires means acts within the powers or stated purposes of a corporation.

investment companies are corporations engaged in the business of investing in securities of other businesses. The most common kind of investment company is the mutual fund. An investment company differs from a holding company in that the latter seeks control of the ventures in which it invests while an investment company seeks the investment for its own benefit and normally diversifies its investments. Investment companies are subdivided into "open end" and "closed end" companies. An "open end" company stands ready at all times to redeem its securities at net asset value and to issue new shares to investors on demand; such an investment company is known as a mutual fund. An investment company that has a fixed capitalization and neither issues new shares nor redeems outstanding shares on request is a "closed end" company. The shares of closed end companies are widely purchased and sold on securities markets.

issued shares are the shares a corporation has outstanding. Issued shares should be contrasted with authorized shares. Issued shares that have been reacquired by the corporation are called treasury shares.

ITSA is the acronym for the Insider Trading Sanctions Act of 1984.

ITSFEA is the acronym for the Insider Trading and Securities Fraud Enforcement Act of 1988.

J

junior securities are debt or equity securities that are subordinate to other issues in terms of dividends, interest, principal, security, or payments upon dissolution.

L

leverage refers to the advantages that may accrue to a business through the use of debt obtained from third persons rather than contributed capital. Leverage is created when the earnings allocable to borrowed capital exceeds the interest cost of borrowing the funds.

leveraged buyout (or "LBO") is a transaction in which an outside entity purchases all the shares of a public corporation primarily with borrowed funds. Ultimately the debt incurred to finance the takeover is assumed by the public corporation. If incumbent management has a financial and participatory interest in the outside entity, the transaction may be referred to as a management buyout or MBO.

leveraged recapitalization is a transaction that involves the substitution of debt for equity in the capital structure of a corporation that fears it may become the subject of a leveraged buyout. A leveraged recapitalization may be undertaken by borrowing funds and distributing them as dividends to shareholders; by distributing evidences of indebtedness to shareholders, by a statutory merger with a subsidiary, and by other methods.

liquidating distribution is a distribution of assets by a corporation that is reducing invested capital or going out of business. Such a payment may arise, for example, if management decides to sell off certain company assets and distribute the proceeds to shareholders.

listed security is a security that is publicly traded on a securities exchange or on NASDAQ. For a security to be listed on an exchange or on NASDAQ, the issuing corporation must meet the requirements established by the exchange or NASDAQ and execute listing agreement.

litigation committee is a committee of the board of directors created to consider demands made by shareholders that suits be brought on corporate claims or derivative litigation that has been filed by shareholders to pursue corporate claims. If the litigation committee is disinterested and makes a decision consistent with the business judgment rule that pursuit of that claim or litigation is not in the best interests of the corporation, the court may accept that conclusion and not review the merits of the claim. The precise effect given to a decision by a litigation committee depends on the nature of the litigation and may vary to some extent from state to state.

lockup is a slang term that refers to a transaction that is designed to defeat one party in a contested takeover. A lockup usually involves setting aside securities for purchase by friendly interests in order to defeat or make more difficult a competitive takeover.

M

management buyout (MBO). See leveraged buyout.

mandatory requirements are substantive statutory requirements that must be substantially complied with in order to create a de jure corporation.

merger is an amalgamation of two corporations pursuant to statutory provision in which one of the corporations survives and the other disappears.

misappropriation theory states that an employee violates federal prohibitions against inside trading if he trades on the basis of information that is not publicly known and the trading is in violation of rules imposed by, or duties owed to, the employer. The information need not come directly or indirectly from the issuer of the securities in which the trading takes place.

mutual fund is a publicly held open end investment company that invests only in readily marketable securities. A mutual fund stands ready at all times to redeem its shares at net asset value. A mutual fund thus provides the advantages of liquidity, diversification of investment, and skilled investment advice for the small investor.

N

NASDAQ stands for National Association of Securities Dealers Automated Quotations. NASDAQ is a computerized trading market in which numerous dealers make markets in specific securities.

negative cash flow arises when the cash disbursements of a business exceed its cash intake. Short periods of negative cash flow create no problem for most businesses; longer periods of negative cash flow may require additional capital investment if the business is to avoid insolvency.

net worth is the amount by which assets exceed liabilities.

nimble dividends are dividends paid out of current earnings at a time when there is a deficit in earned surplus and other financial accounts from which dividends may be paid.

NOBO acronym for non-objecting beneficial owner. The Securities and Exchange Commission requires brokerage firms to provide issuers with the names of beneficial owners of securities held in book entry form who do not object to the disclosure of their names to the issuer. The issuer may thereafter communicate directly with the beneficial owner.

nominal value. See face value; par value.

nominee registration is a form of securities registration widely used by institutional investors and brokerage firms to avoid onerous requirements of establishing the right of registration by a fiduciary.

noncumulative voting or **straight voting** is the traditonal voting system that limits a shareholder to voting no more than the number of shares he owns for a single candidate. Compare: cumulative voting.

no par shares are shares issued under par value statutes that expressly state that they have no par value. Such shares are issued for the consideration designated by the board of directors and the entire consideration is allocated to stated capital unless the directors or shareholders determine to allocate a portion to capital surplus. Shares issued in states that have abolished par value should not be described as "no par shares."

novation is a contract principle that permits a third person to take over the rights and duties of a party to a contract and release the original party from all obligations under the contract. In the law of corporations, the concept may be applied to release a promoter who is personally liable on a preincorporation contract when the corporation is formed and adopts the contract. A novation requires the consent of the other party to the contract, but that consent may be implied from the circumstances.

NSMIA is an acronym for the National Securities Markets Improvement Act of 1996.

O

open end. See investment companies.

oppression in a close corporation involves conduct by the controlling shareholders that deprives minority shareholders of legitimate expectations concerning roles in the corporation, including participation in management and earnings.

outside directors are directors of publicly held corporations who do not hold executive positions with management. Outside directors may include investment bankers, attorneys, or others who provide advice or services to incumbent management and therefor have financial ties with management; the latter are sometimes referred to as "affiliated" outside directors. Compare: independent directors.

P

par value or **stated value** of shares is an arbitrary or nominal value assigned to each class of shares issued under par value statutes. At one time par value represented the selling or issuance price of shares, but in modern corporate practice, par value has virtually no significance or role. The Model Business Corporation Act (1984) and the statutes of many states have eliminated the concept of par value.

participating bonds. See: bonds.

participating preferred shares are preferred shares that, in addition to paying a stipulated dividend, give the holder the right to participate with the common shareholder in additional dividends under specified conditions. Participating preferred shares may be called class A common shares or given a similar designation to reflect their open ended rights.

pendent jurisdiction is a principle applied in federal courts that allows state created causes of action to be joined with a federal cause of action arising out of the same transaction even if diversity of citizenship is not present.

phantom stock plan is an employee benefit plan in which benefits are determined by reference to the performance of the corporation's common shares. For example, a person receiving

benefits based on 1,000 "phantom shares" will have credited to her account each year an amount equal to the dividends declared by the corporation on 1,000 shares; the number of "phantom shares" will also be increased by share dividends or splits actually declared on real shares; on her death or retirement the person will receive a credit equal to the difference between the market price of the "phantom shares" in her account on the date of death or retirement (or a related date) and the market price of the "phantom shares" in her account on the date she was awarded the shares.

poison pill is a special issue of shares by a corporation to protect it against an unwanted takeover bid. A poison pill creates rights of existing shareholders to acquire debt or stock of the target or aggressor upon the occurrence of specified events, such as the announcement of a cash tender offer or the acquisition by an outsider of a specified percentage of the shares of the corporation. A poison pill issues the potential cost of any acquisition, and either deters a takeover bid or compels the aggressor to negotiate with the target in order to persuade it to reduce the terms of the pill or withdraw it entirely.

pooling agreement is a contractual arrangement among shareholders that relates to the voting of their shares.

preemptive rights give existing shareholders the opportunity to purchase or subscribe for a proportionate part of a new issue of shares before the shares are offered to other persons. Preemptive rights are designed to protect shareholders from dilution of value and control when new shares are issued to non-shareholders. In modern statutes, preemptive rights may be limited or denied.

preferred shares are shares that have preferential rights to dividends or to amounts distributable on liquidation, or to both, ahead of common shareholders. Preferred shares are usually entitled only to receive specified limited amounts as dividends or on liquidation.

preferred shareholders' contract refers to the provisions of articles of incorporation, bylaws, or resolutions of the board of directors, that create and define the rights of holders of preferred shares. Preferred shareholders have only very limited statutory or common law rights outside of the preferred shareholders' contract.

preincorporation subscription. See: subscription.

private placement of securities is the sale of securities to sophisticated investors without registration under federal or state securities acts under the private offering exemption or under Regulation D.

promoters are persons who develop or take the initiative in founding and organizing a business venture. Where more than one promoter is involved in a venture, they are described as co-promoters.

prospectus is a document furnished to a potential purchaser of a security that describes the security, the issuer, and the investment or risk characteristics of the security. SEC regulations require a prospectus that meets specified requirements be provided to each purchaser of registered public offerings of securities.

provisional directors are directors appointed by courts pursuant to special close corporation statutes to serve on the board of directors of close corporations with deadlocked boards.

proxy is a person authorized to vote someone else's shares. Depending on the context, the word proxy may refer (1) to the grant of authority itself, (2) to the document granting the authority, or (3) to the person granted the power to vote the shares.

proxy solicitation machinery describes the process by which proxies are obtained from shareholders of publicly held companies.

proxy statement is the document that under SEC regulations must accompany a public solicitation of proxies. The proxy statement provides shareholders with appropriate information with respect to the transaction in question.

PSLRA is an acronym for the Private Securities Litigation Reform Act of 1995.

public offering involves the offerings for sale of securities by an issuer (or a person controlling the issuer) to members of the public. Generally, any offering that is not exempt under Regulation D, (the private offering exemption of the Securities Act of 1933), or a similar exemption is a public offering.

publicly held corporation is a corporation with shares registered under section 12 of the Securities Exchange Act of 1934. Shares of publicly held corporations are usually traded either on a securities exchange or in the over-the-counter market.

Q

qualified stock option is an option to purchase shares awarded to an employee of the corporation under terms that qualify the option for special tax treatment under the Internal Revenue Code.

qualifying share is a share of common stock owned by a person that qualifies him or her to be a director of the issuing corporation in a corporation that requires directors to be shareholders.

quo warranto is a common law writ designed to test whether a person exercising power is legally entitled to do so. In the law of corporations, quo warranto may be used to test whether a corporation was validly organized or whether it has power to engage in the business in which it is involved.

R

raider is a slang term for an aggressor in a takeover attempt: an individual or entity who attempts to take control of a target corporation by buying a controlling interest in its stock.

recapitalization is a restructuring of the capital of the corporation through amendment of its articles of incorporation or a merger with a subsidiary or parent corporation. Recapitalizations usu-ally involve the elimination of unpaid cumulated preferred dividends, and may also involve reduction or elimination of par value, the creation of new classes of senior securities, or similar transactions.

record date is the date that the identity of shareholders entitled to vote, to receive dividends, or to receive notice is ascertained.

record owner of shares is the person in whose name shares are registered on the records of the corporation. A record owner is treated as the owner of the shares by the corporation whether or not that person in his or her name, is the beneficial owner of shares registered.

redemption means the reacquisition of a security by the issuer pursuant to a provision in the security that specifies the terms on which the reacquisition may take place.

registered corporation is a publicly held corporation registered under section 12 of the Securities Exchange Act of 1934. Section 12 may apply to issuers other than corporations. The registration of an issuer under this section of the 1934 Act is independent of the registration of an issue under the Securities Act of 1933.

registration of an issue of securities under the Securities Act of 1933 permits the public sale of those securities in interstate commerce or with the use of the mails. That registration is unrelated to the registration of corporations under the Securities Exchange Act of 1934.

registration statement is the document that must be filed to permit registration of an issue of securities under the Securities Act of 1933. A major component of the registration statement is the prospectus that must be supplied to prospective purchasers of the securities.

regulation A is a small offering exemption to the Securities Act of 1933 that entails the filing and distribution of an offering statement; it is more similar to a simplified registration process than to an exemption.

regulation D is the SEC's principal small offering exemption to the Securities Act of 1933.

reorganization is a general term describing corporate amalgamations or readjustments. The classification of the Internal Revenue Code is widely used in general corporate literature. A "Class A reorganization" is a statutory merger or consolidation pursuant to the business corporation act of a specific state. A "Class B reorganization" is a transaction by which one corporation exchanges its voting shares for the voting shares of another corporation. A "Class C reorganization" is a transaction in which one corporation exchanges its voting shares for the property and assets of another corporation. A "Class D reorganization" is a "spin off" of assets by one corporation to a new corporation. A "Class E reorganization" is a recapitalization. A "Class F reorganization" is a "mere change of identity, form, or place of organization, however effected." A "Class G reorganization" is a "transfer by a corporation of all or part of its assets to another corporation in a title 11 or similar case."

retained earnings are profits accumulated by a corporation after the payment of dividends. Retained earnings are also called "undistributed profits" or "earned surplus."

reverse stock split is an amendment to the articles of incorporation that reduces the number of shares outstanding. The amendment must specify the basis on which holdings of existing shareholders will be adjusted to reflect the smaller number of shares outstanding. Reverse stock splits may create fractional shares and may be used as a device to "go private" by reducing the number of shares outstanding to the point that no public shareholder owns a full share of stock, and then by providing that all fractional shares are to be redeemed for cash.

reverse triangular merger. See triangular merger.

risk arbitrage is a strategy employed in takeover situations in which shares of a corporation that is about to be taken over are purchased, while shares of the acquiring corporation that are to be exchanged are sold short or on a when-issued basis.

S

A major statute, the **Sarbanes Oxley Act of 2002,** imposed sweeping changes in corporate governance and required the SEC to adopt implementing rules and procedures to make effective these changes. These changes, summarized below, impose federal standards on many issues that were formerly the sole responsibility of state law.

Historically, state law controlled corporations formed under the statutes of each state. Though enactment of the Securities Act of 1933 and the Securities Exchange Act of 1934 in the depth of the great depression imposed federal registration of publicly held corporations for the first time, but the detailed rules governing the activities of public corporations, to the extent they existed at all, continued to be supplied by the laws of the state of incorporation of the specific corporation.

This reliance on state law proved inadequate in the period from the late 1990s through 2002, a tumultuous period that involved disclosure of significant misconduct and fraud an the part of many publicly held corporations; Enron, WorldCom, Adelphia, Berlin Metals, Cendant, Computer Associates, Dynegy, Global Crossing, Homestore.com, Reliant Resources, Inc., Rite Aid, Sunbeam, Waste Management, WorldCom, Xerox and others. In January, 2003, the SEC published a report documenting that over 100 blue chip companies had "Cooked their books" during this period.[1]

The result of these disclosures was the enactment of the Sarbanes–Oxley Act in 2003. This statute imposes sweeping changes in corporate governance at the national level for the first time and requires the SEC to adopt implementing rules and procedures to make these changes effective. At the same time, new listing and rating requirements were created by several state agencies, including:

1) New listing requirements for publicly traded corporations governed by the New York Stock Exchange which are described as "Corporate Governance Rules" and often abbreviated as the "NYSE CG Rules;"

2) Detailed and stringent corporate governance rating systems that have been devised by private governance rating agencies and proxy advisor, including International Shareholder services Government Metrics, International ("GMI"), the Corporate Library, Moody's and Standard & Poor's. In addition, agencies such as Glass, Lewis, & Company now provide significant targeted advice when voting issues are to be considered by individual corporations.

3) Changes in the tone and emphasis of judicial opinions, particularly in the Delaware Courts (where more than half of all American publicly held corporations are incorporated).

In addition to these permanent changes, a number of smaller corporations restated downward their announced earnings during this period: Berlin Metals, Computer Associates, Dynegy, HomeStore, Livent, PNC Financial, Reliant Resources, Sunbeam, Waste Management, and others.

In addition, section 201 of Sarbanes–Oxley (which adds section 10A(g) to the 1934 Act), prohibits external audi-

---

1. Securities and Exchange Commission, Report Pursuant to Section 701 of the Sarbanes–Oxley Act of 2002, at 38, (January 24, 2003).

tors from providing a number of traditional business-related services to the companies they are auditing, corporate auditors may not create financial information systems, design, and implementation; they may not help clients in choosing, installing, and operating accounting-related computer and software systems. Furthermore, they are prohibited from providing a number of other services, including provision of book-keeping services, appraisal and evaluation services, actuarial services, internal audit outsourcing services, management functions, human resource sources, investment banking services, and legal and related services. In addition, they must separately hire companies and rating agencies to test their balance-sheet goodwill amounts, pension payments estimates, and review the assumptions used to compute the company's determinations of pension plan assets and liabilities. In connection with these services, public companies must disclose the dollar amount of audit and audit-related services separately from permitted non-audit services. These determinations may be evaluated by governance rating agencies, and investors are advised to taken this data into account when making investments or casting votes. In the current environment, some shareholder activists have sponsored resolutions asking companies to discontinue providing non-audit services.

Section 301 of Sarbanes–Oxley provides that the power to hire, fire, and compensate internal auditors must reside in the corporation's audit committee rather than in the board of directors or in corporate management. Members of this committee must be "independent" under standards set forth by the audit committee. Prior to Sarbanes–Oxley, the usual Practice was to have the board of directors select corporate auditors; under Sarbanes-Oxley, individual auditors who deal with the company's executives must be independent, and furthermore, must be rotated off the engagement after five years. Section 206 further requires the SEC to adopt rules requiring the principal executive and financial officers to certify quarterly and annual reports with respect to the following:

- That they have actually reviewed the report in question;

- That to their knowledge the report does not contain material falsehoods or omissions;

- That the financial statements present the company's condition and operating results in a way that is "fair and complete' in all material respects;

- That they are responsible for, and have evaluated, the adequacy of internal controls;

- That they have disclosed any significant control deficiencies to the external auditors and to the audit committee; and

- That they have disclosed significant changes in controls and corrective actions that have been taken.

Presumably, the intended effect of these statutory certifications is that they will make officers and directors more focused on reports and more diligent and assiduous in their dealings with subordinates. Whether or not this will have the intended effect is probably questionable.

Sarbanes–Oxley sections 301 and 407 also require that at least one member of the audit committee have financial expertise and financial literacy.

Sarbanes–Oxley also requires the creation of a new independent regulatory body, the Public Company Accounting Oversight Board ("PCAOB"), the function of which is to oversee and regulate external auditing firms and their auditing processes. Sections 101–109. Section 404 sets forth the standards for such oversight and regulation. The PCAOB began the process of overseeing and regulating external auditing firms and their auditing processes and experienced decidedly mixed results: On the positive side, a number of CEOs have expressed the view that the process of meeting the requirements of section 404 attestation has improved their management information systems, and have led to better internal controls. On the other hand, there is a real risk that a mandatory attestation requirement will become so routine as to be ineffective.

The risk of potential criminal liability imposed by sections 404 and 906 have led to the development of intensive and expensive evaluations of internal review processes and procedures. The cost of these procedures has been one of the major criticisms of Sarbanes–Oxley. These procedures involve the following steps:

1) Review, and if necessary, adopt new liability assessment and reporting practices;

2) Obtain and evaluate all insurance company risk assessment for company properties

3) Discuss with appropriate corporate officials pending and threatened litigation and regulatory enforcement issues referred to in periodic reports;

4) Include a discussion of environmental matter;

5) Discuss and evaluate potential contingent liability issues in financial statements, including operational, warranty and environmental issues;

6) Implement and periodically evaluate all section 404 controls;

7) Perform periodic actions required by internal controls and procedures, including the evaluation of known problem areas, the search for new-problem areas, and a report of the results to participants in the management chain;

8) Have all of the preceding steps reviewed, evaluated, and certified by appropriate senior managers; and

9) Require a review of the foregoing and its audit by company accountants.

If these steps are consistently followed, they should generate information that is much greater in both quality and reliability than that generally available previously. This information should also be valuable in connection with internal review and the assessment of public information. However, the cost of such an evaluation will be substantial.

The Sarbanes–Oxley Act also contains a number of sections of minor importance: Sections 406–498 requires a code of ethics for senior financial officers, the determination of a financial expert, enhanced review criteria, and a requirement of "real time" disclosures under sections 13(a) and 15(d).

A minor section, section 806 of Title VIII, makes employees, employers, and other specified persons civilly and criminally liable if they retaliate against whistle blowers.

Finally, despite all of these mandated controls, there is always a slight risk that cannot be avoided that trusted corporate officers may have engaged in misconduct ranging from embezzlement of funds from the company, to receipt of improper payments from vendors, or the disclosure of sensitive information to competitors in exchange for cash payments.

S corporation is a corporation that has elected to be taxed under Subchapter S of the Internal Revenue Code. The taxable income of an S corporation is not subject to tax at the corporate level, but is allocated to the shareholders to be taxed at their level. S corporation taxation is similar but not identical to partnership taxation.

scrip is issued in lieu of fractional shares in connection with a stock dividend. Scrip represents the right to receive a portion of a share; scrip is readily trans-

ferable so that it is possible to acquire scrip from several sources and there assemble the right to obtain the issuance of a full additional share.

securities is a general term that covers not only shares of stock, bonds, and debentures, but also a variety of interests that have the basic characteristics of security, i. e., that involve an investment with the return primarily or exclusively dependent on the efforts of a person other than the investor.

security-for-expenses statutes require plaintiffs in a derivative suit to post a bond with sureties from which corporate or other defendants may be reimbursed for their expenses if the defendants prevail. The Model Business Corporation Act (1984) does not impose a security-for-expenses requirement.

senior security is a debt security or preferred stock that has a claim prior to that of common shares to the corporation's assets and earnings.

series of preferred shares are subclasses of preferred shares with differing dividend rates, redemption prices, rights on dissolution, conversion rights and the like. Typically, the terms of a series of preferred shares may be established by the board of directors so that a corporation periodically engaged in preferred shares financing may readily shape its preferred shares offering to market conditions. Series may be created only if a class of shares is created by the articles of incorporation and the board of directors is authorized to create one or more series within that class. If none of the terms of the class of preferred shares are specified in the articles of incorporation, the class of shares is usually called "blank shares."

share dividend is a proportional distribution of shares to existing shareholders.

share split creates a proportional change in the number of shares owned by every shareholder. It differs from a stock dividend in degree; however, typically in a stock dividend no adjustment is made in the dividend rate per share while a dividend adjustment is usually made in a stock split. There are also other technical differences in the handling of stock splits and stock dividends in some states.

shareholders or stockholders are the persons who own shares of stock of the corporation. Modern usage generally prefers "shareholder" to "stockholder" but the latter word is also deeply ingrained in common usage.

shark repellent is a slang term that refers to measures undertaken by a corporation to discourage unwanted takeover attempts. It may also refer to state statutes designed to discourage takeover attempts.

short form merger is a merger of a subsidiary into a parent through a streamlined procedure permitted under the statutes of many states.

sinking fund refers to an obligation of the issuer of debt securities to devote or set aside a certain amount each year to the retirement of the securities when they mature. A sinking fund may also be used each year to redeem a portion of outstanding debt securities.

split is a proportional change in the number of shares owned by every shareholder. Other things being equal, a share split does not affect the aggregate market value of the shares. Share splits differ from a share dividend in degree; typically in a share dividend no adjustment is made in the dividend rate per share while an adjustment is usually made following a share split. There may be other technical differences in the handling of share splits and share dividends in some states.

squeeze outs are techniques by which a minority interest in a corporation is eliminated or reduced. Squeeze outs may occur in a variety of contexts, e.g., in a "going private" transaction in which minority shareholders are compelled to accept cash for their shares, or a proportionate offer of new shares to existing shareholders. Shareholders may also have their proportionate interest in the corporation reduced significantly unless they invest a large amount of additional or new capital over which they have no control and for which they receive little or no return. Squeeze outs may involve the use of cash mergers. Squeeze out is synonymous with freeze out.

staggered board is a classified board of directors in which a fraction of the board is elected each year. In staggered boards, individual members serve two or three years, depending on whether the board is classified into two or three groups.

stated capital in the traditional nomenclature represents the basic capital of the corporation. Technically, it consists of the sum of the par values of all issued shares plus any consideration for no par shares that has been transferred to capital surplus plus other amounts that have been transferred to stated capital from other accounts.

stated value. See: par value.

stock appreciation rights (SARs) are bonus payments to corporate executives based on the growth in value of a predetermined number of hypothetical shares.

stockholders. See: shareholders.

straight voting. See: noncumulative voting.

street name refers to the practice of registering publicly traded securities in the name of one or more brokerage firms with Wall Street offices. Such certificates are endorsed in blank and are essentially bearer certificates transferred between brokerage firms to reflect specific transactions. Street name may also refer to the modern practice of book entry registration of ownership. See book entry.

strike suits is a slang term for derivative litigation instituted for its nuisance value or to compel a favorable settlement.

subchapter S refers to the subchapter of the Internal Revenue Code that regulates the S corporation election. See S corporation.

subordinated. See: junior securities.

subscribers are persons who agree to invest in the corporation by purchasing shares of stock. Historically, subscribers executed individual "subscriptions" or "subscription agreements." The modern practice is to enter into contracts that provide that the purchaser "agrees to purchase and subscribe for the specified shares."

subscription is an individual offer to buy a specified number of unissued shares of a corporation. If the corporation is not yet in existence, a subscription is known as a preincorporation subscription, which is enforceable by the corporation after it has been formed and is irrevocable despite the absence of consideration or the usual elements of a contract.

subsidiary is a corporation that is majority or wholly owned by another corporation.

superfund. See CERCLA.

surplus is a general term in corporate accounting that refers either to the excess of assets over liabilities or that amount reduced by the stated capital. Surplus has a more definite meaning when combined with a descriptive adjective from par value statutes, e.g., earned surplus, capital surplus, or reduction surplus.

T

tainted shares are shares owned by a person who is disqualified for some reason from serving as a plaintiff in a derivative action. If the shares are "tainted", a good faith transferee of shares may also be disqualified from serving as a plaintiff.

takeover attempt or **takeover bid** are generic terms to describe attempts by an outside corporation or group, usually called the "aggressor" or "insurgent," to wrest control away from incumbent management. A takeover attempt may involve an offer to purchase shares, a tender offer, an effort to sell assets, or a proposal that the target merge voluntarily with the aggressor.

target corporation is a corporation the control of which is sought by an aggressor corporation.

temporary insider is a person or firm that receives nonpublic information from an issuer pursuant to duties owed by that person or firm to the issuer. A temporary insider is subject to the same proscriptions against inside trading as an employee or director of the corporation. A temporary insider is not a "tippee."

tender offer is a public invitation by an aggressor to shareholders of a target corporation to tender their shares for purchase by the aggressor at a stated price. A "creeping" tender offer is a series of private acquisitions in the market place and may or may not be treated as a tender offer for regulatory purposes.

thin corporation is a corporation with an excessive amount of debt in its capitalization.

tip is non-public information passed on by one person (a "tipper") to another (a "tippee"). Such information may be of material value and not available to the general public. Securities trading by tippees in some circumstances violates federal law.

transfer agent is an organization, usually a bank, that handles transfers of shares for a publicly held corporation. Generally, a transfer agent assures that certificates submitted for transfer are properly endorsed and that there is appropriate documentation of the right to transfer. The transfer agent also issues new certificates and oversees the cancellation of old ones. Transfer agents also usually maintain the record of shareholders for the corporation and maintain other records to prevent the corporation to distribute checks for dividends and other payments.

treasury shares are shares that were once issued and outstanding but which have been reacquired by the corporation and are "held in its treasury." Treasury shares are economically indistinguishable from authorized but unissued shares but historically have been treated as having an intermediate status. The Model Business Corporation Act eliminates the concept of treasury shares. Reacquired shares automatically have the status of authorized but unissued shares in the MBCA.

triangular merger is a method of amalgamation of two corporations by which an acquired corporation is merged with a subsidiary of the acquiring corporation and is the surviving corporation in the merger. Thus the acquired corporation becomes a wholly owned subsidiary of the acquiring corporation by merger.

U

ultra vires is the common law doctrine relating to the effect of corporate acts that exceed the powers or stated purposes of a corporation.

up stream merger is a merger of a subsidiary corporation into its parent.

V

voting group is a term used to describe the right of shares of different classes or series to vote separately on fundamental corporate changes that adversely affect the rights or privileges of that class or series. The scope of the right to vote by voting groups is defined by statute. Older state statutes may use the terms "class voting" or "voting by class" to refer to essentially the same concept.

voting trust is a formal arrangement by which record title to shares is transferred to trustees who are entitled to exercise the power to vote the shares. Usually, all other incidents of ownership, such as the right to receive dividends, are retained by the beneficial owners of the shares.

voting trust certificates are certificates issued by voting trustees to the beneficial holders of shares held by a voting trust. These certificates may be readily transferable and carry with them all the incidents of ownership of the underly-

ing shares except the power to vote.

W

warrants are a type of option to purchase shares issued by a corporation. Warrants are typically long term options, are freely transferable, and if the underlying shares are listed on a securities exchange, are also publicly traded. The price of warrants of publicly held corporations is a function of the market price of the shares and the option price specified in the warrants.

watered shares are par value shares issued for property which has been overvalued and is not worth the aggregate par value of the issued shares. Watered shares is also a generic term that describes all shares issued for less than par value, including discount and bonus shares.

white knight is a friendly suitor: a potential acquirer usually sought out by the target of an unfriendly takeover to rescue it from the unwanted bidder's takeover.

Z

zeroing out is a slang term that describes the common income tax strategy in C corporations of reducing taxable income to zero by paying out all earnings in the form of tax-deductible payments to the shareholders of the corporation.

APPENDIX C

Table of Cases

†